# CRYING WOLF

# VANORA BENNETT

# CRYING WOLF

## THE RETURN OF WAR TO CHECHNYA

**PICADOR**

First published 1998 by Picador

an imprint of Macmillan Publishers Ltd
25 Eccleston Place, London SW1W 9NF
and Basingstoke

Associated companies throughout the world

ISBN 0 330 35170 2

1 3 5 7 9 8 6 4 2

A CIP catalogue record for this book is available from
the British Library.

Typeset by SetSystems Ltd, Saffron Walden, Essex
Printed and bound in Great Britain by
Mackays of Chatham plc, Chatham, Kent

# Contents

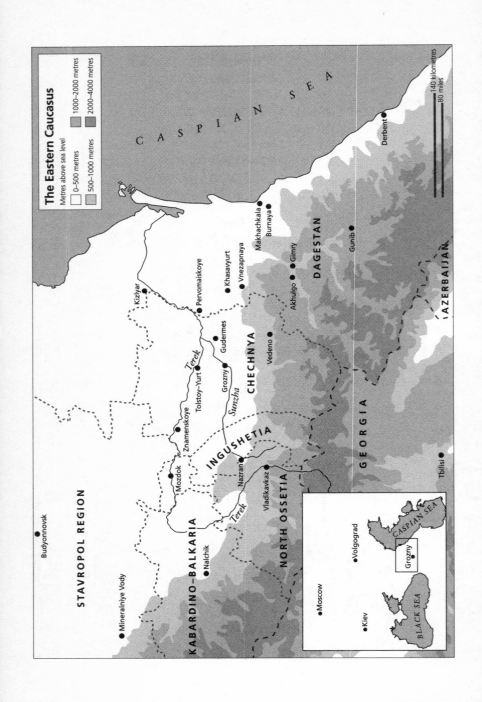

## The Eastern Caucasus

Metres above sea level

0–500 metres
500–1000 metres
1000–2000 metres
2000–4000 metres

140 kilometres
80 miles

C A S P I A N   S E A

Derbent

Makhachkala
Burnaya

Gimry

DAGESTAN

Gunib

Akhulgo

AZERBAIJAN

Kizlyar

Pervomaiskoye

Khasavyurt

Vnezapnaya

Gudermes

Vedeno

Terek

Tolstoy-Yurt

Grozny

CHECHNYA

Znamenskoye

Sunzha

GEORGIA

Mozdok

INGUSHETIA

Tbilisi

STAVROPOL REGION

Nazran

Vladikavkaz

Terek

Budyonnovsk

KABARDINO–BALKARIA

Nalchik

NORTH OSSETIA

Mineralniye Vody

CASPIAN SEA

Volgograd

Grozny

Moscow

Kiev

BLACK SEA

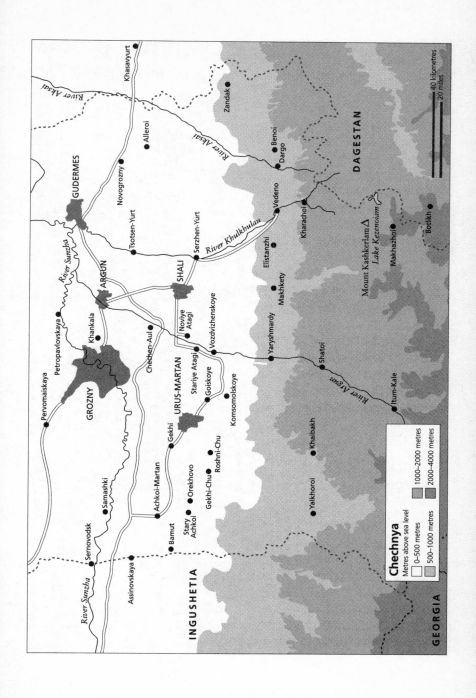

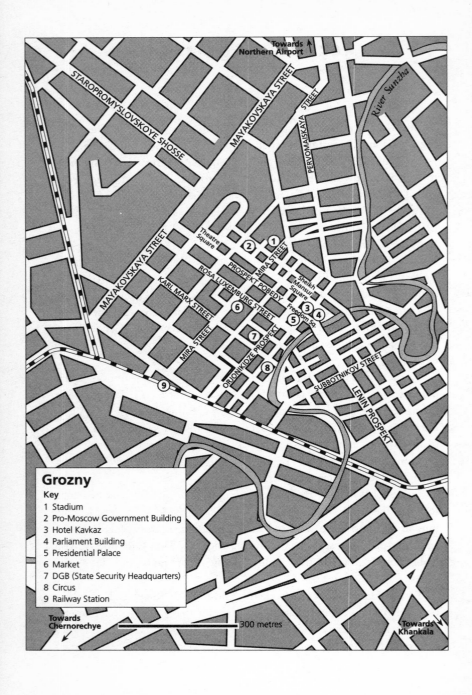

**Towards Northern Airport** ↑

STAROPROMYSLOVSKOYE SHOSSE

MAYAKOVSKAYA STREET

PERVOMAISKAYA STREET

River Sunzha

MAYAKOVSKAYA STREET

KARL MARX STREET

ROSA LUXEMBURG STREET

MIRA STREET

Theatre Square

PROSPEKT POBEDY

MIRA STREET

Sheikh Mansur Square

Freedom Sq.

ORJONIKIDZE PROSPEKT

SUBBOTNIKOV STREET

LENIN PROSPEKT

② ①

③ ④

⑤

⑥

⑦

⑧

⑨

# Grozny

### Key
1 Stadium
2 Pro-Moscow Government Building
3 Hotel Kavkaz
4 Parliament Building
5 Presidential Palace
6 Market
7 DGB (State Security Headquarters)
8 Circus
9 Railway Station

**Towards Chernorechye** ↙

300 metres

**Towards Khankala** ↘

# Acknowledgements

To the Gazgireyevs and Autarkhanovs, and many others in Chechnya, Ingushetia and Dagestan, for their hospitality, friendship and time.

To travelling companions and colleagues: in affectionate memory to Adil Bunyatov and Farkhad kerimov; to Dan Edelman, Hugh Pope and Thomas Goltz; to Lawrence Sheets, Igor Shatalov and Alkhan Tasuyev; to Vitya Korotayev, Grisha Dukor, Sean Ramsay, Kostya Leifer, Peter Andrews and Pyatras Malukas; to Misha Yandiyev; to Elif Kaban, Catherine Eldridge, Sasha Sokolkov, Nick Doughty, and Kostya Trifonov; to Oliver Wates, Tolya Verbin, Oleg Shchedrov, Robert Eksuzyan, Tanya Ustinova and Andrei Shukshin; to Marie Bennigsen Broxup; to Olivia Ward, Maksharip Chadayev, Sonia Mikich, Colin Peck, Andrei Mironov, Carlotta Gall, Tom de Waal, Sebastian Smith, Rick Beeston, Alessandra Stanley and Michael Specter; to Roza, Bilkis and everyone else from Griboyedov Street in Grozny.

To my sister Sophie for making me send off a book proposal; to my parents for their encouragement; and to my brother Timothy for first giving me the idea of writing a book. To Ralph Boulton and Vicky Barrett, with heartfelt thanks for their generosity at difficult moments; to the Karpov family for the Russian newspaper cuttings they sent to London; and to Kostya Bogdanov and Marina Chernykh in St. Petersburg for all their thoughts.

To Carol Williams, for helping me return to Moscow and find time to finish this book, and to her and the rest of the L.A. Times Moscow bureau for putting up with me while I worked on it, especially to the endlessly patient researchers Christine Kiernan, Tina Carr and Marisa Robertson-Textor for their help pinning down facts and dates and times.

To Bill Hamilton at A.M. Heath, and to John Riley, Tania Stobbs, Ursula Doyle and Ann Cooke at Picador, for their support. To Nanette van der Laan, Penny Morrison, my mother Rhuna Martin, Carlotta Lemieux, Mia Foster, and Nick Braden for being kind enough to read my manuscript at different stages, and for their intelligent and helpful advice.

And, most of all, to John Morrison, for ideas, arguments, perspective, historical background, bacon sandwiches and every kind of help from beginning to end.

# Prologue

In the still point at the centre of the world, the Chechens dance.

Old men with tranquil eyes and taut faces form the circle, moving in a dignified shuffle, singing their prayers. Their black coats flap in the black winds, their words are swallowed up by the night, but their stately astrakhan hats bob on in an endless act of worship.

Their prayer-dance, the *zikr*, has gone on for centuries. The Chechens danced before Islam came to the mountains. They embraced the faith of the Sufis – the whirling dervishes of the East – and the dance went on. They have danced throughout the hard years that followed, drawing strength from their prayers to continue the fight against the Russians who invaded their austere home from the plains of the north.

The dance and the faith, which merged at the moment of the first Russian advance, are the most potent symbol of defiance Chechens have against the violent marriage forced on them by the Tsars' big guns. For, like the *zikr*, Chechen history since that marriage has turned in repeating cycles, cycles of war and not-war, suppression and oppression, blood and rebirth. Russians have gone on hating and fearing the one subject people which has never bowed down to their rule, and a Chechen prophecy that their tiny nation will be brought to the brink of extinction at Russian hands every fifty years has come true over and over again.

Yet Chechens still greet each other with the phrase 'be free', still call themselves *uzden* or freemen, and still watch for every possible chance to escape their bonds.

*

I didn't find out any of this at the beginning, when I came to work for Reuters in Moscow as the Soviet Union started to collapse in 1991. What I learned then from my Russian friends was that the Chechens were people to hate, dishonest, bloodthirsty, cut-throat, criminal. Darkies.

I didn't yet realize that this was only Act One of the latest rerun of a historical drama pitting Russians against Chechens, and Tsar against Imam, which was to start unfolding again after seventy history-free Soviet years. I didn't understand that the Russians explaining the Chechens to me were not the chorus and commentators I took them for, but players, with their own dramatic purpose and their own hidden motives.

It was only as the other four acts were played out, and as I began to look backstage in both Moscow and the Caucasus, that I began to understand the truth.

# ACT ONE

# WATCHING THE CHECHEN VILLAINS FROM MOSCOW

# ONE

Sleet was slapping at the windows. It was dark outside, although it was only four o'clock on an autumn afternoon in 1991. But our cosy Moscow office was alive with yellow light and the whirring of faxes. Andrei and I were slumped in front of the television, half-watching the news, but we were both too exhausted by the failed coup two months before and the disintegration of the country which we could only guess at two months ahead to concentrate.

I looked up, and suddenly the television was showing a flickering picture of dark men in tall dark hats, dancing somewhere outside in the night. They were shuffling round in an endless circle, mouths opening and shutting soundlessly. There was no expression on the bony faces, all chiselled cheekbones, hooked noses and white stubble. Their shoulders were hunched forward against the wind. They wore long coats, flapping down to their ankles, like miniature Dostoevskys or Bolshevik activists. They moved purposefully, one behind the other until the first intent face appeared again, but without sound you could only guess at the reason for their dance. They weren't the usual Russian television faces, sly politicians in thick glasses or the glum, broad-cheeked peasants of the perestroika era's incoherent vox pops. They didn't look as though they came from the time of television at all. They looked like ghosts in the machine.

'If this is still the news, who are those men?' I asked, wondering if I'd dozed off and a period film had started. 'Chechens,' Andrei answered, and his mouth twitched up sardonically at one corner. 'Doing a war dance.'

I'd never heard of the Chechens. Andrei said they lived in an autonomous republic in the southern mountains, called Checheno-Ingushetia by its Soviet administrators, about twice the size of Kent, 1,000 miles south of Moscow. They were on television because they were among the many Soviet regions and republics trying to overthrow their local government for supporting the coup in August.

It was the same story all over the country in the autumn of 1991. Every night, the television showed a new region or a new republic somewhere in the Soviet one-sixth of the globe, with a crowd demonstrating in the square in the centre of town. Sometimes the square was called Lenin Square; in more up-to-date places it had been renamed Freedom Square. There was always a great, grey, greasy government building in it, sometimes called the Former Regional Committee building, sometimes something more modern, and there was always a Karl Marx Boulevard stretching off into town. The faces could be Asiatic, Mediterranean or Nordic, a televised testament to Soviet ethnic diversity. But it was always the same demonstration, with the same placards in front of the concrete government block, the same long speeches and the same scruffy, indignant protesters.

The Chechens were the only protesters who danced, though, and it was the dance that intrigued me. Television was keen on the demonstrations, which proved the point of Boris Yeltsin's Russian government that the time for the Soviet Union to end was coming, and every news bulletin that night showed the whirling Chechens in their tall lambskin hats.

'It really is a war dance,' Andrei said as I got ready to leave. 'They're wild men. They go round and round and work themselves up into a frenzy, and the only way to come down off the high is to shed blood. They all carry daggers, you know. They call themselves wolves.'

He grinned mischievously. Everyone enjoyed astonishing newcomers to the Soviet Union with stories about its uniqueness, and the taller the tale the better. That night alone, Andrei and I had discovered grisly news items on the Soviet wires about cannibals in starving Sverdlovsk, the suicide of a poet, police distributing free vodka to rioters in a secret space-industry town in the tulip-strewn desert, and children who had been given transfusions of AIDS-infected blood in one of the northern cities where the sun rises only in summer. If they were true, then why not believe in southern tribesmen performing a dance of death?

Whispers on the wind. It was stout Yevgeniya, a friend of a friend and now my Russian teacher, who reminded me the next morning that I had heard of the Chechens after all. 'Of course you have,' she said chidingly, still in the middle of the ritual of removing her street clothes, unwrapping her second scarf from under her fur coat, unzipping big snow-boots, and pulling her fur hat off. 'Fetch me your Lermontov and I'll show you.'

Lermontov was a Russian officer and poet who fought in Russia's war to conquer the tribes of the Caucasus mountains last century. His only novel, *A Hero of Our Time*, was published in 1840, and has had a chalky afterlife as a set text for all modern Russian students. I vaguely remembered its anti-hero. He was a precocious, precious, glamorous but amoral Russian officer called Pechorin. Pechorin's brain was bigger than his heart and he used his quick understanding of the way other people thought to trick them, humiliate them, and – in the case of the St Petersburg ladies holidaying on the fringes of the war – bed them. I also vaguely remembered Lermontov's rapturous descriptions of the mountains, the snows, and the dark tribesmen galloping in the background. Pechorin was proud of his riding ability, and liked frightening pretty husband-hunters, at the spas behind the front where wounded officers convalesced, by dressing up in Caucasian clothes for his morning gallop and swooping down on them unawares. I didn't remember the enemy he was fighting.

'Here it is, here are your black Chechens,' Yevgeniya said bossily, waving the book at me and stabbing at it with a finger. 'Now, what about a nice cup of tea?'

And there they were, being reminisced over by one of Pechorin's victims-to-be, a Russian Cossack called Maxim Maximych. Yevgeniya patted her hair back into place and rearranged her shawl neatly as she declaimed his rough speech in her correct intellectual's accent. 'Our Chechens, even though they were bandits and cut-throats, at least were daredevils . . . Now, thank God, they're more peaceful, but in the past if you stepped a hundred yards beyond the walls you'd find some wild devil there on watch; and if you dropped your guard for a moment you'd have a lasso round your neck or a bullet in your brain. But they were good lads!'

Scary, but romantic. Why did the tribesmen fight for decades? Yevgeniya paused to inspect the tea-making process and tut-tutted at the absence of sugar. 'Because they're blacks. Violent, ignorant, savage, brutal. They're the same now as they were then, and they'll never change,' she said with considerable venom. 'They have no culture and no civilization.'

# TWO

Blacks. There were a lot of Western taboos that had no place in the Russia of 1991, and I was discovering that queasiness about racism was one. I spent a lot of time in my first months in agonies of embarrassment, helplessly eyeballing any other foreigners around, while people who had seemed perfectly normal and open-minded suddenly launched into what would seem rabid racist rants in England but were taken as part of civilized conversation in Moscow.

Russians don't mean Negro when they sneer out the word 'black'. That kind of black is an *Afrikanets*, whatever part of America or England or the West Indies he might come from. White women who talk to male *Afrikantsy* are automatically labelled prostitutes.

In the southern Russian university of Voronezh, where I studied for a few months in the 1980s, hundreds of mostly male African students from 'friendly socialist countries' spent up to ten years surrounded by pursed lips and unfriendly expressions. Russian students would nudge each other when we passed park benches with Africans sitting talking to blonde girls, smirk knowingly and whisper in each other's ears. When the aptly named Kommendant of our hostel on Fridrikh Engels Street wandered uninvited into the room I shared with three other girls, before we had had time to clear up a party the night before, the sternest rebuke he could think of was: 'Even the Negroes in this hostel don't live in such disorder.'

The *Afrikantsy* shared rooms with each other, made food with each other, had parties with each other. Made nervous by the hostility of the Voronezh doctors, they even treated each other's illnesses with their own medicines and pulled each other's teeth. When one of the Russian students, Lara, a podgy, light-hearted girl with a cynical wit and a flirtatious giggle, discovered she was pregnant, she tried every trick she knew to get an abortion at the hospital without having to give her name on any official forms. It had to be secret: she didn't want the authorities to throw her out of university for being 'morally unreliable' enough to have sex before marriage. But her charm and offers of bribes got her nowhere at the clinic. In the end she sold her white vinyl winter coat and went to the *Afrikantsy* for a botched bucket-of-soapy-water operation. 'I don't mind them; they're not bad lads really,' she explained, then fixed me with a beseeching look, her eyes filling with easy tears. 'Who else can I go to? I just don't want you to think that my going to the *Afrikantsy* means I'm a tart.'

When I returned to work in Russia nearly a decade later, it was from a job in southern Africa which I had been delighted to escape. But all my attempts at explaining the deadly suburban respectability of the white community in my previous home, Harare – their 1970s bleached perms, their bitter little racist jibes over the gin, their stifling nostalgia for the lost glory days of Rhodesia – fell on deaf ears in Russia. 'However did you live there, a white girl alone in the jungle with all those monkeys and chimpanzees and black Africans?' my otherwise charming new friends would marvel. 'Thank God you at least got out of there without marrying an African, or being raped by one.'

The agonizing process of self-censorship and then self-discovery that Germany and the rest of the West went through, after the horrors perpetrated against Jews were made public, never happened in the Soviet Union. Our post-war rejection of the idea of classifying people as members of a race made the old empires of the West slowly collapse after 1945. But Russians remember the Second World War only as their own painful victory over fascism, and their own sufferings against the Nazis, not as a parable about how the racial classification existing inside their own borders could go wrong. So Moscow's empire went on standing until 1991, and Soviet passports went on listing their peoples' ethnic origin as their 'nationality'.

Jews – considered representatives of a nationality rather than a religion in Russia – were officially a race apart from Russians, and registered as alien at point five of their internal passports, where nationality is indicated. Traditional, institutional, organized anti-

Semitism is such a recent memory in Russia that it is hard to say it ever really died.

Under the Tsars, most Jews were forced to live in the village ghettos of the Pale of Settlement on the western reaches of the Empire, a European zone which had been Russia's spoils from the partition of Poland. Policed by the Tsar's Cossacks and suspicious Polish, Russian, Belarussian and Ukrainian peasants, victims of pogroms whenever hardship or xenophobia gripped their neighbours, they had no way of escaping. Jews could not join Russia's mainstream population in their nineteenth-century eastward colonial push into the rich Siberian hinterland, and only a few were allowed to live in St Petersburg and Moscow.

Things did not get any easier in Soviet times. Periodic campaigns against 'cosmopolitanism' fanned nagging suspicions that Jews had loyalties outside Mother Russia and were plotting its downfall. The disgraced Trotsky, once Lenin's co-revolutionary, became the image of the Jewish betrayer. Only Stalin's death in 1953 stopped a full-scale bloodletting of the Jews in the planned second stage of the 'Doctors' Plot', in which a group of doctors were accused of trying to murder the Soviet leader. Thousands of arrests planned for follow-up show trials were shelved as a new struggle began for succession to the Kremlin. But Slavic suspicion of the outsiders persisted.

Not only bureaucracy, history and prejudice condemn Jews and other non-Russians to be perpetual outsiders in the land of their birth. They are also excluded by the Russian majority's anxious self-image as a tight-knit community of 'our people' – *nashi* – surrounded by possible enemies. Partly this mental picture is a reflection of Russia's geography, a large and sprawling state in the middle of a still larger landmass, a place of unstable borders, perpetually expanding in a burst of aggression or contracting under attack by physical enemies outside or inside its territories. Partly it harks back to the closed world of traditional village communes, whose members relied heavily on each other but looked with suspicion on all outsiders. Anyone who does not belong by blood and birth and upbringing can never hope to be fully integrated into this defensive, touchy, spiritual community. The parameters and definitions shift, but everyone concerned always knows whether or not they are being welcomed under the comforting shelter of an umbrella word used far more commonly than any English equivalent. *Nashi* is 'our boys' in the army, fighting the *chuzhiye* or 'aliens'; *nashi* is 'our team' in sports; the phrase '*ona – nasha*', or 'she's one of us', is an open-sesame for the ubiquitous guards and doormen reluctant to let outsiders past their post. The strong approval it expresses for national, military, and team formations reveals a people who yearn passionately to impose order on the chaos they have so often felt engulfing them.

The wars, traumas and upheavals of the twentieth century, and the confusion of Soviet bureaucracy, allowed many thousands of Jews to 'lose' their Jewish nationality by getting new papers and changing their names to Russian ones. Since 1989, when Russian Jews began to be allowed to emigrate to Israel without impediment, the shadow has begun to lift. Overt anti-Semitism is now seen as uncivilized, at least by the cultured middle classes that lament the departure to Israel of writer after musician after artist. In an ironic coda to their history of suffering at Russian hands, Israeli officials now even tell stories of blonde Russians queuing up with fake Jewish papers in the hope of getting permission to emigrate to Israel, where they hope they will make it rich.

But a whole underworld of conspiracy theorists still blames the Jews for destroying the Soviet Union. President Yeltsin's wife is one, these people say. So is new Russia's first economic reform chief, Yegor Gaidar, and a host of other plotters in the suspected international Jewish conspiracy. Vicious lampoons in the far-right press always depict the liberal, democratic politicians of new Russia as thick-lipped, hook-nosed, swively-eyed Shylocks, with sacks of money at their feet. For the readers of these newspapers, the unique destiny of the Russian people remains to be robbed and humiliated by the sly outsiders. *The Protocols of the Elders of Zion*, selling like hot cakes on street corners along with *Mein Kampf* and other bibles of hate, prove their point.

As a jocular insult, Russians will call their Russian friends by imitation Jewish patronymics: Abramovich! Aaronovich! Jewish jokes in Russia are still hostile jokes told by Russians against Jews, not ironical ones told by Jews against themselves – although they are now told in the same furtive, behind-the-bike-sheds spirit that taboo racist jokes are told in the West. Their humour lies in 'revealing' the squalor and money-grabbing of the shtetl.

Although the stigma of Jewishness has lessened, as emigrating to Israel has come to be seen as a prestigious and economically attractive option, it is perhaps unsurprising that Jews are often still embarrassed to admit their nationality to Russians. 'I am from Russia,' some say, hanging their heads in shame at the unnatural-sounding grammatical construction; others answer even more elliptically, with a hint of laughter: 'Fifth point.'

In Russia, people relate to each other not only as individuals but, always, as representatives of a 'nationality'. Generalities about nationality are taken in deadly earnest and deemed always to apply to every individual. In 1991, when Westerners were still a relative rarity in Russia, it was a matter of great surprise, attracting sincerely astonished comment, if a representative of England did not strike a Russian interlocutor as dry, withdrawn and clipped. 'But you're so friendly!' people would say to me. 'Are you really English?' 'Well, my mother is South African,' I would answer, and there would be wise nods all round and a chorus of 'Ah, that explains it.'

Foreigners from outside the Soviet Union were always honoured guests, with a respected place high up in the international pecking order, deferred to to the point of embarrassment – at least if they were from the capitalist world. Americans topped the list; then, in descending order of prestige came Western Europeans, Eastern Europeans, and the many students from the socialist states of the Middle East, Asia and Africa.

At first, I put this simplistic ordering of the outside world down to Soviet lack of exposure to foreigners and travel abroad. Russians who spoke English had often mastered grammar and spelling without ever practising on a native speaker; years of memorizing dull English texts about international workers' holidays on 1 May and the history of trade unions, all in the genteel accents of the British 1920s ('hets', not 'hats'), had left them confused about how the foreign world worked. People in Russia were always asking how much things cost in 'my' currency – by which they meant the US dollar. They only shrugged indulgently if I answered that we didn't use dollars in England, as if I was having an outburst of flouncy nationalism against the dominant American culture. 'No, but seriously,' they would persist, 'how much would it be in your dollars?' Russians who had never learned foreign languages were still more confused about what boundaries might exist in the world outside. One taxi-driver I took a ride with in Moscow had his car plastered with foreign stickers in a language I thought might be Dutch, or Swedish, or Danish. 'Where are these from?' I asked. He looked at me with great suspicion, as though I might be laughing at him. 'Well, you ought to know. They're in foreign, and you're a foreigner,' he answered.

But it gradually became clear to me, as I worried about Yevgeniya's strictures against Chechen 'blacks', that the Russian views on race and affiliation, whites, blacks, Americans and Jews, which struck newcomers with such force, were just a logical extension of the strict racial hierarchy that existed inside the Soviet world.

Under Lenin and Stalin, the many peoples of the Soviet world had been separated into racial territorial units. The Soviet Union became a four-tiered confection, made up of union republics of which the biggest was Russia, which in turn each contained 'autonomous republics' for big ethnic minorities, and 'autonomous regions' and 'autonomous districts' for smaller non-Russian racial groups. These were originally supposed to promote Communist equality between all races, by giving the empire's many 'backward' peoples space in which to speed up their development until they caught up with the 'advanced' Russian majority, first drawing close, *sblizheniye*, before finally losing all their separate national self-consciousness and merging completely, *sliyaniye*, in a single Communist nation. But time and changing circumstances turned this experiment on its head.

Lenin's argument was that, in their own racial enclave, members of backward races could be educated on their own terms, hope for promotion and advancement, and learn the ropes of local government. In practice, this system of *korenizatsiya*, or 'putting down roots', quickly became an excuse not to promote non-Russians outside their ethnic homeland. What resulted was racial segregation in a network of Bantustans. The ethnic areas were not economically self-sufficient. Their assets were stripped and their raw materials used to fuel Moscow's central economy. Nor were they politically self-respecting, as their cardboard castles of 'autonomous' local government remained, in reality, dependent on Moscow.

Under Stalin, a contradictory policy of Russification began in the hope of reintegrating the fragmented Soviet peoples. Throughout the 1930s, laws were passed promoting the Russian language in ethnic areas to a position of primacy, and Moscow sponsored an official attitude giving Russians the favoured status of 'older brother', 'first among equals' and leaders in the Soviet family of nations. This attitude crystallized at the end of the Second World War into the perception that the Russians of the Soviet Union had sacrificed most in defence of the socialist fatherland – although several non-Russian peoples sustained proportionally greater losses. At the end of the Second World War, Stalin toasted the Russian, not the Soviet, people, saying: 'It is the leading nation of all the nations belonging to the Soviet Union,' and 'it earned in this war general recognition as a guiding force of the Soviet Union.' What this translated to in practice was that ethnic Russians, who after the war moved into minority areas in ever greater numbers, could now expect special treatment and easy promotion even in the once-sacrosanct Bantustans.

Deluded by the calm decades of post-war stagnation, Mikhail Gorbachev came to power in 1985 assuming that the process of ethnic blending was virtually completed, and that the non-Russian peoples of the Soviet Union were as happy as their Russian bosses with the way things were. It was only once he started to ease central controls over the Soviet peoples that he discovered, to his distress, that his non-Russian subjects were so far from satisfied with a world in which they were never as equal as their Russian neighbours that they began clamouring to leave the Soviet Union altogether. The cannier Boris Yeltsin, who had slithered back into power as leader of the Russian union republic in 1990 after falling out with the Soviet party hierarchy two years earlier, read the mood of the times more accurately. He promised the ethnic minorities of Russia 'as much sovereignty as you can swallow' if they would vote for him as president. Meanwhile, struggling unsuccessfully to stop the process of national self-expression he had started, Gorbachev – and 150 million Russians – watched bewildered as the multiethnic superpower tore itself apart in riots, revolutions, and wars.

By the autumn of 1991, when the formal end of the Soviet Union was already in the air and the only real question left was when and how, there were plenty of Russians who were angry and disappointed with the ungrateful lesser Soviet peoples for destroying the fatherland. Their faults were much dwelt on, and their ethnic stereotypes much disparaged.

Settled snugly on my sofa, always willing to be distracted from the painstaking reading of Agatha Christie novels in Russian with which we whiled away the months before Gorbachev's resignation, Yevgeniya became my guide to the race snobberies of the Soviet Union. She would quiz me about my travel plans for the week, then fill me in on what I should expect in whichever Soviet republic I was heading for.

Of the lesser, but still 'white', Slavs, Belarussians were dull plodders and Ukrainians (known as *khokhly*, or 'topknots', from their traditional Mohican-style hairdo in which all but a single tuft was shaved off) affable, but lazy and greedy. Out on a limb were the blonde peoples of the three Baltic states, co-opted into the Soviet Union in 1940, not Slavs at all but respected for the wealth and order in their countries which made holidays there almost as good as a trip to the West. But they too came in for a sneer or two from Russians who emigrated there after the war. Natasha Karpova, a twenty-year-old Russian student who lived in Baltic Estonia until she was five, remembered how she had avoided playing with her white-haired Estonian neighbours: 'We weren't supposed to have anything to do with them. We used to call them Kurds,' she said with a half-suppressed giggle.

Then came the 'black' republics: Mediterranean-looking Christians and Muslims from the three Transcaucasus republics over the mountain range on Russia's southern border, or Asiatic-looking visitors from the -stan republics of Central Asia. Yevgeniya had nothing good to say about any of them, though she did concede that Armenians – hard-nosed businessmen, drivers of vicious bargains – and Georgians – expansive, hospitable, macho, feckless wine-drinkers – at least belonged to ancient Christian cultures. The rest, the Azerbaijanis and the Central Asians, with their Turkic talk and Muslim faith, were no better than savages, as far as Yevgeniya was concerned, and nothing good could be expected from them.

Lower still were the 'black' mini-peoples who lived on the northern slopes of the Caucasus mountains and on the southern reaches of the Volga, inside Russia proper, speaking their Turkic or Iranian or Finnic or wild hill tongues in their reservation-style ethnic mini-republics and regions. Violent, primitive, criminal . . . the traditional terms of contempt had been tempered with fear in the years of perestroika as these peoples, including the Chechens, flocked into Russia to carve a niche in the new private markets that were opening up; by 1991, Russians worried about their own worsening poverty in the collapsing state economy had started to fear these strutting Moscow blacks as mafias.

Right at the bottom of the heap, too low to be anything but the butt of contemptuous jokes about their naive stupidity, were the herders and fishermen of the far north and east, with their Eskimo looks and their helplessness, lost in the modern world of cars and colour televisions. Best-known of these peoples were the Chukchi, whose name could hardly be said in Russian without a twitch of the lips; without fail, it prompted the question: 'Have you heard the one about the Chukchi who . . . ?'

An autumn of questions and culture shock left me feeling, rather disappointedly, that there wasn't much to choose between the mindset of the hate-filled, resentful white Rhodesians I had left behind in Africa and the Russians I was meeting in Moscow – except that, here, the basis for racial prejudice was not even skin colour, but hair colour. 'You're such a little whitey, like a real Russian girl,' taxi-drivers would cluck approvingly, patting my fair hair irritatingly as we inched through the sleet and the traffic. Jenny, another reporter in my office, a tiny American with the almond eyes and dark hair of her Lebanese parents, had a different experience of Moscow taxi-drivers. Drenched, freezing and furious, she appeared in the office one evening after waiting forty-five minutes for a car to stop for her. 'In the end I found a helpful traffic cop who forced a car to take me,' she said, with drips of water running out of her hair and into her eyes. 'Once I was in the car, I asked the driver why he hadn't stopped for me himself. He was surprised when he heard my voice and realized I was a foreigner. "I'd have stopped if I'd known you were American," he said. "But I thought you were a black." '

Complacent racism had ripped the Soviet Union to shreds. There was no complacency left, but that didn't mean there was any less racism. Now that almost all the union republics, and a good many autonomous areas too, had declared themselves independent, Russians were trapped, shut out of places they had always thought of as their own, and claustrophobic.

'I used to always go to resorts in the Caucasus for my holidays,' Yevgeniya reminisced. 'It was so beautiful, so romantic . . . there was always snow on the mountaintops, and sunlight, and the air was the purest in the world . . . There were roses and pomegranates growing in the valley, and vineyards everywhere. Pushkin wrote poetry there. They had meat and brandy and flat bread and herbs and spices . . . springs and fountains and courtyards . . . daggers and horsemen. It was our history, our memories, and now it's lost to us. Now it's just abroad.

'And now what do we have instead? Every black nationality from the mountains has crawled into Moscow to rip us off and bring their guns and hoodlum ways to torment us at home. Gorillas. Monkeys. Invading us from their independentistans, freeloading in our streets, shooting innocent old ladies, holding us all to ransom.'

It wasn't just Yevgeniya who felt this way. Her views were those of any moderate, well-educated intellectual. If things went wrong for you in the Moscow of 1991, no one found it offensive if you blamed someone further down the racial hierarchy, kicked a darky scapegoat.

'Why don't these blacks go back to their bloody stans and stay there?' Marina, our office cook, asked petulantly as she flounced round the Central Market, run by Caucasians, where fixed state prices did not apply and so the tables were groaning with expensive, exotic, scented food. The soft-voiced salesmen with their singsong accents and gentle eyelashes could do no right in her eyes. It was their fault prices were high. It was their fault the newer, freer, economy had brought real money, but also violent crime, into streets that were once so safe you could walk around all night without fear. Even her dyed-blonde virtue was not safe. 'They rip you off, then they make passes at you. They have enormous . . . *appetites*,' she added primly, eyes downcast.

The Chechens were the worst of all. Their name was never invoked without a shiver, an unspoken hint of nameless violence and dread. When Yevgeniya and I got lost one day on the way to an exhibition, I was about to ask a passer-by the way. 'He won't know, he's black. Probably a Chechen,' Yevgeniya said, tweaking me. I drew my coat tighter around me, shutting out the man. We passed on over the potholes.

In September 1991, Chechen nationalists took over their ethnic homeland and threw out the old Soviet leader, Doku Zavgayev. An air force general, a Chechen called Dzhokhar Dudayev, was elected president in October. Chechens danced their wild dances on dark Freedom Square. Bodyguards in fedoras fired Kalashnikovs by bonfires. Dudayev's pointy features smiled enigmatically from every television screen. There was a whiff of sulphur in the air as he declared Chechnya independent. Yeltsin's deputy president, Alexander Rutskoi, sent troops to Grozny to restore order on the last Soviet October Revolution holiday. Dudayev's men shut them up at Khankala airport outside Grozny, and politely sent them home after the weekend. Rutskoi was disgraced.

No one in the Kremlin, busy with the end-game of the power struggle between the departing Gorbachev and the ascendant Yeltsin, did anything further to stop him. Yevgeniya fretted about the fate of the 400,000 ethnic Russians in Chechnya, nearly half the population of just over a million people, now under the sway of the wild darkies. The Chechen act of David-and-Goliath defiance was the final, humiliating proof that Russia's old leadership of the

Soviet Union had collapsed and Russian greatness had imploded. It was also the first symbolic defeat for Yeltsin's new Russia.

'Oh, those Chechens!' Andrei said with a mocking smile, as we sat in the office on another night shift, watching the dances and the bonfires again. 'Who but the Chechens could take on the mighty Soviet army, and win?'

# THREE

But Yevgeniya had better things to think about than Chechens, most of the time. The Soviet Union was ending and her hero Boris Yeltsin was about to come to power. She was out on the streets most afternoons with the rest of the middle-aged Moscow intelligentsia, demonstrating for the democrats, sneering at the hapless Communists who still loitered damply on street corners, clinging to their red flags.

What had Boris Yeltsin brought back to life? He had reunited words and meaning after the Soviet years of empty phrases. People were saying what they meant at Yevgeniya's demonstrations, eloquently analysing what had gone wrong in their lives before Yeltsin, lamenting the theft of seventy years of their history by Soviet rulers, scoffing at Gorbachev's failings. Over the road, the bewildered Communists were still mouthing: 'Where is our bright future?', hissing 'provocateurs' at anyone who laughed at them, or bad-mouthing the 'decaying West', waving their dusty red flags. No one listened to their sad nonsense. Everywhere else, people were drunk on truth.

In that time of timeless euphoria, everything suddenly seemed possible. The 50,000 people who had successfully defended the White House parliament building with Yeltsin from an attempted Communist coup in August had given Russians back their self-respect. After a lifetime of grovelling to anyone more powerful in the Soviet hierarchy of deference, they had achieved something dramatic for themselves, with one act of defiance. No one knew that autumn what the consequences would be, but in the weeks immediately after the coup failed – as Yeltsin humiliated Gorbachev and scotched his old rival's hopes of trying to go on working with the Communists – ordinary people felt the effect of this surge of collective self-confidence, in their own lives, in immediate and surprising ways.

For Tanya Ustinova, a darkly beautiful woman in her mid-

thirties, who spoke slow, elegant, thoughtful English in a melli-
fluous voice, what it might all mean was the end of sexual worries
for her compatriots. Tanya was generous and kind and open-
minded. Working with foreigners had taught her an openness
about sex which was still unusual in a buttoned-up country where
physical relationships were little discussed. There were scarcely any
words, bar the brutally scatological which women were in any case
not supposed to know, to discuss them in. It was only a couple of
years since a Soviet woman had announced crossly, on a talk show
broadcast in the United States: 'There is no sex in the Soviet
Union!' But Tanya and her husband wanted their fifteen-year-old
daughter Olya to understand the adult world of sexual relationships; they had got hold of English-language books explaining to
adolescents the changes their bodies undergo, and they were
reading them to her. 'When we started, we realized we had never
known any words for these things ourselves,' she said wonderingly.
'I still wouldn't know how to talk about sex in Russian.' The
question of how Russian men and women related to each other
sexually was much on her mind, and now here was an answer.

'Men here have always felt powerless, humiliated, impotent,'
she said thoughtfully. 'It's natural. How could they feel powerful,
how could they expect even their wives to respect them, after all?
They were always having to scurry round, obeying people, agreeing
to things they didn't want, queuing up. But now everything's
changed. You can see it in the way people walk and talk since the
August events. Men are becoming surer of themselves. Even . . .'
she paused, 'sexually.' Suddenly she smiled the radiant smile that
had men from all over Moscow falling at her feet, and raised her
palms in happy acceptance. 'So you see, these political changes
must be good for us women!'

For Vitya Korotayev, the photographer with whom I often went
to demonstrations, different kinds of freedom had opened up. Out
on the street, where the once-strict police had more or less given
up patrolling the endless little *mitingi* of the democrats and
Communists, we could suddenly do what we liked. We would
perch on pompous statues, jaywalk across main roads and take
short cuts in the car down potholed pavements. Red lights meant

nothing to us. We lit up cigarettes under No Smoking signs and blew smoke in the faces of grumpy guards and grannies. One night, skidding down the pavement between the pedestrians, our head-lights lit up an obstinate elderly man who turned and stared back down the beam at us for a long moment of confrontation. His rabbity teeth and eyeballs gleamed. Then he hunched up tighter and shuffled off again, his feet in their Communist grey slip-on shoes coming down painstakingly one after the other. We crawled along behind him. In the smoky fug of the car, Vitya and his son Dima nudged each other gleefully and laughed at the old man's stubborn refusal to join in the festival of anarchic freedom that had taken over Moscow. 'He's the kind of guy who goes to *mitingi!*' Vitya chortled.

The euphoria lasted through the crisp autumn days of October. But then the long season with no name set in, the time of mists and miseries that linger on endlessly before the sharp frosts and snows and blue skies of a real Russian winter. It was only when the *slyakot'* began, the slimy sleet that seeped inside your boots, the grey wind in your soul, when it was dark on the street at nine in the morning and three in the afternoon and you never saw the sun in the dimness of noon, that the nauseous hangover began too, the nightmare fears of an unknowable future.

Because, after all, the world was about to end. Everyone except the most determined of middle-aged demonstrators was scared of the void opening up ahead, when the inevitable finally happened, when the Soviet Union vanished and history came whistling into people's ears. Gorbachev kept vainly calling meetings of the leaders of the Soviet republics at dachas outside Moscow, hoping to make them agree on a new union; but hardly any of them showed up, and those who did could not agree on anything out in the black countryside, surrounded by white, whispering birch trees. The end was only a question of time. When he appeared on television, exhausted, defeated, wisps of hair trailing, stumbling over his words, people would mimic his hick southern accent and pull disgusted faces. There was no pity, no forgiveness, and no food in the shops.

Some time soon we would be living in Yeltsin's Russia. We all wanted it to work. We all wanted the truth to come back into Soviet life. We mockingly called everything that was Soviet, everything untrue and bureaucratic, *savok* or spade, to show how ugly and artificial it was, how useless in the modern world. Yeltsin astride his tank, resisting the August coup, had become an icon to ward off the darkness closing in. This real honest-to-God man, with a forthright wit that pleased the masses, would make things right. At least, everyone hoped so. But the waiting, and the worrying, wore people down. And would the future get any better?

'What will happen . . .?' Nadya Asanova asked repeatedly, in a little-girl voice, tweaking at the white lace napkins with which she draped the lamps in the sitting-room of her poky flat which cast gentle light over the hard spines of her books in their glass cases. She slept on the sofa here, so her teenage son Danya could have the bedroom and decorate it with punk rock posters. She was a senior lecturer at Patrice Lumumba Friendship University for Third World students. She loved classical music. She was just back from a year's teaching in India, sophisticated, serious, and frightened.

Once the Soviet Union went and Yeltsin was really in charge, he was going to free prices. A 'Kamikaze' government of radical reformers was already waiting in the wings to swoop on the state economy, destroy it and themselves, and leave the way open for capitalism. It was headed by the fat young intellectual Yegor Gaidar, the grandson of Arkady Gaidar, who had been a writer of children's fairy stories. That was the only thing people knew about the future: the subsidies, the symbolic rents and taxes that had always been pegged at the same price would go up, though wages might not. Prices for all but basic foods had already shot through the roof under Gorbachev, but no one could imagine a world in which bread, still the staple of life in Russia, still praised in every numbered restaurant and bread shop with the twee capital-letter slogan 'Bread Is Our Wealth!', did not cost 27 copecks a loaf.

Nadya was hoarding food, just in case. She kept a box with flour and oil and greyish pasta and sugar and tea under her kitchen table. Like everyone else, she talked with a tremble in her voice and a tear in her eye about the new year, when *Golod i Kholod* – Famine and Freezing – would stalk the vanished Fatherland.

'What will happen if you start having to pay for heating and electricity, and someone in your building won't pay? Will they cut off everyone's power anyway and plunge the people that pay into darkness too?' she wondered. Everyone paid the same tiny fee for municipal services in the Soviet Union; flats were heated courtesy of the town council, which switched on the heating for everyone one day in the autumn, in a blast of hot air, and switched it off again some time in the late spring; there was no need for gas or electricity meters. But Nadya only shook her head at the idea meters would be installed. Too expensive. Too much trouble. They wouldn't bother with that kind of finesse if it would be easier just to let people suffer.

Nadya was so polite that she hesitated for months before calling me '*ty*', the friendly way of saying 'you'; she introduced me to her other friends as 'an acquaintance'; yet she would come to my flat and fling herself on foreign cheeses with a starved, anorexic look, half-apologizing through the crumbs: 'It's a long time since I've been able to eat cheese like this.

'I stood in a queue for sausage yesterday, and ordinary sausage cost 15 roubles a stick! The queue went right down the street!' she would lament, legs crossed neatly, fingers plucking. 'But Moscow sausage cost 150 roubles a stick! So there was hardly any queue for it. I was wondering whether I had enough time to queue all morning, or enough money for Moscow sausage, when a little old lady in the long queue saw me. "Get in the queue with me," she said. "The other queue's shorter, but ours has more fellow-feeling."'

There was only one conversation on the street, and it always began in panicky indignation: 'I was standing in a queue for sausage yesterday, and it cost . . .' I would walk from my hotel on former Karl Marx Street, now renamed Hunter's Row, up former Gorky Street, now renamed Tverskaya, listening to the grey-faced shoppers with empty bags. 'What does your milk (or butter, or tinned sardines) cost?' old ladies would ask, when they happened upon something they thought might be edible. But their faces would pucker in despair when they heard the answer. There were shouted arguments. Shop assistants and customers yelled at each other over the ghostly shelves, faces twisted with hatred. Doors slammed, and the biting wind blew.

I came to know all the words for Russian rage, a darker and more subtle palette of negative emotion – touchiness, spleen, bile, spite and injured ego – than exists in English. You weren't just angry or indignant in 1991 Russian: you were offended, or insulted, or injured by the price rises; or you were being hateful, or making a mockery of people, or tormenting them, or killing them, by selling at the new prices.

On one November day, I saw a successful shopper: a shabby middle-aged man emerging from a shop on Tverskaya with a paper parcel. He promptly unwrapped it to reveal a dozen *sosiski*, colourless frankfurter-style sausages, in individual cellophane tubes. With a look of ferocity, he wrenched the wrapping off the first one and stuffed it into his face, without boiling it, without mustard, without horseradish, without bread, swallowing without chewing. He watched me watch, meeting my eye, hating me, daring me to look disgusted.

Larisa Karpova was building herself a dacha in the countryside, or trying to. But every time I phoned her to find out how it was going, the answer was badly. 'I was granted that plot of land two years ago to build my construction of the century on. I got quite a long way at first, too,' she sighed into the receiver. 'But now they're like vultures out there in the dacha territories. Robbers, cut-throats, murderers. They'll strip any plot bare in five minutes flat. Last month, a friend finally managed to get hold of some roofing felt for me. We'd been looking for months. It was a nightmare. So we borrowed a car, took the felt out to the dacha, and what did we find? Someone had stolen all the roof timbers! But now I don't care that I can't find a door for the stove – because the stove has gone. And what does it matter that there aren't any bath tiles, when the bath was nicked in September?'

There was violent crime on the streets already, and there would be more. Society would splinter into rich and poor. The mafia would take over. Andrei bought me a *ballonchik*, a canister of Mace, to keep in my bag in case I was mugged on my way home. Everyone was buying them. You listened for hurrying footsteps behind you. You clutched your *ballonchik* in your hand until it got sticky with fear.

People's most routine phone calls, even work calls made to ministries and government departments, began with hostility and ended in venomous insults and receivers being slammed down. Inflation was eating away at the little nest-eggs people had built up over the years. The respectable were losing their security. Nuclear scientists were reported to be defecting to North Korea. 'The papers used to be full of satire and humour. But there are no jokes any more, have you noticed?' Andrei asked one day, looking up from his desk.

Nadya began divorce proceedings when she came back from India. When I told her I was going to get married, she said, rather wistfully: 'I don't know a single person in Moscow who would have the courage to marry. We're not up to that now. We're too busy surviving.'

But Nadya was the only Russian I knew who could also laugh a little at her country's panic, at the unfolding melodrama of collapse, at the hysteria and exaggeration. 'Have you actually seen people getting thinner?' she asked one day. 'I haven't. I go out to do my shopping on Saturday mornings, and I smell frying everywhere. Then I stand in the queue for my stick of sausage, and everyone's panicking about whether they'll ever see sausage again, so they buy five sticks instead of one, just in case. But they don't store that sausage up, they fry it and eat the lot. People are turning into calorie addicts. When things turn violent, it won't be because there are little old ladies starving on their sofas. They'll stay inside and die quietly. It will be the calorie addicts, the big violent men with red faces and thick muscles, who'll get scared their sausage supplies will run out, who'll pick up their guns and go out to kill for more meat.'

Even people who weren't in mourning for the banned Communist Party and the Soviet political system were grieving for the sunlit certainties of the past. Outside metro stations, under stinging flakes of snow, sad old men in brass bands wrapped themselves in scarves and blew out lugubrious anthems into the dark afternoons. You could hear snatches of the laments of tubas and horns from the street, in traffic jams, through the pipes in your apartment.

It was the evening rush hour at Kropotkinskaya metro, whose underground walls gleamed with precious marble from the Tsarist cathedral which had once stood nearby. Wafts of white steam rose under the spotlights from the open-air swimming pool, built on the vanished cathedral's site in the 1950s, and tiny heads bobbed on the dirty water whenever the mist cleared. By the metro entrance, in a little park of freezing mud and naked trees, a ramshackle kiosk was selling hot chocolate for three roubles a cup. But the raggedy crowd in big boots, pouring into the metro mouth, had no time or money for chocolate. It was four o'clock, and already too dark to make out anything but the silhouettes of the bandsmen as the melancholy music began. I sighed, and blew a puff of white breath onto freezing fingers.

Suddenly – somewhere between the steam from my cup of chocolate, and the steam from the pool, and the gusts of hot air from the banging metro doors – the band was swept by a wild mood of skittish gaiety. It changed from minor to major and speeded up. As the street lights came on, the disconsolate stream of shoppers wavered, and pricked up their ears, and stopped to listen. Before I knew it, strangers had clutched other dumpy strangers to themselves and were waltzing, strange, despairing dances, with their forgotten shopping bags bouncing alongside. I watched for a few entranced moments, then left them at their private wake under the trees, a hectic pink tinging their pinched faces, snatching at happiness.

*

Yeltsin's democrats did not know how to fill the void of the present any better than Gorbachev. They did not know how to stop the fear clutching people by the throat, or how to raise popular hopes for the future. While Gorbachev was there, they still had the automatic trust of the majority. They were still the plucky under-dogs snarling at the Soviet leadership, which everyone knew lied and cheated. But the time would soon come when they would be the only government, and when ordinary people would look at them with the same traditional suspicion and contempt that Soviet citizens had always reserved for their bosses. So they began, hurriedly, to experiment.

Until the coup, the masses had been buoyed up through decades of Soviet rule by hammers, sickles, red flags and bossy slogans. Now Yeltsin had made these politically unacceptable. Yeltsin's electorate, who were against red flags, had liked it when he got rid of some Communist street names, replacing them with their pre-revolutionary alternatives. They had liked it when he raised the old Russian tricolour. But now they needed more morale boosters. So the Russian president's men started casting round for a new kind of politically acceptable pageantry, which would reassure Russians that their country had always been great without referring to the Soviet Union.

The test day that was coming up for them was 7 November, seventy-fourth anniversary of the 1917 Bolshevik Revolution. How should Yeltsin's Russia commemorate it now the Soviet Communist Party had been outlawed and the Soviet state was falling apart? The October Revolution, celebrated on 7 November because the Tsarist calendar had been two weeks behind Western Europe, had been the high day of Soviet Communism for seven decades. It was impossible just to ignore it, and impossible to honour it.

While Chechens routed the Russian forces in Grozny, embarrassing Yeltsin's government which had sent troops down there, the democratic Mayor of Leningrad (a city whose Soviet slogan had been 'Cradle of the Revolution!') was busy cooking up a grand hotchpotch of anti-Soviet symbolism in honour of the great day. Anatoly Sobchak called a huge municipal party, with balloons and bands and speeches on Palace Square, in front of the green Hermitage museum which had once been the Tsars' Winter Palace. The city had just got back its old name, St Petersburg. As star attraction, Sobchak invited the man who would become Tsar if the monarchy were restored, Grand Duke Vladimir Kirillovich Romanov, to pay his first visit to the former Russian imperial capital.

In case anyone was unimpressed by this venture into historical fantasy, Sobchak also asked along Pik Botha, the big, shambling, glad-handing, canny foreign minister of minority-ruled South Africa, the 'racist republic', whose whites-first ideology had made it the enemy of Soviet Moscow for decades.

It was a new festival of the absurd for this bizarre metropolis, dreamed up by Peter the Great three centuries ago as Russia's window on the West, its classical palaces designed by Italians, mocked by Dostoevsky as the 'most abstract and intentional of cities', with its tubercular air, salt fogs, fountains, rivers, canals, floods, glamour, decay and poisonous water.

Vladimir Kirillovich, second cousin a few times removed of the last Tsar, Nicholas II, was an elderly man with splendid eyebrows, a straight back, and the pure Russian of another age. He was accompanied by his large, jolly, dark-complexioned wife, Princess Leonida Bagrationi, whom he would not have been allowed to marry if he had ever really been the Tsar, because her blood was not royal enough.

No one knew what to make of the visitors. There was the odd moment of uneasy awe. When Vladimir Kirillovich held a press conference, spotty child journalists in anoraks, with the nasal, blasé, proletarian drawl and swallowed syllables of the new world, were suddenly at a loss as to what to call him. Some tried simply his name and patronymic, Vladimir Kirillovich (Vl'diiim'r K'riiill'ich!), the usual polite if exclamatory way of addressing a respected adult; but, after a few confused questions, the princely title *Vashe Vysochestvo* (Your Highness) began to gain a hesitant hold. It was almost *Vashe Velichestvo* (Your Majesty), but not quite. But mostly Vladimir Kirillovich and his entourage of fine-boned, Parisian aristocrats – with their haute couture clothes, glamorous mink coats and Russian names – attracted only bewilderment, or gentle mockery. 'Can you imagine any of them living here now, in little Soviet flats, taking out the rubbish bags at night?' whispered my friend Kostya Trifonov, watching in amazement as the foreign Russians filed past him.

And the only question the not-Tsar was asked, phrased many different ways, was: 'Why are you here?' – 'Why are you here now?' 'Why are you here on 7 November?' 'Are you here for a *prazdnik* [holiday] or a *panikhida* [memorial service]?' He had not come to take back the throne, Vladimir Kirillovich answered repeatedly, ramrod straight, without a smile; he just wanted to show his country he was ready to be of service.

Pik Botha had no fewer problems finding a common language with his Russian hosts. When he flitted in for a little chat with officials in the city hall, his words of encouragement for a future of freedom and friendship with Pretoria were translated by an earnest woman with a dyed brown perm who could not make head or tail of his clipped South African accent. When Botha said breezily: 'There'll be some shouting about economic reform; don't let it put you off,' she translated 'shouting' as 'shooting'. There was a respectful silence as officials and journalists bent their heads and scribbled down his prediction of bloodshed in the streets, which coincided perfectly, if accidentally, with their own gloomy expectations for the future.

Sobchak pulled out all the stops for the 'royals'. There was a solemn mass in St Isaac's Cathedral, all frost, stars, candlelight, incense and a Soviet system of passes monitored by the usual policemen. For purely decorative reasons, some young men from southern Russia wearing strangely archaic uniforms were also allowed to stand at the gates. They called themselves Cossacks, like the long-vanished Tsars' crack troops. Their ancestors might or might not have been the real thing, but these were Soviet youths, members of neo-Cossack 'social organizations' formed in a revival not more than a year old. There was a mock-imperial ball in a crumbling palace, where young men with the kind of sharp urban faces that would look most at home above black leather jackets put on frogging and powdered wigs and acted as surly footmen, slipping bottles of erzatz Soviet *shampanskoye* out of the window to their friends on the pavement in full view of the guests.

'Ah . . . They so wanted it to be different this time, but it panned out Soviet-style after all,' Valery Karpov, the scientist whose family I was staying with, said with a malicious little grin. We were on the staircase of an apartment block in Dostoevsky's old district, discussing the day's events over a cigarette. He stubbed the butt out in the communal ashtray, a sardine tin attached to one iron

banister with knotted wire, and we went back inside the cramped
flat to the smell of frying pancakes. The Tsar seemed a long way
away from this urban home: the kitchen had cheerful orange
curtains, pipes gurgled comfortingly behind cupboards, and the
ration coupons – for meat, vodka, and wine – were kept in a saucer
by the teapot. 'You're not taking this Tsarist business seriously, are
you?' Valery asked with a twinkle as he, his wife Larisa and I
perched on stools for midnight tea. I shook my head, not being
very impressed with Sobchak's tacky pastiche of the past. 'It's hard
to know how gullible foreigners are,' Valery went on. 'This is all
just showing off for the outside world, you know. I don't think
anyone except journalists is taking any notice of this Kirill,
Vladimir, whatsisname, Vladimir Kirill'ich. Everyone else is too
worried about making sure they've got enough food.'

Everyone, that is, but one trusting little old lady who served tea
at the House of Scientists, a dark former palace on the Neva
embankment, down the road from the Hermitage. The house had
once belonged to Vladimir Kirillovich's family of Grand Dukes.
While I went to talk to a gathering of Communists, who had been
exiled to a windswept street at the edge of town and were hissing
and snarling under their red flags ('Tsar? What Tsar? It's a
provocation!'), a friend dropped in for coffee and konyak in the
scientists' café. The tea-lady was looking out of the window at the
gleaming spire of the Peter and Paul Fortress on the other side of
the river. There was no heating in the building. 'Will the heating
be repaired soon?' my friend asked. The little old lady only
shrugged, and looked proudly down at a newspaper cutting, with
Vladimir Kirillovich's photograph, which she had put on the
counter.

'Who can say? Now he's back, it will all depend on the Master,'
she answered.

*

Suddenly, Yeltsin decided the waiting was over, the cat-and-mouse
games with Gorbachev and the pantomimes from the past. It was
time for the future. He met the presidents of the other two Slav
states, Ukraine and Belarus, on 8 December, at a hunting lodge in

Belovezhskaya Pushcha, near Brest. The three men decided their countries would not sign any more Soviet treaties but would create their own little commonwealth instead. The other republican leaders started clamouring to join Yeltsin's commonwealth, and were allowed in.

The Soviet Union ended almost at once, in an undignified slither. Gorbachev resigned on television on 25 December, to mournful music and pictures of birch trees in the snow. Yeltsin had him kicked out of his Kremlin office, and the red flag came down from over the ramparts before the due time of midnight on New Year's Eve. Rumour had it that it was stolen.

'It's so strange! We don't even know what our country's called,' Natasha Karpova, the twenty-year-old student daughter of my friends in St Petersburg, said down the phone with devastating understatement and a breathless laugh. But the Russian Soviet Federated Socialist Republic quickly got a new official post-Soviet name: the Russian Federation, or simply Russia. It already had two unofficial names: Absurdistan, and Wonderland.

What Yeltsin started to do to the economy after that was even more painful than what had gone before. Prices went up on 2 January, and up, and up, and up. Inflation in 1992 hit 2,500 per cent. The shops were never empty any more, but only the rich could afford to buy what was in them. Old ladies with genteel accents were begging on the street.

Only Robert Eksuzyan, the chief translator in my office, was briefly happy on 2 January. He came in for his evening shift with his face pink from windburn, having spent the day trudging round the shops in the first real snow of winter inspecting the new goods on offer at new prices. 'There are five different kinds of sausage in the shop nearest my flat! Butter! Cheese!' he said with profound satisfaction. 'There are things to buy, and I have a good salary, and I can afford them!' All the other Russians in the room looked disgusted by his beaming smile and the gleam behind his glasses. He was shushed for heartlessness. 'Think of the hungry pensioners,' people said, and Robert, who was good-hearted and also in his fifties, went silent, hung up his coat, and began to look a little ashamed.

After a month or two, when the prices carried on rising, Robert got as angry as everyone else about the cost of living. He spent his days raging about Yeltsin bringing humankind low, dragging his people's faces in the mud, about the shock reform which the West liked so much but was humiliating and dispossessing his people. New banknotes were printed, first in hundreds of roubles, then thousands, then five thousands and ten thousands. The rouble's value dropped every week, from 27 to the dollar during the August coup to 500 to the dollar in 1992. Who was to blame? people started asking, the classic, if paranoid, question of Soviet political analysis. Who were the salesmen on the streets? Caucasians, black bums, criminals.

The Central Market shut as the Soviet Union collapsed. The Azeri traders who ran it, bringing up exotic watermelons and hot-weather fruit from their southern republic, were shunted with their stalls of pomegranates and pickled garlic on to the pavement nearby. You could hear the lion roar next door at the circus as you haggled over a bag of dates.

People said there was a mafia war on, and the Chechens were taking over Moscow. When their mafias took you on, they didn't mess about. All your people died with knives in their backs. But no one was very sympathetic to the Azeris, who were making money out of Russians. The Azeri traders, famous as the cowards of the Caucasus in the Soviet hierarchy of prejudices, didn't fight back, just quietly sat out the storm. And, sure enough, the Chechens who had locked the doors vanished again and the merry Azeris moved back in.

I loved the cheerful Azeri bustle of the Central Market.

Girl! Young man! Don't you want to buy my fine juicy oranges? Go on, taste a bit. Isn't that delicious? They're fresh, they're straight from the south. Look at them, taste how sweet they are. Young man! Walnuts! Dates! Apricots! Coriander? Saffron? Cumin! Girl, just stop and look at this sturgeon. You've never seen a sturgeon like it. Look at that firm flesh. Pickled garlic! Pickled apples! Sausage! Live crab! Try these almonds. Try these almonds, my beauty. Oh, what white teeth, oh what pink cheeks, oh what lovely blonde hair, my pretty blondie, wouldn't you like a loaf of fresh-baked French bread? Georgian bread! Lavash, lavash! Oh madam, oh missie, young lady, for the love of God spare a copeck or two, God be with you, God bless you. Suckling pig slaughtered this morning? Honeycomb? Cheese fresh from the farm! Young MAN! Buy the girl some red roses! Still full of mountain dew! Plucked from the snow! A fine bottle of Azerbaijani champagne! The best vodka! Ah – a foreign GENTLEMAN! Caviar! The freshest blackest black caviar from the Caspian Sea! At prices you wouldn't believe! Buy mine! Buy mine! Buy mine!

But I could understand why markets were becoming the focus for my Russian friends' hostility, with all their economic and emotional worries. When I saw Marina the cook there, she was stalking disdainfully up and down the aisles, tweaking at herbs and wrinkling her nose over the pickled cabbage. 'Look at the dirt,' she muttered. 'Look at these prices!'

Grey daylight filtered through the grimy glass ceiling. Marina hung at my side, whispering that the Azeris would be bound to rip off a foreigner. I bought a honeycomb from two black-haired urchins in the sleet outside, gave alms to five elderly beggars, and accepted a package of what looked like pickled grass. '*Cherem-SHAH*! My dear, buy this delicious *cherem-SHAH*!' the billowing gipsyish lady in gold hoop ear-rings, bangles and a lurid red-and-orange tent dress had whispered enticingly. Marina shook her head in disbelief.

Another day, I went with Danya, Nadya's son, to the market's front lobby, where young brigands with black curls and gold teeth stared hopefully out over banks of dewy roses. 'Look at these prices,' Danya said, eyes fixed on the two policemen in a corner extracting large numbers of banknotes from an elderly trader. In a way, he was right; the prices were outrageous, but they were open to negotiation to anyone prepared to haggle with the traders.

'Let me buy you a present,' I said, looking at a cluster of brown pods hanging from strings at a flower stall. '*Chuch-KHE-la*! The sweetest from the south!' sang a happy trader, whipping out a grubby blade and slashing dramatically through the strings. I gave him three of the rubbery pods, a honey-and-grape-resin coating over a walnut centre. Danya held his sinewy *chuchkhela* fingers as if they would turn and grasp him by the throat.

It was the poached caviar from the Caspian Sea that annoyed him most. Danya had been poaching himself. It hurt his sixteen-year-old pride that someone else was making money out of it. He wriggled by my side while I tasted five different jam jars of glistening caviar with a dirty teaspoon, asked bright questions about how Caspian Sea sturgeon poachers worked, haggled over the price and demanded the muddy teenage traders throw in a free bottle of Azeri champagne. 'You drive a real hard bargain, missie,' one of them said, jostling the others out of the way to relieve me of a vast sum of money. 'Just like a real Soviet girl.'

He smiled, hissing his 's' sounds and smiling brilliantly.

'Dirty little bastard,' I heard, in a vengeful whisper, from beside me.

When the weather at last began to get warmer, Russians reluctantly began to join the Caucasians selling on the street. The streets were suddenly lined with women with set faces, grudgingly holding out single plastic boots, old anoraks, Thermos flasks, sausage and flowers. The impromptu market – known as a *tolk-uchka*, or scrum – stretched for miles around where I lived, down Tverskaya almost all the way to the Kremlin and back into dozens of streets to left and right. In the long evenings, men in quilted jackets swept up mounds of debris and set fire to them. Against the flames and stinging smoke and sunsets lingering on golden Kremlin roofs, I could imagine myself in a medieval market town.

A few of the women – the kind who only a few months ago would have dressed me down loudly for not wearing a hat on the street – now called out '*Devushka!*' ('Girl!'), with a perky grin, to attract my attention to their salt fish or bottles of cut-price vodka. But most were quiet, sullen, and deeply humiliated by the turn of fate which had forced them on the street and into an activity – selling for personal profit – which their Soviet upbringing had taught them was the crime of speculation. No one knew what constituted an acceptable profit margin. Some sold with virtually no mark-up, wasting their own time. Others demanded such high prices it made me laugh and walk away. But every sale and every commercial transaction was marked by the anxious question, the search for reassurance that no crime was being committed: is that *normalno*?

As it turned out, plenty of crimes were committed at markets. People were marking out their territory. They were nervous, aggressive, uncertain. Russians and Caucasians began settling scores, with fists and then knives. When three Russian taxi-drivers were murdered in April 1992 in the Siberian town of Novosibirsk, suspicion fell on 'black' businessmen from Ingushetia, the statelet next to Chechnya, who worked in a local cooperative firm. Most Russians were anyway deeply suspicious of the new cooperatives – the first officially sanctioned commercial enterprises, which had been allowed to operate since 1988 – and were convinced that anyone connected to a cooperative was also in the criminal underworld. At the third victim's funeral party, the remaining taxi drivers of Novosibirsk worked themselves up into a fury over the vodka, then stormed off to destroy the central market, which was also run by 'blacks' (though not from Ingushetia). The police prevented them from smashing up other, smaller, markets in town; but nothing could stop the taxis crawling threateningly through the streets all afternoon, headlights on, horns blaring. Police guards were maintained for days afterwards on hotels, the central restaurant and the airport, to protect the Caucasian traders who were using them on selling trips.

Russian taxi-drivers went on the rampage again in Bryansk, 250 miles south-west of Moscow, in July. They beat up the 'black' Armenian traders who turned up at the bus station with goods to sell at the market. The Armenians got out their knives, one Russian man ended up in hospital with stab wounds, and several people were arrested. The taxi-drivers took their revenge the next day by destroying Bryansk central market, breaking up stalls and kiosks and beating up the Armenians. While the police were separating the two sides, fighting broke out in a tunnel near the market and another Russian driver was stabbed by an Armenian stallholder. Outraged, 500 taxi-drivers signed a petition demanding that Bryansk be 'purged' of the southerners within two days. A local interior ministry official, Vasily Fesunov, was quoted by Tass news agency as saying Bryansk had always been a hospitable city and had no right to clear out the traders. 'This outburst of race hate is the first of its kind here,' he said. 'But if no immediate action is taken it could prove to be the shape of things to come.'

Despite the fears of a future of poverty and humiliation, despite all the denunciations, despite taking out their terrors on the blacks, who in Moscow was actually starving? Even before the prices were freed, even when there were still queues and copecks and people agonizing about *Golod i Kholod*, you still couldn't go to anyone's flat without a huge, greasy, fattening meal being whisked out and placed before you. Fried potatoes, fried meat, sour cream, pickled cabbage, beetroot, bread, jam with your tea, cake, and fried pancakes was the kind of meal people would tuck into several times a day and not even think about it. The better you got to know people, the easier it was to see they weren't hungry at all.

'Do you know the saying: the shops are empty but the fridges are full?' people who were beginning to become friends would ask, with a wicked smile, when you interrogated them about where they had found some delicious morsel. Although there wasn't much in Soviet shops, everyone had some kind of access to some easy supply of food. Everyone had an uncle in the Party or an aunt who worked in a sausage shop. Perks and privileges and little food parcels constantly being exchanged were the glue holding Soviet life together.

But it didn't stop people complaining with gusto. They weren't quite telling lies about how bad things were, but they pushed the truth to its outermost limits. No one thought that was wrong. It was just a cultural gap. There are two words in Russian which are both translated into English as 'lie': *lozh*, which means much the same as the English word, and *vranyo*, which is closer to the Irish blarney. Spinning a line, and exaggerating a bit to make your good story better or your bad story worse, is fully accepted in the Russian scheme of things. Everyone does it. Russians themselves are prudently sceptical about everything their compatriots tell them. *Vranyo* is almost an art form in Russia. It is only hapless foreign newcomers, who take every word seriously, who fall for it all.

Long after I had got used to his pet lines, I heard Robert reciting his woes to an old English friend, back in Moscow for a few days. He reeled out the whole speech, about Yeltsin bringing humankind low, dragging the Russian people's faces in the mud, about the shock reform which the West liked so much humiliating and dispossessing his people, how he stood in queues for hours for his sausage ... By then, I knew that the mercurial Robert would be as happy as a sandboy again in a few minutes; I knew he earned a fat salary; and I also knew that he did so little shopping himself that he was quite unable to remind me of the prices of basic foodstuffs whenever I was writing a story about price rises. My sympathy for his eloquently expressed fears of starvation had somewhat diminished.

As she was leaving, the friend drew me aside and said: 'Things are really bad. I've never seen Robert so low, so depressed. People really are hungry. It's terrible.' 'Oh, it's nothing,' I said heartlessly. 'That's just how he talks, but he's not getting any thinner, is he?'

Afterwards, when I found Robert chuckling over a cup of tea and a television comedy, I said reproachfully: 'What did you go worrying that poor woman for with all your horror stories? She went off all anxious about you, although I told her you were fine and fat and rich really. She'll be miserable for weeks now, thinking of you starving. You're quite shameless.'

Robert only giggled, though he did have the grace to look a little ashamed of himself. 'Ah, Missis Vanora, you are a hard woman, and you know me too well,' he said happily. 'The trouble is that you English are a dry people, and you take things too seriously. But WE are RUSSIANS, and we need more drama and excitement. You'll never be bored with us.'

'Even the trees are dying, and do you know why?' Yevgeniya asked. The radio was giving yet another report of Russian taxi-drivers destroying a Caucasian street market with chains and clubs, smashing expensive watermelons and black heads, the post-Soviet equivalent of Paki-bashing. She nodded approvingly, half-listening to the report as she spoke.

'Pollution?' I guessed. The air was black with the fumes of neglect: factories in the city centre, dirty petrol, cheap cigarettes, unwashed bodies, uncollected rubbish, drunk tramps, dead dogs. People dropped litter on the street, and no one picked it up. She shook her head. 'No, don't be naive,' she said. 'The trees are dying because of the bad vibes. Everyone's so full of fear and loathing they're emanating death rays. Nothing can live in this atmosphere.' She patted the radio, sighing. 'And the blacks are making vast profits out of our Russian misery. And things will only get worse.'

# FOUR

I didn't go to Chechnya at first; too many small wars broke out on new Russia's perimeter to give me time. These wars were the reason why Russians, if pressed, would say they were scared of the knife-wielding blacks in Moscow. They were right in saying that the blacks' new political leaders were making a chaotic mess of independence in their ethnic homelands. The places where my friends had once taken quiet Soviet seaside or mountain holidays were now angry, impoverished, violent countries where wild-eyed men with guns and gold teeth plotted coups, explosions, riot and revolution.

The Caucasus – the mountain range on Russia's southern border – was always in flames. There was war between Azeris and Armenians in Nagorno-Karabakh. Armenians were starving because the Azeris had cut off their power lines. Azerbaijan changed its president by coup every few months. There had been a putsch in Georgia as the Soviet Union collapsed; it was run by warlords with private armies, a war with separatists had already wrecked the mountain region of South Ossetia and another war was brewing with separatists in the seaside region of Abkhazia. On the northern slopes of the mountains, just inside Russia, trains couldn't go through Chechnya without getting robbed. West of Russia, there was war near the Romanian border between Moldovans and a Slavic minority. East of Russia, civil war was looming on the old Soviet–Afghan border between clans in Tajikistan.

You couldn't switch the television on without being confronted with grisly, incomprehensible footage of corpses, burning villages and tanks. The cameras lingered on severed limbs and charred children in a way that Western television stations would censor. Panicking women, draped in refugee rags, wept into the cameras, mouthing incoherent words of hatred and distress in the pidgin Russian of the south, or east, or west. The brief factoids which accompanied the bloody televised war coverage bristled with

baffling acronyms of parties and guerrilla forces, and place names
no one had ever heard of. They explained nothing. There was little
discussion of the real causes of the wars, of the many territorial
time-bombs Lenin and Stalin and their successors had left by
redrawing and redrawing the Soviet Union's internal borders, by
deporting whole nations to the gulag, or twinning them in single
administrative units with their traditional enemies. No one ever
suggested that any of the causes might be just, or even worth
discussing. There was a quiet assumption, never challenged, that
mindless violence was natural in these places, among these peoples.

So most Muscovites I knew turned off the news when the
bulletins got to the wars – if, that is, they were in the minority of
Russians that still watched the news at all. (Many others had
disgustedly given up following politics, and only watched escapist
television – pop videos, dubbed Mexican soap operas, or ultra-
violent American B-movies.) All the war pictures looked terrifying,
and they all looked alike.

One reason it was hard for Russians to tell the difference
between the wars was that even people who had been to the
Caucasus on half-remembered holidays had memories of them
which didn't include the local people. The Russian word for taking
a holiday, *otdykhat'*, translates directly as 'resting'. It has no
Western-style connotation of having adventures or making discoveries. So Soviet holidays were traditionally taken in *sanatoriyi*,
hypochondriacs' heavens where health treatments were a major
part of the attraction. Spa towns, mountain towns with pure air,
and seaside resorts were the most popular destinations. Most
people did nothing especially healthy when they got to their
*sanatoriyi*. A good many went on holiday for some serious eating,
drinking and flirting; others took holidays to get away from the
spouses and in-laws they lived with, in overcrowded apartments,
for the rest of the year. The resorts were packed all summer long
with Russians of various sizes and shapes taking the sun in their
underwear, striking up new friendships, and admiring the local
*priroda*, or beauties of nature. The young and energetic headed
into the wilds in groups, for the male-bonding diversions of
hunting, shooting, fishing and camping. But few Russian holiday-

makers made an effort to mingle with the natives, whose languages they did not speak and whose quaintly accented Russian they laughed at, or to find out what the places they flitted through so light-heartedly were really like. If the natives nurtured ancient grievances, the holidaymakers knew very little about them. Until the wars started, the blacks had been no more than local colour to Russians.

And Russians were unpleasantly surprised if they discovered that any of the blacks had been cheeky enough to hold up an unflattering mirror to them. Two Moscow journalist friends of mine were comparing notes on their lost childhood summers in Georgia, poking gentle fun at the wild macho Georgians as they went, and laughing even more at Georgia's Abkhazian minority for its language in which almost every word begins with the letter 'a' (*A-bomba! A-respublika!* And they collapsed into giggles again).

'Did you know that Georgians have a kind of generic nickname for Russians? They call you *shapka*s,' I said, meanly trying to burst their bubble. Even in the southern republics, where the cold is not intense, Russians spend their winters with their heads inside their big fur hats, or *shapka*s, trying to avoid putting down the earflaps tied over their heads which would be a sign they had been defeated by the frost. Failure to wear a *shapka* in appropriate weather calls down the wrath of every *babushka* on every passer-by. The *shapka* wreaks such destruction on the elaborate hairdos Russian women favour that a break of several minutes, for 'putting oneself in order', is held to be vital at every complicated disrobing. Large mirrors are available at every cloakroom for this purpose. Many Russian women, however, take the easier option and simply keep their *shapka*s on, even indoors, in offices and corridors, until the spring. Despite all the in-built problems, the *shapka* is an artefact held in almost religious awe, without which it is deemed impossible to survive a Russian winter. Georgians are among the Caucasian peoples who find this funny.

They paused. They were both visibly discomfited.

'What, *all* Russians?' said Andrei. '*Georgians?*'

'*Shapka*s?' said Lena. '*Us? They* call *us* names?'

She shook her head, they exchanged glances, and finally he

shrugged. They weren't really worried; but they were taken aback. Finally, Lena broke into an uneasy smile.

'I didn't know that. How rude of them!' she said lightly.

*

At first it was the sheer scary romance of the mountains that gripped me: snows and crags and grapes, pomegranates and panache, and the ancient drama of a region where Jason and the Argonauts had quested after the Golden Fleece. Coming from Russia, I sometimes also felt a stab of pride that I, one of the naive and gullible foreigners who had to be cosseted like a child when in Moscow, protected from crime and other kinds of post-Soviet reality, and reminded to wear a hat in the street, had made it to a part of the Russian mental map where 'here be dragons' was written everywhere in blood-red ink.

As I travelled more, I grew fascinated by the immense differences between the peoples of different 'black' nations, and the peoples of different areas and even different valleys and villages inside any one tiny Caucasian statelet. There was something appealing about this quarrelsome diversity, something manageably human about the scale of it, in contrast to the monotonous immensity of Russia proper, the endless birch trees, flat snow, and wooden houses – with three elaborately carved windows on each side – stretching across eleven time zones, from Poland to Japan. It became hard to take seriously the Moscow blanket designation of 'Person of Caucasian Nationality', with its suggestion of brute criminality and its colonial undertones of 'I find it hard to tell these people apart.'

And, once I had had a chance to see the south for myself, something else began to become clear. People down there really were living the nightmare of collapse that Russians had only been scared might come to them. In Russia, people always found last-minute, back-alley escape routes away from the disasters threatening them; in the Caucasus, in a flamboyant, comic-opera way that kept veering off into tragedy and terror, life had already become impossible by the time ordinary people started complaining about it. The ordinary citizens who became victims of the wars were trying to make sense of the absurd world of sudden death and dispossession that they had been flung into, often gallantly, but with little real knowledge or understanding. It was easy to feel sympathetic, even if many of them were gripped by passions and hatreds which seemed oddly out of sync with the end of the twentieth century, even if the foolishness of some of their causes made you exasperated.

These people were hunting down invisible enemies: chimeras, wisps of history, and myths from the past, instead of tackling the real cause of their rage – the poverty that gripped them and shook them by the scruff of the neck. The wars brought fanatics, fools, romantics, opportunistic politicians and shameless salesmen to the fore. The former sincerely believed that their traditional ethnic or political enemies must somehow be to blame for all their present woes, and wanted revenge. The latter group were determined to hold on to their influence by prolonging this tension. Like Sobchak in St Petersburg in November 1991, such politicians hoped that offering their voters a heady cocktail of familiar history, legend and prejudice – blaming their next-door-neighbour for everything – would divert the electors' attention from their inability to find answers to the problems of today. Distributors of humanitarian aid, black marketeers, gun-runners and drug dealers completed the picture, trading illegally between war zones, supplying some of the basic human needs which had earlier been supplied at a tenth of the cost, making themselves vast profits, and further firing up ethnic hatreds in the interests of their own bank accounts.

It was only later that another pattern underlying the wars began to emerge, and it was only with the start of war in Chechnya three years later that this pattern was fully revealed. In the chaos of new Russia, where government had splintered into a series of conflicting clans and interest groups and there was no longer any single overarching policy, there were quiet groups in the armed forces, government and security services who regretted the passing of the Soviet Union. Unlike ordinary Russians, watching in bewilderment and distress as their country was torn apart, these people were playing a role of their own in the wars of the south. They covertly supplied support and weapons, whichever warring side was most sympathetic to Russia, they strong-armed desperate local rulers into taking back Russian troops on their soil, and won back Russian control of most ex-Soviet economic assets outside new Russia's borders. In the three years between the Soviet collapse and the Chechen war, the new independence of most non-Russian republics slowly crumbled away. By 1994, the nationalist rulers who had come to power in 1991 had almost all fled their presidential palaces. Pro-Moscow leaders, often the old bosses of the Soviet era, came back in their place.

This Russian contribution to the wars of the south was something my friends in Moscow, except the journalists who went there, had no inkling of. They tended not to believe it if they heard it in conversation. It was natural enough: they had no reason to rethink the traditional Soviet perception that *nashi*, our boys in the army, were an honourable and straightforward caste, or that the blacks were naturally savage. At first, I was equally sceptical of the stories which could be heard on any losing side anywhere in the Caucasus, the accusations that phantom phalanxes of blond Russian tank-drivers, or Russian planes, were helping the other side win. But, gradually, the evidence began to mount up.

That came later. When Vitya Korotayev and I caught a plane to take us 1,200 miles south on 7 January 1992, Russia's old, and now restored, Christmas Day, all I wanted was a brief escape from the relentless gloom of Moscow's type of turmoil and a glimpse of a new world.

*

The driver who took me to the airport at dawn was not as pleased as he might have been at the extra public holiday as well as Soviet New Year, the day traditionally celebrated with fir trees, family gatherings and a red-caped Grandfather Frost. 'What will we do with it?' he asked, shrugging mournfully. 'We've never been taught what to do at Christmas. Our great-grandfathers knew, but they're all dead. I expect I'll just go home later and get drunk.'

I was beginning to feel impatient with all the lamentations. It was only a holiday, after all. The driver reminded me of a conversation I had once read in a Saki story. 'Are the Russians really such a gloomy people?' 'Gloom-loving, but not in the least gloomy. They merely take their sadness pleasurably, just as we are accused of taking our pleasures sadly.'

In the airport, we waited for a plane in a special Intourist lounge, Soviet apartheid for foreigners, where Western visitors were charged more for plane tickets but kept away from the heaving, sweating, parcel-wrapping throng in the ordinary departure lounge. It had a grimy café and a few padded seats. We didn't have any tickets – they had been impossible to find in town – and the ticket office was shut because it was a holiday. So we begged the 'head of the shift', a stout woman in a red hat behind a locked door, to find us seats on the planes because we were VIPs, foreign journalists. (Vitya, my guide in the art of Soviet air travel, counted as foreign because he worked for a foreign company.) In spite of the box of chocolates we gave her, and Vitya's compliments, she wasn't able to find tickets after hours of yelling down an intercom at unseen subordinates. Then the plane was cancelled.

We waited till evening for the next plane. Despite her promises of help, the head of the shift vanished without saying goodbye, locking her office door for the night. 'Don't worry,' Vitya whispered, peering out of the window into the slushy darkness as the plane landed and the crew got out. 'We'll get on this one. I know the pilot.' He sneaked out of an unlocked back door onto the tarmac, clapped the pilot on the back, and they smoked together in the snow next to the plane while it was being refuelled. I shut my eyes and tried not to think about it. Five minutes later, Vitya came back soaked, shivering but all smiles, with a piece of paper in his hand – our 'tickets'. 'He remembered me!' he said triumphantly. 'It cost quite a bit, but pilots have to survive too in these hard times.'

The pilots were Armenian, and kind-hearted. They were also very post-Soviet in their devil-may-care approach to safety rules. We put our heavy satellite phone in the aisle, blocking the emergency exits. There weren't enough seats, so we sat in the cockpit. Then the co-pilot took us off to the galley for a stand-up party with the air hostesses. We drank vodka and ate pistachios and Vitya gently quizzed them about what life was like now in Yerevan.

There was no heating, no light, no food. And there was the war in Karabakh. 'I don't know how many more winters like this we can take,' one of the air hostesses said quietly, in a damp haze, picking at the pistachios. But there were no histrionics either. 'I understand,' Vitya said. The co-pilot patted her shoulder.

We landed after midnight. Another passenger, a cosy middle-aged woman with an enormous handbag and an enormous nose, talked to me for the last part of the flight. She had been to Russia on the way to visit her son at Vilnius University in the Baltic republic of Lithuania. She was very proud of his having got a place there. She leaned forward, pulling a bagful of biscuits out of her bag to feed me, and whispered with a conspiratorial look: 'Lots of our Armenian children have always got places at good universities. But you don't see any Azeris at Vilnius University, or at Moscow University. Oh no. They're all thick (she tapped her head), and do you know why? Because they're Muslims. They think it's OK to marry their first cousins. Naturally it depletes the genetic fund. Naturally their children are half-witted. But they're all too stupid to understand, so it's only our Armenian children that are smart enough to get the scholarships.' For a moment, there was real malice in her laugh. 'Have another biscuit,' she added kindly.

The lights were on at Yerevan airport, but there were no phones and no taxis. Passengers who had pre-arranged lifts were swooped on by unshaven men in long dark coats, and taken off into the darkness. Finally, Vitya found us a pair of swarthy drivers, lurking on the edge of the pool of light by the airport door, waiting for someone who hadn't turned up. It was −25 degrees, and the air bit into your lungs. We drove off into the woods, dark trunks in the headlights, and the headlights were soon the only light anywhere. I began to remember Yevgeniya's scary stories about taxi passengers being murdered in dark forests. But Vitya kept up a constant flow of conversation and cigarettes, mentioning in passing that our satellite phone only worked if the subscriber paid the rental and so wasn't worth stealing, and that we didn't carry much money with us. Even if we were driving deeper and deeper into the darkness of the wild countryside, I decided to follow Vitya's lead and be calm.

'Hotel Ani . . .' the driver said with quiet triumph, and stopped in the thick blackness. It was only then that I realized we had been driving into Yerevan all along, through city streets unrecognizable without streetlights and the orange glow of civilization. The whole city was plunged into darkness.

There was no breakfast at the hotel. We walked through empty streets, past bare trees. The cold still bit into our lungs, and froze the wisps of hair outside my hat, but it was more bearable in the pale morning light. 'How do people live in this?' Vitya asked, but it was a rhetorical question. On the horizon, Mount Ararat gleamed in the sun.

Ararat, visible from every street corner and almost every window, is the Armenians' symbol of loss, the loss of an ancient kingdom which, more than two thousand years ago, was about ten times the size of modern Armenia. The biblical mountain where Noah's Ark landed lies in what was traditionally Armenian land. It fell to the Ottomans in the Russo-Turkish War of the 1870s, and was completely out of reach to Armenians throughout the Soviet period. What used to be Western Armenia, along with its two and a half million Armenians, became eastern Turkey. But its Armenians no longer live there. Their demands for autonomy brought massacre after massacre down on them towards the end of the century, in which thousands of people were killed. In 1915, scared that the Armenian minority would back Christian Russians in the First World War, the Young Turk government in Istanbul ordered almost all of them to be killed or deported into the Syrian deserts. Those who escaped settled in Los Angeles, Syria, Beirut or France, but a million people died.

So who in Armenia, staring up at that shining cap from their tiny kitchens, with the whiff of Turkish coffee drifting over the snow, could forget their endless hatred of the Turks?

*

Herbert was waiting for us at his office, a half-empty suite of rooms over an empty shop. The boss of the Armenian news agency's photo department was white-haired and graceful, wrapped in a long coat and scarf, with white stubble on his chin, white breath on the air, and gentle amusement always on his face. There were bright French-Armenian posters calling for the

salvation of Nagorno-Karabakh on the walls of his office, which
was so big that a once-grand desk, a bookcase and a carpet were
lost in its dusty space. His desk had photos in an in-tray, a
telephone, and a drawer where he kept his coffee-making equipment: a hand grinder like a big square peppermill, a little bag of
beans, and a heating element.

The ritual of coffee-making, the quiet determination of gloved
hands over the mill, the tiny cups with their thick grounds, is what
I remember best from the freezing rooms of Armenia. But Herbert
had something else to offer as well. He looked at us and grinned.
'Cold? You need an Armenian breakfast to warm you up,' he said,
and pulled out three glasses and a bottle with no label. His
breakfast was *cha-cha*, the clear local liqueur made out of grape
skins; we drank three glasses each in our coats and scarves, and it
burned down our throats and warmed us, but didn't fuddle our
brains. 'Are you wondering why?' Herbert asked. 'It's one of the
hidden advantages of extreme cold.'

He started phoning, hands in thick woollen gloves sticking in
the fingerholes of the white plastic telephone, looking for a driver
to take us out of Yerevan. In response to his calls, young men and
women began to wander into the icy room. 'Have you seen Ararat?'
they all asked. 'What do you think of the war in Karabakh?' But
their questions were, at first, as muted as my confused answers. It
was only after more coffee and more *cha-cha* that they began to
talk freely, but their talk made me begin to feel as though, after all,
the *cha-cha* had made me drunk. 'Why did the war in Karabakh
start?' I asked, and they would answer: 'Because we hate the Turk.
Because the Turk has always wanted to finish off the genocide of
our people which was begun in 1915.' But . . . I started wondering
. . . what Turk? Surely the war in Karabakh isn't against the Turk?
Surely it's against Azerbaijan?

That was the way the articles I had read put it. Soviet leaders
who had redrawn the internal borders of their domains had in the
1920s put the Nagorno (Mountainous) Karabakh Autonomous
Region, whose people were almost all Armenian, under the control
of the republic next door, Azerbaijan. The map of Azerbaijan
looked like a fried egg, with Nagorno-Karabakh the yolk; the

map of Armenia looked the same, with a similar Azeri enclave called Nakhichevan tucked away in the furthest corner from Azerbaijan proper. It was Stalin's technique of 'divide and rule' to give everyone in his domains a local enemy minority to take out their discontents on, thus preventing them from hating the 'centre' in Moscow, and the symmetry of the arrangement in Armenia and Azerbaijan was almost perfect. Fighting had begun, in the perestroika era, after the Karabakh Armenians had started demanding independence from Azerbaijan and union with their cousins in Armenia proper. It had carried on sporadically since 1988, along with fighting between villages on the ethnically muddled border, and with pogroms of the ethnic Armenians who lived inside Azerbaijan. Already, at the beginning of 1992, most of the ethnic Armenians who had once lived in Azerbaijan had fled back to their Armenian motherland, and most of the Azeris from the border villages and from elsewhere in Armenia had escaped 'home' to Azerbaijan.

Except for the Armenians of Nagorno-Karabakh, still technically inside Azerbaijan, both republics were painfully and bloodily becoming ethnically 'pure'. Like Turks, Azeris were Muslims. It was also true that their language was a highly Sovietized dialect of Turkish, so archaic and distorted that it made real Turks laugh (the Azeri for 'Stop the car, I want to get out' sounds to a Turk like 'Halt the carriage! I long to throw myself down!'). But that was an accident of the region's confused history, a centuries-long struggle for control of its trade routes between Ottomans, Persians and Russians. The ethnically muddled Azeris, like the Armenians, had lived for two centuries under Russian imperial rule. If they were Turks at all, they were a forgotten tribe. They had no more played a part in the Ottoman massacres of Western Armenians than I had.

'What's the difference?' one of the young men in long coats sniffed. 'They're all Turks. They're all Muslim bastards.' And he lifted his glass in a toast to Armenian Karabakh, known to Armenians as *Artsakh*: 'To *Artsakh*! To the good fight against genocide! To the return of Armenia's historic borders!' More young men and women raised their glasses for the emotional toast.

Herbert ushered us out to the car he had summoned up, waiting on the icy street. 'They're excitable. It's natural,' he said in polite half-apology. 'When people have nothing to eat, they dwell on their grievances. They look for enemies, especially people in our Soviet world where we were brought up to perpetual struggle, against class enemies, anti-Soviet agitators, wreckers, and saboteurs. Looking for enemies . . .' he sighed, and turned to squint up at Ararat. 'I call it the slow AIDS of Communism.'

*

We drove through the rugged mountains of Armenia, all cliffs and frozen waterfalls and austere monasteries, and one great lake with icy trees spreading black fingers into the sky. 'Oh, the *priroda*,' Vitya sighed nostalgically. 'I came to Lake Sevan once for a holiday. The mountain air was so pure, the stars so bright. Perhaps we should just stop here and have a good meal and stay the night?' But he caught himself in mid-flow and laughed his own suggestion off. 'There's probably nowhere you can get a good meal nowadays, and I don't want any more freezing nights like yesterday.'

We were heading for Idzhevan, a town near the Georgian border to which the president of Georgia, Zviad Gamsakhurdia, had fled two nights before. We wanted to interview him. His flight was the culmination of a week-long siege in his capital, Tbilisi, where he had been hiding in the bunker under the parliament building while what the newspapers called the 'gunmen of democracy' prowled the city, laying waste to the show buildings of Rustaveli Avenue with their grenades and mortars and Kalashnikovs, trying to force him out of his underground shelter. At dead of night, in a lull in the fighting, he had escaped in a convoy of cars that drew up unexpectedly in the ruins of the great Stalinist columns. At breakneck speed, he had made it over the Red Bridge out of Georgia, through the disputed Azeri–Armenian border, into neutral territory. He didn't know where to go next.

Gamsakhurdia was as bizarre a figure as any of the new nationalists who had taken power. A tall man with the mournful, twitchy appearance of a bloodhound, he had once been an academic and later an anti-Soviet dissident. He had translated Shake-

speare from English. He had been in and out of prison through the
1970s and 1980s. When he was elected president in May, he had
denounced all half-dozen rival candidates as KGB agents. People
who had lived under Russian rule all their lives were sympathetic
to his paranoia. But, ever since, he had gone on saying that
everyone who stood up to him was a KGB agent, and imprisoning
them. In September he had even jailed Georgy Chanturia, a popular
young opposition politician. In Tbilisi, the intellectuals and the
middle classes had quickly come to despise and hate him. But the
poor and uneducated people of Georgia still adored him, because
he said what they had always thought about Moscow. His most
passionate devotees were women, mockingly called the Black
Stockings by the Russian press, who stood under the red roofs and
wrought-iron balconies of Tbilisi and wept for their vanished
president.

With Gamsakhurdia gone, Georgia was left to the haphazard
control of the Provincial Council that had seized power. Apart
from the urbane Tengiz Sigua, who had the nominal role of prime
minister, this meant gunmen in dark coats. There was Jaba
Ioseliani, a big, shabby, energetic ex-housebreaker, who had done
time in a Leningrad jail for manslaughter and who now ran the
heavily armed Mkhedrioni private army. Its name, romantically,
meant The Horsemen. A second anarchic private army, the
National Guard, was led by Tengiz Kitovani, a plump character
with a loud voice, a determined nose and a peaked De Gaulle hat.
Young men in shades and leather jackets and headbands carried
guns on the street, and traded them behind public buildings
plastered with post-Soviet posters of Rambo, on whom they had
clearly modelled their own image. The centre of Tbilisi was in
ruins. The restaurants and cafés and markets were closed. There
were bread queues in what had been the richest and most carefree
of Soviet republics.

For the moment, to the embarrassment of the Armenians,
Gamsakhurdia had nowhere left to run. Cars came from Yerevan
regularly with government officials to work out what to do next,
but left quietly and without comment. We stopped at Idzhevan's
former District Party Building, where the lights didn't work and

the Lenin plaques were just being taken down from the corridors, to ask where Gamsakhurdia was. The secretaries' offices were full of the ubiquitous men in dark coats, with gold teeth and stubbly chins, clustered round the middle-aged secretaries in scarves, grinding up coffee or drinking it in huddles.

There was the occasional boom from the unlit hills, and now and then a crackle of gunfire. The sounds marked the border with Azerbaijan. A secretary made us coffee, but when Vitya asked where we could buy lunch she shook her head. 'We are offering you all the hospitality we can,' she said, 'but we have nothing. And listen to what we have to put up with,' she added, turning to the window and the latest boom with a watchful look. 'The sounds of fighting never stop. All our misfortunes are their fault.'

Eventually, out of the muddle, came the information we were looking for. Gamsakhurdia was in residence in what had been a holiday sanatorium for writers, a great pink granite palace in Soviet grotesque, a few hairpin bends up the hills outside town. We drove there. A dozen journalists were there already, clinging to the bars, looking at the luxury Georgian cars in the courtyard, or chatting persuasively to the guards who were playing cards in a little wooden hut outside the door in the hopes of getting them to carry notes to Gamsakhurdia and persuade him to come out. But Gamsakhurdia stayed in splendid isolation inside. Vitya and I tried our wiles on the guards, too, but they were only provincial Armenian boys and had no pull with the city Georgians inside, in their sharp tailoring and shades.

It was getting dark before we gave up and left the muddy hillside. We decided, a little nervously, to press on into Georgia by the same road along which Gamsakhurdia had fled. It meant going through the fighting, a few kilometres into Azerbaijan, and then into Georgia over the Red Bridge. The taciturn driver shook his head glumly at our plans. 'I'm not taking you any further,' he said with finality. So Vitya began reminiscing about the glories of Georgian food, in Soviet times, in the days when there were still restaurants. 'Armenian food is no worse than Georgian,' the driver said suddenly, with an unexpected burst of patriotism, and pulled in at a scruffy street in town. Through an unmarked basement door was a canteen, where men sat at Formica tables in groups of three and four, smoking, drinking, and eating vast helpings of kebabs and beans and bread. Food, after all. Vitya winked at me. 'It smells delicious!' he said with a winning smile at the driver. 'Let's order whatever they've got.'

After a steaming, spicy dinner and a couple of rounds of *konyak*, the driver unwound far enough to let himself be persuaded to drive us past the last Armenian guards to the Soviet army border post up the road, at the frontier. 'You'll get a lift there from someone going further,' he said, more kindly. 'But you should be careful of taking a girl into night fighting.'

Vitya shrugged, sneaking an anxious glance at me. I shrugged, determined not to look weak. We drove in the dark, and no one spoke. We all smoked. Our speed slowly dropped.

When an armoured personnel carrier parked across the narrow road blocked our way, the driver stopped. We dragged our belongings out and put them on the side of the road. By the time we looked round, the driver had already turned his car, with much frantic squealing of brakes, and was heading back at a brisk pace towards the distant silhouette of Idzhevan.

It was suddenly very quiet and very chilly. Between the APC and the concrete blocks laid across the road a hundred yards further on, half-a-dozen soldiers were clustered round a bonfire. The shadows danced behind them. There was no other light, just the noises of the night and the noises of distant fighting.

The soldiers warming their hands at the fire had clearly been waiting for a long time. Another armoured personnel carrier would be along in due course to take them away at the end of their shift and bring in the night team instead. They had fresh, unlined faces, but their backs were hunched in miserable acceptance of fate. We joined them, sharing out the last of our cheese. We were given tin mugs full of liquid in return. 'Down in one!' Vitya said encouragingly. More *cha-cha*, then. I drained mine in time with the rest of them, determined not to choke. Vitya looked surprised, then clapped me on the back with a big grin.

There were a couple of Russians and a boy from Central Asia. The duty officer was Ukrainian. None of them knew how much longer they would be serving in the Soviet army, whether it would be disbanded or reconstituted as a series of small national armies or taken over by the new Commonwealth of International States; already, in that little pool of light in their little patch of primal-scream darkness, they were protecting the interests of a state which no longer existed. None of them knew why they were there.

Long silences were broken by short conversations. Words fell away into the night. A shot or a shell would echo back to us. Vitya hacked away at my cheese with a huge army knife, offering round more bits with an easygoing smile, relaxing the tense group with his sympathetic chat about his own past in Central Asia and his military service in quiet Soviet days and the stupidity of *praporshchiki*, the much-mocked corporals of the Soviet army.

A clatter of footsteps. Someone ran up out of the primeval darkness. In the pool of light, the tired boy soldiers had hands on their guns. But it was a woman, wrapped in layers of socks and galoshes and scarves and jerseys, with the panic of the night in her eyes. She rushed to the officer, laying her hands on his arms, tugging at them to acccentuate her whispered words . . . 'not far away . . . down the road . . .' I sat very still, trying to make out what she was saying, and noticed everyone else too was frozen in attitudes of mock-relaxation.

But it was all right. The APC we were waiting for chugged up to us from the opposite direction, roaring comfortably. A new team of anxious boys got out and took their places by the fire, glancing round beyond its limits then staring determinedly into the flames. Vitya and I climbed in with our new friends from our fireside picnic, now all smiles and sleepy contentedness.

At the gates of the barracks not far away, the lights were blazing with cheerful yellow light. The soldiers stopped a heavy goods lorry heading into Georgia and the two Chechens in the cab agreed to take us most of the way to Tbilisi. But when an officer came out of the door and yelled in distress at the sight of me climbing into the cab with Vitya, they all scattered and vanished. The Russian officer, in the Crimplene drab and neatly combed thin hair of his calling, was a family man and distressed at the idea of foreign girls in this risky place.

'Stay the night in the barracks at least,' he said, pleading for the lost decencies of yesterday. 'You should be ashamed to take a girl over a front-line in the middle of the night.'

The two lean Chechens shrugged and waited, not scared like the soldier boys. Not their problem, their faces said. 'You don't want to spend another night in Armenia, do you?' Vitya hissed at me. I shook my head, so used to being talked about as if I wasn't there by now that I was slightly surprised at this direct appeal to my preferences. So Vitya smiled soothingly at the anxious officer. 'I understand, I understand,' he answered. 'But we have to get to Tbilisi tonight. People are waiting for us. That's what our work's like.' He searched for more reassuring explanations, and fell back on his and my favourite argument, about whether it was acceptable to call adult women girls, whether girls could be professional, whether they should be allowed to work at all. In direct contradiction of his usual Soviet-man beliefs, he finished, with a triumphant look at me: 'Anyway, she's not a girl, she's a journalist!'

The officer looked imploringly at us, then shrugged. 'Well, be careful,' he said, defeated.

I didn't understand much of what the Chechen drivers said, squashed up against me in the cab with Vitya on the other side. I was so tired that Russian words were becoming meaningless music to me, the sounds and the sense diverging. But they were angry, their voices rose and rose in a long litany of complaints and everyone smoked furiously. We drove as fast as the rattling of the truck would allow us to. There were no lights anywhere except our headlights and the glowing tips of the cigarettes.

We passed a road sign. Vitya glanced at it. 'So we've crossed the border. This is Azerbaijan,' he said, but the trees and the bumpy road looked just the same. A few minutes later, there was suddenly light again. We were on the ancient Red Bridge into Georgia, and there were grinning men with guns and coats and gleaming teeth on the other side, and buses stopped by the roadside with sleepy, dishevelled people standing beside them. They didn't want us to go any further, but Vitya took their *starshy* (leader) aside for a whispered conversation and a fumble of hands, and we drove away with no more problems.

\*

It wasn't until the next May that I went back to implacable, revenge-driven Armenia. By then, the Armenians were beginning to win their war for Nagorno-Karabakh. I got on the first bus to take the road to Karabakh in four years. It was packed. Women hauled boxes and bags up behind them, pushing and shoving and squeezing against each other in the cramped interior. Men shoved them from behind to make sure they got their place. Children with rings under their eyes sat silently on top of holdalls, watching. Crowds of bystanders loitered on the pavement, watching and smiling and murmuring 'Artsakh!'

There were cherries on sale in the streets of Yerevan, and victory in the air.

The mountain road to Karabakh had been opened, the way through a narrow band of Azeri territory suddenly lay clear, and the refugee women and children who had been evacuated from Karabakh by helicopter while the Azeris were besieging their little capital, Stepanakert, were going home at last. At the same time, Armenian fighters had chased the Azeris away from the area around Stepanakert. The siege was over, and safety had returned.

I didn't expect to be on the bus. I had gone to see a man from the Karabakh committee, a kind of diplomatic-military representation for the Karabakh Armenians whose address was at an Armenian government building near the parked bus. Although Armenia did not recognize Karabakh's claim to independence, which would have been too diplomatically explosive, the Armenians did everything they could to further the cause of their cousins from Karabakh. Karabakh Armenians had offices and homes in Armenia proper, their refugees took shelter in Armenia proper, and romantic Armenian students went to Karabakh in their summer holidays to fight the Turk.

All I wanted to find out at the Karabakh committee was how the road – now known as the Lachin corridor from the town on the edge of Karabakh that straddled it – had been so miraculously cleared. Its representative Volodya Pogosyan, little and dark and handsome, as full of energy as a sparrow, and with the same beady, alert eyes, quizzed me about my attitude to the Armenian cause. I answered, with what by then had become a ritual response, that I had only sympathy for a people that had suffered so much, for so long, though war was a dreadful way to solve his people's problems. 'What can you do?' he shrugged back, but he smiled. 'That's what our life's like. War is war.'

My reply must have satisfied him, though, because he gave me a detailed speech about how the people of Lachin were ethnic Kurds, a minority which like the Karabakh Armenians had been forced to live under the Azeris throughout the Soviet period and were sick of them. Seeing the misery of their Karabakh Armenian neighbours, starving in the Azeri siege of Stepanakert, these Kurds had decided spontaneously that it was time to end the suffering. They had opened the road as a humanitarian corridor so food supplies could get into Karabakh through Lachin. At the same time, the Karabakh Armenians from the valley town of Stepanakert had broken through the siege and chased the Azeris from their hilltop fortress of Shusha. There was peace in Stepanakert, though the people were still suffering unimaginable hardships. The Azeris had all gone. The Karabakh Armenian civilians who had taken refuge in Armenia were free to go home, and they were such patriots, with such a deep love of their country, that they wanted to go now. It was a triumph for man's better nature, a breakthrough in the search for peace.

'The bus is ready. Do you want to go with it?' Pogosyan said, and led me back out of his room, with its military maps with little flags for Karabakh Armenian positions, past the Defence Ministry rooms where government employees were playing war games on computers supplied by international aid organizations, into the warm street.

I sat on a box too, although the kindly mothers all around pressed me to take one of the few seats and old ladies kept getting up to offer me their place. I made myself small, feeling like an intruder as they stared greedily out of the window, drinking in the

landscape of their return. I smiled at the children. They didn't want
to play, didn't want to smile back, but it broke the ice with their
mothers, who started talking to me, hesitantly at first and then
with increasing animation, as the ancient bus shuffled over the high
plateaux home.

'She's only four. And we got out of the siege months ago. But
she's in a bad state still,' Arvush, a young mother sitting on the
next box to me, said in muted apology for her unresponsive child.
'She doesn't speak. When she opens her mouth all that comes out
is explosion noises, "ba-BOOM!" She still starts to tremble when
she hears planes, or even lorries . . . Oh, how the buildings used to
tremble when the Grads exploded. Like an earthquake. Yes . . .'
she paused. 'They say there's nothing left of Stepanakert now, but
we're going home anyway.'

It was enough. The whole bus started talking, not exactly to me,
in reflective, obsessive voices, calling up their nightmare memories,
exorcizing them by putting them in words for a stranger.

. . . They burned the fields all around, we couldn't farm, we
couldn't leave town . . . They shot at us from all the villages all
around. We didn't know which wall to shelter behind . . . They
kept attacking us because we were weak and they were strong and
rich. Now we've had enough. We have started carrying weapons in
our hearts . . .

Gradually a young teacher called Vartush became the channel
for their reflections. She was travelling with her elderly mother and
a baby. She had almond-shaped eyes which bored into me with
hypnotic intensity. She was articulate, clever, and appealing, but
clearly still in a kind of shock which I began to realize was the
norm for people from Karabakh.

'You'll understand why we want to go back when you see
Karabakh; it's like Switzerland. There's nowhere in the Soviet
Union with our mountains, our nature, our pure air. It's in our
souls,' she said enthusiastically.

Even so, Vartush and the women of her family had wheedled
places on a helicopter out of Stepanakert during the spring, at the
height of the siege. It had been too terrifying for the children to
stay there, she said. The Azeris had still been in the hilltop town of

Shusha, and from there they could rain missiles down on Stepanakert in the valley.

'The Grads shattered the glass out of the windows ... there was
broken glass on all the streets and snow on the broken glass ... I
remember one winter day I got out of the cellar and started looking
for food outside, and the bombing started ... I was caught in the
street, in the snow, barefoot on the glass ... I just walked along
with the bombs going off all around me and glass under my feet
and the terrible noise, and prayed to be saved.'

The mothers' dreamlike recollections went on all day, and
through the night at the little Armenian border town of Goris, and
into the next day as we crossed the quiet valley that was now called
the Lachin corridor. But the voices of these passive victims of
catastrophe, the decent ordinary people who didn't understand
what had gone wrong with their lives or how to put it right,
weren't the only ones I heard on that bus, and later all over the
Caucasus. There were also the angry victims, hooked on pain but
no longer ready to have it inflicted on them, ready to actively inflict
it on others instead to restore what they believed was a just balance
in the world. On the bus was a wild-eyed teenage girl called Anahi,
who grinned manically and broke into every conversation with
stories about her fighter brothers, how she had fired their guns,
how I could go out with them and kill Azeris when she got home
and set herself up again. 'We should kill their children,' she said
with what I hoped was only the excessive certainty of extreme
youth. 'Get them young, or they'll grow up to kill us.' The other
women shushed her uncertainly, stealing glances at me from round
their silent children's heads ('You shouldn't say things like that!'
'Shame'), but I wondered how they would have answered if I
hadn't been there.

And there were the manipulators, with watchful eyes assessing
the potential benefits that could accrue to them out of any collective
disaster, showmen trying out the buzzwords and slogans of the day
to see which ones appealed most to the people around them. The
bus's most important passenger was a former deputy from the
Soviet-era Karabakh local parliament, going back from his current
job in the safety of Yerevan to see what had become of his

homeland. The women treated him with awed respect, but I didn't like his smugness and his eagerness to go home only now that it was safe there too. A stout man in a splendid three-piece suit, he had had no qualms about taking the most comfortable seat in the bus. He was a VIP, after all, and it was his due. Stretching his legs, he addressed me in lecture-room language about the sufferings of Stepanakert while he hadn't been there.

'There isn't a single building left undamaged. People hid in their cellars all day long. There are no shops any more, and people have been living on rations of one kilogram of flour a month and whatever they could find or grow or store. Can YOU imagine that?' and he pointed a reproving finger. There were answering murmurs of sorrow from all over the bus.

I asked whether Russia was helping the Armenians in Karabakh, by trying to broker a peace with the Azeris. 'Keeping agreements,' he declaimed mellifluously. 'None of us ever has. We say one thing, do another and think a third. So I have no faith in Russia, I am deeply suspicious about Russia's intentions. A Third World War between the North and South is a real possibility because the Western world has never confronted Islam. Russia is using Armenia as a buffer state . . .' He paused, aware of the bored silence around him, eyeing the mothers who had suddenly all started making sure their children were all right. His alarmist geopolitical chat didn't register with them; it might have gone down better with their husbands or on the more serious kind of television talk show, but it was a world away from these women's practical worries. He dropped it immediately and changed tack.

'What was happening in Stepanakert was genocide,' he said. 'Genocide isn't just the wholesale destruction of a people, not just what we suffered in 1915. It's also putting people in conditions where they can't live like human beings.' And the mothers tuned in again, sighing in respectful agreement, and his chest puffed out a fraction further with satisfaction.

*

In Goris, when we stopped for the night, there were more of the angry ex-victims: 'Karabakh self-defence fighters', armed to the teeth, flushed with victory and spirits, heads filled with slogans, lounging all over the scruffy hotel. They were just back from a stint of fighting. 'Why are you here? Romanticism?' one asked roughly, and I was as scared of them as anyone else in the ramshackle little building. But once I answered: 'No, it's just my job,' they took me off to the room where they were drinking, filled me a tin mug of *cha-cha* and raised a toast to Artsakh, freedom, independence or union with Armenia.

I had discovered before that there was very little sexual danger in any of these encounters. Women who are not the spoils of battle are almost invisible to men at war, who have their heads full of the romance of death and heroism; if they are aware of them at all, they treat women with extreme chivalry, as the symbols of the homes they are fighting to protect. In a strange way, it was a relief to be among them and have the sensation virtually unknown to adult women in peacetime of not being an object of some sort of sexual scrutiny.

But these fighters turned ugly when I only sipped at my mug. 'Don't you believe in the independence of Artsakh?' one asked threateningly, and a dozen pairs of eyes turned on me, in my chair far from the door and the corridor. '. . . It's just . . . I don't drink spirits . . .' I stammered. 'But this is a toast to our independence! You have to drink, out of respect,' the first soldier ordered, slamming his fist on the table. It was a very ordinary dilemma: I didn't like the idea of taking sides, even symbolically, while I was supposed to be neutral and objective and at work, but I didn't want to annoy a dozen men with guns either, especially when they looked ready to force the issue.

'Let me propose a toast,' I said hurriedly, working out how to use the stock phrases for this Soviet ritual to my own best advantage. 'War is a terrible thing. But I've never been among Armenians who have behaved like bastards; I've always been treated with honour and respect here; and I've never heard of Armenians treating their enemies dishonourably. I don't know how your war will end, but I hope you get what you want out of it, and I wish you happiness and peace.' There was a long pause, and slowly approving grins began to appear on the gaunt faces, and the angry first soldier raised his glass and drank. The slogans in their heads had made them slow-witted, and a soft answer had turned away their wrath. 'To happiness,' another murmured. 'To peace,' said a third.

I made my excuses and left before they found out I had never been to Karabakh, but before I had even reached the door they had forgotten me, and peace, and were drinking to the annihilation of the Azeris. Their rage was frightening. I locked my door before going to sleep.

And there were more and more angry ex-victims. By the next day, as we reached the end of the corridor and the bus started twisting up the grey-green hillside to Lachin, even the passive and despairing mothers were transformed into avenging angels.

Smoke smudged the horizon. A joyful whisper eddied through the bus. 'Lachin!'

I stared.

Half a dozen houses on the hill were still on fire. Dozens more were blackened ruins. Smoke wreathed the streets. There was no glass in the windows. Disembowelled sofas were scattered along the roadside, in a litter of chairs, books, kettles and cutlery.

There were no live Kurdish residents to be seen. A beheaded goat lay at one crossroads, and a dog whose body was riddled with bullet holes at another. In the ditch by the highway was a man's corpse, face down, legs in sodden trousers sticking out into the road.

'But where are the Kurds?' I asked, into the sudden buzz of excited, happy conversation around me. 'The ones who live here and took pity on the plight of the suffering Armenians and opened a humanitarian corridor so people in Stepanakert wouldn't starve?'

'They ran away before our boys came,' one of the women ad-libbed, although she knew I knew there was no way she could have found that out in Yerevan. Her face was glowing with happiness, and she was pointing something out in the street to her silent child. She wasn't really paying attention to me.

'When our boys came into town, they found all the inhabitants had fled,' the pompous deputy expanded soothingly.

'But it looks as though there's been fighting here. There

are houses on fire. There was a corpse in the ditch...' I stammered.

'There was no corpse. You must have been mistaken,' Vartush said firmly. She was holding her mother's hand and her lovely almond-shaped eyes glinted with tears of fierce joy.

I saw the corpse again on my way back two days later, when traffic jams of looters were already inspecting the pickings at Lachin, and their carts were being directed around town by dozens of grinning gold-toothed guards. A young journalist travelling with me then saw it too, and put his hands over my eyes as we approached it. 'Don't look now,' he said. 'There are things you shouldn't see, and questions you shouldn't ask.'

But the people in the bus were too blinded by their hatred to even notice.

'The Turks just set their own houses on fire before they ran away, so that our people wouldn't be able to live in them. That's the kind of bastards the Turks are,' Vartush added.

Turks again. It was the deputy who took pity on me and explained. The Kurds of Lachin had always lived here. In the 1920s, their three districts had briefly been given autonomy as 'Red Kurdistan', a status which their overlords in Azerbaijan had soon abolished as the Kurds were incorporated into Azerbaijan proper. Their numbers dwindled from 20,000 in the late 1950s to only 4,000 when the Soviet Union collapsed, mostly because they were forced to re-register as Azeri nationals and use the Azeri Turkish language.

'So you see they're all Azeris really,' Vartush said, breaking across the deputy's monologue, with no fellow-feeling for another little minority deprived of its collective identity in the Soviet nationalities tug-of-war. 'All Turks. All dirty Muslim bastards.'

And the bus murmured approval of her verdict.

But it was hard to censure the mothers for gloating, or the looters for stealing something back for themselves. Once we got out of Lachin and into Karabakh proper – an unforgiving landscape of slatey hills and wet grass and overcast skies – I began to get an inkling of what they had gone through. The debris of war was everywhere.

A bridge had been blown up just outside town. Someone had put a rattling piece of metal over the shallow river instead. We got out of the bus and walked through the river bed. The driver edged backwards and forwards, testing the strength of the metal, getting his nerve together, and finally raced safely across.

Before we could get back inside the bus, there was a buzz in the sky. The women started craning their necks towards the noise, and edging their bodies back under rocky outcrops in the steep hill we were standing on. 'Helicopters,' Vartush said quietly, and everyone shrank further away into the rocks, their faces hard and still as their children's. But it was only the caution of habit. Armenians were safe now on these slopes. The helicopters swooped by, and the women broke out in smiles when they saw the friendly markings on their sides. '*Nashi*,' they started saying in relief. The deputy mopped his plump face.

There was a new spirit of companionship as we drove on, as if I had been let into one of the bus passengers' secrets. We passed a destroyed Azeri tank with the word 'Tural' (translated eagerly for me as 'Great Turkey' by the bus ladies) painted on its side, next to a green flag with a crescent moon and stars. APCs littered the roadside, and more thundered up and down the road, topped by happy fighters yelling 'Artsakh!' The fate of the abandoned vehicles went unremarked; I suspected they weren't designed for the high-speed road travel they were being subjected to by the victorious Armenians and had simply broken down.

The road to Shusha was uphill all the way. 'Shusha is the highest point in Karabakh,' Vartukh told me, as we climbed and climbed. 'Its Azeri name, Shushi, means "glass" in Azeri, because it's naturally so well fortified that you can't even see it until you climb right to the top of the mountain. Historically it was the fortress of Karabakh. The Azeris always wanted it so they could completely control us; but they're not good soldiers like us, they had weapons but our boys were armed in their hearts, and they sneaked up at dead of night and took it back . . . The Azeris just ran away, like the cowards they are . . . and taking Shusha has enriched us with weapons . . . they turned our church there, the church that used to be the centre of Armenian Christianity, into an arms depot. It was full of weapons. Now they're ours.'

Suddenly we were in Shusha, another forlorn ruin. We drove round its outskirts and skated down the opposite hillside on a burst of collective happiness. The women only hissed softly for a moment when we passed the Muslim graveyard, with its small blue and green headstones. For there, in the valley, was the squat silhouette of Stepanakert. They were home.

*

Stepanakert was in a frenzy of spring cleaning. In brilliant sunshine, tiny old women were sweeping up rubble and shifting bits of wall. The crunch of broken glass being dragged over broken pavements was the loudest sound. There were ruined buildings on all sides, and almost every house had some trace of war damage, an exposed roof, bullet holes, cracks, staring windows. There were no shops, no gas, no electricity, no phones, no post, and no cash money.

Everywhere, the victims were trying to come to terms with the devastation of their lives. Women beckoned us into the cellars they had lived in all winter, still damp and smelly, ratholes filled with heaps of mattresses and blankets, with tiny half-windows onto the street blocked by hardened sandbags. A metal box, like a giant biscuit tin, stood in the middle of each cellar, with a lid whose edges turned upwards, and a series of cans welded together into a rough pipe which stretched out of the window onto the street. They had burned fuel inside these *burzhuyka*s, or makeshift stoves, and mixed up their one-kilogram monthly flour ration with water into a paste which they used to make flat bread pancakes on the lid of the oven.

No trains had left Stepanakert station since 1988, and the building was now being used to turn green Grad missile boxes into white-painted coffins.

A makeshift hospital had been set up in the basement of the parliament building during the nine-month siege. There were still a few pathetic bottles of pills and bandages on desks and shelves. A tired woman doctor, Gayana, was on duty. 'We treated war wounds, of course, but do you know what our other main job was during the siege? Performing abortions. We love children, but there wasn't a woman in Stepanakert that wanted to give birth in those conditions. That's how low they brought us.'

I stayed the night with Susanna, who had once been a school physics teacher. But she had two sons, a father and a grandmother to feed, so once the fighting started she had been working part-time as a government typist to be sure of getting her rations.

Her house was untouched. Square, two storeys high, with a long veranda, blossom trees, and a hencoop in the garden, it was like a tiny paradise of peace. But there was almost no food inside. We ate pasta made from her flour ration, with herbs from the garden. There were three eggs, and Susanna, her father and her twelve-year-old son all wanted to give me theirs. Finally, Susanna went back into the kitchen and started fiddling round in cupboards, watched intently by her family, who made no sudden movements as if they didn't want me to see they were surprised. She pulled out a dusty packet. 'Coffee,' she said in quiet triumph. 'I've been waiting for a special occasion to open this packet. I've kept it hidden here since 1990.'

And slowly, the house filled again with the forgotten smell of Soviet peacetime, the tiny cups were rattling on the table, and her father's talk turned to the old subject: the war still raging in other parts of Karabakh, the war against the imaginary Turk.

*

Everywhere, the passive victims were turning angry. 'Come and see us!' quavered one old lady from a fifth-floor balcony, seeing me staring up at her apartment block from the street. Scared the masonry would crumble away altogether, she had plugged a hole about five feet in diameter in her outside wall with a sofa, which stuck right out into the empty air. 'That's what those bastards did to us! I'd kill them with my bare hands if I got half a chance!'

The local prime minister, Oleg Yesoyan, kept a candlestick in his office made out of the casing of a Grad missile.

In Shusha, the looters and refugees showed us the ancient

Christian church, piled high with empty Grad cases, its walls
graffitied with Muslim names. But someone had reverently put an
icon in a corner, scattering plastic tulips and real daffodils around
it and lighting candles underneath. Volodya Babayan, the Armenian restorer who had spent seven years trying to restore the
church under Soviet rule, until the Azeris drove the Armenians out
of Shusha in 1988, was looking at the new damage with his
comfortable face wrinkled in despair. 'It was hard enough before
. . . it was sixty per cent destroyed in 1981, and I had to apply to
Azerbaijan for a visa every time I wanted to come here, and they
never provided us with the supplies they promised, and they never
paid me . . . but now . . .' He shook his head again.

When I went afterwards to the town mosque, to see what the
Armenians had done to it since they took the town back, two
young 'Karabakh self-defence' fighters followed me. The mosque
had some shell damage, and the carpets that must have decorated
it were gone. I climbed to the top of the minaret, stuck my head
out – and a bullet whistled past my ear. I slithered back down the
stairs and found the two youths still taking potshots at the crescent
moon on top and laughing unpleasantly. 'You shouldn't have been
messing around in that dirty Muslim place,' one said. 'You owe me
a cigarette,' I answered crossly, and he cheered up and showed me
how even the mosque's windows had the round arches of Armenian
architecture, not the pointy tops of Muslim tradition. 'Which goes
to show,' he said, 'that this was once a Christian church too, and
the Azeris just stole it and stuck that tower on top. Armenians have
lived in this land for centuries; the Azeris are newcomers. They
know nothing. They just copy us, steal from us and breed like
insects. Well, we've had enough.'

The villagers from near Stepanakert, whose houses and
cowsheds had been clipped by Azeri shells or whose fields had been
burned, were out for revenge against the Turk. So were the self-
defence fighters, some Karabakh Armenians, some Armenian
Armenians, some Los Angeles Armenians waving their American
passports at the first sign of trouble, and even an Armenian colonel
from the old Soviet army who was spending his leave in Karabakh.

They fired themselves up by telling the same atrocity stories, stories originally transmitted by whisper but now passed down the trenches in a shout, and they believed every word.

'They're using chemical weapons against us . . . they scalp our men, and string the scalps from the handles of their tanks . . . The Russians have been helping them, sending blond lads to drive Azeri tanks, but our boys are winning back even against these impossible odds . . . The Turks are such savages that whenever we organize a truce so both sides can collect their dead they don't keep it; they leave their own people lying rotting on the ground . . . They eat babies . . . And do you know how low they have sunk? We have confirmed information that four negro corpses have been picked up, and THAT means they're using black mercenaries. Can you imagine that?'

In the primitive hospitals, scurrying doctors would pause long enough to confirm the atrocity stories, the scalpings, the stabbed babies, the severed fingers and ears, the noses sliced open. The bodies actually in the morgues at any moment I dropped in on these hospitals were those of people who had died in more conventional ways, but the stories were told with such conviction that I almost believed them.

The refugees, wandering through Stepanakert in search of a home, hoping they might be rehoused in Shusha, were consumed and feverish with rage. One of them saw me loitering in the corridor of the parliament building, waiting for an interview, and strode my way.

Stubble grew in the ingrained lines of his face. He was drunk. 'Journalist! You probably want an interview, don't you?' he hissed, sticking his chin out pugnaciously. 'So interview me! I know what's what. I've seen years of fighting and I have nothing to show for it, nothing, I'm a beggar.' Tears started down his face. 'I walked down here from the north alone. The Azeris killed my family and I didn't even have a spade to bury my son with. I had to bury him with my bare hands,' he said, choking on sobs. 'What good does it do for foreigners to come here? You've all been coming here for years to wallow in our misery. Do things get better for us because of your articles? Do they? Why don't you send fighters here from

America? You say you're democrats. You fought for democracy in Kuwait. What's wrong with us? Why don't you help us fight the Christian fight for democracy? Why did you let my son die?' His voice rose in a furious crescendo and one hand clawed at my throat.

A balding parliament aide shushed him and led him downstairs, past the emergency hospital and into the street. The aide came back, adjusting his suit and his thin hair and looking uncomfortable. 'I'm sorry. But it's understandable how he feels. We have been very disappointed that America refuses to help us. Humanitarian aid is all very well when there's an earthquake, but what we need now is troops. This is a righteous war for democracy and for our territory. You Americans have a moral duty to help us.'

*

This aide was only one of many manipulators, one of the comfortably-off Soviet élite with an eye to the main chance, looking at ways to adapt themselves to a changing world so they could keep their old positions of power. Mostly they operated by playing on people's worst instincts, spinning them lines, encouraging their greed or anger, for their own advantage.

It was a given of their Soviet mindset that Westerners were greedy, and that perception had been strengthened by the West's willingness to go to war over oil-rich Kuwait in 1991. I lost count of the number of times I was dragged embarrassingly into dark corners of the parliament building to be told – in strictest confidence – about the untapped oil and mineral resources in the Karabakh mountains. The officials would watch with cunning, beady eyes as I dutifully scribbled down the 'scoop' in my notebook. I didn't mind playing along; it was an understandable enough piece of deception. After all, they badly wanted Western help.

I was so interested in the victims' phantom hatred of the Turk that at first I didn't take very much notice of the way the manipulators whipped up that hatred and paranoia, each playing a lone hand, each trying to convince the simpler people around him that he alone had the lowdown on the full extent of the enemy's villainy, each creating extra panic and distress where none was really necessary. A lot of what they said I simply disregarded at first as too far-fetched for serious attention, along with the fascist-sounding talk from victims on all sides about how the Azeris were so genetically impoverished that they were trying to deplete the Armenian genetic fund too by killing off the flower of Armenia's youth.

When I was briefly arrested in Stepanakert and taken off to the local equivalent of the KGB, for being a suspicious foreigner in a war zone, my interlocutors quickly forgot their suspicions and sat down for a long tea-and-talk session instead. They had something important to tell me, they said. The hatchet-faced commander gave me a photocopy of a hand-drawn map, with a Muslim crescent in its centre, and the title 'Greater Azerbaijan'.

The area it depicted stretched right across most of modern Armenia. Hundreds of maps like this had been found in destroyed Azeri villages, the commander said earnestly as he warmed to his theme; it was clearly cunning Azeri propaganda to stir up bloodlust in the peasantry and convince them to kill innocent Armenians. Who knows? Perhaps he believed the story; but perhaps, too, the map was his own black propaganda project. I thanked him and tucked it away in my notebook next to the unexplored oilfield notes.

After a second trip to Karabakh a month later, I shared a car back to Armenia with a vast Rambo-substitute called Vrej, festooned in headbands and bandoliers of bullets, arms rippling with muscle, heavy gut swinging. Until the war he had been a lowly teacher of Armenian literature in a village school. The war had allowed him to become a powerful man in the Karabakh self-defence forces, carry a gun, issue orders and bully people. He was very pleased with himself, and full of boastful stories about his own derring-do and the bravery of all Karabakh Armenians generally. He obviously didn't want to go back to his peacetime life.

'It's dark in the mountains and the watchman hears footsteps,' ran one of Vrej's self-glorifying anecdotes. '"Who goes there?" he asks nervously. "Don't shoot! I'm an Armenian," quavers a timid voice from behind a rock. Then there's a scuffle and a huge, muscular shape looms up ahead of the guard, silhouetted against the stars. "Don't be afraid!" booms a confident second voice. "He might be just an Armenian – but I am a Karabakh Armenian."'

Vrej was using the lift in our car to sow panic along the road out of Karabakh, stopping every ten minutes to read militiamen the best bits from a crumpled piece of paper covered in red stamps and signatures. It declared a state of emergency and banned would-be refugees from leaving in case the Muslim enemy swept back in ready for a new wave of bloodshed. Between militia posts, Vrej would order the car to stop so he could harangue groups of ragged pedestrians trying to get out to Armenia and safety, ordering them to turn back down the hill road and fight the foe. Most of them ignored him and carried on walking, however much he thrust his gun under their noses. But he had a final argument up his sleeve, which he would yell out in the mixture of archaic Armenian and military Russian words spoken in the mountains, and after that the blank-faced groups would stop and mill around and stare fearfully at the boulder-strewn crags above. After three or four of these stops I asked him why he kept saying 'obstrelivayut', the Russian for 'they're shooting,' in his torrent of guttural explanations and imprecations, when the road ahead was perfectly quiet.

He grinned in delight. 'But there will be shooting. Look, I'll show you,' he said.

He wound down his window and tried to stick his gun barrel outside. Wedged between too much Vrej and a lot of other military equipment, it stayed stubbornly pointed at the ceiling. Krikor stopped the car and Vrej leaped out onto the grey turf and shattered the mountain silence with four or five deafening shots. A scatter of shale tumbled down.

'You see? Now they'll all turn round and go back and fight the Turk,' he said sternly as he got back in. 'It's better to die at home fighting than be a cowardly beggar abroad.'

In the long corridors of the Stepanakert parliament building, I met Khachik Stamboltsyan, the head of the Gtutsyan charity which had channelled aid to the needy ever since the 1988 earthquake. Stamboltsyan shook his beard at me; he was too busy and important to talk. But he stopped for a couple of minutes on the stairs to tell me in tones of ringing sincerity what he thought would come of the wars and natural disasters visited on his people in the last few years: 'Our ancestors said that by the end of the century there would once again be a huge Armenian kingdom and a reawakening of the Christian faith. I believe in both.' Behind him, a man crossed himself reverently.

It was only when I got back to the slightly less paranoid atmosphere of Armenia, and Herbert was making me coffee, that even Stamboltsyan was debunked. Herbert only laughed at the charity chief's speech. 'Yes, I bet he believes in a great Christian crusade, all the better to keep the aid flowing in for years and make him rich,' Herbert said cynically. 'I don't know whether he makes money out of it personally, but do you know, I went into one of their aid distribution offices the other day, and they had got a huge consignment of Bibles from the Los Angeles Armenians . . . think of all those donors in Los Angeles, happy that they're giving their brothers here the comfort of the word of God in their hour of distress . . . and the aid people were SELLING them at five dollars each?' he said.

Herbert was distressed at the hatreds which were splitting his home apart, and distressed by the politicians and power-brokers playing on people's weaknesses to make things worse. He didn't like the black-marketeers in Yerevan who sold illegal Azeri petrol at a mark-up of ten or twenty times its original price (though he bought it, because he had to use his car for work). He didn't like the restaurants where profiteers could eat Azeri sturgeon or caviar for sums equal to several months' average wages in Armenia.

There are four mutually incomprehensible dialects of Armenian. Children schooled in Armenia proper, in the classical language, can communicate. But in Karabakh, where children were educated in Azeri or Russian and only heard their own dialect at home, people had literally stopped understanding one another. The Armenian opposition party was split in two, but neither bitterly opposed group would relinquish the name it shared to the other. The Kurdish ethnic minority had announced it wished to be considered two separate peoples.

'We're fighting ghosts and killing shadows,' Herbert said. 'Ordinary people are suffering and don't understand why. Homo Sovieticus has become a lost soul, looking for a new Big Brother instead of Russia, desperate for America to run things or an enemy to hate so he can avoid taking responsibility for his own life. People are screaming for a new master to save them from the enemy, and our tragedy is that our worst enemy is really ourselves.'

*

Under the shadow of Ararat, covered by the barrage of antique anti-Turk hatred which held ordinary people in a powerful grip, the real geopolitical problem that Armenia's leader was facing was a completely different one – how to deal with new Russia.

The Soviet Union was gone, and Russia was in chaos. But it was still dozens of times bigger and wealthier and more powerful than Armenia, and it still had troops on Armenian soil. The Soviet army, with bases in every outpost of empire, had for a few months been renamed the Commonwealth of Independent States' army, but reality had won out by mid-1992 and it became the Russian army. Tiny Armenia, with seven million people and a crippled economy, urgently needed to accommodate its huge and threatening neighbour.

But Armenians had struggled for their independence from Moscow, and they had elected as President Levon Ter-Petrosyan, an intellectual ex-dissident who symbolized their success in that struggle. Even if they no longer knew what to do with their independence, and even if everything that had followed was a disaster that was destroying their lives, they would feel cheated if they lost the freedom they had only just won. They were suspicious that Russia was manoeuvring to take back control. They were scared Russia favoured Azerbaijan in the war, because Azerbaijan was run by a loyal Communist, Ayaz Mutalibov, who had carried on kowtowing to Moscow even after the Soviet collapse. Every time they lost a battle to the Azeris in Karabakh, more stories would fly around about how blond boys speaking the pure Russian of the north had been driving tanks with Azeri markings. The Turk was the worst enemy, true, but Russia was creeping stealthily around trying to lure them back into slavery. If that happened, they would feel they had elected the wrong president.

Levon Ter-Petrosyan, a reserved intellectual with a big, loose-limbed body and fluent command of ten languages, had not spent his life learning the ways of the Soviet corridors of power, but he turned out to be as good a manipulator of hatreds as the rest of Armenia's ruling class. While Armenians went fighting the Turk in Karabakh, or turned on each other in hysterical fear inside Armenia, Ter-Petrosyan quietly reached an accommodation with Russia that summer – formally agreeing that the troops of the Soviet-turned-Russian army could stay on in Armenia, and opening the way for Russian aid for his stricken economy.

He was lucky twice over. His people were by then so traumatized by the war that they hardly noticed their sovereignty being whittled away by Realpolitik. If they did notice, they had become so obsessed with beating the Turk that any help, even Russian, seemed no bad thing; and in case they got round to changing their minds later Ter-Petrosyan started to clamp down on political dissent like the old Soviet political élite he had never belonged to. Ter-Petrosyan's second piece of luck was that his deal with the Russians coincided with a coup in Azerbaijan. Mutalibov, yesterday's yes-man, was hounded out of office and replaced by a nationalist ex-dissident of the type Moscow found hardest to deal with. Uptight Abulfaz Elchibey, with his brittle limbs and thin goatee beard and bitter memories of KGB prisons, was a passionate pro-Turkish nationalist. He had once visited Ataturk's tomb and signed the visitors' book: 'Your servant, Elchibey'. Elchibey took Azerbaijan out of the post-Soviet Commonwealth and turned his back on Moscow. He replaced the Cyrillic alphabet with Turkish Latin. He introduced a Turkic currency, the manat, instead of the old rouble. For Moscow, he meant trouble.

The balance of power shifted in the Caucasus. Russia now had an ally and a military base for the future in Armenia. Azerbaijan had become an unfriendly country.

From then on, the once-helpless Armenians, with no visible money, their tanks and trucks apparently fuelled by nothing more than rage, surged through Karabakh unimpeded, cleansed all the Azeris and began a relentless surge forward into Azerbaijan proper. They treated their enemy with all the ferocity which had earlier been meted out to them. It was only much later, in 1997, during an army corruption hearing in Moscow, that it emerged that Russia had secretly spent $1 billion on military aid to the Armenians up to 1996. But all that could definitely be said in the summer of 1992 was that there were no more of the stories, which I hadn't really believed anyway when I first heard them in the Armenian trenches, about Russian soldiers covertly helping the Azeris to fight.

But had any of those stories about the Russians ever been true? 'We don't believe in Russian tank stories, do we?' my boss had said comfortably before I went to Armenia. 'Everyone who loses a battle wants to make it seem as though the odds against them were overwhelming ... I think it's just an excuse that the Armenians have been coming up with to justify themselves when they don't win, don't you?'

I agreed with him, and at first treated the tank stories with as much scepticism as the rest of the war stories. Russia seemed too collapsed, too chaotic and too demoralized by the implosion of the Soviet Union to have the time or energy for covert expansion tactics outside its borders. President Yeltsin's energies were all being spent on the fierce domestic struggle with parliament over reform. And, however nostalgic military leaders might be for their lost Soviet empire, they could hardly afford to pay or house their troops inside Russia as it was, or bring home the leftover forces still hanging on in East Germany and the Baltic states, let alone send new forces out on secret missions to the ex-Soviet republics. It was a remote possibility that the odd Russian mercenary had hired himself out to the Azeris, but that was as much as I was prepared to believe, and even then only if there was proof.

I never saw any proof, but on my last day in Yerevan I was told one final tank story that I did believe. I had no particular reason to trust the old man who told it to me, except instinct. He was sincere in a quiet, desperate way that struck a chord with me, he had no reason to lie and, even if he had, he had no imagination.

I met him in a school in Yerevan where refugees from Karabakh were being lodged during the summer holiday. He was living in a sunlit room with six mattresses and more than six children and grandchildren. He was thin, with rough hands, and he sat very upright on his chair. He spoke with the quiet, internalized, reflective voice of real memory.

The old man was seventy, and he was a farmer from a village up in the north of Karabakh, near the border. The Azeris had started shelling the village one night in the spring. His neighbours ran into the street in their nightclothes and decided that the whole village of two hundred people should get away as fast as possible. His wife was seventy-three. She ran out of the house barefoot, in her shawl. She was so scared she wouldn't even stay long enough to get dressed.

The column of villagers walked all night and all day through the hills and trees, hoping to get to Gulustan airport at the very north of Karabakh and catch a plane away. But when they got to the hill overlooking the airport, they saw it had been taken by the Azeris. They turned back and started walking the other way, hoping they might find safety if they made it south as far as Stepanakert. Another night fell.

... They walked with the kind of slowed-down breathless movement which running becomes when you're too tired to go on trying. He and his wife were somewhere in the middle of the stained, exhausted, bobbing group.

Breath was being sucked in and out all around them. It had been dark for a long time. His knobbly bunch of belongings dug into his back. Half-asleep, he was watching and not watching the flickering pale feet of his wife moving in front of him, dusty bare soles up, down, up, down, up, down. The bleeding crack on her right heel was the only syncopation in their staccato rhythm. Breath. Eyeballs. The glow of cigarettes. Feet.

There were someone's children grizzling behind, and somewhere ahead in this alien forest, perhaps over the next hilltop, or another, or another, was the road to safety.

And here was the brow of the hill. A new wooded valley stretched out below, a new hill on the horizon, and the sky lightened a shade with the first glow of the pre-dawn.

A quiet spring dawn, without birds. Without words.

He looked up.

There were darker silhouettes in the dark on that next hill.

There were thirty-five tanks pointing at him.

There were blond boys looking at the group of people coming over the hill at them, diving inside their vehicles. They were as scared as the villagers. They yelled snatches of panicky instruction at each other in the clipped correct Russian of the north.

Suddenly all the tanks were blazing with light and fire and noise, and the earth rose up around him in showers of sparks, and the forest was in flames.

Time stopped. He was running. They were all running. Shadows running, screaming without sound, bleeding, burning, dodging between the shafts of light and the well-shafts of darkness. Mouths open. Eyes open. Running in the wounded spring woods, with their sharp hot stink, bleeding boughs ripped off, sap oozing out. One man's hair was on fire, and he was beating at his head with knobbled hands as he ran. He was running and not breathing, running and not touching the ground, running . . .

The old man didn't even notice the tears flowing down his cheeks when he finished his story. 'Those Russian lads started firing at us,' he said again, and his eyes filled with their own distant terror. He had lost his wife in that distant forest. He had walked on with the survivors, to Stepanakert, to Goris, to Yerevan. He didn't care that the tank-drivers had been Russians, he didn't stress it or comment on it. It was just a fact, just a moment in the cataclysmic disaster that had swallowed his family up. He was still hoping his wife would somehow appear in Yerevan, following the rest of the village's trail, to find out who was still alive and what had happened to her family. But there was no optimism on his face.

I couldn't quite make sense of the old man's story. I didn't want to believe it, however true it rang. And it didn't prove anything. But afterwards, in Moscow, I used to wake up trembling for months afterwards from a recurring nightmare based on what he told me.

Later, when the world began to be interested in how and why

war had begun in former Yugoslavia, it became fashionable to decry the belief that ancient ethnic hatreds had set Yugoslavs at each other's throats and instead to pin the blame on unscrupulous politicians, principally Serbia's Slobodan Milosevic, who had manipulated a gullible population into war on spurious ethnic grounds so they could stay in power after socialism collapsed.

But it seemed to me that things were less clear-cut in the Caucasus in 1992. The manipulators in Armenia – the politicians who wanted to keep their power, the black-market traders who wanted to keep their illegal trade routes and quick wealth, the fighters who found their swashbuckling lives at the front more interesting than their dead-end peacetime jobs, the angry victims hell-bent on revenge, and perhaps even any Russian military groups who might have been helping out – were all in a sense freelance. Many of them really believed the ethnic horror stories they told, at least up to a point. They were not working to a master-plan; they were just anxious, selfish people, each trying to cut the best possible deal for themselves in a hostile new world. Almost accidentally, their different aspirations pushed them, jostling, shoving and squabbling, down the same road, further into war.

*

By the next year, however, it was becoming clearer to me that there were military Russians tampering with the outcome of the Caucasus wars, though no one knew whether they were doing so with the explicit sanction of Yeltsin's government.

Moscow could not make common ground with the new nationalist leader of Azerbaijan. Azerbaijan now held a chunk of the ex-Soviet Caspian Sea in which there were oil reserves worth $9 billion to the foreign oil companies flooding into Baku. Elchibey did not want to include Russian companies in the consortium being put together to extract and sell the oil. So Russia could not get its hands on the oil. And Azerbaijan refused to be in the Commonwealth of Independent States that had taken the Soviet Union's place.

'Moscow will be getting rid of him soon,' a British Helsinki Group election monitor in another ex-Soviet republic told me darkly in the spring of 1993. 'If you want to see the next coup in the Caucasus, go to Azerbaijan.' Sure enough, by the time I went there in the summer, Elchibey was out.

Oil is the first thing you notice in Baku. The Caspian Sea bay glitters dirtily with it. It seeps up out of the ground on the edge of town, where hundreds of old 'nodding donkey' derricks from its first oil boom at the turn of the century still clank forlornly in the sea breeze. And the bars of the hotels were full of men with big hands and British or Texan accents, drinking beer, waiting for their contract. They had waited two years, but Elchibey was due to go to London any day now and sign the deal. He needed the money to finance the war in Karabakh, to stop the endless defeats which were making him so unpopular.

But Elchibey fled town the night I arrived. A rebel army had been advancing on Baku for days from the old Russian military base at the other end of the country, burning posters of him, sticking branches through his mouth, snickering as they called him rude names. He was afraid for his life. The rebel army camped on the edge of Baku, waiting. But no one except Elchibey was scared of them. They slipped in and out of town, grinning, picnicking in restaurant kitchens. The bed-and-breakfast coup was all a huge joke to the people of Baku.

The rebel leader, Suret Huseinov, became prime minister after Elchibey ran away. Azerbaijan's sleek old Soviet leader, Heidar Aliyev, also came back to Baku from the distant province he had retreated to in the years of collapse, and eventually became president. Under his rule, Azerbaijan joined the CIS. The oil contract was renegotiated and, although it was never enough to satisfy the Russian foreign ministry, Russian companies got a share after all.

And how did Suret Huseinov's rebellion start? Stripped of government office by Elchibey in February, in one of an endless series of upheavals over Azeri military losses in Karabakh, the hooknosed young millionaire retreated to his power base at Gyandzha, near the frontline. There he built up his local private army and bided his time. Gyandzha was home to a Russian army garrison, which had promised to pull out of Azerbaijan by the end of 1994.

They unexpectedly speeded up their departure. The 130th brigade left in May from a two-brigade barracks for 20,000 men. Russian troops had let Huseinov's men into the adjoining barracks of the departed 709th brigade, although Huseinov was known to be hostile to Elchibey. For reasons Russia never explained, the ex-Soviet weapons its men left behind were not handed over to government soldiers in the 130th brigade's barracks – but to Huseinov next door. To Elchibey's men, this was proof that Russia was arming the rebels. They said Suret Huseinov was in Moscow's pay.

Huseinov's men only laughed when asked why they, not the government forces, got the Russian guns. 'Funny things happen in the Caucasus,' answered one smug young brave, in the khaki fatigues and striped blue-and-white shirt of a Russian paratrooper. He winked.

*

The Azeris weren't the slavering fanatical Turks who had been described to me by Armenians. The people of Baku, a relaxed old town with a medieval Persian quarter of vines, fountains and bathhouses built centuries before by the Shirvan Shahs, shivered on the edge of the sea, as far away as they could be – across deserts and cotton plantations in central Azerbaijan – from the mountains of Karabakh and Armenia, and the war. Cosmopolitans from Baku, like Herbert in Yerevan, were sorry the violence had sprung up unbidden and torn apart their city life. They missed the shoemakers and artisans who had once lived in the district of Ermenikhend (Armenian Town) but had vanished in terror after Azeri pogroms against Armenians in 1988. They took me to see Armenian wives who lingered on, terrified, under the flimsy protection of their husbands' names and their neighbours' good will.

True, there were manipulators everywhere. There were politicians who fed on hatred, like Elchibey's interior minister, Iskender Gamidov. A man who made his fervent patriotism as public as possible, Gamidov looked like a small-time crook: stubble, sunglasses and gangster suits. He kept a stuffed grey wolf almost as big as himself in his office as a symbol of the struggle of Turkic-speaking peoples. He blamed the Karabakh war on the Russian 7th Army, stationed locally; a familiar nationalist rallying-cry. He told me between clunky videos of what he said were prisoners of war from the Russian KGB that, if the Russians didn't stop interfering, World War Three would begin. 'Speaking as a human being, an Azeri and a nationalist, not as a politician, I say that if the Russians don't stop, there are eleven nuclear power stations in Russia, and I would go and blow them up to stop the Russians.'

And there were profiteers. As well as the sellers of guns and petrol, who were doing nicely out of the twenty-fold mark-up they could charge for getting goods from Baku to Yerevan, Azerbaijan was home to Fantomas, the hostage-swapper. He was named after the killer in the French black comedy film, which was popular in the Soviet Union; the film character's *modus operandi*, leaving rhyming notes on blue paper for his intended victims, was copied in several real Soviet murders, and the authorities banned the film. The real-life Azeri Fantomas hitched round the country, arranging expensive swaps between Azeri prisoners of war held by Armenian families and Armenian boys held prisoner by Azeri families.

Only the hundreds of thousands of peasant refugees pouring out of the distant war zone to escape the advancing Armenians, filling the hospitals and schools and town halls with their parcels and carpets, were angry and wanted revenge. They lived in tent cities and made houses out of containers. They sold the carpets of their grandmothers' dowries, woven with the jagged flame patterns and bright colours of their fire-worshipping history. In the Martyrs' Cemetery, where sad piped music and national flags and plastic flowers were strewn over the graves of teenagers, a mother whose son had been killed by the Armenians had gone to the front for her own savage revenge. She had come back with a dead Armenian soldier's heart, pickled in a jamjar, and laid it on her son's grave. But these people were provincials and peasants. No one important listened to them.

'What do we need this crazy war for?' my grimy, good-hearted driver Suleyman asked plaintively. 'Who needs to be shot dead?

Not Azeris, and not Armenians. This war is just mafias fighting each other and making big profits for themselves and getting us all killed into the bargain.'

Some reluctant soldiers hitched rides away from the front. 'It's impossible to tell how many men have been captured in fighting, and how many are just hiding out with their parents,' a defence ministry official told me. 'Azeris speak a form of Turkish, but it's a mistake to assume they have the toughness of Turks,' a Western diplomat said. 'This is an ethnically muddled region, and what Azeris really are is gentle Persians with Turkish and Russian overlays. They're lovers, not fighters.'

People in Baku were philosophical about the troubles besetting them. Valid, a forty-five-year-old engineer who had turned taxi-driver when his wages stopped coming in 1991, blamed the whole mess on independence and his country's attempt at democracy. 'We're just not ready for democracy,' he said, slicking back thinning hair in the heat as he told his favourite story about why. Valid had watched a recent episode in an American police television serial, in which a pet parrot had sniffed a gas leak in the night and flown round the house squawking so loudly it had woken up the family and saved their lives. 'That American parrot was brought up in democratic conditions,' he said with a sly grin. 'It could fly where it wanted in the house. So it behaved responsibly. Now, I've got a parrot at home, but it's always lived in a cage. It was brought up under developed socialism. If I let it out to fly round my flat now, it would only attack people and rip the curtains to shreds. My parrot couldn't handle democracy, just as no one here can. I reckon it will take a century for us to learn democratic ways. Only our children's children will think that way automatically. So if I get a baby parrot I'll bring it up to fly round the house. But I'm going to keep my old parrot in its cage.'

Despite their carefree appearance, many Azeris in Baku were increasingly fearful. They blamed Elchibey for everything that had gone wrong. They were pinning all their hopes on Aliyev, crossing fingers he could somehow end the war, even if that could only be done by dumping their dreams of independence and moving back into Moscow's embrace. By the summer of 1993, even rule from Moscow seemed an attractive alternative to a violent death.

'Only Aliyev can save us now,' Chingiz, a student, said fatalistically. 'If he doesn't do it fast, there'll be Armenians swimming in the Caspian and we won't have a country to save.'

*

In the autumn, it was the turn of the third Transcaucasian republic, Georgia, for strong-arm treatment from Moscow, when the war at the Abkhazian seaside came to a head.

After Gamsakhurdia fled, the old Soviet foreign minister Eduard Shevardnadze had come back to rule the land of his birth. But he had not been as complaisant as Moscow might have expected. Russia wanted the ex-Soviet republics in the post-Soviet Commonwealth of Independent States, the CIS, but Georgia had never joined and Shevardnadze had not tried to persuade his fiercely independent compatriots to change their minds. Russia wanted its ex-Soviet troops to stay on in the republics, but Shevardnadze didn't want them in Georgia. Russia saw Abkhazia as strategically important, sandwiched between Georgia proper and the southern Russian stretch of the Black Sea at Sochi. There had been Soviet military bases all along the Black Sea coast, and Russian dignitaries had dachas and memories in Abkhazia.

The war had blown up out of nothing in the summer of 1992. Abkhazia was an ethnically muddled place. So many Russians and Georgians and Jews and Armenians and Greeks lived there that the Abkhaz themselves made up only a sixth of the population. But Abkhaz nationalists in parliament began voting for autonomy, and that outraged the Georgian private armies which Shevardnadze had not managed to suppress at home. Their attempts to 'pacify' Abkhazia triggered fighting which raged across the province for another year.

Here was the odd thing: the Abkhaz, with no money, no real state structures, and no real army, suddenly acquired enough heavy weaponry to thrash the Georgians.

By then, the Caucasus was full of illegal weapons, bought from

Russian soldiers or stolen from old Soviet arms depots. The Abkhaz were getting freelance help from other tiny Caucasian peoples, including the Chechen 'Abkhaz battalion' led by Shamil Basayev, who had hijacked a plane to Turkey in the autumn of 1991 in a wild demonstration of Chechen independence. The Georgian army was a mess, its soldiers joined and left the fighting at will, guns were issued to soldiers only to be resold days later on the black market in Tbilisi, and many of the troops were high on home-made poppy mush, cooked up over campfires.

But unmarked warplanes started to bomb Georgian villages in Abkhazia – and the Abkhaz had no planes. Even if the Russian defence ministry issued a statement after every mysterious raid, saying its hands were clean, the Georgians still believed the planes must be Russian, with their markings disguised, flying in from Black Sea bases to help the Abkhaz.

Shevardnadze's pleas to Russia to leave his people alone had no effect. Nor did his raging against the dark forces in Moscow who were trying to revive 'the empire'. So he made peace, persuading the angry Georgian parliament that it was not capitulation but realism to accept Russian guarantees that fighting would stop, and that anyway broken-down Georgia could simply not afford the war any more. He was so convinced that being gentle with the Russian bear would work that he again made the dramatic promise, or threat, that had ended his career as Soviet foreign minister: if peace went wrong, he said, 'I will resign.'

Peace held in Abkhazia for seven weeks, long enough for the Georgians to pull out most of their equipment. Then the Abkhaz started fighting again, and the unmarked planes started flying. A furious Shevardnadze, realizing he had been hoodwinked, flew back to the Georgian-held Abkhaz capital Sukhumi to direct the war effort. He tried every day to call the defence ministry in Moscow, or to get in touch with Yeltsin. But they were ignoring him. No one important would take his calls; they were too busy, and he was out of the access loop.

Sukhumi fell in September 1993, and within twenty-four hours the Georgian army had retreated at a run right out of the province. Shevardnadze flew home to Tbilisi, thunderous and despairing, promising Georgians they would one day get the lost province back and fulminating against 'empire-builders' in Moscow. He still didn't want to accept Moscow's only offer of help – to send more of its own troops to Georgia to keep order. And there was worse to come. Taking advantage of the chaos, Gamsakhurdia crept back into western Georgia from his hideout in Dudayev's Chechnya and began a rerun of the previous year's civil war. He cut Tbilisi off completely from the Black Sea. Georgians got ready to starve.

But, eventually, Shevardnadze too caved in. He accepted the inflow of Russian troops that Moscow proposed, and Georgia joined the CIS. He stopped talking about the menacing rebirth of the Russian-ruled Empire. After that everything went better for Georgia. Gamsakhurdia died in mysterious circumstances, either by suicide or murder, in Chechnya. There were no more wars. The economy began to recover. The private armies were dispersed.

Ever since Georgia has became a friend to Moscow, it is the Abkhaz – clinging to their independence, locked in their claustrophobic little land with no way out through either Georgia or Russia – who have been worrying about whether Russia will now turn on them.

*

'Georgians, Abkhaz . . . they're all a bit crazy down there, aren't they?' asked my painting teacher Valery Geraskevich. 'I don't know why they just can't stop fighting each other.' There were five of us crammed into his studio, and his half-finished pictures hung on the walls – the pictures of a Russian patriot and romantic, onion-domed churches, golden Moscow houses, and angels. The fat model, Natasha, shifted uncomfortably on her chair.

'Well . . .' I was concentrating more on getting the proportions right in my picture without offending Natasha. 'There are plenty of people in the Russian military arming them . . . which doesn't help . . .'

'Surely not!' Valery exclaimed, taking his eyes off Natasha to stare at me in astonishment. 'Not our Russian boys, not *nashi*?' He was a very honest and straightforward man, and he had been fascinated by his trips abroad to Paris and to Serbia. He was always asking interested questions about what we found out on our journalists' travels, or about life abroad, during our disjointed, absent-minded, art-class conversations. But he was a patriot too, and I felt sorry for having distressed him by saying what I had.

Help came from an unexpected quarter. Natasha heaved herself off her chair and put on her robe, and we stopped for a break. 'I go to Abkhazia every summer,' she said suddenly, as Valery filled the kettle. 'I always have.' Valery was still more distressed. 'But there's a war on. How can you have a rest in a war zone?' he said. 'Well, I like it there, and so I've gone on going anyway,' Natasha answered, and I warmed to her unusual independence of spirit. She brought out a sketchbook of watercolours she had done in a quiet village by the sea – a full moon, cypresses, dolphins. Valery's eyes began to sparkle they way they always did when he was finding out about adventures and romance and beauty, and he was impressed at the idea of Natasha having gone and seen it for herself.

'And it's true,' she added, fixing Valery with a firm stare. 'Our Russian boys were down there all right, and they were doing awful things.' Valery looked at her, and nodded slowly, with a different, more accepting, kind of astonishment.

'Well, well,' he said. 'The world's a dirty place. Who would have believed it?' Then he laughed. 'I won't think about it any more, just as long as they don't bring their nasty little wars into Russia.'

# FIVE

How could Yeltsin stop this wave of violence seeping through the porous borders of the CIS and into Russia? The old political power of the state to poke into every aspect of public and private life had been eradicated by the Soviet collapse, and Yeltsin's enthusiastic support for the freedom that would follow had earned him the respect of the West. He had no room for manoeuvre. He could only keep a watchful eye on the likeliest trouble-spots.

*

Many ethnic regions and republics inside Russia took Yeltsin's early promises of sovereignty seriously. In the brave first years of post-Soviet life, they demanded not only a bigger share of the earnings from their local industries, but also more political say in their own affairs than the Soviet Union had allowed them. Of them all, the mini-republics which were initially thought likeliest to be trouble were Chechnya and Tatarstan.

Chechnya and Tatarstan both had oil, Muslim traditions and warrior pasts fighting Russia. A bleakly humorous Russian saying recalled the past: 'An uninvited guest is worse than a Tatar.' Chechnya and Tatarstan were the only two of twenty-odd republics that actually refused to sign the Federal Treaty of 1993, which Moscow devised to draw together the many pieces of Russia after the post-Soviet collapse. The idea behind the treaty was high-minded. It aimed to avoid the lie that had formed the basis of the Soviet Union – that they were free to secede at any time if they preferred full independence. Instead, it wanted to establish a more honest entity whose parts knew they belonged to the whole. This did not suit either the Chechens or the Tatars. Both peoples felt they would be better off controlling their own future, in particular the oil which had been handed over to the centre until now, helping make Moscow rich but leaving them poor.

Nothing much came of the Tatar rebellion.

It had been four centuries since the Tatars' ancestors were defeated in their capital, Kazan, by Ivan the Terrible. They had lived peacefully with Russians ever since. Rates of intermarriage were the highest in the former Soviet Union. No one had personal memories of ethnic persecution, war against Russians, or genocide. Nor was the Tatars' brand of Islam a powerful vehicle for anti-Moscow feeling. The nineteenth century had seen a long period of reformist thinking in their faith; the modernized, moderate Tatar Muslims had then become easy prey for Soviet-era atheist teachings. Nationalism here was an abstract notion, based on resentment over the lack of job advancement for local Tatars in their homeland and a vague historical sense of being a proud people brought low over the centuries by their lazy, feckless, hard-drinking Russian rulers. There was nothing in it to get your teeth into.

Tatarstan, on the Volga River, is surrounded on all sides by hundreds of miles of Russian countryside. It is nowhere near a border with any other state which might have let it sell its oil independently of Moscow. Geographically, it is doomed to deal with Russia.

Even the new nationalist leader of Tatarstan, Mintimer Shaimiyev, was the old Communist Party boss with a new hat on. Shaimiyev was not any kind of revolutionary, just a Soviet bureaucrat who wanted to stay in power and had an acute sense of the politically possible. He had nothing against playing nationalist if it meant a weak Moscow would hand out more money to his republic; but he would also be likely to come running back to Moscow if the Kremlin bear growled. This happened in 1994: Shaimiyev then salvaged the Tatars' pride by signing a special bilateral treaty on Tatarstan's relations with Russia instead of the off-the-peg Federal Treaty which other ethnic minorities had put their names to. But the end result was the same: Tatarstan once again became a cog in the Russian Federation machine.

The Chechen rebellion of 1991 was a more violent affair. Government buildings were seized by men with guns. Convicts were released from prisons in Grozny. Within days, Dudayev claimed to have an armed force of 62,000 men and a home guard of 300,000 ready in case Russia declared war. But, perhaps most importantly, Dudayev scared new Russia's top officials by refusing the chance of a tactful Soviet-style deal with Moscow. Delegations of Russian officials darted to and from Grozny throughout the autumn of 1991, returning to Moscow full of smug smiles, announcing triumphantly that they had sorted everything out. Within days, they all appeared on television screens in Moscow fulminating against the Chechen leader, who had ignored their agreements and carried on with his own separatist agenda. Dudayev was a military man who had never been initiated into the clubby world of Soviet politics. He did not understand its Byzantine rituals, face-saving public agreements, or quiet treacheries. He was not the kind of man Moscow would find it easy to do business with.

Russians also remembered more about Chechen resistance to their rule last century, mostly from their literature. A stock figure was the Chechen bandit, dagger in hand, eager for a chance to sink it into Russian flesh. Dudayev's wild television appearances, and his beefy bodyguards in reflector shades firing Kalashnikovs in the air, were a latter-day reminder of that history. Suspicious Russians and Chechens seldom intermarried.

Dudayev's Chechnya was also close to the southern border of shrunken post-Soviet Russia with its newly independent neighbours, the ex-Soviet republics of Azerbaijan, Armenia and Georgia. If these three states managed to shrug off Russian control – and both Georgia and Azerbaijan spent most of 1992 and 1993 trying to do just that – then Chechnya might also gain a geographical window on the outside world.

The abrupt way in which Dudayev took Chechnya out of the Russian Federation left the south-eastern Russian frontier area highly unstable. The old two-nation administrative unit of Checheno-Ingushetia was disbanded, because Dudayev declared only Chechnya independent. The Ingushi, a small people who spoke a similar language to the Chechens, opted to stay in the Russian Federation for the time being. They had territorial claims on a patch of the neighbouring statelet of North Ossetia, and believed the problem could only be sorted out with Russian good will. The Ingushi were left with no administrative centre, a situation nearly as destabilizing as Chechnya's stab at independence. The regions of the south-east – Chechnya and the statelet of Dagestan, to its east, that bridged the gap to Azerbaijan – had been the focus of last century's Caucasus wars. Their peoples shared the same Muslim, warlike, clannish culture. Now, Russians worried, the narrow hill tracks of the North Caucasus might turn into gun-running routes by which war could be brought into Russia.

*

Yeltsin was too weak and too busy trying to keep control over the changes in the Russian heartland in 1992 to have much time to find practical solutions to the humiliating Chechen problem. With Yegor Gaidar trying out shock economic reforms on the people of Russia, and the phrase 'market economy' the only incantation on the lips of the people in power, his government had no time or energy to spare for the Chechen rebellion. So Yeltsin's young adviser, Sergei Shakhrai, suggested trying on Chechnya the power- ful new magic of an economic blockade. With Russian forces on the roads into Chechnya, hopefully turning back food lorries heading into Grozny, Yeltsin turned his attention back to economic reform at home and hoped the Chechen problem would somehow sort itself out.

But he did cast around for a symbolic way to reassure his voters that they were being protected from the blacks. They desperately needed reassurance. People equated the freedom brought by the collapse of state power with anarchy, and it often came danger- ously close. The word *bezpredel* – limitlessness, of chaos and mess and crime – was on everyone's lips. To counter it, they called repeatedly for the security of *poryadok*, or order – an approving word whose authoritarian overtones are welcomed wholeheartedly in Russian, unlike the English word with its slight sense of unease. Yeltsin did not want to offer them any manifestations of *poryadok* that might smack of red flags, bullying slogans, or the gulags or secret police. Instead, he recalled the success of his earlier exper- iment of references to Tsarist *poryadok*, his revival of the tricolour flag and Sobchak's colourful games with Tsarist imagery on

7 November, and looked for something more historical to calm a nation tormented by economic woes and ethnic fears.

What he found to latch on to and sponsor, in the end, was the revival of the Russian Cossacks, which had already started spontaneously just before he came to power. They had galloped through the steppes for centuries, in shaggy sheepskin hats and curved *shashka* swords, fighting, swearing, laughing and drinking. The Cossacks – descendants of runaway serfs, outlaws, defrocked priests, religious dissidents, and bandits who had fallen foul of authoritarian Muscovy – had once formed the last wild outpost of the Tsars' empire. On the hunt for freedom, these blond Slav rebels had settled in the badlands between Christian Russian territory and the khanates of the Tatars and Turks and mountain peoples to the south and east. They had married local women and spoke a rough Russian liberally sprinkled with Turkic words from the mountain languages; their name was borrowed from the Turkic word for 'horseman' or 'free warrior'. They had adopted Caucasian dress and a Caucasian sense of honour and camaraderie. Their freedom of spirit and suspicion of the Russians of the north had worsened the chaos of the Time of Troubles, which enveloped Russia at the beginning of the seventeenth century, after the death of Ivan the Terrible in 1584 and the rise of the Romanov dynasty. Pretender after pretender marched through the country at the head of army after army, and the Cossacks rode out behind every pretender.

Even after order was restored in Russia, the Cossacks carried on backing rebellions for another two centuries. But, after a final bloody Cossack uprising in 1773 led by the red-bearded Don Cossack Emelyan Pugachev was crushed, the unruly southerners struck a deal of sorts with the Tsars. In return for freedom from the serfdom which held the rest of Russia in sway, and the right to make their own wine, and exemption from taxation, and ownership of their own land, Cossack men would leap on their horses at a whistle from their elected leader, the *ataman*, and ride off from their *stanitsa*s or farm villages to fight the Muslim mountaineers. Although their landholdings were scarcely larger than those of the

peasantry, they had almost as many rights as the nobility; the only
noble privilege this warrior caste was denied was the right to
demand labour obligations from the peasantry. (Later still, élite
troops of Cossacks guarded the monarch in St Petersburg, to whom
they became fanatically and personally devoted, and the rank-and-
file's swords and whips were turned in a more sinister way on the
Jews of the Russian south; but that was in relatively modern times.)
By the 1860s, there were about a million Cossacks, and a dozen
freewheeling armies.

Gradually, as imperial Russia began to expand south in the
eighteenth and nineteenth centuries, troops from the capital St
Petersburg were sent to reinforce the little Cossack *stanitsas* and
fortresses and push forward the Cossack Line that marked the edge
of Russian control against the Caucasus mountain peoples. The
Russian soldiers billeted in Cossack villages romanticized their
hosts, heaping praise on their bravery, their warrior virtues, and
their sense of honour. The Cossacks, with their horizons bounded
by the mountains and steppes of the south, did not return the
compliment.

'Even now the Cossack families claim relationship with the
Chechens, and the love of freedom, of leisure, of plunder and of
war, still form their chief characteristics,' Lev Tolstoy wrote in his
novel *The Cossacks*. 'Only the harmful side of Russian influence
shows itself – by interference at elections, by confiscation of church
bells, and by the troops who are quartered on the country or march
through it. A Cossack is inclined to hate less the *dzhigit* hillsman
who maybe has killed his brother, than the [Russian] soldier
quartered on him to defend his village, but who has defiled his hut
with tobacco-smoke. He respects his enemy the hillsman and
despises the soldier, who is in his eyes an alien and an oppressor.'

The Cossacks were annihilated under Soviet rule. Most of them
picked the wrong side in the civil war that broke out in 1918, just
after the Bolshevik revolution, backing the Tsar to whom they felt
passionate personal loyalty and not the Russian underlings they
despised. But by the autumn of 1920 about 100,000 Whites were
evacuated on Allied ships to Constantinople and the counter-
revolution petered out.

The 1919 Communist constitution vested supreme authority in the All-Russian Congress of Workers', Peasants', (Red) Cossacks' and Red Army Soviets. But the majority of White Cossacks who remained in Russia became targets of Communist reprisals. All Cossack institutions – mainly the dozen regional Cossack armies which had existed until 1917 – were abolished, and the descendants of the Cossacks who escaped prisons, camps and death lived quietly and anonymously in villages dotted about southern Russia for the next seventy years. But many Soviet Russians, bowed down by the endless demands of the state, remembered the free Cossacks with the reverence Americans feel for cowboys or Scandinavians for Vikings.

A picture that hangs in the sedate Russian Museum in St Petersburg captures the swashbuckling image that Russians have of the old Cossacks. The vast canvas of Ilya Repin's *Zaporozhiye Cossacks Write a Mocking Letter to the Turkish Sultan* is filled with big, tanned, bare-armed, muscly men, gathered round their leader who is reading from a parchment. Some of the Cossacks have just a Mohican-style topknot of hair, others have shaggy lambskin hats perched at a rakish angle on their heads. All of them are swathed in unkempt, un-Russian clothes, and festooned with daggers and pistols. There is brilliant sunshine everywhere. And they are clutching their stomachs and rolling their eyes, convulsed with great guffaws of uninhibited mirth. They are splitting their sides laughing.

*

The only pre-revolutionary Cossack I ever met was ninety-five years old and as dried-up as a grasshopper. Colonel Boris Fyodorovich Dubentseff had lived in the bleak Parisian suburb of Asnières since 1925, and his house doubled as a museum of Cossack memorabilia which could be visited by appointment. A glove worn by Catherine the Great was displayed in a glass case on one wall. *Shashka*s and pistols and the epaulettes of the élite Cossack guard from St Petersburg hung on others. The air was full of dust, and Colonel Dubentseff full of regrets. He had escaped to France with what was left of his regiment after the Russian Civil War and bought this house, which had been a textile industry sweatshop. But his comrades-in-arms had gradually died off, and now he was the last Cossack alive who had been personally presented to the Tsar and had the right to be buried in full dress uniform. 'It can be lonely . . .' he sighed, over the teacups. 'My children and grandchildren are more French than Russian. Naturally they don't care about the past. They don't even really understand it. They come and see me and they speak Russian, out of politeness to me, but badly, and when they leave I hear them speaking French.' I began to feel sad for this impeccably polite old man, marooned in a foreign country, the last living remnant of a dead world, who would only wear the tunic he had been so proud of once more when he was in his coffin.

But Colonel Dubentseff was less of a sentimentalist than I was.

'Do you know what the Cossacks REALLY were?' he said with sudden energy, breaking into my silence, putting a withered claw confidingly on my arm. 'The Tsar's honour guard . . . farmer-warriors . . . ?' I answered hesitantly, slightly taken aback by the gleam in his eye. 'Yes, but all that came later,' he answered impatiently, and his face lit up with a fierce smile. 'What we REALLY were, in the beginning, in the good old days, was BANDITS! BRIGANDS! ROBBERS! The Cossacks were runaways from Russia who settled by the Don River, or the Dniepr, and made their living robbing ships and merchants!'

And the claw tightened triumphantly, and visions of the flamboyant crimes and adventures of the past flitted over his happy, wicked face, and his little wizened frame heaved with an echo of those big Zaporozhiye Cossacks' gusts of carefree laughter.

*

When Gorbachev started to ease state control over his people, the romantic young Russian men of the Soviet south began to look nostalgically back to their half-forgotten past. They got their mothers to sew them old-style Cossack uniforms. With a conformist caution which owed more to their Soviet upbringing than any Cossack blood in their veins, they registered themselves in official 'social organizations' of Cossacks through 1990 and 1991. In the summer of 1990 a big gathering of all the Russian Cossack unions was held in Moscow, and regional unions created lists of men ready to rejoin the twelve old Cossack *voiska* or armies. Sergei Meshcheryakov, the new *ataman*, was elected to the Russian parliament. A few canny older Cossacks, hoping that Soviet nationalized land would be privatized under Yeltsin and that perhaps the new Russian government would revert to the old practice of giving Cossacks free parcels of land, prudently set up a bank in southern Russia.

Yeltsin had a short-term political point to make by raising the Cossack profile further.

The drastic economic reform he wanted for Russia was meeting sustained opposition in the parliament in Moscow. Ostensibly over reform, discord between president and parliament turned in 1992 and 1993 into what looked like a naked, personal struggle for power between Yeltsin and the parliament speaker. Ruslan Imranovich Khasbulatov was a Chechen, one of the mountain tribes that the historical Cossacks had policed and brutalized. It made no difference that Khasbulatov was a university professor who had spent most of his life in Russia, or that parliament slavishly obeyed his voting instructions and the nasal whine of his whiplash orders; Russian newspapers still mocked his Muslim past and his impure blood. Putting neo-Cossacks on display in Moscow helped Yeltsin remind his people just how low his enemy Khasbulatov's ancestors had stood in the imperial pecking-order.

In 1992, Yeltsin took to keeping a few tame presidential Cossacks at meetings of the supreme legislature in Moscow. Journalists and deputies snickered at them but, rapt in contemplation of their own splendour, the neo-Cossacks didn't seem to notice. In March 1993, the Russian president went further. He issued a decree that turned the clock back a century by ordering Cossacks to replace ex-Soviet border troops around the Caucasus. The decree didn't work out, like many pieces of legislature. Khasbulatov's parliament vetoed it. But it seemed to me to show that Yeltsin was joining that band of manipulative politicians who were playing with history to divert their people's attention from their modern economic and political problems, not caring about the Pandora's box of old hatreds they were opening by doing so.

Reinventing traditions lost under Soviet rule was big in 1992 Russia, so people were not too unkind about the Cossacks. But the past is dangerous terrain in the lands of the ex-Soviet Union, whose 250 million people are filled with nostalgic yearning for the history they lost in the time of the Bolsheviks. Pre-Communist times were not quite forgotten in the seventy years of Party rule, despite an official 'history' rewritten to serve Communist ends and drummed into reluctant schoolchildren's heads. The memories of the real past, however, underwent a dangerous fragmentation over the four generations when they could not be discussed in public. The true stories of what Grandfather and Great-Grandfather and their grandfathers and grandmothers did carried on being passed down, through the years, in a mutter, in every family kitchen. But these oral histories were pared down to the bone. There was only space to dwell on the heroism, tragedies or lost wealth of the teller's own ancestors, not those of other protagonists in the adventures. There was no equivalent of a friendly modern MacDonald to give the other side of a Campbell account of Glencoe. Nostalgia and isolation bred a harsh egotism. When Soviet controls loosened and these secret histories emerged from the kitchen, every family's view of the past turned out to have diverged from that of every other family. Each rival group clung desperately to its own version, which had sustained it for seven decades. Even for people whose ancestors had avoided personal conflict with the authorities or with other claimants to their land or position, it was easy to get lost in the bristling thickets of rival interpretations and clashing facts.

The Cossacks' whole past had been one of conflict. But now that they were 'revived', most neo-Cossacks didn't know what to do with themselves. Straight out of the Soviet army, or stuck in dead-end jobs, or forming the ranks of the new unemployed of the end of Soviet economics, they couldn't ride (unless they borrowed horses from the local collective farm to learn), or farm, or brew their own alcohol. There was no Tsar to protect, and no one else in the confused world of new Russia really wanted to share their towns with wannabe Cossacks with too much testosterone and too much time on their hands. They hung about on street corners, a little scary but more than a little comical in their home-made military gear, worked themselves up into frenzies of patriotism over the idea of protecting Slav honour, and occasionally got into fights with black-market traders over prices. So it was a godsend for these woebegone Cossacks-without-a-cause when the Soviet Union broke up and the little border wars started. At last, there was something for them to do.

*

The first post-Soviet Cossacks I ever saw were in the ex-Soviet republic of Moldova. They were waking up over a morning meal in the grim, cabbagy canteen of a commandeered school. These Cossacks were ordinary-looking Soviet youths with brutally short hair, sitting at long refectory tables in their Soviet tracksuits (blue, with double white stripes down the arms and legs, standard night clothing for all Soviet men on long train journeys), and they were slurping up the greasy meat stew being dished up out of an iron cauldron by a fearsome babushka. Everyone was grabbing for the bread. They stopped and stood up sheepishly when they saw me come in. One bowed. There was the hint of a clicking of heels.

There were a few dozen neo-Cossacks still sleeping in the school dormitories, on iron bunks. Soviet army kitbags lay in corners. Soviet guns and ammunition were piled up on all sides. But the rumpled tunics hung on the backs of chairs and the trousers dropped on the floor were altogether fussier than Soviet uniforms, with red or gold piping and double-headed eagle insignia. They had hung a black, yellow and white flag over the door. It was the spring of 1992, and it was the Cossacks' first armed sortie out of their traditional homeland.

Moldova was a tiny republic made up of the little chunk of Slavic industrial land where we were and a few Romanian-speaking provinces of historical Bessarabia. Independence from Moscow a few months before had not suited the book of the local Russians and Ukrainians of the factory zone, Pridnestroviye, which was separated from the rest of winegrowing Moldova by the broad

Dnestr River. The Slavs of Pridnestroviye suspected that Moldovan nationalists now ruling the new country, with their dark skins and Italianate language, might force a merger of Moldova and Romania next door, leaving them a shunned minority in a country of hostile blacks. The Communist bosses of Pridnestroviye wanted to keep control of the smoke-stack industry which they hoped, even in the new post-Soviet world, would one day make them rich. The ex-Soviet 14th Army which was stationed in Pridnestroviye was supposed to be neutral and keep the peace between the Pridnestroviye people and the Moldovans. But its Russian and Ukrainian soldiers were mostly recruited from the little Slav towns and villages nearby, so its sympathies were naturally with the Pridnestroviye leaders when they declared their tiny industrial zone independent of Moldova. There had been sporadic fighting along the river. Armed Moldovan police manned one side of the bridges, and armed Pridnestroviye militiamen manned the other.

When I walked over the river to the Pridnestroviye town of Dubossary on an overcast day in March, the shaggy, gruff militiamen had blocked the middle of the bridge with a huge armoured personnel carrier and daubed self-glorifying slogans all over it. A red flag fluttered in the wind. There was a thin stream of civilians crossing the river with me – people who had to get to work, go to the shops or meet their relatives, and were prepared to face the document checks on each side. Mostly depressed-looking young women with babies, they were pushing their prams cautiously between the rows of one-foot-wide anti-tank mines which the militiamen had also seen fit to lay all over the bridge.

Yeltsin was embarrassed by the Pridnestroviye Russians' appeals to Moscow for help, and by the 14th Army's taking their side. Modern Moscow hummed and hawed and did not recognize the Dnestr republic. But the idealistic Cossacks were delighted to rush to their aid.

'If there are threats to the lives of Slavs anywhere on the territory of the former Soviet Union, naturally we must go and protect them,' declaimed Yuri Grigoriyev, a sharp young man with a natty ginger moustache, in a burst of breathy sincerity. He had explained he was the head of the Cossack detachment billeted in the school in Dubossary, and whisked me off into his dormitory to tell me more. I had been expecting the wild belly-laughs of the Repin Cossacks, so I was finding Grigoriyev disappointingly short, spotty and serious. But I couldn't fault his chivalry. For propriety's sake, his number two – a big, shambling, silent, moustachioed man whose paunch made him look middle-aged but who was probably also in his twenties – was sitting in on our conversation as a chaperone, staring at the ceiling and occasionally, very furtively, wiping at his nose.

'A real war is building up here. We are fulfilling the role of a United Nations mission,' Grigoriyev carried on in his public-speaking voice. His greatcoat went down to the floor; much decorated with buttons, straps and pistol holsters, it was far too big for him and he had to push back the sleeves which kept flopping over his hands. It was also too hot for inside, but too complicated to undo without losing his dignity, so he was sweating uncomfortably.

Shy Cossack boys in tracksuits kept peering round the door at us, creeping closer and perching on beds, ready to help explain their sacred mission to me, or to scuttle away if Grigoriyev barked at them. We were beginning to attract a crowd.

When I asked Grigoriyev how many Cossacks were in Dubossary, his moustache began to twitch nervously. 'Oh, our numbers change constantly. There are more than a million and a half Cossacks registered in the Don region alone, and they all want to come here. Now more people – between thirty and forty a day – are arriving,' he said defensively.

(Oh no they weren't, said an exasperated middle-aged man in the local council office, when I dropped in there later: 'There are exactly seventy-two Cossacks in Dubossary, they're all inside that school, and no more are arriving,' Vladislav Finagin snapped.)

Perhaps aware that he was laying himself open to contradiction with these numbers, Grigoriyev began rootling round in his great-coat pockets. Eventually, he found what he was looking for and pulled out a much-folded photocopy of a telegram. 'There . . . you see?' he said triumphantly, spreading it out for me to read. It was from Ivan Kolodnin, the Don Cossacks' religious leader, and it pledged more help. 'We are waiting with all our forces for the order to go on crusade to you in Dubossary,' it said.

I asked the junior Cossacks about their time in Dubossary. They had been eager enough to interrupt Grigoriyev before with boasts about their sacred duty, but suddenly they went bashful and mumbly at the idea of being interviewed themselves.

'It's my wife, you see . . .' explained one youth, who was trying valiantly to grow the prescribed shaggy Cossack moustache. 'She doesn't know I'm here.'

The others scuffed their boots against bedsteads and nodded their shaven heads.

'But you've been here for a month. How did you explain to your wives and mothers that you were going to be away from home for so long?' I asked sternly, secretly entranced.

They livened up again, and there was much prodding of ribs and shamefaced laughter. 'I told mine I had been picked to go on tour for the karate team!' one said with a giggle. 'And I told mine I'd got six weeks' holiday booked through the factory at a sanatorium in Odessa!' smirked another. 'So you mustn't use our names, see, girl, because if you do it will be all up with us. Our wives will kill us!'

After this outburst of confidences, there was no stopping the once-shy junior Cossacks. They still wouldn't tell me their names, but they crowded into the tiny room, perching on beds and kitbags, explaining how they had been issued with their guns when they arrived here and started protecting the Pridnestroviye Russians and their helpless wives and children from the marauding Moldovans whose only thought was to rob and kill and rape.

'You see what filthy swine those Moldovan bastards are?' cried one nameless youth. 'You're a girl, and it's your feast day today. The eighth of March. International Women's Day! And those Moldovan bastards have forced you out to their war, when you should be at home celebrating with your family.'

I adopted a mournful look, and shrugged. 'That's what my work's like,' I said, a phrase I had learned deflected argument.

But an eddy of outrage ran through the group. 'No, no. It's a shame,' they chorused, and a couple of them immediately presented

me with spent bullet cases as improvised Women's Day presents.
'You should have flowers, but this is all we can offer. We Cossacks
are very chivalrous; we know how to behave to women, and you
really should have flowers,' Grigoriyev said. He begged me and my
Moldovan photographer, Tudor, to stay to lunch (which was the
same stew as breakfast), but as I sat down at the table I noticed a
couple of them sneaking off downstairs in their absurdly long
greatcoats, looking intent and purposeful.

Lunch dragged quietly on, and after another hour I stood up to
make my farewells.

'But you can't leave yet!' Grigoriyev said, looking genuinely
upset. 'Some of the boys have gone out to get you a present for
Women's Day, and they should be back any minute. I don't know
what's keeping them.'

'That's what my work's like . . . and I have a lot of people still
to see,' I apologized.

Whispering at each other, he and his silent number two escorted
me to the street and bowed deeply and sorrowfully as Tudor and I
turned the corner.

It was only when we had walked back over the bridge, found
our car, and driven nearly all the way to the Moldovan capital,
Kishinyov, that Tudor turned on the local radio to catch the news.
He listened for a few minutes, then burst out laughing and started
translating from Moldovan: '. . . Armed Cossacks in Dubossary
raided a market-gardening establishment today, and held pistols to
the heads of the workers, demanding that they surrender several
bunches of roses as what they called a gift for International
Women's Day. There are several dozen Cossacks stationed in
Dubossary, fighting alongside the Pridnestroviye militias . . .'

'Do you realize what that means?' Tudor chortled, turning the
radio down. 'Those were your flowers! Those chivalrous Cossacks
who went to get you a Women's Day present as one of their sacred
duties were actually looting them from the people they're supposed
to be protecting . . . Oh, those Cossacks!'

# SIX

It was hard to remember or even imagine the Caucasus from Moscow. In Moscow, the politicians of 1992 were sleek, smooth young men who wore silk ties and whose paeans of praise to democracy and the market economy were lapped up eagerly by Western diplomats. In Moscow, the articles I had written from the south – describing Cossacks and warriors with gold teeth and violent death and illegal gun sales and covert Russian aid and rebuilding the empire – seemed not only far-fetched but impossible. It made me feel schizophrenic even to try to marry up the way life was in the south with the way it was in Moscow. So I took to thinking of my Caucasus trips as completely private experiences, no more appropriate for discussion in the capital than the solitary rituals of applying face-packs and leg-wax are good subjects to talk about on a hot date later, an echo from another world.

In Moscow, the economy was the subject on everyone's lips. Yeltsin's government team were pushing ahead as fast as they dared with their experiments on the economy, and being rewarded on all sides with diplomatic friendships, foreign business interest and fat new loans from the IMF. True, the young men of Gaidar's government didn't actually have control of the levers of economic power that would back up their reforms. The central bank was not in Gaidar's hands, and it carried on churning out paper money, with nothing to back it, to pay wages. So inflation carried on sky-rocketing, and everyone blamed Gaidar's men. So far, it was only the thought of reform that counted.

However much people complained about their new poverty, and about being experimented on, and however many beggars with genteel accents had appeared on the street, there were also signs on the street that Gaidar's attempts at shock reforms were beginning to take. Foreign sweets went on sale everywhere. You measured the level of inflation in a new town, or a new week, by the price of a Snickers bar. The large and threatening men, always in groups of four, who had once squeezed their enormous shoulders and jaws into tiny Soviet toy cars before screeching round Moscow on unspecified but murky-looking business, gradually traded in their Zhigulis for Mercedes and their long black leather coats for cashmere. Luxury car dealerships opened in central Moscow. Private shops opened inside government ministries. Russians in sleek furs began to appear in the 'strictly-credit-card-only' dollar stores, full of luxury imported goods, which had been set up for foreigners in Soviet days. They piled up their trolleys with tropical fruit. Outside, in the jungle of kiosks on every pavement, first the pineapple and then the kiwi replaced the banana as the post-Soviet fruit most in demand. Real money from somewhere began pouring into the Russian economy.

Everyone wanted to get rich quick. Everyone was thinking of a scheme or a scam, even the gloating little girl on the television lottery ad who proclaimed every night, with a triumphant thumbs-up sign, 'I'm going to be SUCH a millionairess!'

Everyone was buying and selling, but not necessarily in the places you would expect. There were never any books any more in the state bookshop down the road from me, for instance. And there were never any state employees inside. They were all outside on the pavement, manning the private stalls they had set up, selling the books from inside at two or three times their official state price. It was a fiddle that drove Yevgeniya to distraction. She had liked shopping at the bookshop but didn't like feeling cheated now.

Most of my friends were beginning to work out how to play the new game. Nadya completed her divorce, keeping the flat. She complained that her salary was only a few thousand roubles a month, scarcely enough for bread and sausage. But she hardly ever went to Patrice Lumumba University to teach. She had found enough private English-teaching work, paid in dollars, for herself and her son Danya to get by very comfortably. She just hadn't yet learned to think of this as real work, to be counted with her official salary as what she was living on, or perhaps she didn't want to be envied, so she never talked about her extra money.

Yevgeniya had found the money somewhere to plan a summer in Sweden.

Andrei was full of wild get-rich-quick schemes on a grand scale. 'What's the point of thinking small?' he said. He went to Turkey and bought 200 leather jackets. He sold them by knocking on the doors of the new private offices opening up all over Moscow. He borrowed my flat and hired two seventeen-year-old girls to model them, wearing nothing but the jackets, lying on my bed with my kitten draped across their crotches or climbing out of the breast pocket. I found the negatives, which he had left lying round the flat. The bed was broken. I was furious, but he was pleased. He had made a huge profit. 'We have to survive somehow. You can see how bad things are here for us Russians,' he said, with practised collective self-pity but no hint of apology. 'Now, will you open a bank account for me in London?'

*

Even if they were starting to do well, most people were still a bit scared of the future, and everyone still played on your heartstrings with their hard-luck stories. Everyone, that is, except Boris the Bandit, the opportunist with a heart of gold.

I followed Boris the Bandit's adventures second-hand, through a young British student called Roderick who was living at a hostel studying Russian for a few months before going home to start university. He would come and eat at my flat every few weeks, and every time he came he would tell me a new instalment in the life of Boris.

Boris the Bandit was a delightfully flamboyant character. He had come to Moscow from the provinces at the end of perestroika, and he shared none of the timid worries of my law-abiding friends. He would take Roderick out of the hostel for walks around the centre of town, marvelling at the big cars and the kiosks, and exclaim: 'The streets here are paved with gold! There's money everywhere, if you only know how to get your hands on it.'

Roderick came to know Boris the Bandit through another student on his course, who had once lived a month with the Russian family of Boris's girlfriend Masha. Now the eighteen-year-old Masha had left her parents' home, to their great anxiety, and moved into a plush downtown flat with her *biznismen* lover.

For a while, Boris the Bandit was doing nicely. He bought a car, and took Roderick and the other students and Masha out to restaurants in it. He gave them money. He bought them bottles of vodka. And he demonstrated to Roderick how best to shoot a person if you wanted to get their wallet without getting blood on it – through the buttock.

Then things went wrong. Masha went home for the weekend to see her parents. When she came back to the flat, the door had been blown away by a bomb and the interior was a smoking ruin. Boris had vanished. It was weeks before he reappeared at Roderick's hostel, slipping the armed guard at the desk downstairs the usual huge tip to be allowed straight upstairs. Roderick was sitting in his room with three of the girls from his course. They were delighted to see him and asked him in for a drink. 'No,' Boris the Bandit replied brusquely. 'I've got to take just Roderick out for a drink. It's men's business.' Roderick followed him out to the car, where two men were sitting in the front seats. Boris and he climbed into the back. Boris opened a bottle of champagne and poured him a glass.

'Now, Roderick, the two of us have to go somewhere. Can you keep an eye on *him*?' Boris said, and he and the front-seat passenger vanished. Roderick was left in the car, with a glass in one hand, a bottle in the other, and a stranger in the front seat staring straight ahead. He was a well-brought-up English boy, and there were plenty of empty glasses on the seat, so he coughed gently and said: 'Er, would you like some champagne?' It was only then that he noticed that the man's wrists were handcuffed to the steering wheel.

'It was so *embarrassing*,' Roderick told me afterwards, with a teenage blush creeping up under his T-shirt. 'I mean, what do you say to a man in handcuffs?' It was only when Boris the Bandit and his silent friend returned to finish the bottle, having made a phone call round the corner, that Roderick heard the full story. Boris the Bandit had persuaded a business contact to lend him $10,000 for a deal, but he hadn't returned it. The contact's gang had firebombed his flat. So Boris was taking his own revenge, he explained cheerfully, by kidnapping a junior member of the gang. 'I got rid of them eventually,' Roderick said, rather mournfully. 'But I don't think I'll be seeing Boris the Bandit again.'

He was wrong. Boris turned up one more time at the hostel, sidekick in tow, wanting Roderick to put them up for the night and ask no questions. The gang was out to get them. They were about to do a disappearing act. Both men had dyed their hair peroxide blonde.

*

The capitalist bacchanalia meant crime. Even if they weren't quite as blatant as Boris the Bandit, almost everyone in the country was on the fiddle. It was hard not to be. There was literally no law any more to define what you could and couldn't do in the new world. Soviet law had strictly forbidden most of what new Russians spent their time doing – buying, selling and earning foreign currency, and the sale of goods on the street. Now there was no Soviet Union any more, and the Russian government was encouraging them to do all these things. Russia needed new laws to regulate those processes.

But Yeltsin and the parliament were so busy battling with each other, vetoing each other's decisions, each trying to impeach or dissolve or somehow silence the other, that the parliament had no time to bother with creating a new base of post-Soviet law. So the old Soviet laws remained on the statute books, so irrelevant that even the police never consulted them, and trade remained technically illegal.

Despairing of getting the parliament to knuckle under, Yeltsin started introducing more daring market reforms by presidential decree. But the courts had no legal basis for interpreting his decrees. He decreed, for instance, that Muscovites could carry gas pistols to protect them against street crime. But the pistols, not yet made in Russia, were confiscated at airports because customs officials regarded them as illegal under a 1982 Soviet law.

Naturally enough, confusion over what should be now considered a crime gripped even the most honest of Russians, brought up in a stable Soviet world where the rank-and-file obeyed authoritarian laws even if the powerful bent all the rules. They felt they were back in the world of the nineteenth-century witticism: 'The harshness of Russian laws is compensated for by the fact that no one need obey them.'

Naturally, too, there was an atmosphere of suspicion, envy and paranoia about anyone who was somehow managing to find a way through this legal muddle and get rich. The envy and hatred of other people's success that runs through Russian society is illustrated by the folk tales which Russians love to tell against themselves. In one, God appears to Vanya, promising to grant him one wish but warning him that He will grant his neighbour Vasya the same wish twice over. The tormented Vanya thinks and thinks and thinks, and can't bear to ask for anything good for himself because he would so hate it if Vasya reaped twice the reward . . . and finally answers sadly: 'God, put out ONE of my eyes.' Another folk tale shows the fear with which good Russians approach any material improvement in their own lives. Ryaba the chicken lays a golden egg. Her owners are so confused over what to do with it, and appalled at the changes wealth might bring to their lives, that they let it drop, break and become worthless. Then they live happily ever after.

This suspicion of wealth makes people look tolerantly on theft from a rich man, saying indulgently that it will help him get to heaven. So when rich people started appearing in the midst of the post-Soviet *bezpredel*, the rest of the country was convinced they must all be criminals. Often, they were right.

Who the first new rich were and how they had got their money was not immediately clear. Anyone who worked for a foreign company, earning an inflation-proof dollar salary, was doing comfortably. Despite their low salaries, people in government quickly got enough money for expensive cars and clothes. The sons of diplomats and party officials, who had been to top schools and belonged to the Moscow old-boy network and spoke foreign languages and understood economics, set up import-export businesses bringing consumer goods to Russia for resale in kiosks and in the huge wholesale markets all over town. Then there were the others, the flashy young millionaires from nowhere who first began to buy Rolls-Royces, emaciated girls with scarlet lips and microskirts, and lobsters and champagne to feed them with, and who all said coyly that they had made their money in metals.

All over the country, a great transfer of wealth was beginning. Privatization of all Russia's state enterprises was planned. Once the sell-offs started, workers and outsiders would be able to own a stake in their country for the first time. Meanwhile, who was better placed than the factory bosses to quietly flog off their enterprise's best assets in advance, and keep the cash for themselves? A brisk and illegal trade began in fake export licences for Russia's valuable raw materials, oil, metals, gas. The people astute or well-placed enough to feather their own nests in time were the Communist-era managers who had always been at the top, or their *nomenklatura* families. Yeltsin and Gaidar turned a blind eye to evidence of corruption. If there was to be instant capitalism, to replace the old economy of fictitious state orders and paper that had existed only a few months before, there had to be money in it. How it got there didn't much matter.

Corruption busters were hired by Yeltsin in a burst of publicity, then fired a few months later if they asked too many questions about the questionable dealings of those too close to the top. Mikhail Gurtovoi, a crime journalist and an outsider to Kremlin wheeler-dealing, was hired briefly in the first flush of enthusiastic democracy of 1992. Later the liberal Yuri Boldyrev – an ex-electrical engineer with an economics degree who got into politics on an anti-Communist ticket in the Soviet elections of 1989 – ran the Presidential Anti-Corruption Unit for a year. But he too was sacked. Boldyrev fled back to a parliamentary career, but he carried on accusing his ex-friends, Gaidar's 'vulgar liberals', of creating a climate of vice and violent confrontation in Russia by condoning theft from the state on a grand scale. Not only did Gaidar's reformists condone corruption, he said, but they dabbled in it themselves while the president turned a blind eye. Boldyrev's corruption probes had been repeatedly stopped from the top. 'I'm not talking about a series of mishaps, or shortcomings, or procrastination, but a completely conscious policy,' Boldyrev said sadly.

'We're being robbed blind,' people who had not made money

kept lamenting. 'We are being deceived.' No wonder the man on the street had given the democratic élite a new name, a pun on the Russian word for theft, *krad*. Yeltsin's men were now known everywhere as the *demokrady*.

It was an investigation into army corruption that finally got Boldyrev the sack at the end of 1992, because the liberals in power were far from the only people taking advantage of *bezpredel*. Boldyrev wrote a report detailing the off-duty activities – car sales, arms sales, and dodgy large-scale barter deals – of generals in the ex-Soviet army stationed in Germany, who were preparing, as slowly as possible, to come home, and wanted to bring a nest-egg with them. He recommended that five of them be stripped of their rank for graft. He handed his findings to Yeltsin personally, expecting heads to roll right up to the level of the defence minister, Pavel Grachev, but the only result was that his own job was organized away.

When the Russian army finally came home from Germany, in the summer of 1994, Yeltsin was still feeling kindly enough disposed towards its chief, General Matvei Burlakov, to reward him with the high-flying new job of deputy defence minister. Boldyrev's report surfaced again only after a young reporter on the same corruption trail was blown to pieces by a bomb a few months later. Amid public uproar and suspicion that Dima Kholodov's death had been ordered by the defence ministry, Yeltsin finally sacked Burlakov.

One piece of shady dealing that went undetected by officials at the time, but assumed dark significance later, was carried out by Burlakov's boss, Defence Minister Grachev. Grachev was a close friend of Yeltsin; he had a round moonlike face, with a beaky nose sticking out of it at an improbable angle and a sly grin.

In 1991 and 1992, Grachev withdrew the Russian army's detachments from Chechnya. But, although Russia had stigmatized Dudayev's Chechnya as an illegal regime, Grachev ordered his men to leave behind half their weaponry in 1992 rather than face a confrontation with the Chechens surrounding their base. Dudayev's Chechens became the proud owners of tanks, troop carriers, artillery and thousands of small arms. Grachev said the army was simply too weak and understaffed to take its weapons away with it.

Did he make a deal with Dudayev? And how much did he get for it? people in Russia wondered later, as the rumours of Grachev's corruption spread. He acquired the nickname 'Pasha Mercedes'. The Chechens kept the guns.

Yeltsin declared public war after war on corruption, but nothing stopped it. Within a couple of years, much of the old *nomenklatura* élite of the Soviet era had equipped itself with the money and possessions it needed to lead the lifestyle it had always been accustomed to, but under the different conditions of capitalism.

If the crimes of the Russian élite went quietly unpunished, so did those of the Russian underworld bosses who ran the regional gangs that had carved Moscow up. The police arrested the small fry, but did cosy deals with the crime leaders. Everyone was happy. It was only the crimes of the upstart outsiders who had muscled in on the new wealth – the Caucasian gangs who had moved north at the end of perestroika and were fighting a turf war for a stake in Moscow, and the yobbish Russian nobodies from the depths of the provinces who had also somehow grabbed a slice of the nation's assets for themselves – which were constantly surrounded with a blaze of publicity. Unlike the familiar old party bosses, these newcomers were not *nashi*. Although police and crime reporters say the Chechen criminals eventually lost this war, and settled down to a small if profitable share in the capital's multiethnic extortion and protection-racket business, their popular reputation for fearsome criminality kept growing and growing.

*

The Chechens weren't the only outsiders who suffered the Russian establishment's hostility. The other upstart outsiders – the now-wealthy Russians from nowhere who were first known as *nuvo-rishy* (*nouveaux riches*) and later simply as *noviye russkiye* (New Russians) – were mocked and detested by the rest of the country. Who did these low-lifes think they were?

They were vulgar. They were criminal. They were showy. They shot each other on street corners. They opened casinos and strip clubs. They drank Amaretto. They drove huge limousines and shiny Japanese jeeps. They clanked with heavy gold jewellery. Their women wore too much skimpy, glittering Versace. They bought mobile phones which rang endlessly at restaurant tables. They held loud conspiratorial conversations on them, disturbing other diners with their uncouth provincial accents: 'Da . . . da . . . ya pod'yedu cherez chas.' 'Yes . . . yes . . . I'll drive over in an hour.'

The New Russians' Bible was the new glossy magazine, Domovoi (House Spirit), which offered advice on how to train your governess, how to buy an island, and what kind of jacuzzi was most chic. The New Russians were the personification of excess and bezpredel. The snickering liberal intelligentsia started making cruel jokes about them, the first jokes of post-Soviet times, tittering at the New Russians' determination to out-spend each other and prove their worth by the size of their wallets. One New Russian says proudly to another: 'Look, I've got a new Armani tie. It cost me $1,000!' His friend looks pityingly back at him. 'You fool,' he answers. 'I've just got a new Armani tie too, but I managed to get mine for $2,000.'

The New Russians offended their compatriots not only by their outrageous vulgarity and their presumed bandit tendencies. As well as robbing someone, somewhere, to get their wealth, the new rich had committed a crime more frightening to the Russian society from which they emerged. It was the conviction of these newcomers to wealth that everything was possible and that whatever they personally set their minds on could be achieved. That conviction had been borne out by their own success. But this arrogant presumption of personal freedom was a denial of the rigid hierarchy of Russian social organization which had existed for hundreds of years, a bulldozer running amok through the carefully laid bricks and cement which had held people together for three centuries.

In the early eighteenth century, Tsar Peter the Great built a complex fifteen-layer bureaucracy as part of his plan to organize, civilize and control the upper layers of a still largely medieval society. Peter had grown up in an age of armed revolt against the monarchy by wild noblemen; he was determined to make the upper layers of society as docile as the courtiers of Versailles. He succeeded brilliantly.

Whether you were a colonel in the army or a paper-pusher in a ministry or a diplomat abroad, if you were Russian and educated you had a grade in this bureaucracy. Everyone knew exactly to whom they had to kowtow and who they could sneer at and ignore. (On the side, it was tacitly accepted that you stole from those above you, or won their sympathy with wildly exaggerated sob stories. Similarly, you took bribes from those below you in exchange for doing them favours, after bullying and browbeating them to extract the nugget of truth from what you knew was the wildly exaggerated sob story they were telling you.) You had no loyalties to your own class in the structure, only to your close circle within it. Your loyalties within the system were to individuals immediately above and below you: the good superior who protected you, or the slavishly loyal subordinate whom you protected. Right at the pinnacle, above the squabbles for power and influence that were an inevitable part of the system, reigned the Good Tsar. Immense personal loyalty to the Tsar was the cement that held the system together: even if the Tsar was harsh to you, it was an article of faith that his bad advisers were plotting against you and were really to blame. Above the Tsar, and also vested in his person since he ruled by divine right, was the God of the Orthodox Church. Russians believed profoundly in this incense-wafting, icon-laden institution, which was also a bulwark of support for the Tsars. This feudal network of patronage and subservience, rising up through society from the lowest peasant to God Himself, was secure, if stifling. It persisted right to the end of the Tsarist era –

– and beyond. After a brief period of Soviet experiment in the 1920s, the hierarchical principle returned in a form only slightly changed from Tsarist days. Moscow was stuffed with ministries, and the ministries were stuffed with people who feared taking decisions, in case they irritated their immediate superiors. The simplest decisions were passed up the hierarchical pyramid to the top by fearful underlings. Orders were obeyed without question. When Stalin absent-mindedly approved two rival designs for the

Hotel Moskva, right outside the Kremlin walls, none of his aides had the nerve to point out his mistake to him – so both façades were built, facing different directions. Although the Communists had come to power on a wave of protest against the Tsars, with the rallying cry of class war, the irony of the system they created to run the Soviet Union was that it was startlingly like the one they overthrew, right up to the authoritarian figure – a General Secretary, not a Tsar – who topped the social pinnacle. The only difference in this system was that the Orthodox Church had been cast aside, and replaced by the canon of Marxism-Leninism. Churches were shut down, but metro stations and political buildings worshipping the new ideology of the machine age were built in shapes reminiscent of the old houses of worship. In the age of the deification of the state, Soviet power was feudalism without God.

Soviet underlings not only didn't take responsibility or answer questions, but also seldom asked them. It was the mark of an intellectual, half opted out of the system, or a boss, high up in the system, to dare ask the question 'Why?', or to interpret or alter any ruling from above to fit in with changing circumstances, just as it was a sign of being a top boss if you dared answer the question. Even in modern times, if you asked a burly guard why he was barring your way to a door you wanted to pass through, he would only shrug, scratch his head, and answer something along the lines of: 'I'm just a footsoldier' or 'I'm only obeying orders.'

It was one of Solzhenitsyn's great complaints, in his massive description of the Soviet prison camps, *The Gulag Archipelago*, that so few people arrested on crowded streets asked why they were being detained, or kicked up a fuss, or shouted that they had done nothing wrong. Instead, they trooped meekly off to the Lubyanka without a word of protest. It was only once they were inside the prisons, being interrogated or sentenced for nonsensical crimes, that they realized they had been excommunicated from the Soviet social hierarchy altogether and began to protect themselves by resisting. By then, it was too late.

Everything in Soviet Russia came down through the system of patronage. Flats, cars and perks were not bought or sold, but 'received' or 'allocated' from above, just as scarce goods were 'acquired' from contacts higher up in the system. Party officials got the best theatre tickets, and their ZiL and Chaika limousines were the only cars allowed in the left-hand lane on the road. Traffic cops shouted and bullied complaisant drivers into parting with fines, but meekly accepted being bullied in their turn by their bosses, who turned the other cheek when they were yelled at in turn by theirs. There is no word in Russian for bullying, a British notion which suggests it is unfair for a powerful person to threaten someone weaker; in Russia, everything that gets done is done by bullying. Like a keystone, the power of the authoritarian ruler held together the hierarchy below. Huge crowds of people who had lost their families to the gulags wept with genuine sorrow when Stalin, the pinnacle of the system, died; they felt bereft, alone, and panicky. There were more red eyes and black armbands – though fewer each time – for Khrushchev, Brezhnev, Andropov, and even the lacklustre Chernenko, who died in 1995.

Soviet social order resembled the seven Stalin skyscrapers, built in the 1950s, which still dominate the Moscow landscape. It was a vast wedding-cake of layers, edged with separate pinnacles, rising into the sky like a church steeple, but not pointing at God. Inside, everyone had his place.

At the ground floor were the rooms of the non-Russian republics, with their 'less civilized' inhabitants. They were the foundation of the Soviet edifice. Each republican room was given its own little imitation-Russian internal structure, and an ethnic boss with a phone line to Moscow to report on and keep order among the savages.

But most of the space was taken up by the huge Russian structure above that. On one layer, you might find the fuggy comfort of the peasant hut, all home-made jams and strings of onions and herbal remedies and cosy superstitions. On the same floor, but in another room, were the quarters of the collective farmers in their crumbling country apartment homes, and the rustic newcomers to towns, packed into dormitories or little flats but still living to the rhythm of the fields, planting their potatoes, tomatoes and radishes at the weekends. On another floor were the rooms of the industrial proletariat, with the clang and scrape of machines echoing through the windows and overalls hung up to dry by the stove, and of the local Party officials they elected with their lists and precepts and slogans and the complete works of Lenin prominently displayed. On another floor, further up, were the rooms of the intellectuals: the cramped, book-lined studies of the academics, the drawing-boards of the engineers, and the musicians' mess of velvet-wrapped violins and scattered sheet music.

The communication channels connecting all these floors to the upper echelons were the Red Nooks – the Party centres in every workplace – with their pictures of Lenin and tractor-building successes, their active workers taking a role in Party affairs and getting themselves inside a lift to the top.

And right at the top were the senior politicians' floors, long corridors for whispered plotting. The uppermost rooms were all marble and glistening wood. Lower down were the teak-finish offices of medium-importance bureaucrats, with the orange curtains and the T-shaped desks and many telephones. Out on the side was the snoops' room with the listening apparatus. At the doors were guards, whose jobs was to keep the masses out. These heights were not for the ordinary person.

For the timid, there was a lot of charm in a system which had a clearly defined place in it for everyone. Whichever room you found yourself in the social edifice, the people closest to you in it would help you keep the masonry from falling on your head with acts of tremendous kindness which most Westerners would never dream of, breaking and twisting the law to keep you safe. It was only the claustrophobics who hit trouble, because no one was allowed to leave their cosy room and find out what was happening elsewhere in the house.

You could visit your neighbours on the same level. Every level had its public meeting rooms. In places everyone could get to there were the Red Nooks, looking out onto green parks with public gymnastics displays under the slogans. There were the hurried, stand-up cafés where you couldn't smoke or drink and where you took whatever food was offered. Shut away in dusty corners were the disreputable beer halls where you couldn't drink beer. Further up were the tinkling chandeliers and delicate plaster of the concert halls and opera houses, the echoing splendour of palaces turned into people's museums, the nostalgic glamour of the second-home country *dacha* with its wood aromas and apple blossom. Further up still were the gold-encrusted official banqueting rooms and special shops for the political élite. If you were an engineer, you might marry a musician, or a writer, or an intellectual, whom you'd met in one of these public rooms of this great collective home, or just on the landing of your floor.

And there were the little side towers, separate from the main social structure. One of these was the sanitized Orthodox Church, which carried on working, in a limited and supervised way, under Soviet rule. Here, you could climb into a different world of incense-scented interiors, icon-hung rooms, choirs, seminaries and religious refectories. But these little towers rose only so high. Once you entered them, you couldn't get back out into the main building again unless you used the secret back door that connected you unseen to the KGB and the power structures.

The main building was dotted with service lifts: you could get into one and swoop painlessly up a few floors by going to university or college or music school, or by being promoted in the army, or the bureaucracy, or the KGB, or, most popularly, the Party.

But the main stairs upwards were closed. Guards were posted at each of the floors to stop cheats sneaking up to the wrong place. You couldn't just walk away from the level you were born into, and experience how other people lived. You couldn't read the books or see the films or visit the countries or listen to the music appropriate to higher floors. People who trespassed outside their proper domain were sent to the underground.

Just like the Stalin skyscrapers, the social structure had many underground floors, stretching down secretly into the depths as far as they rose proudly into the air. In this subterranean world, far from daylight, the only people who could run freely up and down the stairs were the KGB officials who dispensed justice, or mercy, or death.

Students who were expelled from the Komsomol Young Communists' League and therefore from their colleges for immoral behaviour – drinking, having abortions, reading banned literature, flirting with the black market, dodging the draft – were put just one floor down. They were only guilty of adolescent hooliganism, graffiti-ing their names on the walls of their social room. They were often let back above ground if they repented publicly enough.

Dissidents, the inquisitive or the angry who tried to break down the door of the room they had been born in, or to tunnel out to new parts of the building or away altogether – to Israel if they were Jewish, to the West if they tried to marry out – were a more serious threat to the structure. They were guilty of anti-Soviet activity, or wrecking. They were dispatched further down, to the secret world of cells and camps and searchlights which citizens above the ground hardly knew about but which was later described by Alexander Solzhenitsyn.

So were economic speculators, who tried illegally to increase their floorspace with furtive flat swaps, or rip off their workplace to fill their homes with luxury. They were altering the common structure without planning permission or regard for the stability of the whole building; they were destabilizing.

Nationalists and separatists from the non-Russian republics were more threatening still. They were shaking the edifice from the ground level up, setting the chandeliers far above tinkling, their selfish wish for their own freedom threatening the millions of others who lived above them. They too went to the cells.

Down at the very bottom were the pure criminals. In Soviet Russia, the thieves' world was a highly organized but upside-down mirror image of the respectable society above the surface. Interior ministry criminal historians believe it may have been born from White Army officers after they lost the Civil War, turning to crime to survive outside the Red structure being built over their heads. To belong to this world, a fully-fledged thief had to keep aloof from all things Soviet: he must avoid military service in the Soviet army, must not live in state housing, and must serve time in the gulag prison zone. The mark of his craft was skilful pickpocketing. Thieves were initiated into thieves' circles; their leaders had thieves' conventions; and their wise men, the Party members of the under-world, were called thieves-in-law. There was honour among the

Soviet thieves: they looked out for their own and they put a proportion of their swag into their *chornaya kassa* or thieves' bank to support the families of the fallen and the legal expenses of those captured by the state. But their cruelty and hostility to the rest of society, even to the once-respectable surface-dwellers who had been summarily dispatched underground with them, made them the terror of the gulags.

The crime of all these people was to try to knock holes in the social order, one way or another; to assert themselves, their personal wish for freedom or advancement, at the expense of the rest. What they had in common, whatever their crime, was that however much they might be against the system they were still inside it, and of it.

The whole social order was kept together by the secret police, the eyes and ears of the remote leaders at the top, watching and waiting in every nook and cranny all over the building, reporting misdemeanours of thought, word and deed. It was the secret police, too, whose job was to quietly repair any structural faults in this perfect edifice without letting public attention be drawn to them.

To do this, they used the fiction of the External Enemy. This bogeyman of Soviet collective thought was reputed to be somewhere outside the building, tunnelling like a mole to get in and cause whatever damage he could. The defining characteristic of the External Enemy was that he did not recognize this perfect social structure, and would demolish it – and the Russian way of life with it – by bulldozing straight through it. Sometimes the External Enemy was the West, sometimes a hate object closer at hand. Traditionally, in Tsarist as well as in Soviet times, the External Enemy was the Jews, with their possible links to the outside and their possible international conspiracies.

When one part of the building inconveniently sprang a leak, when a ceiling fell in or a floor needed mending, public attention inside the building was diverted by a shouted SOS: the External Enemy has been sighted! If a factory's output was too low, or someone was caught stealing, or the neighbour married a foreigner, the guilty would be arrested to shouts of wrecking or anti-Soviet activity. Good citizens would rush naively to patrol the rooms and corridors in their common home, to keep away the imaginary enemy, while the real damaged part was quietly locked up and repairs carried out by the policemen in the know.

Because all wealth and influence came from being high up in the organizational pyramid, the people at the top fought like rats to stay there. There were cliques and cabals and intrigues and plots. Kremlin life was a naked struggle for power. Political fights were never over principle; no one ever resigned out of shame if he was caught with his hand in the till, but only if his opponents chose to publicize his crime and hound him out of office. There was no absolute morality governing these fights, only the quest for power. Fighting dirty to stay in the same place was socially acceptable, and even necessary in a system where there was no law but the survival of the fittest. But fighting dirty to get ahead was frowned on. The phrase 'making a career for yourself', in Russian, sounds selfish and negative in a way that is hard to convey in English; there is a suggestion in it of dragging yourself up over other people's broken bodies, of brute selfishness, of vicious greed. So the politicians at the top did not want their power struggles made public. They needed to keep public respect. The notion of the External Enemy protected the political élite from prying eyes further down the structure.

But cold cynicism began to damage the edifice as the Soviet order lost its ideological energy. In their hearts, people stopped respecting the principles of the people above them in the late Soviet social order, and no one believed any of the top people would ever dream of doing anything genuine for the common good. When a politician announced a campaign, with a fanfare of noble-sounding explanations of why it would benefit the masses, his announcement was always treated with extreme suspicion and scepticism. 'What's in it for him? It's all just *vranyo*,' they would mutter privately, a nod to high-up spin-doctoring, although in public they too would fulsomely praise the idea. In the case of most Soviet politicians, people were right to be suspicious: the 'campaigns' would peter out, the idealistic phrases that had begun them forgotten, with nothing much accomplished except a bit of extra power or prestige for their initiator. With these politicians, it was the visible search for personal self-advancement behind the disguise of a search for the common good that alienated observers.

People also grew sceptical about the destructive power of the External Enemy. Were the Americans really brutal, greedy capitalists? Were the English still a race of top-hatted oppressors of the poor? They wanted to see for themselves. More and more often, they tried to read banned Western books, buy banned Western goods or sign up for whatever rare foreign trips they could wangle. If they did make it to what their political leaders called the 'decaying West', they usually came back dreaming of the wealth and luxury of abroad. The slogans of the élite became the subject of satirical humour. Only the naive still believed.

In a society full of suspicion, people often felt manipulated by those above them. No one quite dared to accuse high-ups of misbehaviour, so they took refuge in elliptical political analysis by questions. It was always the same three questions, a heritage from early Soviet days: Who is to blame? Who stands to gain? Who is beating whom? Out of the remnants of deference to the hierarchy, the answers were not brutal namings of names – Petrov, Ivanov, Gorbachev; the accusers would usually restrain themselves to pointing above them, and blaming 'certain forces' and 'I think you know quite well who I mean'. Whispers and suppressed rage were everywhere. It was the time of the conspiracy theory.

All that was left of the socialist idea, by the end of the Brezhnev era, was a culture of mendacity. Politicians no longer expected those below them to actually believe their official lies, but they still derived power from making underlings repeat them *as if* they believed them. Out of inertia, the underlings often did. But cracks were appearing everywhere.

When the energetic Mikhail Gorbachev came to power in 1985, he wanted to set this creaking house in order. He exposed some of the cracks – the corruption, the bribe-taking, the failing economy – to public view, believing that all the rooms were full of enthusiasts who would leap forward to suggest imaginative repairs.

Pandemonium ensued. All over the house, people suddenly realized that they had a chance to complain about conditions in their rooms. People from the political upstairs, the *verkhushka* or summit, complained they were losing power. People from the intellectuals' rooms wanted to get abroad and share ideas with their foreign colleagues. People from the republics complained about the bad smells and pollution coming from the Moscow rubbish bins of nuclear waste and factories positioned at their windows – and then, more directly, about the Moscow politicians who had put them there. Holes were knocked in every door and every wall. People talked to and about the castes of society they had never come across, and were outraged at the injustice and inequality they found.

Even the KGB joined in. The younger members of the secret police were highly educated and intelligent, with more informed reasons than most for criticizing the way the Soviet Union was run. Many of them joined the crowds clamouring for change. Underground, all the prisoners and criminals got out. The dissidents walked free. The Jews went to Israel. The speculators openly set up businesses and were given the respectable new name of entrepreneurs. Pornography was sold on street corners. The social structure crumbled, the Soviet Union collapsed, and the republics decamped altogether.

No wonder Gorbachev was bewildered. He never intended to bring the whole social structure tumbling down round his ears. And no wonder ordinary Russians, shivering in the ruins of their once-mighty building, cursed him for destroying their civilization.

Now Yeltsin seemed to be going further still, joyfully clearing away the ruins, watched equally joyfully by Western politicians who were enthusiastic about what they saw as his plans to let every Russian have his own space and build the personal future on it that he chose for himself. This was democracy the way the West understood it, and Yeltsin was rewarded with words of encouragement, promises of friendship, and cash from Western financial organizations and governments to pay for the changes.

In a final farewell to the old order, Yeltsin abolished the KGB. There was no need in a society of equals for an all-powerful secret police, for phone taps, secretive arrests or political surveillance. Governing Russia would be done in full public view from now on, by people-power institutions: an elected parliament, an open government, and an elected president. There would be no more secretive Kremlin cabals. Now everyone could travel where they wanted and say what they thought, there was nothing for the KGB to report on.

Half a dozen little security agencies were set up in its place, separate, uncoordinated and underfunded. Of them, the two biggest were the lowly security ministry, reporting to the prime minister like any ordinary ministry, which took on most domestic counter-intelligence, and a separate foreign intelligence service under Yevgeny Primakov, which ran the remaining spies. The huge statue of Felix Dzerzhinsky, founder of the Soviet secret police, which had stared out over Moscow from a plinth outside the Lubyanka until angry Russians toppled it during the August 1991 coup, was quietly removed to lie round the back of an art gallery.

The once-hated 'cloak-and-dagger knights' of the KGB started trying to be lovable. Agents opened a museum at their Lubyanka headquarters to show the public some of their old tricks – eyeglasses with fatal doses of poison, shoes with hollowed-out heels for carrying secrets in, briefcases that could send satellite messages. My husband made friends with the ex-KGB general, Oleg Kalugin, and used to take him out to tea and feed him and his granddaughters cakes. 'They just hoover up those cakes,' he laughed. He was almost as distressed as the urbane Kalugin himself when the elderly agent was detained, during a trip to London, and questioned about his involvement in the long-ago murder of the Bulgarian secret agent Georgy Markov by poisoned umbrella tip. Other KGB agents slipped around foreign journalists' offices, coat collars turned up, flogging off old secret files from their archives for a few thousand dollars at a time. They had to make ends meet, they muttered pitifully

Getting rid of the KGB was the act most praised by Yevgeniya and her Russian democrat friends. It represented no more worries about meeting their foreign friends, no more sneaking round with banned books wrapped in newspaper, no more careful phone conversations. It meant no more fear.

Andrei Konchalovsky, a Russian film director who had gone into self-imposed exile in Hollywood years before, returned – all charm, baggy linen suits, Western worries about vitamin intake, and sunglasses – soon after the Soviet collapse. He wanted to make a new film, at home, a gently mocking look at people's attitudes to the new freedom, called *Ryaba My Chicken*. He shot most of it in the countryside, and came back to Moscow marvelling at the way his compatriots had changed. 'It's dangerous in Russia now,' he said excitedly. 'In Europe it was dangerous in the sixteenth century, when you had to take bodyguards to go out at night or someone would rob you in the great woods. In Russia now, you can't wire money; you have to carry it with you. So you sit on it and you have guards. It's all danger. Russia's in that medieval time now, and I don't know how long it will last . . .'

And his eyes widened as he described the pirate qualities of his countrymen now they were casting off their unnaturally sedate Soviet selves: 'Much more savage, anarchistic, emotionally unrepressed, wild, beautiful . . . free.'

For a year or so, it looked as though Russia might really become free under Yeltsin. Most intellectuals – traditionally a separate class of people who sat on the sidelines of active life, thinking, but seldom meddled in the practical business of running the country – still met at endless seminars in converted palaces, discussing philosophy and their ever-shrinking salaries. But some went into government as new democratic politicians.

Their initiatives, however, were often muddled and impractical, and they were treated with contempt by the hard core of lifelong bureaucrats. The new boys didn't know how things should be done, they mocked. They had no experience. They weren't business-like. They quarrelled all the time, and they couldn't impose order on the chaos around them.

Gradually, the old class of professional administrators who had run Soviet Russia in the 1980s squeezed out the democratic competition and came back to run their departments with the old mixture of fist-thumping threats and patronage. The sons of KGB generals presented television shows. The sons of Party members ran international companies. The democratic mayor of Moscow, Gavriil Popov, resigned in a huff in 1992 over the pace of economic reform in the Russian capital; his number two, the briskly efficient construction engineer Yuri Luzhkov, ran the city for the next four years without benefit of elections, but voters were heartily relieved their city was back in the hands of a good administrator. The democratic Yegor Gaidar, Russia's acting prime minister, who had begun Russia's economic reforms, was removed at the end of 1992, and replaced by Prime Minister Viktor Chernomyrdin, an avuncular man with a long history in the Soviet energy industry. There were more sighs of relief.

The new bosses were the old bosses reborn, but there was something comforting about that. After a few uncomfortable years of too much freedom and too much fear, many people felt that their fate was now safely back in the hands of people they could leave to take their decisions for them. A structure was beginning to re-emerge from the ruins. The top people drove foreign cars now, and wore silk ties, but they were the same old faces. Once again, people at the bottom of the social heap didn't have to fend or think for themselves too much.

Only the outsiders who had taken advantage of the burst of heady freedom to get rich quick made the 'achievement' of a measure of stability seem hollow. The success of the New Russians – and the Caucasian bosses – who had established themselves in Moscow made the rest of the country suspect that their own failure to get rich might have more to do with their reluctance to work hard than with the way the cards were stacked against them by an unchangeable system. The outsiders might be tacky, and they might have gold teeth; but they now banked in Zurich, shopped in Paris, holidayed in Cyprus and Thailand and partied in New York. And all because they had ridden roughshod over the elaborate code of social organization that bound the rest of Russia together, ignoring their once lowly place in the pyramid and unilaterally declaring themselves free.

At first, the general public hated the New Russian bandits and the Caucasian bandits equally for looting in the Soviet ruins. But, as the reality of the Soviet collapse was gradually overtaken by the beginning of the construction of a Russian state – smaller, more flexible, and with a hierarchy based more simply on wealth – the

New Russians were at least partly forgiven. They might be robbers in a time of chaos, but the idea began to gain hold that these Slavic grabbers of money were the founders of the new dynasties of capitalism, the Rockefellers of tomorrow, and that they would soon slot back into a reviving social order. 'They're bandits now, but they'll send their kids to good schools, and in a generation or two their families will be the most respectable and law-abiding of aristocrats,' my colleague Oleg Shchedrov said philosophically.

This more kindly view of the New Russians left only the Caucasians to hate – the last of the dangerous free radicals who had ignored their proper lowly place in that system, apparently done well out of it, and were destroying other people's sense of well-being by their very existence. Earlier, Russians had perceived their national space as the whole of the Soviet Union, with the Russian Socialist Federation of Soviet Republics – their ethnic homeland – existing only as an administrative entity within that Soviet construct. Now, as they grudgingly adjusted their mental picture of their homeland to the borders of the independent Russian Federation, the Chechens' declaration of independence came to seem more, rather than less, irksome and threatening. No one wanted any more disintegration. No one wanted any more chaos. Russians tired of revolt wanted the Chechens to understand that they must now knuckle under and creep back into their place in the Russian hierarchy. Stubbornly, the Chechens refused. No wonder ordinary Russians loathed them.

*

As 1992 wore on, with its price rises and parliamentary rows, the Moscow papers filled up with more and more lurid Chechen mafia stories, until a newcomer to Moscow might be forgiven for thinking every mugging, fraud and gangland shooting in the city's potholed streets was being carried out by dark-skinned gun nuts from the south with gold teeth, death in their eyes and flashy getaway cars. You might not actually see them at it; you might notice many more wide-cheekboned Slav thugs in the new-rich restaurants and shady casinos that were springing up everywhere; but, you were told, the

Chechen mafia was as omnipresent as the forces of darkness. What had been a general distaste for blacks was sharpening its focus and becoming a specific hostility to Chechens.

Sometimes, people still scratched their heads in bewilderment over the new hatred. 'There wasn't all this fuss about the Chechen mafia before,' Vitya Korotayev told me. When he was young and living in Central Asia, he had had a lot of Chechen neighbours. One of them had been in his teenage gang. 'I knew he was completely reliable and honest; I knew I could trust him. This suspicion just wasn't there in those days.' But most people found this kind of precision uninteresting. It was more fun to gasp and stretch their eyes over the stories.

The Chechens in these Russian crime stories were satisfyingly picturesque villains from the edge of the earth. Dark and lean and sharp-featured, they carried daggers and learned to kill almost in the cradle. They settled scores with vendettas so deadly they could last for generations and wipe out entire villages. The remoteness of their tiny territory, about 100 miles across and surrounded by dramatic snowy mountains, had left them still fanatically Muslim, fanatically loyal to their friends, and fantastically violent to their enemies.

Even the president was picturesque. Dzhokhar Dudayev really did wear sharp pinstripes, a fedora and a pencil moustache, just like the dandyish gangsters in films about Chicago in the 1920s with whom he was regularly compared. In the film clips shown on Russian television, he winked and smirked knowingly as he watched the war dances from a balcony. He was always flanked by spivs in shades, hats and black shirts, who celebrated their moment of televised glory by shooting in the air with the sub-machine-guns they all carried.

Russians believed that most of the Chechens who stayed at home were sunk in a savage tribal past. Russian television regularly illustrated stories about Chechnya with film of village elders with flowing beards and tall lambskin tubes on their heads intently circling public meeting places in a traditional round dance. The Chechens who came to Russia, and the gangsters who had taken over the leadership of Chechnya and were stealing its oil wealth, were also out for blood – it was their nature, they could hardly help themselves – but they were more dangerous because they also wanted money and would stop at nothing to get it.

All the Chechen crime since the Soviet collapse, which the Moscow media suggested was personally masterminded by Dudayev and his government, was ultimately a way of getting the oil out of a tiny region surrounded by Russia, selling it and laundering the profits.

I was most fascinated by the fillers and features on the edges of newspaper pages, each little fragment building up the Russian picture of Chechens as darkness personified, and the snippets of gossip passed on in conversation.

. . . In one newspaper, there was a picture of a dark young man with a beard, hanged from a city lamppost. A Chechen, victim of mafia reprisals or a vendetta, the caption said. No one knew which. Bystanders quoted in the article below said four big Caucasians had screeched up in a tiny Zhiguli, fixed up a noose and held a gun at their prisoner's head. He had climbed up and hanged himself. His tongue lolled out of his head. His name wasn't given. The crime wasn't solved.

. . . At Grozny central market, you could buy a hand-grenade (known as a 'lemon' in Russian slang) with your other fruit and veg, over the counter.

. . . Dudayev, in Grozny, drove sports cars. His bodyguard was made up of his nephews, all gun-toting carbon copies of himself. The Russians who lived in Grozny were leaving; the crime down there was too frightening, and the economy was collapsing.

. . . Russian oil was pumped through Grozny on its way back from oilfields in Central Asia to be sold on world markets. But Dudayev was stealing it. It vanished from Grozny. Where did it vanish to? I asked, with a mental picture of Chechens bowling barrel after barrel of oil down snowy mountain roads. Tsk, don't be naive, the answer came; but there were no explanations.

The most startling of the 1992 stories was not a filler. The story of the Chechen bank fraud made the front pages of all the newspapers for months on end. A group of Chechens visited banks all over Moscow in May 1992, and exchanged standard promissory notes, in this case issued by banks in Grozny and elsewhere in the CIS, for sackfuls of cash. The next day, according to a detailed account in Stephen Handelsman's book *Comrade Criminal*, another group of well-dressed Chechens who identified themselves as police from Chechnya entered the banks and asked to see the notes. Explaining they were conducting an official investigation, they took away the vouchers that were the only evidence of the transaction.

The police got wind of a possible crime when they came across a gang of Chechens dragging sacks full of money right past Moscow's main police headquarters. Seeing a police car, one of the Chechens slipped and dropped his sack, letting heaps of money tumble out into the street. The men were arrested. Phone calls to the Chechen banks revealed that no promissory notes had ever been issued. Phone calls to the Chechen police revealed that no investigators had been sent to Moscow. Security ministry investigators who searched the Hotel Salyut, where the Chechens had been staying in south Moscow, found abandoned blank vouchers with the seals and stamps of the Grozny State Bank.

The scale of the attempted swindle was staggering. Handelsman says forged promissory notes worth about $700 million turned up in hundreds of banks during the early summer. The Russian government, which admitted later that the fraud would have triggered the collapse of the national monetary system if it had not been discovered in time, was deeply embarrassed. But the press was delighted to be able to dwell on Chechen villainy at length, and ran front-page shock-horror coverage of the scandal for months.

Unlike the Russian media, Handelsman suggests Russian crooks should take a big share of the blame. 'Although the Chechen syndicate received most of the attention over the bank scandal in those months, the volume of promissory notes required for the swindle implied collusion with bankers and elsewhere in Russia,' he comments. Within days of the police discovering the first sacks of money, a Russian citizen was arrested heading for Zurich with about $1 million of the illicit profits in an overnight bag. Four officials of the Russian Central Bank were arrested a year later for accepting bribes of millions of roubles and tens of thousands of dollars for helping distribute the forged vouchers. Handelsman says that Sergei Yegorov, head of the Association of Russian Banks, believed the Chechen fraud was only a part of a larger conspiracy by the ex-Soviet *nomenklatura*, still hostile to the private capital the banks represented, to undermine the banking system.

From cliffhanger to cliffhanger: at the beginning of 1993, a still more astonishing and titillating news story broke, so picturesque it almost defied belief. Dudayev sent two Chechen brothers on a mission to London. The older of the two, Ruslan Utsiyev, was to be the informal ambassador for Chechnya, whose claims to statehood had gone unrecognized by the outside world. He was to equip Chechnya with the paraphernalia of statehood. He began negotiating with the Royal Mint to help bring out a Chechen currrency. He also contacted British officials and businessmen to plead the cause of investing in his country's oil. The prospect of Chechnya organizing its own banknotes and foreign trade relationships was bound to infuriate Russia.

But Utsiyev never completed this task. He and his younger brother Nazarbek were murdered, and their bodies disposed of in spectacular fashion. Delivery men who called at the brothers' million-pound Marylebone flat at the end of February to drop off a double bed were asked by two men inside the flat to take on another large box containing antiques to an address in Harrow. The pair went with the van, and directed the delivery men to put the box in the garage. But the delivery men got suspicious. There had been a horrible smell coming from the box. After the weekend, they went to the police. Ruslan Utsiyev's body was found inside the box, wrapped up in a carpet and bound with tape. He had been shot three times in the head with a handgun. The corpse of his brother, also shot with three bullets in the head, was found lying on a bed in the Marylebone flat.

The British press reported the double murder sensationally, with much lingering attention on the lavish lifestyle of the Utsiyev brothers, their £100 tips to waitresses, their frequent visits to

expensive restaurants and their two Armenian bodyguards. The
fact that they were the victims of murder was buried in a welter of
dark, if vague, suggestions that they must have been villains.

'Scotland Yard will be working in liaison with their opposite
numbers in Russia,' announced the *Guardian*, reproducing a
description of the Chechens which could have been written in
Moscow. 'Chechens, who number just over a million people, have
a reputation in Russia for containing the most ruthless of the
criminal elements currently operating protection rackets, drug
running and money laundering in what used to be the Soviet Union.
Chechens are said to have involvement in the increasingly lawless
underworlds of Moscow and St Petersburg and have access to large
quantities of firearms. They are blamed for many of the gangland
killings that have been taking place since the break-up of the Soviet
Union.'

The Armenian bodyguards were duly arrested, and more sensation followed. One of them, Mkrtich Martirossyan, admitted he
was an agent of the Armenian KGB. He carried a KGB phial of
snake poison with him, but after it was taken away he hanged
himself in Belmarsh prison before the trial. The other bodyguard,
Gagik Ter-Ogannasyan, was convicted and jailed. The trial heard
that the Chechens had been killed by their Armenian hangers-on
because the Armenians had discovered Utsiyev was doing his own
private deal on the side – buying weapons for Chechnya's fellow
Muslims in neighbouring Azerbaijan to use in their conflict with
Christian Armenia. The Armenian KGB decided to kill the Chechens in revenge. An alleged hitman hired in Los Angeles, home to
hundreds of thousands of expatriate Armenians, failed to get a
British visa. Instead a KGB colonel known only as Artur – an
Armenian name as common and anonymous as 'Paddy' in Ireland
– slipped into England to carry out the assassination. The British
press speculated meanwhile that the Utsiyev brothers' real job in
London had been to launder Dudayev's illegal profits from stealing
Chechen oil. Journalists later reported that Ruslan Utsiyev had
been trying to buy 2,000 Stinger missiles.

There was a final chapter to the Utsiyev story. Gagik Ter-
Ogannasyan was married to an Englishwoman called Alison

Ponting, whom he had met while they were studying at Voronezh University in Russia several years before. A year after the Utsiyevs were killed, when Gagik was already in prison, Alison Ponting went for the weekend to her sister Karen Reed's house in Surrey. The doorbell rang. Karen Reed opened the door, and was shot dead.

The conclusion everyone drew was that the killing was a professional hit, and that the intended victim had been Alison Ponting. She went into hiding, and still sends her former colleagues at the BBC Russian service the occasional postcard from unidentified locations. The British press again came out with conclusions which leaned heavily on information from Russia: 'The revenge for the brothers' deaths may well have been organised by their "family": like the Sicilians, the Chechen mafia have a reputation for blood loyalty,' said the *Guardian*.

I could just imagine the Russian diplomats and policemen briefing their eager British colleagues, and British reporters hearing the stories second-hand from stolid British policemen, listening with their eyes popping and their pencils in their mouths. The story did make fabulous copy. But it was altogether too much of a good thing.

The layers and layers of romance – the Armenian KGB agents, the snake poison, the Stinger missiles, the Caucasus wars, and the Chechen vendetta – made no sense. Russia and the Caucasus were awash with cheap weapons which could be bought for roubles. Why go all the way to London to waste precious hard currency buying Stingers? (Once, on a trip to Azerbaijan, I had met a smooth Chechen politician in reflector sunglasses, Yaraghi Mamodayev, who boasted that he was just about to clinch a big arms deal. He would probably have jumped at the chance of a trip to London, but it wasn't worth the effort.)

And why try to kill Alison Ponting? Every Russian who has ever discussed the case with me has said: 'Obviously, a Chechen vendetta.' But not a single Chechen has even understood that this is the conclusion they are supposed to draw from the facts, until I explain it to them. Then they just shake their heads and laugh. 'But that's nonsense,' they all say. 'That's not how our customs work.'

Chechens do still have a tradition of blood vengeance to avenge violent death, but it is not the frenzied killing Russians believe. In a slow and legalistic process, the families of victim and aggressor meet; if, at the end of long negotiations, the victim's family cannot forgive the aggressor, he is declared an outlaw and can be killed. Crucially, Chechens never pursue vendettas against women.

When you stripped away the tall tales, all you were left with was the simple story of how two men who were equipping Chechnya with the trappings of statehood had been murdered. The people likeliest to have ordered their killing were the Russians, who did not want Chechnya to acquire that statehood and pull still further away from Moscow. And Alison Ponting was likelier than anyone else still at liberty to have an inkling of that.

Dudayev did accuse the Russian secret services of being behind the Utsiyevs' murders, but he was 'in a far away country, [of which] we know nothing', as Neville Chamberlain famously said of Germany's annexation of the Sudetenland in 1939. The outside world found this accusation paranoid and hysterical. It did not make the British press.

*

Fed on this diet of eye-popping horror stories, people in Moscow were shocked but not surprised to discover that the Chechen Khasbulatov, the parliament leader, had set up a private army of 5,000 men in Moscow, ready to 'protect' strategic objects all over the city if called upon. The discovery was made public just before one of the many knife-edge Congresses at which Khasbulatov and Yeltsin's men each tried every kind of dangerous brinkmanship to unseat the other. Khasbulatov's army was disbanded.

That was the kind of thing Chechens did, Yevgeniya sniffed. If you went to Grozny, you had to stay in a hotel called the French House and pull the bed against the door before you went to sleep. Even then, you weren't safe from gunmen.

By then, I had begun to think seriously about going to Chechnya. I could no longer believe people could be as evil as the Chechens of legend. Now I had discovered that Russians seldom let the truth get in the way of a good story, I wanted to see the bogeyman for myself. But the idea filled everyone I knew with horror. My friends brought out every affectionate blandishment and patronizing diminutive they could think of to dissuade me.

'What would those black savages do to a sweet little white-haired girl like you?' Yevgeniya said. 'They'd rape you. Murder you. Rob you. You simply can't possibly go.'

So we went to a concert at the Conservatoire instead. Yevgeniya told me about the cat-burglars who climbed through Moscow apartment windows, the taxi-drivers who murdered their passengers for their rings and bracelets, and the hoodlums who stole old ladies' mink hats in the metro. There were enemies everywhere, circling, watching, waiting. By the end of the evening I was beginning to wonder whether Chechnya could possibly be any more dangerous than the Russia of Yevgeniya's imagination. But I still shivered at the prospect of going to Grozny, and dropped my travel plans.

# ACT TWO

# ETHNIC CLEANSING AT THE CHECHEN BORDER

It was more than a year before I finally went to the edge of Chechnya myself, and discovered how distorted the view from Moscow was. What drew me were Moscow newspaper reports in the autumn of 1992 about an ethnic clash on Chechnya's western border. It was the first time the fighting from the southern republics had spilled over on to Russian territory to the north of the Caucasus mountains. It might be the beginning of the home bloodshed that Russians in Moscow so dreaded.

The fighting was between two local peoples, the almost-Chechen Ingushi and the pro-Moscow North Ossetians. Fighting was already going on, but the Russian army had been sent to separate the two sides. I remember feeling secretly relieved at the idea of stolid sergeants and colonels being at hand, because the place was so near scary Chechnya and because I already knew before I set off what to think and who to blame.

The papers were quite clear about it. The Ingushi – the Chechens' country cousins whom Dudayev had left behind in Russia when he declared Chechnya independent – were the bad guys. They had been disgruntled for months and had got quarrelsome. All they had left, after Dudayev split the Soviet administrative unit of Checheno-Ingushetia, was three tiny districts of farmland. About a quarter of them had settled outside their own borders in a fourth district, Prigorodny, which was ruled by the neighbouring statelet of North Ossetia. The Ingushi, as wild as the Chechens, wanted to seize Prigorodny for themselves, although the North Ossetians had always let them live there in peace anyway. There had been a couple of unfortunate accidents, including an armoured personnel carrier driven by Ossetians which had run over a little Ingush girl. The conservatives in the Russian parliament, egged on by the cunning Chechen Ruslan Khasbulatov, had provoked the Ingushi further with a decree allowing them to create their own administrative unit, and wishful thinking had made the Ingushi think they could take over Prigorodny district. The fights had got out of control.

President Yeltsin, and the democratic government, whom my Russian friends still supported, had sent the army and appointed a Russian emergency administrator who was based in Christian North Ossetia. Khasbulatov, whom we did not like, had appointed a temporary boss for Muslim Ingushetia from the Russian parliament. Growing hostility in Moscow between Yeltsin and Khasbulatov was finding violent expression in the south. The fighting seemed like a metaphor, with real blood and guns, for the infighting in Moscow.

I flew to Vladikavkaz, the capital of North Ossetia, and spent a day in the corridors of the government building talking to the Russian emergency administrators. But almost at once I felt Vladikavkaz was a nasty little town, sunk in mud and pride. A sharp smell of dead leaves and old snow hung in the morning air, and a hint of river fog. The main street had a strip of wooded parkland running down the middle, and an intersecting main street without trees. One was called former Lenin Street, one was called former Karl Marx Avenue, and both were lined with the long, low, yellowish stucco buildings of Russian garrison towns of the last century. They might not have been unattractive if they had not been so decrepit. There was former Lenin Square, now Freedom Square. And there were sad shops everywhere with mournful dark women half-heartedly selling bread, meat, tinned fish and grey vegetables to depressed customers. That was all there was, except talk and gunmen.

# Ossetians

The Ossetian gunmen were waiting in the twilit hotel. They pawed at my notebook and my legs in the corridor. They guffawed and banged on my bedroom door. One whom I met in the lobby threatened me with his gun when I refused to tell him my room number 'so I can visit you later'. They were drunk in mid-afternoon and very drunk by dinner.

'I'd liketa getta know you. Wouldja liketa get to know me?' slurred another fat 'soldier', smiling down fuzzily over his paunch and bandolier of bullets at my table. The forgotten gun over his shoulder banged against a chair lost in the dusk.

I drew my overcoat tighter around me and watched the man's rank breath cloud upwards, towards the Vladikavkaz Hotel dining-room's cavernous ceiling. There were a few dozen military types in different styles of grubby khaki eating under the puddles of light cast by five naked bulbs. Their weapons swung on straps from chairs or hooks, or were propped against cement pillars, or dumped on the floor next to canvas bags. I thought they must be Russian soldiers, but few of the men were the blond, brutally shaven boys I associated with the Russian army. Several were middle-aged. Most were swarthy and muddy, with dark stubble on their chins. Almost all of them, at eight in the evening, were drunk and jumpy.

'By all means,' I said politely, feeling apprehensive but gesturing at one of the six empty places on the other side of the twilit table.

Skeletal cloud fingers clawed between the stars which were starting to glimmer through a single, endless window. The bright evening star was neatly ringed by a bullet hole in the glass. Outside, the Terek River and a forlorn mosque's enamelled sides sparkled bravely in the headlights of waiting jeeps, but the town was already dark.

'I can see you're a Western journalist,' the fatty said, twisting his squidgy face with its wispy, pubic-hair beard as he concentrated on heaving his bulk downwards into the nearest chair and disengaging the gun from his back. 'I wanted to ask you, sincerely, for God's sake, to only tell the truth, the truth, about what's going on here. Why? Because it's easy to distort the truth. People do . . .' He hiccupped – a tidal shudder ran through his ocean of soft flesh – and fixed melancholy, bloodshot eyes on me. 'Western journalists do.'

Some of the other men in uniform had started to stare and point at my new friend, nudging each other in the ribs and snickering.

'What's your name? Are you all from the Russian army?' I asked. 'Is this all the Russian troops there are?'

The man smiled knowingly. 'Ah, the Russians. No, no. That's not exactly what we are . . .' He scratched himself. A burst of wild laughter from the distant watchers ricocheted off the freezing walls. 'There are all sorts here, but the Russians are billeted in their own places,' he added, turning to give his cronies a withering look before checking his still-empty glass.

'Where are those damned girls? They should have served a Western journalist a bit quicker than this,' the man barked suddenly, waving imperiously at one of the two wispy middle-aged waitresses cowering by the kitchen door. She rushed over, an anxious smile on her face and a menu in her hand. The man clacked out orders in a guttural language, and she bobbed and retreated again. 'That's what you need here, dearie, the knack of command,' the man said with a broad grin, spreading his knees comfortably and planting both elbows on the table.

'Very pleased to meet you. I'm Aslan,' he said. He delved into a breast pocket with a fat, clumsy hand – missing two fingers but with more than enough grime under the remaining spade-like nails to compensate – and yanked out his red identity booklet. He waved it under my nose. 'That's who I am. Aslan Chochiyev. It means "lion", you know. At your service.'

'Very pleased to meet you,' I replied. 'And what was that language you were talking to the waitress just now?'

'Ossetian . . .' the man replied. 'I'm Ossetian myself, Ossetian, look . . . it says so here on my passport, passport. I've got no secrets.' He was beginning to look truculent. I quickly turned a fascinated smile on him and he relaxed again.

Aslan and his friends, it turned out, were self-appointed, part-time peacekeepers from neighbouring South Ossetia. South Ossetia was technically part of Georgia, although it had declared independence two years ago, while Vladikavkaz as the capital of North Ossetia was part of Russia. But both types of Ossetian spoke the same language, an archaic dialect of Persian. 'They're our brothers. So when they started to have a bit of bother with those filthy Ingushi swine, we naturally wanted to help out,' Aslan said. Then the Russians had come along and imposed a state of emergency, bringing their own soldiers and administrators, he added. 'But we've come along too, to see for ourselves that everything's all right. The Russians don't like it much, but you have to look after your own kind, right?' Aslan said, sticking his jaw out. He belched, adding darkly: 'Otherwise God knows what provocations there might be.'

I was only half listening. My attention was fixed behind Aslan's back, on two of his militia who had picked up their guns and were waving them drunkenly in the air . . . at each other . . . in the air again. The waitresses had vanished into the kitchen. I kept my face expressionless and body still, mapping out the quickest path through the tables to the plate-glass door. Aslan slewed round, apparently sensing through his vodka haze that something was amiss, but only rolled his eyes and shrugged when he saw what was happening.

'We had a good day today. And now the radio says a cease-fire has been declared in the villages, so the lads are celebrating. Don't be afraid,' he said calmly, turning back to me and picking up the empty glass in front of him again.

A shot rang out.

I didn't see which of the staggering men fired. But now, slowly, confusedly, in a tumult of breaking glass and china, the mass of camouflaged men stood up, grabbing guns, overturning tables, tripping up on ammunition belts and swiping ineffectually at each other. One bearded brave jumped on a table, waved a gun down at the rest and yelled incomprehensibly. But the group ignored him and moved off unsteadily towards the entrance.

Even more slowly – or, I thought, perhaps my brain has just gone on to emergency time and is working faster than usual – Aslan lumbered to his feet and moved towards them. His feet, small for his fleshy body, almost twinkled under plump legs. He didn't look back.

The locked door tinkled gently, like a chandelier in the breeze, as the first man to it smashed his gun through its eight-foot-high central panel. More echoing yells and groans followed as the gunmen streamed out down the stairs.

I was left alone in the icy restaurant.

The waitresses brought me warm kebab, a local dish which I christened potato pizza, loose herbs and cucumber, vodka and sulphurous mineral water. Now the militiamen had left – and were indulging in a full-scale shoot-out on the dark street outside – the two women became much more openly friendly. They hovered round my table, scurrying to fetch more bread, and smiling gently when I winced at a particularly long and murderous burst of automatic gunfire.

'It's always like this here, now. We're used to it. It used to be such a quiet place before,' the black-haired one said rather sadly, picking up an empty plate. 'Shall I fetch you some tea?' They patted nervously at their piled-up hair, new lipstick gleaming on their anxious mouths. Far away, through the gloom, the doorman who had been standing tut-tutting over the broken glass door but doing nothing to pick up the pieces turned to give them a long, forbidding look. But the two servile, broken-down little women had their own brand of half-conscious defiance. Both kept their backs turned so they couldn't see him.

'You should have come before, when everything was still all right,' the grey-haired waitress said, fiddling with her teaspoon. 'People used to come here from all over the Soviet Union for their holidays, for the peace, for the nature . . . for the mountains . . . But now look at us. Just look what we've become.'

'My son goes out on these militia patrols,' the black-haired one chimed in. 'He's a good boy, too, not scared of anything. But I sit up all night through the curfew, wondering if he'll ever be back or if they'll get him.'

'If who will?' I asked. 'Those bastards! Those provocateurs, of course! . . . the Ingushi,' she answered with a little burst of heat, gold rabbit-teeth flashing, before relapsing into melancholy. 'You should see what they've done to our beautiful countryside, to our peaceful villages . . . there are fields and fields that no one dares plant any more . . . We were so good to them for decades, we let them live there in their thousands and breed like rabbits, and this is how they repaid us. Stabbed us in the back. That's how we live nowadays.'

Both hurried to explain the villainy of the Ingushi, words tumbling out of their mouths and half-surprised looks at their own volubility flashing across their faces. 'They were plotting to take over. Now they're running away because their plot's backfired,' one said. 'Naturally people are angry with them. They've got such guilty consciences that they've just vanished from one day to the next. The Russians have sent troops to protect us. But those bastards will go on sneaking back to make trouble. They've burned down the villages. It's a nightmare out there in the countryside.'

They talked on and on, apparently deaf to the gunfight still going on downstairs. They explained their collective past in repeated phrases, used and dropped by one and picked up again by the other to weave into a new theme. The phrases were so abstract that they sounded like half-remembered slogans. Their softly-furred upper lips would twitch for a few moments each time they fired off an aggressive line, then slip back into slack repose during the lulls which followed. They didn't make much sense to me.

All I could really understand was that North Ossetians had chosen to stop the clock of history in 1944. That was the year when Stalin had deported all the Ingushi, as well as the Chechens further over, to distant Central Asia. He accused them of collaborating with Nazi Germany and he tacked on part of the Ingushi land, Prigorodny District, to North Ossetia. It was not until more than a decade later, after Stalin's death, that the Ingushi and the Chechens had dared to start creeping home. And the Ingushi had found much of their land in foreign hands. Many had settled in Prigorodny District, as if 1944 had never been, and many more had tried to go back there after Khasbulatov's parliament had passed its law rehabilitating them.

'But that land is ours, legally ours,' the grey-haired waitress said, without a scrap of sympathy for her dispossessed neighbours. 'We let them settle here again, the ones that wanted to. We were good to them, more fools us. But you can't rewrite history. You can't gainsay the law. Russia accepts that, and that wild rabble should too.'

'Mmm, yes,' I said, smiling vaguely and getting up, not meeting their eyes. My brief sympathy for the waitresses had long ago evaporated. Now, instead, I could imagine them knitting by the

guillotine, cackling and clucking over lost stitches as heads dropped
unheeded into the basket. I paid and went thoughtfully up to my
room, stepping over the shards of broken glass in the doorway to
reach the empty, clanging lift.

My new room was as familiar as any Soviet hotel room. There
were the orange nylon half-curtain and the grubby net half-curtain,
the decaying balcony, the two narrow beds covered with brown
patterned cloths, the hideous lampshades, the pair of tattered
crimson armchairs, the spiders in the shadows, the cockroaches in
the bath, the unplugged fridge, the non-functioning television and
the assemblage of cut-glass vessels on the coffee table. The phone
didn't work.

The gunfight had stopped, but I still didn't want to venture out
on to the balcony to set up my portable satellite phone. I went to
try phoning from the corridor. As I stepped out of the room, I
noticed that my flimsy door was splintered all up the lock side and
that the current lock was hanging by one nail from its appointed
place.

The floor maid was dozing under her green lamp. 'Excuse me,' I
began, my heart sinking at the thought of the battle to come. But
she shook herself awake like a faithful old guard dog, gave me a
sleepy, suspicious look which quickly melted into a smile, and
gestured towards her own orange phone. 'You're a journalist,
aren't you?' she said through her gums. 'So you'll want to call
Moscow. Pull up that chair and dial from here.'

Nine-for-an-outside-line, I dialled. Eight-for-out-of-town. Zero-
nine-five for Moscow. Nine. Eight. Engaged. Nine, eight, oh-nine-
five. Engaged. Nine, eight . . .

The phone was made of light plastic and I had to hold it down
with one hand, to stop it slipping round the desk, while dialling
with the other hand and crunching the receiver between jaw and
shoulder. My shoulder began to ache. The floor maid bumbled off
into a nearby room and came out with two boiled sweets wrapped
in grease-proof paper and a steaming glass of tea. She gave me a
toothless smile as she pushed her offerings under my nose. 'The
lines aren't very good from here,' she said gently. 'Just keep trying.'

'Sounds as if they've stopped shooting downstairs,' I said, fingers still busy, looking gratefully at her. She clucked and shook her head. 'Oh, those boys! They're murder when they're drunk. We've taken seven of them up to the top floor already with bullets in them. One of them has a nasty stomach wound. I don't know what things are coming to nowadays. It used to be so peaceful. People would come from all over the Soviet Union for their holidays.' She sighed. 'You could tell there was trouble coming long before it started. It began to be easy to buy guns. God knows it was hard enough to find anything else in the shops, but there were guns everywhere. These crooks turned up here, some sort of mafia, and all of a sudden there were bags of bullets under every table. No one was working in the fields and factories any more, but everyone had plenty of money. And the prices! the prices went crazy. And then it all broke out, suddenly, the horrors and the atrocities and the bloodshed, and we woke up into this nightmare.'

The lift door opened, flooding the shadowy lobby with a dazzling burst of light. Three of the boys, one with a bloody bandage on his grazed temple, got out and lumbered over to the floor maid's desk. Two sat down in the red armchairs by her soundless, luridly coloured television, guns by their sides, and stared at the pictures as the third leaned unsteadily over me.

'I need to phone now,' he said.

The floor maid took the phone from me with her liver-spotted left hand and passed it quickly over to the man. 'There you are, lovey,' she said reassuringly. 'You sit down in my chair and make your call.' She winked at me, as the man ignored me and started dialling. 'He's an important man. You can make your call next,' she explained in an undertone.

The man talked for thirty-five minutes. Some of his conversation was in Ossetian, some in Russian. All the parts in Russian seemed to be about bringing in a car over some border without paying tax. He laughed a lot as he spoke.

'Just wait,' one of the others said, as, now standing, I glanced pointedly down at my watch for the sixth time. 'He's finding out what's happened to his family in South Ossetia. There's a war there against the Georgians, you know, and half his family has been forced to leave home. There's genocide going on.'

The man on the phone let loose a huge guffaw, slapping his thighs and sides and slumping down against the desk. Tears of laughter coursed down his stubbly cheeks. 'That's a good one!' he breathed into the receiver between gales of hilarity, before reverting to Ossetian.

'Hey, you! Journalist!' one of his friends said suddenly from the depths of his armchair, rolling bloodshot eyes. 'You must write the truth about what's been going on here!' I nodded without paying much attention. 'You must tell the world objectively about the genocide being perpetrated against Ossetians, Ossetians! You mustn't distort, distort the truth!'

'OK, OK,' I said. The man stood up threateningly. 'Of course I won't distort the truth,' I added hastily, smiling ingratiatingly at the hunk of tattooed muscle towering over me. Were these the same men I had seen downstairs in the dining-room, I wondered? It was hard to tell.

'You can interview me if you like,' the man said, settling himself back down again with a satisfied grunt. 'I was there, in Prigorodny District, when they attacked. I saw what went on.' His friend nodded sagely. I tried to look encouraging and responsive, and not as if my heart was beating too fast for comfort. The floor maid had retreated to her room.

But what followed was just more phrases, delivered with such lip-smacking relish that I found the recital hard to accept as their personal experience. You can't rewrite history, they chorused. Moscow gave us the land in 1944. 1944. It's legally ours. That wild rabble, that scum. They attacked the post office and the local government building in every village in Prigorodny District at five in the morning on the same day. It was obviously a plot. They raped children. They set fire to Ossetian houses. They chopped off people's ears and noses. The atrocities! They kept prisoners in cellars and cow-sheds. They're so vicious and vengeful that they even set fire to their own houses to stop Ossetians moving in afterwards. Can you imagine that? And it was hell stopping the fighting afterwards. You'd clear a street, but there'd still be snipers in some cellar you'd missed. They'd get you from behind. The morgues were full of bodies. They're murderous bastards, one and all. They're so savage they don't even understand you can't rewrite history. But they won't dare come back now. If they do we'll teach them another lesson they won't forget. Oh yes, we'll bloody their noses all right.

The phone man put down the receiver at last.

'May I?' I asked politely. I got through first time. The gunmen didn't feel like going anywhere. They sat and listened as I dictated my first story to my Moscow office. One came and sat next to me on the hard chair, half pushing me off, running his hands up my leg to the appreciative guffaws of his mates. I pushed him away, but he kept coming back. I kept dictating. When I said the word 'Ingush' for the first time, the whole group erupted.

'Ingushi!' the cartoon goons screeched happily from their armchairs. One prodded his sleepy neighbour with a pistol. 'Don't forget to say they're all savage swine! The lowest form of human life! The world has to know the truth about our reality! Savage Muslim swine!'

'All RIGHT!' I answered crossly, irritation overcoming my natural caution. 'I'll tell the world they're all savage swine, don't you worry!' I spoke into the phone again, in English. 'I'll finish up here, then try to get to Ingushetia in a couple of days to hear their side of things,' I told my boss, provoked more by defiance of the Ossetian thugs than any real wish to meet the murderous, treacherous Ingushi. 'Well, be careful,' the crackling voice said from far away. 'Don't do anything unsafe. They sound a nasty lot down there.'

Five Ossetian militiamen were still upstairs with injuries, the floor maid said the next morning. 'I hope you didn't go sticking your nose out on the balcony to see,' she said sharply. 'I hope you locked your door.'

She looked a sensible woman, sagging flesh encased in respectable ancient garments.

'Why are the Ingushi fighting?' I asked, thinking she would have a common-sense explanation. 'Because they're scum, the lowest form of humanity, the dregs,' she answered, her jaw jutting, her face hardening. 'We let them live there, although it was given to us, by Stalin, in 1944, and look how they've repaid us. You can't deny history. Prigorodny is ours.'

There seemed little else to ask. I hadn't expected such a smug recital of this history from her. I turned to go.

'Did you hear what the radio was saying this morning?' she asked from down the corridor. 'In the Prigorodny villages where our boys – and the Russians, they know who's right – have gone in to clean up after the fighting, the Ingushi have gouged out the eyes of all the corpses. Surely human beings would never have done such a thing?'

In the huge grey cube of government building, the Ossetian interior minister, Major-General Georgy Kentimerov, said there was still fighting going on in three villages in Prigorodny, and Cossacks were guarding a fourth village, Redant, home to the waterworks which supplied Vladikavkaz. But the villages would soon be pacified. Kentimerov wasn't pleased that the Russians had come, with 3,000 troops, and that commandos were now loitering on street corners in Vladikavkaz, enforcing a kind of cease-fire, or that they had imposed a month-long state of emergency. He was just cross that they hadn't come before, and very cross that they hadn't been more aggressive in wiping out the Ingush trouble-making before it got out of hand. He had hoped for more protection from the Russians, leaders of the Soviet peoples, first among equals.

'So they're here,' he sniffed. 'But they came very late. We could have used their help earlier.'


# Russians


Yeltsin's temporary Russians were installed in the corridors too. The Russian government man appointed to stop the crisis and run an emergency administration down here, a deputy prime minister called Georgy Khizha, was busy talking to the Ingush about disarming their guerrillas. But his deputy offered tea and talk in another echoing room with damp walls.

Gennady Shoigu was all civilized regrets. He had the strict-but-fair demeanour of a schoolmaster forced to bang naughty children's heads together. The Russians would not be able to leave in a month, he said: it would take far longer than that to heal the spiritual wounds inflicted by the fighting. So the soldiers from Moscow would have to stay on. Also, there was no chance now that the local borders could be redrawn to give Prigorodny back to the Ingushi. They had brought disaster on their own heads by trying to grab too much, too fast. If they'd just been patient before, willing to negotiate instead of ambush, some compromise could have been worked out. Now, with all the bad blood left by the fighting they'd started, there was no hope.

'I can't see a way out of the dead end,' he said, stirring sugar into his tea.

More sugary tea with the Russian commander, Colonel-General Vasily Savvin, a friendly man with Slavic cheekbones and a bright pink bald patch, and more regrets. He was trying to arrange a hostage exchange between Ingushi and Ossetians, but the Ingush side was delaying. His conversation was punctuated with phone calls; his brow was furrowed.

'These Ingushi are impossible . . . Wild men . . .' sighed Savvin. He dropped four grainy lumps into his cup. 'They have no honour. They agree to things, then they don't show up or they ignore our messages. I want to have an equal attitude to both sides; I don't want to believe either side wants war. But I must say I'm starting to have my doubts.'

The local Russian Cossacks, Terek Cossacks, were locked behind their stout door with the double-headed eagle on it. They were drinking tea, but they had no polite regrets. Of course they were helping the Russian troops sort out the Ingushi, they said; that was their historical role. But they also had historical reasons of their own to be furious about the Ingushi claim to land in Prigorodny.

'Because that land was ours, you see,' the plump, jolly Cossack *ataman* said. Like the Ossetians, the Terek Cossacks had stopped the clock of history, but they had chosen the moment of their own glory days last century to stop it at. And, even if they were helping the Moscow Russians now, they were deeply suspicions of Moscow's motives in sending troops.

'Certain forces in Moscow, the forces of Soviet repression reborn, don't want the world to know that land is ours. But it's the truth. All the villages in Prigorodny District were Cossack *stanitsa*s in the nineteenth century. The Ingushi only took over that land when the Communists chased us out. They complain that it was always their land and that it was stolen from them . . . but that's just another Soviet lie. All the land to the north and west of the Terek River has always, historically, belonged to us.'

His side-kick, a raw-boned young man, rootled through cupboards and threw shaggy hats on the floor as he hunted for photocopies of ancient documents about Cossacks. The desk was awash with papers. 'We want to have the honour of explaining history through an exhaustive and objective study,' he said happily. Despite his puppy-like enthusiasm, there was the usual sour smell of wet lambskin and bigotry in the little office.

Back outside, in the modern world of the ex-Soviet Union, I took a deep breath of sleety air to dispel the clouds of clinging history, and set off back down the freezing street towards the ministries built for vanished giants.

That night, I met two young Russian journalists in the hotel who also wanted to go to Ingushetia. They were about twenty, and they were trying to get jobs on a Moscow paper by uncovering a hot story down here. They didn't know whether they'd be paid for their work, so they were hoping to cadge a lift. We teamed up. Sasha had the round pink face, irrepressible air and luxuriant moustache of a southern Russian, Volodya had the diffidently bearded look of the Moscow intellectual. I was glad they were there; they felt like home. We agreed to go together the next day, first to the villages, then on to Ingushetia. Sasha had been born round here, he said; it didn't matter that the road to Ingushetia was shut. If I got a taxi for all of us, he'd guide him on a safe route round the conflict zone and get us all to the other side.

# The Villages

Kentimerov didn't want us to go poking round in the villages. He made us promise to go in an Ossetian interior ministry car, with an escort provided by him, then made us wait five hours for it. We sat on the floor at the interior ministry, outside his office, smoking, telling stories. Journalists came and went. Kentimerov found a car, but then said there was no room for me in it. 'Let's leave the girl behind,' he suggested to the others with misplaced gallantry. 'Wars are no place for women.'

'Nonono,' I protested hastily. 'It's my job. I might not like wars but I have to go. My editor will kill me otherwise.'

Reluctantly he gave way. There was plenty of room in the car.

*

The corpse lay in a puddle, its arms crossed over its chest, a Molotov cocktail next to its arm – and its identification card displayed ostentatiously on its chest, photo upwards. The Prigorodny village of Chermen was still burning, but Ossetian villagers were picking through the mud, red-eyed and coughing from the smoke, tut-tutting over the damage. Cows that hadn't been milked for three days were lowing. Geese splashed in the puddles. More than half the one-storey houses were burned-out shells. There were bits of shattered glass and bloodstained cloth embedded in the mud. The doors of barns and cellars swung open.

There were no Ingushi, although the staccato sounds of automatic gunfire were still coming from the smoke at the other end of the village. It was their homes that were burning. Our interior ministry escort had already tried to make me creep through the mud on my belly, pretending that the sound of blazing, cracking roof timbers nearby was sniper fire. He only shrugged when I said I didn't think those were gun sounds, and strolled down the road whistling. Clearly he didn't, either.

Now he rushed me to the corpse. 'Look what those Ingushi bastards have done to our boys,' he said fiercely. That five hours' wait in Vladikavkaz had left plenty of time to organize a set-up photo opportunity like this. 'Look, that's an Ossetian villager; you can see from the ID.' He waited expectantly for me to examine the ID, or take a picture.

'Why did the person who displayed the ID not take the corpse out of the puddle?' I asked, intrigued. He sighed. 'Don't you have a camera?' he countered.

'Did the Ingushi gouge out the eyes of the people they killed here?' I asked, and he brightened again. 'Oh yes, dozens of them,' he said. 'Can I see the bodies in the morgue?' I asked. He hesitated again. 'They've all been taken away,' he said weakly.

A lanky boy in a padded jacket, about the same age as Sasha and Volodya, attached himself to us as we trudged through the filth.

'That was the police station. That's where they started their attack,' he said, stopping us. His name was Alan, and he was nineteen. He was from another village, and had only just got here, like us, but he seemed to know everything that had gone on here. The building was cracked and fissured. There were scorch marks near the sodden remains of a bonfire.

'I don't know what's happened to my family, but we think my uncle was taken hostage. My auntie decided to stay in her cellar, but I don't know what's become of her. I can't go and find her yet because there's still shooting round our house,' he said. He pointed towards the other end of the village, into the smoke. 'These Ingushi are the lowest form of life imaginable,' he added, his voice expressionless, and everyone nodded, even Sasha and Volodya.

We drove away up a different road. Blond Russian soldiers loomed up in the afternoon mist, behind a razor-wire enclosure and a tank. Eyes and gun barrels peeped out at us.

'Documents. Open the car up for a search.'

On a shallow rise, overlooking the great flat sweep of valley where the villages burned, Russian soldiers had made a car park for their tanks. Dozens of boys mooched miserably about between the rows of big iron carcasses, watching the smoke. When we drew up, more boys popped up from inside, looking curiously at the newcomers. Smiling shyly, a couple offered gifts of apples and spent bullets.

An old man with high cheekbones was watching the villages burn too. He had a tall hat on, and a walking stick, and a distant look in his eyes.

'It's not right,' he was saying calmly to the weary uniformed boys around him. 'It's just not right what you're doing here.' He had obviously been standing there a long time. He was making the boys uncomfortable, and something in their pink cheeks, the way they shuffled and twitched miserably at his words, reminded me of a line of Dylan Thomas, about wild boys in the park, innocent as strawberries. These soldiers were innocents, in a way, and they didn't want to think his difficult thoughts or even watch his dignified face or straight back.

I wanted to hear more, but Sasha drew me away. 'We should go,' he said. 'It's late.' And he put his mouth by my ear to whisper even more quietly: 'He's an Ingush. Best not to meddle.' We drove off back to Vladikavkaz in the failing light. When I looked back, the old man in his high lambskin hat was still there, watching.

As we entered Vladikavkaz, seven Russian armoured vehicles dashed past us in the opposite direction, heading for Dachnoye village in the valley which the interior ministry people said was still in Ingushi hands. Our escort turned on the local radio news: a statement by the Ossetian parliament press office was being read out, saying that all the fighting had completely stopped that morning and the Ingush rebels had been crushed. Sasha and Volodya prodded me in the ribs, pointing towards the radio and raising their eyebrows at this manifestation of the official lie. I grinned back. The Ossetian interior ministry man pretended not to see.

The old man was the only Ingush I'd seen in three days, although nearly 100,000 had been living in Prigorodny until that week. When I asked where they were, both Russians and Ossetians only shrugged. 'Hiding, probably,' they all said. They agreed with each other too much, and the Ossetians were too visibly delighted to have a big brother to protect them. I could smell bullying and collaboration, and I didn't understand why. I wanted to leave. I wanted to find the missing Ingushi.

*

Russian tanks at the villages, Ossetian looters on the roads. Our final encounter with Ossetians, the next morning, was symbolic of the whole trip: highwaymen wanted to rob me until they realized I was foreign, therefore – possibly – important, therefore unbullyable.

Four men were lounging on crates and spare tyres under a road sign reading 'Beslan 3 km', beards bristling, guns ready, threatening looks on their dark faces. The driver started to mutter nervously, feeling along the dashboard, in his pockets, in the sunshield above his eyes, for documents. The car swerved as he searched.

'This road is full of bandits,' he said, hands fastening on his cigarettes and rejecting them again. 'God knows who they all are.' He pulled up and began quiet, anxious negotiations with two of them. Another pair moved round to the passenger door, and barked 'Documents' at me when I opened it. He did a slight double-take when he saw me sitting there, not a man, not a Russian, but stuck to his guns. 'What is your business on this road?' his friend asked sternly.

I got out. They looked puzzled. I showed them my foreign passport and accreditation and told them as impressively as possible that I was a very important foreign correspondent.

They melted, grinned, called off the cronies who were tormenting the driver and clustered round me. 'Are you American?' asked the shortest one with new respect, holding the passport upside-down between two grimy fingers. Further questions about chewing gum, dollar salaries, California and Chevrolets were clearly bubbling up in his brain. But by now I was tired of wasting my charm on Ossetians. It was time to turn Ossetian tactics back on the bullies with no uniform, I thought, and brazen my way out of what looked ominously like an encounter with freelance highwaymen.

'And who, exactly, are you? Why have you stopped us?' I asked, raising my eyebrows haughtily and flaring my nostrils. 'Do you have documents to show us, by any chance? Do you have any official business on this road? Or are you just here . . .' I paused for effect '. . . for FUN?' I snapped my jaw shut and stared sternly at first one, then another, of the young men, noticing with distaste that one had a festering pimple at the corner of his mouth.

Rather to my surprise, they were quelled. They wriggled and cast sidelong glances at each other. They shuffled their feet. Finally, the leader muttered: 'We're picketeers. And we've checked you. There won't be any road tax for a foreign journalist. Have a good journey.'

He swung away, waving his gun as if to bolster his drooping morale. I gave them chewing gum and got back into the car, promising myself never to return.

So our battered taxi left Vladikavkaz, whose name was Tsarist imperial swagger and meant 'Ruler of the Caucasus', without mishaps. We were lucky; later, once they had worked out that foreign journalists weren't that important after all, the 'picketeers' on that stretch of road got bold enough to rob them regularly.

Through the cracked, cardboard-patched windscreen, I watched the fields which stretched away from the pitted road and its scatter of Soviet litter. It had snowed overnight. The Russian driver puffed away in silence at a cardboard tube with a dab of tobacco at the end. A packet marked Belomorsky Canal lay on the dashboard. Thousands more packets, sodden and half-buried, lay on the roadside.

We turned off the main road back to Russia through a pair of white columns. A road sign saying 'Nazran Grozny Baku' was smeared with a red paint line. A low wall topped by snowy trees ran alongside. Empty fields stretched in all directions. An uncanny, birdless silence filled the air. Chermen, the village we had visited, lay to the right. The driver pointed at it.

'All those burned houses are Ingushi houses. They had the best ones everywhere. They worked harder. They built better. They were envied.' He lit another cigarette from the first, throwing the butt out of the window.

'No one said anything like that in Vladikavkaz . . .' I said on a slight rising tone. The man grinned sourly. He was a Caucasian from Kabarda, further west, so he was neutral in this conflict. 'Well, they wouldn't, would they? The Ossetians were practically the first Caucasians to knuckle under to Russia during the great wars last century. That's the kind of people they are. Sneaky. Soft. Stool pigeons. They say what Moscow wants to hear. But I see things from both sides. My wife's mother is Ingushi.'

The sun came out. Far away in the sky, above the clouds, the great Caucasus peaks glittered with brilliant gold-tinted snow.

# To Ingushetia

It took five hours and two changes of taxi to drive to Ingushetia, as the usual 30 km road was shut for battle. Sasha ran round in bedraggled Nalchik, capital of the neighbouring statelet of Kabardino-Balkaria, looking for taxi-drivers with neutral number plates who would feel safe driving into Ingushetia. They had to be ethnically neutral. They had to be well paid. I was delighted Sasha was there to deal with it all.

By late afternoon, we were on the muddy hillside that marked the beginning of Ingushetia. Bleak Russian guards were trying to arrest me for not displaying my British passport when a neat black Volga drew up, interrupting our weary 'Oh-yes-you-do,' 'Oh-no-I-don't' discussion. The Russians drew back respectfully as the neat driver, with thinning black hair slicked back over his head, drew his leather coat around him and got out.

'Do you need a lift?' he asked me politely. 'Yes they do,' our driver said firmly; he was regretting going off the beaten track like this, and he wanted to get home. Wondering whether it was wise, I accepted. The man coughed to get the soldiers' attention. 'When you've quite finished, boys, please put this lady's luggage in my car. I shall be looking after her.'

Isa Eldiyev explained that he was an Ingush businessman who worked in Moscow. He promised to organize transport for me to find out what had happened to the missing 100,000 Ingushi. He had come home from Moscow himself to find out what was going on, because you couldn't trust the Russian newspapers, he said. Perhaps we could pool resources. I was suspicious. I wouldn't have gone with him if I'd been alone. But I was emboldened by having the two Russian boys with me, and flattered by his appeal to me as the leader of the group.

We heaved the satellite phone and our muddy selves into his Volga, and our taxi drove off hastily back to the calm of the Nalchik bus station.

'Do you have any weapons? Guns? Bombs? Grenades?' the border guard asked defeatedly, as Isa shut all the doors and locked the boot. Isa only laughed and raised his shoulders. 'Why would I?' he asked. 'I'm going home, and I'm not planning to shoot my brothers.' The guard waved us on.

*

My apprehension vanished as Isa's car sped away from the checkpoint towards the hills. It climbed effortlessly over rough roads, soaring past old men whose low-slung carts were drawn by ponies, sleepy mud-brick cottages with long verandas and shriv-elled vines, wiry grannies heaving rough-woven sacks into sheds. Wind whistled through Isa's half-open window. The uplands swelled and cracked and billowed around them, rivers and frozen waterfalls, empty plains, sharp deserts of ragged rocks breaking out from under the snow. There were no farm fences to be seen anywhere. There was no Soviet litter of cigarette packets and rusty car parts. I sucked in lungfuls of rushing air and felt the growing exhilaration of speed and freedom.

Born into a wild, monochrome landscape, the villagers had coloured their immediate surroundings with a dramatic palate.

Shapely brown ponies shuffled purposefully away from the road, their front legs hobbled with scarlet twine. Houses were painted lilac, turquoise, blue and green. Cemeteries were filled with bluish headstones. Herds of cows, their left horns painted orange, wan-dered through the snow near one village. At the next village, the left horns were lime green. Silvery filigree work and crescent moons flashed on humble cottage roofs, and gold glittered on human wrists, ears, teeth and fingers.

As Isa leaned forward to fiddle with the stereo, I noticed he was wearing a gold signet ring and what appeared to be a Rolex watch. He turned up the chirpy Arabic-style pop music which had rustled on at low volume since the border check.

'This is my favourite travelling song,' he said, taking off his sunglasses. Ray-Bans? I looked at the logo with disbelief. Isa had deep brown, honest eyes. 'It's Chechen, but we're cousins and we speak more or less the same language. Chechnya's only another couple of hours' drive away ... I always play this music at the border post. It makes me laugh. And those poor boys don't understand why.' He tapped neatly manicured brown fingers on the steering wheel and hummed quietly for a few minutes.

'I'm in Moscow and I'm bored by this little world of rules,' he translated. 'That's more or less how it goes. Then ... Let's put the car roof down, Tamara, and fly to the roof of the world.' He smiled again, a distant look on his gentle face. 'Russian soldiers make a point of searching Ingushi and Chechen cars. They don't like us,' he said meditatively. 'But they're more frightened of us than of fire, and somehow they never dare check our pockets.'

He brought out a tiny pistol and laid it on the dashboard. Its butt was chased with what might have been mother-of-pearl and silver. 'Of course one has to say one has no weapons. But how can one travel the countryside without a gun in these rough times?'

*

Isa turned out to be very rich. Because he travelled the world and wore Italian designer clothes, I guessed that his firm in Moscow was perhaps one of the new not-very-legal mafia-type organizations. But he was polite, soft-spoken, gracious, and as horrified as I was by the discoveries we began to make together about the Ingushi villagers from Prigorodny District.

'My family home is nearby, and I have a van which would be suitable for transporting your equipment. If you would all like to stay for a few days, I would be delighted if we could travel together,' he said. He used the Russian word for van, *furgon*, and I thought rather dejectedly of the decrepit vehicles that came under the heading, and the discomfort of bouncing around between their metal struts. But I was grateful anyway.

He turned off the main road, down a muddy lane lined with small houses. It was deserted except for a few bedraggled hens pecking around a rough fence and two untethered goats skipping over the frozen ruts. He brought the car to a halt and hooted.

A high blue-painted fence in front of us opened up. Double gates swung back and we drove into a neatly concreted courtyard. A dark, handsome young man waved a greeting from the gates. Isa parked the Volga next to a sparkling white Toyota jeep, sitting incongruously in its capitalist splendour under an archway. 'Your *furgon*,' he said with a smile, and my heart lifted. 'Now, let's see if we can find you something to eat before we set off.'

I got out, feeling suddenly grimy in the unexpected elegance of these surroundings. Sasha and Volodya were whispering and prodding each other in badly disguised disbelief. I was glad they were there, but I began to worry that they would not behave with the formal graciousness of this place. They were so Russian, so scruffy yet superior and sneery. Then I looked down at my own muddy jeans, and laughed at my worries.

We stretched and stared. Long buildings of pleasing proportions stretched away down the yard. On one side, loosely-carpeted steps led up to a veranda whose curly wrought-iron railings ran the length of the main house. Several pairs of shoes were laid out on the steps. A second building, identical but for the veranda, stood opposite. A covered colonnade at the far end of the courtyard connected the two buildings, and cars were parked between its arches, by the jeep. The fence at the courtyard's near end, and the three silvery roofs, were edged with narrow bands of filigree work.

'But this is beautiful. What a wonderful house!' I said. My breath had been taken away.

'We do what we can,' Isa answered. 'Come inside and meet my family.'

A group had gathered at the top of the stairs. I looked up, taking in a plump woman in her late thirties with a shadowy chin, a broad smile of welcome and gold teeth. The handsome gate-opener had been joined by a lean, sharp-featured beauty with a sardonic gleam in her eyes. There were two older men in impeccable charcoal suits and silk ties. Three or four children hid behind adult legs. At the back, demurely kitted out in crisp white shirts and dark skirts, were two young women. One might have been twenty, very slim, very elegant, with the curved, aquiline features of her family softened by a gentle smile. The other could be no more than a tall sixteen. She had the long blonde hair of Spanish aristocrats, an apricot bloom to her skin and the awkward grace of a beauty to be.

'It's a bit improvised . . .' Isa said half-apologetically after we had washed (hot water! a bathroom ten paces long! fluffy towels! hairdryers!), changed our clothes and sat down in an airy dining-room to eat the spicy beef, fresh salad, rice, cakes and other dishes which the women wafted in to lay before us. Without the leather coat and dark glasses which made up his travelling wardrobe, he had transformed himself into a faultless Italian-designer aristocrat like his brothers. There was gold leaf picking out the mouldings on the ceiling, and a lustre on the carpet on the main wall, and a choice of champagne, mineral water, Coke and American vodka. The women didn't eat with us. The men ate and drank with restraint, but pressed food on us.

After the impromptu feast, I tried to clear away some of the plates littering the table, but I was stopped. Monty, oldest and goldest of the men, and the blonde teen-aged girl both burst out laughing when I appeared in the kitchen with dirty crockery in my hands. Her laugh was like bells. His was more of a bull's bellow. I stopped uncertainly.

'Zemfira. Run along and clear the table and don't torment our guest,' Monty said, calming himself and hitching up tweedy trousers over his broad stomach.

'Guests are sacred in our houses. We're bound by honour to defend you with our lives while you're under our roof . . . so we can't let you demean yourself by doing housework,' Zemfira explained. 'Sit down instead. I'm going to do everything,' she said, brushing past me into the corridor.

Before we left for work, we set up the satellite phone in a corner
of the courtyard, angling it towards the east. 'So it's Muslim, like
us,' Isa said as I fiddled with cables and dials, with laughter barely
suppressed in his deep voice. 'It prays to Mecca.'

I began to like Isa.

*

We drove to the Ingush capital, Nazran, in the jeep.

Darkness was falling on the road.

Nazran wasn't much of a town. It had never been intended as a
capital, but had been forced to stand in as a kind of administrative
centre for the Ingush lands when Chechnya had pulled out of the
Russian Federation. There was a crumbling two-floor government
building, grey but nicknamed 'the White House', and there was a
square outside, and more crumbling flats with the slogan 'Sixty
Years of the October Revolution' built into the wall in red brick.

The square was packed with people. Old men in tall hats stood
in circles, talking quietly. Around them, uncertain in the foggy
dusk, hundreds of other people hung about.

'They're waiting to hear whether there's been a hostage
exchange,' Isa said. 'Stay here, we'll find out what's going on and
come back for you.'

He fished out a briefcase from the back seat, whistled up one of
the guards lounging nearby and set off through the dense crowd. I
thought there was probably money in the case. I lit a cigarette,
aware of thousands of eyes turning towards me through the misty
black evening, and shrank back into my seat. We had been lucky
to find Isa, but perhaps the Ossetians and Russians in Vladikavkaz
had been right: perhaps the Ingush were the lowest of the low,
bloodthirsty, raging savages, thieves and murderers . . . Sasha and
Volodya, in the back, were also looking nervously out into the
dark. 'Best for Isa to make sure things are safe for us,' Sasha said,
patting me on the shoulder. I didn't mind his being patronizing; I
could see it cheered him up to have someone he felt he could
protect. But the very fact of his pat made me feel I didn't need
protecting by him; after all, it was me who had made the contact
with Isa. 'So what do you think of Isa?' I asked. Four little eyes

lowered and raised themselves again: 'Mafia, of course,' pronounced Sasha with certainty. 'So he'll have the local government
in his pocket. We'll hear things just the way they want them heard.'
He adopted his cynical, hardboiled-journalist look, which sat oddly
on his childlike pink cheeks.

We dozed and smoked. After twenty minutes or so, the door
opened and Isa was looking down gravely at us. He led us through
the shabby crowds towards the White House.

*

Everyone wanted to talk: the refugees on the dark square, the
people crowded into pools of light in the White House corridors,
on the stairs, in the local leader's room. At first, everything I heard
was confusing and frightening. Although they weren't angry with
me, everyone I talked to was angry. They pushed and pulled and
tugged and harangued; sometimes they wept, sometimes they shook
their fists in the air. There was a nightmarish quality to their
accounts, and unexpectedly becoming the focus for so much rage
was dizzying, like being in the centre of a fish-eye lens. Gesticulat-
ing arms and open mouths gleamed and flashed right round my
field of vision in a red haze. Everyone shouted at once. They
couldn't stop themselves. No one had listened to their stories
before. They felt impelled to tell. My hand ached from writing. My
tapes were full. My notebook was full. It was exhausting to be in
the eye of their storm.

The first thing that struck me was that they, like the Ossetians,
referred repeatedly to the deportations of 1944. But they did it in a
different way. To the Ossetians, the date meant rubber-stamped
approval by Moscow for bullying; to these people, it was shorthand
for suffering and injustice that they and their parents had lived
through and that they could not forget. It was also fast becoming a
yardstick to measure the morality of Moscow's behaviour to them
now, and not one that showed modern Russian behaviour in a
good light.

'What happened during the deportations was nothing compared
to this,' said Eset, a distraught mother of three who was taken
from her home in Vladikavkaz and kept in a camp for four days

before being sent to Nazran in a hostage exchange. Her husband was still a prisoner of war, and she was terrified to give her last name in case it stopped his release in another hostage exchange. 'Hitler would be ashamed to carry out the genocide which has been perpetrated against us,' she said, her face twisted, pushing hair back from her face.

But what began slowly to filter through into my brain was that I couldn't detect any Soviet hyperbole in their stories. Each person was telling his or her truth. The violence they described was visited on them from the outside. Most people weren't telling exaggerated horror stories they'd heard about something that might have happened to someone else; the few that did were careful to explain how they'd come to hear the story, and why they thought it was true. Chaotic as the scene seemed, there was an unusual honesty about it.

Eset's account of her last days in Vladikavkaz was measured. She wasn't raped or beaten up. She pointed out other women in the crowd who had been physically mistreated, but didn't try to tell their stories for them. Her story was one of psychological bullying and terror. 'We had to go out to buy bread at gun-point. Those Ossetian guards would sit there on the streets with their weapons and get drunk and chant: "In-GUSH, In-GUSH." Some of them were our neighbours, people we'd lived with for years. We didn't know what was happening.'

When she and her family were carted off to a camp in the villages, they were kept in a cellar with dozens of others. 'We gave them all our money, more than a thousand roubles, for food, but we only got four pieces of bread in exchange. We hardly ate a thing in those four days. Then they let all the women and children go – that's why I'm here now – and they were thrusting down our throats how humane and Christian they were. But they kept the men there, and what kind of humanity is it when they keep our husbands and brothers and we don't know whether they're being killed or tortured or starved or what?

'They opened the cellar door every now and then to yell down. "No one knows you're here, we could finish you all off now, and no one would ever know," and then they'd roar with laughter and shut the door,' whispered another girl, with a pale face and staring eyes.

The old men in astrakhan hats wouldn't let me talk to the women who had been raped. 'The Ossetians have shamed us all,' said one of them, Ortsnapo, whose granddaughter had been molested by three Ossetian men in a cellar. He was blocking out the horrors of today, looking for comfort in the harsh treatment mountain peoples traditionally meted out to their enemies to match the tough rules the Ingush still used for themselves. 'Our Muslim culture says girls must be virgins at marriage. Those raped girls will never marry. But this is the land of blood revenge, and we will get our revenge, however long it takes. In fifteen years, in twenty years, not one of the Ossetian deputies who ordered this will be alive. We will wipe them out, one and all.'

At the doorway of the White House, a Second World War veteran with a chestful of medals and a frost of white stubble on his furrowed skin accosted me. Isa had gathered his own group of lost souls a few feet away. They were absorbed, talking, slowly, gently, in their own language. Heads craned towards Isa for comfort.

'Lieutenant Imagozhev . . . Alaudin,' the old soldier said to me, saluting in forlorn memory of a sprightly Soviet past. 'You must tell the world our story. I've never seen anything like this in all my years as a military man. They're not letting us go to the camps and collect our dead to bury them. They're burning the bodies. The Ossetian leaders say they've buried some but we want them to be given the final rites in our religion and not to be burned or shovelled underground by a bulldozer.

'It's a mockery of our people. We have no artillery and no tanks. It was Stalin's idea to promote the Ossetians at other people's expense, and look at what's happening here now. We don't want other people's land. We just want the place where our ancestors lived.'

We left the grief-stricken crowd swaying outside and went upstairs to meet Isa Kostoyev, the Ingush leader who had been appointed by the Russian parliament as the region's temporary administrator. He had worked for years as an investigator in the Russian justice ministry. He was as measured and moderate as the situation allowed. But it was an extreme situation.

'All the Ingushi from Prigorodny District are now either hostages, refugees or dead,' he said. 'Of about 65,000 people who were living there, practically none are left in their own houses. They were treated with such atrocious cruelty that it would be shocking in a horror film. People have been mutilated, their sexual organs cut off, women have been raped and people have been imprisoned in toilets and forced to eat excrement. It's very hard to establish the number of refugees. A few hundred hostages have been released, but we believe there could be another 10,000 on the other side of the border. What we went through during the deportations is nothing compared to this. Genocide is not the right word. This is murder.'

Kostoyev showed me a telegram sent to Moscow, asking in strong, emotional language for permission for Ingush groups to go to Prigorodny and take the hostages away to safety:

This is the fourth day that the Ingush side has demanded permission to go to Prigorodny District to take out the remaining living old people, women and children. Deputy Prime Minister Khizha, the leader of the Russian troops, and the head of the Ossetian Council of Ministers, Khitogorov, give lying answers to our request and block all our questions. They are gaining time to hide their crimes. There are secret burials going on, burnings and mutilations so as to give the impression that Ossetians are allegedly being killed by Ingushi. Hostages are dying of cold and thirst and there are cases of death by hunger. For every piece of bread, the hostages are forced to pay up to 500 roubles. Ingush houses are being destroyed and burned. There is an unrestrained bacchanal of looting going on. People are being kept in toilets and cattle sheds, in unthinkable conditions. The world has not yet been able to grasp the crimes being committed by Russian troops and all kinds of Ossetian bandit gangs. This is a brutal blow to the naive faith of the Ingush people in the honour of the Russian army and its ability to protect us from Ossetian bandits.

We ask for urgent intervention and help to stop this barbarity and genocide. From the Ingush people's General Tsechoyev, and Beg Abadiyev, member of the People's Council of Ingushetia.

Kostoyev had sent another telegram on Friday, pleading to be allowed into the disputed district to collect the dead. But there had been no answer. Kostoyev was convinced that Moscow was hand in glove with the Ossetians, and deliberately turning a blind eye to his own people's woes. He was trying to sort things out as peaceably as possible, but he wasn't getting any help.

'Galazov [Akhsarbek Galazov, the North Ossetian leader] asked Yeltsin for an *ukaz* declaring a state of emergency, and he got it. But since the beginning of these events I haven't been able to get through to Yeltsin on the phone. And when I try to call Khizha in Vladikavkaz, as soon as his office hears the call is from Nazran, the phone goes dead. I feel very negative towards Khizha,' he said quietly.

I told him about my conversation in Vladikavkaz with the Russian commander Savvin, who had said Ingush militants were obstructing hostage exchanges. Kostoyev only laughed hollowly. 'He hasn't been in touch once,' he said. 'I've got a Moscow phone right here, and I spend my days calling out on it, but no one's calling us back. We'd be delighted if someone would set our people free from there. Whyever would we obstruct hostage exchanges? It wouldn't make sense.'

Was there any hope of peace returning? I asked. Not unless the Russian government changed its ways and began to obey the laws passed by its own parliament, he said wryly: 'Certain Russian apparatchiki don't know how to obey the law.'

Was it true, as the Moscow papers suggested, that an Ingush plot had been hatched in the autumn to organize an uprising in Prigorodny District and seize it back from the Ossetians? Were we seeing the disastrous end of that plot now? He shook his head.

'Discontent has been brewing up for a long time and then suddenly it exploded elementally. That's why it's finished so quickly. If it had been prepared beforehand it would have gone on for much longer.'

And was war going to engulf the North Caucasus now, another worry of Moscow editorial writers? Would the Ingushi turn against Yeltsin, whom they had almost all voted for in presidential elections in 1991, and throw in their lot with Dudayev's freedom-minded Chechens instead?

He shook his head wearily. 'We haven't officially asked Chechnya for military help. My opinion is that we must extinguish the conflict, not fan the flames. Our solution must be within the framework of the law of the Russian Federation . . . and anyway, our people are in mourning. They are not in a state to think about pro-Russian or pro-Chechen moods. The time to do that will be when we have buried our dead and got over this sorrow.'

But Kostoyev and the rest of the men in the little White House, who all looked exhausted under the harsh white lights, weren't very interested in political questions. Their expectations of Moscow had been low from the start, and now they had a far more urgent task on their hands than trying to make Russians act according to their notions of right and wrong. They were trying to absorb nearly 100,000 people into their tiny homeland, whose whole population was less than half a million, and whose people were dirt poor. The Prigorodny people were being fed and clothed as they came in, he said, then most of them were being taken into private homes by relatives and well-wishers. It was a massive exercise in problem-solving.

We went to the hospital, a dark, crowded place, with more weeping relatives crowding the courtyard and corridors. The middle-aged surgeon, Rukhlan Alpagachi, said 500 refugees had been admitted to his hospital and about sixty had died of their wounds.

'In the first couple of days, we were treating people for bullet and shrapnel wounds,' he said. 'But since the Russian troops moved in, the wounds are more serious. People are being admitted with parts of their bodies cut off and worse.'

I asked him to show us the morgue. But there were only two bodies, neither of them victims of Prigorodny. 'They'll have taken today's people away,' he said resignedly. It was ten o'clock at night, and he wasn't planning to go home any time soon.

Sasha and Volodya fidgeted again, with the young Russian journalist's instinct for the official lie of their Soviet-era elders. I didn't know whether to disbelieve him or not. But something about his quiet demeanour made me more inclined to believe him than I had the atrocity-mongers of Vladikavkaz.

We were to go to the mountains to see the refugees coming in the next morning. Late at night, the three of us sat whispering. Isa's family had gone to bed. A dog was barking fitfully in the yard. Sasha and Volodya were sceptical about what we'd seen; I was undecided.

'It's all exaggerated, of course. A few refugees come in from the hills, and there's a lot of weeping and wailing about ethnic cleansing . . . There obviously *was* an Ingush plot, and these guys were in on it too,' Sasha said. 'They got greedy for land. They brought it on themselves. Now they want aid money, and they're Muslims: it's in their nature to exaggerate and tell tall tales. They're primitives.'

'Do you think they'll get much aid?' I asked.

Sasha shrugged and grinned.

'From Russia?' he asked rhetorically.

*

It worried me all night that everyone on the Nazran central square had talked in that realistic way about the deportations to Kazakhstan. Everything I had encountered so far in the former Soviet Union had been make-believe, one way or the other. It seemed impossible that an entire generation of this people, with their appearance of having lived in these hills since time immemorial, had really been exiled to Kazakhstan for thirteen years at the whim of a dictator.

I got up early the next morning. I talked to the women in the kitchen. Then I found Isa, emerging clean-shaven to check the car.

'Isa,' I asked, 'where were you born?'

'Kazakhstan,' he answered with a shrug and a resigned smile.

Isa took a carload of bodyguards with us when we started off for the mountains at dawn. Four men in an elderly Zhiguli set off behind the jeep.

'Don't worry about the bodyguards. It's just that you need

protection on these roads. But we'll be fine now we've got them,' he said, his soft eyes beaming reassurance.

I looked at the flickering dials on the dashboard. Our car had quietly speeded up to 140 km an hour, already, effortlessly. Cars on Soviet roads were not usually capable of exceeding speed limits of 60 or 80 km. There was no way the ancient Zhiguli full of gunmen would be able to keep up, I thought, but was too polite to point that out to my thoughtful host.

I sat back happily, watching the scenery flow by, watching the needle on the speedometer creep up to 160. It was only after about twenty minutes that I looked back down the road. The gunmen waved from the Zhiguli, which had kept its place right behind us. My jaw dropped. What kind of engine could that old rattletrap have? I wondered, then quickly wiped the shocked look off my face as I realized Isa was watching me with amusement and had followed my train of thought. 'Surprised?' he said. 'Don't be. When we do something, it works.'

The Zhiguli was still behind us when we abandoned the car, when the road ran out. The refugees were coming out of a wilderness where no car could follow.

*

What we saw in the mountains between Ingushetia and Ossetia was ethnic cleansing.

Ingushi from Prigorodny were creeping down old hiking trails through the mountains, barefoot, in torn pyjamas, with ripped legs and sodden hair. Two teenage girls were dragging their grand-mother's frozen corpse. Ingushi from Ingushetia were mobilizing en masse to help save them before the first big snowfall, just about to fall from thick grey skies, shut the mountains off for winter.

Lorries lurched up through riverbeds to the highest possible point in the grey-green hills, then edged back down again packed with stoic humanity. Another old military truck turned up, thick with mud, every half an hour or so. Young men paced up into the peaks to guide down the lost and carry the injured. Great tureens of greasy soup boiled over open fires at reception points. Thick mud coated our legs up to the thighs, and everyone avoided noticing the first flakes of snow settling on hair, on bags, on soil. In the valleys, mothers were collecting old clothes to put on the shivering, shocked newcomers.

'The first big snowfall could come any time and then they'll all be trapped up there,' said Fatima, a nurse standing knee-deep in stinking mud at the improvised rescue post we reached, long after we abandoned the jeep and took to the lorries and riverbeds. About 5,000 people had already passed through into their ethnic homeland after days of walking through a roadless gorge from North Ossetia. She and rescue organizer Bagaudin Bogatyrev believed that up to 60,000 more, the entire Ingush population of North Ossetia, were following on their heels.

What I believed I was seeing was Dunkirk spirit with a Caucasian flavour. Obviously, with my cultural baggage, I was more impressed by this manifestation of rough-and-ready damage limitation than the two young Russians, whose expectations of disaster relief were of government trucks and lashings of bureaucracy.

Sasha and Volodya hung about, at a loss as to how to proceed.

'Ask them how they feel about it,' Sasha nudged me, as a trio of girls in nightclothes waded downhill through the mud to the fire. 'You're a foreigner. They'll talk to you.'

I didn't want to torment people with questions unless they wanted to talk, but I approached the three girls. One began to tell me her story in a monotone: locked in a cellar, freed after two days without her brothers and father, a long walk over the mountains, sleeping rough, scared the big snowfall in the heavy skies would begin, scared of everything.

'How do you feel about it?' Sasha broke in impatiently.

Her eyes filled with tears. Her face collapsed. 'How do you think I feel?' she said with unsteady dignity. She didn't want to cry. Another of the girls put a hand on her shoulder. They walked on.

But there were plenty of people who had been given dry clothes, bowls of hot soup and moral support and were ready to talk. While they were waiting for the next lorry to take them swaying down into the valley, they gathered round us and told their stories, as hypnotically as the people in Nazran the night before.

They had fled their homes at 5 a.m., days before, when they heard gunfire and realized the Ossetians were coming for them. Not everyone had been lucky enough to escape. Almost no men were among the refugees. The Ossetians had shut them up in the cellars before they chased the women away.

No one wanted to cry or show weakness. They were too proud. The stories came out in a dreamy monotone.

Fatima, whose job was examining the refugees as they arrived, was not impressed by Sasha and Volodya's wish to see tears and hysteria on all sides.

'You keep those silly Russian boys calm,' she said, giving me a mug of soup. When they rushed to carry my bag or help me climb a steep stretch of hill, she burst out laughing at their out-of-place courtliness. 'She can do fine without you! She's doing her job! She's perfectly good at getting in and out of trucks without you boys helping her!' Fatima scoffed. 'You just get on with your own jobs!'

There was something serious about the Ingush rescuers that made the two Russian boys seem amateurish and comical.

'How much do you think they're getting paid for this?' Sasha whispered later. Fatima had a tideline of mud at mid-thigh, and she was spattered with the thick brown of the rivers up to the waist. I asked, and she shrugged. 'We aren't getting money. This is just something we've got to do,' she said. It was a common-sense answer, but Sasha looked sceptical again.

There was the same air of quiet purposefulness about most of the kindly, dignified helpers. They were helping without fussing, suffering without complaining, doing good where they could without expecting rewards. It was the first time since I'd come to Russia that I'd seen a group of people interacting socially in a constructive way. Only one of the helpers, a boy of about twenty who had spent his day standing shoulder-high in a raging mountain river in a human bridge which the elderly and infirm could cross to get down the hillside to safety, lost his temper when he thought about what was happening. It was worse than Stalin, he said. It was worse than 1944.

'You tell that Yeltsin,' Musa Albakov said, picking up his gun

and stroking it longingly. 'You tell that Yeltsin I'm saving a bullet
for him.'

*

Bogatyrev and Isa were huddled together, deep in mud.

'What we need is a helicopter to spot who's still coming, and
lead them down,' Bogatyrev said. I faded in and out of their
conversation.

Isa gave him money. I didn't see how much. I had $200 on me.
I wanted to give it to Isa to pass on, but I knew I might need it to
pay for Sasha and Volodya's passage back to Russia, because they
had no money to be here. I began to feel irritated with them.

Late in the afternoon, as we were leaving the mountainside, a
helicopter buzzed into view. Isa pointed it out to me, with a big
smile of relief; he didn't mention the money I'd seen him slip
Bogatyrev; he was just pleased that some sort of salvation was on
the way for the people in the hills. I warmed to his generosity even
more.

We hurtled home in the dark that night. Isa's elegant car was
smeared with mud. Everyone was quiet, even Sasha. Isa's features,
lit by the red and green points of light on the dashboard, were
frozen in loss and bewilderment. Starlight on the light dusting of
snow outside gleamed round dark roadside huts. The headlights of
the souped-up Zhiguli glared behind us. Our legs were plastered
uncomfortably to the seats.

'My head's spinning. It's hard to take it all in, isn't it? I can
hardly believe things can be so bad . . .' Isa said. His voice was
ragged. He stared out of the window, into the dark. 'You must be
tired,' he added after a while, with his usual politeness.

We shuffled out of the car, across the dark courtyard, and into
the softly lit house, aching all over. I locked myself in a bathroom
and scrubbed away all the dirt I could until the mirror misted over,
and I was pink, dressed in dry clothes, and profoundly grateful not
to be still in the freezing, draughty shelters in which the refugees
would be curling up together.

Isa and his cousin Musa were waiting, in fresh suits and sharply
pressed shirts and ties, cufflinks gleaming, hair damped back. They

looked drained, but fatigue had done nothing to wipe away their formal dignity. Musa stood up with a tired smile.

'We have been invited to have supper with a neighbour. Shall we go?' he said. 'I think you will enjoy meeting him.' There was nothing to do but accept.

Another mansion, more Japanese luxury jeeps outside, more pedigree dogs, more foreign liquor, more gold leaf and space and chased silver cutlery. Two sucking pigs had pride of place at the long table, flanked by roast game birds and platters of sizzling meat, salads, potatoes, rice, sauces and three different kinds of flat bread. A vast television glowed in the corner, at maximum colour and minimum volume.

Glasses clinked. To Isa, who came home to look after his own. To the journalists who will tell the world what is really happening here. To the ladies (God bless 'em). To the Chechens and the Ingushi. To our fathers who have gone before us and our unborn children. To our host. To our guests' next visit. To the end of our troubles. To a better future.

But the real point of the evening was to gather the local gentry, in this world without telephones, to tell them what Isa had found out about what was happening in the mountains.

'What we have seen today is hard to make sense of. It was horrible up there, wasn't it? What was going on up there was wrong. But at least we've found out the truth for ourselves, and we can start doing something about it,' Isa said, appealing to me with a fatigued smile.

Our host was an old man with white hair, a gold bracelet and a face-splitting smile who fumbled over his own words but listened intently to Isa's simple, shocked description of the day.

Isa's account was detailed but dispassionate. We were each asked to add our impressions. Something else I wasn't used to after my months in Russia: everyone at the table listened to each account, quietly, asking questions that showed they were taking in what had been said. No one interrupted, and no one branched out into a passionate philosophical speech about something only tangentially connected to the issue. I was also personally pleased with the conversation because no one cast doubt on what I said just because I was a woman, or asked me condescendingly for a 'woman's view'. Although the Ingush women sat in the kitchen and not at the dining table with us, the men had quietly taken me at my own valuation and accepted the way I did my job. Once again, I felt Russia was far away and I was in a new country.

'And what do you make of it all?' the old man asked Sasha at one point.

'We have to try to take an objective view,' Sasha answered uncomfortably. 'We are journalists, and we have to be impartial. It's hard to understand a new situation all at once.' He stopped. Volodya was looking down.

'Of course, you have a woman's response to it all,' Sasha added into the silence, turning to me. 'Immediate, emotional . . . but we have to think it all out and be rational.'

There was a pause before a new conversation started.

Sasha and Volodya were happier talking about the flak jackets they had stolen from the Russian military post in Prigorodny while no one was looking. The grown-up Ingushi humoured them, although there had been no need to wear flak jackets on the hillside.

Sasha was less reticent when we got home to Isa's. He and Volodya crept up to me in the courtyard, giggling, as I tried to get through to Moscow on the satphone. 'Did you see the jewellery on that old guy?' Sasha whispered. 'I take it you guessed who he was?' I shook my head, puzzled. They tut-tutted over my naivety. 'This is a black mafia clan we've fallen in with,' they chorused happily. 'It wasn't by chance that we had to go there tonight. He ordered us to be taken over for him to inspect. He was the Godfather.'

I didn't really agree with him any more. 'Wasn't that just Caucasian hospitality? It's natural enough for people to want to find out what's going on. There are no phones that work properly, after all,' I said, feeling disloyal to Isa's family for having this conversation at all.

Sasha lifted his shoulders, grinning. 'They're all the same, these Muslims; desperate to ram down our throats this idea about being mistreated. They just wanted to make sure we'd got the message. They're sure to have some axe to grind themselves.'

But Volodya began looking as uncomfortable as I felt. 'But don't you think what we saw today really was terrible?' I said. 'Those people we saw coming from Prigorodny have all been kicked out of their homes. Surely you're not saying they haven't had a rough deal?'

Unexpectedly, Volodya nodded. 'I suppose they have,' he said, trying out the new idea.

*

We had done enough. It was time to go home. Isa and Monty drove us to Nazran and got us plane tickets after an effortless five-minute conversation inside the airport building. I was sorry to part with them. By now, I felt closer to them – with their warmth for their fellow countrymen, their kindness to us, and their willingness to put themselves out and climb mountains and wade through rivers to find out the truth about the tragedy taking place in their homeland – than I did to the hapless, scrounging, adolescent pair of Russian reporters, full of prejudices that they had accepted without thinking. During the brief period of the trip, without my really being aware of it, my sympathies had changed from Russian to Ingushi.

Later, it became common knowledge that tens of thousands of refugees from Prigorodny did make that mountain crossing. They are still living in Ingushetia today, sharing houses with the Ingushi families that took them in in 1992. They make up a quarter of Ingushetia's population.

Aid agencies called in to preside over later ethnic tragedies in the region describe how Ingush families, like Isa's, offered all the help they could during that winter crossing of the mountains, and absorbed the huge inflow of refugees into their own homes so effectively that surprisingly few of the newcomers needed to throw themselves on the public purse.

But, at the time, the Moscow papers never described their exodus. There was no humanitarian aid from Russia for the homeless. It was history swept under the carpet, a secret event that never officially happened, like so much in Soviet history. It was probably the first such piece of organized blindness in new Russia.

I went back to Moscow full of enthusiasm for my story. 'We got it all wrong!' I told my boss, still in my muddy jeans, as I heaved the satphone through the door. 'If there were ever any good guys, it's the Ingushi. This is an ethnic cleansing story.'

What followed must be what Cassandra must have felt like, with her long hair flowing and her warnings of disaster unheeded. My boss raised an ironic eyebrow, but let me write my stories. 'You were very angry about all that Ingush stuff,' he recalled later.

Four Western television companies called me the next day, politely checking out my stories, asking whether I really thought more than 50,000 people were trying to get to safety. They didn't send crews to film it.

A friend who worked for a British newspaper took me out to lunch. He raised the subject of the story I'd just put out, saying that the situation in the south was an exact parallel of Yeltsin's fight with Khasbulatov in the north, only with real blood and real guns.

'I thought it was interesting – if true,' he said sceptically.

As a story, it was at odds with the orthodoxy of the day, which was that what Yeltsin's men did was almost certainly in the best interests of democracy. No one listened.

Isa telephoned a few days later. He was back in Moscow. I asked him and Musa to supper. They wanted copies of the articles that I and the two Russian boys had written. They were going to get mine translated into Russian and distributed to help raise awareness of the disaster and funds for the refugees. They were charming. They brought expensive wine and flowers with them. Sasha and Volodya, who came too, brought nothing but drank all my brandy. The two Ingushis' heads were still full of the torments in the hills, and they carried on discussing them with me and Volodya and Sasha. I thought we might become friends.

But my husband, by now working in Moscow as a correspondent, didn't approve. He withdrew into himself at dinner, pouring drinks, smiling vaguely, talking only to the other English people there. 'They didn't talk to me,' he said afterwards, only half joking. 'They were only interested in you. They were chatting you up.' I laughed it off, but the idea wouldn't go away. I could see my

husband didn't completely believe Isa and Musa could have helped
a woman unless they had some sexual motivation, just as Russians
couldn't quite believe that the black Ingushi could be anything but
villains. I loved my husband, and I didn't like to think that he
suspected my trips south, which I took very seriously as a great
voyage of discovery, were just sleazy searches for sensation, or
exotic excuses for flirtations. It made me feel bad. So when Isa rang
a few days later to ask us out for a drink, I said with a hint of
regret that we were busy. Isa understood. He never called back.

*

There was an ugly political coda to the North Ossetia fighting.
Belatedly, Russian troops did go into Ingushetia, closer to the
Chechen border, to enforce the state of emergency declared weeks
before and to stop the darkies killing each other. In Chechnya,
Dudayev's government began to suspect this was a ploy masking
preparations for an invasion which would force him to bow down
to Moscow. Dudayev told Moscow to move the troops back from
his borders, or face armed conflict. Sure enough, the discomfited
Russian troops did move back. The whole story vanished from the
press.

The end of fighting in Prigorodny was interpreted in Moscow as
a political victory for Yeltsin's quick thinking against the trouble-
making of Khasbulatov's parliament, a victory for the forces of
progressive good against those of reaction. Dudayev's subsequent
intervention in the row was seen in Moscow as just one more
proof, if one were needed, that southern blacks were wild, aggressive savages.

'It wasn't like that! The Ingushi were being ethnically cleansed,
and Yeltsin's men were encouraging the Ossetians to do it,' I told
Andrei. He looked quizzical. For a Russian, he was very open-
minded, but he was unconvinced. His eyebrow twitched at the
word 'Ingushi'. 'But surely,' he said, 'the Ingushi are just like
Chechens?' It was answer enough.

Even after my day in the mountains, when Isa's cousin Musa, an
ex-deputy of the Checheno-Ingush parliament, had offered to
escort me on to Grozny to introduce me to the Chechen leaders, I

had made my excuses and returned to Moscow. I trusted his family, and I was impressed by the Ingushi, but I was tired. Also, I still couldn't see how the wild Chechens of popular disrepute could possibly be like these phlegmatic, stoical ethnic cousins. The dark power of the Russian legend was still too strong.

# ACT THREE

# JOURNEY INTO THE CHECHEN PAST

# ONE

Everyone I had spoken to in the Caucasus had invoked history to explain themselves and their old hatreds. The past slapped you in the face wherever you went. But what history? Whose past? Now that I had seen that the courtly Ingushi were nothing like the 'black savages' of Russian legend, and wondered why their collective trauma of half a century ago had never been addressed, I began to ask how the legend of savagery arose in the first place.

Back in Moscow, I tried to find out from Russians what they knew about the history of Russian involvement in the Caucasus, but all they remembered from Soviet school was the literature of Lermontov and Pushkin. There was only fiction, or ignorance.

'*Zloi Chechen*,' our translators whispered, with grins and grimaces, widening their eyes in mock-horror. '*Zloi Chechen*,' laughed Natasha Karpova, pulling a horrible face, when I went to St Petersburg for a weekend to reassure her anxious parents that I had survived my latest visit to the south. '*Zloi Chechen*' – 'the wicked Chechen' – was the memorable refrain from a Lermontov poem called 'The Cossack's Lullaby', which every Russian had learned by heart in Soviet school. In it, a Cossack mother lulls her baby to sleep in a Cossack *stanitsa* with stories of her husband's bravery fighting the Chechens, and with promises that when the baby grows up he too will have a sword and a horse with an embroidered saddle and kill infidels. Outside the safety of the village, each verse recalls in a shiver of scared anticipation, the wicked Chechen is prowling along the night river with dagger in hand, ready to attack. But, in every verse, the mother defiantly banishes these uncertain dark forces, waiting and watching for their chance to do evil, with yet more triumphant descriptions of Russian bravery. It was the perfect metaphor for Russians' panicky attitude to their homeland's ever-changing land borders, their historical sense of being surrounded by potential enemies and needing to keep weapons at hand and watch out for trouble from beyond the camp fire. But it didn't reveal much about the Caucasians.

I went back to *A Hero of Our Time*, but that didn't help either. Set against the backdrop of last century's Caucasus Wars, Lermontov's novel focused on a subject far closer to the hearts of intelligent nineteenth-century Russians. This was how intelligent nineteenth-century Russians should, or could, behave in an atmosphere of political repression which gave them no obvious channel for their talents. Russia remained under an autocracy which denied freedom of individual thought while the rest of Europe lived through the age of romanticism and revolutions. For the officer class of Tsarist Russia, there were only two political choices: the gilded cage of court in St Petersburg, toeing the Tsar's line, or exile to the Caucasian front-line where they would die fighting the southern tribes. The cumbersome bureaucracy waited to embrace the young gentry and stifle their spontaneity. Writers were viewed with suspicion. Writings were censored. As the young noblemen whose liberal leanings were exposed in the 1825 Decembrist plot discovered, the punishment for straying from the path of Autocracy, Orthodoxy and Nationalness was death. And so a literary figure came into being, known as the 'superfluous man', who represented the only escape for the spirited youth of the day.

Lermontov's anti-hero Pechorin is the perfect example of the superfluous man. Exiled to the Caucasus after a scandal in St Petersburg, he is revealed as a person of talent and distinction, but trapped by circumstances in the selfishness of perpetual adolescence. He is an idealist gone sour, who never learns to temper his wit with mercy. Pechorin seeks release in wild, dashing, reckless actions, but also in ever crueller manipulation of people who take him for a friend. He takes pleasure in twisting the laws not only of the land but also of morality in a search for excitement which ultimately proves sterile. He views with detachment the courtly world of hierarchies, swank, uniformed splendour, snobbery, and love rivalries, which his Russian acquaintances take seriously, and handles both the rules of this world and the acquaintances with practised contempt. Because he is intelligent, he understands the emptiness of this life; but because he is a Russian gentleman, there is no other way to live. So Pechorin's emotional homeland is a barren terrain of duels, deceit and heartlessness, which he takes refuge in to hide his underlying despair and stifle the melancholy and yearning that torments him for all the things that can never be, a mood known in Russian as *toska*.

If the novel had been set in St Petersburg, it might have been a cruel comedy of manners. What gives it a note of tragedy is its setting in the Caucasus mountains. Pechorin only betrays his hidden capacity for noble feelings, and the man he might have become, through his one uncynical love – for the freedom of his surroundings. Smoking waterfalls, galloping horses, the moon on silver daggers, lyrically described, become shorthand for the romantic sensibilities and the modern individual consciousness sweeping the rest of Europe, but not on offer to Russians such as Pechorin. The mountain peoples, not unsympathetically described, are the noble savages of this mindset. Pechorin admires their simple lives, close to nature; he respects their willingness to die for their honour, he imitates their dress while riding in the dangerous mountains – and he destroys any of them whose path he crosses.

The story of Pechorin mirrored that of many young Russians. Lermontov too was exiled from St Petersburg when he was twenty-one for writing a politically incorrect poem defending his role model, the poet Alexander Pushkin, and spent the rest of his life in the Caucasus. Lermontov died when he was only twenty-six. Like Pechorin, he fought a duel with a friend; unlike his fictional alter ego, Lermontov was mortally wounded in the spa town of Pyatigorsk.

Lermontov's tragic death, as much as his life or writing, put him in the pantheon of Russia's great literary figures. The tragedy of poets, living and dying young under brutal censorship, has been the shadowy main theme of Russian literature until very recently, a Jimi Hendrix syndrome of beyond-the-grave devotion spanning two hundred years. In the middle of this century, the poet Osip Mandelstam described the brutal process of the authoritarian state silencing the poet's voice as 'treading on the nightingale's throat', and the poet's tragedy as knowing this is the price he must pay for singing but being unable to stop:

And there is no hope
For heart still flushed
With nightingale fever.

Mikhail Bulgakov, in his 1930s novel *The Master and Margarita*,
draws the upbeat conclusion, after describing the state's persecution of his writer hero, that 'manuscripts do not burn', suggesting
that a writer's work will survive whatever humiliations are heaped
on its author; but his hero survives only on an imaginary plane
where good and evil exist, far from modern Moscow where, as far
as ordinary people are concerned, he has committed suicide. The
gravel-voiced bard of the Soviet 1970s, Vladimir Vysotsky, wrote
one of his most memorable works in praise of the poets who, like
Christ, die by the age of thirty-three, while a state bureaucracy of
the cowardly and corrupt lives on. But the semi-sacred status
conferred on these tragic poets by their untimely deaths has had
the ugly side-effect of making their every word holy. There is no
arguing with a dead prophet, even if some of his beliefs bear critical
re-examination by later generations.

*

Alexander Pushkin, the first great poet of the Caucasus wars, who
is still revered by Russians today as the father of their national
literature, was also exiled to the Caucasus in his youth and also
died fighting a duel. His writing – playful, witty, ironical – brought
into the Russian domain the great currents of literature sweeping
the rest of Europe. His prototype of the superfluous man, Eugene
Onegin, lives on in a later opera as well as in the original long
poem. The circumstances of Pushkin's own death are more novel-
istic than most novels, enduring proof that truth is stranger than
fiction and the source of many later works of literature (including
the poem which later condemned Lermontov to exile). Recalled
from his 1820–21 exile in the Caucasus, Pushkin was made the
caged songbird of Tsar Nicholas I, who wanted to keep him at
court to inspect the poet's writings himself for signs of dangerous
liberalism. The Tsar also had an interest in keeping Pushkin's
beautiful wife, Natalya, at court. An anonymous writer began to

send Pushkin letters suggesting he was a cuckold. Believing the young French royalist, Baron D'Anthès, adopted son of the Dutch ambassador Baron Heekeren, to be to blame for the letters, Pushkin challenged him to a duel, and died shortly afterwards of his wounds. The burden of Lermontov's poem, 'Death of a Poet', was that a hostile court cabal had plotted to provoke the brilliantly original – and therefore disliked – Pushkin into challenging D'Anthès.

Pushkin's Caucasus writings are among the most famous Russian descriptions of the region. He wrote some of the most quoted lyric verse in the language, extolling the beauties of the snowy peaks and craggy landscapes. But Pushkin's most famous Caucasus writings are the long narrative 'Southern Poems', written during his two-year exile in the south, and the most beloved of these is *The Prisoner of the Caucasus*.

It tells the story of a young Russian prisoner's captivity in a Circassian village, his life in chains, his hopeless longing for the homeland he has lost, his pale, suffering face, and the love he arouses in a young Circassian girl who comes to him every evening with food and drink and pours out her feelings to him in a language he cannot understand. Finally he makes her understand that he cannot love her back, settle happily in the village, and forget his Russian past. She takes his explanation to mean that he loves a woman at home, and retreats, wounded. One evening, while the villagers are all away, she comes to the prisoner as he sits staring mournfully over the Kuban River towards Russia with a dagger in her hand and frees him from the shackles which have prevented his escape. Gratefully, he offers her the chance to run away with him; but she refuses, believing he only wants to be reunited with his Russian love. He is already over the river and climbing the cliffs on the other side when he hears a distant groan and the muffled sound of waves. He looks back; the Circassian girl has vanished into the stormy waters. After a single backward glance at his place of imprisonment, he walks away and, by dawn, reaches the safety of a Cossack patrol.

The themes of pure romanticism are here, but woven into a cloth more serviceable to the Russian empire. Pushkin's Russian hero pines for a lost love, but it is the love of his fatherland. He appropriates the rushing river, galloping stallions and rugged cliffs of the Caucasus – the symbols of freedom which so inspired the poet – as metaphor for his own, Russian, relationship to a liberty which he can see but not touch, and from which he eventually retreats. Despite its Caucasian setting, there is no place in this Russian inner world for the tragic heroine; her perfect love, self-sacrifice and suicide ultimately remove her from the landscape altogether. Through his fiction, Pushkin achieves what the Russian generals of his day were trying to achieve by force of arms. He empties the mountains of their troublesome inhabitants, whose unflinching love of freedom both attracted and repelled Russians because it was so alien to their own conception of order and hierarchy. Pushkin steals the landscape of freedom from its real inhabitants, creating out of it an imaginary terrain whose perfect liberty can easily be colonized by the nearby Cossacks and incorporated into a Russia whose rigidity has until now cast Pushkin himself out.

The conclusion drawn in Pushkin's epilogue is pure imperialism. His Muse, he explains, has been drawn to the edge of Asia, crowned with the wild flowers of the Caucasus, and imprisoned by the bleak tribes who have always lived by war, making him sing the siren songs of the south. But he will soon sing of Russia's imminent victory over the unworthy Caucasus, celebrate the unfurling of the Tsarist double-headed eagle flag, and praise the Russian generals Tsitsiyanov, Kotlyarevsky and Yermolov, whom he calls 'the scourge of the Caucasus', as they carry out their duty to subdue the tribes and, at last, bring peace. 'Submit, Caucasus: Yermolov is coming!' Pushkin declares triumphantly, wrongly predicting that the southern tribes will quietly lay down their weapons, and that remote gorges where the Caucasian tribes have 'nested' until now will soon be safe for Russian visitors to travel.

However much Pushkin's glorification of Russian militarism might stick in the throat of foreign readers, no modern Russian would think to criticize Pushkin on political grounds. During the seven decades of Soviet rule, when writers came under even fiercer censorship than in Tsarist days, Pushkin's very distance from the modern world made him the ultimate 'safe' author, preferred by Soviet school curriculum planners reluctant to be caught napping by changes in political fashion which might make today's favourite author tomorrow's Enemy of the People. Even self-willed nine-teenth-century authors such as Dostoevsky were viewed with suspicion for emphasizing personal free will above the greater social good preferred by the Soviet state. Pushkin and Anton Chekhov, Russia's other great bard of wistfulness, mocking laugh-ter at the human condition, and submission, were the set authors of choice in the monolithic Soviet education system, whose pupils turned the same page of the same textbook on the same day all over one-sixth of the globe. Soviet schools did not encourage too much analysis; the question 'why?' was not favoured. Instead, pupils learned vast numbers of facts by heart: the number of bricks in the Kremlin, the number of pictures in the Hermitage. They also committed to memory huge screeds of literature, which were so effectively drummed into them that every half-educated Moscow taxi-driver today can still recite Pushkin's poems while he idles his car in traffic jams. Soviet ideology may have vanished, but Soviet education has kept alive in Russian minds the imperial ideology of an earlier age, which long ago became distasteful to the rest of modern Europe. It is a leap through time as striking as if every child educated in English schools today was brought up on a literary diet of Rudyard Kipling's writings about the North-West Frontier in British imperial days, without being encouraged to look at the ways in which that world has changed since. Russians who love Lermontov and Pushkin, and who have perhaps visited the Caucasus on a Soviet holiday before the wars all started, feel they have a deep knowledge of and affinity with a part of the world whose landscape still symbolizes everything that is positive about freedom, but whose peoples remain a symbol of all that is bad about untrammelled self-will.

But what can Russians actually learn from their high literature about the Caucasians they have now lived with for centuries? There is virtually no mention in Russian writing of the political or philosophical aims of the Caucasian peoples, or even of their having political leaders who might channel any aspirations they might have. Only at the beginning of the twentieth century did a Russian novel appear which gave a cameo role to Shamil, the leader of the Caucasian fighters in the great nineteenth-century wars against Russia, and a sympathetic hearing to Khadzhi Murad,[1] the Caucasian leader who betrayed Shamil and turned to the Russians, hoping they would rescue his family from captivity in a Caucasian feud. Khadzhi Murad was later killed by the Russians when, having realized they could not save his family, he tried to return to his own people and rescue them himself. *Khadzhi Murad*, one of the last novellas written by Lev Tolstoy, was the work of an elderly man who had turned his own back on the pretensions of aristocratic life in Russia and embraced a life of extravagant austerity comparable to the noble simplicity of the Caucasian leaders he depicted in this fictionalized account of a true story. The book is savagely critical of the autocrat Tsar Nicholas I, depicted as a dull-witted buffoon with delusions of grandeur, immoral ways and a taste for cruelty. Tolstoy shows no more mercy to the fawning Russian aristocrats running the imperial war effort, whose deluges of flattery hide uncomfortable truths from their generals and open the door to abuse and immorality of every kind. He shows the south torn between two tyrannies, Russian and Caucasian, both so cruel and so destructive of the little people under their sway that there is nothing to choose between them. And he betrays a lingering sympathy for his hero, Khadzhi Murad, trapped in an agonizing tug-of-war between the two sides.

The rebellious Tolstoy's affections are for the underdog, whether Russian or Chechen. Describing Chechen villagers' feelings on finding their homes burned after a Russian raid, Tolstoy wrote:

No one spoke of hatred for the Russians. The feeling experienced by all the Chechens from the youngest to the oldest was stronger than hate. It was not hatred, for they did not regard those Russian dogs as human beings, but it was such repulsion, disgust and perplexity at the senseless cruelty of these creatures, that the desire to exterminate them – like the desire to exterminate rats,

---

1. The title of Lev Tolstoy's novella *Khadzhi Murad* is often transliterated into English as *Hadji Murad*; the honorific 'hadji' or 'haji' means 'pilgrim to Mecca'.

poisonous spiders or wolves – was as natural an instinct as that of self-preservation.

When a Russian officer triumphantly produces Khadzhi Murad's severed head at the end of the novella, the attractive and humane Maria Dmitrievna walks away without saying a word. Later, she delivers the moral of Tolstoy's story, saying in disgust: 'You're cut-throats, really . . . War? War indeed! Cut-throats and nothing else. A dead body should be delivered back to the earth, and they're grinning at it in there! Cut-throats, really.'

*Khadzhi Murad*, the bitterest judgement of Russian conduct during the war, was banned for years under the Tsars. As recently as 1988, Caucasus analyst Marie Bennigsen Broxup reports, a production of it by the Avar National Theatre in the North Caucasus was banned by Soviet censors, in what she calls 'an unwitting tribute to Tolstoy's talent' and a sign that Tsarist imperial attitudes persisted to the very end of Soviet rule.

# TWO

Since I couldn't find out about the Caucasian past from Russian literature, I went looking for it elsewhere. A dusty body of foreign books, written by intrepid travellers from Alexandre Dumas onwards, all out of print, circulated like the banned manuscripts of Soviet *samizdat* among a tiny band of foreign Caucasus admirers. It was from them that I dug up the bones of last century's war, the play within the play of this century's hostilities, and a story no less dramatic for having two sides rather than just the one that Russians prefer to dwell on.

*

On one side of the stage is the huge army of the Russian Tsars. The Tsars themselves are far away in the Slavic snows of the north, but they are represented by a shaggy giant of a general in the mountains, the first of a series of commanders aspiring to the title of 'scourge of the Caucasus'. His name is Yermolov; later there will be Paskevich, Rosen, Neidhardt, Vorontsov, and finally Baryatinsky. Even the Tsars shudder at Yermolov's violence against the 'Asiatics' he holds in deep contempt, but Yermolov believes 'there is no other way to destroy the enemy'. He makes and casually breaks treaties with the native princes, interpreting them, by his own admission, 'as Muslims interpret the Quran, namely, according to circumstances'. To his men, he is the Lion of the Caucasus; to the enemy highlanders, he is the Moscow Devil. Thousands – old men, women and children among them – are killed by fire and sword in the hunt for the fighters, but Yermolov is unrepentant. 'I desire that the terror of my name should guard our frontiers more effectively than fortresses and that for the natives my word should be a law more inevitable than death,' he writes. 'In the eyes of Asiatics condescension is a sign of weakness and from pure humanity I am inexorably severe. One execution saves hundreds of Russians from destruction and thousands of Muslims from treason.' Of all the mountain tribes, Yermolov is most suspicious of the Chechens. As early as 1814, he warns the Tsar that the Chechens, 'by their example of independence, can inspire a rebellious spirit and love of freedom even among the most faithful subjects of the empire', and vows to 'find no peace while a single Chechen remains alive'.

On the other side of the stage is a troop of black-robed Muslim warriors, all scholars. Their leader Shamil, the Third Imam of Dagestan and Chechnya, is an ascetic with a lean, stern face and hooded eyes. After Yermolov is disgraced by the terrifying pewter-eyed Tsar Nicholas I, and exiled to the Russian interior, Shamil unites the highland peoples from all over the north slopes of the Caucasus mountain range with his austere and mystical Sufi teachings. As both infidels and conquerors, his reasoning goes, the Russians are evil. Surrendering to them is morally wrong. The internal holy war that Sufis – known in the Caucasus as Murids, or followers of the path – fight against sin must be transformed into an external holy war against the invader. But the Russians keep coming. Since they absorbed the southern Caucasian kingdom of Georgia into their empire in 1801, Russians have surrounded the mountain tribes' hill villages from both north and south. Russia now needs to conquer the tribes to keep the mountain roads open to its new southern lands. The highlanders' holy war or *ghazavat* rages on for two generations, through most of the first half of the nineteenth century. Shamil teaches and dispenses Islamic Sharia law as he travels the remote villages of his Chechen and Dagestani supporters across the eastern stretches of the Caucasus, gradually overlaying the tribes' older *adat* or customary law and marking the beginning of the end of an age of vendetta. He is especially dangerous to the Russians because the Islam he preaches has given the squabbling tribes a cohesion, discipline and rationale for resistance which they have never had before. Their swords, he tells them, are the sabres of Paradise.

Shamil has a Houdini-like knack for escaping at the last minute from certain death. At the 1832 siege of Ghimri, where 500 Murid fighters and the First Imam are surrounded by 10,000 Russian troops and slaughtered, only the young Shamil manages to get away. The story of his disappearance, recalled by a Russian officer, has become a legend:

> It was dark: by the light of the burning thatch we saw a man standing in the doorway of a hut, which stood on raised ground, rather above us. This man, who was very tall and powerfully built, stood quite still, as if giving us time to take aim. Then, suddenly, with the spring of a wild beast, he leapt clean over the heads of the very line of soldiers about to fire on him, and landing behind them, whirling his sword in his left hand, he cut down three of them, but was bayoneted by the fourth, the steel plunging deep into his chest. His face still extraordinary in its immobility, he seized the bayonet, pulled it out of his own flesh, cut down the man and, with another superhuman leap, cleared the wall and vanished into the darkness. We were left absolutely dumbfounded. The whole business had taken, perhaps, a minute and a half.[2]

Shamil hides in the hills and recovers from his wounds, returning healthy to continue fighting and become Imam in 1834. Just as Yermolov proclaimed victory over the Caucasus tribes when he left in 1825, so later Russian generals continue to underestimate their opponent and declare the region pacified, only to be confused by continued resistance. Shamil makes a truce with the Russians after they sack a highland fortress, Akhulgo, in 1837; but the Russians then storm two more fortresses, Ashilta and Tlitl, and invite Tsar Nicholas I to Tiflis[3] to accept the allegiance of the vanquished Caucasian leader. Shamil refuses and Nicholas orders a new, all-out campaign to conquer the region quickly.

Akhulgo is surrounded again, and Shamil forced to agree to surrender and to give up his eight-year-old son, Dzhemmal-Eddin, as a hostage. The Russians promise the child will be brought up by a peaceful local chieftain in a nearby fortress – but they break their word again, and send the child to distant St Petersburg instead. Furious, Shamil withdraws his offer to surrender. The subsequent

---

2. Account of an unnamed Russian officer quoted by Lesley Blanch in *The Sabres of Paradise*, published in London in 1960, p. 74.
3. Tiflis is the old name for Tbilisi, capital of Georgia.

siege of Akhulgo lasts eighty days, and the Russians lose half their forces, but when they finally climb into the shattered mountaintop village:

> victory turned to dust in the Russians' hands, for Shamil had vanished. Every cavern was ransacked, every *saklia* [hut], all the rubble-heaps were uncovered; the putrefying bodies were examined and re-examined. He was nowhere to be found: none of his people could, or would, shed any light on the mystery, and the thwarted [Russian General] Grabbe had to admit that, once again, Shamil had effected an escape as legendary as that when he leapt over the heads of his captors at Ghimri.[4]

Again, Shamil retreats into the impenetrable fastness of the mountains to recover his strength; again, he pieces together an army and returns to harass the Russians.

The war spreads. With Circassian tribes from the west of the Caucasus also fighting advancing Russians, Shamil tries to link up with them by seizing the central territory of Kabarda. He fails; but the Russian generals, hampered by their Tsar's insistence on the full-frontal assaults and flintlock guns of traditional warfare, cannot even begin to stop his Murids' operations across the eastern Caucasus. Russian forces try, but fail, to lure the mountain guerrilla groups into easy defeat in pitched battles in the valleys, and rail against their cowardice when the shadowy highlanders continue to attack by night then fade back into the landscape. (Nicholas I was always impatient for a quick 'one-blow' victory, the historian Moshe Gammer writes: 'He expected the army which had defeated Napoleon – that was how all Russians regarded the matter – and which had dispersed Persian and Turkish armies vastly superior in numbers, to "put a quick end" to a "few bands of robbers".'[5]

After decades of failure, the Russian strategists begin to understand that, to defeat a guerrilla enemy, they must destroy enemy supply bases; they burn lowland villages, destroy crops, and cut

---

4. Blanch, *Sabres of Paradise*, p. 171.
5. Moshe Grammar, *Russian Strategies in the Conquest of Chechnia and Daghestan, 1825–1859*, p. 58, in *The North Caucasus Barrier*, edited by Marie Bennigsen Broxup, published in New York in 1992.

down the beech forests all around. The nature of the war changes at the beginning of the 1850s with the appointment of brilliant young Guards officers to high posts in the Russian command, ending a long period of indecisive leadership. Under Field-Marshal Prince Alexander Baryatinsky, the young Commander of the Left Flank appointed in 1851, the Russian army abandons the Tsar's preferred confrontational military style and reverts to Yermolov's patient tactics: slow sieges and encirclement.

Shamil's fighters retreat into the hills in the south and east; the Tsar's men pursue. Shamil's former Naib, Khadzhi Murad, goes over to the Russians but is killed when he tries to escape. This Russian success is one of many incidents which discourage the Caucasians.

Shamil, whose aim is to unite the Caucasus as a religious caliphate under Ottoman rule, pleads with the Sublime Porte for support, but gets no more than Muslim sympathy. Aware of the Great Game between the nineteenth-century Great Powers – expanding Russia and Britain each protecting itself by building its influence in the shifting borderlands of the old Persian and crumbling Ottoman domains, which are vital for trade and communications with their new imperial possessions – he comes to believe that Britain might help him. In despair, he writes letter after dignified letter to Queen Victoria, hoping that the impending Crimean War against Russia will encourage her to support his separate war against the Russians. 'England,' he writes, 'must know of our ceaseless struggle against Russia . . . we urge you, we beseech you, O Queen, to bring us help.'

England has a burst of enthusiasm for this dream of a Caucasian state – of Shamil's eastern Caucasian Imamate joined to its allies, the Circassians, further west – seeing it as a potential buffer between expanding Russia and British-ruled India. A delegation of Caucasian tribesmen dispatched to London in the 1850s is given an enthusiastic welcome. Shamil's solitary stand against Russian aggression makes him the hero of the hour in public meetings across England. Silver collections are held 'for those poor brave Caucasians'. Journalists and travellers returning from the Caucasus denounce government inactivity. A women's committee sews

Shamil a Caucasus flag of scarlet stars on a white background. The British sea captain James Stanislaus Bell breaks Russian blockades to run ships to Circassians on the Black Sea; with the covert support of the Foreign Office, British advisers help the Circassians frame declarations of defiance to Russia; Bell is among those who fight on the Circassian side against Russian troops. But the private help from England is too little and too late. There is no government answer to Shamil's letters and the state aid he asks for never comes.

The outbreak of the Crimean War in 1854, pitting Turkey and Western Europe against Russia, gives Shamil a breathing space. Russia has to pull some of its forces back from the Caucasus to fight on other fronts. The old Tsar Nicholas I dies with all his plans collapsing around him; the liberal Alexander II comes to the throne. Making the most of the opportunity, Shamil sends his men out into a daring raid into enemy territory. Penetrating into Tsarist Georgia, they kidnap the Princess Anna Chavchavadze, wife of a leading Tsarist officer, and several women and children from her family, and spirit them off to the mountain fastnesses of Vedeno, Shamil's latest mountain headquarters in Chechnya. After eight months of negotiations, which Shamil nearly upset at the last moment by demanding a million roubles ransom which the impoverished Chavchavadzes could not hope to raise, the family is exchanged for Shamil's long-lost son, Dzhemmal-Eddin.

But the improvement in Shamil's fortunes is short-lived. Dzhemmal-Eddin's upbringing at the Tsar's court has turned him into a Russian gentleman. Desperately lonely among the tribesmen of his birth, he pines away and dies. The Crimean War ends in 1856; Russia is the loser but gets off relatively unscathed, and pours its troops back to the Caucasus. The new Tsar promotes the young and energetic Baryatinsky to be Viceroy of the South and control the whole Caucasus campaign. He reforms the southern armies, begins to treat the defeated Caucasians of surrendering villages with mercy, and closes in on Shamil's mountain fortresses. Shamil's men are growing tired of nearly two generations of war, and fatalistic about their imminent defeat at Russian hands. After losing the last *aul*, fortified hilltop village, of Gunib, Shamil hands over his sword in 1859 to Prince Baryatinsky, and lives out the rest of his days in exile in the Russian town of Kaluga. Victory brings Baryatinsky no lasting glory; his philandering with other generals' wives creates a court scandal and he too is exiled.

And what comes to the Caucasus after the war is not real peace. Russian burning, looting and harassment force tens of thousands of western Circassians, and many eastern highlanders, to flee to safety in Ottoman domains. Even before Shamil dies on a pilgrimage to Mecca in 1871, the next uprising is beginning in Chechnya.

*

The first account of this war that I laid hands on was Lesley Blanch's *Sabres of Paradise*, written in 1960. It is based on the memoirs of nineteenth-century travellers, the 1908 chronicle of John Baddeley, *The Russian Conquest of the Caucasus*, and her own research across Russia and the Middle East. Blanch's version of the past, told with gusto and plenty of campfire and seraglio gossip, comes out as half history, half full-blooded historical romance.

Between gripping accounts of battles and negotiations, or breathtaking descriptions of the hidden *aul*s from which Shamil raided the Russian army, she slips in verbal snapshots of a Caucasian fighter galloping through the wilderness half-smothered by the great hoops of a Western crinoline for a lady of the seraglio, or of the rivalries between Shamil's women, or of Russian tongues wagging over General Baryatinsky's long-running affair with Madame Davidova, the wife of a senior officer. Blanch characterizes Shamil, 'the Prophet and Warrior', as 'springing on the scene in a flash of steel, a clap of thunder, like some flamboyant Prince of Darkness, the dramatic nature of his legend and his black banners matched by his back-cloth of towering mountains, perpendicular rock cliffs topped by eagle's-nest *aoul*s [*aoul*s], hung over ravines slit so deep no light ever penetrated the abyss where the torrents raged, and a never-ceasing wind howled down the precipices.' And, she enthuses: 'The Caucasians wrote love poems to their daggers, as to a mistress, and went to battle as to a rendezvous. Fighting was life itself to these darkly beautiful people – the most beautiful people in the world, it was said. They lived and died by the dagger. Battle-thrusts were the pulse of the race. Vengeance was their creed, violence their climate.'[6]

Alexandre Dumas's musings were just as romantic, when he visited the fair at Nizhny Novgorod and dreamed of floating down the Volga to the Caucasus, '. . . where we shall visit Shamil's camp: Shamil the Titan, who struggles from his lair, against the Tsar of all the Russias. Will he know our name? Will he allow us to sleep a night in his tents?'[7]

However overblown, these Western accounts of the Caucasus wars show the themes that were to re-emerge in all future dealings between Russians and Chechens.

First, there was the question of strategy. The Great Caucasian Wars were fought, largely, after the time of the Titan Yermolov. After he vanished into exile, at the very start of the war, his realistic military strategy of slow encirclement and entrapment was abandoned by later generations of generals. They preferred the politically expedient strategy of following the Tsar's unrealistic orders and pushing for a quick victory, with disastrous military results. Russian armies tried to force mountain guerrillas into the classical pitched battles fought by two armies on a field; when they failed, because the mountaineers knew they could not win such battles, the Russians accused the mountaineers of sneaky cowardice, of hiding behind women and children. It was only when, under a new Tsar three decades after Yermolov's disgrace, Baryatinsky reverted to Yermolov's original tactics – cutting down entire forests to remove the guerrillas' cover, and pushing the fighters slowly up into the most remote of mountains for siege after hopeless siege – that the Russians finally won the war.

Another theme that resurfaced in the war that was to engulf Chechnya in the twentieth century was the appalling conditions in which rank-and-file Russian soldiers lived – scarce weapons, food, boots and pay; forced service under often corrupt and incompetent generals.

---

6. Blanch, *Sabres of Paradise*, p. 1.
7. Alexandre Dumas, *Impressions de voyage*, published in Paris in 1868, quoted in Blanch, *Sabres of Paradise*, p. 189.

Perhaps most important was the question of attitude. Russians were sure – mistakenly – that their huge army could quickly pacify the small groups of mountain tribesmen. When they were proved wrong, and the mountaineers carried on fighting even though they knew it was impossible to win, Russians concluded angrily that the highlanders must be savages, in love with war for its own sake. Coming from a strongly hierarchical background, where the weak always bowed down to the strong, they could not think of any other reason why the southerners would not give in. This justified the extreme cruelty with which Russia treated its opponents once it had beaten them: the burning of villages, the hounding of clerics, and the forced emigration to the Ottoman empire of thousands of defeated Circassian and Chechen villagers once last century's war was over. As far as the Russians were concerned, this was a colonial war against inferiors, and their treatment of their defeated opponents was a measure of their contempt for them. Russian motifs in this war were brutality to their own forces and to the enemy, corruption, long years of military incompetence, a final victory flawed by the disgrace of the victorious general, and outbreaks of ethnic cleansing.

What Russians remembered with great bitterness about their enemy in those wars were the dramatic mountain kidnappings which made fools of them more than once, and the mountaineers' relentless bargaining over the price of their hostages.

What struck them with even more force about the mountaineers' behaviour during the Great Caucasian Wars was the unity which the war fostered – among an enemy formed from what had always been squabbling, quarrelsome tribes who should have been easy to divide – and Russia's inability to buy off or even identify an élite within the eastern Caucasian tribes.

Most shocking of all were the moments which seemed, to Russians, almost supernatural: the injured Shamil's two miraculous disappearances from what should have been certain death, and his miraculous reappearances later at the head of a fighting force.

And what memories did the mountaineers retain from the great war that devastated their homeland? A fierce anger over the

Russians' repeated broken promises. A moral refusal to give in to an enemy that, although bigger, they believed to be in the wrong. The war honed their readiness to fight to the death on a point of principle. As Imam Shamil said: 'Weakness and cowardice never saved anyone.'

The highlanders' stern morality in the face of invasion came from the faith that the great wars strengthened across the region, as well as from their traditional social organization.

The Muslim precept that each man is his own 'priest' matched the Chechens' democratic notion of each individual in their own society as *uzden*, or intrinsically free and noble. (Chechens do, however, perceive several other Caucasian peoples as lesser, 'slave' nations, '*lei*,' lacking their own culture of honour and probity.) Even today, Chechens are deeply respectful to their elders – they do not smoke or swear if someone older is present, for instance – but they stress that they themselves choose to make these marks of respect, and are free to decide how to behave to anyone else.

The Islamic notion of holy war sanctified centuries of inter-clan skirmishes; the Sharia gave more sophisticated new legal solutions to old disputes. Islam reinforced and dignified the mountain tribes' already strong identity. It also gave them a moral framework in which they could interpret the Russian invasion as not only dangerous to their way of life but also wrong.

There did not seem much hope of compromise in the two opposing world views. Unlike Russians, who believed society was organized in a great pyramid of power, in which the lowly allowed their superiors to do whatever they wanted and random, absolute exercise of power over dependents was an accepted part of life, Chechens and other eastern mountaineers lived in highly democratic societies where everyone was equal before God. They sorted out their differences by discussion, argument and negotiation, not by the exercise of one person's power over another. They resorted to the dagger only as a last resort, but then took it seriously and pursued the fight to the death, irrespective of their chances of winning. For the Russians of the last century, might was right; for the Caucasian idealists, right was might.

To this day, Russians greet each other with the phrase 'Be healthy'; Chechens, in their own language, prefer to say '*Marsha wooghiil!*' or 'Be free!'

*

A century after the Caucasian wars came the other great confrontation between Russians and Chechens which is still, partially, remembered in Russia: the deportations of 1944. The deportations were Josef Stalin's attempt to rewrite the drama of Russia's relations with the Chechens, adding a darkly fantastical final solution. On 23 February 1944, he ordered Chechens and Ingushi out on to their village squares to celebrate Red Army Day – and had all 600,000 of them rounded up by soldiers and packed off in cattle trucks to exile in the Soviet interior. Those that could not be easily collected were massacred. At Khaibakh, in the mountains, 700 people were herded into a barn and burned to death. Stalin dissolved the administrative entity, the Chechen-Ingush republic, in which they lived. His excuse was that the Chechens had collaborated with Nazi forces, whose path across southern Russia had been blocked two years earlier, and who even then had never reached Chechen-Ingush territory.

Hundreds of thousands of people died of cold, hunger, epidemics or humiliation on their way to the frozen steppes of Kazakhstan, where they stayed for the next thirteen years. Chechens and Ingushi who tell the story of that winter now tell it as a ritualized lament, not their own personal story but that of a national tragedy:

'The winter ... the cattle trucks ... people were packed into them, dying ... the troops wouldn't let us bury them according to Muslim rites, just made us throw them over the side of the truck ... There was no sanitation on the trucks, just a hole in the floorboards ... and there were soldiers watching all the time ... girls who had never seen men from outside their families were suddenly forced to relieve themselves under the gaze of those Russian soldiers ... many of them just couldn't overcome their upbringing: their bladders burst, their internal organs ruptured, or they hanged themselves by their long plaits out of shame.'

There is no film footage of this great movement of peoples, and

few written accounts of individual experiences. But one, published
in a Soviet periodical, is the unemotional story of a student who
helped carry out the deportation:

> In 1943 I arrived from Kokand in Grozny with the Petroleum
> Institute which had been evacuated to Kokand in 1942 at the
> time of the German attack.
>
> No real *kolkhoz* [collective farms] had been established in
> Chechnya though members of *Zagotserno* [the state grain pro-
> duction entity], of *Zagoskot* [the state livestock production
> entity] and even *kolkhoz* presidents were present in the *aul*s. It
> seemed that the peasants remained independent.
>
> Gangs were active in the mountain *aul*s. After the liquidation
> of the Chechen-Ingush republic, the newspaper *Groznenskaya
> Pravda* wrote that since the establishment of the Soviet govern-
> ment, the gangs of Chechnya-Ingushetia had killed nearly 20,000
> Red Army troops and Party members.
>
> During the war, when the Grozny Military School was
> evacuated to the Chechen mountains, the guerrillas killed 200
> students.
>
> At the end of 1943, there were rumours in the city of the
> projected deportation of Chechens and Ingush, but these
> rumours were mere whispers. In the second half of January and
> the first half of February 1944, special detachments of the NKVD
> began to arrive in American Studebaker lorries. The newspapers
> published an appeal to the population: 'Let us make an example
> of our roads and bridges,' and 'Let us help our dear and beloved
> Red Army in its manoeuvres in the mountains!' Thus the army
> occupied the mountains and each *aul* was supplied with its own
> garrisons.
>
> Then came the day of the Red Army: 23 February 1944. In
> the evening, the Red soldiers built blazing fires in the village
> squares and there was singing and dancing. The unsuspecting
> villagers came to see the festivities. When they were assembled
> in the squares all the men were arrested. Some of the Chechens
> had weapons and there was some shooting. But resistance was
> rapidly eliminated. The men were locked up in barns and then a
> hunt began for those who had not gone out. The whole operation

was effected in two or three hours. Women were not arrested but told to pack their belongings and get ready to leave the next day with the children.

At the same time, in Grozny, students and housewives were mobilized. In the evening of 23 February, the director of the Institute came to the students' quarters and told us to assemble at 6 a.m. near the building of the Institute. We were to take some extra underwear, and food for three days. The students of the Pedagogical Institute also showed up. When we had assembled near the Institute we saw many Studebakers half-filled with Red Army soldiers. Then, according to a carefully prepared plan, we were stationed among the *aul*s by groups of twenty to thirty men. When we arrived in the *aul*s we were surprised by the silence. Half an hour after our arrival the lorries were filled with the men arrested the previous day and the women and children. They were then transferred to freight cars in Grozny. All Chechens and Ingush, without exception, were taken away. The Dagestanis were left: there were seven or eight of them in our *aul*.

The students' task was to take care of the farms until the arrival of immigrants from Kursk and Orel regions. We had to assemble and feed the livestock, store the grain, take care of stocks and so on. Things were different in the mountain *aul*s: after the livestock had been evacuated, the *aul*s were set on fire in order to deprive the 'bandits' of their means of subsistence. For days one could see *aul*s burning in the mountains. At the same time, an amnesty was promised to those who had escaped to the mountains if they returned. Some of them did return but they were also deported.[8]

When I got to know him well, an old Ingush man who lives in Grozny, Musa Gazgireyev, moved beyond the general lament and told me his personal memories of being deported. At the time, he and his Ingush family were living in the town of Ordzhonikidze (the Soviet-era name for Vladikavkaz). He was sixteen at the time,

---

8. Abdurakhman Avtorkhanov, *The Chechens and the Ingush during the Soviet Period and its Antecendents*, in *North Caucasus Barrier*, quoting *Prometheus*, No. 3, March 1949.

and the only man in his family not fighting in the Soviet army. He was friendly with the Soviet soldiers arriving in his home town, particularly with a Lieutenant Semyonov. The soldiers would often come to his house and he would entertain them with what food and drink the family had. When Red Army Day came around, he realized the soldiers were going round the houses telling people to get ready for a journey, and taking them away, but no one came to his house till the evening. Then his Russian friend Semyonov appeared, embarrassed, worried, and sweating. 'I don't like to have to do this,' Semyonov said uneasily. 'We're being told to tell people they're leaving temporarily, but I know it's not true. You're my friend, and I'll tell you what I think you should do: prepare your family for a long journey. Take all the clothes and food and drink and money you can carry. You're going to need it.' Astonished and nettled, Musa Gazgireyev refused to pack. 'I'll take my chances like everyone else,' he said proudly. But Semyonov, torn between his personal friendship for the Ingush family and his Russian perception of duty as playing his part in the hierarchical pyramid and obeying orders, insisted that his Ingush friend and his mother and sisters be well provided for. Baffled by the Gazgireyevs' refusal to take the special favour being offered them, the classic Russian gesture of help between good-hearted people powerless to escape orders from on high, Semyonov and his men did the Gazgireyevs' packing for them, then took them away to the trains.

Even in exile, the Russian dissident Alexander Solzhenitsyn wrote with admiration, the Chechens kept their pride: 'Only one nation refused to accept the psychology of submission.' This applied 'not to individuals, not to insurgents, but to the nation as a whole: the Chechens ... No Chechen ever tried to be of service or to please the authorities. Their attitude towards them was proud and even hostile.'[9] They were the only people who never curried favour with the authorities by sneaking on fellow victims of repression.

Musa Gazgireyev has the same story, only his account is earthier

---

9. Alexander Solzhenitsyn, *Arkhipelag Gulag*, YMCA Press, pp. 420–1, quoted in Avtorkhanov, *Chechens and Ingush*.

and full of the black humour with which Chechens and Ingushi recount their past. After a few years of hunger and poverty, he fixed himself up with a job as an accountant on a Kazakh collective farm, where he worked for a decade. 'No one messed with any of us,' he says proudly. 'Anyone who tried to humiliate a Chechen or an Ingush met a nasty end! Sometimes these bosses would try to split up families, or take away our rights ... but then they'd be found dead on the highway ... and after a while they learned to treat us with respect.'

Only after Stalin's death did a gentler ideology take hold in the Kremlin. In 1957, under Nikita Khrushchev, the Chechen and Ingushi survivors and their children were allowed to go home. Even after thirteen years away, the call of the homeland was strong. Even children born in exile wanted to see the mountains of their history. Despite – or, Musa Gazgireyev says with a laugh, because of – a Soviet propaganda campaign encouraging the Chechens and Ingushi to stay in their new homes in Kazakhstan, most of them hurried back to the Caucasus. Once home, they settled down to have as many children as they could as young as possible, rebuilding their numbers until there were about a million Chechens and half a million Ingushis just before the Soviet collapse.

Stalin's final act against the Chechens was deleted from official history after his death. When they reached home, the Chechens and Ingushi found their villages renamed and all references to them written out of the paperwork of their homeland. They had not been deported, because they had never officially existed. Musa Gazgireyev's home in Ordzhonikidze had been given to an Ossetian family, so he moved to Grozny, the region's main urban centre, and started a new life there. A statue of Yermolov now stood on the central square of Grozny, with the Russian general's most notoriously anti-Chechen pronouncement for an inscription: 'I will find no peace while a single Chechen remains alive.' Even in the years of late Soviet crisis, when histories long hidden by officialdom began to come to light and other peoples clamoured for justice, no one made reparations to the Chechens for the wrongs they had suffered. The statue of Yermolov was blown up by unknown attackers several times a year, but replaced regularly by Soviet authorities who continued to complain about Chechen deceitfulness and treachery. It was only taken down for ever in the 1970s, to be replaced by a more neutral Lenin. Moscow had more or less forgotten the deleted act, and did not understand the bitter Chechen expression coined as a result of it, 'to lie like the Soviet Union'.

But Stalin's deportations seemed to be the very end of the historical script of Russian–Chechen conflict, for history was slowly being banished from the quiet life of the late Soviet period. Even if Russian taxi-drivers around the Caucasus still told the story of the Chechen and Ingush betrayal of the Red Army to the hated Germans, Moscow thought it had almost stopped mattering. For decades, the Soviet Union had been replacing the Tsarist past with cheery slogans which praised progress, the future and the friendship of nations. The slogans were everywhere, painted on buildings or concreted into hillsides or tripping off people's lips. There were no mosques left in Chechen lands, and scarcely any teaching in the Chechen language. Seven thousand Russian atheists, known as the Army of the Godless, preached tirelessly to wean the natives off a religion Moscow thought primitive and backward. Although Chechens never got the top jobs in local Party hierarchies or in the oil and chemicals factories springing up across the lowlands, they lived in relative harmony with their Russian immigrant neighbours settling in the urban wastes of Grozny. Moscow began to believe that the wars of the past had finally been consigned to history.

All that was left were the jokes, the comic interludes that have always lightened the drama and which continued to be told by Chechens in the concrete housing estates that began to spread across their homeland.

Packed in smoky cars or stretched out in their airy houses, Chechens like to repeat stories about their jaunty insouciance in the face of Russian bullying. This is one told me by my first Chechen friend, Musa Autarkhanov, when I went to Grozny with him in 1993:

A vast Russian army, bristling with guns and swords, besieged a tiny Chechen village.

'Surrender, or you will all be killed,' the Russian general told the Chechen villagers.

'We need time to think,' the Chechen elders replied. 'Give us until tomorrow.'

The sun set and rose again, and the Russians waited. They could hear the Chechens on their village square, dancing, praying and discussing what to do next, but they could not understand the guttural words of the villagers' language. No one came out to surrender.

'Your time is up! Surrender now!' the Russian general shouted angrily as the sun rose high in the sky. The Chechen elders, in their tall hats, walked out to his tent to calm him.

'We need time to discuss the situation,' they said again. 'Give us till tomorrow.'

The Russian general waited, watching the sun set and the moon sail across the sky. Wolves howled in the mountains. Eagles soared in the dawn, and the endless Chechen talk was still going on in the village square. His patience vanished.

'You have no choice! If you don't surrender now, we will attack and you will all die by the sword! What is there for you to talk about for so long?' the Russian general screamed.

The Chechen elders trooped out of the village square again.

'The problem,' they explained to him courteously, 'is that you have such a big army and we are such a small village. We're worried that there won't be enough of us to give all of you the honourable burial you will deserve, as men of war, after the fighting is over.'

And then the Soviet Union disappeared too, and the curtain was drawn down on all the cruelties and injustices of the past. The slogans which had covered up history vanished. By that time, there had been seventy years of Communism, longer than the average Soviet lifetime. For most of the quarter of a billion Soviet people, the continuum of past, present and future was broken. Hardly anyone remembered any other past than the official version, now discredited, and the stories of a different kind of experience that their grandmothers had whispered long ago, half-understood and only half-heeded, in the privacy of their kitchen.

Huge numbers of people voted for the future when they chose Boris Yeltsin to become president of Russia in June 1991. His promises were better than history. There was something for everyone: wealth if you worked, a chance to join the rest of the modern world in a democratic future, and – the best part for the ethnic minorities of Russia – sovereignty. The eastern nations of the North Caucasus – Chechens, Ingushi, Dagestanis – voted almost unanimously for him and for this vision of a freer post-Soviet future.

When he did not keep this promise, Russia's ethnic minorities were naturally disappointed at being thwarted in their aspirations to sovereignty. Equally naturally, the Chechens were not exactly surprised: to them, it meant only that Yeltsin and his new Russians were liars as bare-faced as their Soviet predecessors. But they were genuinely disappointed and distressed when he began reviving the Tsarist past, even if to most Russians it was a game with costumes and props from a time so distant that no one properly remembered it. To Chechens and other mountain peoples, this imagery recalled painful collective memories of a past at the point of Russian bayonets, a past which, to them, was still within living memory. They did not see it as a game.

# THREE

Coming after this history of Russian repression, General Dzhokhar Dudayev's declaration of Chechen independence in 1991 began to look less surprising. An uprising that was interpreted afterwards in Moscow as an act of defiance, a spiteful attempt to break the unity of the new Russia just as it won independence from the Soviet Union, the Chechen rebellion began very differently – with a burst of enthusiasm for Boris Yeltsin.

Soviet Moscow had never acknowledged the unjust way it had treated the Chechens. When Yeltsin came to the fore, they took his promises of a brave new world at face value. They believed he would let them dismember his Russian Federation – as he was doing, one level up in the hierarchy, with the republics of Gorbachev's Soviet empire – and be free. The Chechens were the first to support Yeltsin in his hour of need, during the coup of August 1991. The rebellion that followed in Grozny was a manifestation of their disappointment at finding out that his Russia was just as quick to rage, threaten, bully and cheat as its Soviet predecessor. It was just too weak to put the boot in as effectively.

When I went back through the newspapers, rereading the story of the Chechen rebellion of 1991 – the events that I had first watched on television with Andrei – what I found was an almost farcical re-enactment of the misunderstandings that had bedevilled the relationship between Russians and Chechens under the Tsars and the General Secretaries. The themes of past conflicts were leaping out from the pages again.

*

On 19 August 1991, a junta of Soviet hard-liners who wanted to get rid of President Mikhail Gorbachev and stop his hesitant attempts to reorganize the superpower's pyramid of power began an ill-fated coup attempt in Moscow. It lasted just three days. Ironically, the failure of their takeover led to the collapse of the

Soviet empire which the putschists had been trying to save, the resignation of Gorbachev four months later, and the emergence of fifteen republics, including a Russia headed by Yeltsin, from the ruins of the superpower.

But when Soviet television first began playing soupy renditions of *Swan Lake*, and the putschists first announced that Gorbachev was 'unwell' and that they would be replacing him, there was panic in every tier of the Soviet power pyramid. No one knew what would happen. No one knew which way to jump. No one knew who would be the most expedient figure to support. Soviet apparatchiks faced the biggest dilemma of their lives. The undecided, the confused, and the cowards got sick, or went into hiding.

The Soviet First Party Secretary of Checheno-Ingushetia, a pop-eyed, balding man called Doku Zavgayev, was one of these. He skulked in Moscow, emerging only after the drunk, panicking putschists had been confronted and beaten. The victor of the day was the Russian republican President Yeltsin, freeze-framed forever in an iconic photograph astride a tank, outside his resistance centre, the White House building which was then home to his Russian republican parliament. Crowds of people gathered in front of the White House, facing down the tanks which were supposed to get rid of them. The Soviet army went over to Yeltsin's side. The putschists were arrested, or jumped out of windows. One putschist, Interior Minister Boris Pugo, shot his wife dead, then shot himself.

After that, the reprisals began. Gorbachev came back from imprisonment at his dacha on the south coast and pleaded ill-advisedly for the continuation of a reformed Soviet Communism. But a people punch-drunk on power after having stood up against dictatorship for the first time had no patience with this sort of talk any more, or with Gorbachev. He was hated. He was disgraced. Power slipped into Yeltsin's hands. Those officials who had failed to pick Yeltsin's winning side at the start rushed to support him once they realized the way things were going. But it was too late. Only leaders who had shown loyalty in the Russian leader's hour of crisis were remembered with honour. The rest were condemned as old-style Communists, not needed by new Russia, and either discarded by officialdom or hounded out of office by their own people. Zavgayev duly returned to Grozny on 21 August, as the coup petered out, and called a parliamentary assembly which condemned the putsch and declared all was quiet in Checheno-Ingushetia. But a great autumn of demonstrations against the backward-looking, morally bankrupt regional leaders of Soviet days had already got underway, and the Chechen Zavgayev, for all his after-the-event protestations of loyalty, was one of the men whose fate was sealed.

*

While the Communist Zavgayev havered and wavered, misreading the revolution breaking out all around him in Moscow, the people of Chechnya were in no doubt about whom to support. Yeltsin's ringing endorsement of the subject Soviet peoples' rights to sovereignty, his promises of a different kind of democratic future, his bluff, straightforward manner – as well as their old distrust of Soviet Communists – made him the obvious choice.

Like most other ethnic territories in Russia, testing the limits of the new freedoms introduced by Gorbachev during the perestroika era, Checheno-Ingushetia had been in the grip of passionate nationalist debates for more than a year. The Chechen National Congress, a broad-based talking-shop for nationalists and democrats, had been formed in 1990, and had been the forum for much emotional discussion of the wrongs of the past and the ways to right them in the future. In June, this national independence movement's leader, General Dzhokhar Dudayev, had demanded a formal peace treaty between Russia and Checheno-Ingushetia before any talks could be held on the future relationship of Moscow with the republic, a public reference to the situation which Chechens felt but Moscow had never acknowledged – that the North Caucasus had been at war with, or in revolt against, Russia since the days of Sheikh Mansur, the first Chechen leader who had fought Yermolov.

Dudayev, born in 1944 and raised in exile in Kazakhstan, had served in the Soviet air force until 1990. His reputation as an honest officer made him popular among his air force colleagues.

He had never lived in his Chechen homeland. He had fought with the Soviet army in Afghanistan, without showing any sympathy for the Afghans' Muslim, nationalist struggle. It was only later, stationed at the Estonian air base of Tartu in the late 1980s, that the general saw the great surge of Baltic nationalism with his own eyes. It was a revelation to him. In the tumult of late Soviet times, he let Estonian nationalists demonstrate on his airbase. Then he took sick leave and went home to Chechnya to try and work the same miracle at home.

Dudayev's emotional speech to the June Congress showed the extent to which he had adopted the new nationalism sweeping the Soviet Union. He celebrated the fall of the Soviet colonial empire which had robbed the Chechen nation of its 'religion, language, education, science, culture, natural resources, ideology, mass media, leadership cadres, and rights to freedom and life'. He pinpointed the Communist Party, the KGB, the interior ministry and the prosecutor's office as the agents of colonial repression. Their goal, he said, was to preserve the empire at all costs; their main method was to fight Islam, which had united the Caucasian peoples; and the Chechen response must be to reject any 'hybrid' version of sovereignty for the sake of economic stability. 'Despite all the aggressiveness and dangers which have always faced the Chechens, we must learn the lesson that a slave who does not wish to free himself of his chains deserves his slavery ... The price of genuine sovereignty is so great that to expect to achieve it cheaply is as absurd as to presume that the Chechens will ever be reconciled with their present miserly colonial freedom ... There is only one question to raise today: do we want to be free or shall we willingly sell our future into serfdom? The time has come to make our choice.'

When the first news of the coup was broadcast on 19 August, Dudayev leapt straight to Yeltsin's defence. He appealed to Chechens to obey the Russian president, not the Soviet putschists, and to begin a campaign of civil disobedience against the coup leaders. 'Let us not be fooled yet again by a corrupt pro-Communist clique,' read one appeal. 'The Executive Committee of the Chechen

National Congress appeals to you personally to follow its instructions and defend democracy in order to avoid bloodshed in our republic.'

Telephone links between Moscow and Grozny had been cut. The Communist leaders of Checheno-Ingushetia were paralysed. The Grozny local parliament leader, A.N. Petrenko, was asked whether he thought the coup constitutional, and could only answer that he did not know. He refused to convene an extraordinary parliament session in Zavgayev's absence.

Meanwhile, Dudayev's Congress did what the local Communists were refusing to do: set up an executive committee in the centre and re-established telephone contact with Moscow. They connected up with Yeltsin through the man who was still, in those early days, Yeltsin's right-hand man among the democrats – the Russified Chechen Ruslan Khasbulatov. They also got in touch with the nearby Ingush, Dagestani and Kabardino-Balkar territories to co-ordinate opposition to the coup.

Democratic groups rallied in central Grozny on 22 August. They condemned the Communist leaders of their republic – including Zavgayev and Petrenko – for their untrustworthiness and ambiguous behaviour during the coup. They resolved to get Zavgayev, who had 'betrayed the people during the days of the failed coup', to resign, to disband the parliament, and to transfer power to Dudayev's Congress.

For the next fortnight, demonstrators milled in their thousands on the streets of Grozny, just as other demonstrators were doing in dozens of other regional centres around Russia. They poured into town from the villages. They took control of the TV and radio stations, the telephone exchange, and other administrative buildings. They blocked the airport to stop Zavgayev running away again.

On 6 September, men from Dudayev's Congress stormed the mainly Communist parliament while it was in session and disbanded it. During the raid, Vitaly Kutsenko, the Russian head of Grozny's city council, fell out of a window; he died in hospital later. Dudayev's men patrolled central Grozny. Green Islamic flags were raised.

Dudayev's followers provided a copybook example of how Yeltsin's Russian democrats wanted the many peoples of Russia to behave during and after the coup. From Moscow, via an interview on Russian television, Ruslan Khasbulatov welcomed the fall of his old Communist enemy Zavgayev, and hoped stability would now return to the corner of Russia that was his own ethnic homeland.

*

The great debate that engulfed Moscow after the coup was over what was to become of the Soviet Union. Its fifteen constituent republics had been arguing for months about whether they could carry on together; it was to prevent the looser, vaguer union treaty they had more or less agreed on from being signed that the putschists had struck. Now even that treaty was a dead letter. Moscow Central Television broadcast a 26 August address to the Soviet parliament by Nursultan Nazarbayev, the president of Kazakhstan and a supporter of some kind of union, in which he insisted that any future relationship between the Soviet republics start from scratch. Instead of the old tight federation of Soviet states, he wanted a looser confederation; he also wanted little internal republics – such as that of the Chechens and the Ingushi – to join as equal members. 'By republics I have in mind all republics, including the autonomous ones which have declared themselves sovereign and those which will want to do so . . . Only then shall we attain genuine equality for the republics,' Nazarbayev said.

But this was too scary a notion for many of the small autonomous ethnic republics inside Russia. On 29 August, Tass news agency published a statement by ten of the sixteen ethnic republics, signing away their rights to this possible greater freedom and calling for the Russian republic to be preserved as a 'single and indivisible' state. Checheno-Ingushetia did not sign.

The changes in Russia had been so swift and intense that no one had had time to notice how strange the bedfellows were that had come together under the democratic blanket: an increasingly powerful Russian president whose closest ally was a Russified Chechen in Moscow, giving slightly tremulous support to a Chechen revolution in Grozny which featured precisely those armed Chechens and public disorders which loomed so terrifyingly in the Russian collective consciousness, all in the name of a vague future state of democracy which no one in Russia could yet define.

But now reaction set in, and things began to go seriously wrong between Yeltsin's Russian democrats and the Chechen democratic forces grouped around Dudayev.

Delegations from Russia started flying to Grozny, to try to calm the Chechens down and to mediate between the old Communists and the new, unruly, empowered forces of the people and Dudayev's Congress. A stalemate had been reached, with Zavgayev refusing to resign as Chechen leader. The disbanded Soviet-era parliament had not formally resigned either, although Dudayev's men had in practice taken over its functions.

The first delegation was led by Gennady Burbulis, Yeltsin's state secretary. After he held talks with all sides, the legislature met on 15 September and formally dissolved itself. Power was temporarily transferred to a new Provisional Council, headed by Husain Akhmadov of Dudayev's Congress. This Council was to hold new elections within two months. That night, Khasbulatov flew down from Moscow and made a speech to the Grozny demonstrators, singing the praises of the democratic forces' victory. Another Moscow politician, Press Minister Mikhail Poltoranin, stayed on in Grozny and negotiated more.

It seemed the Russians had successfully restored calm. The demonstrators dispersed. But, two weeks later, emotional crowds were back on the streets of Grozny, barricades had been thrown up again, and Khasbulatov was sending furious telegrams from Moscow. This spat, it turned out, was caused by an internal quarrel in the new Provisional Council in Grozny: its conservative minority had tried to replace the more radical Husain Akhmadov. Dudayev's Congress thought the conservatives were hand-in-glove with the KGB, and it was trying to reassert its own power; the Congress announced the dismissal of the Provisional Council, arrested the local prosecutor, and blockaded the KGB building.

The delegation that rushed down from Moscow in early October was headed by Yeltsin's vice-president, Alexander Rutskoi. Although he was an Afghan veteran and an ex-air force general, like Dudayev, this hot-headed, Communist-sympathizing, Russian-nationalist patriot was the worst possible choice of mediator. In what already seemed another lifetime, before the Russian elections four months earlier, Yeltsin had picked Rutskoi as his running-mate in the hope of winning votes from Rutskoi's moderate Communist supporters. Since then, events had moved so fast that having even a moderate Communist as vice-president had become an embarrassment. Rutskoi was out of sorts at the unexpected turn events were taking; suspicious of his new democratic colleagues, angry, and ready to lash out. In Grozny, he went out of his way to annoy the Chechens. Tactlessly, he brought the Russian interior minister and KGB head with him, even though Dudayev had said publicly that both these institutions were symbols of colonial repression.

Talks went nowhere. The trip was a failure.

Rutskoi went home in a rage, the very image of the growling Russian bear that had always been anathema to the Chechens. He told Russia that Dudayev was running a gang of criminal brigands who were 'terrorizing the population'. He said Dudayev's men had murdered Kutsenko when they stormed the Grozny parliament. And he got the Russian parliament to condemn 'the escalation of violent actions by illegal formations', and to brusquely order Dudayev's men to accept the Provisional Council and hand in their weapons.

The slanging-match between Russians and Chechens got angrier.

The Chechens did not hand in their weapons; past Russian attempts to disarm them had been followed by repression and deportation. Dudayev said Russia had made 'virtually a declaration of war on the Chechen-Ingush republic', and put his national guard on high alert.

In Moscow, Rutskoi and Khasbulatov said 'very tough measures' were needed to stop Dudayev's Congress, which they now described as two or three hundred desperate terrorists forcing the Chechen people away from the Russian Federation to which the majority wanted to belong. Rutskoi made veiled threats that Russia might use soldiers to get rid of Dudayev.

In Grozny, Dudayev responded melodramatically, but again

defensively. He called on his people to prepare for war. It was inevitable, he believed, 'since hostile forces are massed in North Ossetia and Dagestan preparing to attack the Republic and strangle the revolution'. He did not trust the delegations of Russians who kept coming to Grozny to make peace; they 'speak smoothly but act badly', he said, and each of their visits aggravated the problems of Checheno-Ingushetia. He threatened that any hostile actions by Russia would be seen as 'a continuation of the genocide against the Chechen people'. He reported that 62,000 men had signed up for the Chechen national guard and militia.

In Moscow, Yeltsin joined the verbal attack. On 19 October, he told Dudayev to submit unconditionally within three days. If he did not, 'all measures' would be taken to protect Russia's constitutional order.

Dudayev tried a soft answer. He told Tass he had not yet seen Yeltsin's order personally, but that the wording reported by the media sounded like an ultimatum, suggesting prejudice rather than objectivity. Yeltsin's order had upset the Chechen people, he said, who were following the example set by Russia in their aspiration for democracy and freedom. He said Boris Yeltsin was respected in Checheno-Ingushetia, and opinion in the republic was that the Russian president was being fed a distorted version of the events there. Other Chechens were less tactful. Husain Akhmadov defiantly told local television that Yeltsin's bullying was the 'last belch of the Russian empire'.

Russia's next threat was made by the prosecutor's office, the body in charge of criminal investigations. All groups which might undermine the Russian Federation were illegal, it ruled, and could be banned 'if a court so decides'. 'This statement makes depressing reading,' wrote Marie Bennigsen Broxup, a Western academic:

If one dismisses the legal niceties of the text . . . one is left with the same basic tenet that Russian communists have always striven to apply – unquestioning compliance in thought and action with a dogma imposed from above; previously this was communism, now it is Moscow's own interpretation of democracy. From Kalinin's dream to give everyone in the USSR 'the

psychology and ideals of a Russian industrial worker from
Petrograd' to the later hybrid *Homo Sovieticus*, the Soviet
nationalities have been expected to fit within a mould acceptable
to Russia. The North Caucasians are still expected to conform,
notwithstanding any 'differences', for the sake of Russia, for the
'integrity of the territory of the Russian Federation'.[10]

Dudayev refused to drop his plan to hold a presidential election
on 27 October.

Just before polling day, Russia's parliament denounced the
election as illegal. So did the remnants of Chechnya's Provisional
Council. Yeltsin offered Chechens an alternative to Dudayev by
appointing his own representative, another Chechen called
Akhmad Arsanov, to run the southern territory. Dudayev snapped
back that Russia was not to try to introduce 'governor's rule' in his
land.

*

Grozny's central squares were full of people, arguing over the
political crisis. Those hostile to Dudayev gathered on Sheikh
Mansur (formerly Lenin) Square, where the monument to Yermolov had once stood and where Lenin had more recently been taken
down from his pedestal. Dudayev supporters rallied outside the
government building on Freedom Square. Tass reports from
Grozny referred repeatedly to guns being fired; but, the reports
added endearingly: 'Thank God, at least for now they are being
fired into the air.'

Panic and paranoia, gunfire, and wild rumours: an uneasy
election atmosphere. Bizarrely, Dudayev himself added to the
tensions of October with repeated warnings that an earthquake
was about to engulf his homeland. 'Rumour? our seismologists are
ninety per cent certain of it,' he told *Pravda*. He said earthquakes
sometimes occurred in places where socio-political tensions were
particularly sharp, and reminded listeners of the 1988 earthquake
in nearby Armenia at a time of nationalist passions. He said

---

10. Marie Bennigsen Broxup, *After the Putsch, 1991*, in *North Caucasus
    Barrier*.

earthquakes could be provoked deliberately, a hint at almost supernatural Russian skulduggery. His press aide, Movladi Udugov, spelled out this hint more clearly to an Associated Press correspondent, saying 'experts' believed Russia might use satellites to cause earthquakes on election day.

This rumour gradually took on a life of its own. The head of the local seismic forecasting station in Vladikavkaz, Kyuri Mamatsuyev, was interviewed by Tass on 21 October, saying he was worried about growing seismic activity in the region. 'We are registering continuous weak, so-called background tremors in the region, which are either releasing the tectonic pressure or warning of a powerful shock. In any case, we should be ready for possible consequences,' he said. He said he decided to make his forecasts public after several unsuccessful appeals to his chiefs and government officials. 'I asked to send a group of experts from Moscow to confirm or dispel my doubts. But they refused, because of the unstable social and political situation in the republic.'

It was only much later that I discovered the origin of this rumour: a generations-old folk belief, one of many gloomy forecasts passed down in the villages as 'the predictions of our ancestors'. Among these beliefs was a wistful fantasy that Chechens would one day be ruled by the British, and a sadder but truer estimate that the Chechen people would be brought to the brink of extinction every half-century. The particular belief that Dudayev was nodding towards in these weeks was that one day, at last, Grozny would be free of invaders and would flourish – but would soon afterwards be swallowed up entirely in an earthquake. Was Dudayev deliberately drawing on this folk image to bind the superstitious villagers who were his power base closer to him? Was he, like them, so overwhelmed by a turn of events unforeseeable in Soviet times that he was taking refuge in old folk stories? Or could he just not believe, even now, that the Chechen independence he was aiming at could last?

The election went ahead. Dudayev beat three other candidates to be picked as president of Chechnya on 27 October 1991. The Congress was quick to point out massive support for Dudayev – 99 per cent – among poor rural voters, but slower to give voting figures for urban areas, where middle-class voters were far more ambiguous about their new leader. Official results announced by the Congress on 30 October showed a turnout of 490,000 people, 55 per cent of the electorate, with 85 per cent overall support for Dudayev.

'Intense and chaotic firing was heard last night in Grozny from sub-machine-guns, machine-guns, pistols and hunting rifles. Fortunately it was into the air. This is how Dzhokhar Dudayev's supporters, learning that preliminary figures showed he had been elected the first president of the Chechen republic, gave distinctive expression to their joy,' Tass reported.

Elections were not held in Ingush districts, which opted to stay out of trouble and inside Russia in the hope of getting their own disputed territory back from North Ossetia. Dudayev held out the hand of friendship to the Ingushi, known together with the Chechens in their shared language as 'Vainakh' or 'Our People'. 'As soon as the Ingushi find it necessary and possible to hold presidential and parliamentary elections on their territory, the question of creating a single Vainakh republic will be settled voluntarily,' he said.

In Moscow, Khasbulatov, who was elected chairman of the Russian parliament on 28 October, denounced the elections as undemocratic and illegal and said only 200,000 people out of an electorate of 1.5 million took part. (Since the total population of Chechnya was only 1.3 million people at the time of the 1989 census, Khasbulatov's figures read rather strangely.) Observers from the International Committee on Human Rights, quoted on Russian television on 29 October, did not notice any such violations.

Dudayev declared the Republic of Chechnya a 'sovereign state' from 1 November.

\*

Dudayev had still not won the hearts of all his people. The rival demonstrations ground on into November.

Simple country folk adored him. He was the first leader who had ever publicly referred to their long-ignored sufferings during the deportations. As his parliament convened in the big Soviet administrative buildings on Freedom Square, they could look out of the window and see their rustic protectors dancing and pouring out praise to the new president.

It was the sophisticated urbanites of Grozny who were dismayed, the people who had worked out how to survive in the bigger modern world. Even if they were unenthusiastic about rule from Moscow, they did not want to be shut into a tiny national space full of gunmen. They found Dudayev too confrontational. An outsider brought up in exile, he had never lived at home. He spoke Chechen badly, and his understanding of Chechen feeling was limited. Nationalists were appalled that he was ready to leave out the Ingushi from their broader 'Vainakh' national equation. Intellectuals found his histrionics ridiculous. Thousands of Chechens and Russians who worked in the Grozny oil-refining business, as well as teachers and administrators, wondered where their pay would come from if he annoyed Moscow so much that it stopped the flow of funds southwards.

But, after three months of revolution, everyone was tired. They wanted to leave the squares and go home. Whatever their views, Chechens stressed that their culture was one of consensus. They favoured negotiations. As demonstrators elsewhere put down their placards and vanished, the signs were that the Chechen rebellion would also eventually peter out.

Even Dudayev's military chief, Iles Arsanukayev, had started talking of training future generations of Chechens in Russian military schools, rather than of a totally separate existence. 'Believe me, we will be far more useful to Russia free,' he said.

And even Yeltsin's representative to Grozny, the Moscow Chechen Akhmad Arsanov, whose grandfather had been a revered clergyman, agreed in an interview with *Pravda* that Chechen problems would be more efficiently solved without interference from Moscow. 'It is of course an honour and a responsibility to be the Russian president's representative,' he said, 'but in resolving narrowly ethnic issues we ourselves will choose.'

The Chechens never got a chance to choose for themselves. Russia struck back.

On the day of Dudayev's inauguration, 9 November, Yeltsin took an unexpected leap into Soviet-style military confrontation which destroyed all hope of compromise. He dispatched more than 1,000 Russian troops to Grozny and Vladikavkaz airports, to enforce a presidential decree imposing a state of emergency on Chechnya: a curfew, compulsory gun registration, travel bans. On a day when he knew Grozny would be full of people for Dudayev's swearing-in, he ordered riot-control squads to disperse crowds by force.

Invasion from Russia was the stuff of Chechen nightmares. But Dudayev reacted quickly. Deputies from his parliament went to the airport to negotiate with the commanders of the Russian detachments. His national guardsmen blocked highways and airfields. Chechens closed off the North Caucasus Russian railway running through their territory by putting concrete blocks on the tracks. By the end of the long weekend, the Russian troops, surrounded at the airport, outmanoeuvred and bewildered, meekly got on buses and left Chechnya. It was very polite, and it did not even interrupt the inauguration.

Wearing general's dress, the new president swore his oath of allegiance on the Quran. The ceremony, Tass reported, 'was conducted under bursts of automatic gunfire which was directed, thank God, at the sky'. Flushed with triumph, Dudayev told Tass afterwards: 'I want all the people of the country and the world to know that the Chechens do not want confrontation with anyone. The Russian leadership is wasting time in aggravating the situation in the Chechen republic.' All the Russian soldier boys who didn't know what they had been thrown into were being well fed and would be sent safely home, he added.

Then Dudayev declared martial law. He raged against Yeltsin's decree, calling it 'political provocation and an act of state terrorism to a sovereign republic'. He got a sympathetic hearing in Grozny: even doubters forgot their doubts in the face of a real threat from the old enemy, Russia. Thousands of people poured onto Freedom Square in passionate response. Weapons were distributed. Defence detachments were formed. A group of Chechen men hijacked a plane, a fairly common perestroika-era crime, and diverted it from

Yeltsin's home town of Yekaterinburg to Turkey, so they could publicize the Chechen cause.

There were other disturbances, terrifying to the Russians watching these scenes on television. In the chaos, hundreds of prisoners escaped from the Grozny remand centre and from out-of-town Naurskaya prison. They turned up in the triumphant, nervy crowd on Freedom Square to be greeted with rapture at the bonfires, my photographer friend Vitya Korotayev recalled. To the joy of their audience, the prisoners donned green headbands with Islamic slogans and talked, for the first time, of a new *ghazavat*, or holy war, against Russia.

*

The Russian attack cleared Chechen minds. They united behind Dudayev. The sympathy of last August for Yeltsin vanished; in Chechen eyes, the attempted raid proved that the new Russians were no better than the old ones. They could call themselves democrats, but they were jackbooted liars as oppressive as their Soviet and Tsarist predecessors.

Former foes now spoke with one voice, the voice of opposition to Moscow bullying. The crowd on Freedom Square demanded that the state of emergency be lifted at once. The Chechen interior minister Vakhri Ibragimov, a Yeltsin man who had earlier refused to swear the oath of allegiance to Dudayev, now resigned in protest against Yeltsin's state of emergency. Yeltsin's envoy Arsanov also repeatedly offered his resignation and asked for the state of emergency to be lifted. The Chechen cabinet, a leftover from Zavgayev's days, sent a telegram to Moscow signed by Prime Minister Sergei Bekov demanding that the state of emergency be lifted at once. Moscow Chechens, including the respected General Aslakhanov, spoke against the decree in the Russian parliament.

'Without exaggerating, all the Chechen people have risen to support President Dudayev and the parliament ... An event which at face value may be considered as extraordinary but natural to the Chechen people has taken place. The people have united in the face of danger, and confrontation has gone,' Russian Mayak Radio reported.

But Dudayev had been tipped over by the raid – by what he saw as betrayal from Moscow – into a very emotionally expressed hatred of his former Russian friends. Tass reported him that night appealing 'to all Muslims to turn Moscow into a disaster zone for the sake of our common freedom'. Agence France-Presse reported him saying 'he was going to call on Chechens living in different parts of Russia to commit acts of terrorism, including exploding atomic power stations'. Dudayev talked about documents in his possession which proved the 'provocative role played by the Russian leadership and KGB in these events'.

If Yeltsin's men had fallen into the old Tsarist error of thinking the Chechens would be cowed by a quick show of Russian force, Dudayev in his turn reinforced Moscow's traditional fears – that the Chechen rebellion could spread until it became another Caucasus-wide rebellion like the war of the last century – by making another charged appeal to his neighbours in the mountains. 'It is necessary to turn every metre of land, every village and town into a fortress, and to break off all relations with Russia,' he raged. 'We will turn the united Caucasus into a united fortress.'

The emotion that gripped Grozny was equalled by the pandemonium that broke out in Moscow political circles as news of the botched operation emerged. Russia's democrats, loosely grouped in an entity called Democratic Russia, asked Yeltsin to revoke the decree.

Who was to blame? democratic politicians asked, the classic question of the Russian power hierarchy looking for a scapegoat. The answer, to their great joy, turned out to be Rutskoi, who had prepared the presidential decree, and the occasion the perfect opportunity to disgrace him. Liberals snapped at the ex-pilot as he stumbled through his explanations.

Rutskoi was grilled at an extraordinary parliament presidium session on the night of 9 November. He justified himself only lamely. He and the young lawyer Sergei Shakhrai had prepared the presidential decree because they had got an urgent telegram begging them to do so from Yeltsin's Grozny representative, Akhmad Arsanov. (That night, the Chechen Arsanov announced again that he would resign.) Moscow had not sent a single army soldier to

Chechnya, though, only interior ministry troops, Rutskoi said, as though interior ministry troops somehow didn't count. There were 1,500 of them, enough 'to ensure constitutional order', and they had been ordered not to fire, or at least only in the air, because 'extremists are hiding behind women and children so that they themselves will not be hurt in any way, only the women and children will be'.

Rutskoi circulated a confusing document called 'Chronicle of the Conflict'. Copies of the secret telegram allegedly sent by Arsanov, which had prompted Rutskoi to draw up his plan, also appeared on chairs in the parliament building. Arsanov again offered to resign.

As Rutskoi thrashed angrily about, his former friends in the Moscow power élite deserted him in droves during an emotional two-day parliamentary debate. Shakhrai said the decree must be revoked. The head of the Russian KGB said he had not been informed of the planned attack and would have been against it. He revealed that Rutskoi had sent Deputy Interior Minister General Kommissarov to Chechnya to arrest Dudayev; where the warrant came from remained a mystery, since the prosecutor denied issuing it.

Those democrats who were too radical to be in serious government institutions had a chaotic but enjoyable field day. Plump, wheezing intellectual Valeriya Novodvorskaya led her Democratic Union and the Union of Anarchists out into a central Moscow square in a hilarious protest against their new leaders. A dozen demonstrators carried placards saying: 'We congratulate Foreman Yeltsin and Sergeant Rutskoi on their victory in the Caucasus!' and 'The dystrophic and impotent government must go!'

The Russian political crisis reached a peak. Parliament rejected the presidential decree. A humiliated Yeltsin had to accept that decision. He knuckled under, and agreed to negotiate with Chechnya. But he was left with a gnawing personal hatred of Dudayev.

Punishments were dished out. Arsanov was fired, Rutskoi disgraced. But Russian voters were left with a sour feeling that their violent, quarrelsome new politicians were less competent than the blank-faced men in shiny suits of the Soviet era, who for all their shortcomings had at least ruled the Kremlin with a show of consensus. Yeltsin, Rutskoi, and Khasbulatov – all from outside the Soviet political mainstream – seemed to take perverse pleasure in a visible display of dissent and disloyalty, a demonstrative washing of their dirty linen in public. Their clumsy handling of Dudayev made it clear that they didn't know their political manners. From now on, the Yeltsin team began trying to dignify their reign by identifying it with a revived pastiche of Tsarist history. But that didn't stop Russians from identifying them as people who could not make dignified policy.

Perhaps the most damaging result of this weekend crisis, inside Russia, was the split it caused between Yeltsin and the parliament leader Khasbulatov, until then his ally. Hostility between these two men now became the axis of Russian politics. It distorted the way Russian democracy developed, and it led to armed confrontation in Moscow by 1993.

\*

Chechens were not reassured by Russia's retreat from force of arms. Much of the Moscow criticism of Rutskoi had focused on the failure of his attempted military crackdown, not on whether it had been wrong to attempt it in the first place. 'None of the points of the emergency decree is being implemented,' scoffed *Pravda* on 11 November. It was a moral distinction which Chechens were quick to notice.

Rutskoi's attempt to use military methods to quell the Chechens revived an old template of Russian–Chechen relations as relations of confrontation between armed men. It made that template a basis on which the new peoples of post-Soviet Russia and Chechnya defined themselves. You were Russian, so you disliked Chechens; you were Chechen, so you wanted to be shot of Russia.

Dudayev never forgot how his people had rallied behind him in that moment of danger, the defining moment of his rule. So he maintained martial law. He carried on wearing military uniform. And he refused to disarm his people, saying: 'Weapons will help the Chechen people to preserve their honour and dignity.' As normal life resumed, and his popularity faded, he appealed again and again to Chechen patriotism by warning his people that Russian spies were out to get them, or that Russia was about to invade them.

When crime began to scare people in Grozny, Russia blamed it on the 400-odd escaped prisoners still at large after 9 November. But Dudayev blamed the Russian KGB. The rector of Grozny university, Viktor Kankalik, was kidnapped on 12 November. The prorector, Abdul Khamid Mesliyev, was killed trying to protect him. Staff at the university telephone exchange went on strike, demanding that the hooligans who attacked their colleagues be punished and safe working conditions restored. Schools stopped working. Russian Mayak Radio reported that Dudayev thought the KGB was behind the attack.

The National Guard arrested a KGB major, Viktor Nikolayevich Tolstyonov, on Freedom Square on the same day. He was carrying his KGB card and service pistol, but wearing civilian clothes. Central Moscow television showed a Chechen officer of the tough OMON riot-police squad saying the arrested Tolstyonov would be 'judged by the people'. The next day, his body was dumped in Grozny city morgue. The Russian KGB said he had been lynched by Dudayev's men, and said there was no excuse for 'vandalism and mob law' being turned against its operatives. Dudayev responded by ordering Russian KGB operatives still in Chechnya to register within twenty-four hours, or face the consequences. On 16 November, the Russian *Sovietskaya Rossiya* newspaper published an interview with Dudayev in which he claimed that Tolstyonov 'was detained during an attempt to stage a provocation. Legal medical experts have established that he himself cut his throat with a piece of glass.'

Hard times began in Chechnya. Supplies failed to get down the railway lines. There were bread and sugar shortages, and queues at the shops. Dudayev said he had done deals worth $9 million with Turkey to cover the shortfall. If Russia declared a full economic blockade, he threatened implausibly, 'then we too will announce a blockade and Russia will not only have to drink tea without sugar but will also have to go without the tea itself'. Dudayev appointed

Yaraghi Mamodayev to run an economic management committee. His priority was to ensure food supplies 'during the harsh winter and the blockade by Russia', Tass reported. Emergency supplies of Turkish sugar were distributed in the districts.

When the Soviet Union finally vanished at the end of 1991, Russia became its legal inheritor. It promised to pay wages and pensions to all the millions of ex-Soviet citizens who had worked all their lives in Soviet state enterprises. But the payments it made to Grozny came fitfully, if at all. The people of Chechnya tightened their belts.

It emerged that Dudayev was even shorter on ideas about how to run his new state than Yeltsin. His government was a mixture of Communists, nationalists, and returnees from the diaspora. He appointed Shamseddin Yusuf, a Jordanian of Chechen descent, as his foreign minister. But there was little economic reform and no privatization; his one innovation was a 40 per cent tax on profits. Mafias prospered at the expense of the poor people who formed the basis of Dudayev's support. The Communist *nomenklatura* remained loyal to Zavgayev. Intellectuals remained sceptical about the prospects of independence in isolation. And the Russian blockade dragged on.

Chechens who thought his ambitions unrealistic were embarrassed by Dudayev's wilder utterances: his empty boasts of breaking the Russian blockade, his assurances that there were no shortages in Grozny, and his promises that Chechen oil would make the little statelet a 'second Kuwait', so rich that 'camel's milk would flow from golden taps'. As they pointed out, drily, there had never been any camels in Chechnya, and their home had never been part of the Middle Eastern Arabic world. Dudayev was not only reviving past hatreds they thought best left behind, but 'recreating' an imaginary past which had never existed.

Fantasy and paranoia took Dudayev over. His survival of one confrontation with Russia fed his larger ambition of leading all the Caucasian nations to independence. The Confederation of Mountain Peoples, a body aiming to unite the non-Russian peoples of the North Caucasus, based itself in Grozny. When his Georgian friend, President Gamsakhurdia, was removed from power in a coup at the end of 1991, Dudayev invited him and the exiled Georgian court to live in Grozny. He voiced public support for Saddam Hussein. When deposed East German Communist leader Erich Honecker was looking for a home in exile, at the end of 1991, Dudayev offered him a refuge in Grozny as well. Dudayev, with his sideways grin and his sharp suits, became a dark figure of fun in the Russian media: the crazed don of a mafia republic, constantly threatening to blow things up, trying to make his capital a club for all the world's pariahs.

Dudayev's revolution descended into farce. The patchwork of history and traditional associations he was piecing together had much of the same unintentional humour, the same quality of parody, as the history Yeltsin's men were opportunistically reviving in Russia. It didn't stop at camels' milk. He discussed reshaping the Chechen armed forces of modern street boys with Kalashnikovs and sunglasses into a cavalry regiment from the past. Between mischievously thumbing his nose at Moscow with his invitations to Russian enemies, and posturing about the terror he could unleash on Russia, Dudayev sent Yeltsin flirtatious letters which the Russian president never answered. He flitted about the Baltic States and the Middle East in his plane, mysteriously moving unimpeded through Russian airspace, looking for aid, trade and diplomatic recognition with no visible results. His bodyguard of men in shades and guns, the endless quarrels over money which began to divide his government team, and the criminals still on the run from the Grozny jail (they had mostly been jailed in the first place on weapons-carrying charges, which Dudayev dismissed as a petty Soviet offence, not the kind of thing which should hem in the noble Chechens) all added up to a grotesque parody of the military–religious order which had ruled the North Caucasus in Shamil's time, but they became the outside world's image of modern Chechnya.

# FOUR

This parody of a past of war was already coming back to life all over southern Russia when I drove to Grozny from the southern town of Stavropol in the spring of 1993. Stavropol, Gorbachev's home town, was a sleepy garrison five hours west of Grozny by road. Its heyday had been in the Caucasus wars. It has slowly, gently, been returning to the earth ever since. Poplar trees lined rotting boulevards of golden two-storey houses, and on its fringes the rich farmland, dotted with blossom trees, stretched back to the horizon. By 1993, Stavropol was becoming a behind-the-lines town again. Its streets were filling up with Cossacks and spies, mingling with the dowdy people in Soviet drab and the dark strangers from further east who had lived here during the Communist inter-regnum.

Most noticeable were the Cossacks. They weren't just present in the shape of the big moustaches on otherwise unremarkable middle-aged men in Crimplene, vaguely reminding one of their ancestry. There were also little knots of new-wave Cossacks in old-fashioned uniforms, striking self-conscious poses in the cobbled courtyards, or strutting up and down the sloping boulevard from the hotel to the grey city government building. Eagles, stars on the shoulder and stripes down the leg were much in evidence below their moustaches.

I went to see their boss, the Stavropol Region *ataman* Pyotr Fedosov, to ask what he thought of the decree Yeltsin had just signed reviving Cossack military units. Fedosov could hardly contain his delight at the idea of real power for himself and his subordinates.

'There are some mountain peoples who feel negative about this decree. But most realize we don't want to oppress them any more, we just want to live as we did historically,' he said happily. 'The president is giving us that chance.'

Fedosov entertained me in a dingy local government office at the end of a long corridor. These offices are the same the length and breadth of the former Soviet Union. Thin orange curtains are drawn over the daylight but only half-cover the window. A desk under the window has a table drawn up to it, in a T-shape, for supplicants and petitioners to sit at. Hard chairs line the walls, where a pale square often marks the spot where the Lenin portrait used to hang. The number of light plastic telephones in different colours sitting on the desk gives the only clue to the official's importance.

Fedosov was fat and cheerful and talkative. He had been given this office, he explained with an airy wave of the hand, by friends in official structures. He only waved his hand again, more dismissively this time, when I asked if he too had once been a Party member and worked in the same official structures. He was far more interested in a personal question. My appearance had reminded him of a visit he'd once made to London, where he had lived for three months with a relative in sedate Pinner. It would have been rude to ask how he managed to swing this in Soviet days, without good Party connections, when he had such affectionate memories of the place. Like most Soviet-era travellers to the West, he had come back with an illegal nest-egg. His was forty worn one-pound notes, which he had treasured at home ever since. Now there was no Soviet Union and it was legal to hold foreign currency, he was worried to find only dollars cut the mustard in the street markets of downtown Stavropol. His sterling was worthless here, he said with a crestfallen air.

'Now, you go home to England to see your family, don't you?' he asked, wagging his finger at me admonishingly. I nodded, with a sinking heart, realizing he was going to ask me to change his pounds for dollars. Pound notes had long ago stopped being legal tender in England, but I didn't have the heart to tell him his nest-egg was no longer worth a copeck. I decided just to give him the dollars.

'We could change the money here, at the market rate of course, and everyone would be happy,' Fedosov added wheedlingly, head on one side, assessing my reaction through shrewd eyes. Sighing, I said yes. Would $60 be about right?

Poor Fedosov. The ambush he'd dreamed up didn't work out; he wasn't as efficient as he was cunning. He didn't know how much to exchange his worthless pound notes for, and he got panic-stricken at the thought that the rate I had suggested might be a rip-off. He called in two young men in Cossack uniform who had been lounging in the corridor. They didn't know either. He promised to send them round to my hotel that evening once they had got things worked out. They never showed up.

I walked back to the hotel through the rush-hour, under the black-smeared city trees, laughing. These greedy Soviet timeservers wearing new lambskin hats had none of the religion and morality which had made the old Cossacks a fighting force to be respected. Cossacks like Fedosov made the Cossack revival look like a rather sad joke.

At the check-in desk of the Stavropol Hotel, a grey-haired man with a weaselly face appeared from nowhere and started asking, very politely, in unusually idiomatic English, what I was planning to do in town. Vadim had the wistful look of a retired KGB snoop with no one left to frighten. I felt rather sorry for him. We sat in his office, a narrow space next to the floor maid's ironing room, and drank coffee together. There was no nameplate on his door. Vadim rang round his contacts to try to fix interviews for me.

He was as tricky as a spider with a fly in his parlour. He asked for $120 for a car ride the next day, about six times as much as I would have paid if I hailed a driver on the street. He suggested going to Grozny on the train – the most notoriously dangerous way to travel there – but just smiled and nodded understandingly when I demurred. He talked English at first, then snaked over to Russian in mid-sentence. After I answered without stumbling, he nodded as if I had unwittingly revealed something important and said down the phone: 'Her Russian's not half bad'; after that he insisted on answering any questions I asked in Russian in his flawless English. Wrong-footing, testing, startling; in less friendly days, I had been scared of men like Vadim. But it was 1993, and the Soviet Union was dead, and the KGB had been disbanded (or at least broken up into smaller, friendlier chunks). All there was left for Vadim to do these days was to wring as much money as possible from the hotel guests; the expensiveness of his thick sweater made it clear he was doing well, but it was still rather a comedown. So I smiled, chatted, paid him for his time and trouble, said no to the train ride to Grozny, and went away.

By nightfall, Vadim had remembered he had old Chechen friends staying at the hotel. 'They're Chechens, but they're good people,' he said reassuringly. They would be going to Grozny in two days. They would take me with them.

We set off at dawn. I drove with Musa, the younger of Vadim's two friends, in his sleek white BMW, overtaking the tiny, rattletrap, Soviet cars and big army lorries cluttering up the road with breathtaking ease, talking. Musa, a big man in his early thirties, with a rough edge to his Russian and touches of grey in his dark hair, had a packet of Marlboros open. Two smart suits in plastic casing were hung up from hooks above the back seat. Behind us, Ardi, the second Chechen, and the pair's two Russian guests pounded down the road in a brand-new Japanese jeep. The plastic covering was still in place on the seats. It had no number plates.

The road east runs backwards through the chronology of the Caucasus wars, to the decades when Russian troops in the plains of the south-west were at war with the Caucasian tribes of the south-east, across the great Caucasus mountain barrier which divided Europe from Asia, West from East, Christendom from Islam.

Safely behind the old Terek River Line of Russian imperial defence is a straggle of once-elegant spa towns with names like Pyatigorsk (Five Hills), Mineralniye Vody (Mineral Waters) and Zheleznovodsk (Iron Water), where wounded Russian officers would take the waters. Heavily chaperoned young ladies also visited from St Petersburg, the imperial capital, looking for a hectic social whirl, fresh mountain air, romance, and a shiver of danger.

The main highway through southern Russia, stretching from Rostov in the west to Baku in the east, is the route the Tsarist armies took. There are few other roads.

Towns like Stavropol, in the south-west, are the oldest garrisons. More modern towns mark the Tsarist troops' slow advance on the mountain tribes. Further east, the Russian town names became more aggressive. The whimsical Prokhladny (Cool) gives way to the more firmly ideological Vladikavkaz. Once over the old Line and into enemy territory, the names the Russian soldiers gave their forts were intended to strike fear into Caucasian hearts: Burnaya or Fort Stormy, Vnezapnaya or Fort Surprise, and Grozny – Fort Fearsome.

Even in 1993, it was getting hard to find a Russian driver ready to risk his car heading as far east as Grozny. For history was already repeating itself. A few kilometres past Vladikavkaz, the road began to bristle with barbed wire. Armoured cars were dug into the ditches, with their gun turrets pointed towards approaching traffic. Russian soldiers paced watchfully up and down, guns under their arms. Beyond them lay Dudayev's Chechnya and the Ingush lands he had left behind when he declared his own territory independent. Once again, to all intents and purposes, anywhere east was enemy territory.

*

Our two cars gobbled up the road, doing at least 140 km an hour between stops. But there were plenty of stops. The police stopped us seventeen times in the five-hour drive, tutting over Musa's papers and his Chechen number plates, pocketing their speeding fines and bribes in mournful silence. Musa paid up with a resigned smile on his face. Every time he got out, he turned up the skittish Chechen music a few notches; but he didn't translate it. I guessed it was the same kind of music Isa had played in Ingushetia – mischievous music. 'They stop me all the time because I'm a Chechen,' he said, slamming the door and starting up the engine. 'They're more scared of us than of fire, so they try to push us around.'

Valya, the Russian woman in the other car, stopped us an eighteenth time, demanding lunch in a roadside café. Musa cursed under his breath.

'I don't want to spend hours on the road,' he said impatiently. 'This is business, not a day out.' But Valya tossed her head and pouted. 'You're with ladies now, and you have to behave in a civilized way,' she answered flirtatiously, and flounced into the café. Musa sighed, but followed her in. Ardi ordered tripe soup and cutlets for everyone, but Musa ate nothing himself and waited out the coffee in the car, smoking another cigarette.

'These Chechens are savages,' Valya confided again, putting her arm through mine. 'Valya!' her husband Oleg scolded tolerantly. 'It's you that's a savage. You forced them to stop when they didn't want to. You're their guest, and they couldn't say no. It was highly questionable behaviour.' Valya's eyes and mouth opened wide as she assimilated the new idea. She started to protest, but then only shrugged good-naturedly. 'Oh dear. Perhaps I am a savage,' she said. Under all her mannerisms, she was a nice woman.

We drove on, and I laughed to Musa at the rattling Soviet military lorries clogging up the road, drab olive green, guzzling fuel, canvas covers flapping. 'We have those on the Moscow ring road all the time,' I said. 'And they're always empty. Drivers running errands. People out for a packet of cigarettes. The petrol they waste . . .'

Musa weaved past one and looked at me sharply. There was a hint of laughter in his eyes. 'You think these lorries are empty, do you?' he said.

I began to wonder.

Surely this couldn't be how Dudayev broke the economic blockade, so openly, along the main road with its Russian soldiers dug in threateningly at checkpoints and its Russian traffic police stopping cars at every turn? And if it was, why didn't anyone stop him?

We made a couple more stops without the other car. Musa wanted to look at the bills of goods on sale in the local commodities exchanges which had sprung up everywhere since the start of capitalism. At Pyatigorsk, he ran into a building, picked up a stapled leaflet on cheap paper and flicked through its pages. A consignment of oranges briefly tickled his fancy, but then he wrinkled his nose and grinned.

'Nothing here today,' he said, and we set off again.

Musa's official job was at the Grozny state grain conglomerate. Unofficially, ever since Russia had imposed the blockade the previous year, he had been doing another job too – busting the blockade to bring in enough food to feed his employees and other dependents.

'None of those lorries heading for Grozny are empty. I and people like me have wasted the last year of our lives buying food for Grozny. Someone has to do it, because Dudayev isn't,' he said simply.

But wasn't busting the blockade exactly what Dudayev was doing? I asked, puzzled. If those lorries we were overtaking on the road to Grozny weren't empty, weren't they also being paid for by Dudayev to bring food illegally into Chechnya?

Musa only raised his eyebrows at the mention of Dudayev's name. No, he said. Dudayev had provoked the blockade in the first place by making the break with Russia as aggressive as possible. He'd been pandering to peasant nationalism. But then he had failed to fulfil his obligations to his people by feeding them. Musa had nothing but contempt for Dudayev, whose peasant supporters were suffering.

'It makes me laugh when I turn on the television and I see some government official boasting about how he's organized five trucks of potatoes for Grozny,' he said with a shrug. 'I bring in thirty trucks practically every week, and that's only a start.'

It wasn't the break with Moscow that bothered him, but the manner of Chechnya's going. Musa felt things could have been organized in a civilized way, allowing his people to escape the chaos of Russia's subsequent economic and other reforms peacefully.

'Of course we can live quite happily without Moscow,' he said. 'Russia is one big political blunder these days. Who needs it? But the government should have normalized our economic ties with Russia right at the start and avoided this blockade.'

The logic of the blockade had imposed an impossible situation on Chechnya. Naturally Russians thought it was criminal to break it. Naturally Chechens had to break it to eat. Rich men had always protected their dependants. A feeling of *noblesse oblige* was pushing Musa and people like him to carry on this role in the uncertain post-Soviet world.

Musa used to have one bank account in Grozny, but after the blockade and the Chechen bank fraud, the Russian central bank refused to carry out financial transfers to Chechnya. Musa wasn't worried – he simply opened five new accounts across southern Russia. He travelled between the rich southern farm towns' commodity exchanges, buying food products, cars and mechanical equipment and paying for his deals from the nearest account. When he needed money in Grozny, he put it in his pocket and took it there. Musa didn't worry too much about what Moscow denounced as criminal. His concerns were more pragmatic and common-sense. He had mouths to feed.

'Of course Moscow considers that sort of thing illegal,' he said with a laugh. 'But it's Moscow that's forcing crime on us with this blockade. We Chechens are a hardworking race and their rules won't stop us. They can call it crime if they want. But Moscow will have to accept sooner or later that the south, which has all the farming wealth, is ready to do business with us. Stavropol region ignored the blockade last month and signed a huge agricultural contract, for instance,' he added.

The real problem, he said, was that the leadership had gone to a nobody, a man without that inbred notion of *noblesse oblige* that characterized the men of authority in the Chechen clans. Dudayev was a nobody, and he'd spent his life out of the country. All he wanted now was to get rich quick. 'In any civilized country, let's say America, the president has to be a rich man. Then he has the leisure to help the poor. But if you put a nobody like Dudayev in power, he will spend years accumulating his own wealth before looking after others. That's what's happening with us. It's wrong, but it's only natural.'

The road forked, and we set off down an avenue of trees. Untended fields stretched away to our right. An empty village lay in the middle of them, wreathed in afternoon mist. Some of its roofs were caved in. It was eerily quiet.

Musa turned on another tape of chirpy Chechen pop music and

began whistling. Ahead, straddling the road, was a razor-wire enclosure whose armoured vehicles were topped with gun turrets and blond Russian soldiers' heads. We were back on the Ingush border, but now the fighting was over we could pass through what had been last year's war zone.

A single shot rang out over our heads. My sense of the absurd, my snootiness about the parody of history on this unreal front-line, diminished. My breath shortened. Musa stopped the car gently. We got out. I smiled ingratiatingly, but Musa didn't bother with the usual checkpoint schmoozing.

'Hey, you! Chechen!' an officer shouted sternly, stumping towards the car with his automatic at the ready. 'Are you carrying weapons, explosives or narcotics in this car?'

'No,' came Musa's carefree reply. 'I left them all at home today.'

*

Musa was thoughtful as we drove through the flat plains of lesser Chechnya, past turnings to old Cossack villages with the Slavic names Davidenko and Assinovka, or to peaceful Chechen villages whose names had the exotic endings -yurt and -aul, past villages built on old battlegrounds whose name bore the proud suffix -martan. One of them, Achkhoi-Martan, had been the site of the last battle fought by Imam Shamil and his Muslim warriors on Chechen territory last century, before the final run of defeats in the mountains in which he surrendered his sword to a Russian commander.

'What happened in Ingushetia last year was a tragedy,' Musa said, almost to himself. 'But it was worse than that. It was the start of a war with Russia. They won't rest now until they get us.' It was a widely held opinion in Chechnya. There was a jokey quality of parody about the past coming back, but at the same time a sense of inevitability. The Russians were coming. It was only a question of time, people would say, and shake their heads.

But there was no more gloomy talk when we reached Musa's home. Here, everything was grace and decorum. Hidden behind a metal fence, in a quiet street behind the interior ministry, the single-storey house spread elegantly around a central courtyard. The fence and the roof were capped with silver filigree borders. Lustrous carpets were laid out along the veranda. Quiet children milled around behind their smiling mother Luiza. Musa's niece Sapiyat, a beautiful girl with delicate aquiline features who was finishing a PhD in French and English at Moscow University, talked to me while a lavish meal was laid at the twelve-seater table. A married cousin, Aminat, dropped by. The women, dressed with the expensive simplicity of wealthy Middle East matrons touring London, stayed in the kitchen, but Valya and I were welcomed to the table. The chandelier cast tiny lights around the room as we ate, and Musa's ten-year-old son videoed the toasts for posterity with a hand-held Sony.

Before supper, Musa and Oleg talked money. Oleg brought out the calculator which spoke out loud, pronouncing each number in Japanese-accented English as he pressed the button. They did sums together on little scraps of paper, and reached an agreement. A silent employee came into the room with a plastic bag containing a wad of neatly wrapped banknotes. It was as thick as a couple of bricks. One more sign of the rouble's devaluation, I thought with the beginning of a smirk. The Russian currency had been worth a hundred to the dollar at the beginning of 1992, but inflation since then had climbed 2,500 per cent and was still rocketing up, and you needed wads of roubles to pay your bills. I was wrong, though. When Musa unwrapped the bundles, each note turned out to be a new $100 bill. I tried to work out how many tens of thousands of dollars he was holding in his hand, but gave up. I also tried to work out what deal could be worth so much, but gave up. I found my jaw had dropped, and shut it quickly. 'That's our work done,' Musa said. He turned to me and grinned. 'Tomorrow it'll be time for yours. We'll take you to meet the men who should be running Chechnya. We'll go to the opposition.' He handed the bag of banknotes back to the silent, stubbly lackey, who vanished out of the door. If it hadn't been in Chechnya, this quiet scene of trade and profit would have been the perfect illustration of new capitalism at work, a source of joy to the pro-capitalism politicians in Moscow. Moscow's rich businessmen dealt with wads of cash and weapons. It seemed unfair that, because we were in Chechnya, the association that immediately sprang to mind was with crime.

We didn't go out after dark. 'You can't go anywhere at night any more,' Musa said. 'You never know who you'll meet, and whether they'll be carrying a gun. It's just not safe.' The iron gate clanged shut. Musa put a plank under the stout bolt, so it couldn't be shifted from the outside. We retreated behind the high metal fence into the safety of the house.

Even in this gently lit oasis, eddies of anxiety ran through the Chechen men's conversation, and the imaginary front-line cast its shadow. Dudayev had authorized all Chechen men to carry hand guns; no wonder there was hooliganism. Camel's milk and gold taps in a free Chechnya, what nonsense, but simple people had been foolish enough to believe him. The Utsiyev brothers had been sent to their deaths in England; what had really happened to them? A television set flickered in a corner. When Dudayev's face appeared, moustache over pinstripes, Musa turned the sound up. He and Ardi tut-tutted quietly at the guttural words of Chechen. Ardi turned it off. I asked what Dudayev had been saying, but he only waved a dismissive hand. 'The usual old rubbish,' he said. Silence fell.

'I bet you have guns here,' Oleg said hopefully. It was his first trip to Grozny, and he looked puzzled by the well-bred restraint of Musa's wealth. I'd watched him before supper, looking worriedly around at the perfumed beauties using discreet Western gadgets in the clean, airy kitchen.

Ardi laughed. 'You want to see a gun? I'll show you a gun,' he said. He went outside and came back with a large automatic. Oleg put it under his arm and began pointing it round the room, making Rambo noises. Something clicked.

We all faded back against the walls. 'It's loaded,' Musa said. Oleg's jaw dropped. Musa took it gently away from him.

# FIVE

Chilly early sunlight in a scruffy ex-Soviet town. It was my first visit there, but Grozny didn't look at all unfamiliar after my travels in other parts of the former Soviet Union. Musa lived near the centre where, unusually for a Soviet city, the houses were spacious and private and silver-roofed, spread round courtyards, with vines on the balconies and little gardens. There were a few rows of elegant mansion blocks with arched windows near the centre, built at the turn of the century by British investors in an oil boom. But the rest was the usual: down-at-heel people on endless wide boulevards, the peeling concrete and giant pipes of Soviet housing estates, and a great many oil institutes, colleges and ministry buildings, testament to the city's past role as the Soviet Union's best refinery. There was a huge modern theatre, on Theatre Square. There was a crowded market, filled with the usual post-Soviet mixture of imported plastic knick-knacks, Snickers bars, cigarettes, Turkish clothes, meat, dairy produce and fruit. Leading away from the centre was one boulevard with a narrow strip of parkland down it. There was another boulevard, without trees, which swept past towering ministries to the two big squares of the government district. There were elegant turn-of-the-century buildings on Sheikh Mansur Square, and the naked pedestal where Tsarist and Soviet idols had once been celebrated in stone. Set adjacent to it, on Freedom Square, there were the huge squat blocks in which stodgy Soviet bureaucrats had felt most at home.

The people had pinched faces. A few, but only a few, carried guns. There were some flashy Western cars weaving around on the boulevards, between the battered little Moskviches and Zhigulis in drab colours, but not nearly as many as I had expected from the stories. So far, Grozny was not living up to the menacing charisma of its name and reputation. I was partly relieved, but also a bit disappointed.

The demonstrations of the pro- and anti-Dudayev factions also seemed nothing out of the post-Soviet ordinary, and the probable consequences could easily be imagined. Two banner-waving crowds on two city squares, filled with rage; separated only by an invitingly wide Soviet boulevard down which one crowd, wild with impatience, would sooner or later rush to attack the other crowd. What followed in these crowd scenes typically depended on how much weaponry people from each of the two crowds had managed to lay their hands on in the gestation period, and how much political ill-will motivated the leaders they supported. In the worst case I had seen, in Tajikistan a year earlier, a precise replica of this two-squares-and-two-protests scenario had started a horrifying civil war. Elsewhere, fights between twin crowds had left no worse damage than a few broken windows and broken heads.

The Soviet Union was a seventy-year-long celebration of revolution. Its towns were designed to make mass parades of happy citizens easier. The main streets were usually so wide that a single person walking through them felt lonely and dwarfed. It took a huge crowd, preferably orderly and waving red flags, or a noisy parade of tanks and soldiers, to make sense of them. Their very width makes them a magnet for mass action. In the confused post-Soviet world, where crowds were likelier than not to be angry and out for trouble rather than compliant and radiant with hope for a bright future, this was yet another headache for the local inheritors of Soviet power, already dwarfed by their new offices and the enormity of the task of ruling which now faced them. It was a problem they could do very little to counteract.

The new rulers of Grozny had done what they could. The anti-Dudayev demonstrators had been moved off Sheikh Mansur Square, which was too easily within fighting distance of their opponents on Freedom Square and of Dudayev's government centre. They had been relocated at the other end of the long boulevard on Theatre Square. It gave at least an illusion of distance, air, calm, and safety.

*

The spring air and yawning crowd, stubbly chins and long over-coats, gave Theatre Square the sleepy air of a weekend student

demonstration in England. The opposition had been in the square
for ten days. Over the crowd, home-made banners waved in the
breeze, formalizing and freezing a moment of hot anger with
the neatly uniform lettering of Soviet public meetings. Some of the
bobbing flags called for the sovereignty of Chechnya. The word
Chechnya was decorated with flowers, the word Dudayev with
guns and daggers.

Dudayev, you've got the guns, but we have Allah and the truth!
Robbers and killers should answer for their deeds!

But the people wandering from soapbox to soapbox were
subdued and anxious.

Half a dozen opposition leaders swept me up and took me off
to talk in the car park behind the theatre, perching like friendly
crows on concrete slabs and forgotten tree stumps. They interrupted each other as they talked and broke off into twos and threes
to argue among themselves in Chechen. But everyone deferred to
Salambek Khadzhiyev, a former Soviet petrochemicals minister and
now their leader, standing bright-eyed in the middle of the group.

The people had come to town to air their grievances, Khadzhiyev
said. There were as many grievances as people. No pensions,
salaries or child benefit had been paid since October. The collective
farming system had been smashed but no new system set up. Only
a third of the land was being farmed. Censorship had crippled the
media. Chechnya had oil, but its revenues were mysteriously
vanishing. Khadzhiyev's men wanted the president and the cabinet
to resign and elections to be called.

But the protest was not going well. After three days, Dudayev
dismissed both the cabinet, a concession to the opposition, and the
parliament, a slap in the face. The parliament had turned against
Dudayev. It had called a referendum for June, on whether Dudayev
should continue to rule. The opposition crowd wanted the parliament to stay on until after the referendum. It was furious. It waited
again, while its leaders demanded that parliament, still meeting
despite Dudayev's dismissal, impeach the president. But so many
deputies had been intimidated that the legislature could not get a
quorum to start work. Dudayev grew impatient. He ordered the
interior minister to take the police to disperse the legislature, but

the minister refused. Dudayev sacked him and appointed someone else. But the minister refused to vacate his office, and the police refused to let the newcomer in.

But the protest had to go on, Khadzhiyev said, even if it was getting dangerous. He had united the teachers, intellectuals, doctors, heads of villages and entrepreneurs of Chechnya – 'without undue modesty, the flower of the nation' – to stop Dudayev. Like the ignorant supporters of Dudayev at the other end of town, the thinking class of Chechnya wanted sovereignty and Islam. It just didn't want them to mean beggary and authoritarian rule. That, he said, was all Dudayev was handing out. Chechnya was fast turning into a dictatorship, and Dudayev into a Saddam Hussein, a Muammar Gaddafi or a Fidel Castro.

'There is a crime wave here,' Khadzhiyev said. 'It's being worsened by Dudayev's entourage, which is a Tonton Macoute-style organization run by criminals.' He said there were already three armed groupings being set up to protect Dudayev. No one knew how big they were, or how many weapons they had. Dudayev's cabinet and regional administrators also had their own private armies. 'Dzhokhar's mistake was to take power by force. When you do that you need to live by the gun. You start to steal and rob. Then you find there's no way out of the dead end. Now we go to work with guns because the streets are so unsafe. Our leaders don't fight the criminal underworld, they belong to it. There's a group of people here trying to create a Latin American dictatorship where life is cheap and death is on every corner.'

The lesser opposition leaders nodded dark heads as Khadzhiyev spoke in the confident, simple voice of authority. From time to time, there were respectful murmurs of assent. The starling chatter of argument and counter-argument only started after Khadzhiyev had swept away towards the theatre to address the supporters gathering around the open-air podium. The talk turned again and again, obsessively, to the invisible but omnipresent Dudayev, to his dishonesty and unscrupulousness.

The explosion of public distrust now had come because the Chechen people realized they had been conned when they trusted Dudayev. They were a warrior nation which respected military men, so they assumed Dudayev, Chechnya's first Soviet general, must be honourable. They believed everything he said. And everything he said was a lie. Dudayev came back to Chechnya promising his people would now be able to live by the traditional laws suppressed under Soviet rule. But the Muslim leaders had turned away from him, and Dudayev had sacked the leading religious judge and appointed a tame supporter instead.

'What right does a president have to appoint a religious leader?' Lecha Umkhayev, a lean, hungry man who ran a Grozny opposition centre, asked rhetorically. Umkhayev had an endless stream of stories about his hate object, and now he started chuckling, helplessly, as another one came to mind. His black coat flapped in the breeze as he laughed.

'You know, Dzhokhar convinced people he was a prophet from God, but then he started to make mistakes which made it obvious that he didn't even know the tenets of the faith. He was on telly one night talking about religion and he let slip that Muslims were supposed to pray three times a day. Everyone sitting round him started nudging him and saying: "Dzhokhar, Dzhokhar, surely you mean five times." And do you know what he answered? 'Oh well, the more the merrier."'

Downcast faces at the soapboxes. Some listened to Khadzhiyev. Some muttered among themselves. Knots gathered around me, talking, explaining, lecturing. No one shouted. Everyone was a former professional; they had all stopped practising.

Zargan had been a teacher in town. But anything that wasn't bolted down at her school had been sold or stolen and the salaries had stopped coming. Schools had shut down altogether in the villages. She survived on handouts from her sister in Russia, and she never let her fifteen-year-old daughter out of the house on the mean streets without an escort.

Anatoly Suboten was Russian and worked in the oil refinery. The lads there had protested so much they'd forced the government to pay their wages until January. So he was lucky; his pay was only three months behind. He came straight off his shift every day and joined the protest.

Stout Vakha Saidov had been a Party member and a professor at one of the oil institutes till the pay stopped. He couldn't stop talking about the crime. 'It's a kind of geno-suicide. People are killed here every day. Girls don't dare go on the streets. It's created an image abroad of Chechens as a monstrous mafia. It was never like that before.'

It wasn't just him. Everyone talked about blood. The Theatre Square people all said they didn't want fighting to begin here. They were scared of the history whistling in their ears. A drop of blood shed here might mean a return to the old ways of *krovnaya mest'*, blood vengeance, pitting family against family, clan against clan. 'Once blood starts to flow, it won't take long before there's no Chechen nation at all. Everyone will die,' Vakha said. I thought I detected a touch of relish in his gloom. I couldn't imagine him with a gun.

A lot of people worried over the square's favourite conspiracy theory: that Dudayev had been planted on them by Moscow especially to force such blood feuds, the worst of their old ways, back on them now. They pointed to the flurry of visits by Moscow officials in the autumn of 1991, during the crisis, as a sign that Dudayev had, at least at first, had some sort of secret deal going with Yeltsin's Russia. Most people thought Yeltsin's men had then flown into an uncontrollable rage because Dudayev had reneged on whatever that deal had been. But Vakha, with all the whispered gusto of his own past in the Soviet Communist Party corridors, took this conspiracy theory even further. He thought Dudayev was still in with Moscow.

'I think he's a pawn of the military-industrial complex,' Vakha gabbled. 'They wouldn't bother with us if we only had livestock farming, like in the old days. But now we've got oil, and that's made us important to them. The Russian military has always kept people in strategic places to safeguard their own interests. That's what Dzhokhar is – a mask for Russia's totalitarian regime.'

Common-sense Ardi was walking me round town. He supported the opposition, but he fidgeted through Vakha's wild explanations, and raised his eyes eloquently to the heavens. Seeing his exasperation, passers-by nodded understandingly. Several people grinned at us. One man winked. We extricated ourselves, and went off to visit the rival pro-Dudayev crowd.

*

An armoured vehicle guarded Freedom Square, covered in netting. Sultan Geliskhanov, Dudayev's hatchet-faced security boss, watched from the steps of the presidential palace with narrowed eyes. Below, the loyal peasants were getting food and information handouts from big green army tents. Men with guns and bits of camouflage uniform were everywhere. Some had camouflage trousers. Some had jackets. Some had Makarov pistols or Kalashnikovs. They had left their crops and their cattle and their families to defend Dudayev. Everyone was passionately devoted to him but too inarticulate to explain why. To most of them, it was too obvious to need explaining. Some got angry when asked. Few spoke good Russian.

Those who were old enough to remember the deportation yelled: 'Remember 1944.' So did a good many who weren't old enough. Rage over the deportation had been the main theme of Dudayev's speeches. A flood of television programmes on Chechnya's new independent station backed up the message with horrifying true stories, giving a new boost to Chechens' old hatred of the oppressor and a new energy to their demands for freedom.

'Dudayev's the only man who has fought for our nation,' men would say, struggling to make themselves clear. 'We are Muslims. We don't need Russia. Dudayev spoke out.'

They were blunt about what was wrong with the opposition.

'They're all old Communists. Or Russians. Party fat cats. Of course they hate Dudayev. He took away their fast cars and easy jobs.'

Unlike the middle-class protesters on Theatre Square, none of these people were educated. None had had a foothold in the Soviet power hierarchy. None had any interest in restoring it now. They just wanted to be shot of Russia, and they weren't cudgelling their brains about how practical it might be to do so. 'Dudayev gave us back our nation,' one middle-aged peasant said. It was enough for him.

We walked slowly down the boulevard, halfway back to the anti-Dudayev demonstration, heading for the quiet turn-off where Musa's house stood. Ardi was humming under his breath. And I was beginning to feel puzzled. They looked like the usual post-Soviet protests at first, but there was something subtly different about these Grozny *mitingi* after all.

Neither square was full of the usual raucous rentacrowds who haunted demonstrations in Russia, the bored middle-aged citizens who thought in slogans and who had nothing better to do than spend their afternoons waving banners. Those Russian crowds didn't have much to say about the issues they were protesting over; their thoughts were all waving in neat letters and exclamatory messages over their heads. There was no possibility that they might discuss the problems and, as a result of that discussion, develop or even change their views.

But here, on both Grozny squares, people were talking seriously. The views they expressed were radically different, but they were expressed with genuine concern. And most people didn't indulge in the hysterical yelling I had come to expect from Russian *mitingi*. There was an unexpected sense of restraint here, behind the strong feelings; unusually for a post-Soviet demonstration, it seemed to me people were not just talking, but also listening.

Of course, Ardi agreed calmly. 'People here have always sorted out their problems at public meetings,' he explained. 'That's our tradition. We Chechens go to the village square to talk over our differences. Listen to the elders. Work out together what to do next. There'd be no point in just standing round waving flags.' He paused, and looked gloomy. 'Not that I can see it working this time, though; not that I expect Dzhokhar to listen.'

\*

The most unusual moment of all came when we approached the interior ministry, halfway down the boulevard, and the entrance to Musa's side-street. It wasn't quiet there any more. You could see the silhouettes of sharpshooters on both the high roofs opposite, Dudayev's men on one side, police on the other, eyeing each other down sniper sights.

On the street below, more than a hundred people from both the protest meetings had converged in front of the interior ministry. A wall of riot shields at the door. A dense crowd pressing inwards. A sense of shock in the air. Separately and collectively, the demonstrators were having a fierce argument. Fists waved. Voices were raised. Chechen gutturals gurgled in tense throats. Gold teeth flashed, and so did thoughtful pale blue eyes under dark lashes. There was no Russian sense of deference to bigwigs here. Furious village women in headscarves took on important-looking men in suits; youths in uniform argued with the drivers of flashy cars. Policemen squeezed by the doorway argued with other policemen inside. Staccato Chechen sentences had abusive Russian words thrown in.

I stopped and waited. Anywhere else, this would be the flash-point for a mob rampage. The stronger side would push the weaker side down the boulevard; people would flood to join the fight. But what would happen here?

A couple of young men gave me a leg-up on to the roof of a parked Japanese jeep so I could see what was going on better. 'Chechens have the best cars for this sort of life,' one of them, a wicked-looking boy called Shamkhan Sheimiyev, said with a grin. 'We have the best cars in the Caucasus.'

The hubbub went on and on. Someone had been injured, or perhaps killed, earlier in the crush around the interior ministry door, it seemed; the word was that they had been taken to hospital. People paused in their political wrangling to wonder whether this was the first death they had been dreading, the signal for vendetta ... but then they were off again, all waving fingers, bared teeth and fury.

Solemn old men with beards and tall *papakha* hats stood straight-backed in Musa's street, watching the chaos with impassive faces.

Suddenly, a voice began to speak through the hubbub and the tumult stopped. 'It's prayer time,' Shamkhan muttered. I lowered my head, uncertain what to do. Everyone else lowered their fists and voices as the green-clad mufti climbed the interior ministry steps. Even the guns on the roofs went down. The crowd prayed for peace.

It was the first time I had seen this kind of discipline in any Caucasus hotspot. In other places, men with guns tended to use them first and worry about the consequences later. Drugs and drink and Rambo posters were what guided their hand. But here, killing was a strictly regulated business, not to be undertaken lightly. Chechen blood vengeance draws in many people: families, elders, judges and the community. Chechen traditional courts were not marked by official buildings, but they had quietly survived Russian and Soviet rule anyway, because Chechens did not trust the Russian laws foisted on them from above. So Chechens are constantly aware that they can be judged for their misdeeds by their own people, in a society so close-knit that there is no escape from retribution. Naturally, no one in Grozny wanted to shoot. The risks were too great.

When the prayers finished, the fists and voices were raised as angrily as before. But it was still the most sensible street protest I had ever seen in the former Soviet Union.

# SIX

Of all the practical, humorous, worried and angry people I met in Grozny, only Dudayev's team struck me as remote and strangely out of sync with reality. Ardi and I went later to the president's palace, hoping to meet Dudayev. The enormous building had the usual post-Soviet air of neglect. An aide hurried us inside, into an echoing hall with giant concrete stairs going off it. The lift we called clanked. Somewhere upstairs, we walked up more, smaller steps.

Dudayev's giant bodyguards with calloused knuckles, his judo expertise and lengthy workouts at his basement gym had been much featured in the Moscow press. But, it turned out, that wasn't what I was going to see.

'You can't see Dudayev today,' said the aide. 'There's an emergency situation. He hasn't got time.'

We argued for a while, but I could see he meant it.

'You can meet the foreign minister instead,' he said by way of consolation, and knocked immediately on a door in the corridor. It was where he had been taking me all along.

The foreign minister's impeccably neat office featured a desk with a man in a suit sitting behind it, and a framed photograph of Dudayev smiling enigmatically. The man gave me his business card. Alaudin Shamseddin Yousf, it read, Foreign Minister of the Chechen Republic. It was printed in English as well as Russian and had a satellite phone number.

The card carried the green and red stripe of the Chechen national flag, and the emblem Dudayev had chosen for his people: a lone wolf under a full moon. (People on both squares liked the wolf symbol: they said it represented everything about their national feelings. Wolves were fierce, like Chechens, but they only killed to eat; they never attacked first, but defended themselves bravely if they were hunted; however long you penned up a wolf, it would never be tamed, but would howl at the moon and dream of freedom.)

Another green wolf flag was pinned up behind the desk.

The man who introduced himself as Shamseddin was sleek and smug and breezy about the problems facing his government. What problems? he asked in Russian, with a big smile. He ignored the armoured car right outside the window, and the rumble of the crowd. There was no real problem with the Russian government any more, this Shamseddin said smoothly. Talks were going on with Shakhrai, which would clear the way for Dudayev to meet Yeltsin. Russia understood that Chechnya was a special case, unlike its many other ethnic regions and internal republics. The troops in Ingushetia were being moved back. The airport was being opened.

There were no real problems inside Chechnya, either, except those caused by Russia. Russia had taken over the Soviet mantle but failed to pay Chechen residents their salaries and pensions. It was all part of the imperial ethos. Chechnya had provided oil for decades, while Russia had kept the profits. But the people understood the problem. A year and a half wasn't long to cure all the ills of Soviet rule. Everything would come right in the end.

The opposition demonstration was a mere bagatelle, he said. It had only started for artificial reasons. Pro-Communist deputies in the Russian parliament had lost their right to a mandate when Chechnya became independent; in retaliation, they had told Khadzhiyev (who wasn't even a real Chechen, but hailed from Dagestan, further east) to sow dissent in Grozny. These deputies were furtively helping Khadzhiyev in his fell designs. But it would all be to no avail. Chechens would not shed their brothers' blood. The opposition would go home.

'Today we took steps towards solving this in a way appropriate to a religious society. We have asked the *Mekhkel*, the Council of Elders, to bring things back to normal. The council is made up of respected elders, both from Grozny and the villages. It's an old informal tradition stemming from our time-honoured respect from our elders. We can talk everything out,' he said. But if the people wanted a referendum, or a congress, or the president's resignation, they could have it, he added. Dudayev would submit to the popular will. He was on safe ground. Bread was cheap in Chechnya. Meat was cheap. There was none of the hunger and hardship you saw in Russia. The only real problem was that one man might envy the next man's Mercedes.

And what about the fabled Chechen mafia? Not a problem either, Shamseddin said blithely: 'If you compare Chechnya to other CIS states, we don't have such a high crime rate. There's no more crime here than in Russia. It's just that Chechnya is smaller, and so it's more concentrated here.'

I raised an eyebrow and smiled, not sure whether this extraordinary comment was intended to be a joke. It wasn't. Ardi, who had got more and more restive during the bureaucrat's rosily optimistic speech, began to argue with him. First in Russian, then in Chechen. The man called Shamseddin hushed him back into his corner, then summed up. Dudayev was handling everything in the best possible way. There was no problem, no problem at all. But the president did have his hands full; he would not be able to meet me. The foreign minister was still smiling happily as I left.

It was only much later, when the war in Chechnya was about to begin and Shamseddin began to make frequent appearances on Russian television, that I realized that the sleek, Russian-speaking man I had met at Shamseddin's desk in Grozny was not him. When I went to Grozny, I was already aware that the real Shamseddin was a returned émigré from Jordan; what I only realized afterwards, from the television interviews with an unknown face, was that the real Shamseddin didn't speak Russian. He gave his interviews in English, in Arabic or in Chechen. To this day I have no idea which Dudayev aide sat at Shamseddin's desk impersonating him for me.

'Shamseddin's' aide was sympathetic. 'Look, I can see what you think,' he said in the corridor afterwards. We could hear the crowd outside through the open window. 'I don't think the picture's as rosy as he paints it either. But I'm pinning my hopes on the *Mekhkel*.' Like most things Chechen, he said, the *Mekhkel* had been banned in Soviet times. It was one of Dudayev's many advances that he had re-legalized it. It could solve everything.

Reviving the *Mekhkel* was not the only tradition Dudayev started harking back to, as Chechnya's economic troubles deepened and his own popularity plummeted. He had also put aside his earlier preference for a secular state, moving closer to Shamil's idea of a theocratic state and flirting with the idea of giving Chechnya an Islamic constitution. But the idea had been met unenthusiastically by the mufti, who didn't like the idea of Dudayev taking over religious authority from him. (The idea of the Soviet pilot with his sharp pinstripes standing in as a holy Imam did seem absurd, especially if he didn't even know how many times a day to pray.) The mufti had resigned. Another split in the ranks.

I went home to Musa's.

'Will the Council of Elders solve anything?' I asked.

He looked sharply at me and burst out laughing.

'Dudayev's one? Of course not. It's a puppet organization,' he said. 'If it was a real *Mekhkel*, a real council of elders, of course we would respect it. Chechens have to respect their elders. But this *Mekhkel* is in Dudayev's pocket. No one will take any notice of it.'

Reviving old symbols was romantic, and it filled the gap in people's hearts left by the disappearance of Communist pageantry and steady wages. But it was also dangerous. The imagery both presidents were harking back to was the imagery of an old war. Why were Dudayev and Yeltsin doing it?

'Because neither of them understands what they're doing,' Musa said dismissively. 'They're two Soviet types trying to hide their own incompetence. They're flirting with history to avoid admitting they don't know how to run their economies.' He had no time for either president. Unlike them, he knew his responsibilities.

*

It was easy to agree that Yeltsin, ex-Party boss of Soviet Sverdlovsk, might not understand the danger of flirting with the past. But Dudayev, the Chechen nationalist?

Dudayev came from nowhere in Chechnya, Musa said. He was a living symbol of Chechen dispossession, born in the year of deportation and brought up in Kazakhstan. Although he studied in southern Russia for two years, Dudayev had never lived at home and was not much of a Muslim. He was one of a handful of Sovietized Chechens who had clawed their way to prominence in the Moscow hierarchy but lost their roots. He was full of hurt national pride that the Estonian nationalism experiment, which he had tried to duplicate at home, had met harsh treatment at Moscow's hands and been ignored by the outside world, while the Balts he had copied had won their freedom. But he understood nothing.

All Dudayev had done since he came home had been to immerse himself in Chechen romance, the romance of fedoras and guns and pseudo-noble poses. He didn't know any better: much of what he knew about the Caucasus had been culled from the collected works of Pushkin and Lermontov that he had always kept reverently on hand at his Tallinn barracks. A lot of real Chechens now felt that he was making a mockery of them. As a president, he had not addressed the practical concerns of Chechens. Instead of running the country he had called into existence, he was turning himself into the *zloi Chechen* of Lermontov's poem, the wicked Chechen outsider of the Russian nationalist imagination.

# SEVEN

Much of what was happening in Chechnya was clearly a legacy of Soviet rule. There was something very familiar about the erratic president – part charm and charisma, part shameless demagoguery just like his Russian counterpart – aping Yeltsin's blind love affair with Russia's past in his own blind love affair with a kitsch notion of Chechen-ness. Internally, the quarrel between parliament and president over the formal balance of power in Grozny was also a carbon copy of the Moscow political set-up. So were the dubious top officials – Shamseddin Yusuf, Yaraghi Mamodayev motoring about the Caucasus in his sunglasses and white Rolls-Royce doing arms deals, and slick young Beslan Gantemirov, whose early career as a mobster in Moscow was often darkly hinted at in the Russian press. (The word in town was that Gantemirov had been involved in the Moscow bank fraud in 1992; Chechens in both squares had laughed benevolently at the thought.) The loud accusations of corruption whenever a top official got kicked out of power were also alike: Dudayev accusing Yaraghi Mamodayev, sacked early in 1993 from his job running the Chechen economy, of stealing Chechnya's oil revenues, Mamodayev accusing Dudayev of doing the same, and being triumphantly reappointed prime minister by the mutinous parliament. There was something Soviet about the very existence of this *verkhushka*, or top class, of officials, many of them recent returnees to their homeland, remote from the people they ruled and all scrabbling for power without responsibility.

Another aspect of life in Chechnya which struck me as post-Soviet, though different from Russia's parallel dilemma, was the confusion about what should be considered a crime. Was it criminal to do things that the Soviet Union had deemed criminal and punished Chechens for, partly just because they were Chechens? Were the convicts who had escaped from jail in 1991 wrongfully imprisoned because Soviet officials were scared of Chechens carrying weapons . . . or were they hoodlums who should be locked up again so that ordinary Grozny citizens, many of them Russian, could go safely about their business? Was it wrong to rip off Russian businesses if you got the chance? Was it wrong to break the blockade?

A third impression was that most Chechens I spoke to didn't take this dilemma as seriously as Russians did. Some thought Russia was exaggerating the power of the Chechen mafia; others thought Russians were making up the stories altogether; but everyone chuckled with happy mischief at the idea of annoying Moscow.

The problem that really worried people on the squares in Grozny was closer to home: the possibility of a deep split that could not be healed emerging within their own society, disrupting their tradition of consensus and turning Chechens against Chechens in what everyone threatened would be a deadly, earnest combat. Beyond the antics of Dudayev and his men in defining their relations with Russia, Chechens had a quite separate – and clear – underlying conception of what was acceptable behaviour among themselves, and what was criminal. I didn't know where it came from.

But afterwards, what I remembered best about Grozny were the completely un-Soviet things: the moment of prayer . . . the elders, with their pale, calm eyes, their hats and sticks and steady walks, and the quiet respect in which they were held . . . and the egalitarian quality of the arguments that raged all over town about what Chechnya's future should be.

*

I went back to the history books, looking for explanations.

Another kind of answer, and a more satisfying one than the splendid romanticism of Lesley Blanch, was given in the pages of a different kind of book: academic treatises written by twentieth-century Westerners and Soviet dissidents about Islam under the Communists. Locked away from the peoples they were writing about by strict Soviet travel regulations, these historians grubbed through Soviet court cases and old diaries and forgotten scraps of writing. They held a mirror up to Soviet atheists' denunciation of rural backwardness and criminal behaviour in the mountains, and pieced together theories about the hidden history and religion of the Chechens that were never openly reported and that ordinary Russians still do not know.

What these books revealed was that last century's heady blend of nationalism and faith, which had given Shamil's fighters the will and the iron organization to fight Russia for thirty-eight years, had never died out under Soviet rule. When Dudayev had come to Chechnya, hoping to lead a secular nationalist revolution along the lines of the Baltic ones he had witnessed, he had appealed to a people unlike most other Soviet nations in that they were not groping back through the clouds of history to try to find a lost, pre-Soviet, authentic past. The Chechens had kept their traditions intact despite a history of vicious repression by Russia. It was an unreported history in which phases of war intermingled only with phases of not-war – uneasy truces, mutual suspicion, treachery and black propaganda – stretching back right through Soviet times and Shamil's time, all the way to the first Chechen clash with Russia under Sheikh Mansur Ushurma in the eighteenth century. And the key to their tenacity was their religion.

The peoples of the eastern Caucasus are Sunni Muslims. The faith came to Chechen and Ingush lands in the eighteenth and nineteenth century, part and parcel of the resistance of Sheikh Mansur and Imam Shamil to Russian rule. It came via Dagestan, home to a brilliant Islamic culture since the eighth century, whose religious men spread the word into the wild mountains by the end of the eighteenth. And it came in the mystical form of Sufi brotherhoods.

Sufism was a body of techniques concerning the inner journey of a mystic adept towards God that appeared in the first centuries of Islam. In the beginning, it was a purely individual experience based on the personal relationship between the disciple, or *murid*, and his master, known variously as *sheikh* or *murshid*. The master alone was responsible for the progress of his student along the path, or *tariqat*, to God. But the nature of Sufism changed in the twelfth century, when Islam was threatened for the first time by Crusaders from the West. Sufi orders were formed as defenders of the faith. They became a mass movement of organized brother-hoods, each grouped around a master and bound by rules which

regimented every aspect of their lives. The adept lived in the
brotherhood until he reached a higher level of mystical knowledge.
Only then was he permitted to go out and teach his master's way
to new disciples.[11]

The first sect to penetrate Chechen lands was the Naqshbandiya
order, or *tariquat*, one of many that had originated centuries earlier
in Central Asia. This was the faith of Sheikh Mansur, and later of
Imam Shamil, lending new definition and inspiration to their fight
against Russian conquest. The model of religious organization in
small groups that it offered mirrored the social organization that
already existed in the highlands, a perfect structure for guerrilla
warfare. What tended to happen was that a Sufi group of thirty to
fifty members would include an entire extended family, seamlessly
joining social, clan and religious loyalties. Socially, the North
Caucasus was divided into small family clans, the *teip*s, joined in
turn in larger, looser *tuqum*s or free societies. Among each village's
respected elders, or *baqqi-nakh*, embodying the pillars of family,
tradition and religion, were (and are) the *ailem-nakh*, or 'people of
knowledge', the *yurt-qaid*, or Muslim judge, the *yurt-muall* or
clergyman, or the secular *yurt-da*, or village administrator.[12]
Although they are no longer the only organizational framework
for Chechen society, modern Chechnya has about 130 *teip*s and
nine *tuqum*s.

Sheikh Mansur and Imam Shamil fused their vision of God with
a national resistance movement, declaring *ghazavat* or holy war on
the Russian invaders with a discipline and strength of resistance
which surprised the Russians. But, when Shamil was defeated, the
Naqshbandi *murshid*s were scattered: killed, imprisoned in Russian
jails or abroad. The rank and file of believers, discouraged by
defeat, ruthless repression and the military occupation of the
country by the Russian army, went over to a new brotherhood, the
Qadiriya.

11. Alexandre Bennigsen and S. Enders Wimbush, *Mystics and Commissars:
    Sufism in the Soviet Union*, published in California in 1985, p. 2.
12. Nicholas Awde and Muhammad Galaev, *Chechen: Chechen–English English–
    Chechen dictionary and phrasebook*, published in Great Britain in 1997, p. 127.

The Qadiriya order was brought to Chechnya by a shepherd, Kunta Khadzhi Kishiyev. He was initiated into the order during a pilgrimage to Mecca during the early 1850s, when the Naqshbandiya resistance already seemed doomed. After Shamil's defeat, Kunta Khadzhi began to preach pacifism to the mountain peoples. His slogans – non-resistance to evil and the external acceptance of infidel domination – were popular among the war-weary mountaineers.

Unlike the quiet, intent Naqshbandi, Kunta Khadzhi's followers celebrated their faith with what was known as the 'loud *zikr*' – the ecstatic round dances, with prayers, songs and music, which were banned by the ascetic Shamil and his Naqshbandi warriors. The new *tariqat*, or order, was more mystical, ascetic and detached from worldly problems (the Naqshbandi believed a *murid* should live 'in the world' and take part in normal society) and it was spectacularly successful in Chechnya and northern Dagestan, where the war had been most destructive. From Chechnya, Qadiri *murid*s penetrated into animist Ingushetia and converted it by the 1870s. The 'gay and witty' Chechens and Ingushi, who had always had reservations about the solemnity of the Naqshbandi, loved the dance and drama of the Qadiriya. They liked the practical idea that holy war only had to be declared if the invader tried to wipe out the language, culture and communities that underpinned the faith. They became enthusiastic *zikrist*s.

But his pacifism did Kunta Khadzhi little good with the Russians. In 1862–3 unrest swept over Chechnya, and in 1864 the Russian authorities, frightened by enthusiasm for the Qadiriya movement, deported Kunta Khadzhi. When 4,000 *murid*s gathered in the village of Shali they were dispersed by gunfire; 200 of them were killed, 1,000 wounded, and many more deported.[13] Kunta Khadzhi died in May 1867 in a Russian jail. His *tariqat* was not officially outlawed, but the loud *zikr* was strictly forbidden, and Russian authorities encouraged a massive new emigration of Qadiris to Turkey. Even so, the Qadiriya order continued to expand.

---

13. Bennigsen and Wimbush, *Mystics and Commissars*, p. 21–22.

Another great uprising swept the eastern Caucasus in 1877, with Naqshbandi sheikhs leading the insurgents of Dagestan and Qadiris leading the Chechens. Once again, they were defeated, after a year of battle with fifteen Russian soldiers against each Chechen. Those leaders who were not killed in battle were nearly all hanged, and thousands of *murid*s were deported to Siberia. Dagestan's Arabic culture was systematically wiped out.

When the leaders of this revolt were court-martialled, the presiding Russian general asked whether they considered themselves guilty under the laws of the empire. Ali-Bek Khadzhi replied: 'It is only before God and the Chechen people that we consider ourselves guilty because, in spite of all the sacrifices, we were not able to reconquer the freedom that God gave us!'[14] They were sentenced to death by hanging. Before the execution the condemned were allowed to express their last wish. Seventy-year-old Uma Zumsoevski said: 'It is hard for an old wolf to witness the slaughter of his puppy. I ask to be hanged before my son.' But the Tsar's court denied the old man's request.[15]

There was no open war for the next thirty years, but the Sufi orders flourished underground as secretive, semi-conspiratorial organizations. While mystical orders in other parts of the Muslim world shrivelled away, the Sufi orders of the North Caucasus grew and practically absorbed official Islam. Nearly all the Muslim élite of Dagestan and Chechnya were members of a *tariqat*, and identified themselves with national resistance against Russia.

Hostility between Russian and Chechen is still evident in the 1914 description of Chechen 'bandits of honour' – *abrek*s – by the St Petersburg Professor Kovalyovsky, in a book called *The Peoples of the Caucasus*, based on his experiences during twenty-seven summers in the mountains.

In 1859 the Chechens were conquered but not subjugated. They were subjugated but did not resign themselves. They resigned themselves, but did not make peace. The blaze went out, but in

---

14. Avtorkhanov, *Chechens and Ingush*, p. 146.
15. Avtorkhanov, *Chechens and Ingush*, p. 146.

the ashes a fire was hidden which sent out sparks and even tongues of flame in the seventeen years from the subjugation of Chechnya until the Turkish war of 1877. All the Chechens were unfriendly and even hostile to Russians, but nothing matched the ferocious hatred of the *Abrek*s (highwaymen), who like wild beasts threw over their families, clans, homes and everything close to them and gave their lives to fighting the *giaour* (Russian infidel).

Their vow of allegiance is interesting: 'I, the son of so-and-so, the son of an honourable and glorious *dzhigit* (horseman warrior), swear to the saints to accomplish however many highwayman feats – and during this time not to show mercy to my own blood or to the blood of anyone else, exterminating others as if they were beasts of prey. I swear to take from people everything that is dear to their hearts, their conscience and their courage. I will take the baby from its mother's breast, I will burn the homes of the poor and wherever there is joy I will bring sorrow. If I do not fulfil my vow, if my heart fills with love or pity, let me never see the graves of my ancestors, let my native earth reject me, let water not quench my thirst, bread not feed me, and the blood of unclean animals be poured on my ashes, scattered at the crossroads.' Such were the Chechen *abrek*s. They were wild beasts for all living humankind, to their own people and to others. Soon, however, they turned only on the *giaour*s and became mortal enemies of the Russians. They were the wildest, cruellest beasts of prey, who went to their own deaths for the sake of killing someone else.

A very different view was expressed in 1887 by an outsider to Russia, the French writer Ernest Chantre, who was charmed by the Chechens' and Ingushis' ancient law of legal equality:

Today they [the Chechens] live as people unaware of class distinctions. They are very different from the Cherkess whose gentry occupies a very high place ... The equality among the population of the Eastern Caucasus is clear-cut. They all possess the same rights and enjoy the same social position. The authority with which they invest their tribal chiefs grouped within the framework of an elected council is limited in time and power ...

Chechens are gay and witty. Russian officers nicknamed them the French of the Caucasus.[16]

By August 1917, the Sufi orders were strong enough again to revive the tradition of the North Caucasian Imamate abandoned in 1859 with the capture of Shamil. The Naqshbandi Sheikh Nadzhmuddin Gotsinsky became Imam of Dagestan and Chechnya. Fighting resumed, and went on throughout the Russian revolutionary years of 1917–25. The Naqshbandi movement again wanted to restore a theocratic monarchy governed by Sharia law, to expel the Russians and liquidate 'bad Muslims' committed to infidel rulers. 'With God's will, we shall construct a Sharia monarchy, for, in a Muslim land, there can be no republic. Were we to accept a republic, we would thereby renounce the Caliphate, which would be tantamount to renouncing the Prophet and finally God himself,' said a leading Naqshbandi sheikh, Uzun Khadzhi. 'I am weaving a rope to hang engineers, students, and in general all those who write from left to right.'

In 1918, as the Russian Civil War between Red and White armies got under way after the Bolshevik Revolution of 1917, Imam Nadzhmuddin Gotsinsky and Sheikh Uzun Khadzhi mustered 10,000 Naqshbandi *murids* and defeated General Denikin's White forces. Uzun Khadzhi proclaimed liberated Chechnya and north-west Dagestan a 'North Caucasian Emirate'.

The leader of the Russian Revolution, Vladimir Lenin, was ready to promise the nationalist and religious leaders of the North Caucasus anything in return for their support. 'All you whose mosques and shrines have been destroyed, whose faith and customs have been violated by the Tsars and oppressors of Russia! Henceforward your beliefs and customs, your national and cultural institutions are declared free and inviolable! ... Know that your rights ... will be protected by the might of the Revolution,' he proclaimed. But it was a lie.

After Uzun Khadzhi died in the spring of 1920, Russian Bol-

---

16. Ernest Chantre, *Recherches anthropologiques dans le Caucase*, Paris, 1887, part IV, p. 104, in A. Sanders, *Kaukasien*, quoted in Avtorkhanov, *Chechens and Ingush*, p. 152

sheviks occupied the North Caucasus. Imam Nadzhmuddin Gotsinsky gathered the Naqshbandi sheikhs behind him and led
Chechnya and Dagestan in a new armed uprising against the
Godless Reds. Historian Marie Bennigsen Broxup calls this 'the
last *ghazavat*'.

The revolt was a widespread popular mass movement, resem-
bling a peasant war, but the guerrilla fighters displayed an efficiency
that only a brotherhood leadership like that of Shamil's fighters,
with their total dedication and iron will, could ensure. The Soviet
army conquered Azerbaijan, Georgia and Armenia in a few weeks,
but full-scale resistance in the North Caucasus lasted over a year.
It ended disastrously for the highlanders. Dagestan was destroyed.
The Naqshbandi leaders were exhausted. The Bolsheviks captured
and executed Imam Nadzhmuddin Gotsinsky and two other
Naqshbandi leaders, though it took them till 1925.

*

In 1921, a Soviet-administered Mountain Autonomous Republic
was created which incorporated the Chechens, Ingush, Ossetians,
Karachai, Cherkess, Kabardians and Balkars. Dagestan, in flames
as it struggled with Soviet forces, remained separate. But there was
little pretence that the new republic was a genuine reflection of the
aspirations of the Caucasian nationalities. Its executive committee
had thirteen members: nine Russian, two Ossetian, one Ingush and
one of uncertain origin. Later, the mountain peoples were hived off
into separate provinces in a series of administrative shufflings
which continued throughout the 1920s and 1930s.[17]

After being defeated in Dagestan, the Sufi orders went underground again. But the brotherhoods' numbers kept growing. They
were against Soviet atheism, but many of the *murid*s saw no
conflict between the egalitarianism of Communism itself and their
faith, particularly the Qadiriya, which expanded again while the
Naqshbandi were busy with their last holy war. Qadiri adepts, or
*zikrist*s, joined the Chechen Communist Party. Sheikh Ali Mitayev,

---

17.  Suzanne Goldenberg, *Pride of Small Nations: The Caucasus and post-Soviet
       disorder*, published in London and New Jersey in 1993, p. 180.

son of the founder of a Qadiriya sect, also belonged to the Chechen Revolutionary Committee.

Just as their forebears had misunderstood the basically quietist beliefs of the Qadiriya in the 1870s, and by brutally crushing them turned them into a more secretive version of the deeply anti-Russian Naqshbandi, the new Soviet leaders failed to grasp the sympathy of many mountain peoples for the ascetic ideals of early Communism. As Communist forces gradually established victory in the Civil War, Lenin's promises were forgotten, and a new wave of repression began. Late in 1923, Sharia courts were abolished. The Red Army disarmed the Chechen population and liquidated what it called the 'bandits' nests' – groups of Naqshbandi guerrillas still fighting in the hills, as well as underground Qadiriya groups. Mass purges of Sufis began. In April 1924, Sheikh Ali Mitayev was arrested as a 'clerical bourgeois nationalist' and executed a year later. In 1926, the local Communist parties were purged of 'unreliable elements'. In 1928, when the Bolsheviks also began collectivizing the farmland of the Caucasus region, they stepped up their campaign to liquidate the 'clerical leadership'. Sheikh Solsa Khadzhi Yandarov of Urus-Martan, of the Chechen branch of the Naqshbandiya, was tried in 1928 for 'economic sabotage' and executed the following year.

The purges only led to more rebellions throughout the 1930s, strengthening and blending the political and religious will of the highlanders to resist. This struggle, with its waves of executions and assassinations, lasted almost till the outbreak of the Second World War.

What were the aims, the expectations and the political goals of the highlanders during this inter-war struggle? ask the historians Bennigsen and Wimbush.

Soviet sources tell us Sufi leaders and adepts were 'reactionaries', 'counter-revolutionaries', 'defenders of the clerical-feudal system', 'bourgeois nationalists', and so forth. They were also accused of being 'agents' of various foreign imperialisms: mainly Turkish, British, and, after 1933, Japanese and German. It is more likely the brotherhoods were fighting without any precise goal in mind, except to expel the Russians – simply because they could not submit to the new Soviet regime with its old Russian character and its new militant atheism.[18]

*

The spine-chilling little tales Abdurakhman Avtorkhanov tells flesh out the day-to-day reality of those years: bullying and deception by Soviet Party officials, mind-games and trouble-making by the powerful Soviet secret police, the NKVD, and answering Chechen guerrilla warfare from the hills. Avtorkhanov was shocked by the kind of Russians sent to rule his people in the twentieth century:

> Chivalry, noble feelings, hospitality, honour, faithfulness in friendship, a spirit of self-sacrifice for the common good, courage in war, modesty in everyday life and yet vindictiveness bordering on inhumanity when facing a treacherous enemy – such are the characteristics of the Caucasian Mountaineers ... The former conquerors of the mountains, Russian noblemen, were themselves endowed with many of these qualities, but the [twentieth-century] Russians and Chekists [secret policemen from the NKVD] were absolutely devoid of them. Let us take a common-place example. A Russian might refer to the unfortunate mother of an adversary with abuse of all kinds. In reply, he will hear the same insults and there the matter will end. But the Chechen who has insulted his foe must draw his dagger to protect his life. With Chechens abuse is punishable by death. Such is the code of honour. According to a Chechen saying, 'A wound by the dagger can be cured by the doctor, but a wound by words can be cured only by the dagger.' These characteristics were now described as 'bourgeois-nationalist prejudices' and condemned to disappear for the sake of 'communist re-education'.[19]

Avtorkhanov is not neutral, because he is a Chechen himself. But this grand old man of Soviet dissent, exiled to the West for his writings, is immensely respected by intellectuals all over Russia. His once-banned books on Brezhnev, Stalin and Beria are treasured

---

18. Bennigsen and Wimbush, *Mystics and Commissars*, p. 28–9.
19. Avtorkhanov, *Chechens and Ingush*, pp. 168–9.

by historians, and his personal sufferings during the Stalin years remembered.

One of Avtorkhanov's stories is about the Muscovite Yegorov, head of the regional party committee, who decided to organize a pig-breeding farm at Dargo. His Chechen-Ingush colleagues advised him against this enterprise, knowing that it would irritate the Chechens who, being Muslims, do not eat pork. They were unsuccessful. Yegorov accused his colleagues of nationalist prejudices: 'If Chechens do not eat pork, so much the better for the pigs. No-one will steal them.' The farm was set up and survived for twenty-four hours: pigs were brought during the day and at night the Chechens killed them. Naturally, not one was stolen. Psychologically, this act was easy to understand. The Chechens considered that by bringing pigs into a Muslim village where no one had ever seen them before, the authorities had committed a gross blasphemy. Pigs were never again brought into the mountains, but in response to the killing of the pigs, the NKVD arrested thirty 'bandits' and deported them to Siberia.

Another story recalls the Stalinist purge of 1937. Lorries with human cargoes trundled into Grozny from all over Checheno-Ingushetia. About 5,000 arrestees were crammed into the city's two NKVD prisons, another 5,000 were bundled into the oil concern Grozneft's garage, and 3,000 were locked up at the Stalin club near Bashirov mill. It was the height of the Stalinist terror, and the 'citizens's rights' enshrined in the constitution were routinely ignored: just one arrest warrant was signed to round up 3 per cent of the republic's population. An emergency *troika* of three Russian NKVD officials – Yegorov, first secretary of the regional committee; Dementiev, the NKVD chief; Porubayev, the republican NKVD's special prosecutor – passed sentence. Those who were not sent to concentration camps were shot. According to Avtorkhanov:

It is impossible to say how many were shot, but every night there were mass executions in the cellars of the NKVD to the accompaniment of the roar of motor-cars outside. As it would have been impossible to carry out the death sentences within the assigned time, a special 'execution hall' was established for the extermination of large groups. It was situated in the northern part of the NKVD building facing the Sunzha River. The Chekists called it the 'relay chamber' because the doomed prisoners taken there were told that they were being sent to Siberia by 'relay-stages'. The relay chamber was made of reinforced concrete and hermetically sealed from the outside world ... Firing positions were fitted into the walls and the ceiling from the exterior. The bodies were carried off in lorries under cover of darkness, and taken to a mass grave in a forest at the foot of the Goryachevodskaya mountain.[20]

In retaliation, thousands of Chechens joined guerrilla groups and fought back from the hills: NKVD officials in the mountain districts were assassinated; a military train was derailed.

In 1938, almost every Chechen and Ingush official and intellectual was arrested, in a case so improbable that it was almost impossible to frame. 'How can we arrest a man if we have no evidence?' Avtorkhanov reports an ingenuous NKVD novice asking his boss, Gudasov. 'We can always find evidence against him if he wears a Chechen hat!' Gudasov answered.

In November 1938, the Soviet case against the 137 arrestees, now known as the 'bourgeois-national centre of Chechnya-Ingushetia', was ready. They were accused of counter-revolution, insurrection, Bukharinist-Trotskyist anti-Soviet terrorism, espionage and sabotage. The prosecution claimed the alleged subversive 'centre' had plotted with its mountain neighbours, and been in contact with a 'Muscovite internationalist centre' to set up a North Caucasus republic under the protection of Turkey and England.

The trial was as cruelly absurd as any of the show trials of the day in Moscow. Three of the suspects died under torture during the three-year interrogation period; two committed suicide. Others died waiting for the court case to begin. Only 120 survived long enough to write surreal confessions to crimes they had never committed. One confession, by the republic's former vice-president A. Salamov, 'revealed' that Britain had sent a huge arsenal of weapons via Turkey to help the uprising: 50 guns for mountains

20. Avtorkhanov, *Chechens and Ingush*, p. 175.

use, 1,000 machine-guns, 200,000 rifles, 5 million cartridges, and 10,000 shells and grenades.

But, when the accused finally appeared for court-martial, they bravely turned the normal pattern of the Soviet show trial on its head by rejecting their confessions in public. Only one man out of the 120 pleaded guilty, Mullah Ahmad Tuchayev. The others all said they were accused of fabricated crimes and that their false confessions had been made under torture. They displayed scars, broken teeth and injuries. One had been castrated during his interrogation.

There was no evidence except the confessions, and now even they had been retracted.

Tuchayev was sentenced to death. But, from his death cell, he appealed to Moscow for a reprieve. The secret emerged: he had only stuck to his false confession because the NKVD had promised to free his imprisoned family and spare his life if he did. Even there they had cheated.

The case collapsed: the death sentences were overturned by Moscow, and most of the detainees sent to prison. But the last link between the Chechen people and the authorities was destroyed. The imprisoned local officials were replaced by imported officials from Russia and beyond. According to Avtorkhanov, the new-comers 'neither knew the language nor had any idea of the customs and history of the people entrusted to their care'. Until the Chechen-Ingush Republic was liquidated altogether in 1944, it was the NKVD who ruled the roost.

Avtorkhanov's angriest story is about the full-scale Chechen rebellion that began in 1940 and had the hills in flames for two years. Stalin's response, at a time when the Soviet Union was not using its military aircraft on the front-line with its Nazi enemy, was to bomb Chechnya, in its own rear, to crush the rebellion. In the spring of 1942, there were two Soviet air-raids over the Chechen-Ingush mountains. In the *aul*s of Shato, Itum-kale and Galanchozh, where the rebellion had been strongest, the number of dead was greater than the number of living. 'While Stalin shelled his own people, not a single German had set foot on Caucasian soil,' Avtorkhanov wrote bitterly, 'and when the Germans finally came to the Caucasus in the summer of 1942 they never penetrated into Chechen-Ingush territory.'

But the Chechens and Ingush were accused of collaborating anyway, and sent off into exile. For decades after they came back, the undeserved slur of treachery stuck, and rankled. 'Children were brought to the rich lands of the Caucasus ... made available after the expulsion of the Chechens,' Russian book reviewer G. Murikov wrote in the Leningrad periodical *Star* in 1987. Why were the Chechens deported? 'Mass collaboration with the Germans and treason – a most heinous offence – were the reason for such a radical act.'

Even in the noisy Gorbachev years of lamentation and breast-beating, the late 1980s, when old Soviet scores began to be settled and repressed nationalities to demand justice, the Chechens and Ingushi were never fully cleared of the crimes they had been accused of. 'Even in the period of *glasnost* and denunciation of Stalinism, people who claimed to be internationalists wrote incredible nonsense about the Chechens and Ingush,' Avtorkhanov wrote. 'Stalin – who is accused of all sins, be they his own or those of others – is loudly justified for deporting the North Caucasians. One could almost say that a second genocide, this time a spiritual one, was taking place up to the late 1980s. It was implied that, since time immemorial, the Chechens' favourite pastime was to butcher the Russians, and sadly the Russians believed it.'

*

There was no more fighting after the surviving Chechens and Ingushi came home from exile. But their homecoming was ugly. 'It is said that their vanguards, which left the camps immediately on Stalin's death to reclaim their villages, were preceded by a wind of panic among the Russian rural population,' writes Marie Bennigsen Broxup.[21]

They were met by signs reading 'Keep Chechens and Ingush out of the Caucasus' and a three-day rampage by Russians who had

---

21.  Marie Bennigsen Broxup, *Introduction: Russia and the North Caucasus*, in *North Caucasus Barrier*, p. 15.

been settled on their lands and were now unwilling to leave. The Chechens were forced into second-class accommodation that would not displace the new occupants. Other returnees remained permanently dispossessed by boundary changes.[22] The Chechen-Ingush Republic had been formally dissolved in 1944. Some Chechen land had been given to the Lak people in Dagestan. Some Ingush land had been given to the North Ossetians.

When Musa Gazgireyev and his family, who are ethnic Ingushi, came home from Kazakhstan and tried to reclaim their property in Vladikavkaz, they found Russians living in their apartment. There was nothing they could do. They moved to Chechnya and built their own home in an empty plot on the edge of Grozny, with peach and almond trees in the courtyard.

The trickle of returnees turned into a flood after the little republic was reconstituted in 1968: only half the Chechens had gone home by 1959, but more than four-fifths of Chechens were living on Chechen land by 1979. They raised big families: the total number of Chechens nearly doubled in the twenty years between the two censuses, reaching 755,000 in 1979. Russians, who had made up half the population of Chechnya at the time of the 1959 census, had static birthrates: by 1979, the 350,000 Russians in Chechnya were only 30 per cent of the total population.

With the quiet obsessiveness of returning refugees, every Chechen man built a house. 'I did well,' Abuyezid, an elderly Chechen from the village of Sernovodsk who worked as my driver for a few days in 1995, told me with deep satisfaction. 'I came back home, married straight away – at eighteen – built a good house and had fourteen children. Now they're all married too, and they all have houses of their own, and children. That's how things should be.'

Most people went back to the villages of their past. But some began venturing into the traditionally Russian world of the city. In 1959, only 5 per cent of city people in Checheno-Ingushetia were Chechens, but by 1989 the figure had grown dramatically, to 20 per cent. Grozny was the destination of choice. It was

---

22. Goldenberg, *Pride of Small Nations*, p. 198.

packed with job opportunities in oil refineries, oil institutes, petrochemicals factories, ministries, and state departments. It was the only big city in Checheno-Ingushetia. Argun and Gudermes, where factories were set up after the war, stayed small. The census of 1979 shows the total urban population was 491,000, or 43 per cent of people living in the republic. Of these, 375,000 lived in Grozny.

To cope with the urban challenge, the Chechens educated themselves. Only three people in a thousand had higher education in 1960; a generation later, in 1987, the figure had grown to 43 in every thousand. But unemployment was running at a third of the population, more Chechens than Russians, and the Soviet slogan 'there are no jobless people here, only shirkers' stigmatized those without work. Competition for jobs between Russians and a still tiny class of upwardly mobile, educated Chechen urbanites may have dispelled some national prejudices based on traditional beliefs, but it replaced them with new, economically-based, hostility.[23] In the city, the new indigenous members of the élite tended to be more negative about the Russians in their midst than the blue-collar workers below. The new Chechen intelligentsia had higher expectations of success in their chosen fields than their less qualified compatriots; their sense of relative deprivation when Russians continued to get the best jobs was sharper.

After the war, Moscow tightened the language screws on its subject peoples. The Chechens had returned from exile having learned good Russian – to communicate with the Central Asians they had lived among – though they usually had a guttural accent that echoed their own throaty language. (Neither Chechen nor Ingush had a written form before the October Revolution. Ingush became a written language in 1923, in Latin script, and a lowland dialect of Chechen in 1925. In 1938, both languages were endowed with a modified Cyrillic script.[24] Checheno-Ingushetia was one of

23. Robert J. Kaiser, *The Geography of Nationalism in Russia and the USSR*, published in Princeton in 1994, p. 245.
24. Alexandre Bennigsen and S. Enders Wimbush, *Muslims of the Soviet Empire*, published in the United Kingdom in 1985, p. 185.

the republics in which schools for natives offered instruction in Russian, with the native language studied only as a second subject. This gave locals less access to their native tongues than was offered to national communities on, say, the Volga, who could choose to have their children educated in their native language. This official starvation of the local language was common among all peoples of the North Caucasus. In the 1960s, Chechen was removed altogether from school curricula.

Chechens and Ingushi did not get much chance to read their native languages in the late Soviet era, either. Although there were three republican newspapers in Grozny, the Russian-language one published 90,000 copies a day, the Chechen-language paper had 16,000 copies and the Ingush-language paper just 4,300. Out of eleven local newspapers, four were in Russian, six mostly in Russian with Chechen-language snippets, and only one, the local paper of the mountain *aul* of Vedeno, entirely in Chechen. There were no local Ingush-language papers.

But the Chechen language is spoken all over the republic to this day – a mutilated version of the pure old language, so full of Russian words that a Russian-speaking listener is sometimes lulled by the illusion that, if he only concentrated, he would be able to get the gist of the conversation. Most of the borrowings are modern and nakedly foreign, but a few date back to the last century and have been adapted to a more natural form: the standard Chechen word for the Russian language is 'Orsiin', but a less polite variant is 'Ghaazaqiin' – 'Cossack'.

Although the dominance of Russian as the language of exile, education and prestigious work was increasing, almost all Chechens and Ingushi living inside their home republic doggedly went on considering Russian as only a second language, right up to the end of the Soviet Union. Of Chechens living at home, 98.8 per cent claimed Chechen as their native tongue in 1959 and 99.8 per cent in 1989; in 1989, so did 92.7 per cent of Chechens living abroad.[25] What the Chechens wrote on their census forms was probably as

25. Kaiser, *Geography of Nationalism*, Table 6.5, after p. 272.

much an expression of their anti-Russian feeling, their wish to
remain unassimilated, as of the linguistic truth.

*

Although inter-ethnic marriages were becoming ever more common
elsewhere in the Soviet Union – as ethnic groups were moved,
blended and Russified – the Chechens and other North Caucasus
people did not marry outside their own race much. In the 1970
census, a total of 8.3 per cent of families in Checheno-Ingushetia
were ethnically mixed. But most of these families lived in town, and
the figure probably indicates more mixed marriages between Russians and Ukrainians or Tatars or Armenians than between Chechens and other races. In the rural areas, where Chechens were the
majority population, only 4.3% of families were ethnically mixed.

There was mutual, and slightly amused, contempt between the
Russians and Chechen inhabitants of Grozny whom I met in the
early 1990s – hardly the normal relationship between a colonial
master and a conquered race, and, equally, hardly the stuff that
marriages are made of. 'Our Chechens, *nashi*, are not the villains
Moscow makes them out to be,' Russians would rush to say. 'It's
true they're Muslims. They have their funny customs. But they're
good people really: honourable, punctual, and kind.' 'Russians
generally are a dirty, feckless lot,' Chechens would say in their
turn. 'But our Grozny Russians, *nashi*, the ones that live among us,
try to learn from our example and live decently. True, they eat
pork, and they drink. But they try not to drink too much. And they
try to keep their houses clean, not to litter up their yards, and to
keep their word.' The few marriages between Chechens and
Russian women that I have heard about – including Dudayev's –
were mostly made by the Russified Chechens who had never come
home after the deportations, or (people would say with a sneer) by
ambitious city people trying to marry into the Communist hierarchy in the hope of career advancement.

Instead of blending into the Soviet melting-pot, as Moscow
hoped, the Chechens and their neighbours were becoming more
and more separate. Chechens were unlikely to marry anyone but

Chechens: if they did, their likeliest choice of partner would be a member of another North Caucasian race. But even this kind of intermarriage declined during the 1970s and 1980s, according to ethnographer Robert Kaiser: 'This indicates that, in contrast to the "drawing together" of *ethnies* in Siberia and the Far East, in the Northern Caucasus each ethnic community was becoming a more fully developed nation over time.'[26]

However ethnically separate they felt, political control of their homeland eluded the élite of late-Soviet Chechens. Moscow still suspected them of 'unreliability' and ruled from the centre. Although most other ethnic regions and republics in the Soviet Union were allowed at least a token ethnic leader to run their local Communist Party branch, Checheno-Ingushetia was ruled by Russians right up to the very end of perestroika. Only in 1990 was a Chechen, Doku Zavgayev, finally appointed First Party Secretary of the republic.

The few Chechens who did get anywhere in the Soviet hierarchy tended to be from the plains north of Grozny, a relatively Russianized region known as Nadterechny (Above-the-Terek) District. Doku Zavgayev came from the Nadterechny town of Znamenskoye; so did Umar Avturkhanov, who was briefly appointed by Moscow in 1995 to run Chechnya. Nadterechny District was the base of the Terkhu clan, and the last home of the Naqshbandi movement, whose adepts now number only about 10 per cent of Chechen Sufis. Because they were more tolerant of Soviet reality than the majority Qadiriya, the modern Naqshbandi were the ideal minority élite for Russia to co-opt in the divide-and-rule strategy of imperial tradition.

Anyone who wanted to get ahead in Chechnya, wherever he came from, had somehow to get the blessing of the Party which, in Soviet days, ruled everything. It was a dilemma facing every Chechen with a career to plan. Looking back on his own past, Dudayev recalled: 'It was not possible for anyone in Soviet society to work and earn a livelihood without being a Party member. All of us were Party members. Party membership was a mere passport

---

26. Kaiser, *Geography of Nationalism*, p. 313.

to work and livelihood. We used to bribe our way into Party membership by paying as much as 5,000 roubles (when a good monthly wage was 200 roubles). In no way did this mean that we subscribed to the ideology of the Party. It was a virtual coercion.'

The easiest way to get ahead was to join the armed forces, because Russians found it relatively easy to accept Chechens as good fighters. But, even here, Chechens who made a name for themselves had to prove themselves better than their Russian colleagues. Mild, energetic Hussein Hamidov, the pilot who during the Dudayev era flew his president abroad, lost his usual calm when he described the frustrations of being a Chechen in the Russian hierarchy:

'In the 1970s, before Gorbachev, there weren't even any Chechen drivers on the Number Seven bus route. They weren't taken on because it was the most prestigious route through town, so only Russians could drive there. You couldn't study. I'm an example myself. They wouldn't let me into the Institute, so I lost a year. Then I lost several more years at the [pilots'] Academy because they wouldn't give me the signatures I needed. I was constantly obliged to prove that I could do more than those Russians. They tried to sink me at the exams, but it didn't work: I got the very best results, even if I had to know every paragraph and every comma of the material. I don't want to boast, but I now have all the very best and highest qualifications that it's possible to have in my profession. I'm a first-class pilot . . . We Chechens have to constantly prove that we're better – transcendently better – and only then do they reluctantly show us the way.

'The only other option is to become a being with no backbone, obey all their orders and bow down before them. And the people who do that are the most despicable and unworthy beings, whom even Russia itself despises.'

*

Something more secret was happening in the countryside, while the Chechens and Ingushi visible in town tried, with only limited success, to insert themselves into the Soviet hierarchy. Away from the gaze of Russian administrators, the Sufi religious brotherhoods were gathering thousands of new members, a turning to God fused with quiet resentment.

When the deportations began, all 806 mosques and 427 medressehs (religious schools) in the Chechen-Ingush lands were closed down. Although Soviet authorities constructed a limited, controllable, 'official', brand of Islam, with four supervised centres for the whole country staffed by tame mullahs who preached the Party line, the Chechen and Ingush religious institutions were not reopened when the mountaineers went home. This unique experiment – destroying Islam completely through the suppression of its official organization – did not work. The faithful who were already members of Sufi *tariqa* did not need mosques to pray in; their faith was internalized, expressed in public only in the weekly *zikr* dance of a religious group's adepts and in unobtrusive pilgrimages to the local *ziyarady*, or tombs, of Sufi saints. Even today, when mosques have sprung up again all over Chechen and Ingush lands, believers still pride themselves on their independent, 'beyond-the-mosque', brand of faith. In the 1960s, 'this lack of mosques and of an official establishment of sorts could only contribute to the development of clandestine brotherhoods in the territory,' Bennigsen and Wimbush wrote.[27]

Quietly, more Chechens and Ingushi flocked to join the brotherhoods, lured by the conviction that what was discouraged by Soviet authorities must be worthwhile. The best recruiters were the Qadiriya sects, with their 'loud *zikr*' prayer dances.

After the death in a Russian prison of Kunta Khadzhi, the nineteenth-century mystic who brought the brotherhood to Chechnya, it split into four groups, each called a *wird* in Chechen, rather than the more widespread Arabic word *tariqa*, or 'path', and each led by one of his disciples. As well as the *Kuntakhadzhintsi* proper, there were the Bammat Giray Khadzhi. This group's founder was Bammat Giray Mitayev of the *aul* of Avtura, in Shali district. Initially limited to the Chechen *Gunoy* clan, it later spread through Chechnya and into northern Dagestan. Its leadership is

---

27. Bennigsen and Wimbush, *Muslims of the Soviet Empire*, p. 187.

hereditary within the Mitayev family. The third group, founded by Batal Khadzhi Belhoroyev of Nazran district in Ingushetia, was named Batal Khadzhi, and hereditary leaders from the Belhoroyev family run it. Limited to Ingushetia, it is the most puritan of all Soviet Sufi orders. The fourth group, Chim Mirza (or, in Russian, *barabanshchiki*, The Drummers, for the drum accompaniment to its *zikr*) was founded by Chim Mirza of Mairtup, also in Shali district.

Later a fifth group, Vis Khadzhi (*beloshaposhniki* or The White Caps in Russian, after the special white fur caps worn during the *zikr*, which in this group is accompanied by violins), was founded in the late 1940s in Kazakhstan – during the deportations – by the Chechen Vis Khadzhi Zagiyev. The most modernist in its methods of the four groups, and the most conservative in its doctrine, it has also become the most popular of all *Qadiri* orders from Dagestan right across Chechnya and Ingushetia and westwards into Kabarda.[28]

Although the main aim of each *wird* was for a group of individuals to move along a mystical path towards God, the Sufi brotherhoods were also ideally organized to become a kind of clandestine surrogate political formation, hostile to Russia. Clan and religious groups overlapped, as did loyalties, always anti-Soviet. Sufi orders were meticulously structured, with their own criminal courts and treasury; they collected religious tax and enforced strict discipline. Sufis ran clandestine houses of prayer and Quranic schools, usually near holy places of pilgrimage; they were quick to seize on new ideas to help them spread the word: they took women as sheikhs, let children take part in the *zikr*, and transmitted their teachings by cassette.

Details of the spiritual life of the Sufi brotherhoods under Soviet rule are scanty, because adepts not only practised secrecy but could also turn to the practice of *taqiya* (from the Arabic word for 'caution') and disavow their faith altogether, without being considered sinful.[29]

---

28. Bennigsen and Wimbush, *Muslims of the Soviet Empire*, pp. 187–8.
29. Bennigsen and Wimbush, *Mystics and Commissars*, p. 76.

But the ceremony which has always drawn members of the brotherhoods together is the *zikr*. Over time, the *zikr* has moved on from the silent prayer of the Naqshbandiya to ever more flamboyant and public displays of faith by the different Qadiriya groupings. In some modern ceremonies, the *zikr* loses its mystical, religious character and whole villages are allowed to take part. The ceremony consists of the repeated recital of litanies based on the Quran – beautiful, emotional, and sombre hymns dealing with the theme of death – accompanied by a complicated and exalting technique of posture, breathing control, and, with the Qadiriya groups, dancing.

THE RECITER:
When leaving this world of illusions,
When the tomb-keeper will knock at my door,
When my soul will take leave of my body,
Come to my defence, O blessed master.
THE CHOIR RESPONDS:
In this world of suffering you remain untroubled.
Without knowing what tomorrow will bring,
Your last hour is hidden
So prepare yourself to join your Creator.
Your hand brushes the hour of your death,
The jaws of the tomb are open under your feet,
So collect your thoughts, which are dispersed throughout the
    world,
And prepare yourself to join your Creator.
Hard is the road you must travel,
Your last hour is imminent,
As long as the source of your speech exists,
Prepare yourself to join your Creator.

Thus goes one *zikr* hymn collected by Soviet academic M.M. Mustafinov and published in a 1971 study. *Zikr*s have always been crowd-pullers, as the Chechen anti-religious expert S. Umarov saw during a visit to the village of Kurchaloy in 1979. Although three Soviet dancing parties and a showing of a socialist-realist film had been organized, Umarov reported sorrowfully, locals preferred to participate in the rival Sufi entertainments: a Naqshbandiya *zikr* and four simultaneous Qadiriya *zikr*s.

The Chechen *zikr*s of Soviet times were sometimes highly politicized. Umarov described a Naqshbandi *zikr* which had replaced the tradition of silent prayer with songs, hymns and dialogue which were 'remarkable for their nationalistic bias. Shamil and other Sufi heroes, remembered primarily for their resistance to the Russians, are evoked, and this experience, according to Umarov, leaves a deep impression on all present, even on unbelievers.'[30]

Because religious education was banned in Soviet schools, and classical Arabic was taught only at universities, the 'parallel Islam' of the Sufis had an educational as well as a religious role in Chechen society. Most teaching was done through 'Sufi *samizdat*' – the illegal circulation of forbidden religious manuscripts, documents, and chain letters among the faithful. M.A. Abdullayev lists many discoveries of Sufi *samizdat* in the North Caucasus in a 1973 publication. These include the existence of a *samizdat* publication by a group of clerics in Nazran district in Ingush territory, which explains the Ten Rules of Life according to Islam. The Soviet newspaper *Pravda* commented in 1970 that this piece of *samizdat* was a typical attempt by 'religious fanatics . . . to oppose science and modern life'.

The Sufis adapted to the advances of science and modern life when it suited them. According to Bennigsen and Wimbush:

Soviet sources have begun to denounce what appears to be the extensive use by the brotherhoods of transistor radios, cassettes and recordings. Several examples of recorded samizdat are given by A.M. Tutaev. In this (1975) work, Tutaev examines the use of recordings by adepts of the Batal Khadzhi *wird* in the Chechen-Ingush republic. In an earlier survey Tutaev explained that Soviet radio facilities have been used by adepts of the Batal Khadzhi *tariqat* to broadcast religious preaching. This curious incident took place in the Chechen village of Ekazhevo in 1967 or 1968. (Tutaev also mentions school-age boys who are

---

30. Bennigsen and Wimbush, *Mystics and Commissars*, pp.79–82.

engaged in circulating religious messages and manuscripts.)
Another Chechen anti-religious specialist, N.A. Mamleev, describes the use of tape recorders and recordings of religious texts
by adepts of the Batal Khadzhi and Kunta Khadzhi *tariqa*.

In order to protect the secret, those involved would fill one
side of the record with popular songs, while on the other they
recorded religious hymns and sermons.[31]

Finally, there were the pilgrimages, made both by Sufi adepts
and by ordinary people, believers and unbelievers alike, to the
unobtrusive mausoleums in quiet roadside graveyards that marked
the last resting places of Sufi saints.

And who were these saints? Most of them were none other than
the religious leaders who had fallen in battle with the Russians
since Shamil's war – making this apparently peaceful act of worship
a double slap in the face to Moscow, an act which showed both
that the Chechens had not forgotten their faith.

The most celebrated of all holy places in the North Caucasus is
the *ziyarad* of Sheikh Uzun Khadzhi, the Chechen Naqshbandi
sheikh who died in May 1920 and is now considered a kind of
'patron saint' by the mountaineers. It is in the *aul* of Dyshne-
Vedeno. The founder of the *Qadiriya* movement, Kunta Khadzhi,
died in a Russian prison in 1867, so pilgrims flock instead to his
mother's tomb in Khadzhi Otar *aul*, near Vedeno. 'The Great
Khadzhi' of Chechnya, Sheikh Tasho Khadzhi of Indiri, is buried
and worshipped at the *aul* of Sayasan, in Nozhay-Yurt district. He
was a *naib* of Imam Shamil, and he introduced the Naqshbandiya
*tariqa* into the Chechen country. He remains for Chechens what
Shamil is for Dagestanis – a great spiritual master and the model
of a political and military leader.

There are many more such holy places, some of which are
devoted to more or less mythical figures co-opted by the Sufis:
ancestors, prophets and even pre-Islamic deities. But it was the
tombs of the Sufi warrior sheikhs who fought the Russians that
were most assiduously worshipped in the late Soviet years. Un-
surprisingly, this was a source of never-ending rage from Soviet

31. Bennigsen and Wimbush, *Mystics and Commissars*, pp.92–3.

authorities, who repeatedly closed down the sites, demolished them, and turned them into anti-religious museums, clubs or 'parks of culture'.

Soviet specialists argued that the holy places were not only 'breeding grounds for charlatans, crooks, parasites and criminals', but unsanitary to boot. 'The holy places attract all kinds of persons, including those who have venereal or skin diseases, trachoma, etc. ... Pilgrims eat in the same place, drink from the same pail, sleep in the same beds and make ritual ablutions in the same plates. Some pilgrims bring bedding belonging to the diseased. All this creates favourable conditions for contagious illness,' wrote Zh. Bazarbayev in 1979.

It made no difference. Whatever the authorities did, nothing stopped the clerics restoring the *ziyarad*s, or the pilgrims coming. *Groznensky Rabochy* reported in 1964 that 'in 1960, the assemblies of the villages of Pervomaisk, Dyzhne-Vedeno and Tsa-Vedeno asked [the authorities] to close the *ziyarad* of Uzun Khadzhi and of the mother of Kunta Khadzhi. Years later pilgrims still continue to visit these holy places, especially during the religious festivals.'

Soviet authorities tried several different tactics in response. The once-reviled Shamil began to be rehabilitated, in a post-war revisionist attempt to promote the myth that enmities had never existed among the Soviet nations, as proof of their voluntary entry into Russia. But, writes historian Fanny E.B. Bryan, the official Soviet view of the other Sufi leaders of revolts in the 1920s and 1930s in Chechnya continued to be that they were villains and political bandits.[32]

Another tack: the Soviet propaganda machine cranked into action against the Sufis. From the Second World War onwards, anti-religious propaganda was centralized in and orchestrated by the Association for the Diffusion of Political and Scientific Knowledge (*Znaniye*). This association had branches all over the Soviet Union. Other institutions were created to fight religion, especially

---

32. Fanny E. B. Bryan, *Internationalism, Nationalism and Islam* in *North Caucasus Barrier*, p. 209.

Islam. The media were also involved in anti-religious work, including radio, television, theatre, the press, exhibitions, museums and libraries. These were supplemented by anti-religious clubs, lectures and one-on-one private discussions. At least until the age of *glasnost*, the anti-religious propaganda machine seemed a fearsome foe, but Bryan says that, like other ideologically bankrupt late-Soviet institutions, it turned out to be a dud. Many of the atheist institutions only existed on paper, and the Chechen 'atheists' who drew salaries for preaching Godlessness were often believers themselves.

While Soviet authorities tried to find a way of stopping them, the Qadiriyas insouciantly went their own way. Sufi adepts avoided any participation in collective Soviet life: economic, social, and especially political. But, Soviet anti-religious critics observed, the highly disciplined and hard-working Sufi communities were socially more solid and economically more prosperous than the average kolkhoz state farm. Members of *murid* communities in the North Caucasus, wrote A.M. Tutaev, 'live completely outside the Soviet legal sphere, both in their working activity and in their family sphere'.[33] According to Kyrgyz expert S. Mambetaliev, 'the *tariqa* are active, clandestine, secret societies, hostile to the socialist system and to the Soviet state, and as such they represent a serious social danger'.[34]

Their very inability to uproot the Sufi brotherhoods made the Soviet establishment view them as dangerous. Bennigsen and Wimbush conclude that the real threat the brotherhoods represented to the Soviet Union was the 'eloquent testimony that large, well-organised communities with their own rules and discipline can survive and even expand entirely outside Soviet political control. From this standpoint alone they are intolerable to Soviet power.'[35]

Chechens say that only in 1979 did the last *abrek*, or bandit of

---

33. A. M. Tutaev, *Reaktsionnaia sekta Batal Khadzhi*, Grozny, 1968, p. 23.
34. S. Mambetaliev, *Perezhitka nekotorykh musul'manskikh techenii v Kirghizii i ikh istoriia*, Frunze, 1969, p. 39.
35. Bennigsen and Wimbush, *Mystics and Commissars*, p.108.

honour, die defending the freedom of his mountains with a rifle in his hand. This old man, Khazaki Magomedov, protected by the local population, had escaped the deportations and fought on since the Second World War, 'sowing death and terror' among Soviet officials. He had killed forty Communists. He was labelled a 'Hitlerite bandit' by the Communist press. He was also a Sufi, writes Marie Bennigsen Broxup: 'When he was killed, a small Quran was found on his breast. Perhaps this is the way others will fight and die before the Caucasus is free again.'[36]

\*

This was the people that Dudayev turned to, in 1990 and 1991, with his off-the-peg late-Soviet nationalism and with his demand that Russia admit it had been at war with the Chechens for centuries and sign an honest peace treaty. In Chechnya, unlike other parts of the Soviet Union, no one had forgotten, and history had never died.

Dudayev understood the anti-Russian xenophobia of the new Chechen nationalism developing in the 1980s, with roots in the old holy war tradition. He understood that the Chechens were bound to leap at any chance to establish themselves on an equal footing with Russia. In the idealistic days of *glasnost*, his brand of secular nationalism appealed to their pride. He also understood what made the Chechens and their immediate neighbours in the North Caucasus more difficult for Moscow to manage than the more easily led Azeris and Armenians, or Georgians and Abkhazians. They were too cautious, and too clear-sighted, to get so lost in local enmities that they called in Moscow to mediate. They had long memories of what forms help from Moscow might take. Despite the border problems that Soviet reshuffles had left, Dudayev was prudent enough to make a private deal with the president of Ingushetia, Ruslan Aushev, and agree to leave their frontier undefined for five years. But his idea of creating a secular Chechen nation state, excluding Chechens' co-religionists in Dagestan, Ingushetia and Kabarda, was something completely new to the North Caucasus,

---

36. Bennigsen Broxup, *Introduction: Russia and the North Caucasus*, p. 15.

whose peoples still defined themselves as being from a particular
village, valley or clan, but also as part of a loose group of Muslims
from all over the mountains.

For Dudayev did not know about the spiritual underground that
had flourished after the war, in his absence. Only after he came
home did he begin to realize how important this was to his
compatriots, and to try to assume the mantle of a religious leader;
but it was clear that all he really wanted from this was the political
cachet of being seen as Imam Shamil's successor. With his Soviet
military upbringing, he never understood other Chechens' light
touch, the way God and family and learning and morality and
general good behaviour shaded into each another in an easy
continuum. He hadn't been brought up in the mischievous tradition
of 'home' Chechens, with code words and conspiratorial smiles
flashing though ordinary talk; he hadn't grown up reminding his
siblings five times a day, whenever it was time to pray: 'have you
"washed" yet?'

Once he got into power, Dudayev's style of government turned
out to be as hierarchical, and almost as bullying and arbitrary, as
that of his Soviet predecessors – something the egalitarian Chechens
hadn't expected from one of their own. It provoked almost
immediate rows between the new president and his parliament.

# EIGHT

Neither Dudayev nor Yeltsin knew what to do with the new democracies that their acts of will had called into existence. Somehow, they were supposed to make their homelands flourish economically; they were also supposed to strip away the apparatus of Soviet totalitarianism and let freedom flourish. But the reality of democracy was that the policies they thought up had to be passed by parliaments, and the parliaments in Moscow and Grozny obstructed everything their presidents wanted to do. It was a time of weakness, frustration and stalemate. It wasn't what either president had expected running a country to be like.

The comforting absolutism of the past beckoned. The Tsars and Imams of history would never have stood for this insubordination. Tsar Ivan the Terrible had put out the eyes of the designer of the brightly-coloured St Basil's Cathedral on Red Square – on a whim. Imam Shamil had whipped his mother on a public square when she dared to plead, on behalf of some of his terrified subjects, for surrender to the Russians – because he felt like it.

Perhaps it was inevitable that both the modern presidents would sooner or later start to believe in their own propaganda, looking for comfort to the make-believe roles of all-powerful Tsar and Imam. In 1993, both Yeltsin and Dudayev cracked under the strain of democracy. They opted instead for a tainted form of autocracy, ending conflict with their parliaments by gunning down their opponents.

*

Dudayev went first. He was at the end of his tether. He had stripped parliament of its powers, but now its opposition leaders were planning to hold a referendum on 5 June, to ask the Chechen people whether Chechnya needed a president at all, and, if so, whether they wanted early elections for a more competent president and a new parliament. The republican Constitutional Court denounced Dudayev. His enemy in Moscow, Khasbulatov, urged him to resign.

When Dudayev got out of his car on 2 June, to talk to an angry crowd on Theatre Square, he was greeted by catcalls, abuse and a five-minute volley of shots into the air. One of his guards was shot in the back as Dudayev scuttled back into his car. 'There will be no referendum. All attempts to hold it will be stopped,' Dudayev thundered in a television address. He disbanded the Constitutional Court.

The bloodshed began at dawn on Friday, 4 June, the Muslim holy day. Dudayev's tanks rolled into the centre of Grozny at 06.00. They shelled the internal affairs directorate and city hall, where opposition leaders were based, and smoked them out. Beslan Gantemirov, the rebel mayor, vanished in the confusion and was later reported injured. Troops, including an experienced battalion of Chechen volunteers which had been away fighting in nearby Abkhazia, moved on the opposition rally in Theatre Square. About 10,000 trembling opposition demonstrators scattered to escape the boom and whistle of war. There was serious destruction, and several deaths. Official Chechen figures issued by Dudayev's office said twenty-eight people had been injured, of whom seven had died. But the opposition said Dudayev's men had killed up to a hundred people and dozens more had been thrown into prison.

A bonfire was built on Sheikh Mansur Square, and referendum voting slips were burned. The referendum did not take place.

Dudayev justified his actions by saying the Chechen opposition and Khasbulatov had been plotting to get rid of him and take power themselves. He claimed that they had committed a crime against the Chechen people and invited Russian special forces to come to Chechnya and do the job for them; even now, Russian troops were waiting all along the Chechen border to help the 'bandit' opposition. Russian military sources, quoted by Tass, denied everything.

But most Chechens thought it was Dudayev, not the opposition, who had committed an unforgivable crime against their people. He had shed Chechen blood, their ultimate taboo. He had killed, and on their holy day. He had broken the social rules of consensus and seemed to be trying to turn himself into exactly the type of authoritarian leader they did not want.

Mustafa Edelbiyev, leader of the 'Gulam' opposition group, said Dudayev was now pursuing 'terror promoted to the rank of a state policy', and 'arbitrariness against his own people'. Edelbiyev suggested that Dudayev was trying to provoke Russia into sending troops to Chechnya. It was the only way the Chechen president, 'who has fully discredited himself, can hope to restore his image as a freedom fighter,' he said caustically.

Opposition rallies were held in several districts away from Grozny. Rumours circulated that a blood feud had been declared against Dudayev. Nadterechny District and two other northern areas voted not to recognize his rule. As Dudayev's men arrested and patrolled in Grozny, the opposition regrouped in Nadterechny District and pondered what to do next.

\*

What Russians thought of Dudayev's bloodshed was mostly predictable.

'Oh, those Chechens!' people in distant Moscow exclaimed with a cynical laugh.

Russians in the south were angrier, because they believed Dudayev had attacked their own Russian brothers in Grozny. Mikhail Shatalov, the administrative head of the North Ossetian capital of Vladikavkaz, shouted crossly in an interview on Radio Russia that 15,000 refugees – all ethnic Russians – had fled to his city to escape the fighting, and he was having to find places for them all to stay. 'It is the Cossacks and Russians who are being kicked out,' he said. 'The Cossacks there have been disarmed, their houses and cattle have been taken away, and all of them are being swept out, so to speak.' The Chechen information minister, Movladi Udugov – a young man who spoke unaccented Russian and whose hooded eyes were always calm – was also on this programme. 'As for the information that some refugees have allegedly arrived from Chechnya, I can tell you officially that this is the most blatant misinformation and an absolute lie,' he answered.

The events in Grozny gave creative members of Russia's old

guard a delicious opportunity for *vranyo*. *Pravda*, the newspaper of people nostalgic for the old enemies of the Soviet Union, was quick to say Dudayev had been brainwashed by the West. 'It was in the Baltics that the general's political career began – in the ancient university city of Tartu, a centre of Estonian nationalism ... Tartu was for many decades – and this is no longer concealed – a relay link for Western ideology generated by the émigré intelligentsia who went abroad with Hitler's retreating troops. It was in these historical pockets of blatant anti-Soviets and anti-Communists that a method of brainwashing Soviet army servicemen serving in the Baltic republics was found. The commander of a strategic aviation division stationed in Tartu, Major-General Dzhokhar Dudayev, also found himself among the "guinea pigs". It did not take long to find him, because the military and university campuses were located next to one another,' the piece concluded with a triumphant flourish of logic.

Ruslan Khasbulatov, the Chechen who ran the Russian parliament and was fighting his own political battles in Moscow with President Yeltsin, wrote a message of sympathy to his fellow-countrymen. He blamed Dudayev for everything.

'The tragic events in Grozny on 5 June, 1993 ... led to the deaths of people who were victims of a regime which has tried and is trying to hold on to power with the aid of bayonets and fear. It is to be regretted that the man who organized the bloody reprisals still bears the title of Russian general. I hope that justice will give its assessment of this tragedy and the culprits will receive the punishment they deserve,' he wrote in *Rossiiskaya Gazeta*.

These sentiments did him no political good in Moscow. There, reporting of the latest Chechen crisis had been slanted by the pro-presidential media to demonstrate to Russian voters how the black-skinned gunmen of Khasbulatov's ethnic homeland preferred bullets to ballots when it came to sorting out their problems.

'An armed power crisis,' Channel One's news programme reported on the night of 5 June. 'This is how many observers see the events of the past few days in the Russian Speaker's homeland, the Chechen Republic. The referendum did not take place. The mass meeting on Theatre Square has been dispersed.'

The inference drawn in Moscow was that Khasbulatov, unable to escape the Chechen savagery in his blood, would do the same thing himself given half a chance.

*

But it was Yeltsin who turned the Russian army on his opponents, in the autumn, when a crisis very similar to the Chechen drama of the summer blew up in Moscow. Infuriated by endless bickering over the shape of the future Russian constitution, Yeltsin outlawed the Russian parliament on Tuesday, 21 September, 1993. There was no legal basis for his act, and the Russian Constitutional Court declared it illegal. Yeltsin outlawed the Constitutional Court.

In a night of frost and high drama, Khasbulatov's parliament retaliated by outlawing Yeltsin's presidency. Inside the White House, a blustering Vice-President Alexander Rutskoi was named 'President' in Yeltsin's place. New 'defence' and 'interior' ministers were grouped around him. Yeltsin's opponents gathered around the parliament building which, two years before, had been the Russian president's headquarters during the August 1991 coup.

Soldiers and interior ministry troops were sent into town to protect the president. They sat and smoked, looking bored, in trucks tucked unobtrusively under the bridge by the Yeltsin government buildings at Staraya Square.

The news of a huge political scandal was a shot in the arm for the usually lugubrious crowds of red flag-wavers who sometimes still protested on street corners around Moscow. Outside the enormous parliament, on the ragged waste ground behind the riverside building, they gathered to support Khasbulatov and his 'government' . . . quick-breathed, bright-eyed, and ready for battle. Their weapons were handbags, or walking sticks, or the bits of brick that men were prying out of a crumbling wall by the car park. They whispered excitedly among themselves. Some of them had bull-horns, and yelled orders at the crowds. Out came the piano accordions, sentimental Soviet songs, and placards. They built bonfires. They sat through the night with their vodka bottles and sausage. They were having a field day . . .

. . . and another . . . and another . . . The stalemate dragged on for nearly two weeks. Neither side knew what to do next. The crowd of supporters at the parliament's campfires dwindled. The squeeze-boxes and the clumsy folk-dances petered out. Yeltsin's men cut off light and heat at the White House. Inside, the rebellious deputies and their 'president' shivered by candlelight, fearful, isolated, wondering what would befall them.

Demonstrating the advantages of incumbency, Yeltsin trumped the opposition's folk-dances by appearing at a grand open-air concert on the cobbles of Red Square on Sunday, 26 September. The golden couple of Russian culture – the cellist Mstislav Rostropovich and his wife, the opera singer Galina Vishnevskaya – were the star attractions. The bespectacled, benevolent Rostropovich had returned from abroad in 1991, to join Yeltsin in defending the White House against the Communist hard-liners. Now, his presence on the conductor's podium – and Vishnevskaya's in the audience, flanked by a smiling Yeltsin and Defence Minister Pavel Grachev – was a potent reminder to Russians everywhere that the great and the good of their country were on the president's side. Even the pianist was a political symbol of support for Yeltsin: Ignat, the American-raised son of Soviet dissident writer Alexander Solzhenitsyn. Even the piece they were playing, Tchaikovsky's *1812 Overture*, was a triumphal reminder that Russia always survived invasion, treachery, and times of troubles.

When, at the climax of the performance, the cannons and bells began to thunder out, I glanced over to where Yeltsin and Grachev were standing, whispering and grinning. (Vishnevskaya, looking disapproving, had moved aside.) Grachev was nodding theatrically in the direction of the White House, which cannot be seen from Red Square but from where the protesters must have been able to hear the mighty music of victory. He prodded Yeltsin in the ribs, leaned over and whispered something else in his ear. Both men burst out laughing.

Finally, the opposition cracked. Egged on by a wild speech from the panicking Rutskoi, the crowd outside charged away from the White House on the night of 3 October, seized the old Comecon building next door, and rushed towards the Ostankino tower from which Channel One television broadcast. The television abruptly went off the air. Troops rushed to stop the mob. There was hand-to-hand fighting in the corridors, and sharp-shooters on the roof. About sixty people were killed in the terrifying stampede. Although the rioters were beaten back from Ostankino, they had the initiative and, for that night at least, controlled two buildings in the centre of town. Yeltsin's authority hung by a thread.

The Russian president could expect no practical help from his democratic supporters. He rushed to the defence ministry and spent the night pleading with reluctant generals to back him. Eventually, Grachev agreed to begin a military assault. At dawn the next day, on 4 October, the tanks that had lined up across the river from the White House, in front of the Ukraine Hotel – a Stalin skyscraper – started shelling the parliament building. There were snipers on rooftops, a burning bus or two on the street outside parliament, and journalists wheedling their way into rooms all over the Ukraine Hotel for a grandstand view. The top floors of the battered White House, all shattered masonry and glass, caught fire: thick smoke rose off the blackened stump into the sky.

Something surreal was going on at the fringes of this scene of destruction. A crowd gathered on the bridge connecting the Ukraine Hotel to the White House. One was shot by a sniper, but that didn't deter the rest of the seekers after extreme sensation, post-Soviet style. They were enjoying every moment. Whenever a tank fired into the White House, the disaster tourists cheered and clapped, yelling encouragement as if they were at a football match. 'Whoooo-EEEE! Go for it, boys!' they screamed, oblivious of, or indifferent, to the danger.

By the afternoon, the rebels had had enough. A surrender was negotiated. Terrified, dirty and exhausted, 'President' Rutskoi, Khasbulatov, the 'ministers' and the surviving deputies emerged from the ruins to be handcuffed and led away to jail. A curfew was imposed. Snipers and scuffles were subdued before morning.

The official death toll was 149. But the White House was closed off to public inspection. Panicky rumours did the rounds: there were suggestions that the tunnels under the building were clogged with uncounted bodies, and that Yeltsin's men were covering up the extent of their destruction. People from the defeated opposition whispered that many more – four, five hundred – people had really died. No one ever knew the truth.

# NINE

The fire in the White House went out. The black smoke above was blown away by the wind. But the October Events, as they were always elliptically referred to afterwards in Russia, left a deep pall of gloom in Moscow. People were suddenly ashamed of their own wildness. They looked back at the last two years, and saw nothing but excess. In hushed voices, as another winter deepened, they wondered longingly whether there would ever be peace and quiet in Russia again.

'Look at it,' sighed a taxi driver taking me over the bridge past the ruined, discoloured White House. 'Look what they've done to it . . . No, look what *we've* done to it, with our passions and our politics and our feuds. It's a real shame . . . and to attack the White House is the worst thing of all. It used to be such a beauty.'

I didn't share his architectural tastes – I had always preferred the taxi-driver joke that the squat, overstuffed White House looked like a giant armchair – but I sympathized. I had felt just as shocked and disoriented when I left the office, the morning after the White House siege ended, and found that the janitor in my building had blocked off the street entrance to the courtyard with an improvised barricade of park benches. He'd been right to do it: the Tass building, just up the road, was one of the last to be cleared of snipers. I had no reason to feel so threatened: I'd seen plenty of fighting in the former Soviet Union. But this amateur barricade seemed much more frightening, even though I pushed it aside without much trouble, simply because of where it was: at my home, where my husband lived, where my cats and books and clothes were. It was irrational, and selfish, but it was how I felt.

Moscow in late October was consumed in shame, discomfort and self-criticism. It was the exact opposite of the post-coup euphoria of 1991. You had to go home early because of the curfew. Driving on roads near the White House, you kept being reminded they were all churned up by the tanks' caterpillar tracks. The ruin, visible along the river, was a mute reproach in bricks and mortar.

'Tanks in Moscow . . . It's hard to take it in,' Tanya, my cleaner, muttered when she turned up for work again a few days later. We were standing at the window, watching the grumpy janitor dragging back the benches to their proper places, on the grassless soil, under the bare trees. 'How could we Russians do such things to each other? This is a civilized country, right? But suddenly we're behaving as crazily as the blacks in the republics.'

*

Shooting and locking up his political opponents did Yeltsin no long-term harm. Russians found the months that followed the crisis unexpectedly reassuring. The frightening time of *dvoyevlastiye* – divided power – in which no one knew whether the president or the parliament was really in charge, was over. Yeltsin was now really becoming the strong ruler of Russia, the *khozyayin*, or master, that he wanted to be. With a single man at the top, and the Chechen Khasbulatov in prison, the old hierarchy of power slotted back into place. Yeltsin concentrated power in his own hands.

Sorrowfully, Yeltsin told the world that the attack on the White House had been a tragic necessity, a one-off act that had saved the democracy he had brought to Russia. Russia's Western aid donors and allies took a deep breath and fell in behind him. They didn't much like the debt Yeltsin had incurred to Grachev and the conservative, anti-Western military. They were worried about what kind of payment the military would demand in return, and which way Russian politics would develop. Disappointed in their bright 1991 hopes that Russia would emerge from the Soviet ruins a normal, peaceable, Western-style democracy, they now acknowledged that Yeltsin's notion of democracy was flawed; but, diplomats and politicians said resignedly, they didn't have anyone else to hang their Russia policy on.

Yeltsin outraged Russian Communists by removing the goose-stepping honour guard from 'Post Number One', Lenin's tomb. Instead, slovenly, gum-chewing, fag-smoking cops were set to loiter under the red marble archway of the Communist holy place on

Red Square. The clock turned backwards towards more authoritarian times. The first television channel's nine o'clock news broadcast got back its old Soviet name, Vremya. Newscasters dropped the grand new names of countries or aspiring countries in the post-Soviet world – Kyrgyzstan and Tatarstan – and went back to calling them by old regional names, Kyrgyzia and Tatariya. Yeltsin was not reverting to Soviet Communism, but these changes did indicate he was beginning to look for a more effective model of strong rule to keep Russia together.

Seeing which way the wind was blowing, Russian regions and ethnic republics suddenly stopped demanding more power, money and freedom. Hostile regional bosses were sacked and their organizations dispersed. Even mutinous little Tatarstan scuttled meekly back into the fold by February 1994. Only Chechnya ignored the pull back towards Moscow.

A new constitution was approved by referendum in December 1993. Written by Yeltsin, the constitution gave the president much more power than before, and parliaments of the future much less. Russians didn't care that it was not very democratic to concentrate power in one man's hands; what they wanted at the moment was stability.

A new parliament was elected at the same time, and given the Tsarist-era name of State Duma. Most of the anti-Yeltsin deputies from the old parliament were banned from running for re-election. This limitation on freedom was ignored by the majority of Russians who by now would do anything for a quiet life. Voters who supported Yeltsin and democracy tried to vote for democratic candidates, but the democratic politicians, who had come to represent the chaos of the last two years in many Russians' eyes, couldn't stop quarrelling even now. So many rival democrats stood for each seat that the pro-Yeltsin vote was split. Voters who disliked Yeltsin cast their ballots for Vladimir Zhirinovsky, a wise-cracking nationalist with a bash-the-blacks, hang-the-criminals programme. He did well, and the new parliament filled up again with deputies hostile to liberal reform. It mattered less than before, because the new parliament had less power. But the age of the liberals was ending.

After the elections, the liberal ministers that the West liked resigned or were sacked. They were replaced by more old-fashioned administrative types, the sleek butlers of the Soviet edifice. These new ministers promised what the people wanted, stability, and sneered that the chaotic economic reforms of the past two years had been 'market romanticism'.

After the elections, Yeltsin also reorganized the secret police. He presented the changes as a reform, designed to make the KGB successor bodies more liberal. In fact, all it did was reunite more of them under his control and increase his personal power. Yeltsin abolished the weak post-Soviet security ministry, which had answered to the prime minister, calling it the 'last bulwark of the totalitarian system'. He replaced it with a new Federal Counter-Intelligence Service (known in Russian as the FSK) that reported directly to him. He said the FSK was quite different from the old KGB: its 75,000 operatives could not police ordinary Russians, and it would not interfere in politics.

But sceptics thought the real reason for the reshuffle was that the security ministry had proved too weak to help Yeltsin defeat the parliamentary opposition; he wanted to make sure it was never so weak again. Their suspicion that the Russian president wanted more, not less, surveillance of his people was reinforced when he appointed a tough old KGB man, the former security minister Nikolai Golushko, to head the FSK, instead of a new-style liberal. Golushko had run the Ukrainian KGB before Ukraine became independent; he had spent most of his thirty-year career in the notorious Fifth Directorate, hunting dissidents.

This 'reform' added the FSK to two ex-KGB directorates already under Yeltsin's direct control: the Eighth Directorate, now known as FAPSI (Federal Agency for Government Communications and Information), whose job was still to gather intelligence by electronic eavesdropping on top politicians, and the Ninth Directorate that ran Kremlin security. The 30,000-man Ninth Directorate, now called the Main Guards Division, was still run by its old KGB boss, General Mikhail Barsukov; it also controlled the ex-KGB Alpha and Vympel anti-terrorist units. Yeltsin also had a personal bodyguard of a few thousand men, headed by another ex-Ninth Directorate general, Alexander Korzhakov.

The secret police began months of reorganization in the early spring of 1994. It ended by reinstating all but a dozen of the KGB's two hundred top officials. Although Yeltsin was trying hard to be a democrat, wrote one expert on the KGB, Yevgeniya Albats, he 'simply could not imagine a government structure in which the KGB was absent'.[37]

Yeltsin's enemies had one last burst of defiance. In February, the new parliament voted to amnesty all the leaders of the October rebellion. Yeltsin ordered his law-and-order bosses to ignore the parliament and keep the prisoners in Lefortovo jail, but his plea to obey the president rather than the law was ignored. Khasbulatov, Rutskoi and the rest of his enemies walked jauntily to freedom two days later.

Yeltsin blamed the new FSK boss, Nikolai Golushko, and sacked him.

The lesson Sergei Stepashin, Golushko's deputy, learned as he took over the FSK at the young age of forty-two was that personal loyalty to the president, however illegal his demands might be, was the only quality that mattered in the new Russia taking shape.

*

After two years of dangerous chaos, Russians were more than willing to believe that strengthening the state, and its leader, was a good thing. Most people preferred the idea of a strong president who could control his country, and impose reform from above, to the quagmire of democratic quarrels they had been living in until now. They explained rather sadly that it was hard for 'slaves' or 'half-slaves' of the Soviet hierarchy to cope with complete freedom all at once, and that they needed what he was now offering, *poryadok*: order, a firm hand from on high to prevent them from

---

37. Yevgeniya Albats, *The State Within a State: The KGB and Its Hold on Russia – Past, Present and Future*, published in the USA in 1994, quoted in *New York Times*, section 7, p. 11, in a book review by Glenn Garclik.

giving way to excess and emotion, a chance to feel themselves a great nation again, a return to normality.

The act which best symbolized this back-to-the-future new order was the expulsion of the 'blacks' from Moscow by Yuri Luzhkov, the squat, businesslike, immensely wealthy mayor. While the Russian capital was still in the grip of curfew, and shock, Luzhkov's men swooped on the street market traders and arrested the lot of them. The markets were shut down. Caucasians were kicked out of Moscow *en masse*. A compulsory registration system was set up for those that plucked up the courage to return. There must be *poryadok*, thundered Luzhkov; it was high time to crack down on Caucasian crime.

To foreigners living in Moscow, this onslaught on the hapless Caucasians seemed, at best, a bizarre way of diverting public attention from Yeltsin's dubious role in the October Events. At worst, it was interpreted as a sign that the racist Zhirinovsky's Russia-for-the-Russians extremist agenda had moved into the political mainstream, and that the persecution of Azeris, Dagestanis or Chechens was now officially sanctioned.

But Russians, whatever their political views, were delighted. 'Luzhkov is quite right. It's time to crack down on these black criminals,' Yevgeniya told me firmly over tea. When I told her that Western newspapers were comparing Luzhkov's raids on the market with Nazi persecution of Jews in the 1930s, she grew indignant. 'Nonsense!' she said robustly. 'It's quite different. These blacks are not at the same level of development as us Russians. They're robbing us, ripping us off, committing rapes and murders. They've got to be stopped.'

Anatoly the driver put it more simply. As we idled at an autumn traffic jam, watching policemen bundle two miserable dark-skinned youths into the back of a car and drive off down the middle of the road, sirens screaming, he turned to me and grinned.

'Luzhkov's a great guy,' he said with satisfaction.

*

Everything was back in its proper place in the scaled-down Russian remake of the Soviet hierarchy of power – except the Chechens.

This defiant absence was further proof to Russians that Chechens were destructive and dangerous to their state. The wolf was prowling in the darkness outside. Since it was no longer really acceptable to hate Jews, or Americans, the Chechens took their place as the External Enemy of the new Russian order.

# TEN

Dudayev was less lucky than Yeltsin. His people had different ideas about how they wanted to be ruled. After he cracked down on dissent, they turned away from him in distaste.

*

As soon as Grozny was back under the armed control of his National Guardsmen, Dudayev flew nonchalantly off on a tour of France, Germany and Austria. A *Le Monde* correspondent spotted him emerging from the Royal Monceau Hotel in Paris, where he spent four days dining with oil, defence and industry contacts and tested out the French Mirage-2000 jet. In Vienna, he told journalists he had introduced direct presidential rule at home out of 'a desire to prevent an escalation of violence, not out of dictatorial ambitions'.

But violence escalated anyway. Unidentified gunmen used grenade-launchers to blow up twelve transformer stations around Grozny in mid-October during five hours of fighting, leaving the city without electricity or water for twenty-four hours. Unclaimed bombs damaged Grozny government buildings in late November. In December 1993, the presidential palace in Grozny was evacuated as hundreds of opposition gunmen waiting on Sheikh Mansur Square threatened to attack. There were assassination attempts against Dudayev. He blamed them on the Russian secret police.

Dudayev ruled Grozny with a mixture of authoritarianism and incompetence. When a gathering of more than 1,000 clan elders, Ruslan Kutayev's Council of *Teips*, resolved to meet in December 1993 at the huge Grozny theatre to discuss whether to hold more parliamentary elections, Dudayev was desperate to stop it. Not only did the Council rival his own *Mekhkel* and command equal respect from the Chechens, but it had also won the support of key elements in his own armed forces: the commanders of the Chechen *spetsnaz* unit, the Grozny Police Task Force, the Shali tank regiment, and Ibragim Suleimenov, commander of a large armed unit. 'The republic's leadership is in panic,' Kutayev announced, saying Dudayev would do his utmost to disrupt the congress. He was right. First, the Mufti appointed by Dudayev, Mukhamad Khusein Khadzhi Aslanbekov, declared it inadmissible to divide Muslims by clan. Then Dudayev surrounded the city centre with loyal National Guardsmen. The council meeting was postponed.

Also in December, the only opposition newspaper that functioned in Grozny was raided by four armed policemen. They trashed the office of Yaraghi Mamodayev's *Justice* and confiscated its computers and papers. Mamodayev, the Chechen official who had risen from Oudayev's deputy premier to premier, had been sacked in the spring of 1993 and later set up a rival 'government of national trust' in Moscow. *Justice* had devoted its last three issues to an explanation of Mamodayev's Moscow 'government'.

Grozny's official economy shrank and its miseries increased. Armoured personnel carriers rolled over the potholed streets every night as residents hurried home before evening curfew deadlines. Many schools closed. Pensions went unpaid for months. Dudayev urged his people to be 'as vigilant as spies'. Thousands of people, Russians but also Chechens, left.

Many Chechens blamed Dudayev, and the close circle of relatives and allies whom he had appointed to run the economy, for letting the economy collapse to line their own pockets. When Grozny oil workers went on strike in the spring of 1994, strike committee chairman Akhmad Abdulkhanov said oil workers had not been paid for more than six months. At the same time, he added, 'a full-flowing river of oil has gone out of the Chechen republic. Fantastic quantities of hard currency are going into someone's pockets.' Dudayev blamed Russia. He said Chechnya had gone on refining oil and shipping it to Moscow, but Moscow hadn't paid.

The Chechen president tried to restart talks with Russia, but his envoys were repeatedly snubbed in Moscow. He reacted in extravagant fashion, extending the hand of friendship instead to extreme nationalists in Russia such as General Alexander Sterligov and making declarations favouring the 'restoration of the Soviet Union'

– on the grounds that it had been easier to live under Soviet rule than it was proving to live as Russia's neighbour.

*

Chechnya's official economy might be grinding to a halt, but the unofficial economy was flourishing. 'A sort of criminal "free economic zone" has formed and functions actively in Chechnya,' Sergei Shakhrai complained in the weekly *Argumenty i Fakty* in July 1994, soon after being removed from a job as Russian nationalities minister in which he had studied the problem from close up. What annoyed Shakhrai most was the huge instant profits made by private traders importing cheap consumer goods into Russia from abroad, via Grozny, without paying a penny in tariffs to the Russian state.

Every trader in Russia knew that Chechnya's twilight status – its non-existent republican tax system, and the lack of customs controls at its borders because Russia still considered it a part of its own territories – made it a perfect place to import goods through. Up to 150 planes, hired privately from companies like Air Azerbaijan and Air Ukraine, landed in Grozny airport every month. Because they were not monitored, the planes broke international aviation guidelines. The traders who rented the planes took them shopping to the Middle East or China, coming home with holds stuffed full of cheap consumer goods for resale. The English-language newspaper *The Moscow Times* quoted one Grozny trader, Ruslan, as saying each flight brought in at least $200,000 worth of goods, and a trader working full-time could earn between $100,000 and $150,000 a year. Prices at Grozny's packed markets, where everything from video recorders and French perfume to Kalashnikov sub-machine-guns could be bought, were much lower than elsewhere in Russia. Russian import tariffs at the time ranged from 20 per cent to 30 per cent. The trade was so profitable that as many as 40 per cent of the working population of Chechnya was involved in it – especially since wages and pensions in Chechnya now came months late, if they came at all. Despite the lack of official money, Mercedes without number-plates purred through the bankrupt city.

The traders were not all Chechens. Russians, Ukrainians and Caucasians flocked in to do business without interference from Moscow. 'Grozny has become the wholesale market of the Caucasus,' said Ruslan, with sly Chechen enjoyment of pulling a fast one on Russia.

As well as the plane scam, there were also the train robberies in eastern Chechnya. Local men stopped Russian trains travelling through their territory and 'liberated' their cargoes. The liberal *Moscow News* weekly said Russian train teams working on the stretch of the North Caucasus line running through Chechnya were too scared of possible Chechen vengeance to testify about repeated gangster raids. But it quoted an unnamed chief of the train network's paramilitary guard unit at its Russian base in Mineralniye Vody as saying: 'We register cargo train robberies almost daily. In Chechnya, there is a no-man's-land where bandits enjoy free reign. Carriages are robbed all over Chechnya. This is done most brazenly on the road section between Gudermes and Khasavyurt [in Dagestan]. Whole villages, from young to old, take part in robberies, and particularly noteworthy in this respect is the Chechen village of Kadi-yurt, where such thefts are practised by the whole population who approach the train together with motor vehicles, tractors and hoists. In half an hour they unload a whole carload of sheet steel.'

Even people from neighbouring Caucasian statelets were angered by the increasingly impudent train robberies. 'Hold on, I'm a Caucasian too!' alarmed Dagestani train passengers would cry as their wallets were removed by gun-toting hoodlums. 'Those people had no respect for anyone, even their Caucasian brothers,' recalled Timur Dzhafarov, a journalist from Dagestan. 'It was a chaotic time when they felt they could get away with anything.'

The trade routes running south-east out of crime-ridden Russia went through Chechnya. But there was also a huge crime wave on the roads and railway lines running north-west out of Russia, over the porous borders of the Baltic states, and into Europe. Hold-ups and train robberies were a danger all around the north-western border. Russian metals, minerals and consumer goods were vanishing in all directions. However, Shakhrai's catchy phrase about the 'criminal free trade zone' in Chechnya, which chimed with their existing suspicion of blacks, focused Russian attention almost exclusively on crime in the south.

With gloomy relish, Moscow chewed over both the factual stories of Chechen crime and the lurid rehashes offered up by their own press. 'Chechnya is called a republic without prisons,' ranted the conservative Russian army paper *Krasnaya Zvezda* (Red Star).

> When Dzhokhar Dudayev came to power, he disbanded all jails. As a result over 4,000 criminals were set free and formed into units of 'fighters for Chechen freedom'. The worst criminals, such as the serial murderer Supyan Khamzatov, became the president's bodyguards. By a special decree, the president legalized the possession and bearing of rifles, regardless of their origin. According to conservative estimates, individuals hold more than 41,000 firearms today. This works out at one gun per Chechen family. By another decree, inhabitants of Chechnya who have committed crimes outside the republic are not subject to extradition. Overnight, Chechnya has turned into a safe haven for criminals. Car thieves register their stolen Mercedes or Volvos for 500,000 roubles in Grozny and enjoy their new possessions unhindered ... Chechnya is under the sway of criminals. The Russian-speaking population is hardest hit: no police protection, no tribal ties. Kidnapping and other forms of blackmail are the order of the day ...

Crime stories began to govern Russian policy towards Chechnya. Just before Russian parliamentary elections in December 1993, Yeltsin addressed his compatriots' fears with a stinging rebuke to Dudayev for provoking instability in the south. The Russian president ordered his government to 'delineate the Chechen borders and take them under control'. Dudayev took this, not as a piece of electioneering, but as a veiled declaration of war. The Russian media had been paying far too much attention to the security of railroad traffic, he said; it was part of a new anti-Chechen campaign: 'Under the pretext of guarding railway trains, Russia is planning to ensure the presence of its troops in Chechnya.'

Dudayev answered threat with threat, warning that Russia's 'behind-the-scenes preparations for a new Caucasus war' would culminate in disaster for Russia itself. For all the heated words on both sides, nothing was actually done to seal off Chechnya's borders.

The outcry in Russia against Dudayev's 'Chechen mafia' grew so vociferous that one wealthy Moscow Chechen tried to explain his belief that the organization which so terrified Russians did not exist. He suggested that what Russians really felt threatened by was not a Chechen mafia of mythological proportions, but simply Chechnya's assumption of nationhood. 'There never was such a thing as the Chechen mafia,' the businessman, who did not give his name, told *Argumenty i Fakty*. 'It was dreamed up by promotion-hungry officials of law-enforcement agencies and sensation-seeking journalists . . . With the current total chaos and widespread corruption on virtually all levels [in Russia], it is very convenient to have a scapegoat. In this respect, if I may say so, the Chechens have been equated with the Jews. It was the Jews who used to be responsible for everything, not so long ago . . .

'What is a mafia? An organization with a rigidly structured hierarchy which affects all spheres of activity in the state, including politics. A mafia must have a coordinating council, headed by a "godfather" . . . In addition, a mafia has funds of its own. But we don't have anything of the sort. We don't live by gangsterish laws. Authoritarianism as such is alien to Chechens. Leaders are usually elected spontaneously, but you can lose this leadership at any moment . . . After being elected president, Dudayev apparently forgot how Chechens relate to one another. He has forgotten about the Chechens' reluctance to submit to authoritarianism. This is one of the reasons the conflict arose in the republic.'

No one in Russia wanted to listen to explanations like this.

Newspaper readers in Russia were so outraged at the Chechen antics they read about in the press that they responded with disproportionate violence. The Chechenpress news agency said in March 1994 that ten coffins containing the bodies of Chechen victims of Russian attack had been shipped home in the month of February alone. Chechenpress blamed the race-hate killings on the

Russian secret service, but what struck me as scary about this snippet of news was the whiff of pogrom that came off it.

\*

The number of Chechens willing to take over from Dudayev grew fast. The opposition that had been gunned out of Grozny in 1993 fled to Nadterechny District, in the north-west. There, or in Moscow, they were joined by others who fell out with Dudayev. Nadterechny District was unlike the rest of Chechnya in many ways. It was flat, not hilly, and it had a lot of Russian Cossack villages. It had never had much to do with Dudayev. The presidential election of 1991, which had brought Dudayev to power, had not been held here. Local Russians wouldn't have voted for Dudayev, and Nadterechny Chechens had old loyalties to their kinsman, the Communist boss Doku Zavgayev. Here was a natural focus for opposition forces.

But not all the Dudayev opponents who passed through Nadterechny District had the kind of ideas that Russia wanted to encourage. The ex-Soviet petrochemicals minister Salambek Khadzhiyev and the Daimokhk (Fatherland) opposition movement's leader Lecha Umkhayev told Russian newspapers that it would be good for Chechnya if Dudayev's rule ended, but bad for Chechnya to become part of Russia by signing the Federation Treaty. 'We are in favour of the closest possible economic relations with Russia, of warm relations with our great neighbour – but political independence and national sovereignty are the dream and the goal of an absolute majority of the Chechen people,' Khadzhiyev told the weekly paper *Moscow News*.

At first, Moscow flirted with Yaraghi Mamodayev. They held talks on a compromise treaty which would give Chechnya 'special status' inside Russia. But Mamodayev's lack of support inside Chechnya gradually became clear, and his influence with Moscow waned. In early 1994, the Kremlin began to look favourably on a more provincial Chechen leader, the mayor of Nadterechny District. Umar Avturkhanov, a stooped man with a mean pursed mouth, was an ex-policeman who had been elected to run his district in 1991. He had exactly the right kind of background –

years of service to the state, a commitment to law and order, an understanding of the Soviet hierarchy – that the Russian security élite liked in a subordinate local leader. Avturkhanov endeared himself further to the Russian establishment by his tough descriptions of clashes with Dudayev's forces. In August 1993, he told a local paper, *Severny Kavkaz* (North Caucasus), how he had ordered 350 policemen to arrest a 'criminal gang' that Dudayev had sent to Nadterechny in 'just another attempt by official Grozny to finish off the opposition'. He said the heavily armed Grozny troops had fought for a week on the edge of Nadterechny District before being forced to withdraw. They wanted to force him to surrender the district's weapons, but he refused. 'We've never given up our weapons and are not going to,' Avturkhanov said. 'It's not that we are going to wage a war: we just do not trust them.'

In the spring of 1994, more Dudayev enemies materialized at the head of small armed groups. The Chechen president quarrelled with his bodyguard, Ruslan Labazanov, who went into opposition with a force of 500 men. The ex-mayor of Grozny, Beslan Gantemirov, out on a limb but also operating from Nadterechny, fielded a separate group of hundreds of fighters.

Chechnya was slipping out of Dudayev's control. He ruled Grozny itself, though with difficulty. He also ran the south-western plains and the south-eastern hills, where his family came from and where blood loyalties bound the villagers to him. But he had no control over the north-west and little over several parts of central Chechnya. Elections were due in a year.

If Russia had had the patience to carry on waiting, as it had since 1991, Dudayev's growing unpopularity would probably have finished his political career off by itself. But Russia by now had a more macho agenda than in the confused days of the Soviet break-up. The military and security officials who were in the ascendant in Moscow after helping Yeltsin put down the parliamentary rebellion were rebuilding national pride. They wanted to purge Russia of all the humiliations of radical democracy, and reimpose order on the chaos. They had two targets: the criminal new rich of Russia, and Dudayev's Chechnya.

# ACT FOUR

# WAR

# ONE

While Yeltsin was still looking for ways of restoring stability and *poryadok* in Russia, at the end of 1993, and the new FSK police was still in the throes of reorganization, the whole country was shocked by a crime that seemed to symbolize the worst of post-Soviet excess. It featured marauding darkies attacking innocent Russians, guns, violence, AIDS, a whiff of Islamic fundamentalism, and unbelievable quantities of stolen money being literally thrown away – all the worst nightmares of the fearful Russian television viewer.

On 24 December, four masked men raided a secondary school in the southern town of Rostov-on-Don. They commandeered a bus, then a helicopter, then flew from one town to the next around southern Russia for four days. They said the helicopter was packed with explosives. They wanted to be flown to Iran for medical treatment because they had AIDS. They demanded, and got, $10 million in ransom. They released some hostages, but kept the Russian helicopter pilots. They were picked up on 28 December on their last moonlit flit – which they thought was to Khasavyurt, a town in Dagestan just near the Chechen border – after the pilots redirected the helicopter in bad weather to the Dagestani capital, Makhachkala. The masked gunmen didn't notice they were going to the wrong place. They were arrested when the helicopter landed. The hostages were freed, to sighs of relief all round and pats on the back from Defence Minister Grachev for the quick-witted Russian pilots. Dagestani interior ministry officials said there would only have been 'minimal' chances of catching the robbers at Khasavyurt, which because it was near Chechnya was known as a den of thieves.

The explosives turned out to be fakes, and the kidnappers didn't have AIDS. 'Most' of the money was recovered, but Major-General Gennady Chebotaryov, the policeman who headed the rescue operation, said the men had thrown a million dollars out of the helicopter over Dagestan. 'The terrorists decided to part with the dollars not only for psychological reasons but also for physical reasons. The dollars weighed 180 kg,' he said. He pleaded with people living under the flight path to return this 'unusual form of material evidence'.

Christmas was more or less cancelled in my office. The story came at just the right time to catch the press in the Western holiday lull and fill world newspapers. Grumbling, I left the idyllic country dacha where my husband was looking after our visiting families, leaving them building snowmen and skiing under the pines, and started commuting through the snowy fields every day to write my share of the reports. It cheered me up to think of sinewy Dagestani and Chechen villagers looking up at the night sky as the helicopter passed overhead and catching the $100 bills raining down on their heads.

The hijackers were later officially identified as a Russian army flight navigator who had been sacked for drunkenness, an Uzbek, a Kazakh, and an Azeri.

But who cared what officials said after the event? Marina Vassiliyevna, the housekeeper at the dacha, had a mellow grin on her face when I came back. After brandy and her first English mince pies, she was hovering by the radio with her assortment of stray dogs. She was thrilled by the news drama, and had drawn her own conclusions about who to blame.

'Oh, those Chechens!' she said appreciatively. 'You'll never be bored here.'

*

The perception that the December hijacking was the fault of Chechens was widespread in Russia. This was exactly the kind of post-Soviet crime that Yeltsin's tough new law-and-order bosses were determined to stop.

In March, the secret police boss Sergei Stepashin and Yuri Baturin, Yeltsin's overall national security adviser, announced that the reorganization of the FSK was finished. So, they said, were two years of upheaval and 'emotional, incompetent, politically prompted changes'.

In May, Yeltsin gave the FSK *carte blanche* to sort out border conflicts. He made a speech to the security agency, saying: 'The armed conflicts near the Russian border, which threaten to spill over on to Russian territory in certain areas, constitute an immediate threat to Russia. It will take a great deal of effort to find ways to neutralize conflicts in countries adjacent to Russia. The intelligence services must discover in good time the driving force behind any conflict and the chances of a political settlement based on compromise.'

He did not specifically name Chechnya as an FSK target, but it was so widely understood that the troublesome little southern republic was to blame for the crime spreading across Russia that he hardly needed to.

*

Dudayev spent the spring of 1994 asking for negotiations, but only with Yeltsin himself. He raged against Russian imperialism, but at the same time deluged the Russian president with wheedling personal letters asking for a face-to-face meeting and offering advice on how Yeltsin should sort out his domestic problems.

But Yeltsin had an almost chemical aversion to Dudayev. He ignored the letters, and refused a meeting. It might have been unwise for him to hold personal talks with the Chechen leader, since that would suggest he recognized Dudayev as the legitimate ruler of Chechnya. But the only explanation Yeltsin ever gave, two years later, in May 1996, was Tsarishly grandiloquent: 'I could not negotiate with Dudayev. Dudayev was a man the president could not meet.'

Lower-level negotiations never got off the ground, partly because of Yeltsin's choice of Sergei Shakhrai, a man Dudayev detested, as Russia's negotiator. Variously nationalities minister, presidential negotiator, MP and deputy prime minister in 1994, Shakhrai was young and looked harmless, with fluffy hair and innocent pink cheeks and the thick moustache of his Cossack inheritance. But he was not harmless at all, and he had a long list of enemies to prove it: Communists and democrats in Moscow, and leaders of ethnic élites elsewhere. Shakhrai was a subtle and pitiless exponent of the imperial motto 'divide and rule'; his genius was for exacerbating ethnic problems between regions until Moscow could justify stepping in and taking direct control. In early 1994, he listed as his achievements the restoration of Russian rule in Tatarstan, peacemaking in Ingushetia – when peace had not been made, but Russian troops had been installed – and the revival of the Cossacks, which had created new tensions all over the southern regions bordering Chechnya. Dudayev blamed Shakhrai for causing the fighting between Ingushi and Ossetians in 1992, and had denounced the Russian negotiator as an 'enemy of the Chechen people'. Shakhrai now confirmed his suspicions by doing all he could to hinder the cause of reconciliation with Chechnya.

When Russia's parliament voted for talks with Chechnya, in March, Shakhrai slipped a clause into their declaration that he knew Dudayev would reject. The talks were shelved. When Yeltsin ordered the Russian government to hold talks with Chechnya, in April, the government took three months to put together a negotiating team – and then appointed Shakhrai to run it. The talks were shelved.

Emil Payin, head of the presidential think-tank that had innocently drawn up policy proposals for the second lot of talks that never took place, now began to smell a rat. 'Why this big practical joke of preparing "consultations with Grozny" and a "draft delimitation agreement"?' Payin wrote later. 'With hindsight, we can suggest that . . . this was all being done to give the appearance of a negotiating process . . . Russian political reality at that time became such that the president was *obliged to create the appearance of talks*.'[1]

\*

At the same time, but secretly, Shakhrai and Stepashin were picking a Chechen opposition leader for Russia to back to overthrow Dudayev. They chose Umar Avturkhanov, after he came to Moscow in June, met them both, and won the Russian secret police

---

1. Emil Payin, *Izvestia*, 10 Feb. 1995.

chief's support.[2] In the time-honoured fashion of Soviet-sponsored factions in every proxy conflict of Cold War days, Avturkhanov's Provisional Council then began publicly lobbying in Moscow for recognition by Russia as the official Chechen government.

Avturkhanov did not have to wait long. Three more hijackings in the south, just like the December one except that they were now really led by Chechens, raised anti-Dudayev feeling in Russia to fever pitch over the next three months. By August, Yeltsin had officially recognized Avturkhanov and threatened, for the first time, to send troops to Chechnya.

These new copycat hijackings were handled by Stepashin and the FSK immediately after they got Yeltsin's permission to deal with border conflicts. They were all so similar that liberal deputies from the State Duma began, much later, to suspect that they might actually have been organized by the FSK, to discredit Dudayev and justify a tougher Russian policy against him; but such suspicions have been impossible to prove.

At the end of May, four masked men seized a bus with twenty-six people on board on the Rostov–Baku highway that runs across southern Russia. They drove to Mineralniye Vody airport and released all but four hostages during twenty hours of negotiations. Then they took a helicopter and flew to Chechnya, again with $10 million ransom, followed by Russian military helicopters. They landed east of Grozny. Dudayev, apparently anxious about the political capital Moscow could make out of these hijackers' Chechen destination, told his police to cooperate. Chechen special forces arrested three of the robbers. The fourth vanished into the forest. Somewhere along the way, $47,000 also vanished.

At the end of June, more gunmen – according to the Russian government 'mostly Chechens' like the previous group – struck at another bus on the same highway. This time, they took forty hostages and a $6 million ransom. Dudayev ordered his police to cooperate. The hijackers were arrested in Chechnya and flown back to Russia. By now, the terror Russian television watchers had felt in December had dissipated; these hijackings, in which no one

---

2. *Handelsblatt* and *Le Monde*, June 1994.

was hurt and the Chechen bad guys were always captured, were beginning to seem farcical.

At the end of July, four Chechens in their twenties, wearing black masks and armed with pistols and hand-grenades, seized a bus with forty-one passengers on board outside Mineralniye Vody and drove straight to the airport. They wanted $15 million and two helicopters. Unlike the others, this attack ended in tragedy. For the first time, Stepashin and the FSK imposed a news blackout, on the grounds that the Chechens had radios. Stepashin and Viktor Yerin, the hard-line interior minister, quarrelled about how to handle the crisis. Confusion descended on the airport, teeming with police squads, ambulances and officials. Before dawn, as the helicopters were preparing for take-off, the script everyone had got so used to changed. The Chechens withdrew their good will. Their information minister, Movladi Udugov, said more than 200,000 extra Russian troops had recently been deployed near Chechnya to intimidate it. Chechnya would shoot down any Russian helicopter that entered its airspace now, he said.

Russian forces attacked the hijackers before they left Mineralniye Vody airport. Five hostages and one hijacker were killed in the resulting blood-bath. Russia blamed the killings on one of the hijackers, whom they said had detonated a grenade in the cockpit of the getaway helicopter as Moscow's forces stormed it. Nineteen people were injured in the blast. An FSK spokesman said the Chechen miscreant was probably on drugs. Russian television showed chaotic pictures of bloodstained tarmac, a charred helicopter, and armoured personnel carriers racing up and down the airstrip. Two female hostages, apparently dead, were lying on the ground with blood drying on their faces. Two dark-haired Chechens, hands tied behind their backs, faces and shirts all blood and mud, lay in the darkened fields by the runway.

'There is no law left in Mineralniye Vody,' an exhausted FSK spokesman said.

Russia's political élite took two days to react. Then, on 31 July, television broadcasts were interrupted for a government statement. It said the bloodshed was Dudayev's fault, and threatened to use force to protect its citizens in Chechnya:

The policy of the current Chechen leadership has become the main destabilizing factor in the North Caucasus ... Organized criminal groups are perpetually infiltrating from Chechnya to commit dangerous crimes ... The Russian government states that if Russian citizens in Chechnya, whether ethnic Chechens or Russians, are subjected to violence, it will be forced to protect them in accordance with the Russian constitution.

The government praised Avturkhanov's opposition as 'sound forces which are struggling to restore the constitutional system and good relations with Russia'. Avturkhanov was wheeled out on television to appeal to Russia to recognize his Provisional Council as the legitimate government of Chechnya. He denied that he was asking for military help.

There were a few days of hysteria. Cossacks from Stavropol sent telegrams demanding a blockade against Chechnya, their eastern neighbour. Prime Minister Chernomyrdin said Chechnya was Russia's worst headache. Russia suspended flights to Grozny. Yeltsin's chief of staff accused Dudayev of beheading his opponents and putting the heads on public display. The tough deputy interior minister, Anatoly Kulikov, displayed grisly pictures of heads in pools of blood, and of headless corpses, and told journalists the dead men were policemen whom Dudayev had punished for helping Russia arrest the May hijackers.

Finally, in the middle of August, Yeltsin made a pronouncement. He promised solemnly that Russian troops would not go to Chechnya. 'Intervention by force is not permissible and will not be undertaken. Were we to apply pressure by force against Chechnya, it would rouse the whole Caucasus. There would be such a commotion, there would be so much blood, that no one would ever forgive us. It is absolutely impossible.'

The crisis subsided. But, despite Yeltsin's soft words, what it had shown was that Russia was at last ready for tough action after three years of indecision on Chechnya. Although the shape of the action to come was not yet clear, a style was beginning to emerge. The security and military chiefs who ran Russia in 1994 were not going to acknowledge the political dimension of the Chechen rebellion. What they saw in Chechnya was not separatists, but criminals, and what they had in mind to stop them was a cops-and-robbers operation.

Avturkhanov announced in August that the Provisional Council had formed a parallel government in Nadterechny District. Implausibly, he claimed it controlled all of Chechnya except Grozny and the surrounding districts. Avturkhanov said Russia had given him 1.5 billion roubles, so he could pay wages and pensions to the inhabitants of districts loyal to Russia. He did not admit what Khasbulatov told Czech television in September – that Russia was also giving him money for tanks and weapons – but soon afterwards he announced that his men had bought a large batch of Mi-24 and Mi-28 helicopters 'from a CIS republic'.

If Russia was now covertly arming Avturkhanov, that didn't stop other Chechen leaders from claiming Moscow's support too. Khasbulatov has also described how Salambek Khadzhiyev, the ex-petrochemicals minister and now the head of another Moscow-based government-in-exile, boasted of being backed by Russian Prime Minister Chernomyrdin.[3]

But a more entertaining opposition figure, who got more play in the Russian press over the summer, was the comic warlord Ruslan Labazanov. Dudayev's ex-minder was one of the few people that the Chechen president, himself so short he wore height extenders in his shoes, could honestly patronize because of his height; in more friendly days, Dudayev had called Labazanov 'my little bandit'. Labazanov changed sides: on 13 June, he attacked Grozny from the eastern town of Argun. Up to a hundred people were killed. He was driven out.

The stocky robber baron, who liked to call himself 'Robin Hood', was a blue-eyed twenty-seven. He was one of the Chechen jailbirds who had escaped in 1991, while serving a sentence for murder. Surrounded by stubbly fighters wielding rocket-launchers and machine-guns, he gave press interviews lolling on his bed, barefoot, caressing a revolver with his toes. He boasted that he

---

3. Ruslan Khasbulatov, *Chechnya: Mne Ne Dali Ostanovit' Voinu* (Chechnya: They Stopped Me Stopping the War), published in Moscow in 1995.

robbed the rich to feed the poor, and protected starving mothers and orphans; he carried a fat wad of $100 notes in his camouflage jacket and enjoyed peeling off handfuls of them to give to his warriors. After the June battle in Grozny, Labazanov declared blood vengeance on Dudayev and dressed his merry men up in black headbands signifying vendetta. Then he took them off to live at Khasbulatov's family village, Tolstoy-Yurt.

I loved the almost-too-good-to-be-true stories about Labazanov that appeared in the Moscow press, but it was no surprise that he came to a nasty end. He and two of his bodyguards were killed in June 1996 in a brawl at his mock fortress at Tolstoy-Yurt, which started when he tried to beat one of them up for drinking. By that time, Labazanov had been nominated a colonel in the Russian army, and, according to the *Moscow Times* newspaper, was said to work for Russia's security services.

As the summer of 1994 drew to a close, neither Avturkhanov nor any of the other opposition leaders were having much success in removing Dudayev, or even in attracting mass support for the kind of civil war that, with a bit of help from Moscow, had engulfed the rest of the Caucasus in recent years. The Chechens were too wary of Moscow for that. All that developed was what the Russian press called a 'weekend war', in which bands of armed men met, took potshots at each other, and went home again.

*

Suddenly, in August, a new unknown was added to the Chechen equation. Ruslan Khasbulatov, the disgraced former speaker of the old Russian parliament, had been commuting between Moscow and his Chechen family home at Tolstoy-Yurt ever since he was released from jail in February. In August, he announced formally that he was making his home in Chechnya. He obviously had his eye on taking power in Dudayev's place. He promised to make peace between all the rival factions, held talks with Avturkhanov on coordinating strategy, and formed a thirteen-man peacemaking group of religious leaders and elders, including the Mufti who had fallen out with Dudayev, Magomed-bashir-Khadzhi Arsanukayev. Big crowds gathered to hear the energetic Khasbulatov speak.

Whether Khasbulatov could have taken Dudayev's place is unclear, but what soon became clear was that Yeltsin could not tolerate the idea of his old Chechen enemy from Moscow digging into a new position of power – even if by doing so Khasbulatov removed Yeltsin's other old Chechen enemy, Dudayev. Yeltsin's hatred of Khasbulatov was as personal, and intense, as his hatred of Dudayev. In his self-justifying second autobiography, *Against the Grain*, in which he describes the parliament siege of October 1993 and explains why he ordered troops to shell the White House, Yeltsin rages against what he calls Khasbulatov's 'devious Oriental mind'. He wanted Khasbulatov in jail or, if not in jail, in disgrace. Khasbulatov's return to his homeland sent the president hurrying to find a way of sorting out the Chechen problem fast.

Suddenly, Yeltsin had no patience with the wait-and-see tactics of his think-tanks. He had even less time for the devious long-term strategies of Shakhrai. Shakhrai had already annoyed him by helping free Khasbulatov in February; in August, he had also dared suggest that, since Khasbulatov was now upstaging the feeble Avturkhanov, he might be Moscow's best chance to unseat Dudayev. In November, Yeltsin took the Chechen portfolio away from Shakhrai and gave it to Nationalities Minister Nikolai Yegorov, a dusty provincial hard-liner.

What Yeltsin wanted to hear now was that there was a short, sharp solution that would get both troublesome Chechens out of his life for good. This search for the simplistic answer was becoming characteristic of the president, who had become more remote from his people since October 1993 and seemed to be losing his old earthy grip on political reality. At the pinnacle of power on which his new hard-line allies had placed him, he now breathed the rarefied air of courtiers' flattery and artful improvements on the truth. (The elderly Yeltsin's drinking habits, health and mental powers had also been causing concern in Russia since, in April, he had failed to get off a plane in Dublin to meet the Irish prime minister. Was the president drunk? hung over? ill? people wondered. In August, he got drunk during a state visit to Germany. To hoots of laughter from bystanders, the stumbling president insisted on conducting an oompah band through a confused rendering of the Russian folk song 'Kalinka'.) When he made his rare television appearances in Russia these days, his voice was often rough and thick and his puffy eyes watchful and angry.

Yeltsin turned to the military and security strongmen whom he had promoted after they helped him ensure Khasbulatov's downfall, hoping they would tell him that the best way to get rid of Dudayev was by force. If the public comments they made a few months later, as war started in Chechnya, are anything to go by, that is exactly what Defence Minister Pavel Grachev and Security Council Secretary Oleg Lobov did. Encouraging Yeltsin to put himself further in debt to the military and security establishment was, after all, in their own interests. Lobov was a leading supporter of what Yeltsin's inner circle enthusiastically predicted would be a vote-winning 'small, victorious war' along the lines of the United States' engagement in Haiti.

But the new idea of war with Chechnya was kept secret, even from the people who had formulated Russia's Chechen policy until then. They were not told that their services were no longer required; they were not told that Chechnya policy was being decided instead by the army, the FSK, and the ex-KGB generals who were now Yeltsin's closest advisers. Emil Payin, head of the liberal Presidential Analytical Centre think-tank, was bewildered as he gradually became aware that a 'conspiracy-adventurist' solution to the Chechen problem was replacing his idea of feeding the opposition and letting Dudayev's regime collapse by itself. 'From September 1994 Russian politicians drew down a heavy curtain of secrecy over the Chechen stage,' he wrote after the war began. 'Our analytical centre stopped getting any instructions on the whole spectrum connected with these political questions, and the channels of information it received dried up too. After some time Shakhrai was also removed from the Chechen case, and his functions were given to a completely new man in this sphere, Yegorov. It became clear that a new "top secret" stage in Chechen policy was beginning, that boded ill.'[4]

---

4. Emil Payin, *Izvestia*, 11 Feb. 1995.

There was one last factor in the Chechen equation: oil. In September, Azerbaijan finally signed a multi-billion-dollar contract with a Western consortium to drill crude off its Caspian Sea shore. Russia's once meek foreign policy was getting angry and assertive; it declared the contract illegal and began a campaign to have the Caspian recognized in international law as a lake. This would give other littoral states – that is, Russia – part-control of the oil. If that didn't work, the only other way Russia could hope to control Caspian oil would be to get the contract for transporting it back through Russia to the West. But the main oil pipeline from Azerbaijan into Russia ran through Grozny. As long as the hostile Dudayev was in power, that would be impossible, and Russia would be kept out of the 'deal of the century'.

*

By late summer, there was a stronger whiff of repressiveness in the air in Russia. Like all bureaucracies, the FSK security police that Yeltsin had created needed to justify its existence, and its share of the national budget, by being seen to be working hard. In the FSK's case, this meant fighting the enemies of Russia as actively and visibly as possible. As 1994 wore on, the number of shadowy enemies apparently threatening Russia multiplied rapidly. In July, for instance, the agency announced it had uncovered a pro-fascist secret group called 'Werewolf', which was planning politically motivated terrorist activities. No one had ever heard of 'Werewolf', and the liberal press suggested Stepashin was deliberately reviving old KGB scare tactics. That story faded, but the sense of paranoia remained.

The politicians who flitted across television screens these days were slab-faced, brutal, military types: Stepashin, Grachev, Interior Minister Yerin, and Yeltsin's smirking bodyguard, ex-KGB General Alexander Korzhakov. The civilians, Shakhrai or Lobov, were almost as intimidating. The new élite was not very united; its members feuded among themselves; but they shared a tough vision of what a state's structure should be: hierarchical, with a strong leader, themselves in key positions, and a fearful, rigidly policed population below.

While few Russians were very bothered about the comic-opera goings-on in Chechnya, my liberal friends in Moscow were getting alarmed at the growing influence of these hard-line politicians inside Russia. Although they were pleased that a measure of old-fashioned *poryadok* had been reintroduced after October 1993, and liked the idea of less crime that the Kremlin was now promising, they were now beginning to suspect that these political disciplinarians wanted far more. Instead of just attacking post-Soviet abuses, it was beginning to seem that they wanted to destroy the new freedoms as well, and to reassert the old control of the Soviet ruling class over every aspect of their subjects' lives.

The new élite was already behaving as though it was above the law.

When a young reporter at the mass-market daily paper *Moskovsky Komsomolets* got too close to uncomfortable truths about top-level Russian army corruption in Germany, he was killed. Dima Kholodov was blown to pieces in his newsroom as he opened a suitcase he thought contained documents from an FSK source proving his case. Yeltsin, who had stifled an earlier report on the same army corruption, showed little regret. Under pressure, he got rid of the deputy defence minister at the heart of the case, but he insisted that the army could not be behind Kholodov's murder, and he clung on to Grachev.

On the day of Kholodov's funeral, the once liberal Yeltsin raged against 'irresponsible' journalists for reporting unfavourably on politicians, and suggested giving journalists licences which would be withdrawn if they failed to toe the government line. Journalists worried about their future freedom. They gave slightly tremulous thanks that there was now a private press; if they worked in the state media, they thought about moving.

Yeltsin's hatchet-faced élite began to hunt down the new rich. Armed tax police in black ski masks – another arm of the dismembered KGB – abseiled into the apartment of the most notorious New Russian, Sergei Mavrodi, and arrested him. The operation was shown on national television. Mavrodi ran MMM, a huge pyramid-scheme company which had lured millions of people into parting with their savings. MMM shares suddenly stopped trading, after rising for months in an apparently endless spiral of increasing wealth. Long queues of would-be millionaires hung round disconsolately outside MMM offices, fretting in the sticky clouds of summer pollution, desperate to get their money back. But it was gone forever. The arrest made Yeltsin's men less, not more, popular.

When the rouble's value suddenly halved, on 11 October, 1994, Yeltsin did not listen to economists who said the fall was a natural consequence of widening the money supply. He blamed 'sabotage', old Soviet terminology unheard for years. He called together his powerful but unelected inner Kremlin cabinet, the Security Council, and ordered the FSK to investigate who was guilty of the secret machinations that had caused 'Black Tuesday'.

The president's hard-line security chiefs, Generals Barsukov and Korzhakov, then launched a startling attack on a free-market banking friend of Moscow mayor Yuri Luzhkov, who was their rival for the president's ear. They sent armed men, with black masks and no badges, to arrest and beat up the security guards of Luzhkov's favourite banker, Vladimir Gusinsky, outside his Most Group's offices in a part of the mayor's administrative complex. Gusinsky, whose empire also included the private NTV television station and the liberal newspaper *Sevodnya*, complained. But when Korzhakov joked that his hobby was 'hunting geese' – a bleak pun on Gusinsky's name – the financier beat a hasty retreat to England.

On 24 November, Yeltsin gave the FSK the old investigative functions of the KGB, to help them 'fight crime'. The new security police were now allowed to break in without warrants to private homes, offices and factories, tap phones, and detain citizens. 'The security system has chosen the wrong road,' lamented the FSK's token liberal, deputy director and Moscow boss Yevgeny Savostyanov. A fortnight later, Savostyanov was fired.

'Who needs a coup these days? The bad guys have taken over anyway,' said Tolya Verbin, Reuter's top Russian political reporter, elbow-deep in newspapers, shaking his head in disbelief.

*

It was in this uneasy climate that the war in Chechnya began. Turmoil inside Russia had stopped most people taking notice of a Chechen opposition attack on Grozny in October, which Dudayev's men had defeated. But there was no way that journalists in Russia could ignore the next attack, on 26 November. The Russian news agency TASS announced it before it happened, repeating the same item several times: 'The Chechen opposition assault on Grozny will begin at 21.30 Moscow time.'

That night, Tass and Ostankino television (the first channel, which had been the official Moscow Central Television in Soviet times) said the onslaught had started twenty minutes early, at 21.10. There was no further information that night, but the next morning Tass put out a plausible follow-up script. It said Dudayev's presidential palace had fallen and his forces were retreating. It quoted Avturkhanov, speaking on Grozny television, claiming victory.

There was only one thing wrong with the Tass story: it wasn't true. When my colleagues from Reuters Television got to Grozny that night, Dudayev was very much in charge, in his palace, ringed by artillery pieces. There were signs of fighting everywhere: piles of wreckage scattered on the streets, a tank turret on a roadside, and flames spouting from broken gas mains. But there was no fighting. The opposition had fled. Movladi Udugov, the Chechen information minister, had just one piece of advice for our cameraman: 'You should cancel your subscription to Tass.'

But it was only the next day that the full embarrassment of Russia's position became apparent. Among the prisoners taken by Dudayev's men were seventy-six *bona fide* Chechens – and twenty-one Russian tank-drivers. The Russians were not mercenaries, and not freelancers. They were fully paid up serving members of the Russian army, seconded from their regiments by the FSK to beef up the ineffective Chechen opposition forces. Dudayev rang Moscow to gloat, delighted to be able to catch the Russian FSK red-handed at last. He told Russia that it must claim the captives as its own soldiers, in which case they would be treated with honour as prisoners of war. If Russia denied them, they might be executed as mercenaries.

Without a moment's hesitation, Grachev denied his soldiers. It was 'nonsense' to suggest Russia was militarily involved in Chechnya, he spluttered. Any Russian troops who might have been captured in Chechnya must have gone there voluntarily, while 'on leave'. If Russia had intervened in Chechnya, he added with characteristic bombast, 'one parachute regiment would have been enough to settle all questions in two hours'.

Yeltsin gave the Chechens an ultimatum. They were to hand in their weapons and release their prisoners within forty-eight hours. 'If the deadline is not met, a state of emergency will be introduced on the territory of the Chechen Republic and all the forces and means at the disposal of the state will be used to put a stop to the bloodshed,' he threatened. Russians and Chechens alike took this as a threat of war.

On 29 November, the Russian president called together the thirteen members of his unelected inner cabinet, the Security Council, for a meeting behind closed doors. What members of the Security Council may have expected from that session was that they would slowly reach a decision on Chechnya by 'consensus', the Communist Party's old tactic for shirking individual responsibility. What actually happened was different: the council was immediately presented with a plan for war. A belligerent Yeltsin told council members to approve it, without discussion.

Yuri Kalmykov, the justice minister who knew Chechnya better than anyone else in the room, sensed an oddly brusque formality about the proceedings, as if President Yeltsin had not really come for advice. 'I want to discuss another way, a peaceful way,' Kalmykov said. Yeltsin cut him off sharply. 'We'll talk about it later,' Kalmykov recalls the president insisting. 'Let's vote on what we have.' Without argument, the council then approved a four-stage military assault. Kalmykov's idea – to delay the war and negotiate on Chechnya's status – was then discussed, but the inconclusive debate petered out. Kalmykov went home and drafted his resignation.[5]

In the weeks that followed, Yeltsin remained so aloof from the

5. *Los Angeles Times*, 3 April 1995.

beginning of the war that many Russians wondered whether he even knew what was happening. They clung to the comforting illusion, traditional to subjects of both Soviet and imperial rulers, that their leader was a 'good Tsar' being led astray by bad advisers. In fact, it was Yeltsin himself who pushed for the war, to satisfy his personal animosity against two prominent Chechens rather than for sound reasons of state. By doing so, he pushed modern Russia into a rerun of one of the most botched military campaigns of the Tsars, whose authoritarian political style he was reviving and whose pageantry he had already appropriated.

It took months for the truth about the Security Council meeting to leak out into the press. Just three years into what Yeltsin called Russian democracy, the country's leaders had abandoned their commitment to open government to the point where they did not feel it was necessary to pass on to the man in the street a decision that would affect thousands of soldiers and millions of tax-payers. After the council members dispersed, the only result of the meeting that Yeltsin made public was a decree naming Nikolai Yegorov envoy to Chechnya.

Unidentified planes began to bomb Grozny. Daily bombing raids mangled the civilian airport and the military airport, and even the disused airfield outside Grozny near Dudayev's house. Planes bombed houses in Argun and Shali, east of the capital. One missile exploded in a crowd of people who had just got off a bus, cutting a woman in half and seriously injuring two children. The arbitrary raids picked off at least nine people in the first week; in the second week, an orphanage in Grozny was hit. Every night, the planes buzzed low over the city, sometimes dropping bombs and some-times not, while people in the houses and apartment blocks listened to the screams of the engines and waited for death. Every morning, one of our reporters would phone from Grozny, and his voice grew quieter, more tense, and more tired with every call. 'It's hard to sleep,' he said.

Back in Moscow, Grachev denied that the mystery bombers were Russian. Perhaps he was expecting the common people of Russia to behave as passively as they had in Soviet times and accept the official line without any – visible – display of disbelief. But, as he quickly found out, it was harder to intimidate people in 1994, and harder to limit the information they received. He had not reckoned with the power of a free press.

Journalists rushed to interview the Russian prisoners in Grozny. When pictures of the young boys' scared faces came out, they provoked an indignant public revolt against the unpopular Grachev, who had so blithely abandoned them to their fate. Members of parliament began to commute to Chechnya to negotiate the soldiers' release. Once in Grozny, parliamentarians quickly realized the air-raids were real. Cowering in bunkers, they appealed directly to the Russian president to 'please do anything to stop the bombing'. When liberal economist Grigory Yavlinsky made a dramatic mercy dash to Grozny and offered himself and his delegation as a 'hostage swap' for the imprisoned soldiers, Dudayev's foreign minister Shamseddin Yusuf turned them down with exquisite politeness. 'We welcome the noble desire of Grigory Yavlinsky,' he said. 'But we are not going to keep him or anyone else hostage, even if they want us to.'

One by one, Dudayev released the prisoners, who all came home telling the same story: they had been paid and recruited by the FSK. Counter-intelligence officers had had them seconded away from their Russian army tank divisions, and promised them payments of about $1,000 each to help the Chechen opposition. They said a contingent of about eighty Russians had been assembled to man twenty-six Russian tanks. Lieutenant Dmitry Volfovich of the Kantemirov Tank Division near Moscow and Private Alexander Danilov, two of the first soldiers to tell their story to Russian television journalists, waved a mocking on-camera greeting to Grachev and Stepashin.

Grachev carried on insisting that the defence ministry had had no idea the FSK was recruiting army troops to attack Grozny in November. But, on 5 December, he admitted at last that the mystery planes bombing Grozny were Russian.

*

Although they had taken the secret decision to send in the troops, the Russian élite spent the next few days maintaining the public's illusion that peace was still possible. Grachev even held peace talks with Dudayev on 6 December. The Chechen president said gravely that his 'main aim was to make use of the last chance to avoid war'. The talks ended in smiles and promises. Grachev promised not to make war on Chechnya. Looking delighted, Dudayev promised in return to free the remaining Russian soldiers.

Dudayev kept his word. Two days later, all the remaining prisoners were sent back home except one man who was too badly wounded to be moved. But Russia did not keep its promise about refraining from war. On 7 December, the Security Council issued a harsh new public ultimatum, ordering 'all constitutional measures' to be employed to disarm 'illegal armed bands'. The warplanes returned to Grozny, dropping bombs on the outskirts of town.

Dudayev's men took the new warning seriously, and told Chechens to get ready to defend themselves. 'If Russia wants to wage war, we will have to defend ourselves. We offer peace, and Russia wages war. They are liars all the time. This is the liar again,' said the foreign minister, Shamseddin Yusuf. Alcohol sales were banned in state shops in Chechnya, and a military edict was issued for thieves and looters to be shot on sight. 'It is very dangerous for Muslims to drink during war,' information minister Movladi Udugov said. 'If you die drunk during battle, you go to hell.'

On 9 December, Yeltsin formalized the Security Council resolution with a decree ordering force, or 'all measures available to the state', to disarm Chechnya. Stepashin and Yegorov were already at the military base of Mozdok, nerve centre of the planned operation, which lay just north-west of Chechnya. Grachev and Yerin flew off there to join them.

On Saturday, 10 December, Tass reported that Russia was sealing off Chechnya's borders and airspace. More bombs were dropped on Grozny; but, from Mozdok, Yegorov denied everything. 'Rumours about alleged air strikes in Grozny are a downright lie,' he said. 'They bear the clear mark of a provocation ... evidently [by] someone who wants to destabilize the situation in Russia as a whole and in Moscow in particular.' In the classic gesture of a puppet leader inviting imperial forces to fight 'his' battle, Chechen opposition leader Umar Avturkhanov urged Russia to disarm Dudayev's 'armed bands', and threatened to order his forces to advance on Grozny alone if the Russians didn't hurry up.

Russian–Chechen talks were scheduled for the following Monday in Vladikavkaz. Even Vyacheslav Mikhailov, who was to be deputy chief negotiator for the Russians, had not been let into the secret that the war would begin before the talks could start. He spent his day talking to officials in Grozny by phone, and reported to Moscow that Dudayev's men were keen to settle the conflict through negotiations. But, in Grozny, Dudayev's chief aide Movlen Salamo was pessimistic about the outcome: 'I don't think so far that there is even the slightest chance anything good will come from the talks. To be honest, we expect a war.'

'I'm afraid the situation has already gone way beyond my control,' Dudayev told *Izvestia*. 'Islamic battalions formed in every village have been reinforced by Islamic fighters and instructors from all over the world. When our general staff gives them orders, they reply: "We are God's warriors, not yours."'

Russian liberals were alarmed by the Kremlin's open preparations for war. 'Chechnya is an inalienable part of Russia. But we are categorically against using fire and the sword on it,' said Yegor Gaidar. He believed the consequences would be disastrous for Russia: 'A military action in Chechnya means a war. A war means bigger military spending, a state of emergency all over Russia, and finally a police state.' But it was too late. Yeltsin was not listening to liberals any more. The day before Russian troops went into Chechnya, he checked into hospital for a minor nose operation.

Even as the tanks prepared to set off, *Izvestia* was predicting that Yeltsin could not really mean to use force. The liberal paper believed the president was performing 'a balancing act on the edge of war' – an act of brinksmanship – in the hope that Dudayev and the Chechens would be cowed enough by a display of superior Russian military might to knuckle under.

*

At dawn on 11 December, three columns of Russian troops poured over the border into Chechnya. One line moved in from the south-west – from Vladikavkaz and through Ingushetia. Another came from Dagestan in the east. The third moved down through Nadterechny from Mozdok in the north-west. Each column was made up of hundreds of armoured vehicles, and was protected from the air by helicopter gunships. They all headed towards Grozny.

What the Russian tank-drivers saw as they headed across the Chechen plains was a primitive part of the former Soviet Union, a sinister ghetto where the niggers and villains of their imagination lived. In it, they recognized only what was familiar to them: towns fringed with the rotting housing estates of the Brezhnev era, factories called October or Red Hammer, mud on the roads, rural poverty, men with gold teeth, fedoras and guns.

Most Chechens are peasants, living in a land watered by shallow, rocky rivers and edged by mountains in the south and east. It is a stark land of eagles, mists and wolves, whose lean human inhabitants have aquiline noses, black hair and thoughtful eyes. Men drink, but seldom to excess; women cover their heads, but only against the cold, with Russian headscarves. Its tiny villages of one-storey houses nestle by rivers, painted from a palette of cool blue and green and lilac shades. Fences mark off the homes of the wealthy, whose roofs are edged in silver filigree and topped by crescent moons. Grapes hang from wrought-iron balconies. Chickens cluck in the road. Sheep are tethered at the roadside to abandoned car tyres, waiting for the call 'Let's slaughter a lamb!' from families planning their next decorously hospitable party. Women collect water in buckets from springs, and old men with haughty noses drive along the roads in low pony-carts like wheelbarrows, sitting on hauls of hay or firewood or fruit. Every village has a mosque and a blue and green graveyard.

What the Russians did not see was the hidden landscape of defiance, in which almost every stone is a secret memorial to the Chechen history of struggle. They did not understand the suffix -*martan*, battlefield, added to the names of the places they were passing, because Russians do not bother with the languages of conquered peoples. They did not understand that the modern silver-roofed mosques, rebuilt in every village since 1978, were another gesture of defiance to a Russia which had knocked down the mosques that still survived at the time of the deportations. They drove blindly past the holy *ziyarad*s at the roadside.

But, for the inhabitants of this spiritual landscape, there was no mistaking what Russian tanks pounding down their roads signified. Historical play-acting by Yeltsin and Dudayev, and self-conscious attempts by Moscow liberals to restore peace, had no place in their scenery. They had ignored it all. But Chechens who saw Russian troops arriving now perceived them, without irony, as the start of Moscow's next attempt to wipe them from the face of the earth. The history they had gone on living throughout the twentieth century gave them no reason to think otherwise.

Crowds of Chechens went out into the roads and stood in front of the tanks, trying to talk the Russian drivers into turning back and avoiding a repeat of the historical cycle of death. When that failed, they went to their clergy, who stopped short of declaring a full-scale new *ghazavat*, but told them they had a right to shoot back if Russians fired on them. Chechens who had been attacked went home, got their guns, prayed and prepared for war.

# TWO

The troops were finally on the march into Chechnya . . . or were they?

The first news of the intervention was a terse dawn announcement by Tass news agency on 11 December, 1994. It said Russian forces had entered Chechnya. An hour later, Tass killed its dispatch. 'The story is being withdrawn,' an even terser advisory message said. I phoned Tass, hoping someone there would explain why the story had been issued, why it had been cancelled, and where the Russian army really was. 'Wrong number,' said the nervous voice that answered the overnight desk phone. 'This is the photo department.' He wouldn't transfer me. The phone slammed down. One by one, I tried all the Tass numbers. 'Wrong number. This is the security guard,' the same voice said on my second call. 'Wrong number. I'm the cleaner,' he essayed on my third call. I fetched a cup of coffee to dispel my growing sense of unreality, and tried again. This time, the voice was marginally more helpful: 'No one will be in to answer your question until ten o'clock.'

By ten o'clock, the invasion was officially on again. Tass reissued its dispatch, but this time added the crucial phrase that had apparently been missing before: Russian forces had now entered Chechnya 'to restore constitutional order' and 'disarm illegal band formations'.

Later, a journalist on the Tass day shift whispered an explanation. The night duty editor had put out the pre-prepared story at the appointed time. But whoever had written it had left out the phrase that Russia was using to justify its military campaign as a crackdown on Chechen crime, rather than an invasion. When Valentin Sergeyev, the spokesman of a new Russian government press centre for Chechnya, saw the story on the Tass wire, he was furious. He rang Tass and gave the night man such a roasting that he cowered, shaking and helpless, at his desk for the rest of his shift. It had been up to the first person in that morning to rescue him from his terror, and transmit a corrected version of the news item.

Sergeyev was on equally assertive form with us all day. When Andrei first rang him at mid-morning to find out where the troops had got to, and when they might reach Grozny, Sergeyev bawled at him for asking questions. 'Don't bug me with your picky questions,' he yelled confidently. 'Just get your pen and write down the news I dictate to tell the world!'

'That was very strange,' Andrei said thoughtfully, replacing the receiver. 'He's all happy ... He was acting as if it were Soviet times again. He thinks he's got all the power in the world.'

What Sergeyev was dictating was the FSK's official version of the truth. The intervention would be a quick scoot down the three highways to the edge of Grozny. Each of the three armoured columns had a drive ahead of less than fifty miles. The city would be encircled by 2 p.m. But the Russian forces would not attack Grozny itself, or its civilians. They would just smoke out the 'illegal armed bands' loyal to Dudayev.

Sergeyev said 30,000 Russian saviours were coming to rescue the Chechens from their lords of misrule. 'The defence and interior ministries are ... not only busy with troops but also bringing foodstuffs into Chechnya: medicine, fuel, and fodder for cattle. The Chechen republic is being supplied with 50,000 tonnes of grain, 9,000 tonnes of macaroni and semolina, 6,500 tonnes of sausage, 1,500 tonnes of butter, and 8,000 tonnes of sugar.'

Tanya, the afternoon translator, got the rough end of Sergeyev's tongue when she phoned later to ask whether the troops had reached their destination. 'If I were your father I'd know how to discipline you, young lady,' he screeched. She held the receiver fastidiously away from her ear, and his angry voice crackled round the newsroom.

*

What Sergeyev was telling us in Moscow was nothing like what correspondents in Chechnya were seeing on the ground. The three advancing columns were running into unexpected resistance – in the shape of villagers whose only weapon was their indignation.

'This is our land. Get out!' shouted a gold-toothed Chechen in a tall fur hat, standing eyeball to eyeball with Colonel Ivan Gromov, a commander of an armoured column of the Russian interior ministry in the farming village of Chervlyonnaya.[6]

'Could you move your crowd back off this bridge,' Gromov ordered in a booming voice. 'Move your soldiers back,' retorted the man with the gold teeth, as about 150 Chechens around him stood their ground. 'Did we ever invade Russia with weapons? No. We're defending our homeland and we have nowhere to retreat.'

This north-western Russian column was making its way through supposedly docile opposition-controlled land. The line of 200 tanks, followed by at least 200 other armoured vehicles an hour later, was thundering down the long flat road towards Khasbulatov's home, Tolstoy-Yurt, just outside Grozny. As the column passed through Avturkhanov's tumbledown town, Znamenskoye, it came upon a tinny little Zhiguli. A Russian armoured personnel carrier opened fire on the car for blocking its way, wounding two people inside. It took the column till nightfall to reach Tolstoy-Yurt.

Things went worse for the second Russian column, advancing through Dagestan in the east. It was blocked by residents before it got into Chechnya. In Gerzel-Aul, forty-seven soldiers were taken prisoner by locals. When this column reached the eastern Chechen town of Gudermes, six Russian APCs were seized.

In Ingushetia, to the south-west, fighting broke out as the third Russian column passed through. According to Grachev, villagers attacked and burned thirty vehicles. According to the Chechen main staff, Russia responded by launching a missile strike from helicopters, destroying a mosque in Gazi-Yurt village and killing fifteen civilians.[7]

The column inched down the valley road the next day, to the muddy little town of Karabulak. There, again, it was confronted by a group of women and elderly men. 'Go to your commander and tell him to turn back. Are you really that sick of life?' a woman

6. *Los Angeles Times*, 12 Dec. 1994.
7. *Ekho Moskvy* radio station, 11 Dec. 1994.

yelled at a soldier standing by a tank. One of the men asked a
soldier to name his home town, saying: 'I want to write your
address on your coffin.'[8]

The Russian column only managed to get into western Chechnya
at all on its third day on the road. Russian soldiers dug in at
Davidenko, a Cossack settlement 25 miles away from Grozny,
after another confrontation with unarmed villagers waving banners
appealing: 'General Grachev, do not spill the blood of our people.'
'This isn't your land, it's our land,' called people in the crowd,
appealing to Major-General Ivan Babichev, in charge of the Russian formation. 'Don't turn this into another Afghanistan.'

The Russian high command ordered Babichev to open fire on
the obstructors, but Babichev had had enough. In the first of many
highly publicized acts of military insubordination which would
come to characterize the war, he refused. He said his men intended
to move no further towards Grozny. They would not shoot
civilians.

News of Babichev's moment of mutiny was read out all over
Russia on television that night – one of many pieces of information
about the war that the Russian authorities would have preferred
the world not to know. In their little kitchens spread over thousands of miles, Russians cutting up sausage or spooning sour cream
on their supper gasped at his bravery in defying unpopular orders.

It was the first time a war in which they knew their own troops
were fighting had been flashed immediately onto Russians' television screens. To the rage of Sergeyev and his colleagues, every
grisly moment of the campaign was shown to the public.

First the viewers saw the bogged-down Russian advance. Then,
for the next fortnight, they watched their troops digging in and
waiting outside Grozny, the planes swooping over the centre and
the armed skirmishes on the edges of town.

On New Year's Eve, hundreds of Russian tanks did storm
Grozny – despite Moscow's assurances that this would never
happen. The assault went disastrously wrong. In the deadly streets,
by night, the 250 tanks got separated from their accompanying

8. Reuters, 12 Dec. 1994.

infantry. The forward group of tanks lost radio contact with their command. They were abandoned to their fate. Chechens who could not believe their luck in being presented with such an easy target immediately surrounded them. A hundred tanks were destroyed, and most of the rest were captured and used by the Chechens. Chechens claimed that 600 Russian troops were killed in the assault. The next day, viewers saw the black metal hulks of the burned-out vehicles, and the bodies in Russian uniform piled up nearby. They drew their own conclusions about the Russian military commanders' competence.

Nightmarish weeks of urban battle followed. The Russian army seized the north of the city. From there, it attacked the presidential palace which had become the television symbol of Chechen separatist rule. Shells and bombs rained down on Dudayev's head-quarters and all around. But his men took to the bunkers, and fought on.

With them in the bunkers was an elderly Russian MP, Sergei Kovalyov, who had come to Grozny at the same time as the Russian army to protest against the war. His worried, bespectacled face filled the TV screens. His gentle voice, describing the damage done by Russian air raids and the high civilian death tolls, echoed round viewers' living-rooms.

But it was the interviews with the Russians who lived in Grozny that shocked the viewers most. If they weren't finding guns and going off to fight, Chechen civilians were slipping out of town to take refuge with their families in the villages. But the Russians of Chechnya were city creatures, with no country cousins to run to, or no money to get away. They were trapped in Grozny, under the relentless Russian bombs. Even in the flailing of elbows and carrier bags, it was easy to see that the pale, scared faces fighting for food handouts from trucks in Grozny were mostly Russian. *Nashi.* Shocked into immobility, bewildered Russian men sat on park benches under artillery assaults. Stooped old Russian ladies cursed Moscow for attacking their own people.

Things were no better in the Russian troop encampments. Horrified mothers saw the deprivations of army life: teenage soldiers who could be their sons chipping ice from armoured troop-carriers with shovels, ragged men keeping warm round primitive cast-iron stoves and bonfires, no soap, ice-cold water, tents, mud and litter.

The footage they watched revealed to the Russian masses the cruel ironies of the war their leaders were pursuing. For the first time in history, the actions of the top people in the Russian hierarchy were stripped of secrecy and exposed for inspection by the people they ruled – and the people didn't like what they saw. A *Moscow News* poll found that the 58 per cent of respondents who opposed the use of force in Chechnya on 6 December had swelled to 70 per cent a week later. Yeltsin's popularity plummeted from 28 per cent to 14 per cent.

Sophisticated modern Russians realized that the unpopular hard-liners in the Kremlin were now treating them with as much contempt as if they were serfs. 'They clearly take Russians for dimwits,' *Izvestia* commented sourly.[9] Members of Russia's ruling élite, now collectively nicknamed the 'Party of War', were shown to be ready to lie, censor, and sacrifice thousands of Russian lives on a whim.

Russians began to perceive the Chechen war as an attack on them, an extension of the autumn crackdowns in Moscow and part of a grand design by the neo-Soviet authoritarians in the Kremlin to take total power and crush freedom in Russia. The war showed 'the adventurism of the military path that has been chosen and . . . sharply exacerbates the threat of a military-authoritarian regime being formed,' Gaidar said on 5 January. 'The possibility of such a regime being formed in Russia has never been so real.'

To save themselves from the threat from above, Russians started fighting back.

*

The most public of the battles fought in Russia was for freedom of speech. Russian journalists were insulted at being told to publish the Kremlin's absurd official propaganda, which alleged that the Chechen fighting force was packed with Arab, Azeri and Afghan

9. *Izvestia*, 30 Dec. 1994.

mercenaries and Baltic women snipers in white stockings. If they could, journalists ignored the propaganda and showed the harrowing truth instead. The independent channel NTV, owned by Gusinsky's Most Group, led the anti-war crusade.

The 'Party of War' tried to muzzle the Russian media. The Kremlin threatened to take away NTV's licence for allegedly spreading 'misinformation'. Yeltsin accused the media of being in the pay of Chechnya. Sergeyev complained that the media had become 'Dudayev's megaphone', that Chechen fighters who had reportedly condemned him to death in Grozny had all his family's phone numbers – and he was sure they had got them from Moscow journalists. The unsophisticated Yegorov went furthest of all. Once troops had subdued the rebels, he suggested, they should 'turn their guns on Russian journalists'.

This Kremlin onslaught had no effect on NTV. Gusinsky's television defiantly carried on reporting whatever it wanted. But the government media were forced to toe the line. Sullen presenters at Ostankino read out what they were told to. At the more independent-minded Russian television channel, the presenters continued to defy the censors. Staring down at their desk, they would rattle blank-faced through the optimistic nonsense-speak of the official statements, so fast and monotonously that you could scarcely follow them. Then, suddenly, their body language would change. They would lift their eyes to the camera, with significant shakes of the head and theatrically raised eyebrows, and enunciate with dramatic clarity: 'That's what the Russian government centre says. HOWEVER, it is NOT what Western television footage transmitted today shows!' ... and pictures of the horrific reality would flicker across the screen again.

'With a few exceptions, the Russian press is behaving with great dignity,' said Pavel Gutiontov, secretary of the Russian Journalists' Union. 'People who give orders to bomb their own citizens' homes have no moral right to accuse the press of anything. They want objectivity, they say. Well, they're getting plenty of it. The problem is they don't like it. But that's their problem.'

Russian mothers fought their own battle with the Kremlin leaders, to save their soldier sons' lives. They believed what the independent media were saying – that the army was giving false death tolls to gloss over huge Russian losses, that the military was failing to collect the bodies of troops slaughtered in Grozny so that they could tell parents their boys had deserted and leave them out of the official death tallies, that Russian soldiers' bodies were being buried in pits in Chechnya to help cover up the truth.

Most of the Russian soldiers being sent to Chechnya had less than one year's experience. Many were the rawest of new recruits. Parents were not informed when their children were sent to the war. If they tried to find out, they ran into a wall of institutional silence. Galina Sidova, deputy head of the Mothers' Committee, returned from Grozny on 16 January with a horrifying description of what she had seen. 'There are piles of bodies everywhere. It is impossible to describe. It is impossible to recognize most of them. They are burned beyond recognition. It is terrible, terrible.'

The mothers of young soldiers started sneaking off to the conscript camps where their sons had been taken, and helping them to escape. Sergei Sorokin, of the Movement against Violence, said 3,000 troops deserted in the first six weeks of war.

The only generals whose popularity grew in the first days of the war were those who were perceived to care for Russian soldiers in the field, and who therefore denounced the hostilities as militarism gone mad. The two leading doves, both rated more popular than Grachev in a 1994 poll, were his most prominent critics in the defence ministry.[10] One was Boris Gromov, the general who led Soviet soldiers out of Afghanistan. The other was Alexander Lebed, the commander of the Russian 14th Army who had ended a war in Moldova.

Lebed condemned the invasion, called the army 'a shapeless and disorganized group of men that does not know where it is going', and said troops on the ground were 'untrained kids'. He caught the mood of hostility to the Kremlin élite's abuse of power when he said he would only command a regiment in Chechnya 'if it is

---

10. 1994 poll by the Friedrich Ebert Stiftung, a German Social Democratic research institute.

made up of the children and grandchildren of our deputies and the children and grandchildren of our cabinet members'.

*

The anger of Russians against the Kremlin grew so intense that it began to make Yeltsin uneasy. His spokesman said he was 'deeply upset' by negative media reports. In an otherwise aggressive speech on 27 December, Yeltsin ordered a halt to Russian air-raids on Grozny. 'To preserve lives, I have given an order to stop bombing raids, which can lead to civilian casualties,' he said earnestly. But the bombing continued. On 4 January, Yeltsin said again that he was stopping the air-raids. Still they went on.

Yeltsin's anxiety peaked when the liberal MP Sergei Kovalyov returned briefly to Moscow from the bombed-out heart of Grozny to appeal to the president's conscience. Kovalyov had spent three weeks in the bunkers under Russian bombardment. The ex-dissident's courage had made him a more potent symbol of public resistance to the 'Party of War' than any other liberal politician. Kovalyov was a national hero. Photographs of his careworn face, framed by thinning, flyaway hair, flashed almost every day from television screens and newspapers, his calm recitals of unpleasant truths juxtaposed with the increasingly wild and untruthful official dispatches. *Moscow News* showed his picture alongside one of Yeltsin in military fatigues, under a front-page headline: '1995 – Russia Has A Choice'. *Izvestia* named him Man of the Year. Its editorial said: 'In the most terrible tragedy of the year, Sergei Kovalyov's personality and his actions have brought hope to hearts filled with pain and alarm.'

At New Year, as tankfuls of Russian soldiers rolled into central Grozny to die, Kovalyov appealed to Yeltsin on Chechen television. 'From the basement of the heavily-shelled residence of Dzhokhar Dudayev, we who fought with you for democracy in Russia from 1991 to 1994 tell you that we are on opposite side of the barricades today,' he said. 'We are not for Dudayev. But we are against the war launched against the entire Chechen people and, unfortunately, you are the commander-in-chief of this war. The problem today is not about Chechnya, but rather about the democratic future of Russia.'

The voice of conscience had always been the sixty-four-year-old Kovalyov's guide. For seven years, he was a political prisoner at the Perm-35 camp. After three more years in exile, he was allowed to return to Moscow. There, he got caught up in the swing of perestroika, became an activist, an MP, and then the legislature's human rights spokesman. His mentor, the dissident Andrei Sakharov, had been Mikhail Gorbachev's official conscience in the perestroika era. Kovalyov hoped to work the same magic with Yeltsin now.

Hundreds of adoring journalists jammed into the Duma building on 5 January to hear what Kovalyov wanted to tell the president. Kovalyov wasn't a natural public speaker. Perhaps it was age – he looked old for sixty-four – or perhaps it was fatigue, or shock, or stress, or just the close heat of the packed hall and the television lights. He rambled a bit, and sometimes got lost in his subordinate clauses. But the sincerity of his message made up for its awkward delivery. He had walked into the biggest lie of his life. He wanted to find out who was to blame.

'As regards lies, we have surpassed the communists and even Goebbels,' Kovalyov said, blinking and searching for words. 'We understand . . . that you can't live in a state whose leaders are liars. You can't live in a country run by bastards.' There was a quiver in the hall. This wasn't the language of polite debate, and it didn't match his quiet, determined air. Kovalyov looked round. 'I insist on that last word, and I ask you not to change it,' he clarified. He had only come to Moscow, he said, to look into his leader's eyes and see where the 'gigantic lie' was coming from.

Kovalyov's presence in Moscow tweaked Yeltsin's conscience even before they talked the next afternoon. When the Security Council gathered in the Kremlin on the morning of 6 January, the president accused the military of disobeying his order to stop bombing Grozny. It was vital to examine why there was a 'two-faced' treatment of the air-raids, he said. Yeltsin also demanded to be told when the fighting in Grozny would be wrapped up.

Vladimir Shumeiko, president of the upper house of parliament and a new recruit to the Security Council, told journalists after the meeting that Grachev swore blind there had been no air-raids on Grozny since December 23 – an implausible four days before Yeltsin's first order. The defence minister said he had documents proving this, which he could submit immediately, but that the media 'do not want to use them, for some reason'.

Kovalyov met the president. Later, tired and dispirited, he met the press again. There was only one real question: What had he seen in the president's eyes?

'I couldn't make out what I saw,' Kovalyov answered sadly. 'I am a bad reader of faces, and Boris Nikolayevich [Yeltsin] was quite off-hand. I can only say that, to me, his face seemed worried and at times very dissatisfied. He was very dissatisfied with what I was saying, and he was dissatisfied with the whole situation. What is there to be happy about, after all? It's hard to say.'

Kovalyov had asked Yeltsin whether he really understood what was happening and was being properly informed. Yeltsin insisted he was. 'But he immediately gave the lie to this statement, since he said that he was quite convinced there had been no more bombing raids on Grozny after his speech to the nation on 27 December,' Kovalyov went on. 'I asked him: "What, don't you believe me? I saw those planes with my own eyes, saw how they dropped the rockets from the planes, leaving traces. I heard the explosion of aerial bombardment with my own ears after the planes flew over."

'"No, I believe you," Boris Nikolayevich said.'

Kovalyov went back to Grozny. His mission to end the air-raids and save Chechen civilian lives had failed. The war went on; Yeltsin had no intention of stopping Kremlin hard-liners pursuing the hostilities that he himself had ordered. But talking to Kovalyov seems to have jolted Yeltsin into understanding that the Russian revolt against current Kremlin policy was a response, not to the Chechen war itself, but to the hard-liners' accompanying attacks on the institutions of Russian democracy. He realized that his mistake until now had been to let the 'Party of War' show its brutal side to his Russian voters, a mistake so serious that it could cause power to slip out of his hands unless he corrected it quickly. He set out to reassure the people of Russia that their own civic rights were not under threat, and that they had nothing to fear from the war.

From 7 January, the 'Party of War' all but vanished from Russian television screens. Its information centre vanished too, and Sergeyev checked into hospital. Soft-spoken centrists and administrators took centre stage instead, to explain to Russians why the war was necessary and to promise that it would not affect their own future. Shakhrai took charge of a new government information and analysis commission. Sweet-faced and smiling, he promised his commission would help the media work freely. 'This commission has no censorship function,' he said. The Kremlin corridors were suddenly full of journalist-loving bureaucrats. 'The government is to blame for the way the press has treated it,' said Yeltsin's chief of staff, Sergei Filatov. 'The press is society's eyes and ears. It should be helped, not hindered.'

The avuncular Prime Minister Viktor Chernomyrdin, who had been silent but disapproving of the war until now, reassured the rest of society that it was protected against abuse by the security-and-military clique in the Kremlin. He met soldiers' mothers; he told them the war was necessary because Dudayev had abused human rights in Chechnya, but promised that the families of soldiers would be looked after. In a show of care for rank-and-file Russians, emergencies minister Sergei Shoigu went to Grozny with a twenty-member team to evacuate the bodies of dead Russian soldiers at last.

Grachev was made the scapegoat, taking public blame for the start of the war. To appease widespread anger against the 'Party of War', an investigation began into army bosses' misdeeds. It rumbled on through February, unearthing evidence of corruption, insubordination and feuding among the generals. Although Yeltsin refused to fire his defence minister, this public carpeting satisfied most Russians. The FSK escaped blame altogether.

*

The crisis in Russia passed. Most of Yeltsin's subjects were relieved at the president's easing of the recent harsh and unwanted restrictions, and their fear that the 'Party of War' would impose a military dictatorship on them subsided.

After the middle of January, people in Russia stopped worrying too much about the war itself, although they knew it was still being pursued with maximum brutality by Grachev, Stepashin, Yerin, and the Russian commanders in the south. Horrific film of the fighting was shown every day on television, but Chechnya was quickly coming to seem distant, savage, and unimportant again; viewers switched off when the war news started. The image of the dark Chechen outsider – armed, violent and malevolent – was by now so deeply ingrained in the Russian psyche that most people thought the Chechens deserved everything they got. 'What can you do with the Chechens?' asked my friend Lena, an economist in shoulder pads. 'A nation of bandits. I can quite see they have to be wiped from the face of the earth.'

In America in the 1970s, ordinary people had taken to the streets in protest when they saw horrifying television footage and photographs of the sufferings of Vietnamese war victims: villagers escaping into the jungle as US napalm bombing destroyed their homes, a little girl running naked and screaming down an empty road. The demonstrations helped force an end to the Vietnam War. Russians had the opposite response. While the Russian army bombed Chechnya, civilians in Russia were terrified they would be attacked in their own homes by Chechens. One of the few pieces of FSK propaganda that had gone unquestioned by Russian voters was that Chechen terrorists were coming to get them. Security in Russian cities was increased, just in case the dark outsiders struck. APCs were parked beside police checkpoints on the main highways into Moscow and next to the Moscow traffic police headquarters. Young soldiers, heavily wrapped up against the winter, checked drivers' documents. In nervous groups of three, policemen patrolled metro stations and public buildings.

Sergei Kovalyov was almost the only Russian to continue speaking out on behalf of the Chechens after the crisis of December and January passed, but he was no longer adored for doing so. Even so, liberals were shocked when, in late January, a dishevelled

and pugnacious Grachev went on television to call Kovalyov's
liberal friend Sergei Yushenkov a 'sleazebag', and Kovalyov himself
an 'enemy of Russia'.

*

On 19 January, Russia said its forces had captured the presidential
palace. The Chechens admitted that their last 300 fighters had left
the building, but denied that this meant even a symbolic defeat for
Dudayev's forces. The palace had simply stopped being a useful
shelter, they said, because Russian bombing had left only the walls
standing.

The military phase of the Chechen operation was 'almost
complete', Yeltsin said. The Russian defence ministry said heavy-
weapons bombardment in Grozny had stopped. The troops were
trying to restore ordinary life in the battered city. Soldiers were
clearing rubble and trying to restore electricity and gas supplies.
Interior ministry troops were pushing out the last of the rebels.
Everything was returning to normal, and the Russian flag had been
hoisted over the ruins of the palace.

To prove this, the official *Rossiiskiye Vesti* newspaper published a
Reuters picture of the palace the next morning, topped by a Russian
flag. But the picture wasn't real proof. Our photographers emerged
furious from their smoky cubby-hole, stabbing angry fingers at the
photo. *Rossiiskiye Vesti* had cheated. It had published a flagless
Reuters picture of the ruined palace, and drawn the flag in on top.
I looked again. It was a very obvious fake. The flag was drawn in
biro, over a layer of Tipp-Ex. There was nothing to do but laugh.

*

I was going to leave Russia in a month. I'd found an editing job in
London. It would only pay half my salary in Moscow and I was
worried it might be boring, but the good thing about it was that I
would be able to rejoin my husband, who had left Russia six
months before. I should have been wading through the bureaucracy
of departure, but this final piece of Moscow propaganda made me
curious. For old times' sake, I decided to make a last trip to the
Caucasus, to look at the ruins of the city Russia said it had beaten.

# THREE

You couldn't take planes to Grozny any more. Instead, I flew to Mineralniye Vody, now hijacker-free, and took a five-hour taxi ride across southern Russia. My original idea had been to find Musa and stay with his family in Grozny, but someone returning from a Christmas stint at the war said that would be impossible. When I showed her where Musa's house was on the map, she shook her head. 'That area was right near the palace,' she said. 'It's completely destroyed. It doesn't even exist any more.' I only really began to believe her when I drove to Grozny and saw the punishment that the 'Party of War', thwarted of power in Moscow, was meting out to the Chechens.

*

Chilly mist. Thin snow on the ground. We walked through a suburban housing estate, beside a frozen dam, looking towards the fuzzy centre of Grozny. In there, columns of black smoke rose into the fog. When the wind shifted, opening a gap in the white-out, there was a brief glint of fire. The deep rumble of explosions rattled windows even out here, vibrating nauseously in my gut. The answering dut-dut-dut of automatic weapons echoed against buildings. It was hard to tell where the noises came from. Musa's house was there somewhere. It was hard to believe people could still be living in that.

While the Russian army had been attacking the presidential palace, journalists had gone further into Grozny. They left their drivers and cars safely at Minutka roundabout in the south, next to another housing estate and market. It was still quiet there. Fighters would come out to Minutka for a break, and tell the journalists where the worst of the fighting was. Then some of the journalists, mostly photographers, would creep further in on foot.

But all that changed when the palace fell two days ago. Now

Minutka was being shelled. Now the Chechen fighters had abandoned the railway station north of the Sunzha River and were defending the bus station in the south. Now Chernorechiye (Black Waters), where we were standing, was the last safe place on the edge of Grozny. The war wasn't over. It was just spreading outwards.

Chernorechiye was a dormitory district of tired nine-floor apartment blocks for the oil, chemical and cement workers of Factory District up the road. Built in squares around scrubby courtyards, its brute concrete buildings stretched back from one side of the south-western highway into Grozny. On the other side of the highway was the dam. Tiny women, shapeless in their many layers of clothing, skittered around at the edge of the dam, a joyless parody of Renaissance paintings of Flemish fairs. They were pulling buckets of polluted water up the banks. Municipal water had been cut off long ago. Over the sheet of ice, far away, rose the rooftops of the village of Aldy.

Up at the top of the dam was a junction marked by two columns and a mess of tram tracks. Here, you could cross the water and approach the centre of Grozny from the side. Or you could carry straight on, past the factories, over another bridge, to the fighting.

Chernorechiye had a little market, known by its affectionate diminutive as the *bazarchik*. The official shops were barred and shuttered. The kiosks weren't working. But a dozen tables were set out by the junction, in front of the buildings, looking out over the dam. The women standing behind the tables wore socks and leggings and tights and galoshes under flowery dresses, and jackets over cardigans over sweaters, and hat and scarves and gloves. The municipal heating had gone off at the beginning of the war, and it was freezing. They were selling packet soups, canned meat, jam and pickled tomatoes. Sunflower seeds. Sweets. Soap. Candles, kerosene and cigarettes. The sweepings of cupboards. Emergency rations. A little crowd eddied past the tables, picking over the goods and talking.

Escapees from the centre stopped here, to catch their breath or to arrange transport out to safety. Fighters came for a rest. The mournful cars and carts of people leaving Chernorechiye for the villages made their farewells here, watched curiously by the people who had opted to stay on. Then they set off down the road out of town, past a mile of buildings to the big *profilaktoriya* (rest home) where sick state workers had once been cosseted, and on through a sweep of thin forest that took them to the police checkpoint at a clearing on the very edge of town, where two highways met. The word 'GROZNY' was spelled out here in great concrete letters, each sunk separately into the ground. A tattered Soviet-era sign nearby said: 'The City of Grozny Welcomes Careful Drivers!' Beyond that was the safety of the villages.

Even in Chernorechiye, the planes had been flying. Some of the buildings were only walls. Off the main road, people had dragged the broken glass and shattered concrete left by the hits into the middle of courtyards, leaving clear paths round the edges of the buildings so you could run fast if you needed to. Neat signs chalked on the walls told people which basements had been turned into bomb shelters. A lot of people spent their nights in the cellars. A lot of windows had huge crosses of sticky-tape on them, to stop glass flying in and killing the people sleeping inside if there was an explosion.

People talked knowledgeably about bombs that sprayed out metal needles when they exploded, depth bombs that cut neat round holes through nine storeys of masonry and only detonated in the basement, shrapnel, howitzers, mines, mortars, and snipers. Children with no school to go to played in the dangerous rubble, running over broken glass. Flocks of pigeons rose and fell over the debris. Abandoned pet dogs and cats with bleeding paws sniffed anxiously around for food and companionship. There were stories from the centre that stray dogs were eating corpses.

But the market women, some Chechen, some Russian, were determinedly cheerful. They didn't want war. They were happy to see people come into town. It gave them a sense of normality. Lena and Lyuba, two Russians, were carrying their babies with them. Did the babies sleep at night, when the shelling was loudest? 'Oh, kids are always all right if their parents are calm,' Lena said, and smiled.

Marina, a Russian ex-hairdresser who had lived twenty years in Grozny, had worked as a trader since money dried up a year or so before. She didn't think anything but bad would happen to Chernorechiye, but she didn't plan to leave. 'I sent my mother and daughter off to Stavropol yesterday. But someone's got to stay and look after the flat . . . I don't know when this will finish: the sooner the better, because my hair's already going grey!' she said with a dour little cackle, wrapping up a paper cone of sunflower seeds for me.

Her daughter didn't speak Chechen, and nor did she, but Chernorechiye was home. They had thought of leaving last year because the schools in Grozny had stopped working, but never got round to it. Part of their family was still here.

'We've got an aunt, my mum's big sister, here. But her family's at Minutka. They went into the cellar in December. Her husband's blind. God knows how they're doing now.'

'The important thing is not to give way to panic,' chipped in Tamara, the friendly Chechen woman at the next table. 'We've got to look after our flats, never mind what those bastards out there decide to do. We can't just leave our homes and let the looters clear us out.'

There was a chorus of agreement.

*

The new war in Chechnya was one which Imam Shamil, or General Yermolov, might have recognized more easily than the hopeful electorate of 1991. The bleak jokes of the Chechens were turning back from fable to fact in a claustrophobic landscape of snow and fire. But it was also utterly different from the wars of the past. Vast armies of tow-headed Russian troops were fighting under the banner of a new Russian ruler – the old double-headed eagle of the Tsars. But their weaponry was that of the Soviet army: tanks and long-range missiles. Although their army was in chaos, their planes and helicopters ruled the skies.

At first, some of the Chechens were armed only with the long daggers and the prayers of their ancestors. But they quickly found guns and grenades to carry, and many had rocket-propelled grenade-launchers slung across their backs like giant pea-shooters. In the white boiler suits they called their 'dressing-gowns', the fighters faded away into the snow. All you could see of them was their boots, dark eyes which occasionally flashed with laughter even now, and the green headbands under their white hoods.

Most of the Russian troops were more invisible still, manning the heavy guns pointed at you from somewhere far away behind the cloud cover; but scared, surly blond boys in uniform inspected the documents of travellers at two checkpoints along the road to Grozny. Their modern tanks were hidden too, half-buried in the wasteland of unfarmed fields.

In the south of Grozny, you never saw a Russian soldier, but you heard their bombs and bullets. There was no escape from the huge noise of death: the juicy snap of birch trees splintering under attack, the whistle of mortars, and the shiver of buildings disintegrating.

The sounds and sights of history were all here: the joyous echo of the warcry 'Allahu AkBAAAR!' as the fighters rush to the attack, the keening of wet-faced women burying sons and husbands under the ice, and the shock of red blossoming on bodies suddenly still.

But, however ancient the model for the war might be, what was taking place in Grozny now was an ugly modern conflict. Lying between these Chechen fighters and these Russian soldiers was a twentieth-century city, a big, messy, heavily populated terrain with no ethnic divides. Its victims, Russians as much as Chechens, were mostly civilians.

Despite Chechens' dislike of rule by Moscow, most people in Grozny were at first reluctant to go to war. Dudayev's commander Aslan Maskhadov led about 5,000 trained fighters, including the Abkhaz battalion of Shamil Basayev. There were a few romantics – boys out for a scrap, men with a grudge – who quickly attached themselves to this tiny force as part-time volunteers. But most of the extra part-time fighters who gradually joined up did so, not out of fanatical devotion to Dudayev, but only after they had been personally attacked by the Russians: after their house was burned down, or someone in their family killed.

The fighters running through the streets now might be yelling 'Allahu Akbar!' but they knew only the basics of Islam. The subtleties of the faith had been knocked out of them by Soviet rule.

They fasted at Ramadan, married and buried their dead according to Islamic rites; they applied to their elders for legal and moral judgements; they had mostly been on some sort of pilgramage to a *ziyarad*. But they were far from the purist *murid* ascetics of the previous century. They had been brought up watching television; they weren't against a good meal and sometimes a few drinks. They smoked and joked.

They were going to war to defend what they remembered of their faith, the central nugget of thought they had clung on to through the years of spiritual destruction. Chechens remember Kunta Khadzhi's pacifist philosophy as a prescription that Chechen Muslims should live in peaceful Muslim communities, surrounded by their relatives and their language and their faith; the only justification for fighting a war would be if those communities were attacked by an infidel. And now they were being attacked.

District by urban district, Grozny was dragged into the war by the Russians; district by rural district, so was the countryside.

If this was a rerun of the old conflict, it was a case of tragedy being repeated as farce.

*

We started commuting into Grozny every morning, across the flat white plains of western Chechnya. Our bosses had told the big team of Reuter cameramen, photographers and writers not to risk sleeping in Chechnya, so we spent our nights just outside, in the sleepy town of Sleptsovsk over the Ingushi border, at a shabby house known as the 'Foreign Trade Ministry Hotel'. It had electricity, hot water in the communal shower-room, an outside toilet, and a cafeteria where three women would dish up *plov* (pilau) and meat-and-potato stew all day. At one end of the corridor was the *lyuks* suite, with a sitting-room, bedroom and separate bathroom which the photographers commandeered to develop their films in. At the other end was Room 16, with two iron beds and a mirror. Outside was a courtyard with frozen vines. The women ran a kiosk by the gate, selling sticky champagne and cigarettes. Batyr, the doe-eyed administrator, sat in the back office playing cards, drinking tea and giving out keys.

We spent studenty evenings there, wearing sloppy jerseys and big socks, setting up the satellites, taking them down, preparing our material, eating biscuits, wandering in and out of each other's rooms, climbing over the heaps of generators and flak jackets we had been sent. The cameramen drove forty minutes to Nazran every evening, to transmit their film from the local TV station. The photographers made coffee and instant soup and sandwiches in their sitting-room, and drank gently from dusk onwards.

It was friendly, and I liked it, although the journalists who had come to Chechnya from Sarajevo were snooty about its lack of amenities. 'A war without real hotels,' lamented one, only half joking. 'In Sarajevo, the war was terrible; but at least you could come in at night and a waiter with a linen napkin on his arm would bring you a martini with an olive.'

I travelled with a big, ambling, bearded Lithuanian photographer called Pyatras Malukas, and with Misha Yandiyev, a wiry Ingush driver with an elegant nose and calm eyes. Misha's car was a white four-wheel-drive Niva with a tasselled crescent moon ornament bobbing under the mirror. It only had two doors. I sat in the back, so Pyatras could take pictures from the front, wondering uneasily how fast I would be able to get out if a helicopter came after us. We made a point of being very calm in the car. We didn't plan to take stupid risks, but we didn't plan to be scared away either. 'The important thing is to be intelligently scared, scared with your brain,' Pyatras said. Every day, we laughed over the same ritual joke, that between the three of us we were everything most reviled by Russian propaganda – a Balt, a woman, and a Muslim outsider. And, every day, we told each other reassuringly that it was *nelyotnaya pogoda* again – non-flying weather.

But we were fooling ourselves. Every day, the white-out that kept Russian planes away, and the traffic safe, cleared a bit more. And it was always flying weather for Russian helicopters. Every day, groups of three or four helicopters loaded with bombs flew along the highway, just to our side, at the height of the telegraph poles, heading for Grozny. They looked like giant wasps. 'Those little bastards again,' Misha would say, and we would drive slowly,

watching them until they buzzed up ahead of us and we were safe
again.

We would spend a couple of hours a day in town, then start for
home by lunchtime. In theory, it was an hour's drive each way. In
practice, getting to Grozny took longer every day. We would drive
in and out of the city with an empty petrol tank – in case the car
was hit – and fill up at the roadside market a few miles on, at the
Urus-Martan crossroads, where there was a tanker and where you
could buy everything from meat to Mars Bars. There was no war
at Urus-Martan. It was a district run by the anti-Dudayev opposition. They had done a deal with the Russians. It was packed with
refugees.

We would stop again, looking for more stories: sometimes at
the hospital in Urus-Martan, sometimes at the long public meetings
in Samashki, and sometimes at the Dudayevite stronghold of
Achkhoi-Martan where a prisoner exchange was endlessly being
prepared. We would stop for the brisk Chechen checkpoints that
appeared and disappeared at the roadside, explain to the common-
sense fighters where we were going, and be waved on.

We would stop off at the bigger Russian checkpoint near
Samashki, where scared boys with guns lurked behind their dug-in
tanks, and traffic jams built up on the roads as the soldiers searched
little Chechen cars for weapons. They closed the roads at six, but
we were only ever there during daylight – long before the Chechen
'ghosts' they were scared of started rustling in the bushes. Still, we
had to spend more time charming these soldiers – taking their
pictures, giving them cigarettes and newspapers and apples, flirting
– hoping they would let us jump the queues and be on our way.
They usually did: they were clunkingly gallant whenever they saw
me in the back of the car. 'Look, a *devushka*!' they cried to each
other, and a little crowd would gather round the car, staring at my
upside-down press card, staring at me. 'A girl shouldn't be in a war
zone,' they said, and I shrugged and gave them more cigarettes.
They stared so long and hard at me that they never noticed our
secret worry – Pyatras had no accreditation. 'You're our strategic
weapon,' Pyatras and Misha would grin as we were waved on. But
others were not so lucky. Sometimes, we would see miserable-

looking Chechen men being hauled off from their cars to the submerged tents and shelters for questioning. 'He had a grenade in his car,' the boss soldier would say dismissively. Or a pistol, or a knife. The man would vanish underground.

More and more often, we would stop because the road had been attacked in a new place. The highway was becoming a patchwork of obstructions and uncertainties.

From the very beginning, we would drive down the highway through Sernovodsk, then turn off by Samashki, and rejoin it later; fighting around Assinkovka and Bamut had shut off part of the road. But every day another bridge over another shallow river somewhere would be mysteriously blown up in the night, and another part of the highway would be put out of action. Who had done it? we asked the calm fighters melting in and out of the mist. 'The opposition,' they always answered.

It wasn't safe to wait too long at a broken bridge. The helicopters which were always flying by might spot the traffic jams building up, and come to shoot. So cars would rev up at the top of the muddy river bank, and try to speed through the water. If they got stuck, the drivers rolled up their trousers and waded over the pebbles to the bank to get help. There always was help in Chechen villages. People doggedly turned out in spite of the helicopters. A man with a truck and tow-rope was usually waiting at one side of the water. Locals brought earth-moving trucks and tractors to the river bank and patiently smoothed over the rutted sides. Or they balanced planks and sheets of metal over what remained of the bridge, making it more or less usable again.

Looking for another way through, we would join the other little civilian cars bobbing down ever more meandering routes along country lanes, skirting the war.

One morning, we were forced as far off-course as the little village of Katyr-Yurt in search of a passable bridge. Even here . . . The bridge had exploded at 3.45 a.m. Four or five of its central columns had vanished. There was a big crater on the muddy far bank. The silver roofs had been blown off the buildings behind it, and their windows had shattered. A quiet crowd of people was out looking curiously at the damage. No one had been hurt in the blast. The villagers said it must have been the opposition. People were already starting repairs. From now on, they were going to guard the bridge overnight.

The toy-town scale of things kept surprising me. Country men driving pony carts, or riding horses, shared the roads with Russian APCs. Grozny was a war zone, but five minutes away was the cheerful bustle of the Urus-Martan market. A bridge would blow up, but the little cars of civilians would just find the next un-damaged bridge and go on with their daily business. Helicopters flew over the highway, but straight-backed men with cows walked underneath them, in the white fields. You could get away from danger in a few minutes . . .

. . . but it could also creep up on you when you least expected it.

Every few days, a new column of between 100 and 200 tanks and armoured cars rolled into Grozny along the south-western road. It crossed the fields to the Samashki checkpoint, then skirted Samashki and climbed up to the ridge of hills edging the flat bowl of western Chechnya. It made its way into town from the safety of the hilltops. If you came across a Russian column, you waited. Almost every column that passed into Chechnya from Ingushetia took potshots at the Ingush villages along the highway. The house nearest the road at Gazi-Yurt, just over the border, was riddled with holes. 'You don't want to get those bastards angry with you,' Misha would say philosophically, pulling the car into the roadside. But you could never be sure they wouldn't turn on you, just for the hell of it.

Trapped in a river on another afternoon, we were waiting for the tow-truck to rescue us when three helicopters flew slowly off the road and up to us. They were so close we could almost see the pilots' faces. Pyatras and Misha were already squelching round in the water; I was on the front seat, besides Pyatras's camera bag, with my boots off. We stared. There was nowhere we could hide. The white sky pressed in on us. I felt sick with claustrophobia.

But they flew off again.

The truck lumbered out into mid-stream, tied us behind him, and pulled us ashore. I went on watching the helicopters. They had veered off to the other side of the highway, to a village near the ridge of hills. They circled over it. Brown puffs of mud rose up from the village. 'Look, they're attacking it,' Misha said, with nothing in his voice. 'We were lucky.'

Pyatras walked around with his head cocked on one side, listening for helicopters. Whenever we heard their clatter, we would run for the car and drive off at high speed. Adrenaline kept us light on our feet. Claustrophobia kept us moving. We were lucky. We were outsiders. We could escape at the end of every day. Only the Chechens couldn't.

*

During that week, Russian troops brought the war slowly to Chernorechiye.

# The Weekend

On my first couple of days there, it was quiet. Just gunfire in the distance, and the occasional boom of a far-off shell. Watchful people slipped out of their apartment blocks in search of food and water. We parked the car safely round the back of the buildings, and left Misha guarding it. Families with buckets were going to the dam, slipping on mud under the thin snow. They paused at every explosion, turned round to stare expressionlessly at the centre, then went back to their task. Pyatras, bigger than most of the Chechens, hauled up a few buckets to help one taut-faced woman, and asked her what had gone on since yesterday.

'It's quiet today. But last night they bombed just up the road and two people were killed,' she said. She didn't want to talk. Her sons hurried to take the buckets.

There were very few fighters about. We met two scared sixteen-year-olds, Dzhemail and Umar, sheltering by a closed kiosk, not talking to anyone. They had fuzzy chins and spots. They said they had come from Ingushetia to help the fighters for a week. Now they were going home to rest. They had huge bags with them, set down inconspicuously against the kiosk. We asked them where they'd been fighting, and what with. 'Oh, they give you guns,' Dzhemail said uneasily. 'We were in the centre . . .' he gestured vaguely back towards the smoke '. . . with Shamil's battalion.'

We left them hitching a lift, feeling hot and uncomfortable in our bulky, heavy, superfluous flak jackets and helmets.

'I don't believe they'd been fighting,' Pyatras said. 'I think they were looters.'

Later, a pair of real fighters came out of town over the dam. They were wearing white *khalatiki* – 'dressing-gowns' – over their clothes. Only their green headbands showed against the snow. It was a quiet day today, they said. Not much shelling. Not flying weather for the Russian planes: too much fog and cloud. They said the Chechens held positions in or around Minutka. The bus station was in their hands.

Another fighter, a handsome young man called Adam, was just coming out to go to battle. He stopped us on the dam. 'Have you been in the centre?' he asked eagerly. 'Not today,' answered Pyatras. 'Well, yesterday, then; did you see any Russian tanks?' persisted Adam. Pyatras said he'd seen a couple near the station the day before. Adam looked pleased. 'I want to get a tank, and I've looked and looked for two days and haven't found a single one. I'm off to get one of those two now!' he chirped, and ran off across the ice, his gun slung across his back, turning every now and then to wave back at us.

People were more expansive at the market. Antonina Petrovna, a stout Russian pensioner who had fled the city centre a week before for the peace of her daughter's apartment here, was prowling the stalls, looking tearful. She turned to me in despair. 'I've got no bread, no salt, nothing,' she said, her voice breaking. 'Hussssh,' broke in one of the Chechen stall-holders, Tamara, with a grin. 'You'll be looked after. Here, take this,' and she passed the elderly Russian woman a hunk of bread. Without a word of thanks, Antonina Petrovna shoved it in her string bag and made off hungrily along the icy pavement. The stall-holder looked at me and shrugged. An old Chechen woman in a flapping black coat sidled up to me with the beginning of a hard-luck story. The stall-holder gave her an icy look. She backed away. But I saw Pyatras slip her a bit of money.

Everyone was kind to Andrei and pigtailed Alyona, a pair of Russian kids who dragged their little sledge everywhere with them and pestered foreigners for chewing-gum and chocolate. Andrei was thirteen, and Alyona twelve. They were neighbours, and they were bored. They hadn't gone to school for a year. Most of their Chechen friends had left for the villages. They hated the cellar where their scared mothers spent days as well as nights. They got out all the time to play and to talk to people. 'God knows what will become of us all if the war comes here,' Andrei said lugubriously the first time I met him, and I detected an echo of his mother's voice. But he cheered up quickly when Pyatras gave him a square of chocolate. Five minutes later, he and Alyona were whooping and shrieking on their sledge again.

If I asked a question about what 'the Russians' were doing, meaning 'the Russian military' or 'Moscow's army', Chechens stopped and looked worriedly at my lips, trying to make out the sense of what I was saying as anxiously as if I had suddenly started talking a foreign language. To them, 'the Russians' meant only the locals they lived with, their neighbours, fellow victims of Moscow. They didn't confuse the two, and didn't make the mistake of turning on local Russians as envoys of Moscow. Light would only slowly dawn in their eyes. 'Oh . . . you mean the *military*,' people would say eventually, and spit on the ground or look disgusted. 'Not *our* Russians, *nashi*. Our people here might be Russians, but they're as brave as the Chechens.' I resolved not to make the same mistake again.

*

It was a weekend of bravado . . .

A layer of ice had already formed on his two pails of water since Alek, bent double by their weight and his seventy-seven years, started the slow shuffle back from the dam to his one-roomed apartment. 'I hardly remember when there was running water or electricity here,' he said, putting down the pails for a breather. 'But I'm glad our boys are still fighting on. Chechens want independence, or death.'

A crowd of men gathered around him in the calm of a courtyard. No one in it wanted to hear anything about bowing down to superior Russian strength, about being beaten, or about giving up. The voices chorused defiance. Stubbly chins jutted out.

'What do you mean, this can't go on much longer? We've already won. We've kept the Russian army at bay for six weeks. The mightiest army in the world. Whatever happens after this, they can't take that away from us.'

'This is the army the Americans were so scared of for fifty years. But we're not scared. Their army has more generals than any other army in the world. But look at their fat bellies. Are those fighting generals? No, they're sitting-at-table generals. Vodka generals. No wonder they're doing so badly.'

'They've brought so much stuff here it would be enough for any war in the world. Defence ministry troops, interior ministry troops, FSK, and all this firepower,' said one wizened little man, with a wicked grin. 'All they've forgotten is the cosmonauts.'

. . . and doubts.

'God knows things were bad enough here before, under Dudayev, when we didn't get paid for thirteen months at a time. But now they're getting even worse,' Tamara said.

'I don't like the fighters coming here. They'll bring the war to us,' the woman next to her added with foreboding.

There were accusations . . .

The two fighters watching the city from the market were full of contempt for the Russian troops. 'Of course, what they're doing isn't really fighting. They shoot into residential districts with long-range artillery. What kind of fighting's that? They wouldn't dare fight us hand to hand with their infantry. They're cowards, and they have no honour.'

. . . and mocking laughter . . .

'Where did you get your weapons from?' I asked the fighters.

'From the Russians, during the New Year fighting!' answered Mukhtar, with a grin.

'From Urus-Martan,' answered Lechi, with a bigger grin. He had a grenade-launcher slung over his back. He had spent his savings, nearly $1,000, on one of the many weapons of Russian origin being sold on the sly by the Russian soldiers through middlemen at markets in Chechen opposition territory. It hadn't been a good bargain, Lechi said regretfully; he had found out afterwards that a lot of fighters were buying arms direct from the enemy and making huge savings. 'Still, it shows what kind of people these Russian soldiers are; not bothered we might use our weapons to kill their comrades, so corrupt they'd sell their own granny if they could make a quick profit.'

. . . and counter-accusations.

Dusk at the Russian checkpoint on the road home, and the nervous soldiers had vanished below ground. Only three of them were still at their post, smoking nervously and glancing at the long shadows in the hedgerows. 'I hate night-time,' one young boy confided, peeping over my shoulder. 'They shoot at you in the dark and you can't see where the attack's coming from. Chechens are cowards. They won't fight like men, they just ambush you and melt back into the villages to hide behind their families. They use their mothers and their children as human shields. And then what? They get a good sleep while we're out here freezing, then they come back for another sneaky potshot, the bloody black cowards.'

But everything stayed quiet.

# Monday

At Sleptsovsk, we came across two busloads of Russian mothers, about to set off for Grozny. The mothers had tight perms, neat coats and red eyes. They carried rolled-up banners with handles attached to the sides, ready to be unfurled when they got out into town. The banners said things like 'Grachev is a butcher'. The mothers, and the few quiet fathers travelling with them, clearly thought they would be able to hold a demonstration in Grozny, then go home with their sons.

The Ingush emergencies ministry staff were supposed to be organizing the mothers' passage. But there was a lot of waiting going on. We sensed reluctance in the air. Mink-hatted officials dithered around the nearest bus, which was festooned with white flags and a banner with the sentimental appeal 'Soldiers! Don't Shoot Your Mothers!' in red lettering.

'They're supposed to guarantee the safety of the mothers. But how can they? I don't think they really want them to go. Look at them, poor dears. They've got no clue what it's like out there,' Misha said with a half-sad smile. We lurked for a bit, waiting to see them off.

A crowd of Ingushi also gathered in the middle of Sleptsovsk to wish the mothers good luck. But the mothers, proudly Russian, weren't speaking to darkies. They stared stonily into the distance when people came up to them, or looked tearful. They did talk to me, though, because of my fair hair and Western looks. A mother in a red fur-trimmed coat, Alla Filippova, burst into tears and I did what I could to comfort her.

'Who wants this war? What good is it to anyone? I want my son back,' she sobbed. Her eighteen-year-old Roma had been called up in Lipetsk in the autumn and been sent off to Chechnya almost at once. 'They tricked my son.' Blindly, she took my tissues.

One of the buses finally set off. We followed it for a bit. Then, before we'd even got to the Chechen border, it pulled in by a tanker. 'I don't believe it,' Misha said with a laugh. 'Surely they haven't forgotten to get petrol?' But they had.

We passed that bus later on. It had got stuck in mud at the side of a road. The mothers looked helplessly out of the windows as a truck struggled to tow it out of its rut. 'No, they're definitely not trying,' Misha chuckled. But he was sorry for the Russian mothers. He was thirty-six, and he had six kids of his own.

But we had only just arrived in Chernorechiye ourselves when the second bus showed up. It stopped right at the top of the market, on the main road. The Ingushi emergencies ministry men went off with a waiting group of fighters to find some official Chechens who could be entrusted with helping the mothers find their captive sons.

The Chechen stall-holders were delighted the mothers had come all the way to Grozny on their gallant, if chaotic trip. A big crowd of people gathered round the bus, smiling and waving encouragement at the mothers. But the Russian mothers were scared of the Chechen faces at the window. They stared tight-lipped into space. They wouldn't get off the bus.

No one outside took any notice of the mothers' pinched faces and forbidding looks.

'I think they're great,' enthused Tamara. Her surname was Bezurkayeva. She was fifty. Like everyone else in Chechnya, she was convinced the war only served the interests of the Russian military mafia. 'They're showing the world – and Moscow – that no one wants this war, that ordinary Russians don't want it any more than Chechens. They're showing we all want the same thing: peace. Good for them!'

The crowd at the water's edge grew bigger and more boisterous. Everyone wanted to congratulate the shy mothers. Everyone hoped they would find their sons.

'We should keep back a bit. The Russians will see the crowd and shell it,' Pyatras said cautiously. 'It's a disaster waiting to happen.'

We moved off to the side of a nearby building, lit cigarettes, and shooed away the inquisitive Andrei and Alyona.

Suddenly a great boom close to shattered the calm of the foggy morning.

'See?' I saw the word on Pyatras's lips, but I couldn't hear it.

We dodged round the back of the building.

The crowd scattered within seconds. The cars that had assembled near the bus screeched away from the exposed junction.

'Look what filthy swine those Russian soldiers are,' yelled one Chechen man through dirty gold teeth, as he ran for cover. 'It's just like them to shoot at their own mothers.'

The mothers poured out of the bus and fled in panic behind the shelter of the block of flats, clutching their hats and handbags. With a scream of brakes and jamming gears, the bus turned round in the road and hurried round the corner after them.

A measure of calm returned as they regrouped in the sheltered courtyard. They clustered together, some angry, some crying. Deprived of the shield of their bus windows, one or two of the braver mothers dared to strike up conversations with the phlegmatic Chechen women who were gathering around them again to make sure they were all right.

'I had no idea you had to live in these conditions, facing all this bombing,' one plump Russian matron said in wonder, as the thunderclaps of shell fire rolled on.

'Oh, there's not a day goes without something like this,' Tamara answered breezily. 'We don't even think about it any more. What worries me more is the bloody awful cold. There's been no heating or light for days.'

Less courageous Russian mothers huddled around a staircase at the edge of the snowy courtyard, wincing at the sounds, and at the sight of the rubble piled up in front of them.

One was angry. 'I'm not leaving until I get my son back, even if I have to sleep in cellars till I find him,' she said, tears and rage mingling on her big square face.

Others were in a softer panic. 'I've never been in anything like this,' another whimpered helplessly, with wet eyes. 'I don't know what to do next.'

But even the most frightened mothers got their courage back when the emergencies ministry men from Ingushetia reappeared a few minutes later. The bus started, they scurried into it, and they drove off to the *profilaktoriya* to work out what to do next. They left one of their banners behind, still neatly rolled up, against a courtyard wall.

We didn't chance it on the open road beside the dam. We walked back through the courtyards. Misha was already running the car by the time we reached it.

*

By the time I met the Russian parents again – a week later in Nazran – they had retrieved six of their missing sons and stopped being scared of Chechens.

They'd spent one night at the *profilaktoriya*. The next morning, Chechen fighters had taken them into the city to search for their children. The Russian bombardment was so intense it was impossible to reach and rescue some boys, hiding in cellars with the locals. A schoolteacher father from Rostov, with metal-rimmed glasses and a neat Lenin beard, had found out which cellar his son was in, but had to leave him behind. 'We ran from cellar to cellar. But it was too dangerous to get to the one he was in. There were rooftop snipers.'

Thin and blonde and tense, Nina Davidova, an engineer from Moscow, had not found her nineteen-year-old son Sasha either, after two nights in the cellars. But she spoke warmly of the Chechens who had helped her try, and was horrified by the Russian-inflicted violence she had seen. Her sympathies had completely changed. She was now angrily convinced that the Moscow troops had deliberately shot at the mothers. And she was astonished to find how untrue the official information from Moscow had been all along.

'They were saying in the Russian parliament that there would be provocations if we went to Grozny. They said Chechen fighters would kill us, and blame our deaths on the Russians. In actual fact, it was completely the other way around . . . We have the impression that the Russian troops knew where we were staying, and that's why they shelled those houses. All the Chechens looking after us in the cellars said we were in the heaviest attacks of the war. The Chechen fighters *helped* us under fire. And when we showed them our photos of our boys, they all gathered round, trying to remember where they'd seen them and which cellar they might be in. The policy being made by those in power in Russia is a criminal policy. The people who are making it are criminals.'

She was planning to go to Mozdok the next day with other unsuccessful members of the group. They wanted to lobby the generals to stop killing people in Grozny.

# Tuesday

Small, grimy and wrinkled, Ruslan Galayev was loading the last of 2,000 square brown loaves into his truck outside the Sleptsovsk bread factory. They were a daily free gift from the factory in Ingushetia to the people of southern Grozny. For hungry people in cellars, they were a lifesaver. Galayev had been going in every morning for a month, rattling through the icy no-man's-land of the countryside, touring the southern city districts, and distributing two free loaves to all comers. The white hanky tied to the side of his truck didn't stop anyone shooting, he said. 'Any villain can wave a white flag.' But nothing bothered Galayev.

'No one else wants to take the risk, but I'm not scared,' the Ingush truck-driver said, a game smile cracking his tough little face. 'People in Grozny need me, and somebody's got to take their bread to them.'

He was thirty-eight, he had four children, he'd been married three times. 'So I can go on doing this right to the end. I've had my fun and I've got my heirs. What have I got to lose?'

Galayev's pride and joy was the bullet hole which damaged his truck but left him unscathed when a rooftop sniper tried to finish him off at the height of the city-centre fighting in early January. The entry hole went through the windscreen, in front of the driver's seat, at head height. The exit hole went through the driver's seat. By rights, the bullet should have killed him. Only his smoking habit saved his life, he chuckled.

'I was already past Minutka and opening a packet of cigarettes with one hand. I got the first cigarette out of it, and then I leaned right over to get some matches out of the glove compartment. I took my eyes off the road for a split second, and when I looked back ahead there was that bullet hole and the noise of things breaking right near me. That's what saved me,' Galayev said. He had kept the matches and the packet of cigarettes, still with all but one cigarette inside, as a lucky mascot.

'I've seen him giving out the bread,' Misha said as we set off. 'It's not a pretty sight watching people go after him, grannies grabbing and pushing, everyone desperate for an extra loaf. It's Stalingrad all over again.'

We often saw Galayev's truck after that. He always waved, and hooted cheerily.

There wasn't much good cheer left at Chernorechiye that Tuesday morning. The market was crowded when we arrived at ten o'clock, but not with shoppers. Traffic jams of people were leaving, some in trucks weighed down with tattered furniture, some in horse-drawn carts with cows tied to their axles, some on foot, carrying sacks on their backs. Disconsolate boys shuffled behind. Confused dogs barked at the trucks. There had been more shelling overnight, at 2 a.m. and then at seven. There was new debris in the courtyards.

'They don't want to let us sleep. They won't let us sleep at night,' Musa, an engineer with wild eyes, a long overcoat, and stubble, told me when I asked what had been happening.

Only Antonina Petrovna was still turning over packets of soup at one market stall, with a discouraged air. 'The prices have gone right up,' she said, looking at me in horror before scuttling off back to her cellar. She was right to take shelter.

At twenty to eleven, the shelling began, and it had got uncomfortably close. By the middle of the day, the long rumble of Grad multiple rocket-launchers was shaking the city, and the boom of artillery. From next door in Factory District, just over the tram tracks, came the brisk answering rattle of automatic fire from the Chechen fighters' guns.

'Have you noticed,' Pyatras said, lighting a cigarette, 'how quiet it always is until just after half-past ten?'

'Do you think,' I answered, wrapping my scarf tighter round my neck to stop the white cold seeping in, 'that the Russian military finish breakfast at half-past ten, and then have a quick fag-break before they start firing?'

'How much longer,' said Pyatras, not laughing, 'do you think it will be before they start on Chernorechiye?'

\*

I could see that the front-lines had shifted, because dozens of newcomers from the centre were appearing at the market today, petrified people with empty eyes who had at last managed to escape. They all told the same story: Russian snipers on the roofs, picking off civilians who ventured out of their freezing holes in the ground for water or scraps of food; dogs eating bodies in the streets. Anyone in Chernorechiye who had a car was bringing it to the market and ferrying these people on out of town, either for money or just out of pity.

Zemfira clawed at my coat sleeve. She and the three silent children behind her had run to Chernorechiye, half-blind with terror, from the cellar they had been hiding in for three weeks. When she made her dash for it that morning, she saw that her apartment block had been destroyed over her head.

'My two sisters are still there. They saw the snipers on the rooftop. They didn't dare come out,' she quavered. She couldn't keep her thoughts together. Her sheepskin coat was filthy and she was clutching just one tattered plastic bag in her hand. 'Look at me, look at me! I worked for years for my flat. Now I've got nothing. I'm like a gypsy.'

She was going to take her children on foot to their mother's house in a village a day's walk from Grozny. They set off down the highway, trotting light on their feet with panic.

The old couple could hardly walk. They clung feebly together. They had stayed in their flat until their front room had blown away during the night. Waking up in the dust and wind and noise, Tonya called for her husband but there was no answer. She thought he was dead, but he was only deaf. She felt along the floor in the dark and found him, trapped under a cupboard, once he came to and began calling her name. Somehow, she found the strength to pull the cupboard off him and help him up. They made up a bag of belongings to carry away on foot, but looters stopped them in the night and stole everything at knife-point.

I bought them the first food I found at Tamara's stall, biscuits. Tonya was frail and genteel with shock. 'He can't eat them because of his teeth, dear,' she said apologetically. 'We left his teeth behind.' I found him some chocolate instead. He sat on a bench, sucking quietly at it with his bare gums, hands as pink and tentative as a white mouse's paws. Pyatras found them a car. They were Russian. They had nowhere to go, but they had nowhere to stay here either. Pyatras gave Tonya $100. She took it quietly. There was no fight in her.

Mazhit Makhmetov was a businessman gone to seed: white shirt torn and crumpled, one cufflink, slept-in cashmere coat, accidental beard, eyes red with fatigue and stress. The cellar he had escaped from that morning was near the post office. He was strangely calm, but he had seen horrors he'd never imagined possible on his lone walk to safety: drunken Russian soldiers prowling from house to house, thieving, ransacking cupboards, ordering any Chechens they found in cellars to bring out their vodka and sausage, yelling and swearing.

'They're killing people for refusing to bring them vodka,' he said. 'They're killing people for not having vodka to bring them. The worst possible kind of looting is going on. They punish the least disobedience with execution.'

Ruslan Galayev's truck was empty. He'd given out all his bread. He loaded it up with refugees instead, and set off for Ingushetia.

*

Pyatras and I went to a funeral.

We were down at the other end of the road, near the *profilaktoriya*, when the little cortège shuffled slowly out of the thin white mist to the quiet sound of sobbing, making for the neglected Russian Orthodox cemetery in a field by the water's edge. The coffin was a makeshift affair of old cupboard doors. The woman in it had been dead for a week. She and her brother were killed in their flat when one of the first night shells exploded in Chernorechiye. They had shrapnel wounds everywhere. Their doctor neighbour had done emergency operations on both of them, but couldn't save them. The brother had been buried on Monday. Both corpses had been kept in a cellar, along with many others, until boxes could be found or made to bury them in. The new fighting around Factory District meant that the Christians of Grozny couldn't get coffins any more. Muslims were cut off from their cemeteries.

An elderly Russian woman at the roadside was sobbing on Antonina Petrovna's arm. She was Raya, an engineer, a neighbour of the dead woman. 'We can't even bury our dead properly, that's how low they've brought us. The Russian army aren't attacking military people, they're massacring civilians.' She pulled her threadbare coat tighter round her short body. 'These aren't just my tears. They're the tears of a million people for a great tragedy.'

It was true, even if it was Russian hyperbole. Musa the Chechen engineer, another neighbour of the dead woman, had recovered the poise lost during his sleepless night enough to come along and pay his last respects. He couldn't match Raya's tearful rhetoric but, in a lower key, he agreed. 'We've had to bury our dead in courtyards, without the ceremonies due to them,' he said. They nodded at each other.

Pyatras came back from the graveside. 'Look over there. Someone's waving at you,' he said to me, 'and we should go soon. I thought I heard helicopters just now.'

I looked up. There were about a dozen fighters in white, with grenade-launchers and Kalashnikovs on their backs, lugging big sacks of ammunition down the road towards the *profilaktoriya*. One of them was staring at me and waving.

I didn't recognize him. I went closer. He was a big man, and there was something familiar about his face. He hugged me sideways, Chechen horseback style, his left arm to my right. 'Shamkhan ... Shamkhan Sheimiyev,' he prompted. 'We're old friends. I met you at the interior ministry in 1993. The protest meeting. I gave you a leg-up on to a car roof.'

He'd changed, but suddenly I saw in this adult face, its expression pared down to the caution of wartime, the rough youth Shamkhan I had met two springs ago. I smiled and hugged him back. Now he had an interior ministry uniform on under his *khalatik*, and a knife at his belt. 'I'd forgotten that demonstration,' I said, to make up for my non-recognition. 'Quite right too. Just

another stupid quarrel, and there've been so many of them since
. . . and now all this,' he answered sombrely.

Where had he been fighting? Up the road in Factory District, he
said. They'd moved back there yesterday. Now they were moving
their supplies back to the *profilaktoriya*, just to be on the safe side.
The nearest front-line had come very close – to 500 yards up the
road, to the near side of Factory District.

His eyes shifted up, away from my face. I looked round too.
The mist was thinning, and anyway the sound was unmistakeable.
Ghostly helicopters, on the other side of the dam, were hovering
over Aldy. Shamkhan froze. 'My aunt lives in Aldy,' he said. He
took out the two-foot-long *kindzhal* of tradition from his belt and
looked longingly at its gleaming, useless blade. 'They're too scared
of us to face us like men. If only the bastards would come down
and fight instead of hiding behind their bombs and missiles, we'd
show them.'

Our car was in front of the *profilaktoriya*. 'Helicopter!' Pyatras
shouted, holding open the front door for me. 'Want a lift?' I asked
Shamkhan. He shook his head. I ran off.


# Wednesday


More refugees streaming away down the road. Thick fog. From
twenty to eleven onwards, the thunder and whistle of battle in
Factory District.

It was the attack on Aldy the previous evening that had made
up Umar Rasayev's mind to get his family out. Armchair legs stuck
out of the window of the oil worker's tiny car. There were three
kids in the back seat, half-buried in blankets and saucepans. In the
passenger seat, with three smaller children on top of her, his wife's
face was set. She didn't seem to notice the tears on her cheeks.
'They're moving further and further out every night,' Umar
Rasayev said, stroking his long beard as he waited for the traffic

ahead to clear. 'Our house has no cellar. I've got to take my family to the village. But then I'll come back and fight.'

Fighters stalked through Chernorechiye all day, polite if spoken to, disciplined and orderly, busy about their private business. 'Did you hear the news last night?' one asked me, with a grim little smile. 'Grachev said the city was completely taken and only isolated pockets of resistance remained. Typical. We'll show him how things really are.'

A furtive man whom I had noticed hanging round on previous days finally plucked up the courage to sidle up to me. His name was Vakha, and he had a problem, he said with a gold-tooth smile. Perhaps I could help? He wanted to fight, but he didn't know who for. Obviously, he didn't like the Russian troops. He couldn't run away to the opposition, who were national betrayers. But he couldn't fight for Dudayev either. Why not? I asked. Men from Chernorechiye had been saying all morning that they were going to join the fighters as soon as their families were safe. Because, he said, Dudayev's men had put him in prison and he'd only just got out when the war began. 'It was a trumped-up charge. They're a bunch of bastards, and I'm not going in with them.' He paused, then added in a confiding rush: 'My real problem is, I can see Chernorechiye's about to be taken, and my flat's full of weapons! Whoever finds them will be sure to execute me if I'm not on their side. What should I do?'

Antonina Petrovna didn't care about Vakha's dilemma. She swooped and dragged me away. Now she was genuinely in danger, she'd stopped weeping about shopping. Instead, she was hopping mad, shaking her fist in my face. It wasn't me she was angry with. It was Yeltsin. 'We slept in the cellar for the first time last night,' she howled. 'I'd like to strangle that Yeltsin with my bare hands. He and his generals should be here suffering this instead of us.'

There was hardly anything left to buy at the *bazarchik*, and prices had doubled. Chernorechiye was emptying out. But Tamara was still at her table with a few packet soups, talking to a calm old man selling kerosene whom she introduced as Lyoma Makhkhad-zhiyev.

Lyoma took us home with him. We walked through the courtyards, over the tramlines, into the borderline area with Factory District. Andrei and Alyona jogged along behind, bumping their sledge. 'Last night's work,' Lyoma said with detachment, pointing up at an apartment block. The last foot or so of a Russian missile stuck out of the wall five floors up. It hadn't exploded.

'Wow,' said Alyona, impressed. Andrei whistled.

Lyoma lived on the other side of the courtyard. Since last night, his home had become the cellar under his apartment block. He had gone down there to take soup to the six old Russian ladies from the upstairs flats. The six Russian women, all doctors, had retreated underground days before, and Lyoma had chosen to stay on in Grozny to look after them. While he was in the cellar talking to them a shell had blown away his flat on the ground floor.

There was something comforting about the fuzzy blackness of these shelters, the endless escapist thinking aloud by the invisible strangers all around, the illusion of safety behind breeze-block walls and fat pipes. But even the cellars would offer no real protection from the planes, once the fog cleared.

'We just sit here, night and day, alone with each other and our thoughts,' Irina Fyodorovna said gloomily. Sitting on a stool with a blanket over her knees, she poured out an anxious stream of consciousness into the dark. The only subject she avoided was the fact that she could not escape death at the hands of her own countrymen. It was too terrible to face.

She was worried looters would burgle her flat. She was resentful that looters had stolen most of the medicine from the polyclinic and that her job had vanished. She was scared that the boys upstairs, who had hung a green Chechen flag from their window, would get the whole apartment block destroyed when there were families still living in it. She fretted that the stress of the siege would send cancer rates up. She mourned for the lost era when all the Soviet nationalities lived in peace together. The other voices murmured a lullaby of assent.

'I'm sixty-five years old, and I've always worked here in Checheno-Ingushetia, and they'll have to carry me out of here dead or alive. I don't know what to do,' she said, and suddenly her voice broke, 'whether to go or stay.'

'Don't cry, Irina Fyodorovna,' quavered the other women's voices. I lit a match and held it to a cigarette, and saw the gleam of tears down their crumpled cheeks.

'Stay, Irina Fyodorovna,' said Lyoma's voice, with a hint of kindly laughter in it. He knew it was a choice she had no power to make. 'There's nowhere to go. But I'm here to look after you all.' But Irina Fyodorovna was not comforted.

'Who needs this war? Who needs this crazy, senseless war?' she asked on a rising note of hysteria, and the dark air around her was filled with the weeping of her colleagues.

Outside, blinking in the white snow, Lyoma only laughed when I ducked a bullet which hit the pipe running across the courtyard over my head. It landed, flattened, at my feet. 'Don't worry. You're safe with me,' he said, kindly if unrealistically. We walked slowly back through the estate to the market, a dozen open-air tables where he went every day to sell his kerosene store to make enough money to feed the old ladies. Without drawing attention to it, Lyoma swapped sides to shield me from the nearby firing. 'To be honest, I don't know what will happen here,' he thought aloud, his elderly face as tranquil as ever. 'Only God knows. But I wonder if even He knows what those bastards are thinking.' He laughed. 'My children wanted me to leave Grozny with them. Don't stay here, Dad, they said. But my wife understood. Someone's got to take care of the old dears. And I've had my life, had my kids. Everything's in the hands of God now.'

He nodded courteously as we reached the first stall. 'Come again,' he said. 'We'll be happy to see you, and we'll show you round Grozny properly when this craziness is all over.'

But I didn't see Lyoma again. The next morning, the Russian army moved in to wipe his suburb off the face of the earth.

*

There was an ugly last fuss at the market before we left. About twenty fighters were tying on their headbands, laughing quietly, and waiting for the order to go into Factory District. One was smoking. It was too much for Antonina Petrovna. She stormed up, shouting.

'You boys! You boys with your guns and your green and your war! I've had enough! I've had enough of Yeltsin, and Dudayev, and you, and the whole thing!' she yelled.

They patted her arm. They tried to comfort her. They were very calm.

'We're defending you, granny,' they said. 'You'll be safe in your cellar.'

No one noticed the breeze blowing the fog clear – until a Russian sniper's bullet, fired from over the dam, hit the tallest bearded fighter in the back of the shoulder. His flak jacket saved him. But the crowd scattered on the hissed word '*sssnai-per*', heads down.

Pyatras and I paused behind a disused kiosk, then slipped round the side of a big building, making for the car. Andrei and Alyona were still with us. So was the sledge.

'Aww. Everyone's going, and we'll be bored,' Alyona said.

Misha was starting up the engine.

'Children,' I said. 'You've got to go straight back to your mothers, and stay safely in your cellar. Now. It's not a good idea to be outside any more. Your mothers will be worried about you. Do you promise?'

'All right,' they said reluctantly as I got into the car. But they hadn't gone anywhere by the time we turned out on to the main road. There was a mutinous lift to both little chins.


# Thursday


The sun came out on Thursday morning. 'Flying weather,' Pyatras said. Sure enough, there were helicopters all along the road. At the Russian checkpoint near Samashki, the soldier who looked at our papers every day had got friendly. He shook his head doubtfully and asked: 'Are you sure you want to go to Grozny today?'

'It's our job,' we said, all together, but no one sounded very sure. He shrugged.

'Well, be careful,' he said, shaking his head, and waved us on.

It was deathly quiet in Chernorechiye. The market had vanished. There was new broken glass everywhere, no one on the street, and only one silhouette woman at the dam. I walked around the courtyards with Pyatras for a few minutes. We saw an old man wheezing as he slopped a pail of water round the side of a building, and two unfamiliar youths in a doorway. There had been shelling all night, they said, and the planes had flown over at dawn.

Then we saw the fighters, whisking through the courtyards. They had borrowed a couple of tiny children's sledges. They were pulling two corpses back through the courtyards on them, wrapped in white sheets. The dead heads and limbs were roped loosely together.

They had no time for us today. 'Show respect: don't photograph the dead,' one of them said. A few minutes later, they were back, busy as white ants, dragging more bodies off to the *profilaktoriya* to await burial.

'Let's go,' I said, being cowardly. 'Today's got a feeling of doom about it.'

'We've come too far to just leave. I can't go home without pictures,' Pyatras said. 'You go and sit with Misha for a few minutes, and I'll scout around up by the junction.'

He loped off, his dark pirate beard sticking out with determination.

Misha and I stood in a doorway, safely round the back of an apartment block, smoking. There was fighting just a couple of courtyards away. On the other side of our courtyard, three women had crept out to peer round the corner and see how close it was.

'This bloody cold,' Misha grumbled. 'Let's sit in the car and put the heater on.'

It was warmer in the car. We blew on our fingers. The women over the courtyard were craned right round their corner. I made the kind of sexist joke that I would never find English words for, about feminine curiosity, and Misha laughed. It was twenty to eleven.

*

The first artillery shell landed at the top of our building. In thunderous slow motion, part of the top floor slid down towards our car. I found myself staring, open-mouthed, fingers spread in front of me like a black-and-white minstrel. I looked round and found Misha doing the same. The three women were flat on their faces, and slow fountains of red sparks were rising from the courtyard.

Misha fumbled with the ignition. Bits of the building were hitting the roof as we pulled away; but the only way back was along the exposed dam road. The shell had come from there. Our eyebrows agreed there was no choice.

Misha's lumbering Niva hadn't ever flown so fast over an icy road. Behind us there were more red fountains and five explosions in quick succession. An old man who had slipped on the ice was lying in the road in a puddle of icy water, next to an upturned bucket. He turned and waved his arms imploringly at the heavens, or at us. We couldn't stop.

There was a sixth explosion, this time in front of us.

'They're hunting us,' Misha muttered. 'Get out of here, quick.'

We were in front of the long white *profilaktoriya*. There was a flimsy metal hut in front. We threw ourselves down by it. So did the frightened middle-aged driver of an aged ochre Zhiguli, who abandoned his car behind us. We clung to each other.

It was the wrong place to stop. From over the dam, the *profilaktoriya* was an easy target on a clear morning. It had a gate of two tall pink pillars, flanked by dead hedges. It was the obvious place to shoot at, too: the fighters had left bodies and probably weapons there, and the mothers had used it to sleep in. But we didn't have a choice.

An explosion just in front of Misha's beloved car, the symbol of middle-class Soviet respectability, cracked its windscreen and buckled the doors. All the glass in the flimsier Zhiguli shattered, and its doors blew off. Trees in the forest splintered and snapped. The missiles whistled by, chipping holes and tears in the masonry behind us.

There were pauses, when we would stand up, embarrassed, and begin to brush ourselves down and eye our cars longingly; but then another slow whistle in our ears would have us crouched back down in the snow. Misha, who had refused all offers of a flak jacket on fatalistic grounds, kept exposing his back to the blast to protect my ceramic-plated torso.

Stupid thoughts flashed through my brain: admiration for Misha's bravery, panic in case he died and I didn't know which pocket to find his car keys in, fear for Pyatras, interest at how few of the whistling mortars actually exploded, worry about making my boss pay for Misha's car repairs, interest at how little damage each hit did to the *profilaktoriya's* façade, terror at the soft weakness of human flesh ... It was when I caught myself in the girlish inner wail, 'I can't die in Armani jeans!' – and laughed – that I realized a new lull was beginning.

'Let's go,' I whispered. The other driver ran to his car, and we jumped into the Niva. It started. But Misha's crescent moon with its little green tassel had disintegrated. The safety of the woods enveloped us.

We stopped at the traffic police point on the edge of town to wait for Pyatras. It was eleven o'clock. Getting colder under the planes which swooped low over the woods, we waited, and smoked, and waited, and tried not to watch the clock, for the rest of the day.

For the rest of the day, people left Chernorechiye. The cars which crept out during the morning, during the full fury of the assault, had all been battered on the road. After one o'clock, the planes stopped flying for a couple of hours, the noise of battle died down, and the flow of traffic speeded up. Cars and coaches poured out. Tow-trucks ventured back to help broken-down vehicles. But most people left on foot, cautiously, through the woods.

A lot of people said they'd seen a big bearded photographer. He'd been in their cellar, or somewhere near; he was on the road; he was coming. Then an American journalist with a dark beard and camera came out. A false alarm. I cursed the lack of communications. We couldn't go back into Grozny; we couldn't leave; we didn't know whether Pyatras was alive or dead. Suddenly we weren't observers: we were in the same position as everyone else.

A friend of Misha's, a fat man called Umar, waited with us for a while, shaking his head at the bedraggled crowds emerging from the trees. 'This isn't war, it's butchery. We're ordinary peaceable people, and they're crushing us underfoot like cockroaches.'

One young man walked out with a single carrier bag, whistling. As he passed me, the bag stirred and mewed. There was a kitten in it. 'I'm taking it to the village,' he said, answering my raised eyebrow. 'Then I'm coming back here to join the fighters.'

Only one car went into Grozny that afternoon, against all the traffic heading for Urus-Martan and beyond. It was a sleek black BMW, the kind of Chechen car I hadn't seen since the war began. It purred up and glided to a halt beside me. Its driver was a sleek, handsome, laughing man in cashmere and a mink hat. I hadn't seen anyone like him in Grozny for a while either. I wondered if I was dreaming. 'What's the road like up ahead?' he asked.

'Not very safe when we came out,' I stammered. 'But we've been here a while. We're waiting for a friend. You should ask someone who's just been on the road.'

'Cheer up,' he said kindly. 'Your friend will get out. And I'm going in anyway, because my mother's sick and I've come all the way from Moscow to fetch her. I'm not scared of Russian troops. I've got a gun.' He made me guess where he had hidden it from the Russian checkpoints on the way in. The hub-caps of the wheels? I suggested. Under the seats? Taped to the underneath of the chassis? 'No, no,' he said, immensely pleased with himself. 'You're not even warm.' And he levered the plastic cover off the front of the steering wheel to show me. There, instead of a horn motor, was a deep empty hole with a pearl-handled pistol in it. I laughed in spite of myself. He waved and glided off towards Chernorechiye.

*

Pyatras turned up at four o'clock, long after I had convinced myself he was dead.

The shadows were getting long. Misha and I had silently smoked almost all the cigarettes. It was cold. The outward-bound traffic had almost stopped. A truckload of fighters had roared up from outside town and was unloading weapons. The planes were flying again.

A Zhiguli overloaded with big bearded fighters in green head-bands pulled up by the truck. I was too miserable even to look at it.

'*There* he is,' Misha said. I looked up, and he was right: Pyatras was disentangling his legs from the car. I hugged him, and our breast-plates clashed noisily, and we all laughed. We hurried him off to the battered Niva.

Pyatras had dived into the nearest cellar when the bombardment started. It was under an old people's home. Everyone in the cellar was frail and ill already, and the stress and darkness made them iller. The women prayed and wept as the planes roared overhead. One old man had a heart attack. 'But when it eased up at lunchtime they made me tea and invited me to stay,' Pyatras said. 'They were so sweet that I would have spent the night there if I hadn't thought you'd be worried.'

Warm with relief, we all told our stories several times, too loud and fast and with many repetitions of the word 'ba-BOOM!'. We tut-tutted over the damage to the car, whose straight lines had all gone wavy but which was mercifully still running anyway. Finally, our flood of words ran out.

'I hope those kids are all right,' I said into a long pause. 'Andrei and Alyona.'

'I was just thinking the same thing. Poor little scraps,' said Pyatras, who had two children.

Another long silence.

'Well, that's Russian soldiers for you. Attacking a place with no military positions. Attacking a suburb full of ordinary people,' Misha said.

'Yes,' Pyatras answered.

'Yes,' I answered.

'And that's it for Grozny,' Pyatras concluded. We nodded.

*

It wasn't quite the end for Grozny. The Chechen chief of staff, Aslan Maskhadov, announced that: 'Nobody intends to give up the city. In the near future, the fighting will move closer to the borders and beyond the borders of Chechnya.' His fighters slugged it out for most of the next month before disbanding their Grozny operation one night at the end of February and slipping out of town. By then, the city was a graveyard of mud and ruins.

Even then, the relentless shelling of Chernorechiye still hadn't let up. Khasan, a Chechen man, and a Russian woman reporter escaped through the woods on 26 February to try and arrange evacuation of the sick and wounded. The reporter had been trapped in the cellars there for a week. 'Conditions in Chernorechiye are the worst of the war,' Khasan said.

The massive Russian military punishment of Grozny was only the first of many to be meted out to the Chechens, both to small groups of fighters and much larger groups of bewildered civilians, as the war went on. The strategy taking shape was one of overkill.

# FOUR

Fifteen thousand Russian interior ministry troops came to Grozny as the battle died down. Drunk, scared and jeering, they went on the rampage for weeks. Moscow smugly said it controlled two-thirds of the city. The reality was different. The troops lived to the jerky rhythm of shell thud and gun crack, they raced nervously through the streets in APCs, they slept behind barbed wire. Shadowy night resistance was everywhere.

Some Russian soldiers shared their bread and cans of *tushyonka* stew with the people around them, but others got their revenge. They did what they pleased with the helpless civilians. The mental picture of the enemy imprinted on their brains seemed not to be the fighter, with gun and green suicide headband, but any Chechen.

*

One dying man I talked to was still so scared of what else Russian troops might do to him that he did not want his name published. 'Magomed' was skinny, thirty, and an ex-traffic cop from Stary Posyolok on Grozny's northern edge. He was greenish with pain; he had horrific shrapnel wounds up both legs, an ankle stripped down to the bone, and a knife slash in his left arm. Russian interior ministry troops had broken into his apartment building on the night of 31 January. They had herded 'Magomed', his family and all his neighbours out on to the dark street, where they separated the men and the women into two groups. 'Magomed' didn't know what had become of the women. The Russian troops had tortured the men, he whispered. 'They beat us round the legs, on the kidneys. I said we weren't fighters. But they were holding knives to our bellies and telling us to give them money. I have no money, I said. So they beat me more.' What 'Magomed' remembered most clearly from that brutal night was the handsome boy next to him in the crowded street, begging for mercy as Russian troops laid into him with fists, gun butts and sticks. 'They beat and beat him. Then the Russian officer took a swig out of his vodka bottle and said: "Finish him off." They shot him with a big-calibre armoured car gun, at close range. His chest disintegrated.' When the troops had had their fill of torturing 'Magomed', they threw him into a cellar, tossed five other men down on top, lobbed in two hand-grenades and raked the cellar with automatic gunfire. 'Magomed', at the bottom of the heap of bodies which included his brother, was the only survivor.

Two open mass graves were filled with about 1,000 bodies – unidentified and unidentifiable. Russian officers told a correspondent from *The Observer* in February that most were the bodies of Chechen fighters, but the bodies she saw, some newly dead, some already decomposing, were in civilian clothes. Many were women and children. Later the graves, filled with more bodies dragged out from the cellars, became a cause for health worries; as the weather warmed up, people grew scared that the fields of corpses would spread disease.

Wherever you went, anxious dark men fluttered up to you with stories of Russian abuse. In a sad display of faith in the machinery of the law, they sometimes pressed handwritten statements on you, headed 'STATEMENT' and addressed to the United Nations Human Rights Commissioner or the Chechen prosecutor-general, or the Russian newspapers.

'I feel everything's useless, but I have to do what I can,' said Khavazh Zhurtshchaliyev, a defeated-looking fifty-one-year-old public transport supervisor from northern Grozny who had escaped to Ingushetia. He gave me one of six neat copies of his detailed STATEMENT. 'If you can, please try to publish it.'

He and his brother Isa had worked at the local transport depot since 1964. The pair spent most of January in their cellar, hiding from the war. But calm fell on the morning of 31 January. They ventured out to check whether their workplace had been shelled or looted. They were stopped by a group of Russian *spetsnaz*. 'They started to beat us up with their gun butts. They beat us cruelly for a long time. As far as I understood, these people didn't want to go to the conflict zone, they were obviously scared and were venting all their rage on peaceful people. They took 120,000 roubles from me, my birth certificate, my military service certificate, my driving licence and the papers for my Moskvich 412 car. They took the same documents from my brother. They forced us to open the garage, threw us into the observation pit and threw a grenade in after us. I had seven shrapnel wounds. My brother had one serious wound in his left leg. We shammed dead. The soldiers locked the garage and left. We bound up the wounds which were bleeding fastest. We managed to get out four hours later with the help of our relatives and were given first aid. I demand an explanation from the legal structures as to why we had to suffer, and why such barbarity is possible in our state.'

In Moscow, Yeltsin's new human rights commissioner and justice minister, Valentin Kovalyov, said politely on Russian television that he was sorry if some civilians in Chechnya had been injured by 'stray bullets and chance shrapnel'.

'These practices are inducing dozens of new volunteers, who until now have been loyal to the federal authorities, to take up arms,' the opposition's Provisional Council was bold enough to say of its Moscow mentor.

*

Men like kindly, stolid Akhad Mutalipov – a thirty-five-year-old ticket inspector living in a one-storey house with a struggling apricot orchard in northern Grozny – had no doubt about what to do after two houses in their street in Michurin district were set on fire by drunken Russian troops. He and a couple of neighbours went to join the fighters.

Other matter-of-fact fighters were taxi drivers, teachers, farmers, accountants, shepherds or bureaucrats. They went out fighting in groups of twenty or thirty or forty. Each group had a boss who was in touch with the Chechen command. They kept loosely in touch, but the fighters trusted each other; there was no elaborate system of control. They could stay as long as they had the strength. They got their weapons from the command, or bought them from the Russians, or found them heaped up in places where Russians who had moved on had just abandoned them. With a visible sense of moral superiority, they told stories of Russian soldiers paying for their bottles of vodka at markets by flinging down a Makarov pistol.

Akhad came home to rest for a couple of days every week or ten days, but he never boasted about that other life facing tanks, snipers and helicopters. If he talked at all, it was about the slow overcoming of fear: the noisy terror of the first plane diving over his position on a hillside, the quiet surprise when his first sniper target fell down in the distance. With held breath and soft footfalls, he had learned to stand in the dark between two Russian posts and fire both ways, to hoodwink them into shooting at each other. He reminded me of elderly uncles in Britain, talking with acceptance about the war effort in the 1940s. When his father died, and he was the only man left in a family of five sisters, he came home to look after them. There was no bravado about him, just a sense of duty, and a gleam of mischief.

'Now that we have upset the hive, we have to catch all the bees,' said General Yevgeny Podkolzin.

As on-the-spot punishment petered out in Grozny, and the power élite in Moscow came to terms with the fact that the war would be likely to carry on for some time, three different hazy patterns of further Russian punishment for the disobedient natives began to appear.

All the 'answers' to the 'Chechen problem' were based on the same notion – that Chechen life was worth less than Russian. But otherwise they were very different.

Shakhrai's vision of creating a sense of Russian ethnic together-ness – by recalling last century's Caucasus-wide war between highlanders and Cossacks – swam in and out of focus.

So did the army's more brutal modern vision of a total military defeat for the enemy inside Chechnya, to be won by wiping out whole villages and towns at a time.

So did a separate police vision of a tiny land of Soviet-style concentration camps, in which disobedience was crushed by random arrests, torture and violence in uniform.

Eventually, Shakhrai's vision faded out. The other two remained.

*

All dressed up with nowhere to go, the Cossacks whom Shakhrai had helped call back into existence had trained and waited and watched for three years. But no one called on them to help when fighting started against the Muslim infidel. The Russian army and the interior ministry had no illusions about the usefulness of the neo-Cossacks. No one could think of a role for them. This wasn't the same war as last century's; concentrated in the tiny territory of Chechnya, it was explicitly about the aspirations of Dzhokhar Dudayev to secede from the Russian state. The image of the galloping all-Russian Cossack didn't fit in here. The romantic imagery of the old war was redundant now the unimaginative military had moved in.

Half a dozen neglected Cossacks hung about in Nazran, in the 'White House' city hall, changing into their Cossack uniforms in side-rooms next to the press office, appearing at conferences and meetings, hopefully clicking their spurs. And, perhaps with the parallel of the old war in mind, Russia made what seemed to be deliberate attempts, early in the war, to draw both Ingushetia and Dagestan into the modern fighting.

I watched from Ingushetia, which had no intention of going to war against Russia. President Ruslan Aushev had condemned the war, taken in 90,000 extra refugees from Chechnya, and offered to mediate between Yeltsin and Dudayev. His peacemaking efforts were ignored in Moscow, but Ingush officials quickly grew scared the little republic would be dragged into the conflict because Russia was annoyed by his dogged search for justice.

'We took the moral high ground from the start . . . we told the truth. These days, you get punished for that,' Ingushetia's vice-president, Boris Agapov – solidly built, blunt, reassuring, an ethnic Russian and Soviet ex-soldier – said with a wry grin.

A campaign of intimidation began, orchestrated by Shakhrai in Moscow.

In the last week of January, Shakhrai turned Moscow's propaganda machine on Ingushetia, saying first that Chechen fighters were setting up bases there, then that Dudayev was sheltering in Ingushetia, and finally that Ingushetia should be rejoined to Chechnya as it had been in Soviet times. Russian convoys passing through the main valley of Ingushetia shot up the houses they passed every few days, not caring that they were outside the official war zone. They did the same in Dagestan.

When I came out of the Ingush 'White House' government building, after talking to Agapov, three Russian helicopters were bearing down on the building. They swooped so low over it that one nearly hit the television aerial. 'That's not threatening, it's just stupid,' Misha muttered. 'And it's the third time they've done it this morning.'

Only the remotely intellectual, or the foolish, in the highlands responded to Shakhrai's Russian challenge with equally far-fetched promises of all-out war across the Caucasus. One of them was Salyakh Khamkhoyev, the young director of the Imam Ash-Shafii Islamic Institute in Nazran. Ingushetia was too quiet by far for him. Sitting very upright at his desk, with burning eyes and a birdlike touch of yellow at his breast, Khamkhoyev was waiting eagerly for a new religious war to engulf the whole Caucasus.

'You can call them liberators or nationalists, but all the Caucasian warriors who ever battled against Russia – Sheikh Mansur, Imam Shamil, and those that came afterwards – were fighting a *murid* war for their faith,' Khamkhoyev said with conviction, his neat hands passing abstemiously over tiny coffee cups and biscuits. 'It was in the name of *muridism* that the great Caucasus war of last century was fought, and it is that *murid* war which is being repeated at the moment in Chechnya. Of course. Dudayev's first slogan about the autonomy of the Chechen republic has been put on the back burner. It is no longer the national idea that is uniting people against the Russians; the war is already on the basis of *muridism*.'

It was the first time I had found someone in the North Caucasus who could talk coherently about religion. At quiet moments, I'd been asking everyone who had time to tell me about their faith. People had looked pleased, but also bashful and faintly surprised;

their Russian words blurred as they tried to convey meaning to me. 'Hmm, so you want to know about *murid*s and *murshid*s! . . . well, let's see, how to explain?' they would hesitate. They could tell me only vaguely that there were differences between the Naqshbandiya and the Qadiri Kuntakhadzhintsy, but they didn't know how to make me understand the differences. 'I know how to tell you,' Batyr, our hotel administrator said after long reflection. 'When someone dies who's a Naqshbandi believer, his family fasts for a week. But the Kuntakhadzhintsy are more open; they bring meat and have a feast and dance and sing for a week.'

They could tell me the names of the little sects they belonged to, but they were names which meant nothing to me. All I had really found out was that everyone I'd talked to did belong to one of many mystical religious groups, just as everyone was observing a daylight fast now Ramadan had begun. But the rest was a vague fumble with the resistant Russian language. We were all foreigners in Russian; I could see I didn't know precise enough words to ask the right questions in an immediately understandable way, and I also quickly realized that most Chechens probably never talked about their religious beliefs in Russian.

With Khamkhoyev, however, there was only dazzling clarity. Born to a religious family, the son and grandson of clerics repressed under Soviet rule, he had trained in a Muslim academy in distant Tashkent before coming home in 1990 to open his own medresseh with financial help from Egypt. He had all the learned idealism of the bearded students who padded over the carpets in their socks, and all the relentless logic of the teacher.

'*Muridism* isn't taught but passed down orally. A person belongs to a sect from birth. There are some sects which only exist here and others which are stronger in Chechnya, but the Naqshbandiya and Qadiriya are the most important everywhere,' he said. 'Now our peoples are being united by *muridism* again. The Chechens and Ingush and Dagestanis are all being drawn together by *muridism*. No borders and no talk of rival sovereignty claims can pull us apart. Our aims and our concerns are shared. Specific religious advances are already going on to support the *murids*. I have taken part myself in secret and open meetings in Dagestan, Kabarda,

Karachayevo-Cherkessia and Ingushetia. When this acquires a legal form it will have spread right across the whole North Caucasus. An unquenchable war will begin.'

It was said with passion, but Khamkhoyev's dream of responding to the Russian invasion with an all-out religious war was only wishful thinking. The North Caucasus republics around Chechnya were doing everything they could to stay out of trouble with modern Russia. No one wanted to be dragged into the fighting.

The level-headed, diplomatic Ingushi were too canny to be drawn into war. Aushev and Agapov kept their homeland's plight in the Russian limelight with a stream of interviews, making a careful distinction between the warmongers, whom they condemned, and the Moscow leadership, which they depicted as benign. 'We'd like to separate ourselves from the group of people making Russia's current policy – and notably from Shakhrai – but not from Russia itself,' Agapov said firmly.

Shakhrai's dream faded, and only the disconsolate Cossacks were left in Nazran, with their uniforms packed neatly into bags, waiting for a chance to dress up and defend their country.

*

The army's solution, having more or less captured Grozny, was to crush and destroy all resistance in the villages – by crushing and destroying the villages.

The people of Samashki, the big village near the Russian checkpoint in south-western Chechnya, were in turmoil in the first weeks of the war. They stood and talked for hours on their village square, debating whether to make a deal with the Russians or to fight. The old men, who remembered the brutality of Russia during the deportations, were scared and wanted to make a deal. The young men, full of dreams, wanted to fight. Every few days, the Russian tank columns rumbled past the edge of their village and over their fields, up to the ridge of hills, making for Grozny. The tanks didn't enter Samashki; the villagers let them be.

Then, one day in late January, a Russian tank column took a new route – through Samashki itself. A fight broke out. Some of the young men attacked the tank convoy. We saw a burned-out

Russian vehicle as we headed home from Grozny that evening. Crowds of angry men were standing in the road. 'Elders waving their sticks; it's a bad sign,' Misha said.

A few days later, Russia's first punishment materialized. Samashki was sheltering fighters, the Russian command said. Tanks, artillery and helicopters surrounded the village on three sides. They bombarded it all night. Samashki's population had swelled to 20,000 with all the newcomers from Grozny. Dozens of people were killed. As their families buried them, Russian helicopters returned two days running to fire on the mourners.

Russian troops also set up checkpoints on all roads leading to the village. Men who wanted to enter or leave had to pay between 10,000 and 50,000 roubles (or the equivalent in vodka). These checkpoints were not attacked. On 12 February, an OMON interior ministry riot police unit demanded entry to the village, which was granted. Once inside, they started shooting, and drunken soldiers abused women, an offence to which Chechen society is particularly sensitive. The men of Samashki returned their fire and the Russians retreated. Afterwards, the elders of Samashki decided not to allow Russian troops in any more, and the village entrances were guarded by armed men.

The original Russian pretext for attack was a self-fulfilling prophecy. The closed village started to attract Chechen fighters retreating from Grozny. By March, according to the human rights group Pax Christi, there were about 400 armed men around Samashki, operating out of a base in a forest just outside the village.

*

My hotel window rattled all through the night with the thunder of artillery, and, many slow seconds later, the muffled sound of distant explosions. From somewhere nearby, Russian forces were shelling the forests around Bamut. A village which began in orchards, it spread from the plain up a steep hillside; in the craggy woods above it was an abandoned Soviet rocket silo. In Moscow, legend had it the fighters there were invincible, because they holed up in the reinforced concrete passages underground and escaped the Russian air and Grad multiple-launcher rocket strikes that followed the early shelling. But the fighters said they were out on the hillside, taking their chances; there would have been no time to run to the distant shelters. The Russian punishment went on and on. Villagers fled. But the fighters around Bamut wouldn't give in.

*

Fighters moved to Argun and Shali. Russian forces shelled the town of Argun in February, but not its front-line positions along the river. Instead, they destroyed buildings in the centre of town. The Russian planes streaked so low over southern Shali that watchers thought the pilots could see the children running round in a playground. They bombed the playground, killing two children and their parents and wounding fifteen other people. Bits of hair and flesh were spattered over nearby fences. One boy's head was blown down the street.

*

Sernovodsk, a Chechen village on the unclear border with Ingush-etia, wasn't fighting. In January, Khizar Vitayev at the town council had locked up everyone's weapons in the administrative building just in case. But the 12,000 people living there still went in terror that Russia would find an excuse to punish them.

Sernovodsk's decrepit hillside hotels, intended for tourists to take fresh air and the local spring waters, were packed with an extra 8,000 refugees from Grozny. Sickly children swarmed around. Refugee laundry flapped from every balcony. There was no heat or light, and not much food. But people who had escaped Grozny without their passports could go no further; Russian border guards had set up a checkpoint a mile away at the start of February, and troops in two armoured cars were turning back anyone without identification documents. Zara and Zura, two sisters from Grozny who shared a room with their bony children, were among those trapped in Sernovodsk. They were convinced that the Russian helicopters always hovering overhead were looking for a pretext to attack and kill off the refugees.

Leaflets fluttered down over Sernovodsk, signed by Viktor Chernomyrdin, the Russian prime minister. 'People of Sernovodsk! You have been betrayed!' they read:

> The people around Dudayev are already saying he and his family have fled abroad. Dudayev's closest aides are driving off in Kamaz trucks property looted from the Chechen people. They are calling on you to resist so they can have time to get out as much as possible. DON'T BELIEVE THEM. Those of you who continue to carry weapons will be strictly dealt with if a single shot is fired. We will answer any provocations with mighty rocket-bombing strikes. YOUR LIFE AND THE LIVES OF YOUR CHILDREN ARE IN YOUR HANDS!

'That's not all the helicopters have been doing,' said Rumi, the head cook, a no-nonsense woman in her fifties. 'I was walking down the hill two days ago when I came across a neat pile of weapons, just sitting there. There were grenades and grenade-launchers and guns. I got two other women to help and we took them to the council and handed them in. No one knew where they came from. Then, yesterday, one of the Russian helicopters landed on the hill again. We sent a couple of men over to see what they were up to. They came back with another load of weapons, which the helicopter had left behind in another neat pile.'

Rumi believed the Russians were deliberately providing Serno-vodsk with a few guns to provoke some local hothead into taking a potshot at one of them. 'That would be all the excuse they need to move in and finish us all off,' she said nervously.

*

The most cautious of Chechen district administrations, in Urus-Martan, tried to avoid the possibility of Russian retaliation right at the start by making a deal with Moscow.

Urus-Martan had refused to recognize Dudayev's rule since August 1994. Its administration chief, Yusup Elmurzayev, a soft-spoken ex-history teacher in his late thirties, blamed Dudayev, not Russia, for the carnage in Grozny. He said attempts to reason with Dudayev had been a waste of time. 'I know the pen is mightier than the sword, but we tried for three and a half years to sort things out peacefully with Dudayev, and we only ever got one answer – "Obey me".' So Elmurzayev invited Russia's Yegorov and Stepashin to his quiet town just outside Grozny at the beginning of January 1995, and got security guarantees from them. His local government mustered a self-defence force of about 13,000 men, and armed them 'from several channels; not from Russia, but I have to be honest with you and say that some of the channels aren't strictly legal,' he said with a grin. But Elmurzayev said he still wanted Chechen independence, and he denied his little opposition army was behind the mysterious blowing up of bridges all around Urus-Martan district, widely blamed on 'the opposition'. His constituents were not fighting other Chechens, either on their own behalf or on Russia's. 'We are not Russia's fifth column,' he insisted.

Some of the men on the scruffy square outside his government building were disparaging about Elmurzayev's cowardice. But refugees desperate for safety flooded into Urus-Martan district, swelling its population from 110,000 to 370,000 by January 1995.

*

Even taking the Russian side didn't always work. Chechens who opted for peace at any price had no guarantee Russian punishment would not be unleashed anyway. Even the opposition centre, Nadterechny District, which had let the vast flow of Russian troops and equipment into Chechnya to attack Dudayev in Grozny, was not exempt from retribution.

The Russians were everywhere here. An endless flow of muddy army lorries and armoured vehicles crawled down the highway, to and from Mozdok, from checkpoint to sodden checkpoint. Drab tents flowered in the fields.

In the windswept local capital, Znamenskoye, the rough government building housed Avturkhanov's men on one floor and those of Gantemirov – now named as the future mayor of Grozny – on another. They weren't speaking to each other. Gantemirov flitted about in smart suits and cars, smooth-featured and young and busy; Avturkhanov swept grandly in and out of his shabby office, talking for hours every day to Mozdok by phone and to a stream of Russian visitors from Mozdok in person.

Outside, an unhappy crowd gathered every day on the square to complain about the Russians' abuse of power. 'Under Dzhokhar, we didn't fight for three years, although we never recognized his power. But as soon as the Russians came we started losing ten to fifteen people a day,' cried an angry man in a flapping coat. All stories told on the square were ugly.

Everything happening in Nadterechny was ugly. When the Russians came, they had ordered the villages of the opposition-held north to hand over their weapons. Ramzan Tokayev, prefect of Naurskaya village, personally persuaded the villagers of Naurskaya and nearby Ishcherskaya to hand over their 142 guns, 127 grenades and 21 mini-grenades 'so that our people should not be regarded as bandit formations'.

Their act of submission did them no good. The very next day, 16 January, masked Russian interior ministry troops burst into both villages.[11] They blew up four houses in Ishcherskaya and stole a car trailer. In Naurskaya, they stole wristwatches from five men and 'confiscated' two television sets and five tape recorders from the houses they searched. They killed nine people, and arrested twenty-three more.

Nervously, Tokayev complained to the interior ministry General Alexei Katsibailo. He got nowhere. 'I will not stand slander! Give me names, surnames!' the general yelled. But, stammered Tokayev, all the Russian troops were wearing masks, and they were carrying guns without identifying marks ... He was rudely interrupted by the general.

'I know that myself,' Katsibailo snapped. 'Ask Dudayev's marauders about it. My men had nothing to do with this.'

Frightened by the Russian soldiers' pillaging, villagers in nearby Nikolayevskaya, Severnaya and Savelyovskaya flatly refused to hand over their weapons. They insisted on guarding their villages and the local Fifteenth Dairy Farm themselves. But Russian troops attacked the dairy farm on the night of 20 January. They captured

11. *Moscow News*, No. 4, 27 Jan.–2 Feb. 1995.

nineteen people and killed three of them as they drove them off to
Mozdok. One Russian villager, Pyotr Paramonov, was killed for
the indignant remark: 'What are you doing?' as the prisoners were
being tied up, and two Chechens were killed for moving. The
Znamenskoye administration chief, Zaindi Choltayev, demanded
that the Russian military raiders be punished. But Yegorov's local
Russian representative would only identify the gunmen as 'an
unidentified special unit or some other force' . . . and let the
investigation drop.

Small detachments of Dudayev's white-robed fighters came to
Nadterechny in the New Year. They commandeered houses from
the locals, demanded maintenance, and shot at the Russians. The
locals didn't want them there. But when Zaindi Choltayev sent out
his anti-Dudayev guard to tackle the newcomers, the Russians
turned angrily on him. As far as the military was concerned, any
armed Chechen, even a loyally anti-Dudayev one, was a threat. 'As
soon as we put out our guard, we were warned that we too would
be regarded as a bandit formation, and that our villages would be
razed to the ground. The situation has become heated. No one
knows who to support any more.'

The Provisional Council admitted in January that support for
Dudayev was growing, and that at least 15 per cent of local people
had gone over to the fighters' side. In early February, it accused the
Russian military of killing innocent people, looting, and 'barbaric
bombardment' of Grozny. The complaints went on and on, but the
military took no notice.

'We thought it was time to get rid of Dudayev, but letting the
Russians in was perhaps not very honourable . . . and now they're
here, we find they're even worse,' Lecha, a young clerk in the
freezing administrative building, said sadly, twisting a paper clip.
'We've let the enemy take control. Now we're under an occupying
army which bludgeons entire residential districts to kill off single
snipers. Of all possible solutions, this one now seems the worst'.
The next time I passed through Znamenskoye, Lecha wasn't at his
seat. 'He's gone to join the fighters,' whispered his neighbour.

'The Russian tactics appeared to serve other purposes besides
military victory. They seemed aimed at achieving the displacement

of as many Chechens as possible, and at impeding a return to
normal life. The bombardments, the atrocities, the killing of cattle
and the deliberate damage done to local industries forced half of
the population to flee their homes for a longer or shorter time,'
wrote Pax Christi.

Anatoly Shabad, an outspoken Russian liberal MP with a shock
of grey hair, said the goal of the killing was 'the intimidation of the
Chechen population to break its will to resist'.

*

A more sinister and systematic type of punishment for individuals,
reminiscent of Stalinist police-state days, was also being established
in early 1995. Chechen civilians began disappearing into a secret
network of Russian prison camps, and not coming out.

Two young Ingush brothers with worried faces approached me
hesitantly in the central square of Nazran, one day in late January,
asking for advice. When Sulumbek and Murat Sakayev had realized
a couple of weeks before that their mother was dying, they had
gone to Grozny, where their third brother Ramazan lived, to bring
him home to her deathbed. On the way back from Grozny, Russian
soldiers had arrested Ramazan at the checkpoint near Samashki.
'They wouldn't say why. His papers were all in order,' Sulumbek
said. So he and Murat had returned to Nazran alone to try and
clear up the mistake and get Ramazan released. But they had been
back for five days, their mother had died, and no one would tell
them anything. 'We're really worried,' Murat said. 'But the
Russians have all the advantages; we don't know what to do next.'

I wrote down their names in my notebook, remembering uneasily the miserable-looking Chechen men we saw, almost every day,
being dragged off into Russian checkpoint dugouts for interrogation. We had often asked the shaven-headed soldiers what these
men's crimes were. Sometimes they answered that the men were
Chechen terrorists. Sometimes they said a detainee had a grenade
or that his papers weren't in order. Sometimes they just shrugged.
They never let Pyatras take pictures of the arrests.

A few nights later, I hitched a ride into Nazran. One of the other
passengers in the car that picked me up was a hollow-eyed young

Ingush journalist. Ibragim Ugurchiyev had a gashed temple and winced when other people on the crowded back seat jarred his broken ribs. But he was in a good mood: by a miracle, he had escaped from the Russian military prison network. He was going out to celebrate.

Clever and well-spoken and well-groomed, Ibragim Ugurchiyev didn't look at all like a 'Chechen terrorist'. He had gone to Grozny in the middle of January to see whether the printing press that published his Nazran newspaper, *Serdalo*, was still working. On his way back out of town, he had been taken off the bus to be questioned – probably, he said with an ironic lift of the eyebrow, just because his interrogator had taken a fancy to the gold wristwatch he was wearing. The interrogator piled up his watch, his tape recorder, his money and his documents on the table between them, then told him to get into an armoured car and go to Mozdok for further questioning.

'But there's nothing wrong with my documents!' Ugurchiyev had protested.

'What documents?' the man answered, and dropped the passport in the bin.

In Mozdok, Ugurchiyev was taken to the railway station. He was imprisoned alone in one windowless carriage for two days, and with seven Chechen prisoners in another carriage for several more. Then he was put in a bigger group, which began a passage through the prisons of southern Russia, first Pyatigorsk, then Stavropol. There was no attempt at interrogation, he said. His warders weren't interested in any crimes he might have committed. They didn't care that he was Ingush, not Chechen. They just wanted to hit him.

'Each new shift of Russians would begin by beating you up. The only questions they asked were with truncheons. They beat us and beat us and beat us.'

But Ugurchiyev was lucky. He had friends in high places, who were kicking up a fuss about his three-week disappearance. They pulled strings, and arranged Ugurchiyev's release.

'The Russians told me not to talk about it, but I don't see why people shouldn't know,' Ugurchiyev said boldly. 'Not one of the

people I shared a cell with had done anything illegal. It's wrong
that they should be imprisoned, and I think it's wrong to hold my
tongue.'

There were no explanations and no apologies from Colonel
Solobyov, the head of Stavropol prison No. 21/1 where Ugurchiyev
had last been detained. He didn't like Chechens, and that was that.
'What are you taking their side for? They should all be shot on the
spot for what they've been up to for the last three years! Every last
one of them, and no quibbling!'

*

From his bedroom in the government hotel in Nazran, Sergei
Sirotkin, a member of Sergei Kovalyov's human rights commission,
was gathering information on human rights abuses against
Chechen civilians. He was coming up against strong resistance
from the Russian army at Mozdok. He was also trying to liaise
with the Russian military at Mozdok on fixing up talks with the
Chechen commander Aslan Maskhadov – which Mozdok was
ignoring – and on drawing up lists of prisoners of war for
exchanges – which Mozdok was being deceitful about – and
compiling statistics from the hundreds of refugees he was interview-
ing which might give a first realistic idea of how many people had
been killed in six weeks of war – a figure he provisionally put at
about 22,000 people. 'No, things aren't going well,' Sirotkin said,
but there was a dogged look about his pale, bearded face.

Sirotkin had collected plenty of information about the railway
station at Mozdok. He called it a 'filtration point'. People – mostly
young Chechen men – were being picked up at military checkpoints
all over the war zone and arrested. It didn't matter whether their
documents were in order or not. They were taken off to Mozdok
'for further interrogation', but what happened next was not
interrogation. 'There is a sound basis for calling what happens
there torture,' Sirotkin said. After days of beatings inside the
railway carriages, the prisoners were filtered out into the prison
system of southern Russia: Pyatigorsk, Stavropol, Vladikavkaz,
Krasnodar or Astrakhan.

Torturing young men for the crime of being Chechen was the

logical extension of the nationalist Russian belief that the Chechens were a bandit nation. But it was also officially sanctioned racism, and an abuse of the human rights agreements Russia was a signatory to. Sirotkin was on to Mozdok about it, but they were stonewalling. 'I've tried twice to talk to the military authorities in Mozdok about it. But they refuse to discuss it with us at all.'

I went to Mozdok with a Chechen driver and two other journalists to try to find out more about the filtration point. We got nowhere.

Usually a grimy little nothing of a town, all mud and market, Mozdok had been caught up in the huge machine of the Russian army. Tanks and jeeps and trucks moved to and from the military base in an endless procession. Off-duty soldiers with fiercely shaven heads toured the market. Televisions and electrical equipment were marked down in the second-hand shops. 'We've had lots in recently,' a salesman said, a glut I presumed was caused by looting.

Remembering Shakhrai's promise that a press centre would be set up at the military base, I presented myself at the entrance: a Portakabin, wrapped in camouflage netting, garlanded with razor wire, full of blank-faced men with small hair and big boots. They let me phone inside, but not go inside; down a wind-up field telephone, an angry voice shouted at me that I could only come to Mozdok if I got special papers from the defence ministry in Moscow. So much for Shakhrai, I thought; we stopped off at the railway station.

More razor wire. A murderous fence stretched round the sidings, protecting the dozens of carriages all around from intruders. There were young military men living in one train. They wouldn't say what kind of unit they were from. They wore black sweaters with no insignia. They were bored, and asked us in through the fence to tea, but their boss caught us. He took us off to another boss, who took us back to another boss. He was convinced we were spies, especially when he discovered that our driver, Abuyezid, a chirpy pensioner from Sernovodsk, was a Chechen. He packed the four of us into an army car and took us back to military headquarters, where we had to switch on our radios and tape recorders and cameras to prove they weren't bombs. Then we waited with a polite FSK officer while the granite-faced boss discussed us inside the Portakabin. Abuyezid sat at the back of the car, with his head bowed, fearing the worst. The rest of us worried silently that the soldiers might decide to set us free but keep Abuyezid, and wondering what we could do if they did.

After an hour, the security-conscious boss let us all go; if nothing else, it appeared, my earlier phone call to the 'information' officer had at least established our bona fides. 'We have to be vigilant,' he said sternly. 'Hostile journalists are writing bad things about Mozdok.' What was there to write about the railway station at Mozdok? I asked, wide-eyed. 'The railway station is a strategic object. There must be order,' he answered stiffly. He took us back to our car, whose doors had been sealed with string and yellow wax in our absence, and watched us leave. Abuyezid sang the same cheerful ditty – 'I'm not, I'm not, going back to Mozdok!' – all the way home.

Refugees spoke of strip searches at the checkpoints. Young Chechen men with calloused knees or shoulders were hauled off on suspicion of being snipers, although thousands of people by then had calluses from the endless dragging of sacks and furniture and belongings that made up a refugee's life. They vanished, presumably heading for Mozdok.

Later in 1995, after I left Russia, the network of 'filtration camps' was extended. The four main camps were in Mozdok, Grozny, Pyatigorsk and Stavropol. Smaller camps were set up around the Chechen countryside. In May, Kovalyov presented a report accusing the Russian troops of severe and systematic torture of civilian detainees. By then, thousands of prisoners had passed through the camps, but formal charges had been brought against only twenty or thirty people. Kovalyov estimated 1,000 Chechens were being held prisoner in the filtration camps that month alone.

*

What followed the arbitrary arrest of a Chechen man bound for a camp was always unpredictable, but always nightmarish. Human rights reports routinely talk of torture and mock executions. The most terrifying of real executions also took place.

'My cousin, Alladin Shamayev, and his father Magomed were arrested and taken away by helicopter, together with thirty other men from Assinkovskaya,' said one man interviewed by Pax Christi in April 1995. 'I was out in the fields that day, and saw the helicopter coming over. When it flew over the woods, I saw a person falling down. I know he was alive, because he moved his legs and his arms as he fell. I went to look for the body, but couldn't find it.

'After Alladin and Magomed were released [as part of a prisoner exchange of six Chechens for five Russians], they told me that ten out of the thirty prisoners had been thrown out of the helicopter on the way to Mozdok.'

Fear of the filtration camps was so intense that the Russian bosses could easily extort money from their prisoners' Chechen relatives. People asking for information about a vanished son or husband almost always had to pay. They had to pay again if they wanted the prisoner set free. Arresting a Chechen men to collect a ransom from his relatives became a nice little earner for the Russian camp guards. Pax Christi says the average size of 'ransoms' mentioned in the testimonies it collected in 1995 was a million roubles: two or three months' average salary in Russia, and a fortune in Chechnya where there was virtually no work.

A Chechen missing persons service was set up under the new pro-Moscow authorities in Grozny. It was run by Khusein Khamidov, Chechnya's top pilot, whose own two sons had vanished at the start of the war and turned up, dead, in a heap of corpses. Articulate and unintimidated, Khamidov made it his business to speak for the disappearing. He dug up mass graves around Chechnya, exhuming bodies and returning them to their relatives. In late 1995, Khamidov described a secret holding-pen for checkpoint detainees between Samashki and Zakan-Yurt. He was allowed to inspect it only after going to the top of the Russian hierarchy, to General Kulikov when he headed Russian forces in Chechnya, for permission.

'We were shown these pits and we made them admit that people had really been kept in them: a common pit, dug in the ground, covered by bars on top. A man cannot escape from it. They fixed up the pits for our visit, and put in a mattress and a pillow, but I have visited the "official" filtration point in Grozny many times. There is not a single bed there, and there has never been one. There are no pillows or mattresses, only bare walls, a bare floor, and a hole with a radius of ten to fifteen centimetres instead of a window. Between fifteen and twenty people were kept in a cell only twelve to twenty square metres big.'

The main camp in Grozny, known as 'PAP-1', was finally shut in 1996. After the war ended, a shrivelled Chechen watchman showed me round it, holding up the razor wire of the gate, lighting matches to guide me down the dark corridors, brushing aside the naked electric wires that hung from the walls. The building, which used to be a bus station, was huge and airless and freezing cold. The bottom two floors had been turned into cells, lined on all sides with a thick metal lattice of bars. The windowless inner rooms with bare concrete walls had been torture chambers, he said; he pointed out the holes in the walls where prisoners had been pegged out, as if being crucified, for electrocution.

The Russian guards had lived on the top floor. The floor up here was still covered with a mess of beer cans and empty cigarette packs. On the walls were innocent chalky calendars, with days crossed off and the end of assignments heavily ringed. Sandbags and breeze-blocks narrowed the windows to a slit, but the Chechen houses over the road were clearly visible. It made me feel queasy to imagine people living in those little houses, hearing the noises of death on the air, and knowing all the time that they were being watched.

Round the back was the old bus repair shed: a flimsy roof over pillars, wind against concrete, with three long inspection pits six feet deep stretching back yards into the dark interior. One of the inspection pits had been filled up with earth, a huge and apparently pointless undertaking.

'We don't know why they did that,' the old watchman quavered. 'We're going to dig it up once it gets warm enough. But we think it's probably full of human bodies.'

*

In Moscow, another famous Russian journalist was murdered in April 1995. Vladislav Listyev, a popular television presenter and executive, was assassinated in the middle of a political row over advertising profits for the first channel. After the funeral, Alexander Minkin, Russia's leading investigative reporter, wrote a bitter comment on the state of Russian democracy. 'Democracy does not protect people from killers,' Minkin wrote in *Moskovsky Komsomolets*. 'It only protects society from concentration camps.'

In Chechnya, even that was no longer true.

# FIVE

Snow and sunlight, silver roofs and the regretful bleat of a sheep in a courtyard somewhere nearby. It was 13 February, 1995, my quiet last day in Nazran, before returning to Moscow, packing up and emigrating back to England. I spent it sitting in an unheated room with the refugee historian Bashir Chakhkiyev, taking stock of the war.

'People are fighting now, but the war isn't really for Dudayev,' Chakhkiyev was saying. 'It's more for the burned-down house, for injured honour, for the murdered brother, the raped sister, or the shattered street. Those are more important to us now.'

Bashir Chakhkiyev's eager smile and neat, if threadbare, suit, masked a private sorrow that he was trying to bear lightly. The academic who had run for the Chechen presidency against Dudayev in 1991 had escaped from Grozny at New Year with his life. But his house had been burned down, his library robbed, and almost all the precious archive of Chechen-Ingush history he had spent two years compiling destroyed. All that was left was a pair of antique maps, propped against the bare wall of the room he'd been allotted in Nazran. He consulted them all the time, touching them lovingly.

'There are copies of some documents in Moscow and St Petersburg, but it's a terrible tragedy,' he said, keeping his voice even. 'A nation is nothing without its history, and now everything is destroyed. My archive was quite unique. What a tragedy.'

He hurried back to the safer ground of an indignant lament over Yeltsin's, and Dudayev's, wilful conjuring up of a modern war through their irresponsible games of historical revival.

'Tsar Nicholas's Russia is surely not the same as Yeltsin's Russia, even if some features of it are now being repeated, and the old traditions are being brought back. It's just crazy for Dudayev to have said "We never submitted before, so we're not going to submit now"; he just shouldn't have done it. Dudayev wasn't born under the Tsars, was he? He became a general thanks to Yeltsin, didn't he? And even if the pair of them fell out afterwards, if things didn't work out for them, they still shouldn't have taken things as far as war!'

'They shouldn't have put all of us in this terrible situation,' he added sadly.

\*

Back in the brute cold of Moscow, where every traffic cop was on the take and every knowing bureaucrat wanted his palm crossed with silver, I packed up my flat and watched Russian television. Nothing here was as simple as it had been in the south. In Russia, the truth was now operating on several different levels. You could choose how much you wanted to know, and most people chose not to know much.

Chechnya had slipped off the top of the news. NTV reports were still full of reality, but most film from Chechnya nowadays was wobbly shots from tanks on the Russian side, the sizzle of planes taking off from Mozdok, thin white trails in the sky, and thin white grannies on the ground weeping their gratitude to the troops.

If you waited for the war news, you could see that the 'Party of War' was doing everything it could to avoid peace talks. Yegorov said it would be 'blasphemous' to negotiate with Dudayev. Stepashin said the FSK was hunting him down. Anatoly Kulikov, now heading the war effort, went through the motions of talks with the Chechen commander Aslan Maskhadov, but then said: 'All existing possibilities for ceasing armed confrontation have been exhausted by the joint command and it has been forced to adopt appropriate measures.'

But many Russians preferred to listen only to what was said in Moscow, near the top of the news, where the peaceable Chernomyrdin was promising at the same time that the Russian government would try to find a political solution. Others preferred not to listen at all.

Clever people who had once hungered for knowledge and information, who had secretly listened to the BBC Russian service or read foreign books to find out what the Soviet-era government wasn't telling them, now switched off completely. With my head still full of shocking memories from the south, I found it hard to believe that so many of my friends in Moscow could be voluntarily choosing complacent ignorance about what was going on in Chechnya even though it was not being forced on them. It seemed to me they were retreating back into their old lowly places in the Soviet hierarchy, lazily shutting their eyes to the reality outside, not realizing that they were abdicating their freedom by their indifference.

Two of these Russians were Alla and Vitya, who turned up giggling one morning, clutching a bottle of vodka, saying they would help me pack. First, however, Vitya wanted to drink a toast. It was 23 February, 1995, Red Army Day. It was also the fifty-first anniversary of the Chechen deportation of 1944.

'To our great Soviet army, which has suffered so much and fought so valiantly,' Vitya began. I laughed. 'I'm not that keen on drinking to them at the moment, but I'll drink your toast if you'll drink a toast in memory of the Chechen deportation afterwards,' I said.

Vitya looked astonished. 'Whatever for? Chechens are a bunch of bandits,' he said.

Seryozha was a more unexpected convert to great-Russian pressure on the weak. He was a doctor, a Jew, a humane man, an intellectual, and had been a passionate supporter of the democratic movement. When I went to supper with him and his wife Nadya, my theatre-going companions, it never crossed my mind to hide my thoughts about what I had seen in Chechnya for fear of offending their national sensibilities. They had always been against state bullying of dissidents, Jews, and Russians. I assumed they would feel the same now.

'It was terrible, unbelievable,' I said. 'The Chechens are always talking about how Russia wants to wipe them from the face of the earth, but keep their land . . . It was the first time I could see why they say that; it's hard to explain the viciousness or even the disproportionate size of the Russian attacks; down there, it really does feel as though the Russian troops want to wipe everyone in Chechnya off the face of the earth . . . Seeing people sitting in their villages, waiting for the Russians to come, was how I imagine it must have been to see the Jewish ghettos in the 1930s, waiting for the Nazis and not knowing what to do.'

I stopped my flood of speech, gradually becoming aware of the chill in the room. A gaffe. A *faux pas*. A cold, harsh look from Seryozha. Then, tapping his knife meditatively against his glass, he began his angry counter-arguments. They went on all evening.

It didn't matter that I had been in Grozny. I had obviously been fooled by the cunning Chechen. The Russian army was reimposing constitutional order. They were all criminals, a natural state for a race which collectively had not reached the same level of development as Russians. I obviously hadn't seen the truth if I hadn't seen the 50,000-strong army that Dudayev was fielding against Russia, packed with thousands of mercenaries from all over the Muslim world; it was a direct threat to Russia, just as the imminent prospect of Chechen terrorists destroying strategic objects all around the country was a direct threat. He denounced Sergei Kovalyov, who had been everyone's liberal hero only a month or two before, as a 'clown'. What did he think he was doing, complaining about human rights abuses, trying to stop Russia getting the huge new IMF loan which had been threatened by the start of war?

I had never heard Seryozha defending the Russian state with such passion; in fact, I had never heard Seryozha defending the Russian state at all. Like every other reflex denial of the Chechens as ordinary post-Soviet people, with the same rights as the Russians or anybody else, Seryozha's endorsement of the Russian élite's war seemed to me to be conjuring back into existence the spiritual hierarchy of 'more equal' people ruling the 'less equal' – an implicit endorsement of the very inequalities which Seryozha had always wanted to escape.

I had no idea how to respond. My mouth opened and shut, but even if I had been able to think of something to say that would get through to him, I couldn't get a word in edgeways. It was a sad farewell evening. I left early, feeling shocked, disappointed and miserable.

After that, I tried not to talk about Chechnya with Russians. I didn't know how to describe the people I'd met there so that my Russian friends would think of them as people, rather than a dark icon of un-Russian-ness and enmity. I felt a coward, but I didn't know how to explain my beliefs; I didn't want to lose them just as I was leaving; I kept quiet.

*

But anyone could find the different layers of the truth, even in Moscow, if they bothered to look.

I started to wonder whom the Russians would eventually choose as the ruler of Chechnya if the current opposition did fall apart. If the logic of other Caucasus wars in which nationalist leaders had been violently removed was applied to Chechnya, I guessed that power would eventually return to the last Soviet leader of Grozny. On 17 February, 1995, I went to find Doku Zavgayev. He was surprisingly easy to track down. To my astonishment, he turned out to work from a grand office in the presidential administration. Three years before, he had been Yeltsin's Communist enemy; now politics had been turned on its head so dramatically that he was advising Yeltsin on Chechen politics.

Balding, plump, smug, and fifty-four, Zavgayev was watching from a grandstand seat as the Russian army smashed the nationalists who had driven him from power in 1991 and the Russian bureaucrats searched for a reasonably credible replacement for Dudayev. Not that he personally had any claim on his old job running Chechnya, he said hastily. 'I don't want it. I've worked there. I've seen it all. It doesn't interest me.'

I didn't believe him. Zavgayev was vague as to who else might do. He didn't have a good word to say for any of the other politicians who had surfaced in Chechnya since 1991. He made no secret of his delight at Dudayev's downfall. Dudayev should come out of his secret headquarters, he said, with the relaxed charm of the successful Party bureaucrat. Dudayev was 'a crook – he should be talking to the prosecutor's office. Nothing depends on him now. He's a zero. He has no one behind him. He's alone, hiding somewhere in those nooks and crannies. He's a general, isn't he? He should come out and take what's coming to him like a man.'

The Nadterechny opposition also got the rough end of Zavgayev's tongue. 'They're no opposition,' he said, gently stroking his gold wristwatch with a well-manicured hand. 'They're the same kind of crooks as Dudayev. They were all in it together until 1993, hiding behind nationalist slogans and stealing Chechen oil. Then they fell out with Dudayev because they couldn't share out the swag. The prosecutor should be talking to them too.' And he loathed Khasbulatov. None of these politicians could possibly win elections, Zavgayev said. 'They can stand, but they won't win. You can't force people to vote for them.'

He wouldn't say who could run Chechnya instead, just wagged his head knowingly.

His vision of the best future for Chechnya was strangely reminiscent of its Soviet-era past, which he had lived through as he climbed the career ladder from metalworker to state farm boss, agriculture minister to second secretary of the Communist Party, before making it to the top of the political tree in 1990. He wanted to reunite Chechnya with Ingushetia. He wanted to return to the political and economic reforms he said were being carried out in those days. He insisted that, under Soviet rule, Chechens 'used to have independence, real sovereignty, and freedom of worship'. And, again unlike most of his compatriots, he was happy for the army to stay on indefinitely in Chechnya. 'It's normal,' he said. 'We don't need to dramatize it. It's our Russian army, which has the right to stay anywhere it wants.'

The hand he offered me as he left was soft and slightly oily.

\*

Chernomyrdin offered people all over Russia a soothing version of the truth; in Moscow, Mayor Yuri Luzhkov was making the same peaceable noises for Muscovites. Luzhkov smoothed the ruffled feelings of anxious Chechens in Moscow, promising there would be no racial discrimination against them. 'Moscow has not seen

the syndrome of enmity or hostility that some people were antici-
pating, and that some people even wanted,' he said. 'We consider
the situation absolutely normal.'

The Chechen mafia wasn't as big or as scary as Russian legend
had it, a senior policeman at the heavily guarded headquarters of
the Regional Directorate for the Fight with Organized Crime
(RUOP) told me. Mikhail Suntsev was the deputy head of RUOP's
'ethnic crimes unit'. Its job was to deal with law-breaking Caucasians in general and the Chechen mafia in particular. The Chechen
mafia was way down the pecking order of crime, below Russian
mafia groups, the Georgian mafia and even the humble Azeri fruit-
and-veg merchants, Suntsev said. His unit kept about 2,000 of the
50,000 Chechens in Moscow under observation. But its targets
included Chechen students suspected of petty theft in their dormitories and any Chechen political opposition leaders who lived in
the capital. The number of actual mafia bosses and 'fighters' was
much smaller. Suntsev said the Chechen mafia's fearsome reputation had been forged in the turf wars of the early 1990s. Now
they had settled down to a quiet life running protection and
extortion rackets on the fringes of Moscow's bustling crime world.
'The words "Chechen" and "criminal" became synonyms years
ago, but Chechen criminal activity has dropped sharply,' he said
soothingly.

Those were the words. But the facts were different: the APCs
were still lurking under bridges, waiting to turn on Chechen
terrorists if ever they came to Moscow. Police-and-army patrols
were still tramping through the metro at night, hunting for darkies
with mischief in mind. Men with sallow skins were still being
bundled into police cars everywhere, with the same look of helpless
misery to be seen at any checkpoint in Chechnya.

Had this expensive security operation, which had now gone on
for two months, actually caught any vengeful terrorists from
Chechnya? No. Not a single one, Suntsev said with a smile. 'But
we can't guarantee that this is completely impossible, so we've
geared up to prevent such things from happening.'

\*

These anodyne official versions of the truth reassured Muscovites, but they were nothing like the real experience of Chechen people living in Moscow.

On one of my last winter afternoons there, when the television news was showing the usual footage of grim-faced Russian soldiers advancing towards an unseen enemy with tanks and planes, I left my empty flat and went to meet one of the Moscow Chechens who represented the essence of crime to peaceable Russians. But the *biznismen* waiting to meet me in a suburban street of crumbling concrete and frozen puddles wasn't the sinister mafioso of Russian legend. There was no sharp Italian suit here, no suspicious bulge under the arm, no gleaming shades. Mayerbek Magomadov was an ex-actor who had fallen in with the opposition in Grozny when they demonstrated outside Theatre Square in 1993, fled to Moscow later to avoid reprisals by Dudayev's police, and set himself up in business. He had prematurely greying black hair over anxious eyes, and he was easy to like on sight. His smile had just a hint of reserve. There might have been suppressed tension in the way he pushed his tall, rangy body up the stairs to his fourth-floor apartment two or three steps at a time, but his voice was calm, his words politely welcoming, and his expression phlegmatic. He behaved more like a slightly nervous young diplomat than a shady salesman. And he was wearing nothing more threatening than a sweatshirt and jeans.

It didn't matter. Mayerbek was in the same trap as every Moscow Chechen. Suspicion, humiliation, street searches and the ever-present possibility of arrest were his daily lot. When he went out on the street, he disguised his dark looks with a scarf, a hat, and a pair of thick pink-rimmed spectacles. He didn't need the spectacles to see. His eyesight was perfect.

'Basically they stop anyone who looks too dark to be Russian. I'm lucky that my hair's going grey and I'm quite pale for a Chechen. With that and the spectacles I can pass for a Russian, so I get searched less often than most Chechens I know here,' he said with resignation. 'But it's still unbearable. They stop you all the time, they take your car apart, they insult you. And they only give your papers back if you put money in their paws.'

There were tens of thousands of Chechens slinking round
Moscow like him, so many that he sometimes looked at the familiar
dark faces on the street and felt as though he was in Grozny again.
Many of them, like him, had come in the last three years to escape
from Dudayev. Others, like his family, had turned up in the last
two months to escape Yeltsin's soldiers. And they were all hiding
from the law.

Mayerbek's wife Liza and their children, eleven-year-old Laila
and thirteen-year-old Ibragim, had escaped from their cellar in
Grozny as the Russian bombardment eased off. Hunched over a
notebook in front of the television, Laila still had the dazed, sickly
look of a child of war. Her mother said she had screaming
nightmares. All three still turned blank, fearful faces towards the
window when they heard a plane or even a lorry approach.

The children were not going to school in Moscow. The local
headmistress had refused to take them when she realized they were
Chechens. 'She got very embarrassed and stiff after she saw my
documents, which give my nationality as Chechen, and said there
were no places at the school,' Mayerbek said. 'We're second-class
citizens here. So here we are – the Chechen mafia!' he added, with
more despair than irony in the twist of his lips and eyebrows. 'If
you believe what those Russians out there say, that is – and they'll
say anything – it's us: my wife, my son, my little girl and me!'

There was nowhere in Moscow for Chechen civilians to register
as refugees. Chechens who registered as refugees in southern Russia
were being given a lump sum of about $4, a fraction of the official
poverty-line wage of $65 a month. Down there, they were housed
in squalid emergency camps for a while, in schools or hospitals or
railway carriages. But no one in the Russian government wanted
any more Chechens coming to Moscow.

Nor had Mayerbek's family registered as new residents, as they
should legally have done. They were too scared to let the police
know his address. So were his friend Sultan's family, crammed five
to a room down the corridor. Under Luzhkov's rules, every 'person
of Caucasian nationality' had to register with the police in
Moscow, stay at an approved address and get official permission
to move into a flat – if they could find one in a city where the line

'Persons of Caucasian nationality need not apply' is included on almost all flat rental adverts.

For Mayerbek's family to get the right documents to live with him, they would have to get the local council's permission for four people to live in a single room. Refusal was a foregone conclusion. If the family didn't move on after that, the police would be round to throw them out. The atmosphere was hostile. No one would help. It wasn't worth trying.

Liza was about thirty, like Mayerbek, and there were wisps of grey in her black bun. She left the tiny kitchen where we were talking at seven o'clock to turn up the television sound, hoping for some snippet on the news that would show the world was taking notice of Chechnya's plight, sure at the same time that there would be nothing. Every time the phone rang, Mayerbek jumped. Chechens in Moscow were always on the phone to each other, anxiously asking any newcomers from the war zone for information about their relatives still trapped inside. Liza spoke into the receiver many times that evening, sadly, shaking her head.

Mayerbek was hoping someone would have news of his seventy-year-old father. The old man had been out when the shelling started which sent Liza and the children scurrying into the cellar. They hadn't seen him since. Someone might remember seeing his body. Someone might have buried him. Someone might have sheltered in a cellar with him, somewhere.

'I'm afraid for him,' Mayerbek said, with the sombre understatement that characterized the whole family's way of talking. 'What's happening there is worse than here. I don't like to think about it. Of course, you can't think of anything else.'

Since the war began, he had even come to admire Dudayev's courage in standing up to the Russians. 'I couldn't bear the man before. But now I would die for him. He's a good man and . . .' he shrugged '. . . we have no choice.'

It was a big change of heart. Because of Dudayev, Mayerbek had fled Grozny and for two years had only been able to see his family on brief holidays. After the violence in Grozny in 1993, he had decided it would be safer to leave rather than wait to be hunted down by Dudayev's police. He left Liza and the children behind in their flat. To keep them safe from retribution aimed at him, he went through a formal divorce. So did his neighbour, Sultan. Once everything was sorted out and the fictitious documents were in Liza's hands, Mayerbek and Sultan came to Russia to look for work.

They found jobs in a building brigade with a group of other Chechens, putting up country houses for New Russians. They quickly realized that their Chechen brigade wasn't like the Russian ones working nearby. While the Chechens worked eighteen-hour days, the Russian teams stopped for endless cigarette and meal breaks. The Chechens finished their building in a month, while, Mayerbek said, Russian teams were taking up to eighteen. Naturally, there was hostility. They moved on.

With a bit of cash in hand, Mayerbek and Sultan reached Moscow and found two one-roomed flats in unfashionable Varshavskaya district. From there, they moved into middleman business – buying wholesale from someone who'd been abroad, selling to retailers. If they ran into trouble collecting debts from their partners, they sent in the muscle, Mayerbek said. And the best unofficial debt collectors were Chechens.

'Let's say we do a deal and you don't pay. We each go to a "shadow man" to enforce our side of things. If they're Russian, they stand round bargaining and making offers to do a deal, to give them a cut for helping. They get nowhere. They're all talk. Go to a Chechen hood and he'll be straight. He'll send his man to get the money. One man. One meeting. The money gets paid. People are so scared of Chechens that they pay up and ask no questions.'

Mayerbek said Chechens took as many short cuts as the next man in Moscow's quicksand of contradictory laws, grasping bureaucrats, and hoods. But they weren't more criminal than Russians, just more loyal to each other. 'That stubbornness and single-mindedness of ours is what they're scared of,' he said. 'All this Russian fuss and fantasy about the power of the Chechen mafia only started when Dudayev came to power. Whoever heard of the Chechen mafia before that? The Russians just wanted an excuse to get him.'

He shut the door on the television and the children before whispering his reservations about risking looking for more schools for them. Even in Grozny, he said, Russian and Chechen children didn't play together by choice. Russians were foul-mouthed and had foul habits from infancy. Modest Chechen children, versed in the strict disciplines of Islam, were scared of their dirty, sloppy, bullying ways. Ibragim had annoyed Russian teachers at his primary school in Grozny by refusing to speak Russian in his first term. The teacher asked Mayerbek to make his son comply with the rules. When Mayerbek asked the little boy why he didn't try talking to the Russian children in his second language, Ibragim replied that it was because their fathers drank and their sisters swore and went around half-naked at home. He didn't want to be friends with people like that.

'Eventually, though, he did agree. The teachers were pleased. We were pleased. But he came back very quiet from his first day talking Russian there with the Russian kids and the first thing he asked me was: "Dad, what does 'fucking Chechen' mean?"'

'I'm scared they'll be corrupted at school in Moscow, if they get in. I mean, Russian kids ... excuse my language, but at school here they're screwing in basements by the time they're thirteen. They smoke in the street. They go out boozing and vandalizing ...'

He put his head in his hands.

It had been dark for hours by the time Mayerbek walked me back to the metro, through the slush and puddles, past the kiosks with their New Russian displays of fags and booze. He was wearing the spectacles, and the hat and scarf. Every now and then, he nodded almost curtly at another wrapped-up figure hurrying by, and got a similar nod in reply.

'Chechen,' he said quietly. I didn't want to make him talk on the street, if he was worried his accent or mine would draw attention to us. We walked companionably, arms linked, like Russians. On a dark stretch of road, he suddenly spoke again.

'We have a tradition that our nation will suffer nine catastrophes, bringing us to the verge of extinction. The deportations were the eighth. Perhaps this is the ninth.'

We reached the lights at the mouth of the metro. There were people around us again, and Mayerbek's voice was so quiet I had to lean forward to catch what he was saying.

'The thing is, we don't know where we can run to next.'

He gave me a sideways half-embrace, his left arm crossing my right shoulder, whispered 'All the best,' and was gone.

The war went Russia's way for months. The destruction that accompanied each Russian victory sent a few more angry Chechen men off to join the fighters; Russian soldiers in towns and at roadside checkpoints went in terror of the ghostly night raids which still picked off several servicemen a day. But fear of Russia's disproportionate punishments gradually set in. Slowly, the soldiers took control of more and more Chechen territory.

In Russia, it was as if the war was invisible. No one saw the Chechens. It took half a year of defeat for the Chechens to learn how to fight back.

*

In the long soft rains of springtime London, I scoured papers and televisions for news about Chechnya. I called journalist friends in Moscow who had just come back from the mountains, went to conferences, read human rights reports, and bought Russian newspapers. At work, I watched Russian television. I even pored over the Tass dispatches on my office computer, trying to decode what was really happening from the baffling utterances of the Russian generals it quoted. I memorized the grainy newsprint pictures: the neat, careful features of Aslan Maskhadov; Grachev's smirk, the pudgy solemnity of Kulikov. But it wasn't like being there: the politicians and warriors moved across the pages and screens like chess pieces, iconic and impersonal. Suddenly, I was cut off in a different world.

'Bloody rain. Wettest spring since the war. If it goes on much longer we'll get webbed feet,' grumbled the taxi-driver who picked me up from the airport on my first night home. 'Can you even remember the last time it didn't rain?'

'I've just come back,' I said apologetically. Where from? Chechnya.

'Chechnya, oh yeah,' he said knowledgeably. 'Saw it on the

news at Christmas, when they had all that fighting there for a bit. And the weather was bloody 'orrible there too.'

# Punishment

Chechnya's three remaining small cities – Gudermes, Shali and Argun – fell by the end of March 1995. In February, the elders of Gudermes had made an anxious pilgrimage to Russian interior minister Viktor Yerin to beg him not to attack their homes and shed their neighbours' blood. They were treated with scant respect. They waited for hours in a cold corridor, in their tall hats and long coats, while he talked behind closed doors. They clustered around as he left. Adam Khadzhiyev, their dignified spokesman, made a long plea in Chechen for moderation.

'What's the problem?' Yerin answered roughly. He scratched at himself with his long arms and added, enunciating his words slowly so the old men could understand and patting them patronizingly on the back: 'You impose order in Gudermes over the next week, so that no illegal armed bands can stay there. We'll go to Gudermes together, drive round it and see where to put the necessary protection so no fighters can get in.' And he strode off.

Under pressure from the elders, the fighters did move out of the towns. But small units remained outside, supported by what fighting vehicles and mortars were left after the loss of Grozny. Heavy machine-guns had to be fired as one-shots. The only tank defending Argun had a broken engine and was towed by a tractor.

The federal forces used massive artillery and air power against the towns for weeks before entering the cities with infantry. Shali was hardly touched, but several areas of Gudermes were badly damaged, and Argun's western outskirts were virtually annihilated.

Dudayev's headquarters left Shali. The fighters moved on.

*

Spring in Chechnya meant fruit blossom and bombing. The Russian forces started flushing fighters out of the southern and western villages they had rushed through in December. Now they were in a hurry to subdue them. Yeltsin had invited a huge party of world leaders to Moscow on 9 May to celebrate the end of the Second World War in Europe – VE Day – with him. He wanted to declare the war over before the foreign presidents and prime ministers turned up. Russian forces announced victories, rather in the Soviet way of 'fulfilling their plan', even if some of the precise statistics now offered masked empty victories.

After two weeks of heavy shelling, Russian troops entered Bamut on 16 March. The fighters had retreated to the surrounding hills.

The Russians left. The fighters returned.

In mid-April, Russia was once again poised for victory – 'in the final phase of the operation'. Two days later, the Russian commander Anatoly Kulikov announced victory, the death of 400 Chechen fighters for fifteen Russians. The capture of Bamut gave him control of 80 per cent of Chechen territory and 90 per cent of the Chechen population, he said.

But his own deputy had a different tale to tell. Colonel-General Mikhail Yegorov said fighters up on the hill positions had shelled the Russians into retreat. By the end of 1995, the Chechens still held their hillside positions near the Soviet-era Strategic Rocket Forces base.

*

Cautious village elders elsewhere in the south and west tried to negotiate with the Russian interior ministry troops. The soldiers were losing their uniforms and inhibitions with the warm weather; many of them now went around in sneakers, with bright cloths tied pirate-style on their heads. The elders of Samashki agreed that the Russian interior ministry troops based nearby could come in and check that their fighters had all cleared out. It was 7 April, and the fighters had been dispatched to Bamut or other hotspots. The elders were pleased: they thought the Russians would now leave their village in peace.

But they were tragically mistaken.

Soldiers told the Samashki elders to hand over 265 automatics by nine in the evening. Bewildered, the elders said they didn't know where to find so many weapons, since the fighters had gone away with their guns. Falling into the absurd logic of the ultimatum, they asked for more time, so they could sell cattle, buy weapons, and give them to the Russians.

Mounting panic: women and children packed off out of the village, men driving off their cows to sell, frantic consultations on the square. There were still 3,500 people in Samashki at seven in the evening, when the Russians grew impatient with waiting.

Intense shelling began two hours before the deadline. Women and children who had not got away in time were turned back by Russian patrols. The attack went on all night. In the morning, the OMON stormed in, shooting, looting, burning houses and people with flame-throwers. Masked 'special police' stalked into houses, dragging out men, killing some, beating others, rounding up more for the filtration camps. Refugees said the soldiers 'shot at everything that moved', screamed obscenities and nationalist slogans, had the kind of tattoos sported by ex-convicts, and injected themselves with drugs. 'They were all shooting up drugs,' said survivor Fatima Zagayeva. 'It was as if they were in a trance.' Afterwards, the ground was littered with broken ampoules and syringes.

The troops rampaged through Samashki for three days. For another three days, they wouldn't let the group of anxious relatives, aid workers, and journalists waiting at the highway checkpoint, staring at the smouldering ruins, go in to help. Survivors trickled out down the road. Some wept. Some, beyond tears, described the atrocities they had seen with the clarity of shock.

Ria Unorova's description of what had happened to her was very simple: she opened her cardigan. The camisole underneath was caked in her sixteen-year-old son's blood. The troops shot him, then grabbed her seven-year-old and threw him under a tank in the road. 'They were going to run over him. I threw myself down beside him and they stopped,' she told the waiting Canadian journalist Olivia Ward.

Stories in the smoke:

Raisa Nasrudiyev, eighteen years old, was alone in her house with her sick father. 'The OMON entered the house. The daughter wanted to block their way but was pushed aside. When they left the house again, they lobbed grenades inside and the house caught fire,' a neighbour said. 'That afternoon, when there were no Russians around any more, I found the dead body of Raisa in front of the door. She had been shot. We found the burned body of Mr Nasrudiyev in his bed.

'The next day my other neighbour, Zakhar Khabilov, an old man of sixty-eight, was killed by passing soldiers. They saw him looking at them from his garden, and shot him casually, as if they were killing a dog that happened to cross their road.'

More than 300 houses were destroyed. No one ever counted all the dead. The Russian human rights group Memorial published a list of 107 names. Two men who were allowed in on 10 April to collect corpses say they carried 248 bodies to the mosque. They saw new graves in courtyards. About 250 men were sent to concentration camps.

Everyone escaping Samashki understood that Russia was trying to crush all resistance in Chechnya before the Victory Day celebrations in Moscow. Junsei Terawawa, a Buddhist monk who organized two peace marches against the war, was waiting and watching, with Olivia Ward, over the shoulders of the troops barring the way in.

'They're celebrating the victory over fascism, but this is fascism. Russia shouldn't be congratulated, it should be thrown out of the league of civilized nations,' he said.

Olivia Ward took out her radio to catch the BBC World Service news. Escapees gathered around, watching her listen. 'What are they saying about us? Surely *this* will shock them. Surely *this* will make the world help us at last,' she remembers them asking.

But the quiet voice of Britain had nothing to say about Samashki. The big news of the day was about Russia. After months of delay, the IMF had granted Russia a huge new loan of $6.8 billion to close Russia's budget deficit – in essence, picking up the bill for the war.

Olivia translated. Hope faded from the faces all around her.

'We were always alone,' someone in the little crowd said sadly. 'But now we know we *really* can't depend on anyone to help us.'

The way the Russians saw it, terrorism should make the Chechens rush to surrender. But Chechens reasoned differently. What was the the point of sending away their fighters, the elders reasoned, if the troops slaughtered harmless villagers anyway? As the rights group Pax Christi said: 'The punishment of Samashki explains the stubbornness of Bamut.'

The Russians didn't make any military gains from the massacre of Samashki. When the troops finally let the villagers who had been evacuated go home, they were frightened that some Chechens might take guns and get revenge. So the Russians retreated to their initial positions outside the village. A tactical full circle: except for the new graves and the hatred, it was as if the attack had never been.

# Propaganda

The streets had been scrubbed and painted and tarmacked for weeks. Fighter-bombers screamed over Moscow, practising their display. Park benches were painted and tulips planted in what Muscovites cynically called *pokazukha* – making things look better than they really were. Yeltsin was pulling out all the stops to impress the foreign leaders who were about to descend on his capital.

To match the flurry of urban spring-cleaning, the Russian president declared a cease-fire in Chechnya on 28 April. His order didn't seem to apply to Russian planes: in the villages, random death still rained down from the skies. But soldiers in Grozny were ordered not to shoot first. Dudayev had no interest in saving Yeltsin's face: he refused to reciprocate by ordering his own fighters to cease fire. In Grozny, the stealthy snipers picked up their guns again. Russian soldiers said Chechen guerrillas struck 105 times in the week before 9 May.

9 May, 1995. For the first time since Soviet days, a triumphal parade of tanks and military hardware was paraded through the streets of the Russian capital. The queasy presidents and prime ministers of the Western world, whose hesitant disapproval of the Chechen war had not prevented them from coming to Moscow for the two-day festivities, asked for a minimum concession to their sensitivities – military units from Chechnya must be kept out of the parade. Of course, they were told. But what was a promise? Units coming back from the war marched by Bill Clinton and the other presidents anyway.

When it emerged that the Russian authorities had lied to them, President Vaclav Havel of the Czech Republic complained. The rest of the presidents kept quiet.

As soon as the presidents had gone home, the Russian military forgot its cease-fire. Having done what he could to subdue the plains, driving most of Dudayev's forces back into the hills, Kulikov took a leaf out of the nineteenth-century generals' book. He began a full-scale assault on the mountain fastnesses.

# Punishment

On 11 May, federal forces started bombing foothills villages in the south. By the time they finished with Serzhen-Yurt, entry to one of the main valleys in the south-west highlands, more than a thousand homes had been destroyed and only thirteen houses were still habitable. Bombardment of the foothills villages was so intense it rattled windows 8,200 feet above sea level in mountainous Vedeno, the new Chechen headquarters, the Russians' goal.

Vedeno was more than a town and a district. It was a manifestation in stone of the Chechens' spirit of independence. Their traditions of guerrilla warfare had been honed up here among the sheer cliffs, narrow gorges and wooded ravines of the highlands. There was shelter from planes in the thick beech forests, and safety from Russian tank attacks in the winding roads. Rustic, hardy people were well armed with hunting guns and Kalashnikovs. The new Chechen headquarters was inside the 20-foot-high white walls of a ruined nineteenth-century fortress, built by Imam Shamil.

Refugees from Grozny and the lowlands jammed the road to Vedeno all spring. The district was full of people suffering the after-effects of bombardment: children who wept at the sound of machines, adults who remembered clutching their stomachs and praying as planes swept through the skies and black depression swept their helpless bodies.

Once their homes had been destroyed and their families done to death, some of these formerly neutral people were ready to take up arms themselves. They felt safer with a gun in their hands.

From Vedeno, shifts of volunteers in pickup trucks, battered cars and later jeeps and armoured cars, had since December shuttled down the icy road to fight, and back up through the steep valley to rest. They bought weapons from the Russians, and they shot with machine guns at the low-flying Russian aircraft that screamed over their heads. Some of the volunteers were graduates of Dudayev's Chechen military academy, where they had been trained by veterans of Soviet army campaigns. Many more were Soviet army veterans of the Afghan campaign, with their own memories of the guerrilla tactics of the mujahideen.

The commander of Vedeno was twenty-five years old, with a reddish beard and a bashful look. His name was Shirvani Basayev, and his older brother, one of the leading commanders in Grozny, was called Shamil, like the great warrior of history. The family had lived in Vedeno for centuries. The farmhouse where Shirvani Basayev lived was still on the site of the home built by his ancestors in 1010, and meals were presided over by the family patriarch, Suleyman. Warrior blood ran in their veins. One ancestor defended the building from the military advances of the fourteenth-century Mongol conqueror Tamerlane. A great-great-great-grandfather served Imam Shamil as a deputy and died in battle against the

Tsars. A great-grandfather was killed in the war against the
Bolsheviks, and his son died in the deportations.[12]

Shamil Basayev's Abkhaz battalion of 500 men was drawn from
these hills; the Basayevs had been preparing for a new war ever
since Dudayev first challenged Russian control of Chechnya. If the
Russians ever tried to storm Vedeno, Shirvani Basayev said, 'that's
the end of them. We're on our land, which feeds and nourishes us.
And we have nowhere to retreat.'

But, by May, the Basayevs' fervour was no longer matched by
the people of the villages elsewhere on the Caucasus slopes. Filled
with foreboding that the war was all but lost, civilians in the
highlands negotiated as desperately as their lowland brothers for
grass-roots truces with the nearest Russian forces. The bloodshed
had gone on too long. They wanted to be neutral. They pleaded
with the fighters to stay away.

'Everybody had this idea in the beginning that we could win if
we didn't let Russia scare us,' Gilani Eldarov, a fifty-nine-year-old
truck driver, said as he watched two Russian jets on a midday air
raid on his home village of Duba-Yurt, which severely wounded a
woman in her garden. 'But then they started using their air force,
their bombs, their Grad missiles . . . Now I tell our fighters to shave
their beards and go back to work before the Russians finish us off.
This war is becoming senseless. It is time to save the Chechens as a
people.'[13]

In a rare admission that his ranks were dwindling, the chief
commander, Aslan Maskhadov, asked in a radio broadcast in May:
'Why are there no more volunteers?'

The bombs struck Vedeno again and again, destroying its
school, bakery, textile factory, telephone exchange, police station,
bank, and parts of a hospital. One of the many houses flattened
was the home of Shamil Basayev's uncle. Eleven family members,
including one of Basayev's sisters and five young nephews, were
killed when the two-floor building was flattened on 23 May.
Dozens of other Vedeno residents were killed.

12. *Los Angeles Times*, 22 Jan. 1995.
13. *Los Angeles Times*, 20 May 1995.

The Chechen high command and several hundred fighters withdrew from Vedeno at the end of May to defend a hill overlooking the town. They were learning the lesson of their recent loss of popularity, and limiting themselves to defensive positions outside villages. The last mountain towns and villages were packed with refugees who had nowhere left to run. It made logistical sense for people to stay; it just might save the villagers if the fighters left.

At the beginning of June, Russian forces opened up safe corridors to let women, children and the elderly escape the fierce fighting at Alleroi, Meskety, Agishty and Yarysh-martan. Buses brought down more than 5,000 people in a single day.

While Dudayev negotiated unsuccessfully at his hideout in Shatoi with Sandor Meszaros, the recently arrived representative of the Organization for Security and Cooperation in Europe (OSCE) – whom Moscow had grudgingly let into Chechnya to try and mediate – the Russian forces were gearing up to attack.

On the night of 3 June, Russian paratroopers seized Vedeno. Its command post had been destroyed days earlier by Russian jets. The troops took Shatoi and Nozhay-Yurt, the last Chechen strongholds, a week later. Russian television showed Kulikov climbing down from a helicopter in Vedeno and talking to people from the town. He said his troops had come into town 'practically without resistance or bloodshed'. He promised to send humanitarian aid to the residents. A Russian flag flew over the bus station. Yeltsin, in Moscow, said the war was all but over.

Kulikov looked magnanimous in victory. The Russians spared the civilians of the hill towns. But this was partly because they knew the fighters had pulled out before they entered, and partly for strategic reasons of their own. The posts Russian troops manned in the unfriendly mountains territory were easy to attack; Russian commanders wanted inhabited villages nearby – a vulnerable civilian population – as hostages whose safety they could still threaten if their own forces were attacked.

Losing Vedeno was the defeat of all defeats for the Chechen high command. Usually quick and trustworthy in their reports of fighting, it took them a day to accept their loss enough to admit it publicly. Afterwards, Ruslan Galayev, a Chechen commander interviewed by Tass, said Dudayev and his commanders were still controlling their forces from a secret location. But losing Vedeno was the end of six months of direct confrontations, he admitted; from now on, the Chechen fighters would be forced into a hit-and-run guerrilla war.

'The days after the loss of Vedeno and Shatoi were terrible for Chechnya, terrible . . . For Vedeno to fall in three days, for Vedeno to be impossible to defend, for it to be impossible to stop them going further into the mountains, seemed to signify the end of everyone's hopes,' Mayerbek Vachagayev, a Chechen academic visiting London for a conference, told me in a steamy coffee bar in Earl's Court. He had been in the mountains at the time, he said with an elusive half-smile, working with a correspondent from *Le Monde*. He had seen the shocked days of reassessment, the lengthy discussions, and the misery.

Shamil Basayev decided it was time to retaliate, Vachagayev told me.

'He gathered a hundred men around him. He wanted to do something that would make the world remember the plight of the Chechens. He was sure none of his men would ever come back alive. But even though the course of action they chose led them hundreds of kilometres outside Chechnya, somehow, against all the odds, they did return.

'It was easy to get through the Russian military checkpoints. They bribed the guards.

'The place they chose to attack was a Russian military air force base from which the planes had been bombing Chechnya. They seized it and they shot forty-two officers; then they waited for a reaction. There was silence from Moscow. And then more silence.' Mayerbek grinned. 'They hadn't expected that. They didn't know what to do; so Basayev took his men into the nearby town . . .'

# Retaliation

As usual, it was a quiet morning in the sleepy southern Russian town of Budyonnovsk: a few weekday shoppers on the streets, a few gossips in the courtyards, a hot breeze fanning the flat cornfields outside.

Everything changed at midday. Spraying gunfire, scores of gunmen in camouflage and black headbands stormed through Budyonnovsk's town centre. They were armed with assault rifles, grenade-launchers and mortars. They blew up a bus, ran over pedestrians and set houses and cars alight. They shot at firemen trying to put out the flames. They grabbed hostages on the street. Operating in small groups with two-way radios, they put the telephone exchange out of action, then stormed the town hall, police headquarters, bank and a hospital. They hoisted a Chechen flag. By evening, they had shut themselves into the hospital with more than 1,000 hostages, and installed a machine-gun on the roof.

Bodies lying in a glittering sea of broken glass, government helicopters and tanks moving through the smoke: the scenes shown on Russian television on 14 June made Budyonnovsk look like any urban battlefield in Chechnya. The mystery gunmen had reproduced in a Russian town much of the damage done by Russian planes to Vedeno.

But nothing like this had ever happened in Russia. The country went into shock.

The FSK boss, Sergei Stepashin, and Viktor Yerin, the interior minister, flew to Budyonnovsk to supervise anti-terrorist units arriving there. The entire regional army, the North Caucasus Military District, was put on alert. Roads and airports were closed. The bodies were counted. At least sixty people had been killed in the swift, deadly raid: thirty-seven policemen and soldiers, seventeen civilians and six guerrillas. Many more were wounded.

No one knew who the gunmen were. In Moscow, officials blamed Dudayev's forces. But the Chechen spokesman, Khamad Kurbanov, denied everything, telling Russian news agencies it was a 'provocation by Moscow' and saying: 'Chechens would never spill the blood of innocents.'

When Thursday dawned, the three-floor hospital was ringed with Russian tanks, flak-jacketed soldiers and snipers. But Russian officials said they had no plans to storm the building. Negotiations opened; Russians bussed in elders from Chechnya to help the mediator, General Vakha Ibragimov, a former Chechen interior minister. The gunmen threatened to blow up the hospital with mines. They wanted the press called into the hospital so they could explain their aims. Russian officials resisted. The talks stopped, and there was the brief sound of gunfire inside the hospital. The talks resumed. Journalists were allowed in.

Shown on Russian television: hundreds of scared people inside the hospital, sitting and lying close together on the floor on mattresses and in corridors. Most were calm, but a few yelled: 'Let us out!'

On Russian television, the identity of the guerrilla leader was revealed for the first time. Shamil Basayev's face appeared, with sweat on his brow. 'Let them come and storm the place. It does not matter to us when we die. What matters is how we die. We must die with dignity,' he said. Basayev told the reporters he had summarily executed five hostages – three air force pilots and two police officers – to persuade reluctant Russian officials to let the news conference go ahead. He had let two women go, but he would kill more hostages if his demands were not met. No one in Russia had heeded these demands when they had been made from inside Chechnya, but Basayev now made them again in a blaze of Russian publicity: Russian forces must get out of Chechnya. Peace talks must start.

The only answer the 'Party of War' had for Chechens was violent punishment. Stepashin ignored Basayev's demands. Budyonnovsk woke up at five in the morning to the sound of intense fighting. Against bitter opposition from relatives of the hostages, Russian Alpha Group troops had launched a misconceived assault on the hospital. They had heavy machine-guns, rocket-propelled grenades, cannon fire and helicopters. Terrified hostages hung white sheets out of hospital windows and yelled 'Don't shoot!' into the deafening noise. About two hundred people got out. The Chechen fighters beat back the Russian troops, but only briefly; in the early afternoon, they tried to storm the hospital again.

'I would not call it storming,' Stepashin said. 'It's called freeing the people.'

But it was a blood-bath. Instead of saving the hostages, the Russian artillery attacks set the hospital on fire and killed more than a hundred civilians. Hostages who escaped, and two hundred more who were freed in on-and-off negotiations which resumed on Saturday, said they had been more afraid of being killed in the Russian attack than being executed by the Chechens. Basayev's men stayed inside the hospital, with hundreds of hostages.

Violent punishment might be acceptable when applied only to Chechens, but Stepashin's brutality here was targeting Russian citizens too. It went down badly. They didn't appreciate being pointlessly sacrificed. Nor did they appreciate Yeltsin blithely going off to Canada, to meet the presidents of the G7, and sending word he wouldn't be home early.

The people of Budyonnovsk felt betrayed and abandoned. Their leaders had failed in their promise to protect Russians from the Chechen bandits. Remote and powerful, the élite of Russia was showing its old contempt for the people it ruled.

'All this is due to the negligence of our leaders. For half a year it's been dragging on in Chechnya. Couldn't they have stopped it spreading over the border?' said Valentina Lazareva, a retired woman of fifty-seven. 'They should never have started this war,' said thirty-three-year-old Svetlana Shakhsadova. 'They should have shut our border tight against the Chechens and let them eat each other.'[14]

'Russia's weakness . . . is not in the absence of an "iron hand", but in its total indifference to the fate of its citizens,' *Izvestia*'s editorial said.

---

14. *Los Angeles Times*, 18 June 1995.

'They're always saying that Chechnya has been sealed off and the situation is completely under control, but now they've been shown up as liars – again,' the mother of my old fixer, Alla Bogomolova, said down the phone with a tremble in her voice. 'It's a nightmare come true. I expect only the very worst now. The Chechens can get out wherever they want. They can bring the war to us any time they want.'

The Russian prime minister listened to the voices of Russian distress. Chernomyrdin overrode Stepashin. He called in the TV cameras and started negotiating with Basayev by phone as they rolled. He agreed to everything: peace talks in Chechnya by Monday morning, a cease-fire now, and getaway transport for Basayev, his guerrillas and the same number of hostages.

The peace talks in Grozny started even before Basayev's seven busloads of live people – 73 guerrillas and 139 hostages – and a freezer truck of corpses set off for home, trailed by Russian helicopters. As the last 700 people in the hospital tumbled weeping out to freedom, Chernomyrdin promised them that there would be no attacks on Basayev's convoy and that the last prisoners would also be set loose.

It was not the ending that Kulikov wanted. The angry military leader refused to endorse Chernomyrdin's promise not to attack the Chechens and their prisoners, and the hostage caravan zigzagged across the south for two days to avoid ambush by Russian troops. Basayev freed his prisoners on a dark road outside the Chechen village of Zandak, and vanished.

To the astonishment of their comforters, the last captives to be released blamed Russian leaders, not their Chechen jailers, for the crisis. Some had never fully realized the brutality of the Russian campaign in Chechnya until they heard their captors explain what had happened to themselves and their families. Many of them said they had volunteered to ride the rebel buses. They defended Basayev's Chechen group so ardently that local doctors thought they must have been mentally unbalanced by the siege. They were diagnosed as suffering from 'Stockholm Syndrome', named after the Swedish hostages in 1972 who sympathized with their

terrorist jailers and grew hostile to the authorities trying to free
them.

*

Basayev's attack on Budyonnovsk changed the course of the war.
For six months, the Chechens had hoped the human suffering in
their land would evoke some sort of sympathetic response from
outside. It hadn't come. Now, instead of hoping they could find a
resolution to the war by appealing to Russians' or foreigners'
nobler feelings, Basayev had taken the opposite course – playing
on Russia's superstitious dread of the raiding black bandit.

Basayev's attack was uncharacteristic for Chechens, who only
fight defensive wars. But it had one parallel in history, from
another time when the southern highlanders believed all was lost
and they were in danger of extinction. Basayev's namesake, Imam
Shamil, had ordered a similar raid more than a century earlier,
sending fighters into Russian Imperial territory to kidnap the family
of Prince Chavchavadze and force the Russians to negotiate. Both
raids were a recognition of the same truth: in the Russian hierarchy,
a Russian life counts for more than a Chechen one and is worth
negotiating over. The attack on Budyonnovsk made the thirty-
year-old commander a terrifying bogeyman to many Russians, who
blamed him for the loss of dozens of Russian lives. It also made
him a hero to Chechens, who believe he saved thousands of
Chechen lives by forcing Russia to start peace talks.

Terror tactics worked. Chechen voices raised in fear and pain
had gone unheard; the separatist leaders could not negotiate with
the generals of the 'Party of War', who refused to recognize them
as a side to talk to. But when Russian voices were raised in fear
and pain, the war came back to the attention of a higher level of
Russian politician. Basayev's raid provoked the first popular debate
inside Russia since the New Year about how to deal with
Chechnya. Because Russians inside Russia wanted a say, the debate
slipped out of the control of the generals who had free rein inside
Chechnya, and into the hands of Chernomyrdin, whose job was to
deal more humanely with Russians.

Unlike the generals, Chernomyrdin was willing to promise

peace, if only to avoid further distress to Russian voters. By 3 July, to the fury of the generals, a cease-fire was in place in Chechnya. The Chechens agreed to disarm. The Russians agreed to withdraw. Peace talks continued. The Chechen separatists noted for future reference that retaliatory attack might occasionally be the best form of defence.

'The war in Chechnya reflects the principle shared by the Czarist, Soviet and the "democratic" Russian governments alike that the only way to deal with the "disobedience" of national provinces is punishment, and the more severe the punishment the less likely they would be to disobey,' Magomed Galayev, a Chechen academic at Oxford, wrote in the 1995 War Report on Chechnya. 'However, if this principle was viable, Chechnya would have been the last place to defy the central authorities in Moscow, rather than one of the first.'[15]

*

Russians were terrified that their nightmare imaginings had come true. The Chechens really were coming. Where would the terrorists turn up next? Moscow turned into a fortress, all military patrols, APCs on street corners, and anxious eyes.

Stepashin left his job running Russia's main security agency in disgrace, but the disgrace was personal. The agency itself – now called the Federal Security Service (FSB in Russian) to reflect the broader investigative powers it had been given at the end of 1994 – had, unlike the army, been thriving on the tense atmosphere created by the war. The latest amendments to the law governing it had given it extra rights to set up its own jails, install more agents, and penetrate the computer networks and databases of all organizations. 'Despite the inability of the KGB [sic] to set up a puppet regime in Chechnya or later to anticipate the fury of the Chechen resistance to invasion,' the *New York Times* reported in May 1995,

---

15. Magomed Galaev, *The Cycle of Repression*, p. 35, article published in *War Report*, the bulletin for the Institute for War and Peace Reporting (IWPR), an independent conflict monitoring charity. Its June 1995 issue, No. 34, was devoted to Chechnya.

'morale is said to be as high as that of the CIA is low.'[16] The article quoted Alexander Mikhailov, the FSB's press officer, shrugging off press criticisms of the agency's increasing powers with the comment: 'They write what they like, and we do what we like.'

Heightened Russian fears of Chechen terrorism after Budyonnovsk gave the FSB a chance to lobby for yet more powers. An anonymous high-ranking FSB member explained that the failure of Stepashin's forces 'was a natural result of the systematic disintegration of the special services which began after the 1991 coup attempt'.[17] Liberals were scared that the head of the Kremlin guard, Lieutenant-General Mikhail Barsukov, would take over the FSB. If he did, said the MP Sergei Yushenkov, 'the FSB will become an extension of the Kremlin and everything will be decided behind closed doors by a handful of unaccountable officers. It would be monstrous.'[18]

Barsukov was appointed on 24 July, after being made a colonel-general. A slew of extra first-deputy jobs were created, bringing the agency's top executive jobs up to levels not seen since Soviet days. Barsukov brought the former KGB Alpha division back to rejoin the FSB from the presidential guards. By the end of the summer, even close presidential advisers were saying they feared their phones and offices were bugged.

Worries about Barsukov's appointment as Russia's security chief were based on two assumptions.[19] 'It is believed that, since he is the strongest security chief Russia has had for a decade, General Barsukov may try to restore the former might of the notorious KGB. He has also spent his life protecting the rights and privileges of top state officials, rather than the rights and independence of individual citizens,' *Rossiiskaya Gazeta* wrote.

There were eddies of public unease in Russia about Barsukov's activities. In January 1996, the Jewish newspaper *Yevreiskaya Gazeta* asked Yeltsin to dismiss Barsukov after the security chief

16. *New York Times*, 8 June 1995, Section A, p. 29. *Lubyanka Lullaby* by
    William Safire.
17. *Komsomolskaya Pravda*, 4 July 1995.
18. *The Times*, 3 July 1995.
19. *Rossiiskaya Gazeta*, August 1995.

made a blatantly racist anti-Chechen remark on television. Saying he was quoting the words of a Chechen, Barsukov told journalists: 'A Chechen can only be a murderer, or a robber, or at least a thief. There is no other Chechen.' Challenging the president to ask his subordinates to 'respect the peoples of the country that you lead', editor Tankred Golenpolsky said that the memory of the Jewish holocaust impelled him to protest against Barsukov's statement, for which 'in any civilized country he would be dismissed'.

But Barsukov stayed on.

*

As public fearfulness and officials' opportunism pushed Russia closer and closer to authoritarianism, a kind of *perpetuum mobile* of Russian punishment and Chechen retaliation was establishing itself in the south. The cease-fire and peace talks of the summer of 1995 broke down by autumn. Sporadic fighting continued. The Chechen separatists only partly disarmed; the Russian troops only slowly pulled back. Russian public attention lapsed, and the generals took charge again.

'Bands in Chechnya are slowly coming back to life, becoming more active, and we cannot allow them to crawl into the lowlands and into Grozny and resume their bandit operations,' Yeltsin warned in August.

In October, the doveish new commander of the joint group of federal forces in Chechnya, Lieutenant-General Anatoly Romanov, was seriously injured in a bomb attack in Grozny. Russia blamed Chechen terrorists, and the Chechens blamed Russian hawks trying to start the war again. Romanov was replaced by a hawk, Lieutenant-General Nikolai Shkirko.

Two days later, planes attacked the villages of Mesker-Yurt and Roshni-Chu, killing forty civilians. A Russian air force spokesman denied the planes were Russian, suggesting implausibly that the raids were carried out by Azeri or Georgian aircraft. The Chechen side pulled out of the peace talks, saying the bombings proved Russian dishonesty. The talks were blocked anyway, since both sides were sticking to their negotiating positions. The window of opportunity for peace closed.

The weak Chechen puppet government in Grozny was dismissed. Doku Zavgayev, the wily last Soviet leader, came back to rule in their place. He resurrected the old Supreme Soviet of the Chechen-Ingush Autonomous Soviet Socialist Republic as his parliament. Dudayev's negotiator, Khodzh-Akhmed Yarikhanov, denounced Zavgayev as the 'puppet' of an 'occupation regime'. But Anatoly Kulikov, now the interior minister, declared that Russian-Chechen negotiations could now only be conducted with Zavgayev. Dudayev's men were shut out of talks, and silenced again.

Russia was going to have parliamentary elections on 17 December. Zavgayev insisted on holding them in Chechnya too.

So the Chechen separatist forces retaliated again. Salman Raduyev, head of a band of fighters based near the Dagestani border and Dudayev's nephew by marriage, stormed the city of Gudermes and attacked Russian troops there in mid-December. Human Rights Watch/Helsinki accused Russian forces of using indiscriminate and disproportionate force to clear Raduyev's unit out of town in ten days of fighting – killing at least 267 civilians, wounding many others and forcing tens of thousands of civilians to flee their homes.

Communists did well in the Russian elections. Yeltsin's supporters did not.

In January 1996, Raduyev struck again. This raid was an exact copy of Budyonnovsk – attacks on an airport, railway station and Russian barracks, seizure of 2,000 hostages, and retreat with them to a hospital. But Raduyev, a young commander with no particular standing among the Chechen separatists, had not understood the secret of Basayev's success at Budyonnovsk. Raduyev's copycat raid was not on a Russian town, but just over the border with Dagestan in the town of Kizlyar.

To Russians, an attack by one armed group of 'black bandits' on another 'black' mountain area did not have the same immediate emotional resonance as Basayev's incursion inside Russia proper. After negotiations with local Dagestani officials, the rebels released all but about 160 hostages in exchange for safe passage back to

Chechnya. But Russian forces commanded by Barsukov, the FSB chief, and Kulikov, the interior minister, stopped them at the Dagestani village of Pervomaiskoye, just next to the Chechen border. The 1,000 villagers fled as the Chechens and their hostages arrived.

Russian punishment began, unimpeded by the anguished voices of ethnic Russian victms. A force of several thousand men surrounded the village. They waited four days, then pounded Pervomaiskoye, the Chechen fighters, and the hostages they were supposed to be rescuing with artillery and helicopter-launched shelling for another three days. Raduyev, some of his fighters and several dozen hostages were rescued at dawn on 19 January by a Chechen relief column which attacked the Russian forces' rear. They broke out of encirclement and escaped to the Chechen mountains. But the Russian bombardment destroyed the village entirely. The number of dead was never known; Russian figures were contradictory.

'The generals' statements made it clear from the first day that their overriding objective was to "punish" and kill the captors even at the cost of the hostages' lives,' wrote Vladimir Socor of the Jamestown Foundation:

> The events served to expose the pervasive dysfunctionality, lawlessness and lack of accountability which characterizes Russia's political system. The president gave the 'power' ministries a blank check, publicly justifying and encouraging the massive use of military force against the country's citizens. Russia's political and military leadership appears to have drawn all the wrong conclusions from this crisis. The spiral of retaliation and counter-retaliation looks set to continue. The role of bellicose elements around Yeltsin will increase and his isolation from reformers will deepen.[20]

By the time Yeltsin had to stand for re-election in June, some analysts now believed that Russians would not want any more of

---

20. Vladimir Socor, *Permovomaiskoye: Yeltsin's Military and Political Debacle*, published in *Prism*, 26 Jan. 1996, Vol. 2, No. 2, pp. 2–4.

their bloodstained president, and would vote in droves to return Communists to the Kremlin.

*

The Chechen saga made depressing reading in London. So did the saga of Russia's slow lurch away from freedom. But I was still following them, and still nostalgic for that distant world. I was living a very different kind of life in the West from the one I had envisaged. I now worked for exactly eight hours a day, adding commas and full stops and dropped verbs to agency copy about foreign politics, in an office with no windows. My colleagues were thirteen mostly older men, who liked to talk about how best to time their early retirement. There was one other woman, much younger than me, who was living with an ex-lover of mine. She was cautious around me. The older men called us both 'the girls'.

My marriage had ended. For months, I went from flat to flat, carting three cats and dozens of cardboard boxes of belongings everywhere with me. I came to hate cardboard boxes. Friends could only find out where I was staying by calling me at work.

A woman I met at a party told me I should write book reviews in my spare time. Nervously, I presented myself at a literary magazine's office in Soho. It was just as she had said it would be – they showed me a crowded bookcase, and told me to pick a book to review. I opened the first one that came to hand, which had a black-and-white cover and the half-joking title *If You Leave Me, Can I Come Too?* It was by Cynthia Heimel. I read:

> A major player in the back-to-nature motif is the wolf. He used to be a big, bad guy. Now he wears a white hat. Now we decry ranchers who shoot wolves. The wolf is a symbol of freedom, instinct, wildness. The wolf is our new superstar. We had *Dances with Wolves*, now we have *Women Who Run with the Wolves*, a book by Clarissa Pinkola Estes, which has been at the top of the best-seller lists for weeks. Every woman I know has bought this book. The title cried out to our secret longings. Every secretary, every waitress, every dry-cleaning clerk in the world is dying to chew up her steno pad or receipt book, grow a tail and fangs, and make a run for it. We want to go wild, have fantastic

adventures, lick our genitals and howl. When the boss asks us to bring him coffee, we want to snarl and go for his throat.[21]

The wolves were a good sign. The passage made me laugh. 'I'll take this one,' I said. I began to freelance on the side, for the review, for newspapers, and other magazines.

*

Yeltsin announced in February that he would run for re-election. He put his campaign in the hands of First Deputy Prime Minister Oleg Soskovets, from the 'Party of War'. But his ratings were dismal. Largely because of the perception in Russia that the Chechen war he had begun had brought suffering to Russians, the president had become far less popular than his warty, uncharismatic Communist rival, Gennady Zyuganov. The Communist Party that people remembered from the Brezhnev era had never been so brutal as Yeltsin had turned out to be. In an early poll, Zyuganov was favoured by 20 per cent of Russians; Yeltsin scored just 6 per cent.

The war was 'maybe one of our mistakes', Yeltsin said nervously.

But a new element was entering Russian politics. The new-rich tycoons who had been outside the hierarchy in the first post-Soviet years now wanted to take their place at the top. They wanted to rescue Yeltsin and make him re-electable. The prospect of a Communist presidency was unbearable to the New Russian millionaires, who had accumulated enormous economic power in the free-wheeling first years of Yeltsin's rule and wanted to hang on to their wealth. A group of these tycoons decided in the spring that the return of Communism would represent a 'deadly danger' to their interests. They combined forces – becoming, for the first time, a political pressure group – to bankroll Yeltsin's campaign and change his image.

The millionaires included Vladimir Gusinsky of the powerful Most Group; Vladimir Potanin of Uneximbank; Mikhail

---

21. Cynthia Heimel, *If You Leave Me, Can I Come Too?*, published in London in 1995, p. 32.

Khodorkovsky of the Menatep financial empire; former liberal foreign trade minister Pyotr Aven; Mikhail Friedman of Alpha Bank; Alexander Smolensky of Stolichny Savings Bank.

The seventh millionaire was Boris Berezovsky, a wealthy car dealer whose $500-million-a-year flagship company, Logovaz, also owned Russia's seventh biggest oil company, Sibneft, and a slice of the liberal media – Russian Public Television, the liberal newspaper *Nezavissimaya Gazeta* and the liberal magazine *Ogonyok*. Berezovsky was a scandalous figure. He had been the victim of a car bomb attack in 1994 that beheaded his driver; he lived behind bullet-proof glass; and he was questioned by the police after the murder in 1995 of Vladislav Listyev, the Russian Public Television executive who tried to ban advertising on the channel. Berezovsky's empire was one of the few business conglomerates allowed to advertise on the channel once Listyev was dead.

This business coterie, nicknamed the 'Big Seven' in the Russian press, persuaded Yeltsin to bring back the energetic ginger-haired politician Anatoly Chubais – an economic reformer from the early days, and their ally – to head his re-election effort. Chubais set up a ten-strong campaign team, which included Yeltsin's daughter, Tatyana Dyachenko.

The 'Big Seven's' opponents, from human rights activists to Communists, said the millionaires were driven by the desire to place the Kremlin under a closed oligarchy, primarily concerned with furthering its own interests. Reformist legislator Grigory Yavlinsky, a rival presidential candidate, said they were creating 'an over-monopolized, oligarchical, partly criminalized state'. But the strategy gradually began to work. Yeltsin's popularity ratings crept slowly up again. The millionaires' media empires blasted Russian voters with blatantly pro-Yeltsin messages. Candidates for the presidency were allowed by law to spend up to $3 million each on their campaigns. Yeltsin's campaign is estimated to have cost anywhere up to $140 million. By the time the election came around in June, the president had been expertly repackaged as the anti-Communist best hope for Russia's future as a thriving liberal state.

To succeed fully, however, Russians needed to be shown a serious attempt to pull their troops out of Chechnya. Popular liberal politicians, such as the handsome young Nizhny Novgorod regional governor Boris Nemtsov, were saying they would only back Yeltsin in the election if he began talks with Dudayev. The dusty, unsophisticated, unpopular 'Party of War' – led now by Defence Minister Grachev, ex-federal commander Kulikov, now the interior minister, and the new commander of the Russian forces in Chechnya, Lieutenant-General Vyacheslav Tikhomirov – was uncomfortably aware that it had not delivered on that original promise to Yeltsin of a quick victory in Chechnya. As far as the 'Warriors' could see, their only hope of political survival now was to crush the Chechens altogether, winning the war before election time.

The president didn't know which way to turn: whether to stick with the 'Party of War' or go over fully to the new 'Party of Capital'. He wanted to be re-elected, but it had always been his way to keep rival cliques at court, playing them off against each other to ensure his own power. Still reluctant to negotiate with Dudayev, he now wavered between all-out war, and victory before the elections, or all-out peace. Yeltsin's dithering and changes of heart were smoothly explained to the Russian public by the urbane Chernomyrdin, leader of the sleek administrative 'party of power' that was the Kremlin's public face.

*

For Chechen consumption, the latest Russian commander, Tikhomirov, offered the usual punishment of the 'Party of War' – a repeat of 1995's spring offensive. In the lowlands, Russian forces massacred villagers at Sernovodsk and, again, at Samashki. There were battles for Orekhovo and, again, Bamut. The Ingush village of Arshty was bombed, and fears that Ingushetia would be dragged unwillingly into the war were aired again. Federal planes targeted Chechen mountain villages.

Simultaneously, but for Russian consumption, there was much public discussion in February and March 1996 of a new peace plan for Chechnya. Seven options were laid out. Both Chernomyrdin and Emil Payin were charged with making viable plans. Grachev flew to Grozny on 5 March, announcing that he was ready to talk peace with Dudayev. Tass announced on 7 March that Russia had made a new peace plan, though its details were still under wraps.

Chechen fighters ignored the meaningless talk of peace from the north, but gave a stinging response to the actions of war they had seen from the Russian military in the south. On 6 March, 700 fighters slipped into Grozny and captured large chunks of it with little apparent effort, surrounding Russian military command posts and killing ninety-one soldiers. At the end of three days, once their attack was in all the Russian media, they slipped away again.

'We have repeatedly warned: if the federals act using such barbarous methods against us, we will take appropriate measures. If the Russian leadership had heeded our words, none of the people of Grozny would have suffered. The operation to seize the city was named "Wolf". We wanted it to be a lesson to the federal forces,' Ruslan Gelayev, the commander of south-western Chechen forces, told *Obshchaya Gazeta* afterwards.

Lending Gelayev's message extra force, a film of the Russian military's latest massacre, shot by the Russian human rights group Memorial, got a prime-time spot on Russian television. Millions of viewers were shown harrowing pictures of Chechen women weeping over charred, legless bodies in the ruins of their homes at Sernovodsk.

Mastering the art of the spectacular counter-attack – spectacular enough to make Chechen reality briefly visible to a Russian audience – kept boosting the fighters' morale.

A story in the *New York Times* described Maskhadov, Basayev and other Chechen commanders, Russia's most wanted men, strolling insouciantly around an eastern village in February, talking into mobile phones, distributing their satellite phone numbers to inquirers, holding press conferences and discussing the release of hostages from Pervomaiskoye.

A story in the *Los Angeles Times* described the Chechen villages' breezy response to the latest Russian peacemaking tactic, prodding the 350 village mayors into signing 'peace protocols' – in which they promised to expel fighters and disarm – or shelling their villages. The mayors had revived a Chechen tactic dating back to Stalinist times: instead of disarming people, the elders went from door to door collecting money to buy weapons on the black market. 'Anyone who tells you he disarmed is lying,' laughed one pistol-toting village man.

An envoy from Tatarstan, Rafail Khakimov, visited Chechnya in April to try to arrange peace talks. He came back saying Dudayev's forces clearly had the run of the republic even in the villages which had promised to turn themselves into 'islands of peace'. 'This is a real army with high morale, rather than "bandit formations",' he said. It was only the Russian federal forces that were 'totally demoralized'.

Yeltsin announced a peace plan on 30 March: a cease-fire from midnight, a partial withdrawal of Russian troops, and – for the first time – indirect talks with Dudayev. Lawrence Sheets, a Reuters correspondent, remembers the scepticism with which the plan was met by the group of Chechen fighters he was with. Eating and drinking tea in a room plastered with Dudayev posters, they watched Yeltsin's speech on television. Some laughed. Others cursed. Outside, they could hear the Russian helicopters bombing Goiskoye.

The plan was met with equal scepticism by the Russian 'Party of War'. Grachev was publicly contemptuous of it. The next morning, Tikhomirov said firmly that the only talks would be negotiations on unconditional Chechen surrender; then he resumed his military offensive with even more ferocity. Two divisions of troops were pulled out of Chechnya, but, on 9 April, Tikhomirov's forces seized Vedeno again. The Chechens attacked a Russian military convoy, killing at least twenty-six Russians. The 'cease-fire' lapsed, but the OSCE's latest representative, the Swiss diplomat Tim Guldimann, said he was still hopeful. The most important part of the deal was that Moscow should talk with Dudayev.

The capricious Dudayev understood the electoral pressure Yeltsin was under to make peace. He blew hot and cold about talking to the Russian leader. In March, he called in six foreign journalists to his latest secret home, the village of Shalazhi, and told them: 'It would be better to have the Communists in power. The Communists would be a gift from heaven compared to the criminal regime that is now destroying our people . . . What they are offering us is to sit in a cage with a hungry bear, shake his paw, and ask for reconciliation.'

Two weeks later, he said he wanted direct talks with Yeltsin, but was snubbed. A week after that, he said he wanted negotiations with Yeltsin through a third party. And a week after that, he said he was ready to go on the offensive.

On 21 April, Dudayev was killed in a Russian rocket attack. He was standing by his car, making a satellite phone call. The Chechen commanders admitted they had lost the symbol of their clandestine statehood. For more than a year, they had kept to their gentleman's agreement to support in public a leader who had become so wildly erratic that one aide to Maskhadov called him 'that complete idiot Dudayev'. But now, without him, it seemed likely that the independent-minded commanders would pull in different directions, becoming no more than warlords heading the armed bandit forces of Moscow's phraseology.

The commanders confounded those expectations. With rumours still rife that Dudayev had somehow survived, they buried him in a secret place. They announced that Dudayev's vice-president, Zelimkhan Yandarbiyev, was now their leader under the Chechen constitution. Yandarbiyev, a poet in soldier's clothing, was a colourless figure among the tough commanders, but not a push-over. Moscow heard his first statement with dismay. Dudayev had been assassinated by a specially targeted Russian rocket, Yandarbiyev said. There could be no peace talks until his killers were brought to book.

The next announcement on Tass was that Yandarbiyev, too, had been killed – this time in a shootout between rival groups of Chechens at the opposition town of Urus-Martan. But it was only misinformation, or wishful thinking. Yandarbiyev emerged with a quip from Mark Twain on his lips, saying: 'Rumours of my death have been greatly exaggerated.'

# SEVEN

'I don't know why people talk about the Chechens in Russia as if they were criminals,' Ghaith Mismar, a young Jordanian judge I had got to know in London, said as he looked at the cuttings scattered over my desk. 'I don't see how they can be. There are thousands of Chechens in my country, and they're famous as the most honest people in Jordan. Not aristocratic, but with this great reputation for honour: so much so that people are proud to have Chechen blood. They boast about their Chechen ancestry.'

I couldn't imagine Chechens living outside Russian control who didn't define themselves first and foremost by their collective disdain for Moscow. But, with the war running on and on, and the Chechens seeming unlikely to escape the brutal regime Moscow wanted to impose on them, the idea of Russia-free Chechen zones elsewhere was appealing. I started finding out about the diaspora Chechens.

There are tens of thousands of ethnic Chechens in Jordan, Turkey and Syria, the descendants of people who fled Russian ethnic cleansing at the end of the great war last century. A much larger number of people from the Circassian regions of the western Caucasus escaped to the Ottoman Empire at the same time: Abkhaz, Adygei and Nogai. In Turkey and the Middle East, where they have lost their language, Chechens from the east were assimilated by the Circassian westerners. In Turkey, Chechens and Circassians alike later found themselves in the huge and ethnically diverse nation Kemal Ataturk welded together this century, and were actively encouraged to forget their mountain traditions and their languages and to become the idealized Turks of the future their leader envisaged. But the Chechens of happy-go-lucky Jordan, who were among the founders of the capital, Amman, kept themselves to themselves on the pale, dusty hills they settled. They still speak the language of their ancestors, separate from the western Caucasian tongue still spoken by their Circassian cousins.

Many of them are called 'Shashani', or other surnames which indicate their ancestry to Jordanian Arabs. Even more than the uprooted Chechens elsewhere in the Middle East, the Chechens of Jordan are filled with the romantic nostalgia of the diaspora.

Most of the newspaper reports about the diaspora were from Turkey. When the war began, crowds of indignant Chechens and Circassians demonstrated outside the Russian embassy in Turkey. They wanted the war to be called off. They wanted their governments to protect the Chechens. They wanted to send arms, or if not arms then medicine and food. Some of the more idealistic young men wanted to go and join the fighting themselves, though most were stopped in time by their more practical parents.

The Turkish police, stern enough when it came to dispersing Kurdish dissent, took a milder view of the Chechen protests. Ethnic Turks were also sympathetic to the Chechens, viewing them as persecuted almost-Turks, warming to their warrior image and lone wolf symbol which was reminiscent of the grey wolf of Turkish nationalism.

The Turkish government, Russia's traditional rival in the Caucasus, had plans to extend its own influence into the Turkic-speaking parts of the former Soviet Union after 1991. It had always been quietly sympathetic to Dudayev. Dudayev had received food aid from Turkey, and had tried to introduce the Turkish version of the Latin alphabet as the Chechen language's writing. (Chechens laugh at the story that the Turkish ambassador in Moscow even suggested Dudayev should make Turkish the official language of Chechnya, blissfully unaware that non-emigrant Chechens spoke a language that was not even closely related to his mother tongue.)

But the Turkish government quickly came to realize it made more economic sense to do business with Russia than support the little peoples of the Caucasus. Turkey was in a double bind, unable to support separatism in Russia's Chechnya while cracking down on it with troops among the Kurds at home. When the war began, both Turkey and Jordan were left balancing official pragmatism with the pro-Chechen sympathies of their people.

The sympathies of the Turkish Circassians for their Chechen brethren were dramatically revealed to the world in January 1996, in a protest against the Russian army siege of Pervomaiskoye. To force the Russians to call off their attack, a group of Turks of Caucasian origin hijacked a ferry boat on the Black Sea. The *Avrasiya*, which was heading for Russia, had two hundred Russian passengers. Gunmen suddenly appeared among them, threatening to blow up the ship and all its passengers. It was four days before the group – six Turks, two Chechens and one ethnic Abkhaz from Georgia – gave themselves up and set the hostages free.

The hijackers' leader, twenty-eight-year-old Muhammed Tokcan, turned out to be a fourth-generation Turkish Circassian whose family had originally come from Abkhazia. Like many Circassians, he felt deeply involved in the wars around the Caucasus. Like just a few, he had personally gone to do battle in Abkhazia's war against Georgia in 1993, when he had joined Shamil Basayev's 'Abkhaz battalion' of Chechen fighters. After the Black Sea hijacking, he was arrested. But he was still regarded as a hero all over Turkey.

In Moscow, Yeltsin growled for four days that he could not understand why the Turkish authorities 'were not doing anything' to free the hostages on board the *Avrasiya*, nor how the gunmen had got on the ferry in the first place – a dig at Turkey for the covert military aid Russia suspected it might be sending to the rebels. Those were four embarrassing days for the Turkish government, unable to decide how to treat the incident. Mindful of public sympathies, no official would condemn the attack. One minister said the gang were 'not terrorists'. Turkish Prime Minister Tansu Ciller used the tense time of waiting to offer sympathy, if not support, to the Chechens. 'The attention of the world public should be drawn to the human tragedy under way in the Caucasus,' she said. 'A massacre is continuing in that region. Women and children are being killed . . . The real problem lies in the Caucasus. A lasting solution can only be reached with full respect for human rights.'

Another sympathizer – this time a twenty-year-old Turkish waiter with a fake gun – struck in early March, holding up a plane bound for Istanbul at Munich airport. He too wanted to draw world attention to the Chechen tragedy, but he gave himself up after eleven hours and released his 109 hostages. The young man dropped his demands for a televised press conference and settled for a brief chat with a German journalist. Newspapers in Turkey again focused on public outrage over the Kremlin's mistreatment of Chechnya, under headlines such as 'The Chechens Again' and 'Russian tyranny caused the plane hijacking'.

Newspaper reports in the West started to speculate that the Chechen war would spread to Eurasia, with the usual dark Western warnings of impending Islamic fundamentalism, but the historian Marie Bennigsen Broxup, who went on visiting Chechnya during the war, accompanied by Mayerbek Vachagayev, didn't think this was very likely. Sitting in her London mews house, she wrinkled her nose over the reports. The idea of Algerian-style Islamic fundamentalism breaking out among the Chechens just made her laugh. Fundamentalists hated Sufism and the traditional national Islam of the Chechens, she said; fundamentalists and Chechens were opposite poles of an old conflict between the jurists of Islam and the mystics. If anything, the Chechens and the mysticism their faith was imbued with were a bulwark against fundamentalism. 'Of course people in Chechnya have become more religious in the course of the war. Naturally it makes them think about God and death. Chechens are quietly convinced they're the best Muslims in the world. But they believe with the humaneness and common sense that you know.'

Nor was there much chance of the war spreading out of Chechnya. Any ties that existed between the diaspora and the Chechens had only been resurrected in the last ten years, she said; they were minimal. There was widespread sympathy for the Chechens in the diaspora, a feeling that all Caucasians had the same beliefs, the same history, and had fought the same war against Russia – even though the Circassians had never really fought very hard for Shamil. But that feeling had never translated into active Muslim help. The diaspora collected money for the Chechens, though the Jordanian diaspora's money never seemed to get through. A few dozen Chechens from Jordan had gone to fight in the war, including one who had set himself up as a commander and was now 'agitating somewhere in the mountains' and making himself unpopular. 'Chechens find now that they just can't get on with their diaspora,' she said. 'The diaspora is so romantic.'

Shortly before his death, Dudayev sacked Shamseddin Yusuf, the foreign minister from Jordan whom I had once 'met', who had raised funds abroad for the cause. Shamseddin was floating round now in Jordan or perhaps Turkey.

The Turks of Caucasian ancestry sounded like armchair Chechens, their interest in Chechnya a combination of theoretical fascination with a Muslim war outside their borders and a nostalgia for the roots they had lost – more an expression of the rediscovery inside modern Turkey of the ethnic mosaic that made it up than to do with Chechnya itself. It was the Jordanian ones I was most interested in, the Chechens who still spoke their old language and had kept their old society together.

'You should go and see them. You'd like them,' Ghaith told me. I flew away.

*

A chilly wind blew through the red-light district in Istanbul. The taxi-driver had driven up and down the same few narrow alleys for half an hour, hunting for the North Caucasus Solidarity Committee among cheap cinemas and gaudy street stalls. When we finally found it, up an unlit flight of stairs, it turned out to be plastered with the same posters I had seen on walls all over the city: exclamatory Turkish slogans over photos of Shamil Basayev and Dzhokhar Dudayev. There was shabby furniture, a pool table and a huge colour photocopier. The air was thick with smoke and conspiratorial whispers.

Fazil Ozen's group was a sort of clearing house for refugee aid and volunteer referral all over the North Caucasus. We didn't share a language, but it turned out not to matter; two young Russian-speaking Chechens, students at college in Istanbul, were hanging around in the scruffy corridor and translated into Russian and Turkish through the evening, over pizza. Dzhambulat and Shoto were puppylike and enthusiastic; Fazil Ozen was neat, courteous, and wary. The walls have ears, his body language said. There are spies everywhere.

Fazil Ozen had good reason to be cautious about unannounced, fair-haired, Russian-speaking visitors asking too many questions. His friend Said-Emmin Ibragimov, an ex-transport minister from Chechnya who was now running the Chechnya human rights committee in Turkey, had attracted too much attention with his hunger strike and his book denouncing the war. Just before I showed up, Said-Emmin Ibragimov had been stabbed.

First it had been voices. Said-Emmin was pushing through a rush-hour crowd on his way home to Taksim district one night, when someone cried out behind him, in Russian: 'What's the situation in Chechnya?' Said-Emmin looked round, but the person had vanished.

Said-Emmin was scared; he phoned Fazil Ozen to say he thought that Russians might be after him. 'We didn't take it very seriously at the time,' Fazil Ozen said regretfully. 'But we've learned our lesson now.'

The attack came three days later, outside Said-Emmin's front door. As he fiddled with the key, three blond men appeared. One yelled to the others in Russian: 'Quick, grab him.' They tried to garrotte him, and left a wire mark on his neck. But he was fit, and fought back; his attackers bashed him on the head and knocked him out instead. They stabbed him in the back, then they turned him round and stabbed at his heart. Then they ran away.

It was cold, and Said-Emmin was wearing a thick coat and several layers of warm clothes. The knife went through them, but only hit his ribs. As soon as he got out of hospital, he went on Turkish television to say publicly that he was staying in his job and that he would fight to the end, wherever he was. For the moment, however, he was in hiding . . .

. . . and so was Salman Raduyev, the 'Lone Wolf' leader who had escaped the Russian siege at Pervomaiskoye in January, but been reported killed two months later.

Reports of Raduyev's death appeared in the Russian press in early March. Tass quoted the pro-Moscow Grozny government as saying Raduyev had died at Urus-Martan of head wounds inflicted when unknown attackers opened fire on his car. He had been heading from the village of Stariye Atagi to Sovetskoye. According

to another report, this time sourced to General Vyacheslav Tikhomirov, the commander of the Russian forces in Chechnya, Raduyev
had been killed fighting miles away in Sernovodsk. Unnamed
officials at the Russian power ministries suggested Raduyev had
been killed as a result of infighting among Dudayev's supporters,
after he stole $1.5 million that should have been distributed among
his followers. A murky tale of thieves falling out. A mysterious
crime.

Except that Raduyev wasn't dead at all, Fazil Ozen said; he had
just lost an eye. He was being nursed back to health at a secret
location in Istanbul.

Fazil Ozen couldn't afford to annoy the Turkish government,
which let him work without asking too many questions, so he was
cautious about how he described the aid he collected for the
Chechens. Medicine and food went to Chechnya, he said. Hospital
beds for the wounded were found in Istanbul. He was very insistent
that there was no traffic in guns on the secret mountain routes
along which [he said] people slipped in and out of Chechnya.
People did use them, but there were also easier ways to get to
Chechnya than mysterious mountain routes: direct flights from
Turkey to southern Russian towns, and then a bus or taxi. There
was no need to send weapons to Chechnya. It made much more
sense to send money to Russia, so the Chechens could pick it up
and buy their weaponry direct from the Russian army.

So there was a lot of nervous throat-clearing, as I contemplated
his overblown romanticism, imagining diaspora Chechens like him
sneaking around the hills of Dagestan reliving their collective past.
He watched me. Cigarettes were lit, pizza passed around.

Where was Shamseddin? I asked. 'I don't know,' Fazil Ozen
said, and his lips pursed tight. 'He's been sacked. We've heard he's
here, but we have nothing to do with him.'

It was late at night by the time we left the committee building.
Fazil gave me a lift back to the friends I was staying with, and
played me one of the many cassettes of Chechen music he had
brought back. As we pulled out into the main road, a police car
stopped us. If this had been Moscow, they would have been
checking us because there were suspicious Chechens in the car. But

crime, like beauty, is in the eye of the beholder. In Istanbul, it turned out, what the police checked on late at night in the red light district was suspicious blonde women, believing they were all part of the army of Russian prostitutes which had descended on Turkey since the borders opened.

'They think you're a Natasha!' chuckled Fazil.

Mystified at our secretive laughter, the police waved us on.

*

There was no air of stifled conspiracy in Amman. In this white, modern city, the Chechens were quiet villagers long established on the dusty hills of Zarqa and Sweileh, with two Chechen and two Circassian MPs to represent them in parliament and a network of clubs to represent them in society. Caucasian culture was out in the open here.

But I had been wrong to think that living outside Russia for a century might have healed old wounds. Everyone remembered the flight that had brought their ancestors here. The trauma of surviving ethnic cleansing had been passed down the generations. They kept the signs of sorrow posted up everywhere. An etching of a weeping, bedraggled crowd in rags, fording a river with hunted looks on their faces, was the first thing I saw when I walked into a quiet Chechen youth club. One of the boys playing pool – paler-skinned than Jordanian Arabs, pale-eyed, with the reddish hair of mountain Chechens – saw me staring. 'That's our grandparents and great grandparents escaping the Tsar's soldiers,' he said. 'That's how brutal Russia was in the past. And it's just as brutal today.'

It was her grandmother's story, but Zokhra Mohamedov described the escape from the Russians last century as vividly as if she had lived through it herself. It was only when I added up the dates later that I realized her story must come from at least a generation earlier than she said. Thin and grey-haired, she wore jeans and a thoughtful look. Zokhra spoke slow English with the dreamy tone of the refugee.

'My grandmother was a small child at the time. She remembered walking through the forest with her family for a long time – seven days, eight days – always scared, always hurrying, always looking back over their shoulders. Then they reached the sea, and took a small boat. The seas were very rough, and she was frightened that they would sink.

'They were at sea for three or four days with many other families, lying close together in the hold. Many of them got sick with vomiting and diarrhoea. I think it must have been cholera. Every night, my grandmother would wake up to the sound of quiet prayers on the deck above, then the terrible plopping sound of a body being thrown overboard. In the morning, there would always be someone missing. One of the families would be weeping. And even when they reached the safety of a Turkish port, they couldn't go on land for forty days, because the Turks quarantined the ship.

'Since the time of those terrible sea crossings, none of the Caucasians who escaped has ever eaten fish. They couldn't bear to touch it. I'm modern, and I like the taste of fish; but I don't know how to cook it, because my mother and grandmother never taught me.'

Zokhra's family stayed in Ottoman Turkey until the local Turkish governor tried to buy her grandmother's pretty sister as a bride for his son. The girls' father pretended he might accept the offer of a capful of gold coins for his oldest daughter, but after the governor had left, he called the other Caucasian villagers together and hastily married the daughter off, by night, to one of her own kind. Then he fled Turkey, taking only Zokhra's grandmother with him. They settled in Jordan; Zokhra's grandmother never saw her sister again.

Every Chechen and Circassian in Jordan had learned these stories of terror, flight and dispossession at their mother's knee. Their home-in-exile was arid and sandy, but they all felt they knew the great green mountains of home. They yearned for the land-scapes of their past. Like many others, Zokhra went back to Russia when the borders opened after 1991 to see the beauty of the hills for herself – and, almost by accident, stumbled across her cousins too. 'I was there for three weeks, and it was so beautiful. I felt at home in my genes. The landscape was in my genes, in my hidden brain. I wanted to describe its beauty to my children . . .

'I didn't expect to find any relatives, though I did ask at the hotel where the people of my name lived. But one day three men came up to me outside the hotel and shook my hand. I didn't know who they were, but I knew and felt they were my family. One of them was an old man of seventy: he was as fit as a dancer and he had my father's face. Then they said they were from the Mohamedov family, and we hugged. It was very dramatic. I cried, and they cried.'

Everyone was fascinated by the idea of seeing the homeland. After 1991, it became fashionable for Jordanian Chechen youths to go and live in Grozny for a while. Some of the boys at the youth clubs spoke a bit of Russian which they had learned on these roots trips. Many of them had set up as mechanics in Grozny, servicing the flashy cars which Chechens liked to drive but didn't know how to mend.

Adnan Yunis Madheb was small and merry and Circassian. He lived on the top floor of his parents' home in Zarqa, where he had spent fifteen years building up a huge home library of books and cuttings about the Caucasian peoples. He loved Circassian dancers and lovingly dusted down the traditional Caucasian coat he had hanging up in his room – a knee-length tunic, buttoned down the front, with two line of little pouches sewn diagonally across the breast for bullets. When Chechnya declared independence, he had enthusiastically adopted the cause. He printed and distributed T-shirts and stickers and posters, all green and all covered with leaping Circassian dancers and bearded, dagger-wielding Chechens.

Mohamed Bino was a witty, urbane Chechen who worked in the prime minister's office. His beautiful wife had gone back to the mountains before the war, and found her family. She returned with armfuls of the chased silver bracelets of the hills bordering Dagestan. The Binos laughed a little at the language of their Chechen cousins, full of Russian words, and at their religious practices: 'They're deeply religious, honest, good people; but after seventy years without proper education some of their prayers have got a bit muddled. They say meaningless things in what they think is Arabic. They dance those old dances. None of us mind their mumbo-jumbo, though; we appreciate it's a sign of good faith preserved in difficult conditions . . . You know what we Chechens say about our faith?' Mohamed Bino asked. 'We say: Mohammed was an Arab – but Allah is Chechen.' The Binos were reverent about their past. They still kept the huge bread-oven of Chechen tradition, with an old wooden paddle to pull out loaves, in a shed beside their spacious home. It had been built when their family first reached Jordan.

Dudayev had come visiting before the war, en route for other countries in the Middle East. He had promoted Jordanian Chechens to government posts for helping him travel. Shamseddin Yusuf, who had been working on the waterways of Saudi Arabia (some Chechens mockingly called him a plumber), had fixed Dudayev's first Middle Eastern trip; he was rewarded with the office of Chechen foreign minister. Later, Dudayev appointed as his ambassador in Jordan the only ethnic Chechen working at Amman airport: Farouk Toboulat, an air traffic controller, a well-meaning amateur with eyes hugely magnified by his spectacles and boundless enthusiasm for the Chechen cause.

Chechens here remembered Dudayev with affection.

'I liked him. He was good and simple,' Farouk Toboulat said.

*

When the modern Chechen war started, Chechens, Circassians and Arabs alike protested furiously against Russia. Passionate discussions broke out at the Chechen charity society in Zarqa, at its branches in Sweileh, Sokhna and Azraq, and at the Chechen–Jordan friendship association in Sweileh, a bare building over a garage.

Some boys went to fight, and four were quickly killed. The Chechens didn't want them. 'News came from Chechnya that they didn't want our fighters. They said: "We know the land. Your people don't. Leave the fighting to us,"' said the Circassian MP Tujan Faisal.

She was a controversial politician: glamorous, miniskirted and frank. She'd been drawn into the Chechen sympathy effort; she was kindly but a bit snooty about her fellow Caucasians, who didn't have quite the snob value of her own Circassian people.

Circassians had the top jobs in the army and formed an honour guard for the king, but most Jordanian Chechens, she said, were lower-middle-class and 'a bit rustic'.

Instead of fighting, the young Chechen hotheads were encouraged to be practical and donate blood. Jordan's anti-war feeling was given decorous expression. No one at the top blamed the government for keeping up relations with Russia while the war was going on: little Jordan, with its Palestinian refugees and its delicate position in the Middle East, couldn't be expected to get into more international trouble. A Jordanian committee for the support of Chechnya was set up to coordinate fund-raising for the Chechens, and registered with the interior ministry and the government. Jordan gave medical care to some wounded Chechen civilians and fighters; it also offered to evacuate Chechen children, but Dudayev's men refused. Jordanian Chechens on the street collected money for the cause from their relatives. For the élite, there were charity dinners and genteel auctions of people's treasured Caucasian family heirlooms: silver wedding bodices, silver belts, antique daggers.

At first sight, these were orderly, decent expressions of sympathy and sorrow. Beneath the surface, however, the local Jordanian Chechen politicians were all at each other's throats over the war. The grand old man of the Chechen community, the leading MP, Sheikh Abdul Barghi Jamo, hated Dudayev and was now trying to limit the Chechen president's popularity among the Arabs of Jordan by suggesting that he was really a Jew. To the rage of Dudayev's many supporters, Abdul Barghi was backing Khasbulatov instead. Abdul Barghi was very grand indeed. There was iron order in his office; he had a solemn, statesmanlike mien born of four decades in parliament. But he bitterly resented Dudayev's refusal to make his son, Omar Barghi Jamo, a minister in Chechnya. Omar, who was forty, had spent a few months in Chechnya before the war but been kicked out under a cloud.

Money was behind most of the quiet feuds. The vanishing Shamseddin Yusuf was easy to blame. The diaspora had raised from $150,000 to $1.2 million dollars for their brothers inside Russia, but the money was missing. The scandal over where it had gone was embarrassing the honest Jordanian Chechen MP Said Bino, who fronted the Chechen support committee. He had never got around to publishing accounts of the money raised in the newspapers, and now his good name was besmirched.

Shamseddin was supposed to have paid a salary to Dudayev's ambassador, Farouk Toboulat. But he had left without paying. Good-hearted, idealistic Farouk Toboulat had been forced to sell his plot of land to make ends meet. His wife was in despair. Farouk Toboulat, still devoted to Dudayev, still poring over his Chechen genealogy tables in his friendly, cluttered Zarqa apartment, was so upset with Shamseddin that it had made him ill. He had spent days in hospital. He was padding round in dressing-gown and bedroom slippers.

Shamseddin was in Turkey, but his wife Wahida was still in Amman. In February, she invited a group of wounded Chechen fighters who were convalescing in Jordan to her house for dinner. When talk turned to the missing diaspora funds, Jordanian Chechens said, the fighters had heard accusations against Dr Yusuf Bilto, who owned the garage next door to the Chechen club at Sweileh. Filled with rumour, indignation and Wahida's wine, the fighters went on the rampage. They beat up Dr Yusuf, trashed his garage, and dropped heavy objects out of the club windows on astonished passers-by. The government quietly shipped the fighters back to Chechnya. 'They were good guests, but not good diplomats; they listened to too many whispers,' one official said resignedly.

And now the number of dubious Chechen envoys fishing for the diaspora's money was growing every day. My guide to the Chechens, the Caucasian researcher Adnan Yunis Madheb, called them 'fox'; the most cunning ones, whose antics made him slap his forehead in comic despair, were 'very fox'. After being sacked, Shamseddin had 'appointed' his own friend, Walid Shashani, as fund-raising 'ambassador at large' in Jordan, a rival to Farouk Toboulat. Now the black sheep son of another respected Jordanian Chechen family, also a friend of Shamseddin's, was also starting down the same road.

'We saw him on television; he was in Indonesia, then Pakistan, and now Saudi Arabia, weeping over the sufferings of the Chechens whom he'd seen in Grozny and asking for money to help. But he's never been to Chechnya and that money will never go there either,' Adnan said, screwing up his eyes. 'That man is *more fox* than Walid and Wahida put together. Most Chechens are wolves: honourable, decent, simple and brave. I like the wolves. But what should we do about these sly foxes, *wallahi*?'

Nothing, was the Jordanian answer. Everyone accepted that the Chechens were too democratic to be able to take wealth with equanimity. Given money, they argued with each other, and sometimes stole from each other. But they kept their quarrels to themselves. They weren't a threat to anyone else.

'We don't have many Chechen tycoons here; the few that do exist have probably made their money through corruption. The Chechens struggle endlessly among themselves,' Tujan Faisal said. 'But they're very closed, they keep themselves segregated and, when they have differences among themselves, they always try to keep them internal and present a united front to the world. So we just try not to interfere with the power struggles of the Chechens.'

It was an exact parallel of the situation that, in Russia, had led to war. A few rich Chechens – the foxes – were squabbling over the money they had got their hands on by fair means or foul; the poor and honest majority – the wolves – were trying to do the right thing. But the response was different. While politicians in mighty Russia felt so threatened that they wrote off the whole Chechen nation as bandits and invaded, little Jordan had enough confidence in the good faith and honour of its Chechen 'wolf' majority that it could shrug off the shady activities of the 'foxes'.

# EIGHT

The election clock was ticking, and even in harsh Russia politicians were now looking urgently for ways of patching things up with the Chechens. Dudayev's death opened the way for the peacemakers. With the personal animosity Yeltsin felt for the dead Chechen president no longer a factor to be reckoned with, Chernomyrdin contacted Maskhadov for talks. Maskhadov said he was ready to negotiate about the military situation, though not about the political question of Chechnya's status. Hesitantly, Yandarbiyev also said he might be willing to negotiate if what Yeltsin was offering was 'true peace, not just pre-election propaganda'.

It was far from clear whether true peace was on Yeltsin's mind. Now that Dudayev – 'a man the president could not meet' – was dead, the Russian president said he was ready to 'meet the opposition . . . to demonstrate our good-will'. He proposed three-sided talks between Russia, the Chechen commanders and the puppet Chechen government in Grozny. But what was clearly uppermost on Yeltsin's mind was the face-saving campaign stump of a lifetime that he announced at the same time. He wanted to press the flesh of the thousands of Russian soldiers miserably stationed in the south, an important symbolic gesture from a president who had never been to the war. Before the end of May, he said, he was going to Chechnya.

The Chechens were suspicious of Russian motives, and divided among themselves about how to respond. It was a dilemma. If they went along with Yeltsin, the man who had brought modern warfare to their land would probably be re-elected Russian president; if they didn't, the Communists who had deported the Chechens in 1944 would come back to power.

Basayev refused to even contemplate talks with Yeltsin, saying: 'I have no interest in talking with this butcher and murderer of the Chechen people for the sake of his election campaign.' If Yeltsin came to Chechnya, Basayev said, he would get 'a warm welcome;

we will try to make sure he never leaves'. But the moderate commanders decided to take Yeltsin's overtures on good faith. Stopping the war was the most important goal, Maskhadov said; it made sense to push for peace while Yeltsin needed to listen. They dropped their demand that Dudayev's killers be brought to justice. Most of them agreed that Yandarbiyev should meet Yeltsin, while keeping a watchful eye on whether the Russians were sincere. 'If we have any doubt,' Maskhadov warned, 'then we will help the Communists.'

Yandarbiyev went to the Kremlin on 26 May, and signed a preliminary deal with Yeltsin agreeing to a cease-fire from 1 June. For the Chechens, it was important to be recognized as a political side to negotiate with, not dismissed as a bunch of shadowy criminals. Yeltsin was delighted. He left Yandarbiyev in the Kremlin as a *de facto* hostage, and flew to Chechnya for a few hours to talk to the Russian troops at the heavily fortified military airport in Grozny. With scant regard for the delicate peace process begun in Moscow, he triumphantly told the soldiers: 'You have crushed the rebels.'

There were more gestures of bad faith from warriors on both sides. Fighting carried on after 1 June, despite the cease-fire. There were clashes in Shali, and Russian APCs blown up by mines in Grozny. There were harsh words from Tikhomirov: 'I state with full responsibility that I will order troops to destroy, resolutely and with hatred, all those bandit groups that do not want peace.'

But the peace process inched forward anyway. Russian and Chechen separatist negotiators, and Tim Guldimann from the OSCE, began talks in Nazran on 4 June.

Russian military attacks did not stop altogether during the talks. Vedeno and Nozhai-Yurt districts were bombed. But, in a sign that the military was coming under pressure from Moscow to restrain itself, the Russian air force angrily denied it was responsible, saying the reports of bombings were 'lies for propaganda purposes, aimed at discrediting the army'.

By the time a deal was reached at Nazran, on 10 June, 1966, the Chechen side had been promised everything it wanted. There would be no more fighting. Russian troops and roadblocks would start packing up the next day, and leave Chechnya altogether by the end of August. All prisoners of war would be exchanged, and the filtration camps shut down. The local elections that Zavgayev had wanted to hold in Chechnya on 16 June, to legitimize his own hold on power, would be postponed until the Russian troops left.

The Chechen separatist convoy that pulled out of Nazran was euphoric, all happy headlights and horns and yells of 'Allahu Akbar!', the fighters in the forty cars waving at the excited crowds that gathered along the road. At Samashki, Maskhadov stood on his car with a loudspeaker, proclaiming: 'The war is over. There will be no more Russian planes and helicopters bombing your homes. There will be no more tanks on your streets.'

But the 'Party of War' hated the deal. Sullen Russian military leaders – who could only lose politically by being forced to stop the war without winning it – had shown their displeasure at the talks by fudging a goodwill exchange of prisoners. The Chechens had handed over first two, then fourteen more Russians, in Nazran; the Russians alleged they too had freed fourteen Chechens – but elsewhere. They offered no proof. The 'freed' men never turned up.

In Grozny, Zavgayev was furious at the implication he would soon become politically irrelevant. He declared Tim Guldimann *persona non grata* and ordered him out of Chechnya.

And even the Chechen commanders' euphoria dissipated when huge explosions broke up their cavalcade, filling the sky with red flashes, throwing cars across the road, and injuring several by-standers. The first remote-controlled mines exploded just beyond Samashki, the second near Grozny. Russian television showed Tim Guldimann from the OSCE, who had been in the direct path of the second blast, sitting shocked and quiet by the roadside, with thick black smoke rising behind him. He blamed 'those who are against the peace process', but wouldn't name names. Stepashin, a delegate at the talks, denied Russian responsibility.

One more mysterious crime marred the day, in Moscow: a bomb exploded under a metro train seat in the evening, killing four passengers. No one claimed responsibility, but many Russians suspected Chechen terrorists were out to stop the election. No one in Chechnya bothered to make the routine counter-accusation that the FSB was to blame.

There was nothing for the Russian and Chechen peacemakers to gain by reacting angrily to these explosions. Despite behind-the-scenes attempts to disrupt the peace process by mysterious acts of violence, the 'Party of War' was banned from open hostilities. Yeltsin had made it clear that the unpopular sounds and sights of battle must be kept off Russian television while his voters made up their minds. The Nazran agreement was an election fiction, but at least for the moment it represented a hope for peace and a chance for the Chechens to be recognized in Russia as ordinary men and women, not bogeymen.

My luck changed; I got a new job in Moscow working for the *Los Angeles Times*. I left London on 2 June 1995. By the time voting started in the presidential elections, I was back in Chechnya.

# NINE

Sunlight, new shops and colourful advertising billboards every-where: Moscow just before the election was brighter and richer than the city I had left fifteen months earlier. There was a new-capitalist construction boom. Huge glittering buildings were rising into the sky. They were made of fashionable glass and steel, but their style – towers and turrets and massive guarded doorways – was oddly reminiscent of the hierarchical Stalin Gothic of an earlier era of consolidation. Flashy jeeps and Mercedes raced up the fast lane on the highways – the 'ZiL lane' which in Communist times had been reserved for Party limousines. The new upper class were everywhere: men in smart suits and leggy girls in expensive clothes chattering into mobile phones. When you switched on the radio now, cheerful women's voices were explaining how to serve foreign delicacies like taramasalata, which everyone ate on their holidays abroad. When you switched on the television, white teeth glittered in an endless series of toothpaste ads, almost as frequent as the election ads – grim scenes of Communist concentration camps from history, exhortations not to let Russia slide back into that darkness.

Even the new underclass of Yeltsin's Russia – the unpaid – were getting happier. For months, state workers had not got their salaries. Sleek government officials had had other priorities, includ-ing the Chechen war; and the time when the government élite had to listen to the opinions of scruffy provincial teachers and miners had passed long ago, as Russia's elected parliament lost its real power. Briefly, however, the complaints of the underclass were now being heard on high, amplified by Yeltsin's electoral needs. The administration was spending millions of dollars on vote-catching sweeteners at the end of Yeltsin's re-election campaign; it suddenly found it could, after all, afford to pay its huge backlog of wages and pensions to the unimportant. Yuri, an eighty-year-old who had retired from being a scientific research director twenty-five years before, was beaming as he pocketed his pension. 'It's great that Yeltsin has come out of the shadow of his bad advisers at last, and is showing his own true worth,' he said happily. Yeltsin's little pre-election miracles got results: less than a week before the first round of voting, the president's popularity rating crept level with Zyuganov's.

There were still beggars everywhere. Beggars on crutches and wheelchairs lurched dangerously around traffic lights, hoping to ambush rich motorists. Ragged, homeless drunks lolled in corners. But if they didn't have a registered home, they couldn't vote. No one in government cared about the underclass. They were too far down the new hierarchy.

*

Sunlight, dust and scorching heat: what the 'Party of War' had left of Grozny was dizzying, unbelievable. The remains of the president's palace had been dynamited away; a heap of girders and rubble, as improbably small as cremation ashes, was the only reminder it had ever existed. Sickening empty spaces stretched out in all directions. Daylight shone through unsteady brick façades, somehow still standing although the buildings behind them were no longer there. Shattered masonry, blackened ruins, cratered roads: there was a random, drunken quality about the devastation. Whole boulevards were punched with a lacy tracery of holes. Whole districts of one-storey houses were damaged, but people still lived inside many of them, behind locked gates scrawled with a pathetic plea to looters: 'People Live Here'.

There were no phones, no light, and no tap water. The reconstruction money Moscow said it had poured into Grozny had vanished. The Grozny government said only Russian federal agencies had handled the money, but the Russian police clapped the Chechen Gantemirov in jail for embezzling it anyway.

I wandered about, staring.

At Chernorechiye, there was thick greenery on all sides: the thin trees I had hardly noticed in winter were flourishing, and people were gathered again at the little *bazarchik*. But the buildings were half empty and horribly smashed. Signs hanging on some ruins read: 'Mines'. My roadside hut was still there, a bit battered; but all that was left of the *profilaktoriya* behind it was a skeleton of wire. I saw no familiar faces.

Not everyone I remembered had disappeared, though. On the road back to the centre, I half-recognized a ruined ministry building. Behind it was Red Front Street, where Musa Autarkhanov and his family had once lived. What people had told me about the street being destroyed was true. Every house was hit, splintered or smashed. But a few were still standing, and the high fence in front of the Autarkhanovs' home was intact. I couldn't see what was inside. The gate was locked; I banged, and a tall, nervous youth stuck his head out – still recognizably the little boy Magomed who had videoed his father Musa, Ardi, me and the two Russian guests at dinner in the house three years before. The house was still standing. Hovering anxiously on the veranda, in case of trouble, was his mother, Luiza, in slippers and a flowered robe. We looked at each other in joy and disbelief, with huge smiles spreading over our faces as realization dawned.

'You're alive!' I exclaimed.

'You're back!' she cried.

She hugged me sideways, Chechen style, and drew me inside to tell me her story. The house had been stripped almost bare, and bare plaster still marked the huge hole a shell had blown in the sitting-room. But the whole family had survived. They escaped to Moscow at the beginning of the war and waited out the siege of Grozny. After things quietened down, Luiza and the children came back to protect the house from looters. She was too late: the looters had been, but she fixed up the structural damage in case, one day, it became possible to sell the house. Musa was in Russia. He was setting himself up in business in the town of Vologda. He was going to take them away at the end of the summer.

She kept stopping her matter-of-fact recital, and looking at me with astonishment. She patted my shoulder, then my hair, as if checking I was flesh and blood. 'And what's been happening to you in all this time?' she said hastily, as though she felt she had spent too long talking about her own troubles.

'Nothing like this,' I answered, shy of talking about anything more trivial than the colossal upheavals in her life. 'I came at the beginning of the war; I wanted to find you then, but people said your district was destroyed ... I went back to England, got divorced ... started a new job in Moscow last week. And now I'm here; and I'm so happy to have found you.'

She hugged me again.

'I've thought about you a lot; about those normal days before the war when people came visiting,' she said. 'I was thinking about you just today. I can't believe you're really here. It makes it seem as though normal times might be coming back for everyone.'

All over Grozny, people were using the electoral lull in fighting to repair their homes. Women dug bricks out of ruins, and cleaned off the old cement. Neat heaps grew at roadsides. But no one believed the war was over. 'The dangerous days are over for the moment, thank God, but how long will it last? They'll be back,' said Yeva Avetisova, an eighty-year-old cleaner, when I stopped in at her hairdresser's shop. It had no roof or windows any more. A mirror and a pair of scissors were its Armenian boss's only assets. But she was dutifully sweeping the floor.

A woman rushed up to me in the street, and tugged urgently at my arm. 'You're a foreigner,' she said. 'So you might know. I've asked everyone, but even the medium I went to can't tell me. Do you think the Russians will ever leave us in peace?' Then she shrugged, and looked bleak. 'Why even ask? I know myself that the answer's no,' she carried on.

*

I admired the undaunted way people were getting on with their lives.

The central market was packed with people, selling every kind of food, cigarettes, alcohol, cheap Turkish clothes, electrical goods and cassettes of Chechen music. The walls and arched windows of what had once been mansion blocks near it were crumbling away. Without warning, a window-sill crashed down on the shoulder of a young man passing by. He jumped back, cursing, and brushed the masonry dust off his dark shirt. Then he sauntered on.

The elegance of the people emerging from these ruins surprised me. Young women in high-heeled sandals and lacy Spanish-dancer dresses picked their way down the streets. Some men wore silk shirts. Street cafés sold kebab and garlicky pasta.

The music of defiance, drifting out of cars and houses, surprised me too. '*Oglya-niiiis, Shamil, oglya-niiiis,*' went one speeded-up refrain: 'Turn around, Shamil, turn around.' The song told the story from last century of Imam Shamil's lieutenant, Baisamgur of Benoi, a Chechen so bitterly opposed to Russia that he wanted to fight on even when all was lost and the Caucasian leader was walking away to surrender his sword. Baisamgur wanted to kill Shamil to stop him surrendering, but honour only allowed him to kill in face-to-face combat. So he called to Shamil to turn around and die; but Shamil refused, and gave up the Caucasus.

A city still alive with the words of Baisamgur didn't seem like a conquered city.

\*

Only Doku Zavgayev's puppet government went in terror in the ruins it theoretically ruled. Sandbags and razor wire, APCs and heavily armed sentries and paranoia surrounded the administrative compound. Central Grozny wasn't safe enough for Zavgayev; he spent so much of his time hiding out in the Russian military aeroport, Khankala, that people in Grozny had unkindly nick-named him 'Doku Aeroportovich'.

Pop-eyed Doku Aeroportovich had good reason to be scared at the moment. To save his own little bit of power, he was taking a big risk. He was holding not just Russian presidential elections in Chechnya but also local elections to justify his continued rule – which the Nazran agreement had said would not be held. Politi-cians in Moscow were worried Zavgayev's election shenanigans would provoke the Chechen separatists into dropping the truce, and that war would break out again before voting had finished in Russia. They growled and threatened, but the usually obedient Zavgayev ignored his protectors.

It turned out, though, that Yeltsin's men were more worried about the disruptiveness of Zavgayev's election than most Che-chens. Hardly anyone in Chechnya intended to vote. 'Elections?

What elections?' was the usual disgusted response. Everyone knew that results which suited Moscow would be announced anyway, since Russia took no notice of what Chechens really said or thought. Most people thought federal troops would attack them again as soon as the second round of voting finished and peace stopped being expedient. 'It's obvious you can't force elections on people down the barrel of a gun. People here won't vote, but the results are a foregone conclusion anyway,' said Raya Khamuradova, a sensible middle-aged doctor. 'I'm just worried about what horrors they'll inflict on us afterwards.'

For form's sake, I went the next day to get accredited with the Zavgayev administration before seeing whether any voting had started in the villages. But the officials dithered endlessly. Bored, I started eavesdropping on the Russian conversation behind me: a man's voice saying he was a correspondent for *Le Monde*. It reminded me of Mayerbek Vachagayev, the Chechen academic I had met months before in London, who had sat in an Earl's Court coffee bar telling me the story of Budyonnovsk that he had heard while taking a *Le Monde* correspondent to Chechnya. I turned round. It *was* Mayerbek Vachagayev, now back in his own world. My jaw dropped, and I would have rushed to greet him, but he raised a warning eyebrow and finished his discussion. Then we both slipped quietly outside.

In the dusty yard, where yet another APC was parking to protect the government compound, Mayerbek said he was in Grozny 'incognito', on behalf of Maskhadov's men, keeping an eye on the election. He had spent yesterday – the first of three election days in Chechnya – on a tour of inspection of village ballot-boxes. He presented me with a typed list of ten districts in which no elections were being held at all. Many of them were in the separatist mountains. I thanked him, and tucked it away.

'There's no point waiting for that Zavgayev accreditation, is there?' I said.

Mayerbek raised his arms eloquently.

'It's the MOST unnecessary accreditation!' he said, and disappeared into the crowd.

On the edge of town, and on the roads to the villages, were

Russian military checkpoints. 'Checkpoint' – a friendly English word, suggesting guidance, a firm but kindly hand on your documents, a helpful finger pointing you forward. '*Blokpost*', its Russian equivalent, has more authoritarian connotations: a place to be searched, questioned and prevented from moving on; in Chechnya, by now, also a place to be arrested, imprisoned, and tortured. With your documents out, you curved around the chicane of concrete blocks they'd laid in the road to where the soldiers waited. 'Slooowly, now,' drivers hissed cautiously.

But the Russian soldiers on the roads now weren't the buttoned-up professionals they had been at the beginning of the war. They were scared boys in rags, hiding behind their guns in their dug-outs in enemy territory. They wore bright bandannas over torn T-shirts, and there were scraps of laundry waving on strings in the grass behind. They peered nervously into the car, found in me a traveller they needn't be scared of, and gathered shyly around with rough, gap-toothed smiles.

'Gotta fag, girl?' one wheedled. 'We've been here for over a week. I've run out.'

Then they were all clamouring: for newspapers, biscuits, or cash.

We gave them cigarettes from the carton in the back, and 10,000 roubles – a couple of dollars. They had the right to vote in Chechnya, so we asked them who they would choose. 'Zyuganov, of course,' they chorused. 'Who needs Yeltsin's wars?'

'I feel sorry for them,' Alkhan the driver said as we pulled away. 'Conscripts. Treated like dirt. They didn't want to come here any more than we want them. Poor little bastards.'

Alkhan was big and thick-set, with a gravelly voice and a twisted arm. He had seven children, and he joked that he now had eight because he was 'honorary father' to Igor, the skinny local Russian boy, a TV cameraman, whom he usually drove with. Alkhan had gone to join the fighters for three months from January; his home village, Gekhi, was Doka the commander's base; he still treasured his scrapbook full of snapshots of him with Maskhadov, him with Basayev, him hovering protectively behind Dudayev.

But none of that stopped him feeling sorry for the Russian

conscripts. 'Now, the other bastards I do hate,' he said, with his sideways grin. 'The mercenaries. The *kontraktniki*. The professionals, who sign up specially to come here. They deserve everything they get. But not these kids. I hope their mothers come and take them home where they belong.'

*

The election was a mockery. It was almost impossible to find voters. Village streets were deserted. Dogs lay around asleep in the fierce heat.

'What elections?' growled one old man at a roadside in sleepy Alkhan-Yurt. 'What polling station?' Then he unbent a bit: 'There aren't any real elections, but I think they've got ballot boxes hidden away somewhere underground. They'll stuff them with votes for Zavgayev, and hand them in. But they're not elections for real people.'

In another village, I was told by the watchman at the administrative building that the election had finished. We were only half-way through the threeday voting period. I asked to see ballot-boxes, lists of voters, or electoral officials. 'Oh, you can't do that,' he said. 'The officials have taken them away and gone out to lunch.'

Elsewhere, there were problems: skirmishes at ballot-boxes, drive-by shootings, explosions. Women in Chernorechiye held a demonstration demanding that Russian troops withdraw from Chechnya, then they invaded the polling station and stole the green ballot-box.

Elections were going on in parts of Grozny, though it was still hard to find active polling stations. There were no voters' registers. There were no crowds. In one quiet office, the hospitable middle-aged women guarding ballot papers offered me a vote. 'You're our guest!' they said innocently. I refused, but several visiting foreign journalists did vote.

The few Chechens and local Russians who cast a vote were by and large voting for a Communist president, in spite of Stalin's deportations. 'The deportations are history. They would never happen again in the modern world,' explained Elbrus Menkailov. He was forty, and had run a literary magazine till Dudayev had shut it down. Like almost everyone else in Grozny, he was now unemployed. 'But look what that swine Yeltsin is doing to the Chechen people now. We'd be crazy to want him back.'

Electoral officials were humping flying ballot boxes around the housing estates, catching pensioners in whom the Soviet electoral habit of casting a meaningless vote was ingrained. Groups of boys loitered around the voting grannies, sneering. One took the ballot papers offered to him, and borrowed my notebook to fill them in. 'Look,' he whispered, with a snicker. He hadn't ticked any candidates. He'd just written 'Dudayev Is Alive.' He folded the papers and popped them in the box and sauntered off, whistling. Umar, his grandfather, a sixty-five-year-old ex-plumber, was voting, but only for Zyuganov. 'Under Communism, at least we got paid and got our pensions and had a bit of peace. And now what? Nothing. All we have now is Boris Nikolayevich, who comes to us, cares for us – and kills us.' Laughing darkly, he walked away after his grandson.

The cameramen who wanted to film a crowd were reduced to shooting at Polling Station No. 12, the undamaged showcase building inside the government compound, where Zavgayev's government and plump Russian matrons from nearby queued up to cast their ballots. 'For Yeltsin!' 'For Yeltsin!' 'For Yeltsin!' they answered the journalists' questions as they trooped in and out. In good Soviet style, subsidized sweets and biscuits were on sale outside to reward the dutiful.

I felt sorry for Yakub Sabirov, at Zavgayev's central electoral commission, wringing his hands and bemoaning the lack of telephones, the bad roads and disinformation that the election had been cancelled, excuses for why he didn't have turnout figures for most of the districts. They were all voting, though, he added hastily. Well . . . except perhaps Vedeno . . .

There were no international observers. Even the OSCE wasn't around. Only two OSCE diplomats were working at their heavily guarded building in a residential street. A cagey Scandinavian, Lennart Kroon, said he had only been in Grozny for two weeks. He couldn't talk about Zavgayev's election. 'We do not have the task of monitoring this election,' he said politely. Afterwards, people from the OSCE said Zavgayev had warned Tim Guldimann, whom he had already declared *persona non grata*, to get out of town, saying: 'I cannot guarantee your safety if you stay in Grozny this weekend.' So Guldimann beat a tactful retreat to the separatist hills.

Early on the third day, Zavgayev swept into Polling Station No. 12. He voted. Outside, with a hot breeze ruffling his combover, he pronounced the elections a triumph for Yeltsin and himself. There were still hours to go before voting was officially over.

'Are you worried that the elections won't be considered valid because there are no observers?' I asked.

'But there *are* observers. Of course!' he squawked back. 'Dozens of international journalists! All of you are observers! And the OSCE are observers!'

'But the OSCE isn't observing, and there are only two of them in Grozny,' I said.

'Oh well, I don't know about that,' answered Zavgayev.

\*

By day, the scared Russian soldiers stayed locked up in their *kommendatura*s around Grozny, and you hardly saw them. But not after dark. Then they were filled with Dutch courage. There were crackles of gunfire somewhere every night. On election Saturday, mortars whistled over the centre, and tracers flooded the half-ruined home I was staying in with ghostly light. Automatic gunfire echoed through the streets till dawn. 'A normal Saturday night; normal drunken troop tricks,' old Bilkiss and her sick daughter Marina said calmly, and went to bed by tracer light.

Some of the bedraggled victims turned up the next morning at our house on Griboyedov Street, where a lot of journalists were staying, to tell their story. No one else would listen: Zavgayev's Chechen district police had refused to help. I went with them to their apartment block in Leninsky district, overlooking a Russian *kommendatura*. A balcony had been blown away, a big hole knocked into the room behind. Skinny Magomed Mutsurov, an unemployed building supervisor, had been asleep in that room with his three-year-old daughter Asya at nine o'clock when the Russians started shooting outwards from the *kommendatura*. They had both escaped to a neighbour's flat which, mercifully, faced away from the *kommendatura*, and spent the rest of the night in safety.

The people next door, in the little private houses of Kashavoi Street, weren't so lucky. Drunk Russian soldiers had prowled up and down their street for hours, demanding the residents bring them out sausage and vodka, taking potshots through windows, and mockingly yelling 'Allahu Akbar!' Then they retreated, and mortar bombs started raining down on the little courtyards. House No. 3 was burned out, and its two inhabitants, thirty-four-year-old Tamara Khumparova and her tall husband Usman, in hospital with shrapnel wounds.

Tamara had lost an eye. Usman was heavily bandaged, but could walk. He said he had woken up to a huge explosion right next to him. He could hear Tamara screaming in the darkness, but the shooting was so heavy that he couldn't crawl over to help her for hours.

'They say the war's over, but this is the kind of present Boris Nikolayevich sends us. It's anarchy, it's a mockery. From now on I'll be twenty times angrier with the Russians,' he said. He hadn't voted.

'We can't sleep. They're shooting and crackling away the whole time, and no one's doing anything to deal with it,' Khusein Khamidov told me. 'The Russians don't seem to realize that they're violating the Nazran agreement, or to care.' His missing persons committee was a couple of tiny rooms in the centre. It was crammed with videos and photographs of the hundreds of corpses he'd dug up in the Russians' mass graves, all neatly numbered so relatives could come and identify their dead. Khusein Khamidov had luminous eyes and immense charm, but he was indignant.

It wasn't just Zavgayev's election, which he dismissed as the 'purest falsification'. He said the Russians were making a mockery of every detail of the Nazran agreement. Under its terms, he and his Russian counterparts had exchanged lists of missing people – 1,322 Chechens, 1,119 Russians – but the Russians were dragging their heels about giving their prisoners back. 'They constantly cheat us, they try to bog us down in trivialities so they don't have to give us anything. They keep asking us for gestures of good faith, and we give and give and give, but they just spit on us and never reciprocate.'

His recital went on and on. 'The Nazran agreement said no one should be detained after the first of June without due process of law. But we're going to protest now because they've actually detained three thousand more people. We can't find those people. The Nazran agreement said the filtration camps should all be shut down, but many are still working.'

One of the latest victims, who had managed to get away, was in the room with us. He was a skinny boy with a bruised face and a bandage over his right eye. Ruslan Uzhakhov was seventeen, and trying to be brave, but he could only speak through tears. He had been arrested a week before – after the Nazran agreement came into force – for having no documents.

'Tell her why you didn't have any documents,' prompted Khusein Khamidov.

A gulp, and a flow of misery. 'Because they burned down my house and killed my parents. On 3 January, 1995. My brother and I have been living rough ever since. He had documents but mine were burned. So they took me to the prison camp on the Kapinsky Crossroads. At night, they beat me up. There were two other people in the cell with me. One had broken ribs sticking out. Then a bloke came along and kicked me out.'

Ruslan's brother had gone to Khusein Khamidov for help; he freed the child.

'Now we're getting documents for him, and keeping him at home so no one picks him up again,' Khusein Khamidov said. 'But it's no easy thing getting documents these days, because so many of the registration offices have been destroyed.'

The little office was packed with people in mourning. Khusein Khamidov's two sons had been picked out of a heap of mutilated bodies after the siege of Grozny ended. His lawyer assistant had lost her three brothers and had her flat looted. And then there were the relatives, picking over the photos of rotting flesh, looking for their missing children. A room full of ghosts, in a city full of ghosts and anger.

'Our children, even our toddlers, are full of hatred for the Russian soldier. Full of hatred,' Khusein Khamidov said meditatively. 'The old men were cowed years ago by the deportations to Kazakhstan; they were destroyed by the might of Russia. But young Chechens today are a strike force for tomorrow. They've lost all fear. You see tiny kids of five or six now, going up to the Russian checkpoints, and yelling 'Allahu Akbar!' right at the soldiers. There's the nine-year-old whose father, mother and aunt were killed, and his house burned down; he took an automatic and went down to the checkpoint and destroyed it, killing five soldiers. The generation that's grown up in this horror will never forgive the Russian aggressor for their murdered relatives, their destroyed hearths and villages. Never.

'And when the question comes up – how many fighters does Shamil Basayev have? – the answer is: as many as he needs. If he needs ten, he'll get them; if he needs a hundred, they'll come, because people are just sitting and waiting to be called to him. The Chechen people won't give up their fight for freedom.'

*

Discovering my own new freedom, I went on my last day in Chechnya to find the separatist leaders. Commuting round the villages after commanders was a novelty for me; when I'd been here at the beginning of the war, they'd still been based in the heart of Grozny. While I was in England, I'd missed the months when fighters took journalists, in cars with no headlights, across bumpy fields, through villages, to the safe houses where Dudayev was living; all that was just stories to me. But Mayerbek Vachagayev said it was simple. All you had to do was go out of town, find a separatist checkpoint by the road, and get the boys to ask on their short-wave radio where you had to go; the fighters were everywhere. The nearest ones were at Stariye Atagi or at Gekhi. I set off to see.

Sure enough, not far south of Grozny, I found a tent at the side of the road with a green Chechen flag fluttering above it. There were half a dozen fighters lounging around in the sun. 'You don't need to go any further,' one of them said, and sent me into the village of Stariye Atagi right behind his tent.

It was a peaceful place. Gleaming silver roofs, well-kept houses, and silver drainpipes that ended in elegantly fashioned crocodile heads. Girls swayed arm-in-arm down the neat roads. Young men gave directions. It wasn't long before I found Ruslan Chimayev, the separatists' foreign minister, relaxing in tracksuit pants in the dewy rose garden outside his home. Big and bearded, with a calm demeanour, he gave me tea and settled down to talk.

If this truce was a cynical election-time trick, if Zavgayev's election had been held and the Russian side was ignoring half its promises already, why hadn't the Chechens fought back as they had threatened to?

Ruslan Chimayev shook his head. The separatist leaders' State Defence Committee had had a pow-wow on Saturday, and decided it would be more sensible to take the moral high ground than to disrupt the Zavgayev election, he said.

'We analysed the situation and realized the Russians probably wanted us to start fighting again to give them a pretext to send in more troops as what they would call "peacemakers' to separate "the warring sides" – us and Zavgayev. We also realized there was no point in disrupting the voting when the elections were so obviously rigged that people wouldn't bother with them anyway.

'So we decided to keep to all the positions in the agreement, and try to get the Russians to keep their word too. It's our bitter experience – each of us has personal bitter experiences, and there's the experience of our ancestors too, because Russian and Chechen relations have lasted for centuries – that we shouldn't expect the best from Russia. Russia never keeps its obligations. Today it's expedient for them to have an agreement. But as soon as it becomes expedient to break it, they'll break it. We are an inexperienced nation in these paper matters, so we say: "All right, we'll keep our word"; and we do, and we always lose out.

'We have no interest in the endless war they're waging against us,' he said over tea. 'We're a tiny country, and we've already lost a tenth of our people, but Russia is huge and hasn't lost a tenth of a per cent of its people. Why would I want a war, when you think I could be here cultivating my garden?'

More signs the Nazran agreement wouldn't survive the Russian election: Russian commanders wouldn't agree to start the promised disarmament talks – except inside their own military base at Khankala airport in Grozny. More delays. More disillusionment.

'We think that the Russians will only keep up these talks for long enough to put fresh troops in Chechnya, and then they'll come back to kill us again,' Chimayev said. 'Even now, last night, all night, we heard the aviation bombing the mountain villages. But, for the moment, they're keeping their word – more or less. So we'll keep ours.'

Somewhere far away, closer to the hazy mountains, there was the echo of shelling.

*

After the first round of the Russian presidential election, Yeltsin and Zyuganov were level-pegging with about 30 per cent of support each nationwide. A run-off second round was announced for 3 July. Strangely, the official results from Chechnya showed Yeltsin did a lot better there than elsewhere in Russia. He scored 64.11 per cent, while Zyuganov only got 16.1 per cent.

In Moscow, Yeltsin energetically reshuffled his Kremlin kitchen cabinet to make the Russian leadership look more liberal and more visibly anti-Communist before the second round of voting. There was a flurry of coup warnings and hysteria, sweaty press conferences and slanderous newspaper smears. Out went Alexander Korzhakov, Mikhail Barsukov, Oleg Soskovets, Oleg Lobov and Pavel Grachev – almost all the leaders of the 'Party of War'. In came Anatoly Chubais, liberal reformer, top economist, and now Yeltsin's chief of staff – an opponent of the Chechen war. In with him came Vladimir Potanin, head of Uneximbank and now deputy prime minister, one of the 'Big Seven' of new millionaires who had backed Yeltsin's campaign. The other millionaires had picked him to take public office on their behalf because, unlike most of the rest of them, he was a pure-blooded ethnic Russian and his appointment would not arouse any anti-Semitic opposition from the voters.

And in came Alexander Lebed, the charismatic Russian general who had been publicly against the stupidity of sending Russian boys to die in Chechnya in the first place. He had run for president in the first round on a law-and-order ticket, and won 11 per cent of the vote. He made no secret of his intention of becoming president by the year 2000. Yeltsin appointed the troublesome, loud-mouthed military man to the dizzy heights of political power, making him secretary of the Security Council. The millionaire Boris Berezovsky said his 'Big Seven' coterie had persuaded Yeltsin to make the appointment, and he had personally conducted many of the negotiations. No one knew whether the president was making Lebed his heir apparent, or just setting him up for a fall later. But it was an electoral master-stroke: a few Lebed voters were disgusted that their incorruptible hero had joined the murky Yeltsin camp, but many more gave their support to Yeltsin in the second round.

With most of the 'Party of War' gone, and Lebed in power, the reshuffles reassured most Russian voters that the truce already begun in Chechnya would become permanent. Their soldiers would soon come home, they believed. They were encouraged in that belief by three promises from the top.

Lebed, also appointed to Russia's State Commission on Chechnya – a body filled with 'Warriors' but supposed to be making peace – immediately spoke in favour of peace. 'It's crazy to let an enclave exist in your own land whose population hates its own so-called country from the bottom of its heart, despises its own laws, and pays no taxes,' he said.

Tikhomirov announced on 24 June that the 245th mechanized infantry regiment, one of the main units in Chechnya, would begin to withdraw in a few days.

Yeltsin signed a decree on 25 June ordering the withdrawal to begin.

When Russians voted again, on 3 July, they chose Yeltsin. The official results gave him 53.82 per cent of the ballots, and his inauguration was set for 9 August.

# TEN

# The Last Punishment

The official Russian election results came out on 9 July. The two days before that were an anxious time for Chechnya. The Russian military was only beginning to dismantle four of the thirty-two checkpoints it had promised would be gone by 7 July. Prisoner swaps had stalled. On 7 July, Tikhomirov issued 'Mr Bandit Yandarbiyev' with an ultimatum to let all Russian prisoners out within twenty-four hours, or be bombed. He also called Yeltsin's re-election a mandate to block Chechnya's political aim of seceding.

On 9 July, Tikhomirov ordered new Russian artillery and plane attacks on two Chechen villages, saying he was taking 'the most resolute action against armed banditry'. The 'pinpoint strike' on Meskhety was to flush out the Chechen separatists' leader Yandarbiyev, who had set up a new headquarters there; the 'pinpoint strike' on Gekhi was to flush out rebels, he said. Vakha Eldarkhanov, the mayor of Gekhi, had a different story: he said thirty-five of the forty-three people killed in the first hours of shelling were civilians. It was the start of a major new Russian offensive, which quickly spread all over Chechnya. Mountain villages were blockaded and bombed. Within a week, Russia's military announced it had killed 470 rebels.

The Chechens saw that the Russian peace overtures had been just a trick, after all. So did one Russian. 'You resumed the war in Chechnya right after the official election results were announced. It was promising to end the war that ensured your victory at the polls. I knew your promises were a lie . . . but the country believed you,' Sergei Kovalyov wrote in an angry open letter to Yeltsin. But most people in Russia had long ago written Kovalyov off as a crazy dissident with a bee in his bonnet about Chechnya. Why make a fuss? They knew politicians were all liars. But Chechens were all bandits, too. And it was sultry dacha season. Plums and cherries were on sale in a Moscow heat wave.

*

Why start the war again now? Yeltsin's long-ago debt to the 'Party of War' for their help beating parliament in 1993 was paid; he had nearly lost the election by continuing to protect its leaders. The alternative vision of a forward-looking liberal democracy had just been endorsed at the polls, and he had put liberals back running Russia. It made no sense, except that the strict hierarchy of Soviet deference had now been fully restored, and every cautious member of the political élite was looking for cues from the person above.

And the person at the top, Yeltsin, vanished right after the election. Later, it emerged he had collapsed with serious heart trouble. At the time, his aides insisted, Soviet-style, he was in perfect health – just absent. So the war started again almost by accident, in a chain reaction of conditioned responses.

*

In Yeltsin's absence, Moscow's many analysts and pundits saw three separate centres of power emerging: Chernomyrdin, running the government; the liberal Chubais, running the president's administration; and Lebed. No one knew which of them would come out on top.

Lebed, still trailing clouds of glory after the election and supremely confident he was now president-in-waiting, ran the powerful Security Council. The way he described his new job, it included almost every aspect of governance. He was going to reform the army, sort out the economy, and stop corruption. 'I have no fears, only a feeling of reality,' he said grandly. The doubters thought this naive and touchy outsider was going to be eaten alive by the subtle, envious courtiers of the Kremlin. A brash military type with a strong sense of his own honour and few diplomatic skills was also going to find it hard to swallow the humiliations that were the daily lot of Kremlin courtiers. Yeltsin 'will never accept treating another person as an equal. Whether

Lebed can stand it or not, I don't know,' speculated Zyuganov's ideological strategist, Alexei Podberyozkin.

Whatever their doubts, for the moment Lebed was the Kremlin's rising star.

Famous for his old anti-war outbursts, Lebed was much too busy at the moment trying to understand the complexities of Kremlin politics to have time to think about Chechnya. His election-time statements on the war had been contradictory: first he had been completely against it; then he wanted to either win or withdraw; later he wanted a referendum. But it was tacitly accepted now that Chechnya was his political baby.

So it was to Lebed that the surviving members of the 'Party of War' looked for a ruling on how to behave in Chechnya. Most of the 'Warriors' had been sacked from their most visible Moscow jobs, but many still had influence over Chechnya. Lobov had lost control of the Security Council in Moscow, but he was still Yeltsin's envoy to Chechnya: Stepashin was no longer head of the Counter-Intelligence service in Russia, but he was still secretary of the State Commission on Chechnya, which was still packed with warriors. The two generals leading the war effort had kept their jobs: Interior Minister Anatoly Kulikov, who labelled the Chechen separatists 'medieval savages' who could not be trusted, and Tikhomirov. Tikhomirov was Lebed's former army colleague, his chief of staff at the 14th Army base in Moldova. Lebed had no reason to distrust the hawkish Chechnya commander's advice.

Before issuing his post-election ultimatum to the Chechens, Tikhomirov consulted Lebed in the Kremlin on 5 July. He got the go-ahead to renew the campaign. A few days later, Lebed took a public line on Chechnya which was as hawkish and militaristic as Tikhomirov's: Chechnya was part of Russia, he said, and it was foolish to talk of its independence. The fighting was starting again 'because there has not been a day that bandits have not shot at and killed Russian forces there'. As far as Tikhomirov was concerned, if the voice on high was saying this kind of thing, it meant the softly-softly election approach could safely be dropped. It was business as usual in the Kremlin, and punishment as usual for disobedient Chechnya.

The post-Soviet hierarchy was now so entrenched that, once the cue had been given, everyone in the 'party of power' remembered their lines. Chubais, who had been out of power for much of the war, had no lines and kept quiet; so did his millionaire backers. Tikhomirov and Chernomyrdin played 'good cop, bad cop'. While Tikhomirov raged against bandits, Chernomyrdin brought out the soft soap to reassure Russians: 'Someone has been acting more and more impudently, I mean some of the fighters and their leaders. But everything there is under control now. We will sort it out, and there will be no war.'

In Moscow, there were two new mysterious crimes: small bombs exploded in trolleybuses, injuring a total of thirty people. No one claimed responsibility, but Muscovites assumed Chechen guilt. Russian fear of Chechens was winched up another notch. No one listened when a Chechen separatist spokesman said the bombings were the work of Russian counter-intelligence 'to justify the federal forces' actions in Chechnya, and convince Russian and world opinion of the need to use force against us'.

Yeltsin's veteran courtiers tied their tongues in knots making public statements that would please everyone, but offend no one later if the Kremlin's stated policy changed. Presidential aide Georgy Satarov said the Kremlin's tactic of bombing and shelling Chechen villages was 'not annihilation so much as coercion to peace'.

Late as ever, the Duma voted almost unanimously, two weeks after the new campaign began, to stop military action at once. But the Duma had no power. As ever, it was ignored.

*

The war took a turn for the surreal when, on 18 July, rebel leader Salman Raduyev, the 'Lone Wolf' leader of the ill-fated Pervomais-koye siege, returned from the dead. Since Russia announced his death in March, Raduyev had been recovering in Turkey from the ambush that hadn't killed him. He had got a new plastic-surgery face. He wore big sunglasses to hide his hacked-about eye and the sewn-up hole where the other one had been. He also sported a jaunty Che Guevara beret and a trim new beard. He grinned all the time, and uttered wild threats.

Touching the raw nerve of Russia's almost supernatural historical fear of Chechens, Raduyev said he was not the only hated rebel on the way back to haunt Russia. He swore on the Quran that Dudayev, his relative by marriage, was also alive and would also return.

'I will not swear on the Quran but I can tell you with 100 per cent certainty that Dzhokhar Dudayev is not alive,' Sergei Stepashin said. Raduyev was just boasting, because his standing among the separatist commanders was low; the Chechen's other claim, that he had been responsible for the Moscow trolleybus bombings was also no more than 'self-aggrandizement, and an attempt to catch the limelight'.

But Raduyev's dramatic reappearance, with its echo of Imam Shamil's improbable returns from the dead, caught the imagination of the Russian media. TV talk-show presenters had a field day speculating about whether the returned Raduyev was really the same man as the old Raduyev. Might he be a double? Might he be a Russian intelligence agent? Finally, interior ministry officials did a comparative study of old and new photographs for Kulikov and concluded – from the growth line of his beard and the alignment of his teeth – that the new Raduyev was genuine. The questions went on. Could Dudayev also be alive? His burial place was still secret – if he had been buried. No one knew; Izvestia reported from Chechnya that people who had never believed the reports of Dudayev's death were now arguing about the date of his return. Moscow officials were rattled, while Russians shivered enjoyably over the high-publicity tall tales and *vranyo*, so much more interesting than the news reports about more bandits in places whose names they couldn't pronounce.

Down south, the fighting worsened. Even Zavgayev's puppet government complained about a Russian atrocity in Grozny, where there were no official hostilities. Soldiers in two Russian APCs went on the rampage in broad daylight. Watched by dozens of bystanders, they shot at three passing cars, stabbed the survivors to death, soaked the corpses in petrol and set them on fire.

Zavgayev's Deputy Prime Minister Abdullah Bugayev demanded exemplary punishment for the perpetrators. The Russian military command in Chechnya confirmed its men were responsible for the killings, but said the victims were separatist rebels who had attacked a *kommendatura*.

The tireless Tim Guldimann at the OSCE in Grozny was unusually pessimistic. The sides had lost trust in each other, he said: 'I wouldn't say it's the end of all hope, but it will be very difficult to re-establish even the imperfect cease-fire we had before the election.'

Peaceful Stariye Atagi was hit by Russian missiles. One of the damaged houses belonged to Yandarbiyev's brother Suleiman. 'This is state terrorism,' Suleiman said. 'When a trolleybus gets blown up in Moscow, it's a tragedy for Russia. But when they bomb villages and kill civilians in Chechnya, it's just the fight against terrorism. They treat us like animals.'

# The Last Retaliation

They had been punished enough and cheated enough. Three days before Yeltsin was due to be inaugurated, when world attention would be focused on Russia, the Chechen separatist fighters retaliated – and more spectacularly than ever before. At dawn on 6 August, they stormed back into Grozny.

On television, I watched Russian tanks and APCs scuttle out of the city's scorched ruins as the gaunt fighters seized administrative buildings in most of the districts. Squat Russian attack helicopters circled above the railway station, market and central food warehouses, firing missiles into the city. The television said the rebels were closing in on the government compound, where at least a dozen journalists were trapped, talking to Moscow by satellite phone. The rebels were shelling the road to the Russian military airport.

If they could, ordinary people ran away. The television showed barefoot parents and children, clutching bags of food, sandals and bottles of water, stumbling away from the deafening noise of war in the city. 'Bombs, rockets, helicopters, death,' panted one ragged father. 'I have to save the kids.'

Movladi Udugov, the Chechen spokesman, appeared on NTV to drive the separatists' point home to Russians. Ironically reversing the cops-and-robbers terminology that the Russian 'Party of War' had often used to explain its own operations in Chechnya, Udugov described the separatist assault as a police-style 'special operation' to neutralize the Russian 'illegal armed bands' roaming his homeland. 'This is a natural response to the large-scale military actions that Russia resumed unilaterally right after the election,' he said, deadpan.

I had lunch the next day with two friends from Grozny. Bashir and Oleg were in Moscow to buy goods for the little retail business they had started setting up in the spring, selling clothes, with their supplies kept right by the central market. Polite, stressed boys, with earnest faces, they were worried about the fighters' latest raid. They were worried about their wives and Oleg's baby, back in Grozny; they were worried about their stock, which was hard enough to get intact into Chechnya by train anyway these days, being destroyed; they were worried generally about the idea of more bloodshed.

But they weren't too distressed. They thought the fighters would stay for three days, as they had in March, then vanish after spoiling Yeltsin's inauguration and robbing the banks.

'Everyone knew the next dollop of reconstruction money from Moscow was coming into the banks in Grozny about now,' Bashir said, looking quizzically at me through his magnifying spectacles. 'The fighters will rob the banks, then get out of town. That's what they did in March. This is a commercial war, and everyone's out for money.'

Bashir was wrong. The fighters stayed on. Every night, Russian television channels pumped out more pictures of Russian helicopters shooting into the city. Every night, the official statements about the city quietening down and 'clean-up operations' beginning were

denied from Grozny by the dozen-odd Russian reporters trapped
in the little government compound's hotel basement, surrounded
by death, telephoning breathlessly from the damaged roof, their
voices bravely calm. This audible Russian presence in the heart of
darkness gave the conflict shape and focus for Russian viewers.
The public was horrified.

The government building burned down under shelling.
Hundreds of civilians took refuge at the Red Cross near the market.
Hospitals ran out of supplies, or were evacuated. The attack by
4,000 fighters was led by Shamil Basayev, whose very name
terrified Russians.

Stiff-backed and mumbling, Yeltsin came out of the seclusion of
his sanatorium at Barvikha to be inaugurated. He was obviously
ill. The initial plan for a grand coronation-style cocktail of democratic and Tsarist ritual – bells, anthems, odes to the leader and a
ceremony on the Kremlin square where the Tsars had always been
crowned – had been cancelled. So had the plan for Yeltsin to give
a speech to his nation. All the president could manage was to blur
his way through a forty-five-second vow to serve his country,
before vanishing again for a long holiday. But there was nothing
wrong with his health, officials insisted desperately. The inauguration ended on an imploring note, with Ivan Glinka's operatic
theme, 'Life for the Tsar'.

Who was running Russia? Nobody knew, even if, that night,
Yeltsin's office issued a harsh statement on Chechnya which it said
the president himself had made: 'Terrorist raids will be decisively
put down. I will not allow anyone to talk to the federal authorities
in the language of blackmail.'

The Russian high command admitted to the Russian public, via
Interfax, that the situation in Grozny was 'totally out of control'.
The Russian commander in Chechnya, Vyacheslav Tikhomirov,
had gone on holiday before the Chechens stormed Grozny. He had
stayed tactfully away ever since, leaving control of the armed forces
in the hands of Lieutenant-General Konstantin Pulikovsky, a man
with a shaven head and angry eyebrows who had lost a son in the
war. He had reason to hate the Chechens. But he couldn't beat
them.

Seven thousand troops in Grozny were encircled by separatists. The column of interior ministry APCS that was reported, day after day, rolling into the burning government compound on a rescue mission to save the Russian journalists was nowhere to be seen.

'We get the impression we have been forgotten,' Vladimir Trushkovsky, of Radio Russia, said in one of a series of increasingly desperate calls broadcast on television, his voice punctuated by the crash of shell fire.

It was a psychological victory for the Chechens, and a disaster for Russian pride.

# ACT FIVE

# ENDING THE WAR

# ONE

Yeltsin was ill, but he was still a consummate politician. He knew that what Russians feared above all else was a power vacuum, a visible empty space at the top of the hierarchy. It hadn't yet been publicly announced, but Yeltsin was going to have heart bypass surgery. He would be away for some time. He needed to keep his people calm and loyal in his absence.

The remaining members of the 'Party of War' were not helping. They had failed to stop the Chechens spoiling his already truncated inauguration. The strongmen's powerlessness was reinforcing Russian fears that no one was running the Kremlin.

The next morning, the president sacked the veteran 'Warrior' Oleg Lobov as his envoy to Chechnya. Instead, he appointed Lebed, the good soldier who had ended war in Moldova; Lebed, the irritatingly self-assured would-be president; Lebed, the man of action; Lebed, who said he had all the answers; Lebed, now confused and directionless in his first month in the Kremlin.

It was a clever presidential repair job to the crumbling Kremlin façade. In the short term, while Yeltsin was out of action, Russians would be reassured by seeing Lebed's hand on the helm. Lebed had the rare reputation of incorruptibility, so there would be no more cynical talk about the Russian élite deliberately keeping the war going and making soldiers suffer for their own profit – dirty oil deals, dirty arms deals, dirty extortion deals. And Lebed's few words on Chechnya since taking the security job had shown he was ready to be tough.

It was just possible that Lebed might manage to find an acceptable solution to a conflict so intractable that no other Russian politician had come close – in which case he would get all the domestic blame that would follow for giving into separatism, while Yeltsin would reap the rewards of better relations with Russia's Western allies. But it was more likely that Lebed would eventually come a cropper over Chechnya, like everyone else. Then the cocky general would also lose his popularity with the people. When Yeltsin got better, it would be easy to get rid of Lebed altogether.

But Lebed liked risk. He was delighted at the chance to get out of the alien Kremlin world of innuendo and intrigue and prove himself on the battleground, where he belonged. He took the Chechnya job and, like a good soldier, he wanted to see the terrain being fought over. So he did something no other Russian politician had done – he went to Chechnya to beard the bogeyman separatists in their lair.

It was an astonishing journey, kept top secret until he was already in enemy territory. Lebed flew to Dagestan. He drove over the border. Like any journalist or refugee, he took his chances with the Russian checkpoints, helicopters and guns on the road. He went to Noviye Atagi and talked to Maskhadov. Unlike the nervous Russian generals during their occasional negotiations, he didn't sit in a dug-out in a neutral field, protected by comforting Russian tanks, troops and helicopters. He went right into the village; he stayed the night in the huge silver-roofed house of Rizvan Lorsanov, a portly local businessman who had early on in the war negotiated a local truce with the nearest Russian base; he ate, he drank, and he played chess with villagers between negotiations.

Lebed broke through the cloak of darkness surrounding the Chechens. On that trip, he made the same discovery as all the Russian and foreign journalists who had confronted their fear of the Chechens' terrifying reputation in Russia and gone to see for themselves. The fighters were not evil bandits, but ordinary ex-Soviet people who would respond to reasonable treatment; the Chechens' ever-strengthening aspirations for freedom were a natural response to the police-state punishment being meted out by the Russian military; the depressed and demoralized Russian soldiers on the ground had not lost, but could not win. If the Chechens were not the External Enemy, the whole basis of Moscow's war was false.

Lebed and Maskhadov made plans for a cease-fire.

*

Shock waves in Moscow: slab-faced, Soviet-looking Lebed, onstage at a press conference, telling Russia that the war waged by the Kremlin he represented was a fallacy. For the first time, Russians heard the truth from a high-up official they trusted, a straight army man now standing before them saying he was 'fed up with war' and it was time for peace.

Russian soldiers were helpless: 'puny creatures at checkpoints – hungry, lice-ridden and naked'. Russia was 'a pauper country with a doddering economy', which could 'not afford the luxury of fighting a war'.

Zavgayev was a puppet, 'stranded in the airport, and it's only that airport that is under his control. He doesn't control the situation, does he?'

The Chechens were 'wolves', people 'absolutely confident that they are fighting for their freedom, people who have lost their relatives; in short, people who have very good reason to fight very seriously'.

'Should hundreds of thousands of lives be sacrificed to achieve this Pyrrhic victory?' boomed Lebed. 'All wars, even if they are hundred-year wars, end in negotiations. So why fight a hundred years? Perhaps we should start with a negotiated settlement.'

They were words of peace, but Lebed was declaring war on the 'Party of War'. To the sedate administrative élite, the 'party of power', Lebed's words also sounded like an attack on the whole Kremlin establishment. The outsider in their midst was making them look foolish. His frankness was a threat to the revived élite's revived habit of stage-managing the truth, showing the ignorant public only what was good for it, while real policy was worked out quietly behind the scenes. Chubais and the millionaires remained silent; Chernomyrdin and other neutrals fumed, and bided their time.

The 'Party of War' regrouped for battle. Once again, a Russian political war broke out over Chechnya. Its verbal thrusts and parries in Moscow were matched again, with real blood and real guns, in Grozny.

I was in Chechnya by this time, on the edge of northern Grozny, where the muffled boom of shelling still echoed out of the centre, and sniper fire cracked from buildings nearby. The fighters, jaunty in green velvet headgear, said they controlled most of the city. But there was heavy shelling, and the Russian planes were out. The refugees who had escaped this far didn't expect the new man in the Kremlin to beat the 'Party of War'. Experience had taught them that truth was no defence against the powerful of Moscow. Adam Khuzgov, one of an angry group gathered round me at a bus stop, said bleakly: 'Lebed may have learned to live with the wolves of Chechnya, but the wolves of the Kremlin will rip him apart.'

*

Red-faced and angry, Pulikovsky flew to meet Maskhadov at the Russian checkpoint outside Noviye Atagi and grudgingly agreed that the cease-fire Lebed had ordered would start at midday the next day. The idea was to let the hundreds of thousands of Grozny civilians, who had been cowering in their basements for a week, get out and get away. The cease-fire time was announced on radios and televisions, but Pulikovsky still believed he could cheat on it. Maskhadov ordered the Chechen fighters to lay down their guns four hours earlier, from eight in the morning. But gruff Russian soldiers at checkpoints on the perimeter of Grozny on Wednesday morning said they had no orders to cease fire. Then they scrounged cigarettes off me, and hassled my Chechen driver. There were helicopters buzzing about overhead, and planes ahead. The roads out of Grozny were streaming with refugees, the usual sad procession of lorries and cars crammed with people, blankets, saucepans, and anxious children. White rags fluttered from aerials.

Midday came and went.

In brilliant sunshine, the two SU-25 planes wheeling over the road ahead bombed the refugees and flew away. The blazing remains of a white Kamaz pickup truck and a passenger car, reduced to ash and twisted metal, were scattered over the steep hillside on the southern edge of Grozny. No one was injured; the passengers all jumped clear in time. Children scrambled down shepherd trails towards the valley settlement of Gikalo to regroup, followed more slowly by adults. The refugee traffic jam on the road kept moving, although passengers craned their necks out of their cars to watch the Russian helicopters which were now circling threateningly overhead.

Lyalya Eldarova, a middle-aged woman who had heard about the cease-fire on her transistor and crept out of the cellar to make her dash for freedom, was breathless and on the verge of tears by the time she got down to Gekalo. 'How we ran, shouting that at twelve o'clock we would at last manage to squeeze out of town! And now a plane has gone and bombed a place where there were only ordinary people!' she panted.

Under the trees of Gekalo's town square, against the buzzing of the helicopters, a crowd gathered, full of sympathy and anger. 'They say there's a cease-fire, and then, exactly when the refugee rush hour's on, they bomb us,' Tamara Magomadova, a local official, said bitterly. The people leaving Grozny said the fighting was less intense than on previous days. But it was still going on. You could hear it everywhere.

Cease-fire? What cease-fire? Pulikovsky said later. He hadn't agreed to a cease-fire with Maskhadov. All he had agreed to was to meet Maskhadov again, and carry on talking. He had unilaterally ordered his men not to shoot first, but the Chechens had gone on attacking. What could you do against the trigger-happy savages?

*

But Yeltsin was still on Lebed's side. That night, the president dismantled the last Moscow power base of the 'Party of War' – the State Commission on Chechnya – and gave Lebed solo power to settle the war. Lebed flew back to Chechnya the next day, with enough extra authority to stop all foot-dragging by the Russian commander.

Lebed and Yandarbiyev agreed to end military confrontation.

Lebed gathered the Russian generals at Khankala, their military airport base on the edge of Grozny, for an hour of plain talking. He was having no more truck with the racism underpinning the war, he said. 'The first thing we have to do is stop killing people – and I don't care what ethnic group they're from.' He was also going to blow the whistle on the dodgy business dealings which the war masked, he told reporters as he left. The war was being dragged out for 'commercial reasons', he said, and he would name what he contemptuously called the 'heroes' the next day, in Moscow, at a press conference.

While Lebed lectured his compatriots, the battle died down in the city. The separatists were in control, the civilians free to escape. Euphoric men in green velvet headgear guided the traffic out from the centre through the twists and turns of Factory District, a huge maze of ruined oil installations, storage tanks, alleyways and waste dumps. Watchful and disciplined, they didn't want cigarettes, because they were still on battle alert; but they did want to celebrate. When more jeeploads of fighters swept into town, moving against the outward flow of refugees, they yelled 'Allahu Akbar!' and fists, guns and smiles flashed in answering salute.

A broken bridge in this no-man's-land had been haphazardly repaired with loose sheets of metal. The plates creaked and clanked as buses, trucks, pedestrians and jeeps clanked over them. The civilians were hungry, angry and scared. A lot of people grabbed me and yelled furious denunciations. Why hadn't the West done anything? Why did journalists come and come but never make things any better? Were we just here to make a profit out of their misery? Were we all agents of the FSB? I gently disengaged myself. There was another broken bridge, and more traffic jams, and more rage, at Chernorechiye.

The fighters were all over the middle of town, in Leninsky district, Oktyabrsky, and Chernorechiye. It was as though, by sheer willpower, they had turned time backwards to the very start of the war, wiping out all the defeats and punishments the Chechens had suffered since – except that then they had been losing, and now they were winning. I was travelling that day with my ex-colleagues from the job at Reuters that had brought me to Grozny at the start of the war; Alkhan the driver was humming cheerfully; it was hard to believe that nearly two years separated Grozny then from Grozny now.

Not that quiet had completely returned to the streets; as I stood in the wasteland that had recently been the central market, shelling still echoed from the east, where trapped Russian troops were shooting from inside their *kommendatura*, and sniper fire was rattling down a nearby avenue. But the fighters from Basayev's new headquarters on the edge of the market were purposefully ignoring the sounds. With a clanging and scraping that set your teeth on edge, some of them were nudging a damaged Russian tank from out of the debris. Others were moving cautiously about in the shelter of ruined buildings, clutching grenade-launchers, or trotting cautiously across the stinking heaps of garbage and stattered stalls. They were gathering up all the equipment abandoned by the Russians, commander Isa Astaminov said, in case of new attacks by the Russian military. 'I am just hoping, not particularly that Lebed and Yeltsin will do anything, but just that common sense will prevail,' he said tiredly.

Apart from fighters, the centre looked eerily empty of people. Only two tearful old Russian women looking for food were picking their way through the market. But many more frightened people were still in the city, hiding in their houses or cellars, peeping out from behind doors and windows. They slipped out to stare curiously at the occasional passing car, but dodged back behind their gates when the rattle of fighting got too near.

The Autarkhanovs' house was deserted. The OSCE house was locked. The Reuters house was deserted, though intact (Alkhan said smugly that he had done a deal with the fighters to guard it from looters). But at Griboyedov Street, the journalists' lodgings of the summer, we found Natasha, an elderly Russian woman, still wandering around alone in her corner of the shabby courtyard which had once housed six Chechen families. Tiny and tearful, she wept over the sleepless nights in the cellar – although she cheered up when she started describing the pickings of a day of genteel looting: boots, cans of fish and meat, and jars of cooking oil. The neighbours slid in and out with whispered snippets of information: 'Roza's been seriously injured,' or 'There's a sniper in the next street.' When shooting began a few streets away, everyone squatted down by a wall. But they went on talking.

Natasha was going to come away with us. She fluttered around in the courtyard, picking over her tins of goodies, wondering what to take. Alkhan and I waited outside, by the car. He was still humming: 'We're walking into Chechnya, we're walking into Chechnya.'

From round a corner, a group of thirty fighters appeared, guns out. The housewives melted back into their courtyards, with dread on their faces. The fighters stalked on, and vanished round another corner. There was a loud explosion somewhere very close. Alkhan and I squatted down behind the car. He looked up, pulled a comic face, and started singing: 'We're walking OUT of Chechnya, we're walking OUT of Chechnya.'

We left town, over the broken bridges, in the refugee traffic. We drove Natasha out of Chechnya, and put her on a bus to Stavropol, where she had relatives.

Shamil Basayev said he was personally against the truce, but he obeyed Maskhadov. The cease-fire went on holding in Grozny, more or less, while the victorious Lebed tackled the 'Warriors' back in Moscow.

*

Lebed had won his first battle against the 'Party of War' in Chechnya, but, flushed with triumph and forgetting his ignorance of Kremlin ways, he now grew overconfident as he tried to pursue his advantage in Russia. He turned savagely on the interior minister, Anatoly Kulikov, the last Moscow representative of the 'Party of War', accusing him of being an inept Napoleon bent on more death and destruction. Kulikov had known days before 6 August that the separatists were planning to seize Grozny back, he said, but had done nothing to stop the attack. Lebed demanded that Kulikov be fired. 'The interior minister did not fulfil his duty to Russia. I am completely certain he cannot remain interior minister any longer.'

This public outburst broke every rule of Kremlin etiquette. First, Lebed had no power to hire or fire ministers, which was the prerogative of the president and prime minister. Second, he was showing he had no caste loyalty to other members of the élite he had just joined, an offence against the 'party of power'. Third, he was trampling on Chernomyrdin's careful two-tier PR structure for discussing Chechnya. Chernomyrdin did not object to rough treat-ment of the Chechens, but he did demand consideration for Russian citizens' sensibilities in the shape of frequent reassurances to them that a united Russian leadership was protecting them from bandits. Lebed had already annoyed him by saying the Chechens weren't bandits. Now he was revealing to the public that the Russian leadership wasn't united, either.

On the same day, Yeltsin's office had admitted in public for the first time that the president was going to have intensive medical treatment. Leaders of the political élite were suddenly eyeing each other nervously as potential competitors for a presidency which might fall vacant in just a few weeks. Lebed's words were now a direct challenge not only to the 'Party of War' but to the whole neutral Kremlin establishment, a sign he was trying to set himself up above the rules of the 'party of power'. He was trying to snatch the next presidency from out of their grasp, they concluded.

'They think they have lassoed me and that I have to obey and play by their rules,' trumpeted Lebed. 'But I am not a clerk. Eleven million voters are behind me. They trust me. And it is their sons who are dying in this crazy war.'

It was unbearable that Lebed was boasting about his previous electoral experience. Neither the urbane Chernomyrdin – Yeltsin's caretaker number two under the constitution – nor the ginger-haired Chubais – running Yeltsin's administration and speaking for the president in his absence – had nearly as much voter appeal as the earthy, charismatic general. So they joined forces. To defeat the interloper in their midst, they took up the cause of the 'Party of War'. There was no response from the absentee Yeltsin to Lebed's demands, and Kulikov was not sacked.

Lebed only realized how big a mistake he had made when he saw the establishment unite, over the next two days, to blast him with demands made in the president's name. He must drop his independent line on Chechnya, show loyalty, and go along with Kremlin policy. For the purposes of humiliating Lebed, that now meant the policy of the 'Party of War'.

The policy that the ranking 'Warrior' on the ground came up with now was monstrous. On 19 August, the acting Russian commander in Chechnya, Konstantin Pulikovsky, ordered between 200,000 and 300,000 people still living in Grozny to leave their homes within forty-eight hours – before he carpet-bombed the whole city. Pulikovsky announced:

> The separatist leadership, true to its tactics, has decided to take hostage not just a group of people but the whole population of an entire city and thus dictate conditions to the federal command. So without issuing an ultimatum I appeal to the civilian population of Grozny to leave the city within 48 hours, starting from the morning of 20 August, along the corridor which will be specially opened by federal troops through Staraya Sunzha to Petropavlovskoye and Argun. I ask that only this route be used, as all other directions are blockaded by troops and mined. After the deadline expires, I exercise the right to use all forces and measures, including air bombardment and also reactive systems of heavy bombardment and artillery, to strike blows at guerrilla positions. If this happens, it will be the fault of the opposition leadership.

A kind of collective madness took over the Kremlin, in which the massacre of hundreds of thousands of people in Grozny could be justified by a political in-fight against Lebed in Moscow. It was still recognizably the earlier Kremlin logic – in which Russian lives were counted as more valuable than Chechen ones. But now it was stretched to a horrific degree, just as the institutionalized anti-Semitism of the 1930s later found absurd and monstrous expression in Hitler's Final Solution.

Despite protests, threats and pleas from good-hearted Russians who were not in the élite, Kremlin leaders fell in, one by one, with the policy Pulikovsky had set.

The real Russian commander in Chechnya, Vyacheslav Tikhomirov, hurried back at last from his extended holidays to take charge. The carpet-bombing order had been given by a subordinate, a temporary commander whose judgement could conceivably have been swayed by emotion over the death of his son at the war. Tikhomirov, not gripped by personal grief, could have countermanded the order. But he did not. It had been backed by the top of the hierarchy, so he backed it too, pledging to 'free Grozny from separatist militants'.

The new defence minister, Igor Rodionov, supposedly an ally of Lebed and Pulikovsky's ultimate boss, said Pulikovsky had been acting on his own initiative when he issued the ultimatum, and had been 'reprimanded'. But Rodionov did not cancel the order.

Boris Gromov, the anti-war general who led the Soviet army home from Afghanistan, said only Yeltsin had the power to stop the 'mindless and gruesome bloodshed'. But Yeltsin was nowhere to be seen. His office first said he was out of town inspecting a possible vacation site, and then said he would be back at work the next day. He did not appear. Instead, the president's office, run by Chubais, issued another presidential statement saying federal authorities would not knuckle under to gun-toting rebels. Lebed was under orders to fall in. He was issued with instructions from Yeltsin's office, run by Chubais, 'to restore order in Grozny as it was before 6 August' by the end of the month.

Lebed compounded his earlier offence of caste disloyalty with more blundering bluntness. He had not been consulted about this, he said. The instructions, above a facsimile signature, were hasty, contradictory, and did not look like Yeltsin's own work – a suggestion which only heightened public anxiety over how ill the president was. The president's office snapped back another statement: Yeltsin didn't have to consult before issuing instructions.

Pulikovsky was asked on television how civilians would get out of Grozny before the deadline. 'That,' he answered, 'is not my problem.'

Confusion reigned in the Chechen capital as crowds stumbled out of their cellars and ruined homes to risk an afternoon of shelling and Russian air strikes, in the hope of saving themselves from the threat of even more deadly bombing the next day. Many of the terrified people left behind in Grozny were old or ill. Broken bridges, sniping and artillery attacks slowed down their escape. The corridor Pulikovsky said he had opened through the north of Grozny was a narrow road. It quickly jammed up with the bullet-riddled, pitiful cars of the latest exodus. From time to time, Russian forces shelled it.

From Chechnya, Maskhadov begged Lebed to use his influence to 'stop the coming madness'. But what did Lebed's influence count for now, against the combined might of the Kremlin and the armed forces?

*

Against all the odds, Lebed did avert the blitz hours before it was supposed to begin. He flew to Chechnya. He talked to the Russian generals at Khankala, and persuaded them to drop their assault plan; he went to Noviye Atagi to meet Maskhadov. 'We will no longer speak the language of ultimatums,' he said as he arrived. 'We will resolve this problem by the morning . . . We will be guided by humaneness and reason.'

Maskhadov agreed to a new cease-fire. Sanity prevailed. The truce took hold. Although the Russian generals in Chechnya were still prone to delay, the fight went out of them and they started obeying Lebed's orders. A breathtakingly fast Russian troop withdrawal began. As the cease-fire went into effect, Maskhadov and Tikhomirov agreed that joint patrols – 270 Russian soldiers and 270 Chechen fighters – would patrol Grozny for the next five days to prevent looting. After that, 11,000 Russian troops would pull out from the Chechen capital Grozny by the end of August. The rest would be gone from Chechnya by the end of the year. Zavgayev took up residence in Moscow. The 'Party of War' withdrew from the battlefield.

Lebed was allowed to complete the peace initiative by negotiating a political agreement with the Chechens, though with none of the praise or recognition from Moscow he might have expected for his unexpected success. He flew home from Chechnya, expecting praise and a briefing with the president, but Yeltsin, who had made his only television appearance in weeks as Lebed set off for Chechnya – to make the point that he was 'not quite satisfied' with his envoy's work on Chechnya – now had no time to see Lebed. NTV reported dismissively that Lebed would be required to make a written report of his whirlwind peace process before gaining access to the president. Just before midnight, when no attention would be attracted to his politically ambitious envoy, Yeltsin's office issued a terse statement saying the president had telephoned Lebed, 'listened to his report, and in general approved of his first steps towards a peaceful resolution of the Chechen conflict'. He authorized Lebed to hold more talks with the Chechen leaders and sign a political agreement with them that would keep Chechnya inside the Russian Federation.

Lebed returned to Chechnya and worked out a political draft with Maskhadov by the end of the weekend. Both men agreed to consult their presidents before rushing into a final agreement. Lebed shuttled back to Moscow again, urging the Chechens to be 'sensible and patient'. In a characteristic piece of earthy humour that, as usual, went down badly with the Kremlin, he added: 'A proverb goes that a war is unleashed by one fool and cannot be stopped by dozens of wise men.'

A genuine warmth and respect had grown up between Lebed and Maskhadov. The Chechen commander worried now that Lebed's many enemies in Moscow would kill the Russian nego-tiator, as Chechens believe the FSK seriously injured a peace-minded negotiator, Lieutenant-General Anatoly Romanov, a year earlier. 'This time, there is the certainty that negotiations will be successful – if Lebed can stop the forces that are in favour of war. But if anything happens to Lebed, there will be more fighting in Chechnya. What I fear most is that Lebed will suffer the same fate as General Romanov,' he said.

Lebed survived. That Friday, he and Maskhadov talked until after midnight in the border town of Khasavyurt, then signed their political deal. It was the simplest of agreements: it put off a final decision on Chechnya's future relationship with Russia for the next five years. With breathtaking simplicity, the reason for twenty months of fighting was withdrawn from the agenda until 'with cool heads, calmly and soberly, we can sort out our relations'.

'That's it. We've had enough of fighting,' a triumphant Lebed told the cheering crowd waiting in the night outside. 'The war is over.'

*

Luiza Autarkhanova and her children escaped from the second siege of Grozny. Her Moscow sister-in-law Aminat, an anxious voice down the phone, called as soon as I got back from Chechnya to find out if I knew where the family was. I didn't. But they turned up in Moscow a few days later, with hacking coughs from the cellar, screaming nightmares about the planes, and one sister still missing in the urban wastelands of the Chechen capital. They counted themselves lucky to be alive.

Aminat's tiny two-room flat, where Luiza, four children, and her mother were now crammed in with Aminat and her husband, was full of rolled-up bedding and the edgy laughter of relief. Hoarse-voiced and plucking nervously at a borrowed dress made of cheap flowered fabric, Luiza blamed herself for getting caught in the latest onslaught. 'My mother told me two days running about rumours the fighters were coming back, and said we should be very careful or perhaps leave town altogether. But I thought they'd just whisk in and out, like they did in March. I never imagined that the city would be subjected to complete destruction a second time.'

At first, Luiza and the children – thirteen-year-old Magomed, nine-year-old Liza, seven-year-old Saida and two-year-old Umar – weren't too worried. The sounds of shelling and shooting were far away. It was only on the second or third day, when the helicopters began flying overhead and a house nearby was destroyed, that they crept down into the relative safety of their cellar. 'It was fun in the cellar at first,' Luiza said. 'The neighbours all came down too – you remember Musa's alcohol collection! We had the best cellar for miles around. We played games. We had food – flour, sugar, bread – and we dragged down boards and mattresses to make a bedroom for the children in the corner. We would even go up into the courtyard whenever the shooting stopped and cook in the open air. It only got really scary when we realized that, this time, it wasn't going to stop.'

Luiza's tiny, wizened and grimly cheery mother, Belila Anzorova, chuckled. 'And then the shells started going right over our heads, whistling, "whoo-OOO!" and you'd just sit in the cellar and bow your head – as if that would help if they blew your head off.'

It was impossible to escape for several days. The shelling was too heavy. The fighters were all around, and helicopters filled the skies. It was only when Lebed's cease-fire began to work that the neighbours agreed it was time to flee into the lull. Bringing only a change of clothes for the children, seven families packed themselves into nine cars and set off for safety.

The fighters they met on the way turned out to be both friend and foe. 'They showed us the way out through the back of Factory District,' Luiza said admiringly. 'I'd never even seen it before. And they were incredibly calm – they don't seem to know the meaning of fear. They warned us against stopping. They said the Russians would shell any crowd they saw.'

Luiza's mother fixed her with a beady gaze. 'And once we got out of town, the fighters took our cars, so we had no transport to get out of Chechnya with,' she reminded her daughter tartly. She had no time for either side in the battle. She just wanted to live in peace. 'If they want to fight, why don't they find some open ground and go off and fight to their hearts' content – only not near me? That's what I kept telling those Chechen fighter lads when they were hanging around the house. "Go ahead and fight each other if you want, one on one, but stop sneaking round shooting from behind other people's backs. We've had enough of you. We should get the police on you."'

The families walked west until they found lifts out to the airport at Sleptsovsk, and flew to the safety of Moscow.

Luiza and the children were now planning to move on again, to join Musa in another cramped flat in Vologda. She knew about the institutionalized racism of Russians towards 'Persons of Caucasian Nationality', especially Chechens. But she said that was infinitely preferable to the constant threat of annihilation hanging over Chechens who stayed in their homeland. 'Of course, it's better to live the way we used to, but now – since we have to – we'll get used to living this way,' she said philosophically. 'The problems will iron themselves out.'

One thing she was absolutely sure of. She was never going back to Grozny.

*

Six weeks after making peace, Lebed was sacked.

Yeltsin was pleased that a neat way had been found to end the war. With his plans for heart surgery now out in the open, he made an announcement taking the credit for making peace on himself. 'My aide, Alexander Lebed, fulfilled my instructions and stopped the military conflict. The most important thing is that he succeeded in stopping the bloodshed.'

But now it was open season on Lebed in the Kremlin.

The president heaped public humiliations on his uppity Security Council chief. 'What Lebed needs now is to get down to work, to carry out instructions, to work more reliably with the prime minister and other services, and to stop squabbling with everyone,' Yeltsin said, thick-voiced, finger raised threateningly, describing one row he had had with Lebed on prime-time television. 'That's not how things work in our state apparatus. You have to live in peace. That's what I told him to do.'

Chernomyrdin couldn't forgive Lebed for breaking the etiquette of the 'party of power' with his uncomfortable truth-telling. The prime minister made his disapproval plain with a separate series of complaints and public dressings-down. More dangerously, for more than a month, he neatly sidestepped Lebed's requests to endorse the Chechen peace process and join the talks with the separatists. Chernomyrdin still saw the fate of the Chechens as a tool which could be used to bludgeon Lebed with later, if the opportunity arose. It was only Yeltsin's public endorsement of peace in Chechnya that forced Chernomyrdin to go along with it too: within hours, the prime minister had obediently met the Chechen president Yandarbiyev in Moscow and signed a new statement on the next steps towards lasting peace.

Kulikov also fought Lebed, in the old-fashioned language of statist paranoia favoured by the 'Party of War'. He accused Lebed of being so impatient to seize power that he couldn't wait for the president to die but was plotting a 'creeping coup' at once. He said Lebed had secret plans to create a 50,000-strong 'Russian legion'. 'Strange questions' had been asked about the defensibility of the main television station in Moscow. And, of course, the separatists in Chechnya had been plotting with Lebed to back his alleged coup. Lebed laughed off the charges. 'The poor guy has let his tongue run away with him,' he said, and filed a slander suit against Kulikov demanding symbolic damages of one rouble.

But, the next afternoon, Yeltsin went on television again and announced he was stripping Lebed of public office. 'I cannot tolerate this situation any longer and am obliged to relieve General Lebed of his duties as secretary of the Security Council,' the puffy-faced, ponderous president said. He signed the decree firing Lebed on-camera.

Lebed himself publicized what he thought was the real reason for his sacking. At a dramatic evening press conference, he said the Kremlin was now being run, not by the enfeebled Yeltsin but by his shadowy 'regent', the liberal Chubais; Lebed had been in the way of Chubais's attempts to build up a powerful regency in Yeltsin's absence. Lebed also revealed that his peace agreement for Chechnya made him yet another powerful enemy in the Chubais camp – Boris Berezovsky, the millionaire. He said Berezovsky had ordered him to rip up the Khasavyurt peace agreement, because it was fouling up Berezovsky's private business interests in Chechnya. 'He tried to scare me,' Lebed said. 'When he found he could not scare me, he just said: "What a good business you have broken up! Everything went so well ... Well, a few people were killed, but people have always killed each other and will continue to do so."' Berezovsky flatly denied the charges. At the end of October, Berezovsky was vaulted into public office himself to fill the gap left by Lebed's departure: he became deputy head of the Security Council, with special responsibility for Chechnya.

The ugly settling of Moscow political scores was over. Russia's peacemaker had been removed. But, for the first time, the bosses of the defence and security agencies which had made up the 'Party of War' did not seize the chance of renewing hostilities in Chechnya.

The clan allegiances of the Kremlin had shifted, and the powerful new group – the politicized tycoons and liberals of the new 'Party of Capital' – was now firmly on top.

Their hold on power had Yeltsin's blessing and was tolerated by Chernomyrdin's administrators. The man appointed to replace Lebed at the top of the Security Council, a conciliatory ex-parliament speaker called Ivan Rybkin, was a colourless figure, but he went quietly on with smoothing over the conflict. Converted to the cause of Chechen peace by his own appointment to the Security Council, the more dynamic Berezovsky started shuttling around the Caucasus, trying enthusiastically to guarantee that oil from the Caspian would flow back to world markets through Russian pipelines via Novorossiisk – where his financial empire owned big oil interests.

The peace in Chechnya held.

*

Down on the street, many ordinary Russians were distressed by the vague peace agreement for Chechnya. They were horrified that a weak, helpless Russia had capitulated to the black bandits' armed blackmail. And they blamed Lebed.

'I voted for Lebed,' Vitya, my driver, said crossly. 'What a waste. He's a traitor to the motherland. He sold out our national interests to the Chechen bandits. He can forget my vote next time.'

But the number of people who believed that Chechnya should be allowed to become independent doubled – from 17 per cent to 35 per cent – over the summer. The organizer of one Moscow poll comparing opinions in May and opinions at the end of September explained what had brought about the change: not compassion for the people in Chechnya, or horror at the idea of carpet-bombing Grozny. Ironically, people in Moscow had so been terrified by the two mysterious trolleybus bombings that had injured more than two dozen shoppers in the summer that they were now ready to cut the black bandits loose rather than face more of what they suspected was Chechen terrorism in their own capital.

# TWO

A bittersweet day of remembrance. Thousands of people came to the ruins of Freedom Square to commemorate Independence Day on 6 September 1996, the fifth anniversary of Dudayev's takeover of power in Chechnya. Many of them carried portraits of Dudayev. They danced. They prayed. They were celebrating independence, but their mood was muted.

Mostly, it was a day for remembering the dead. Between 80,000 and 100,000 Chechens, a tenth of the Chechen people and almost all civilians, were killed in the war.

'This is a very remarkable day, a very difficult day,' President Yandarbiyev, still in fatigues, still surrounded by fighters, told the crowd. 'We're very glad the war stopped. Allah didn't let us down. But we're still suffering.'

Russia also remembered its dead. The army newspaper *Krasnaya Zvezda* filled five closely-printed pages with the names of 2,941 Russian soldiers who had died in the war. 'Remember Them By Name,' read its banner headline on 12 October. 'Those who died in the bitter Chechen war, forgive us who are alive. May your souls rest in peace.'

Through the autumn, Russian soldiers moved slowly out of Chechnya. By December, General Vladimir Sukhorenko, the new commander of Russian troops in Chechnya, said the withdrawal was ahead of schedule. It finished in the first days of January.

Tentatively at first, the arrangements of peacetime were laid out. The Chechen separatists met at Argun in mid-October, and Yandarbiyev appointed Maskhadov as prime minister of a temporary coalition government. Elections were scheduled for a peacetime president and parliament, and a date of 27 January named.

*

Elections didn't seem possible, in a land of ruins with no real government, no money, no electricity, no water, no phones, no

post, no newspapers, no voters' lists and a third of the surviving
Chechens away from their old peacetime homes.

But – as if by sheer willpower – a semblance of normality did
quickly return to the autumn streets of Grozny. Traffic cops in
Soviet uniforms appeared from nowhere and started flagging down
battered cars. There was quite often light and water in the houses I
stayed in. Three local TV stations were on the air with a touchingly
amateur combination of headscarved women, endlessly reading
news, and Indian films, dubbed into Russian, that filled the
evenings. Cassettes of freedom songs were sold in the market again,
but now they were no longer anonymously labelled 'Chechnya in
Flames – 95' or 'Wolf Trails'. For the first time, they carried
singers' names. Cafés opened up, with patriotic names like 'Daimokhk' (Fatherland) and 'Vainakh' (Our People). Somewhere in
town, I saw a café called 'Nostalgia'.

There was immense pride in the green election posters and
banners hanging from the crippled buildings everywhere, and
immense hope that peace was really here. Sixteen candidates put
themselves up, all separatist leaders. All the commanders – except
the wild Raduyev, still waiting on the Dagestani border for
Dudayev to return from the dead – were supporting the elections.
No one in Grozny cared much that Khasbulatov, whose brother
had just been mysteriously kidnapped, was not standing, though in
Moscow politicians were tut-tutting over the absence of pro-
Russian candidates, and over the post-war crime wave they said
had hit Grozny.

By December, you could fly directly into Grozny again. By
chance, I met Alkhan and his Russian 'extra son' Igor when I
landed at the cold, damp airport. They took me off to stay with
one of Alkhan's many friends and relatives from Gekhi, next door
to the Reuters house where they were all living. Igor, until now a
sombre, taciturn boy, whose sweet smile had had to be coaxed out
of him, was suddenly transformed: all electric energy and twitchy
limbs, dancing about and eager to be off somewhere. 'Peace: I
drove around all last night, listening to music, dropping in on
friends; it's great,' he said excitedly. 'But what about the crime? Is
it safe?' I asked. 'Oh . . . *safe*,' he answered, and a wild, adrenaline-

charged light came into his eyes. 'Not very. A couple of people get
blown away by looters every night. But so what?'

Crime was a new kind of fear to confront. The men with guns
in the streets might be fighters, whom everyone respected for their
honour and their patriotism – but they might be anyone. The gun
sellers were back in the central market. In the middle of town,
where children played on the streets at night, and the neighbours
knew each other and muttered quiet greetings on street corners,
you felt safe. But not in the quiet, half-abandoned districts.

Most of my friends from the Gazgireyev family had escaped to
Moscow in August, but their father, Musa, was still at his home
near the old airport, and one widowed daughter, Lyalya, had
stayed on to look after him. The street was empty apart from them,
the other houses abandoned. They wanted to leave too, but there
was no point in dreaming about it; you couldn't sell houses in
Grozny, and they had no money. So they heaved a chest of drawers
up against the gate at night, and kept the shutters shut so no one
outside could see whether there were lights on. They locked the
doors and windows. 'You never know who's coming,' Musa said,
prodding me with a bony finger. Nights locked up inside their
house – on the comfortable Soviet settee, by the glass bookcase full
of Russian books and family photos, illusions of a cosy past – were
deadly quiet. No streetlights. No sounds of life. You heard every
distant car, or pop of a gun, or footstep.

Travellers were kidnapped on the roads.

*

There was no work, and no one knew what to do with the rest of
their lives. 'It was simple two years ago. We knew what to do
then,' said Maksharip Chadayev, who had started fighting when
the Russian tanks appeared in Grozny at New Year's Eve. 'We had
a goal. Now, what to do next? It's becoming a difficult question.'
Maksharip spoke fluent English; he had to finish off a cure for TB
which the war had interrupted, and some time in the future he
wanted to go to America. But, like almost every other ex-fighter, his
first thought now was to get some sort of job as a guard with a gun,
at a ministry, an oil installation, or a business. His brother, who

had been a commander at Stary Achkoi, was already guarding for the oil minister. Being a guard with a gun was the best job going.

There was no money. Chernomyrdin had promised the Russian government would send 40 billion roubles for wages and pensions, but by the time of the elections only 5 billion had actually been disbursed. There was no official oil; the refineries were hardly working; in his unheated office, the peace-negotiator-turned-oil-minister Khozh-Akhmed Karikhanov complained Russia was stalling on the talks it had promised, on reimbursing Chechnya for letting Caspian oil flow through its pipelines to Russia. The only people making money from oil were the traders on the road, selling jars of golden liquid they had refined themselves after drilling holes in the pipelines and siphoning out the oil.

And, coming to the surface, hatred . . .'Want to see a great film?' whispered Alkhan's son Arbi. He was seventeen, but with the childish limbs and smooth cheeks of a twelve-year-old; his eyes were gleaming. He put it in the Reuters video machine.

It was a kind of snuff movie about the Russian massacre of Samashki: pounding music mixed with the heavy rhythm of Russian shelling, shots of houses burning, women weeping hysterically, gunmen. A female body in the mud, her underwear dragged off, her genitals slashed, her throat cut; a close-up of a hand with three fingers chopped off. Enemies: drunkenly, Yeltsin raised a champagne glass; hazily, Khasbulatov smiled at a crowd. More thumping music, more weeping women, more atrocities, Yeltsin raising his glass again. The mutilated hand.

It went on for hours, with the same shots repeated over and over again. It finished with a screenful of wobbly typed letters: 'Pass this video on. Don't let the world forget the horrors of Samashki.' I understood the good intention, but the amateur video would never go outside Chechnya. Inside Chechnya, it would have the same morbid effect on thousands of children – who had lived for years without schools or normal homes – as it was having on Arbi now. He had his penknife blade out and was tapping it on the table in time to the music, grinning with glazed eyes. 'We should slit all their throats,' he said, rhythmically. 'I'll know what to do with them when they come back.'

There were more snuff videos. They were sold in the market, next to the cassettes of freedom songs, of Muslim teachings, of prayers, *zikr* music and lectures on morality. The only other one I watched was the execution video. It showed stolen television footage of a man waiting to be shot in Beirut, his face pale grey-green with fear; the rattle of gunfire; the body unmoving on the hot pavement. Then it showed a jerky home video of Shamil Basayev and a group of fighters, sitting under summer trees; a man standing nervously in front of them talked in Chechen and gesticulated; he was being tried for treason. In the next shot, he was tied to a tree, blindfolded . . . and I stopped watching.

The freedom songs blaring out from market stalls had the same melodies of loss, but I noticed harsher words when I stopped to listen now . . . 'Why do you Russians tell untruths? The whole world knows you'll never conquer Chechnya. You won't make your homes here, that was ordained long ago. Come here, and you'll die like dogs, and you'll die when you're drunk. The Chechens have always lived here, and they'll go on living here, and there's nothing you ugly boozers can do about it.'

In a tiny home recording studio, I found Khasmagomed Khadzhimradov, a handsome man with sad eyes who sang the most famous song, 'Freedom or Death', at the start of the war. He was in his forties, like the rest of the underground music fraternity; a kind of Chechen hippy movement that had been secretly taping the songs of resistance ever since they grew up under KGB surveillance at the end of the 1960s. Now he and his colleagues could perform in the open, at election rallies, at freedom parties. But Khasmagomed said there was no call yet for anything but war songs, and he didn't think there would be any time soon. People wanted a finger stuck up at Russia; they loved the music of defiance.

There were plenty of reasons to hate what Russia had done here. Unwilling tears came to the eyes of Makkal Sabdullayev – who was acting culture minister while his boss, actor-turned-field-commander Akhmed Zakayev, ran for president – when he started listing all the museums, theatres, and libraries that Russian troops had destroyed after storming Grozny in 1995. Makkal believed these buildings had been deliberately destroyed to wipe out the

Chechens' national culture. 'They came in and went round systematically finishing off any cultural centres still standing – deliberately, cold-bloodedly, as a primary objective.' He had just come
back from rescuing the pictures the Russians had stolen from the
museums, before blowing up the museums. They had hung the
canvases up at Khankala and used them for target practice.
Makkal's gentle composure dropped away when he remembered
it; his eyes flashed with rage. 'Every empire lives through three
stages. It rises, it flourishes and it falls. Our victory in this war
against Russia shows the Russian empire is in that final stage of
decline,' he said. 'I hope I live to see its final collapse.'

But it wasn't just Moscow and the Russian military that were
hated. People in the ruins were looking suspiciously at each other
too. The remaining Russians in Grozny kept a low profile these
days; too many Chechens suspected they had collaborated. Even
among Chechens, people were asking 'What did you, he, she, do
during the war?' with narrowed eyes. In Grozny, people called the
people of the northern districts – who had let the Russians in at the
beginning of the war – the National Betrayers. Bilkiss and her
neighbour on Griboyedov Street had a quarrel over lodgers, and
Bilkiss complained to me afterwards: 'She's always been a sneaky
one; we were all for freedom and Dudayev, but *she* was a cowardly,
vicious little *opposition* supporter. She's a national betrayer.'

Maskhadov's government was doing its best to keep down the
hatred, and the crime. Men who had really fought in the war could
get special military ID cards; anyone else carrying a gun was
suspect. Alcohol sales were banned (although it still wasn't difficult
to get hold of a bottle of vodka or beer, after a whispered
conversation with a trader somewhere).

Islamic courts were operating, meting out tough punishments of
flogging and imprisonment for drunkenness. They were trying to
impose strict laws on people who had grown up thinking that
disobeying Soviet authorities was a sign of conformity to their own
culture and community, a people filled with hatred of Russia, in a
land still full of guns, after a war.

They were trying to make people who had never really obeyed
Moscow's laws understand that it was now vital to obey theirs.

The Islamic courts had only mixed success. Many of the judges were traditional elders, but the courts weren't relying only on the Sufi traditions of Chechnya. Contact with the Jordanian Chechens and Arabs who had come to Chechnya before and during the war, and more moral support from Middle Eastern countries now, was encouraging them to bring in stricter elements of Sharia law. The Mufti of Chechnya, Akhmed-Khodzha Kadyrov, rather apologetically refused to shake my hand; a big, jolly man, he said it was impossible to impose the full Sharia all at once on the Chechens. 'Cutting things off, or whatever,' would have to wait, 'because our people were brought up under lax Soviet ideology, and a new generation must be brought up to see Islam in all its beauty.'

One experimental sentence provoked much mockery in the Russian media, and was later cancelled. A judge who had just finished a two-month course in Islamic law, taught by a Jordanian-born judge, ordered Ali Khasiyev to pay sixty-three camels to the family of a person he had killed in a traffic accident. There are no camels in Chechnya, so Khasiyev was later let off with a fine of $360. In another case before Court Number One, a man found guilty of wartime atrocities – torturing and murdering three people – was sentenced to be killed in the same way his victims had died: by being hit on the head with an axe handle, stabbed in the back with scissors, and having his throat cut. Relatives of the victims agreed to carry out the first two punishments and hired a professional killer from Russia to slit the prisoner's throat. But the judges rethought the punishment at the last minute. The case was back under consideration. For the moment, civil and Islamic courts offered two parallel types of judgement. No one knew what law would operate after the election.

*

The two leading candidates of the separatist field of sixteen were Aslan Maskhadov, the man of peace with whom Moscow could deal, and Shamil Basayev, the man of war, Russia's Public Enemy Number One, with a warrant out for his arrest. Politicians in Russia were terrified the Chechens would elect Basayev, who they suspected would bring back last century's war. 'I cannot imagine

how we could deal with an international terrorist like Shamil
Basayev, who has so much blood on his hands,' said parliament
speaker Gennady Seleznyov.

Gleeful anti-Russian mischief, quiet chuckles everywhere in the
dark room. A whole evening of Russian television broadcasting in
Grozny had the words 'Shamil Basayev' printed at the bottom of
the screen, an illegal election ad which must have been fixed up by
sleight of hand at the local transmission station. 'How they'd hate
to see that in Moscow,' Alkhan said, shaking his head.

No one knew who to vote for. In a culture which places great
emphasis on consensus, negotiation and respect, people were
troubled by the idea of picking a favourite out of the close-knit
team that had won the war for them and, by implication, snubbing
the others.

'How can I choose just one of these men as the best president
when they've all been through fire and they're all great men?' asked
Izmail Visayev, Alkhan's unemployed neighbour from Gekhi,
whose family of five lived off their earnings from selling sweets and
cigarettes out of a bedroom window. His private sympathy, and
the private sympathies of many more Chechens, for the serious,
thoughtful Maskhadov didn't add up to a voting choice.

Nor did other people's private sympathies for Basayev. Basayev
was the most natural politician of the lot. His rallies were enthusiastic affairs of off-the-cuff repartee, shared beliefs, and hope.
Watchers hung on his words, and warmed to his bashful smile. He
was studying statecraft, reading international law, preparing hard
for the presidency. He explained his views to the Russian press
with engaging clarity, and what he said sounded moderate and
well thought out. In Russian eyes, he was still damned for having
shed Russian blood at Budyonnovsk, but he was still a hero to
Chechens.

'I don't think I'll vote at all unless the candidates join forces and
nominate just one person to represent them all,' Maksharip said.
'My sympathies are with Basayev, because I was a fighter; but it
seems wrong to suggest that he was more right than everyone else.'

In deference to this feeling, the top five candidates were holding
fitful discussions about putting up a joint candidate to represent all

of them, but the idea was going nowhere. I went to ask why at
Maskhadov's campaign headquarters, a shabby building by the
market at Minutka. I found Mayerbek Vachagayev there; this time,
he was one of Maskhadov's spokesmen. He grinned happily at the
latest turnaround. 'I hope you're accredited this time,' he said,
'because *our* accreditation is good accreditation.' He didn't think
there'd be a joint candidate. Only Zelimkhan Yandarbiyev wanted
this – because he thought he might be picked as the neutral
figurehead, but he wouldn't win the election by competition. 'It's
all inside Zelim's head,' Mayerbek said. He laughed. He wasn't
taking it very seriously.

In Russia, officials suggested crossly that the Chechens' inability
to pick a single candidate proved there was a deep split in separatist
ranks.

# THREE

While the Chechens faced their new problems of peace and poverty, I drew up a table of Russia's post-war winners and losers.

The Russian army was the big loser of the war. Discredited and shamed by defeat, its weaknesses were exposed to merciless public censure. After he returned to the Kremlin in early 1997, having recovered from his heart operation, Yeltsin reshuffled its leaders every few months. But attempts to reform, streamline, cut, and improve it all came to nothing.

Down but not out – most of the individual leaders from, or sponsored by, the 'Party of War' quickly found new niches at the top of the Russian administrative hierarchy. Sergei Shakhrai became Yeltsin's representative to the Russian Constitutional Court. Sergei Stepashin became the head of the administrative department of the Russian government. Oleg Soskovets was the head of the Association of Financial and Industrial Groups. Alexander Korzhakov was MP for Tula. Viktor Yerin was a deputy director of the Foreign Intelligence Service. Vyacheslav Tikhomirov was the chief of staff of the Urals Military District of the Russian armed forces. Doku Zavgayev was Russia's ambassador to Tanzania. Salambek Khadzhiyev ran a Russian state committee for industrial policy. Umar Avturkhanov was the deputy director of Russia's tax police. Tass reported that Pavel Grachev would soon be nominated Russia's representative at NATO headquarters in Brussels. Konstantin Pulikovsky was still a lieutenant-general in the Russian army's North Caucasus Military District. Vyacheslav Mikhailov was still nationalities minister. Anatoly Kulikov was still interior minister; in February 1997, he was given a second, more senior, job as deputy prime minister with special responsibility for the fight against organized crime.

Nikolai Yegorov was dead. But most of the military and security types who made up the 'Party of War', the post-Soviet 'Warrior' aristocracy that had been replaced as the favourites of Yeltsin's court by the new mercantile aristocracy, got a soft landing. A gesture from Yeltsin – a change of mood or circumstances – could bring them back to power.

If anyone in Russia did well out of the Chechen war – apart from the commercial profit to be gained from the undercover trading that goes with any conflict – it was the successor agencies to the Soviet KGB. Russia's security services went from strength to strength since just before the start of the war. By the time fighting ended in Chechnya, they were more powerful than at any time since Soviet days. They kept that strength up afterwards. They are protected from public scrutiny and still answerable only to the Russian president.

After Barsukov was sacked in June 1996, the FSB was quietly run by one of his ex-deputies, Colonel-General Nikolai Kovalyov, another career KGB officer who had worked at Lubyanka Square since 1974. The agency's powers were strengthened again: in July 1996, Yeltsin listed sweeping priorities of combating terrorism and espionage inside Russia, fighting corruption and ensuring economic security – tasks that portray a Russia under siege by unprincipled elements and external enemies.

After the notorious Korzhakov was sacked from leadership of the Presidential Guard in June 1996, it too went unreformed. It has several thousand operatives. As well as security structures, it includes a group of analysts, a counter-intelligence service, a presidential regiment with a guard of honour company, a band, a garage, a group of art critics, restorers and construction workers, numerous auxiliary services and a press service. It is now quietly run by the little-known Anatoly Kuznetsov. Little information has been published about the GRU, a separate military intelligence service that, unlike the ex-KGB, was never reformed when the Soviet Union collapsed.

'A KGB skeleton is still intact and is essentially being reassembled. It is incorrect, however, to assume that the new structure is a direct continuation of the KGB. More than in the past, there is a hand on the leash of Russia's new security organs: the hand of direct presidentital control,' the journal *Transition* commented. 'It must be remembered that Russia has a long tradition of powerful secret police who maintain a political role and are responsible only to the highest political authority, if even that. There seems to be no question that this tendency still exists. The question is whether it can be prevented in the future.'[1]

Each time the security forces have been strengthened, the Russian élite has explained to the public that there is a need for more surveillance of their daily lives – because of the omnipresent threat of Chechen terrorism. Russians have made no particular effort to question their superstitious dread of the Chechens, which has been reinforced at every turn by propaganda from on high. A people that used to be sceptical of every propaganda trick their Soviet leaders pulled on them has proved surprisingly gullible and easily led by race fear. Hardly anyone in Russia has protested as the freedoms they once expected from post-Soviet life are whittled away.

*

One Russian who refused to give up the freedom to speak her mind was Valeriya Novodvorskaya, a plump, hoarse, appealing woman whose ample bosom was always heaving with secret laughter and whose eyes twinkled kindly behind thick glasses. Novodvorskaya was an intellectual, writer, wit, democratic politician and ex-dissident, who suffered years of harassment and on-and-off imprisonment by the KGB in the 1970s and 1980s. Her tiny band of political supporters were out on the streets regularly during the war, protesting against the idiocy of Russian policy and the slaughter of the Chechens.

To her astonishment, Novodvorskaya found herself, once again, threatened with jail under a nonsensical charge brought by the FSB's deputy director, General Trofimov, her old tormentor from Soviet days. In 1996, five years after the Soviet Union vanished, the man nicknamed 'The Grand Inquisitor' of the 1970s dissident trials was back in power.

---

1. Michael Joseph Kozakavich, *The Skeleton in Russian President's Closet*, article published in the English-language journal *Transition* in Prague in edition of 1 Nov. 1996, pp. 14 and 18.

'Trofimov...' Novodvorskaya mused throatily, in a chilly sitting-room at the office of the *Novoye Vremya* journal where she works. 'The former persecutor of dissidents, a most terrifying figure ... a powerful employee of the Ministry of Love.'

Trofimov wanted to put her in jail for eighteen months for writing two articles – one defending the Chechens, another criticizing Russian emotional excess. The second piece said Russians had a 'manic-depressive psychosis' and kowtowed to strong authority, but that they became 'unbridled anarchists, robbers, thieves, rising up in permanent outsiders' revolts', whenever strict control over them was relaxed. Trofimov accused Novodvorskaya of inciting interracial hatred, invoking an article of the penal code designed to protect ethnic minorities from prejudice. She said robustly that the charge was nonsense and it was 'absurd' to invoke it to protect majority Russians from her light-hearted abstractions.

Novodvorskaya's case had echoes of the institutionalized anti-Semitism of the Soviet era. Word got about after proceedings opened that Novodvorskaya was not an ethnic Russian, but a Jew. 'The FSB put it about that she was a "Person of Jewish Nationality", an attempt to appeal to prejudice and xenophobia,' Novodvorskaya's lawyer, Genri Reznik, told me. Two of the FSB experts brought in to handle her case – Yuri Biryukov and Stanislav Roshchin – were veteran investigators from Stalin's days; they worked on the 'Doctors' Plot', a planned anti-Semitic purge that was interrupted only by the death of the Soviet dictator in 1953.

The case, begun in February 1996 – when the FSB's powers had just been expanded to include control of intelligence monitoring, at the start of the presidential election campaign, while Yeltsin was still favouring old-fashioned hard-liners – was finally dropped at the end of 1996. Once Yeltsin was re-elected, and had restocked his Kremlin with forward-looking liberals, there was in principle no reason to pursue a backward-looking political prosecution any longer. But Novodvorskaya believes her judges were scared that Yeltsin's illness might mean a new president, and perhaps a more authoritarian one. So they dithered over letting her off until Yeltsin came back to work at the Kremlin and political tension eased.

To Novodvorskaya, the 'show trial' proves that the legal system in post-Soviet Russia has not become strong enough to protect ordinary citizens against the revival of the old-style secret police. 'We now have the institutions of democracy, but people don't really understand them and the institutions don't work in a cultural vacuum,' she said.

Novodvorskaya was lucky: she was the articulate, adored, eccentric darling of the Moscow intelligentsia. Her ironical smile and cultured voice were constantly broadcast on television, so the noisy post-Soviet press took up her cause. So did liberal MPs in the Duma. So did a couple of top lawyers. So did dozens of human rights workers, all warning that Big Brother of Soviet days was watching them again. In a cluttered office filled with long photocopied petitions, Lev Timofeyev listed seven or eight other cases of writers called in for FSB questioning in the last year about the political content of their work. It was a way for the secret police to 'show its teeth', he said angrily. By the autumn the foolishness of the case against Novodvorskaya had been made so public that it became clear it would soon have to be dropped. One of her main supporters, MP Konstantin Borovoi, laughed and said: 'I think we have to look at this as an FSB provocation that just didn't work out.'

*

Three big crimes were reported from Chechnya during the run-up to the elections on 27 January. All of them threatened to unsettle the tense peace in the south enough to disrupt the elections and put Chechens and Russians back on the road to war – an outcome that remained to the taste of hard-liners in both Russia and Chechnya. One was openly carried out by a Chechen. Another remained a mysterious crime, dense and insoluble; Chechnya blamed the Russian FSB, while Russians believed Chechens had committed it. The third crime bore the clear signature of the Russian secret police.

The wild man of the Chechen separatists, Salman Raduyev, took twenty-two Russian OMON troops hostage on 14 December. They had tried to stop forty of Raduyev's fighting men walking into Dagestan with their guns. Raduyev refused to release any of the hostages until he got an apology from the local Russian commander. He said he was protesting against the elections.

Swaggering Salman Raduyev didn't like the deal Aslan Maskhadov had done with Russia – peace now, and maybe freedom later. The 'back-from-the-dead' guerrilla leader, still recruiting men to a shaggy fighting force he called General Dudayev's Army, wanted freedom now, or no peace at all. Nor did Raduyev approve of Chechnya voting for a new president, since he believed President Dzhokhar Dudayev was still alive. Raduyev's prediction that Dudayev would be back in Chechnya by September had not come true, but Raduyev was now saying the president would return three days before the elections.

Some Russian generals wanted to halt the Russian troop withdrawal; others said in public that Raduyev was an eccentric outsider among the Chechens, and should be ignored. From Grozny, Maskhadov ordered Raduyev to set the prisoners free. From Moscow, Berezovsky flew south to ensure he did.

Five days later, Raduyev let his prisoners go. In the end, no harm was done to the peace process. But another crime in Chechnya, committed a day before the OMON troops walked free, had grabbed world headlines. Six Western medical workers were murdered in their beds, at a hospital which the International Committee of the Red Cross had set up in Noviye Atagi after the August siege of Grozny. It was the deadliest single attack against the Red Cross in its 133-year existence.

A group of fifteen unidentified masked men entered the hospital at 4 a.m. on 17 December, bashed down the doors to the bedrooms where the foreigners were sleeping, and shot seven of them in cold blood. One of the seven survived. The ICRC immediately pulled out its remaining seventy staff from Chechnya. Other Western aid agencies also rushed to leave. The murders deprived Chechens of desperately needed humanitarian aid, added weight to Russia's contention that the region was a den of murderous thieves, and nearly scared off the foreign observers who were due to monitor the elections.

People in the rest of Russia had no difficulty in believing that fly-by-night Chechen gunmen crept in off the streets to murder the wealthy foreigners. In support of this theory, survivors of the hospital massacre said the killers spoke Chechen to each other and spared a Chechen translator and Chechen guards while they hunted down their expatriate victims.

Chechens found it equally easy to believe that Russian secret service agents killed the medical staff, in the hope of discrediting the Chechens and letting hard-liners in Moscow begin a new, more successful war. They said the fact that the killers carried professionals' guns, with silencers, and left behind the expatriates' money and jewellery proves they were not crazy ex-fighters hunting instant wealth. They believed the gunmen were carrying out a contract, and the obvious fact that chasing away the Red Cross was not in Chechnya's interests proved the contract was not taken out by a Chechen.

Movladi Udugov accused the FSB of sending a death squad in to do the killings. 'The structures of the Russian special forces and the FSB are engaged in financing and preparing terrorist acts on Chechen territory,' he said. 'There is a third force which does not want peace in Chechnya, those known as the "Party of War".'

The FSB denied it.

Echoes of historical conflicts grew louder as Russia panicked over the idea that Shamil Basayev might win the election. By early January, the Cossacks of southern Russia were growing restive. Reports were circulating all over southern Russia that Chechen thugs were committing race-hate murders of the Cossack Russians who lived among them in the three flat districts of northern Chechnya – Nadterechny, Naursky and Shelkovsky. A list of twenty-three Russians who had been murdered in these districts was circulated at a Cossack conference in Stavropol on 5 January. It matched Russian preconceptions of Chechen savagery so well that its provenance, or veracity, were not questioned. The list provoked an emotional war cry, full of the resonance of last century's battle between Cossacks and Imam Shamil. The irate Cossacks demanded that Naursky and Shelkovsky districts, which had been part of Russia until Stalin's last redrawing of ethnic boundaries, should be administered from Stavropol again. And they demanded to be armed.

Who had ever taken the Cossacks seriously, until now? Only President Yeltsin, in his brief pre-war flirtation with reviving them as a fighting force. The rest of Russia still regarded them as something of a joke. But suddenly, their war cries got unexpected backing from a very high Russian politician – no less than Boris Berezovsky. He dropped his peaceable attitude towards the Chechens. Impeccable as ever in his handmade shoes and designer suit, Berezovsky urged on an angry roomful of Cossacks in improvised historical costumes and *shashkas*. 'When you say: "Give us weapons, because the Chechens have weapons," I can tell you that I support you 100 per cent,' he said.

The atmosphere of costume drama and hysteria turned menacing when Anatoly Kulikov, the interior minister and last acting member of the 'Party of War', joined in. Cossacks should not meddle, he said; real Russian troops should re-enter Chechnya and 'protect people' if 'genocide against Russians' erupted there.

With tensions running at fever pitch, Maskhadov stepped in to mediate a few days before the election, saying he wanted to 'stop the forces of evil involving Cossacks in confrontation'. He called an emergency meeting between the Cossack leaders and police chiefs of Stavropol, and the local Cossacks and Chechen police of northern Chechnya. As soon as the two sides met, what had looked like an impending tragedy turned into farce. Brandishing their list of Russian murder victims, the Stavropol Cossacks angrily demanded that Chechens stop killing the innocent. The Chechen police chief of Naursky district, Nurdi Eldarov, took a look at the list. 'The Russians were yelling that we were riding roughshod over the law. They gave us this list of twenty-three crimes, probably compiled by the KGB. When I looked at the list, I was quite astonished: it was full of my neighbours' names,' he said. Every one of the 'victims' was alive and well.

'I told them they should be riding roughshod over whoever compiled that list, because I could put all those alleged victims on a bus and send them to Stavropol Territory right now,' he went on, with deep satisfaction. 'The Stavropol authorities published an apology in the newspaper, saying it was all a mistake.'

Maskhadov said he was relieved that the crisis had been averted. The Cossack story was dropped from Russian television news.

*

But tension in northern Chechnya did not dissipate. By the time of the elections, it was a place of fear and suspicion. Russians and Chechens scuttled past each other in village squares, with their eyes lowered. Real ethnic crimes began to replace imaginary ones. Youths from each ethnic group threatened 'betrayers' from the other with fists and grenades. A fifty-five-year-old Russian in Naur tossed a grenade into a police car, seriously injuring two Chechen police officers. The rise and fall of the original 'provocation', the list of imaginary murders, left northern Chechnya a fertile breeding ground for genuine new race conflicts.

A Chechen policeman in Naur, Magomed Murtiyev, took me to see his old Russian schoolfriend Liza Mikhailenko. She was a Russian agronomist whose name had topped the list of murder victims – along with her teenage daughter, she was supposed to have been raped and murdered. She was plump, pink-cheeked and anxious, wrapped in a fluffy hat and scarf outside the collective farm she had worked on all her life. No one had laid a finger on anyone in her family, she said, patting the uniformed Magomed on the shoulder.

But both of them were terrified of the stream of exaggerated reports of Chechen-on-Russian violence that were getting into the Russian papers now the war was over and independence within Chechnya's grasp. They believed the FSB was trying to create ethnic tension here as a pretext for more Russian military intervention later. 'There are third forces at work here, and they're cooking up these dirty tricks whose consequences are too scary to even think about,' Mrs Mikhailenko said. 'It's true that things are hard here, especially for us Russians. But I think it's completely wrong to make up fake lists and stir things up by writing down things that are untrue.'

The local Cossack leader, a quiet man in a check shirt and another old schoolfriend of Magomed the policeman, was also trying to keep a lid on the growing tension. 'We Russians who live inside Chechnya want to go on being at peace with our neighbours,' Vladimir Kashlyunov said. 'The most important thing is not to turn the clock back. That's dangerous, especially when you remember that our history is one of war and violence. There were a lot of these mysterious crimes before the war. Now there's been a new spurt of them since the war ended. These crimes suit the book of someone in Moscow, and I think you know who as well as I do.'

# FOUR

From Moscow, the final days before the Chechen elections looked fraught with every kind of tension and hostility. The Russian parliament refused to amnesty Shamil Basayev for the crimes committed at Budyonnovsk. Apparently preparing the ground in case Basayev won the election, Russian officials started casting doubt over whether fair elections could be carried out at all in a republic whose hundreds of thousands of refugees would not get the chance of a postal vote.

Chechnya touchily refused a Russian offer of money to fund technical support for the elections – but later accepted a similar offer from Tim Guldimann at the OSCE. The Swiss diplomat raised nearly half a million dollars, which provided mobile phones, ballot boxes, voting slips, ultra-violet markers and transport to overcome the logistical difficulties of the election. The Russian parliament was outraged. It voted to throw Guldimann out of his job, and out of Russia. He ignored them, and stayed in Chechnya.

A spate of high-profile kidnappings – including those of two Russian television journalists and an Orthodox priest – worried observers and journalists making their way south for the election. Russia denied Chechen allegations that it was behind them. The Russian press aired counter-suspicions that an aide of Maskhadov's, Vakha Arsanov, was to blame. The president of Ingushetia, Ruslan Aushev, said he thought most of the kidnappings were not political at all. They were the work of criminals, out for dirty money.

'Rather you than me,' Vitya the driver said unkindly, helping me with my bag at the airport on the way to Grozny. 'Now, be careful.'

But all the dark imaginings came to nothing. The elections were a triumph. There was sun on the frost, and the polling stations were packed. Everyone wanted to vote, and everyone was smiling. Most people said they were voting for Maskhadov, and peace.

Fighters were offering a romantic vote for Basayev. It was the happiest day I'd seen in Chechnya.

'What I hope above all else is that after these elections there will be no more war,' Lyalya Gazgireyeva said, as she began preparing her father Musa's evening meal of lamb and pasta. 'God willing, we'll finally be able to put all this horror behind us and get on with living again.' Lyalya and Musa had voted for Maskhadov, because they knew he stood for peace. Lyalya wanted to bring home her two little girls, whom she had evacuated to stay in Central Asia with her sister when the house was hit by a shell in August. She couldn't bear to keep them with her any longer; the oldest child, Asya, had sat in the cellar for three days, repeating 'Mama, I'm frightened', every few minutes, in a monotone. She was eleven. 'I had to send her to Raya in Frunze,' Lyalya said apologetically. 'She'd have gone mad if she'd stayed here any longer. But I miss them.'

Maksharip, staying on his brother's floor on the edge of Factory District, agonized all day, but finally voted for Basayev.

With Chechnya's telephone network taken out by the war, vote-counting was a painstaking, time-consuming business. Walkie-talkie radios supplied by the OSCE helped the Central Electoral Commission compile results from the remote hill districts. Tim Guldimann's seventy-two OSCE observers, and the Russian human rights representatives monitoring voting, pronounced the election free and fair.

Ancient, podgy Bilkiss had borrowed a Kalashnikov to protect the journalists staying in her house. She kept it behind the curtain outside her bedroom. She displayed it proudly to visitors. 'Oh yes, I'd chase off any rascals that came sniffing after trouble here soon enough,' she said. 'I know how to shoot.' But there were no shootings, no kidnappings and no atrocities. Instead, in a land that had officially banned alcohol for itself, the government opened a little bar at the election centre, as a courtesy to foreign visitors.

And Maskhadov won, with 64.8 per cent of the vote.

The day after the voting, before any official results were out, he called a post-election meeting for journalists. He sat, under his grey *papakha*, listening impassively as Mayerbek Vachagayev smilingly announced: 'Today we start the first press conference with Mr Aslan Maskhadov in his capacity as president of the Chechen Republic of Ichkeria' (the Chechen's own name for their land).

Maskhadov immediately made it clear he was not the political pushover Moscow wanted to do business with, but the inheritor of separatists. He politely pooh-poohed Russia's hopes that the five-year wait – before a decision on how to 'define the relationship' with Chechnya – could be considered a cooling-off period in which to rebuild economic ties, let Russia route Caspian oil through Chechnya, and let the issue of Chechen independence be quietly forgotten. He said firmly that Chechen independence was a done deal.

'The first and second steps were taken in 1991,' he said. 'Chechnya became an independent state and its sovereignty was declared. Now there is just one task left – to get our independence recognized by everyone, including Russia – which we will achieve by political means. There are five years to consider this in a sober way, but we want to define our relations with Russia as soon as possible. Everything now depends on Moscow.'

The other presidential candidates conceded defeat. Yandarbiyev called a whimsical press conference in which he didn't quite admit he knew he'd lost, but praised the victory of the separatist cause anyway. Basayev vanished for a day, nettled by Maskhadov's hasty assumption of the presidency, but his aide said he would, of course, not dispute the election results once they were published. Later Basayev took office under President Maskhadov.

Moscow was pleased that Basayev was out. Yeltsin announced he was 'fully satisfied' with the way the elections were run, and no more was heard of the long list of quibbles that Russia had raised about electoral procedures during the campaign. To Moscow, Maskhadov represented evolution, not revolution. He was not going to rush for foreign recognition of Chechen independence, or hastily introduce the insignia of full statehood – currency and passports. He wanted war reparations and a cut of the profits from the Russian oil pipelines running through his land, but he wasn't threatening to divert the oil away from Russia altogether. Most of all, his neat grey hair, measured voice and Soviet-colonel ways reassured Moscow that it need not take fright, or take to arms again, over his demands.

*

In February 1997, Maskhadov was sworn in as president. Even if it found him the least objectionable of the Chechen separatists, Russia treated the occasion with scant grace.

The only undamaged building in Grozny big enough to fit all the guests was the Soviet Chemists' Palace of Culture. Throngs of religious and political leaders crammed in to watch Maskhadov, in a statesman's silk tie – and a *papakha* – swear his oath of allegiance on the Quran. Outside, hundreds of bearded ex-fighters fired guns triumphantly in the air.

Maskhadov made an emotional promise to bring his people the freedom for which they and their ancestors had fought:

> Now it is the duty of every one of us to realize the expectations of our ancestors, our heroes fallen in holy war, of the right to live freely and independently. For hundreds of years, our people were not allowed to be masters of their land ... [they were] killed when the Russians wanted to kill, burned when the Russians felt like it, labelled bandits when Russia felt like it, and deported when Russia felt like it.

I didn't hear him make this speech, although I was in Moscow watching the inauguration on television. I had to read it in news agency reports. Russia's prime-time news broadcast, Vremya, made it clear to Russian viewers that the Chechen president's inauguration was a matter of no importance to them. It broadcast a report of it in the twenty-first minute of the programme, after describing every parliamentary committee meeting and regional hiccup in Russia. It transmitted pictures of the guns firing, but it left out Maskhadov's speech.

Delegations from Lithuania and Ukraine were prevented from attending the ceremony by the antics of Russian air traffic controllers. Ivan Rybkin was the only official Russian representative at the inauguration, though Lebed turned up too, all bluff charm in a dark overcoat. Yeltsin was incapable of controlling the situation in

Chechnya, he said, and should be put on a pension so there could
be a younger, more capable president – like Lebed himself. 'I can
settle things with anyone,' he growled.

*

Trouble didn't end with the successful elections in Chechnya.
Many crimes and upsets followed. Some of the crime seemed to be
genuine and spontaneous, others had the poisoned-umbrella-tip
feel that signalled FSB involvement. With time, the distinction
started blurring.

Russian journalists, foreign journalists and Chechen nationals
were kidnapped. Yelena Masyuk, the gutsy Chechnya war reporter
from NTV, who more than any other Russian journalist had
fearlessly publicized the reality of the fighting for her compatriots,
was one of the many victims. Andrei Mironov – a Russian ex-
dissident, human rights activist and journalist who has spent much
of the past two years in Chechnya – said about four hundred
people had been kidnapped in all in the first six months of peace.

Kidnapping turned into a murky big business. Maskhadov
imposed the death penalty as a punishment for it, and tried to
discourage the payment of ransoms. But not everyone played by
the rules. Although no one admitted publicly they were paying, the
size of the ransoms that were unofficially acknowledged quickly
went up from a few thousand dollars at the end of the war to
around $1 million for a few high-profile victims.

'The tragedy of it all is that if people are paying these huge
ransoms, it will encourage people with no money, but with guns,
in Chechnya to go kidnapping,' Andrei Mironov said. 'People who
would never have thought of it will suddenly see kidnapping as a
way of making money beyond their wildest dreams.'

Saludi Abdurzakov, a Chechen businessman who set up a
satellite phone business in Grozny after the war, often acted as
unofficial broker in arranging hostage releases. One of the people
involved in negotiating the releases said Abdurzakov's phone
operated from a Russian military satellite. There was no other
suggestion of Russian involvement.

Negotiations on a Russian–Chechen friendship treaty – the first step towards a full political agreement – went nowhere for months. An increasingly despairing Maskhadov repeated that the Russians weren't trying. Talks on the oil pipeline were stuck. Talks on politics were stuck. Maskhadov went to Saudi Arabia on a Muslim *haj* pilgrimage; he said at first that he would leave Basayev in charge of Chechnya in his absence, but the squawks of Russian protest were so loud that he changed his mind. There was a spate of ultimatums, assassinations of minor officials, and drive-by shootings; an atmosphere of panic.

Two mysterious crimes inside Russia suddenly had Russians on the edge of their seats again. On 23 April, a bomb exploded in Armavir railway station in southern Russia. Two people were killed. No one claimed responsibility. On 28 April, another bomb went off in the south, killing two more people. The second attack was at the railway station in Pyatigorsk – a popular tourist spot for Russians taking spa waters and looking at the woodland glade where the writer Lermontov fought a duel and died last century. Two Chechen women suspects were detained, and the FSB blamed the bombings on 'Chechen terrorism'.

Suddenly, the 'Warrior' interior minister Anatoly Kulikov was back, breathing fire. He circulated a photo of two Chechen women, saying this was the pair who had 'confessed' to planting explosives at Pyatigorsk and taking part in the wartime raid on Budyonnovsk. 'These are not rebels. This is not a political struggle, this is banditry,' Kulikov said. 'We will catch and destroy those criminals' – a sinister echo of the language Russian officials had used to justify using the army to clean up Dudayev's 'haven for criminals'.

But, this time, Kulikov was pushed aside. The photograph he was circulating turned out to be a picture from Zelimkhan Yandarbiyev's recently published book; one of the women in the photograph was living in Grozny, another had been dead for a year. It was embarrassing for Kulikov, and embarrassing for the Russians who were now trying to consolidate peace. Ivan Rybkin, who had been holding peace talks in Grozny, slapped Kulikov down. 'Irrespective of the number of stars on their epaulettes, people should not get drowned in their own ambitions,' he said. Peace-makers on both sides disassociated themselves from the sabre-rattling of the hard-liners, and pushed ahead with the talks.

Russia and Chechnya signed a treaty of peace and friendship on 10 May, 1997 – the first such treaty in centuries of hostile relations.

Maskhadov and a delegation of Chechen politicians, all dark suits, *papakha*s, and sobriety, met Yeltsin in the Kremlin to sign the documents. The huge Russian president towered over the neat, nervous Chechen leader, but treated him with respect. For the first time, Yeltsin referred to Maskhadov as the 'President of Ichkeria'. Afterwards, Movladi Udugov was interviewed on Russian tele-vision. Sitting on a park bench in the dusty spring sunshine of Moscow, he said, without a smile: 'This is a victory for Russia and for Chechnya over the Party of War.'

The treaty did not recognize Chechen independence. As far as Russia was concerned, it had five years in which to decide on Chechnya's political status. But it was, at last, a symbolic gesture of good faith.

*

What Yeltsin started in 1991 was a game with history, a revival of the gilded trappings of imperial pageantry – double-headed eagles, shadowy enemies and dressed-up Cossack defenders. What Russia ended up with five years later, by the time it made peace with the Chechens, was something far closer to the empires of the past. Russia was no longer run by a tiny Communist élite, but – after a brief period of confusion, labelled democracy – it turned itself back into a state almost as stratified as its predecessors, run by a tiny court, a powerful police and an autocrat. After two years as a growling warrior Tsar, Yeltsin later reinvented himself as a benign democratic leader to win re-election in 1996. He removed from direct power the court clique which pursued the war, and replaced it with a rival mercantile clique whose interests lay in peace. But it was Yeltsin himself, not the 'Party of War', who ordered the assault on Chechnya. A ruthless enough politician to return to bloodshed if he judged it necessary, he had concentrated enough of Russia's state power in his own hands to be able to do so without impediment.

Chechnya had another cause for anxiety over the shape Russian statehood finally took. The five-year deadline for deciding Chechnya's fate was set for one year after Yeltsin's own term in office expires. Who will have inherited the immense powers of Yeltsin's Tsarist-style presidency by then, and what they will do with Chechnya, is anybody's guess.

*

Chechnya after the war was full of people whose long-ago folk or family memories of historical Russian mistreatment had been replaced with their own agonizing recollections. Russia built up its new ruling structure in faraway Moscow on the bones of the Chechens, and the sufferings of people in Chechnya went virtually unnoticed by the outside world. It was hard to imagine that Chechens who had lived through nearly two years of the war would willingly accept Russian rule again. President Maskhadov proved moderate, but he was under pressure from more radical politicians to press for full independence. Meanwhile, Chechnya was poor, unstable, and dangerous. The government was not easily able to reintegrate the armed men irreconcilably opposed to any ties to Russia, who were nicknamed 'Indians', or to stop crime by armed men with no political motives. Chechnya's traditional, mystical Islam was hardening under Middle Eastern influence. As a result of the war, the hostile criminal ghetto of Russia's dark imaginings may have taken real shape.

Many of my friends from Chechnya left, or were trying to leave. They didn't want Chechnya to be ruled by Russia, but the kind of freedom they found now was more ambiguous, brutal and frightening than they expected. Besides, they were scared the Russians would be back.

Southern Russia remained on battle alert. The Russian army withdrew from Chechnya, but not very far. The units that left in the autumn and winter of 1996 dug themselves in at a new camp in Budyonnovsk, a day's journey from Chechnya. They quickly made themselves unpopular with the largely unemployed Russians of Budyonnovsk by throwing grenades when they got drunk. Miserable in their tents and temporary dorms, they hated Chechens; they spent their nights reliving horror stories about slit throats and death.

The Cossacks of the south spent the spring of 1997 agitating. They were scared the Chechens would come raiding, knives in hand. They wanted to dig a huge trench along the border between Stavropol Territory and Chechnya, to keep the darkies out.

Even after the war ended, I tried never to talk about Chechnya with Russian friends. My heart sank at the abyss of misunderstanding which always opened up with people whose every other opinion I found stimulating and sophisticated. The last conversation I did, reluctantly, enter into, at a cosy New Year party with half-a-dozen close friends, ended just as badly as the rest. 'No really, tell us, what is the Chechen people like? What are its characteristics?' Mariya's mother urged, kindly, ladling out cake. 'Well, it's hard to generalize about a whole people,' I stammered, unhappily. 'All different; good, bad, funny, serious, criminal, honest, smart, stupid . . .' But it was a provocation to say even that, even in a roomful of multilingual, well-travelled, university lecturer friends. Mariya's eyes flashed; Kolya, her boyfriend, scowled. 'No. They're all the same – a bandit nation,' Mariya said.

It seemed unlikely that this Russia, and this Chechnya, could make and keep a lasting agreement on a peaceful future.

\*

When I think of Chechnya now, what I prefer to remember is Shamil Basayev looking watchfully over a snowy cemetery into a future as difficult as the past.

There is frost on the roads, and frost on the breath of the people walking quietly round the graves at Tsotsen-Yurt: grieving mothers in headscarves, veteran fighters in *papakha* hats and combat fatigues, elders with long jackets and silver-topped sticks, children. There are few guns, and no sounds of weeping, but the faces on all sides are sombre. There are touches of blue and green in the metal fence. Each of the neat mounds is marked by a tall metal pole. All the people buried here are fighters who died under Russian bombardment, at Pervomaiskoye.

Basayev tours the graves, then gathers the hushed crowd. The latest war is over, the January 1997 election is still a few weeks ahead, and it is time to draw conclusions.

'The war has shown we must not let ourselves be subjugated on the path to *ghazavat*. We must not let them turn us from the true path we have chosen,' he says, so quietly that the intent elders shuffle closer. (This is a private speech, in Chechen, for Chechens, but Maksharip is whispering a translation in my ear.) 'Look at these graves. They show that our people have proved their worth on the path to *ghazavat*. These graves will be an example to the next generation, who will draw strength from our struggle and learn from it how they can also be true sons of their homeland.

'The Russian army has left. We must use this opportunity wisely, or things will go badly for us. And we must not forget what was done to us, for he who forgets his past forgets his future.'

Basayev finishes speaking, and the old men sigh. Somewhere behind the graves is the first whisper of *zikr*. Another dance is about to begin.

# Glossary

**Abkhazia** – Separatist region in Georgia, whose capital is Sukhumi.

**Abrek** – (Caucasian) outlaw or highwayman of honour, who attacked Russians.

**Adat** – Caucasian mountain tribes' old customary law.

Boris **Agapov** – Vice-President of Ingushetia.

Heidar **Aliyev** – Ex-Soviet Politburo and ex-leader of Soviet Azerbaijan, whose career began in the NKVD secret police. Aliyev took back power in post-Soviet Azerbaijan after President Abulfaz Elchibey was ousted in 1993.

**Armenia** – Ex-Soviet Transcaucasian republic, whose capital is Yerevan.

**Artsakh** – Armenian word for the disputed Armenian-majority territory of Nagorny Karabakh; Karabakh lies outside Armenian territory, in neighbouring Azerbaijan, and fighting broke out over it in the late 1980s.

**Apparatchik** – Soviet bureaucrat.

**Ataman** – Cossack leader.

**Aul** – Caucasian mountain village.

Ruslan **Aushev** – President of Ingushetia.

Umar **Avturkhanov** – Soviet interior ministry official and, after 1991, mayor of the Chechen district of Nadterechny where opponents to Chechen President Dzhokhar Dudayev began to gather. In 1994, Moscow recognized his opposition Provisional Council as Chechnya's rightful government, and aid and weapons were channelled to it in the hope of dislodging Dudayev. Avturkhanov was later discarded.

**Azerbaijan** – Ex-Soviet Transcaucasian republic, whose capital is Baku.

**Babushka** – granny, or any woman over fifty.

**Baku** – Capital of Azerbaijan.

**Ballonchik** – Mace canister.

Field-Marshal Prince Alexander **Baryatinsky** – Appointed to command left flank of the Tsarist army in the Caucasus in 1851, later appointed Viceroy of the South, received Shamil's sword in 1859 at the successful end of the Caucasian Wars; later disgraced for womanizing.

Shamil **Basayev** – Leading Chechen separatist, colleague of Dzhokhar Dudayev. Before the war in Chechnya began, Basayev took a group of men who became known as the 'Abkhaz battalion' to fight alongside the Abkhazians for freedom from Georgia. His family is from Vedeno, in Chechnya's south-eastern highlands.

Mikhail **Barsukov** – An ex-KGB general, he ran what used to be the 30,000-man KGB Ninth Directorate after it was renamed Main Guards Division at the time of the Soviet collapse. He was appointed head of the FSB (new Federal Security Service) in July 1995, and strengthened it. Sacked in mid-1996.

**Bazarchik** – small street market.

Boris **Berezovsky** – Car-sales millionaire, one of 'Big Seven' bankers who bankrolled Yeltsin's re-election in 1996; appointed Deputy Secretary of the Russian Security Council, in charge of Chechnya, in October 1996.

**Bezpredel** – Limitless chaos, crime and disorder.

**Biznismen** – Soviet-era businessman, crook.

Gennady **Burbulis** – Yeltsin's state secretary in 1991.

General Matvei **Burlakov** – Until 1994 head of ex-Soviet troops in Germany, then briefly Deputy Defence Minister in Moscow; sacked in late 1994 in a scandal over the murder of journalist Dmitry Kholodov, who was investigating army corruption.

**Burzhuyka** – Improvised stove, looking like a biscuit tin with an exit pipe for smoke leading out of the window.

**Caspian Sea** – Once shared between the Soviet Union and Iran. The Soviet collapse meant that Iran had to share the sea with four partners after 1991: Russia, Azerbaijan, Kazakhstan and Turkmenistan. A big oil find off Azerbaijan's coastline has since made Russia explore ways of regaining its old control over the sea's resources.

**Cha-cha** – Armenian grappa.

**Chechnya** – Area in the eastern part of the North Caucasus region, home to just over a million people at the time of the Soviet collapse in 1991. During the late Soviet era, when its main industry was oil refining, Chechnya was joined with its western neighbour Ingushetia in a single administrative entity, Checheno–Ingushetia.

**Chekist** – Secret policeman of the Cheka, an early Soviet predecessor of the KGB.

**Cheremshah** – Georgian pickled greens.

Victor **Chernomyrdin** – Russian Prime Minister since 1992; earlier a leading light in the huge gas conglomerate Gazprom. Seen as a moderate.

Anatoly **Chubais** – A leading Russian liberal and economic reformer, Chubais ran a huge privatization programme after the Soviet Union collapsed but was sidelined during the war in Chechnya. Having said firmly he was happier in the private sector, the unpopular red-headed Chubais re-emerged after Yeltsin was re-elected president in June 1996 and became first Yeltsin's chief of staff and then First Deputy Prime Minister.

**Chuchkela** – A Georgian sweet made of walnuts and grapeskin resin.

**Circassians** – The peoples who live along the Western stretches of the Russian north Caucasus. Many of them emigrated to the Ottoman empire after last century's Caucasus Wars.

**Commonwealth of Independent States (CIS)** – Founded in 1991 at a meeting at Belovezhskaya Pushcha by Boris Yeltsin, president of Russia, and the presidents of Belarus and Ukraine; almost joined by most other former Soviet republics, except the three Baltic states and, initially, Georgia.

**Dagestan** – Area neighbouring Chechnya to the east. Dagestan is the easternmost part of the North Caucasus, and runs down to the Caspian Sea shore. Some of its mountain peoples are ethnically, religiously and historically close to the Chechens.

**Demokrad** – A thieving democrat, pun on *krad* (theft).

**Devushka** – Girl (or any female between the ages of about fifteen and about fifty).

**Dubossary** – Town in Pridnestroviye, the part of Moldova held by a Slav separatist minority.

**Dvoyevlastiye** – Divided power, struggle for power between two rival Russian leaders.

**Dzhigit** – Caucasian horseman.

Abulfaz **Elchibey** – Ex-dissident, President of Azerbaijan from 1992 until ousted in 1993.

**FSB** – More powerful Russian security service that replaced the FSK counter-intelligence service in 1995. Its first chief was ex-KGB General Mikhail Barsukov, who was fired in the summer of 1996.

**FSK** – Russian counter-intelligence agency in 1993–5. It replaced the Russian security ministry in one of a series of post-Soviet reshuffles of the KGB. Its first boss was Nikolai Golushko, ex-chief of Soviet Ukraine's KGB, who was a product of the dissident-hunting Fifth Directorate. Golushko was sacked in early 1994, and his deputy Sergei Stepashin took over. The agency was later expanded and renamed the FSB.

Yegor **Gaidar** – Young economist who started Russia's post-Soviet economic reform; at various times in 1992 and 1993 he was a deputy prime minister and acting prime minister.

Zviad **Gamsakhurdia** – Ex-dissident and first post-Soviet President of Georgia. He was ousted in a coup in January 1992.

Beslan **Gantemirov** – Mayor of Dudayev's Grozny until fighting broke out between president and opposition in 1993. He fell in with Chechen opposition groups gathering in Nadterechny District. He returned to become Mayor of Grozny again after Russian troops took the city in 1995, but was later jailed for embezzlement.

Ruslan **Gelayev** – Commander of south-western Chechen forces during the war.

**Georgia** – Ex-Soviet Transcaucasian republic, whose capital is Tbilisi.

**Ghazavat** – (Chechen) holy war.

**Giaour** – (Caucasian) Russian infidel.

**Golod i Kholod** – Famine and Freezing, the future Russians feared as the Soviet Union collapsed.

Nikolai **Golushko** – First head of the Russian FSK counter-intelligence agency. Sacked in early 1994.

Defence Minister Pavel **Grachev** – Remained close to Yeltsin until he was sacked in 1996, despite long-running rumours of corruption which led to his nickname 'Pasha Mercedes'. Hawkish on Chechnya.

Vladimir **Gusinsky** – Head of the powerful Russian media and business conglomerate Most Group; friendly with Moscow Mayor Yuri

Luzhkov, and at odds with the Moscow hardline officials known as the 'Party of War' who were close to Yeltsin at the start of the Chechen war. After he clashed with these officials on the eve of the war, Gusinsky's commercial NTV television channel helped expose distortions in official reports of the war. In 1996, Gusinsky was one of the 'Big Seven' group of bankers who joined forces to bankroll Yeltsin's re-election.

Suret **Huseinov** – Millionaire and leader of Azeri rebel army that ousted Azerbaijan's president Abulfaz Elchibey in 1993; later Prime Minister of Azerbaijan under President Heidar Aliyev; later sacked.

**Ingushetia** – Area neighbouring Chechnya in the eastern part of the North Caucasus region. It was joined together with Chechnya, to its east, until Dzhokhar Dudayev declared Chechnya independent of Russia in 1991.

**Khadzhi Murad** – A Caucasian leader close to Imam Shamil during the nineteeth-century Caucasian Wars, who briefly went over to the Russian side and was killed by Russians as he later tried to escape them. His death was described in Lev Tolstoy's novella *Khadzhi Murad*.

Salambek **Khadzhiyev** – Ex-Soviet petrochemicals minister, a leader of the anti-Dudayev Chechen opposition who was briefly installed by Moscow in Grozny during the war.

**Khalatik** – Dressing-gown, or white overalls worn by Chechen fighters to camouflage themselves in snowy weather.

Khusein **Khamidov** – Before the war, he was Dudayev's pilot. Later, after his sons were killed in the war, he ran a missing persons' organization to trace Chechens killed in fighting or arrested and sent to Russian filtration camps, arrange their release if possible or return their bodies to their relatives if not.

Ruslan **Khasbulatov** – A university professor who turned to politics during the perestroika era, Khasbulatov was a displaced Chechen who had spent his childhood in exile in Kazakhstan and made a career in Russia. He became speaker of the Russian Supreme Soviet parliament from 1991 to 1993. At first a close democratic ally of Yeltsin, his parliament later opposed many of Yeltsin's plans. Khasbulatov was also the enemy of Dudayev, in Chechnya, who declared the Russian parliament leader an enemy of the Chechen people. In 1993, after a two-week siege at the White House parliament ended in bloodshed, Khasbulatov and other leaders of an attempt to replace Yeltsin were jailed. After a new parliament amnestied him, Khasbulatov returned to Chechnya and spent much of 1994 mediating between different Chechen factions. Yeltsin's fear that Khasbulatov might replace Dudayev as leader of Chechnya helped tip the Russian president towards war.

**Khokhly** – (Lit. topknots) Russian slang for Ukrainians, who traditionally shaved all but a tuft of hair from their heads.

**Khozyayin** – Master.

**Kindzhal** – Long Caucasian dagger.

**Kishinyov** – Capital of Moldova, the ex-Soviet republic next to Romania.

Sergei **Kovalyov** – An ex-Soviet dissident and prisoner, the friend of dissident physicist Andrei Sakharov, and Russian parliamentary and presidential human rights commissioner at the start of the war; replaced in both jobs because of his public criticism of the war.

**Kommendatura** – Russian command post.

**Konyak** – Cognac.

**Korenizatsiya** – (Lit. putting down roots) The process Lenin hoped would take place in the small ethnic regions created under Soviet rule, in which more 'backward' peoples of the Soviet Union would have time and space to catch up with their more 'advanced' Russian fellow-citizens.

Alexander **Korzhakov** – An ex-general from the ex-KGB Ninth Directorate. He ran Yeltsin's personal bodyguard of a few thousand men until mid-1996.

**Krovnaya mest'** – blood vengeance, vendetta.

Anatoly **Kulikov** – Hardline Russian deputy interior minister before the war, leader of combined Russian interior and defence ministry forces in Chechnya in early 1995, then interior ministry after his predecessor Viktor Yerin was fired.

**Kuntakhadzhinets** – Russian word to describe Chechen adherents of the Qadiriya Sufi order, taken from the name of the nineteenth-century shepherd Kunta Khadzhi Kishiyev who brought the order to Chechnya.

Ruslan **Labazanov** – Dudayev's bodyguard, who fell out with the

Chechen president in 1994 and went into opposition; he was killed at the Chechen town of Tolstoy-Yurt in June 1996 in a brawl among his guards; he was possibly connected to the Russian security services.

**Lachin** – Town in ethnically Kurdish area of Azerbaijan, on the edge of Nagorny Karabakh; Lachin fell under Karabakh Armenian control in 1992, allowing Armenians from Nagorny Karabakh to open a road to Armenia.

Alexander **Lebed** – Ex-general of the Soviet 14th Army in Moldova, from where he quarrelled with Defence Minister Pavel Grachev. A critic of the Chechen war. He ran for president in June 1996 and came in third after a first round of voting; he joined up with Yeltsin for the second round and was rewarded with the job of Security Council Secretary. Before he was sacked in October 1996, he negotiated an end to fighting in Chechnya.

**Lei** – (Chechen) Slave, ignoble.

Oleg **Lobov** – Hardline Russian Security Council Secretary before and during the war.

**Lozh** – Lie.

Yuri **Luzhkov** – Post-Soviet Mayor of Moscow.

Yaragi **Mamodayev** – In the early part of Dudayev's reign, Mamodayev was a deputy premier who ran the Chechen economy; he fell out with Dudayev in 1993 and ran a rival 'government of national trust' from Moscow.

Sheikh **Mansur** Ushurma – Leader of the first Chechen uprising against Russia in the late eighteenth century.

Aslan **Maskhadov** – Ex-Soviet colonel; later commander of Dudayev's forces fighting Moscow; after the war he became Prime Minister of a temporary government under Zelimkhan Yandarbiyev; he was elected President of Chechnya in January 1997.

**Medresseh** – Islamic religious school.

**Mekhkel** – (Chechen) Council of elders.

**Mineralniye Vody** – Airport town in southern Russia.

**Miting** – Political demonstration.

**Murid** – (Sufi) disciple.

**Murshid** – (Sufi) master.

Ayaz **Mutalibov** – Communist President of Azerbaijan until ousted in 1992.

**Nadterechny District** – (Above-the-Terek-River) The quietist area of north-eastern Chechnya which, before the war, became the focal point for pro-Moscow political opponents of Dudayev.

Sheikh **Nadzhmuddin** Gotsinsky – Naqshbandi Imam of Dagestan and Chechnya during fighting with Russia after the 1917 Revolution; executed in 1925.

**Nagorny Karabakh** – A region inside Azerbaijan whose people are ethnically Armenian. Disputed since the late 1980s.

**Naib** – Senior military/religious aide under Imam Shamil.

**Nalchik** – Capital of the North Caucasus region of Kabardino-Balkaria, west of North Ossetia.

**Naqshbandiya** – Sufi order of Imam Shamil, dominant in Chechnya in nineteenth century.

**Nashi** – Ours; widely used in Russian to mean 'our team' 'our boys' 'our side' and 'our army.' Contrasted with *chuzhiye* – or aliens.

**Nazran** – Capital of the region of Ingushetia, Chechnya's western neighbour.

**NKVD** – A Soviet predecessor of the KGB.

**Nomenklatura** – Soviet 'aristocracy' of privileged top officials and their families.

**North Caucasus** – The region on the north side of the Caucasus mountain range, on Russia's southern border; home to dozens of separate small peoples, speaking mutually incomprehensible languages. They were conquered by Russia in the early nineteenth century, as the Tsars expanded their empire southwards. There are two main groups: the Circassian peoples of the western regions, and the Chechens, Ingush and Dagestanis to the east.

**North Ossetia** – Region in southern Russia; its people speak a language related to Persian. North Ossetians are traditionally hostile to their Ingushi neighbours, and historically have been supportive of Russia's advances in the region.

**Noviye Russkiye** – New Russians, the post-Soviet class of new-money millionaires.

Valeriya **Novodvorskaya** – A radical pro-capitalist Russian politician and commentator, who believes most Western politicians, except possibly Margaret Thatcher, are not quite right-wing enough. She was a vocal opponent of the war in Chechnya from the start; she fell foul of the FSB in 1996.

**Nuvo-richy** – The new rich.

**Ossetia** – (See South Ossetia and North Ossetia).

**Otdykhat'** – to rest, or to have a holiday.

**Panikhida** – A memorial service.

**Papakha** – Chechen tall lambskin hat, worn mostly by older men.

Emil **Payin** – Liberal consultant who advised Yeltsin on Chechnya.

**Pokazukha** – Showing off, making things look better than they really are.

Mikhail **Poltoranin** – Yeltsin's press minister in 1991 and 1992.

**Poryadok** – Order; sounds more approving in Russian than in English.

**Praporshchiki** – Corporals, mocked for their stupidity in the Soviet army.

**Prazdnik** – Holiday, festivity.

**Pridnestroviye** – Moldova's industrial area, east of the Dnestr river.

**Prigorodny District** – A district in the North Caucasus that was populated by Ingushi until 1944, when Josef Stalin deported many peoples of the North Caucasus to internal exile. Prigorodny district was tacked on to North Ossetia after the Ingushi had been taken away, fuelling a persistent rumour in the Caucasus that Stalin, who was a Georgian, favoured the Ossetians so much that he was perhaps of Ossetian extraction himself. A quarrel that arose in 1992 over whether Prigorodny District should be given back to the Ingushi led to bloodshed.

Yevgeny **Primakov** – Head of the post-Soviet foreign intelligence service; became Foreign Minister in 1995.

**Priroda** – Beauties of nature.

**Profilaktoriya** – Preventative medicine centre.

Lieutenant-General Konstantin **Pulikovsky** – Deputy head of the Russian North Caucasus Military District; briefly ran the Russian war effort in August 1996 while his boss, Tikhomirov, remained on holiday as Chechen separatists took back Grozny.

Alexander **Pushkin** – Founding father of classical Russian literature, exiled to the Caucasus in the 1820s; wrote about the war in the south before being recalled to St Petersburg and dying in a duel.

**Qadiriya** – Sufi order dominant in Chechnya in twentieth century; its adherents are also known in Russian as *Kuntakhadzhintsi* – after its founder in Chechnya, nineteenth-century shepherd Kunta Khadzhi Kishiyev, or as *zikristi* for the ecstatic prayer dance they perform out loud.

Salman **Raduyev** – Dudayev's nephew by marriage, and the head of a group of Chechen fighters based near the Dagestan border. In December 1995 he stormed and held Gudermes for several days. In January 1996 he stormed the Dagestani town of Kizlyar and escaped the ensuing Russian siege of nearby Pervomaiskoye. He was reported dead in March 1996, but reappeared in Chechnya after Dudayev's death with a rebuilt face and refused to recognize subsequent presidential elections on the grounds that Dudayev was still alive and would return.

Lieutenant-General Anatoly **Romanov** – The doveish Russian commander of the Joint Group of Federal Forces in the summer of 1995. He was seriously injured in a mystery bomb attack in Grozny in October 1995, and is still in a coma.

Alexander **Rutskoi** – A reformist Communist and Afghan war veteran picked by Yeltsin as his running-mate in the Russian presidential election of 1991. Once he became Vice-President, Rutskoi quickly fell out with Yeltsin and flirted with different opposition figures including parliament chairman Ruslan Khasbulatov. In September 1993, Rutskoi was named 'President' by Khasbulatov as hostility between president and parliament came to the boil. He was arrested and spent several months in Lefortovo jail after the revolt was crushed, but was amnestied in February 1994.

Ivan **Rybkin** – Secretary of the Russian Security Council since October 1996. From 1994 until this appointment, he was speaker of the State Duma (Russian lower house of parliament).

**Sanatoriya** – Sanatorium, or place where Soviet citizens traditionally took their holidays.

**Savok** – (Lit. spade) A mocking word for entrenched Soviet attitudes: unhelpfulness, laziness, petty-minded stubbornness, refusal to think for oneself, selfishness, shoddy workmanship.

**Sblizheniye** – The process of 'drawing together' that Lenin envisaged gradually uniting the many peoples of the Soviet Union under

Communism. It was supposed to be followed by *sliyaniye* or total ethnic merging to create Homo Sovieticus.

Valentin **Sergeyev** – Spokesman of a special Russian government press centre on Chechnya which operated briefly at the start of the war to feed journalists Moscow's official version of the truth.

Sergei **Shakhrai** – Russian minister and lawyer, a leading maker of North Caucasus policy. Hostile to Dudayev, and hawkish on Chechnya.

Mintimer **Shaimiyev** – President of Tatarstan, signed agreement with Russia defining Tatarstan's status as part of the Russian Federation in February 1994, after refusing to sign the Federal Treaty of 1993.

Imam **Shamil** – Third Imam of Dagestan and Chechnya from 1834, an Avar who became the most famous leader of Caucasians fighting Russia in the nineteenth century. Surrendered to Russia's General Baryatinsky in 1859, lived in exile in the Russian town of Kaluga, and died in 1871.

**Shampanskoye** – Champagne.

**Shapka** – Russian fur hat, usually with ear-flaps.

**Shariat** – System of Islamic law.

**Shashka** – Curved sword worn by Cossacks.

**Sheikh** – (Sufi) master.

Eduard **Shevardnadze** – Ex-Soviet Foreign Minister; took power in his Georgian birthplace after post-Soviet President Zviad Gamsakhurdia was ousted in 1992.

**Sliyaniye** – the total ethnic and ideological merging of the Soviet Union's many peoples that Lenin envisaged after a period of slow drawing together.

**Slyakot'** – Wet, sleety, almost wintry weather.

Anatoly **Sobchak** – Liberal Mayor of St Petersburg until 1996.

Oleg **Soskovets** – Hardline First Deputy Prime Minister, industrialist from the aluminium sector.

**South Ossetia** – Separatist region in Georgia; wanted to unite with North Ossetia.

**Stanitsa** – Cossack village.

**Starshy** – Elder, head of a team, leader of a group.

**Stavropol** – Gorbachev's home town in southern Russia.

**Stepanakert** – Capital of Nagorny Karabakh, a separatist ethnic Armenian region in Azerbaijan.

Sergei **Stepashin** – Second head of the Russian FSK counter-intelligence agency. Sacked in July 1995.

**Sukhumi** – Capital of the separatist region of Abkhazia in Georgia. A war for control of Abkhazia ended soon after Sukhumi fell to Abkhazian forces in September 1993, forcing its Georgian population to flee.

**Tariqat** – (Arabic) path towards God; Sufi movement, known in Chechnya as *wird*.

**Tatarstan** – An oil-rich, traditionally Muslim autonomous region of Russia on the Volga river.

**Tbilisi** – Capital of Georgia.

**Teip** – (Chechen) clan.

Levon **Ter-petrosyan** – Ex-dissident, President of Armenia.

Lieutenant-General Vyacheslav **Tikhomirov** – Commander of Russian forces in Chechnya for the last few months of the war.

**Tolkuchka** – Unofficial street market, scrum.

**Transcaucasus** – The region beyond Russia's southern border, on the far side of the Caucasus mountains from Moscow. It stretches from the Black Sea in the West to the Caspian in the East and encompasses the former Soviet republics of Georgia, Armenia and Azerbaijan, which all became independent in 1991.

**Tuqum** – (Chechen) free society made up of several *teips*, or clans. There are nine in Chechnya.

Movladi **Udugov** – Chechen Information Minister under Dudayev, became Deputy Prime Minister after the war.

**Uzden** – (Chechen) free man, noble.

Ruslan and Nazarbek **Utsiyev** – Two Chechen brothers murdered in London while on a mission from Dudayev to equip Chechnya with its own currency and passports.

Sheikh **Uzun Khadzhi** – A Naqshbandi leader who died in 1920 during fighting with Russia after the 1917 Revolution.

**Vainakh** – (Chechen) 'our people'; the collective name that Chechens and Ingushi give to themselves.

**Vashe Velichestvo** – Your Majesty.

**Vashe Vysochestvo** – Your Highness.

**Vedeno** – Chechen hill settlement; one of Imam Shamil's strongholds last century; the home base of Shamil Basayev and his family this century.

**Verkhushka** – Summit, top people in the political hierarchy.

**Vladikavkaz** – Capital of North Ossetia, a quietist, pro-Moscow North Caucasus region that divides the traditionally rebellious Circassian peoples in the western stretches of the hills from the rebellious Chechens and Dagestanis in the east.

**Vranyo** – Lie, exaggerated story, blarney.

**Wird** – (Chechen) path towards God; Sufi movement.

Khozh-Akhmed **Yarikhanov** – Chechen negotiator; after the war, became head of the Chechen oil company Yunko, effectively Chechnya's oil minister.

Grigory **Yavlinsky** – Russian liberal economist, democratic politician and presidential candidate in 1996.

Zelimkhan **Yandarbiyev** – Dudayev's deputy until the Chechen president's death; Yandarbiyev then became interim president. He lost elections for a new presidency in January 1997.

Nikolai **Yegorov** – An ex-Soviet collective farm boss, then hardline post-Soviet nationalities minister; Yeltsin gave Yegorov the Chechen portfolio in late November 1994, just before the start of war.

Viktor **Yerin** – hardline Russian Interior Minister; he was sacked after failing to prevent a Chechen attack on the Russian town of Budyonnovsk in the summer of 1995.

General **Yermolov** – Won fame fighting Napoleon's armies advancing on Moscow in 1812; later led Tsarist campaign in the Caucasus.

Shamseddin **Yusuf** – Jordanian Chechen foreign minister under Dudayev, dismissed in 1996.

Doku **Zavgayev** – Ex-leader of Soviet Checheno-Ingushetia; displaced in 1991 by Dudayev's nationalist forces. Worked for Yeltsin in Moscow as adviser on Chechnya at the start of the war. In the autum of 1995, he resurrected the old Supreme Soviet of Checheno-Ingushetia and went back to run Grozny. He was denounced by many Chechens as Moscow's puppet. After the war, he became Russian ambassador to Tanzania.

Vladimir **Zhirinovsky** – Ultra-nationalist leader of the oddly named

Liberal Democratic Party of Russia, which did well in Russian parliamentary elections in December 1993.

**Zikr** – Chechen prayer-dance.

**Zikrist** – Russian word to describe Chechen adherents of the Qadiriya Sufi order, taken from the word *zikr* or Chechen prayer dance which Qadiri sects performed aloud.

**Ziyarad** – (Chechen) tomb of Sufi saint, place of pilgrimage.

# Index